# BUTTERWORTHS ANNOTATED LEGISLATION SERVICE

## STATUTES SUPPLEMENT No. 220

# CONSUMER CREDIT ACT 1974

By

**R. M. GOODE, O.B.E., LL.B.**

*Solicitor, Crowther Professor of Credit and Commercial Law, Queen Mary College, University of London*

with annotations by

A. P. O'DOWD, B.A., LL.B.,

*of the South African Bar*

LONDON

BUTTERWORTHS

1974

| | |
|---|---|
| *ENGLAND:* | BUTTERWORTH & CO. (PUBLISHERS) LTD.<br>LONDON: 88 KINGSWAY, WC2B 6AB |
| *AUSTRALIA:* | BUTTERWORTHS PTY. LTD.<br>SYDNEY: 586 PACIFIC HIGHWAY, CHATSWOOD, NSW 2067<br>MELBOURNE: 343 LITTLE COLLINS STREET, 3000<br>BRISBANE: 240 QUEEN STREET, 4000 |
| *CANADA:* | BUTTERWORTH & CO. (CANADA) LTD.<br>TORONTO: 2265 MIDLAND AVENUE, SCARBOROUGH, M1P 4S1 |
| *NEW ZEALAND:* | BUTTERWORTHS OF NEW ZEALAND LTD.<br>WELLINGTON: 26–28 WARING TAYLOR STREET, 1 |
| *SOUTH AFRICA:* | BUTTERWORTH & CO. (SOUTH AFRICA) (PTY) LTD.<br>DURBAN: 152–154 GALE STREET |





ISBN: 0 406 54731 9





MADE AND PRINTED IN GREAT BRITAIN BY
BUTLER AND TANNER LTD
FROME AND LONDON

# PREFACE

"He that practiseth usury goeth to Hell; and he that practiseth it not tendeth to destitution." Thus spoke Benvenuto da Imola some six hundred years ago, neatly pinpointing one of the many problems with which the Committee on Consumer Credit, under its outstanding chairman Lord Crowther, had to grapple during the two and a half years preceding the publication of its Report in March 1971.

The Consumer Credit Bill, having fallen with the advent of the General Election in February, rose like a phoenix from the ashes of the previous Administration and after many vicissitudes reached the statute book on 31st July 1974, a date that will be indelibly engraved on every financier's heart. The Act implements almost in their entirety those recommendations of the Crowther Committee relating to the reform of the law of *consumer* credit. The equally radical proposals of the Committee for restructuring of the general law affecting security in personal property, strongly influenced by Article 9 of the American Uniform Commercial Code, have not as yet been adopted. They are receiving further study from the Government, which is expected in due course to engage in consultations with interested parties. There can be little doubt of the need for reform of English personal property security law, which remains in a parlous state and is certainly no model to offer to Britain's partners in Europe.

The consumer credit industry is complex and sophisticated. It offers a wide range of credit facilities, and utilises an extraordinary diversity of legal instruments—hire-purchase, conditional sale, credit sale, rental, trading checks, credit cards, secured and unsecured loans and overdrafts. Hitherto, each of these legal forms has been subjected to different rules of law. One set of statutes has regulated hire-purchase and instalment sales contracts; another set has governed loans and security. Some hybrid forms, such as check trading and credit cards, have occupied a twilight zone, stealing within the penumbra of the Moneylenders Acts whilst never conclusively subjugated by them. Certain lenders, notably banks, have been free altogether from the shackles of moneylending legislation.

The Consumer Credit Act, when fully operative, will sweep away this fragmented legislation, replacing it with what is probably the most advanced, and certainly the most comprehensive, Code ever to be enacted in any country in the sphere of consumer credit. The Act draws into its net all types of consumer credit, of whatever legal form, and applies to them and to consumer hire a comprehensive licensing system, to be administered by the Director General of Fair Trading, and a detailed set of provisions regulating the conduct of business, entry into agreements and the rights and duties of the parties. The old legalistic distinctions between loan credit and sale credit are discarded, and all forms of consumer credit are subjected to a unified system of control, save only for such variations in treatment as reflect differences of practical importance in the nature, function and mechanics of the various types of credit.

It cannot be said that the Consumer Credit Act is a simple enactment. To expect simplicity in the regulation of activities so complex and variegated would be to ask the impossible. What is important is that the underlying concepts shall be soundly based and logically expressed. The draftsman, faced with formidable problems of analysis and presentation and obliged to engage in massive amendment in the short period allowed by the Parliamentary timetable, has performed his task with consummate skill. Many of the defects in the original version of the Bill have been eliminated. These included a small omission that would have resulted in the repeal of all the existing legislation before most of the new statutory provisions had been brought into force, thus producing a glorious interregnum in which creditors' rights would be altogether free of statutory control! Happily (or otherwise, depending on your viewpoint) this was picked up at an early stage, together with various other points of difficulty, so that whilst the Act remains far from perfect it is none the less both sound and imaginative, and when backed by regulations should substantially achieve the desired objectives. A brief historical introduction to the Act will be found in chapter 1, and a bird's eye view of the statutory provisions in chapter 2.

This book is designed to meet the immediate need of an introductory guide to what is undoubtedly a most complex piece of legislation. Necessarily, therefore, it has been written at speed, and though reasonably detailed it does not purport to be an exhaustive analysis of the new Act, which requires closer acquaintanceship and reflection over a period of time before the many underlying problems and subtleties begin to surface. Within this limitation I have endeavoured to provide not a literal translation of the statutory provisions—which could be done by the intelligent reader himself and might leave him just as mystified at the end—but an insight into the structure of the Act, the purpose and significance of its elaborate classification of credit agreements and the impact of the various provisions on specific types of transaction. To that end, I have treated the various aspects of regulation in an order somewhat different from that adopted by the draftsman, examining these in the sequence in which they would normally appear in a typical transaction, whilst at the same time bringing together widely separated sections that require to be read in conjunction. Wherever possible, I have indicated not merely the general effect of a statutory provision but its particular relevance to different types of consumer credit agreement, illustrating this with numerous examples.

Whilst the Act itself is obviously the central feature of the book, many of the statutory provisions can only be understood in the context of the existing law, whether the common law or another statute. Moreover, the Act does not provide a complete code of rights. Other statutes confer rights on parties to a credit agreement, or restrict the exclusion of liability under such an agreement, and the common law also imposes certain restraints on freedom of contract. I have therefore woven into the analysis of the Consumer Credit Act concise expositions of the remedies for breach of duty available at common law, the common law doctrine of fundamental breach and the rule against penalties, and have summarised relevant provisions of various statutes, including the Misrepresentation Act 1967, the Trade Descriptions Act 1968 and the Supply of

Goods (Implied Terms) Act 1973. I have also given as detailed a picture as I can of the likely shape of regulations to be made under the Act, in the light of the very informative White Paper on the *Reform of the Law on Consumer Credit* and such other information as was available to me. The regulations will be phased, and it is the intention to keep the book up to date with supplements as appropriate.

A number of provisions of the Consumer Credit Act reproduce, albeit in somewhat different form, existing provisions of the Hire-Purchase Act 1965. These I have analysed in such detail as is appropriate for a book of this kind. For a comprehensive study of the current hire-purchase legislation, and of the common law rules governing hire-purchase, instalment sale and leasing agreements, the reader is referred to my text book *Hire-Purchase Law and Practice* (2nd Edition), where these are exhaustively examined.

As so often in the past, my warm thanks are due to Mr. C. McNeil Greig, Director of the Hire Purchase Trade Association, for his illuminating comments on various problems and for supplying me so rapidly with details of amendments to the Bill which due to printing problems were not available through the ordinary channels. Mr. Derek Hyde, the Assistant Secretary of the Department of Prices and Consumer Protection having charge of the Bill, was kind enough to read the proofs and save me from various errors I should otherwise have committed. His remarkable mastery of the statutory provisions has been of the greatest value to me, and I am deeply grateful. I should also like to thank my colleague, Mr. John Yelland, who performed a similar proof-reading service and whose lively and penetrating comments on the proofs, and on the Bill itself, have been most helpful.

For the typing of the manuscript, carried out impeccably at lightning speed, my warm thanks are due first to my wonderfully efficient secretary Mrs. Wendy Mann, and secondly to Mrs. Kathleen Gerroll and Mrs. Mary Griffin of the Rushgrove Secretarial Agency.

Finally, I should like to thank the publishers, Messrs. Butterworths, for the efficiency and speed with which they handled the production of the book; and to add a special word of appreciation to the printers, Messrs. Butler and Tanner, who laboured with such skill and perseverance to ensure its prompt publication.

The Consumer Credit Act is a landmark in the regulation of consumer credit which is likely to influence developments not only in this country but overseas. It is also a further monument to Geoffrey Crowther, whose inspired chairmanship of the Committee on Consumer Credit brought the reform of consumer credit law to fruition.

*October* 1974 R. M. GOODE

# TABLE OF CONTENTS

# TABLE OF STATUTES

**References in the right-hand column are to paragraph numbers. Paragraph numbers printed in bold type indicate where the Consumer Credit Act 1974 is set out in full. References to "*Statutes*" are to Halsbury's Statutes of England (Third Edition) showing the volume and page at which the annotated text of the Act will be found.**

## *Table of Statutes*

# *Table of Statutes*

# TABLE OF CASES

**References in the right-hand column are to paragraph numbers.**

# CHAPTER 1

# HOW IT ALL BEGAN

## EARLY HISTORY

[**1.1**] For nearly 800 years consumer credit as a subject of regulation was almost entirely ignored by successive monarchs, by Parliament and by the common law. Apart from enactments controlling interest rates and pawnbrokers, and scattered statutory provisions relating to loans to infants, the intervention of the legislature prior to 1854 was virtually non-existent. The courts themselves stood back and, though willing on occasion to grant relief to the hard pressed baronet's son who had mortgaged his inheritance, saw little reason to interfere with freely concluded contracts. "The Chancery mends no man's bargain," said Lord Nottingham in 1676 and few dissented from so self-evident a truth.

[**1.2**] In 1854, the first Bills of Sale Act was passed, requiring registration of written bills of sale. In the same year, removing with one hand what had been given with the other, Parliament abolished all existing usury legislation. The 1854 Act was amended in 1866 and replaced in 1878; and four years later a further Act was passed regulating security bills of sale (*i.e.* written chattel mortgages) and conferring a measure of protection on the debtor who mortgaged his goods, as by nullifying bills of sale for which the consideration did not exceed £30 or which sought to give security over the debtor's after acquired property. The Bills of Sale Acts, though giving some protection to the consumer, were not confined to consumer transactions. Even commercial agreements were caught unless the debtor was a registered company.

## THE MONEYLENDERS ACTS

[**1.3**] Apart from the Bills of Sale Acts and pawnbroking legislation, the lenders of money enjoyed an unparalleled era of freedom and prosperity between 1854 and 1900, and serious abuses resulted. Trickery and extortion were rampant and borrowers suffered misery and hardship through ruthless enforcement of security. The report of the House of Commons Select Committee on Money-Lending, published in 1898, showed that one lender had admitted charging on occasion interest at rates as high as 3,000 per cent, while another confessed that to avoid the notoriety likely to result from his activities he had traded under no less than 34 different aliases. It was therefore scarcely surprising that two years later the first Moneylenders Act was passed, providing for registration (but not licensing) of moneylenders and empowering the courts to re-open harsh and unconscionable moneylending transactions. The Act of 1900, though a step in the right direction, was not a very effective piece of legislation. The absence of any licensing system meant that control of moneylenders was left to the civil courts, acting on the individual initiative of an aggrieved borrower. But most borrowers in the category for whose protection the Act was designed were unlikely to be able to afford the luxury of legal representation, even if they would otherwise have been willing to involve themselves in litigious procedures.

**[1.4]** The Money-lenders Act 1900 had a further curious weakness, the full impact of which was not to become apparent for some considerable time. Instead of delineating the boundary of protection for the debtor according to the purpose, size or type of the transaction, the Act concentrated on the status of the lender. Lending by a moneylender was within the Act; lending by an exempted category such as a bank was not. Conversely, the Act, though designed as a source of consumer protection, was not confined to consumer transactions. It applied equally to commercial loans, even if to registered companies. This situation was to continue unchanged for the next 74 years.

**[1.5]** Moneylending legislation, after amendment of the 1900 Act in 1911 was substantially strengthened by the passing of the Moneylenders Act 1927, which substituted annual licensing for registration and imposed severe restrictions on methods by which a moneylender could seek business. In particular, he was not permitted to employ agents or canvassers or to send out unsolicited circulars or advertisements, and even the right to advertise in newspapers was closely circumscribed. The loan contract had to be evidenced by a note or memorandum in writing and a copy supplied to the borrower; and other detailed requirements were imposed. Unfortunately, the 1927 Act, though going a considerable way towards protection for the small borrower, also seriously inhibited legitimate business transactions. Those engaged in granting commercial loans who were not bankers or otherwise within an exempt category were controlled by the Act in the same way as the small loan business; and since the slightest infraction of a minute technicality would render a loan irrecoverable, with no power in the court to grant relief, very sizable loans—sometimes as high as £50,000 or more—might be placed at risk through a technical defence by a corporate borrower which was wholly lacking in merit.

**[1.6]** These difficulties with moneylending legislation had two consequences. First, they were a major factor in the development of instalment selling and hire-purchase, a form of credit which by-passed the Moneylenders Acts. Secondly—and this was a post-war development—they led companies to explore other methods of escape, particularly by the formation of banking companies, so that a completely new system of secondary banking developed, enjoying the same immunity from the Moneylenders Acts as was possessed by the clearing banks. Initially, these banks suffered the disadvantage that there was no official machinery by which their banking status could be established for the purpose of the Moneylenders Acts without their having to prove such status in a court of law. This was to some extent remedied by s. 123 of the Companies Act 1967, which empowered the Board of Trade to issue a certificate on application that the applicant could properly be treated as carrying on the business of banking for the purpose of the Moneylenders Acts. Early applicants who thought that such certificates were designed to allow non-banking hire-purchase companies to obtain a recognition of banking status were speedily disillusioned. The Board of Trade insisted that banking activities had to be carried on which fulfilled the criteria for banking laid down by the Court of Appeal in *United Dominions Trust, Ltd.* v. *Kirkwood*, [1966] 2 Q.B. 431; [1966] 1 All E.R. 968 and also satisfied other, rather imprecise, criteria developed by the Board to ensure that certificates were limited to companies that were reputable and financially sound. Even so, s. 123 certificates were granted too freely in the early years of the new system, and following serious abuses by certain s. 123 banks, applications for certificates were temporarily frozen in April 1973, pending the formulation of much more stringent criteria, which came into operation in August of that year. It was during this period that the government asked leading finance houses to adhere to a Voluntary Code providing for such matters as disclosure of the true rate of borrowing, a cooling off period and restrictions on sales by mortgagees.

## INSTALMENT SALE AND HIRE-PURCHASE

[1.7] English law in the credit field has always been characterised by a sharp distinction between the regulation of loan credit on the one hand and that of sale credit on the other. The lending of money, as we have seen, was subject to usury legislation prior to 1854, and from 1900 was controlled by the money-lending legislation referred to above. The rights of the mortgagee under a written chattel mortgage, or security bill of sale, were governed by the Bills of Sale Acts 1878 and 1882 and by the small amending Acts of 1890 and 1891. But the sale of goods on credit has never been considered as constituting a loan in English law and thus did not attract the operation of the Moneylenders Acts. Similarly, the reservation of title under a conditional sale or hire-purchase agreement is not a security for a loan and is thus outside the Bills of Sale Acts.

[1.8] The general statute dealing with contracts of sale is the Sale of Goods Act 1893, which (*inter alia*) sets out a range of implied terms in favour of the buyer. This enactment was originally a permissive statute in that the parties were free to contract out of its provisions. The Supply of Goods (Implied Terms) Act 1973 drastically changed this *laissez-faire* approach by making void exemption clauses in consumer sales and consumer hire-purchase agreements and by controlling such clauses even in non-consumer transactions.

[1.9] The first enactment dealing specifically with hire-purchase was the Hire-Purchase and Small Debt (Scotland) Act 1932. England followed with the Hire-Purchase Act 1938, which was subsequently amended by the Hire-Purchase Acts 1954 and 1964 and later replaced in a consolidating enactment, the Hire-Purchase Act 1965. The 1965 Act applied to all hire-purchase and instalment sale agreements under which the hire-purchase price or total purchase price did not exceed £2,000 and the hirer or buyer was not a body corporate. It contained provisions regulating the formalities of contract, the right of cancellation of a hirer or buyer signing the agreement elsewhere than at appropriate trade premises, the non-excludable terms implied in favour of the hirer or conditional buyer and a range of matters designed for his protection, including a prohibition against enforcement of a right to recover the goods from him when one-third of the hire-purchase price or total purchase price had been paid or tendered and the agreement had not been terminated by him.

[**1.10**] The advertising of goods as available for disposal on hire-purchase or instalment sale was regulated by the Advertisements (Hire-Purchase) Act 1967, a measure that represented a consolidation of the Advertisements (Hire-Purchase) Act 1957 and amendments made to that Act by the Hire-Purchase Act 1964.

[**1.11**] In addition, there have been several provisions of different statutes dealing with the effect of a wrongful disposition of goods held by the disposer on hire-purchase or conditional sale. These are still in force. Section 9 of the Factors Act 1889 and s. 25 (2) of the Sale of Goods Act 1893 provide in effect that in given conditions the delivery of goods by a conditional buyer to a *bona fide* purchaser can pass title to that purchaser, even though the conditional buyer has not yet become the owner. These provisions never applied to hire-purchase agreements, and were also made inapplicable to conditional sale agreements within the Hire-Purchase Act 1965, an exemption continued by the Consumer Credit Act in paragraphs 2 and 4 of the Fourth Schedule.

[**1.12**] By Part III of the Hire-Purchase Act 1964 (which is still in force) a disposition of a motor vehicle by a hirer under a hire-purchase agreement or a buyer under a conditional sale agreement, if made to a *bona fide* private purchaser without notice of the hire-purchase or conditional sale agreement, was made effective to transfer to the purchaser the title of the person who had let the vehicle on hire-purchase or agreed to sell it on conditional sale. This was so whether or not the hire-purchase or conditional sale agreement was within the limits of the Hire-Purchase Act 1965.

[**1.13**] Finally, by s. 1 of the Emergency Laws (Re-enactments and Repeals) Act 1964—embodying in permanent statutory form powers originally conferred by regulation 55 of the Defence (General) Regulations 1939—the Board of Trade (later the Department of Trade and Industry and now the Department of Prices and Consumer Protection) was empowered to make orders restricting the disposal of goods by way of hire-purchase or instalment sale. Such orders were designed not as a measure of consumer protection but to protect the economy from becoming overheated by inflationary tendencies supposedly generated by consumer credit. The orders provided minimum down-payments and maximum payment periods for hire-purchase and instalment sale agreements covering a range of goods—mainly, though not exclusively, consumer goods. Rental agreements were regulated by parallel orders requiring advance rentals and controlling the period of hire and spread of rental payments. The orders current at the time of the Crowther Report (referred to below) were the Hire-Purchase and Credit Sale Agreements (Control) Order 1969 and the Control of Hiring Order 1969. These were revoked in July 1971 but were restored on the 18th December 1973 as the Hire-Purchase and Credit Sale Agreements (Control) Order 1973 and the Control of Hiring Order 1973.

### THE CROWTHER REPORT

[**1.14**] The Committee on Consumer Credit, under the chairmanship of Lord Crowther, was appointed in September 1968, when it embarked on what was to become the most wide-ranging review of consumer credit ever undertaken in this country—indeed, the first comprehensive government study of this important subject. For various reasons the Committee felt it impracticable to examine the law of consumer credit in isolation—particularly since the Bills of Sale Acts and the Moneylenders Acts were not confined to consumer transactions, and they extended their study to encompass the general legal framework within which the granting of credit and the taking of security were required to operate. The Committee's Report, published in March 1971, covered the entire field of consumer credit in Britain. After discussing at length the social and economic implications of credit and recommending that terms control (see para. [**1.13**]) should be abolished, the Report proceeded to a detailed evaluation of the law relating to credit transactions. The Committee concluded that the existing law was gravely defective, the most serious weaknesses being the following:

(*a*) *The regulation of transactions according to their form instead of according to their substance and function.* This was reflected in the sharp distinction drawn between loans for the purchase of goods and the extension of credit by deferment of the price under a hire-purchase or instalment sale agreement. One set of statutes governed the lending of money, another the taking of security for repayment. Sale credit, however, was not considered to involve the making of a loan, and the reservation of title was not in law equated with a security interest, so that hire-purchase and instalment sale transactions were altogether outside the above two sets of statutes and were regulated independently by a third set, whose provisions were completely different.

(*b*) *The failure to distinguish consumer from commercial transactions.* Thus, the Moneylenders Acts, though designed as a measure of consumer protection, were equally applicable to loans to companies for business purposes. Similarly, the Bills of Sale Acts, though not according protection to companies, did not draw any other distinction between consumer and commercial transactions.

(*c*) *The artificial separation of the law relating to lending from the law relating to security for loans.* In particular, there was no link between the Bills of Sale Acts and the Moneylenders Acts, Parliament having evidently failed to appreciate that the security for a loan was an integral part of the loan transaction itself.

(*d*) *The absence of any rational policy in relation to third party rights.* Thus, the buyer under a conditional sale agreement (but not a hirer under a hire-purchase agreement) could in certain circumstances pass a good title to an innocent third party under the Factors Act 1889, but not if the conditional sale agreement was within the Hire-Purchase Act 1965. Both a conditional buyer and a hirer under a hire-purchase agreement could pass a good title to a *bona fide* private purchaser of a motor vehicle, pursuant to Part III of the Hire-Purchase Act 1964. The grantor of a duly registered mortgage bill of sale could not transfer a good title under either of the above Acts. Quite apart from these anomalies, there was no official machinery for registering the reservation of title under a conditional sale or hire-purchase agreement.

(*e*) *Excessive technicality.* The slightest infraction of the Moneylenders Acts, however technical, would deprive the lender of his right to recover the loan, however large. Similarly, infringement of the fearsome technicalities of the Bills of Sale Acts might invalidate the security.

(*f*) *Inadequate protection for the consumer in credit transactions.* This was due to various factors, in particular:

- (i) the distinction previously mentioned between sale credit and loan credit;
- (ii) the absence of statutory control of the cost of credit in transactions outside the Moneylenders Acts;
- (iii) the absence of any requirement that the consumer should be informed of the true cost of borrowing;
- (iv) the absence of any legal requirement to give a rebate for early settlement;
- (v) the use of negotiable instruments to defeat defences that the the consumer might otherwise have been able to raise;
- (vi) the total freedom of rental transactions from legislative control;
- (vii) inadequate protection for those entering into contracts of guarantee and indemnity in relation to consumer credit transactions;
- (viii) the absence of any effective machinery for enforcing compliance with the legislation.

**[1.15]** The Crowther Committee considered the law to be so unsatisfactory that it was useless to tinker about further with piecemeal amendments. They therefore recommended repeal of the entire range of existing legislation affecting credit and security in personal property—the Hire-Purchase Acts, the Bills of Sale Acts, the Moneylenders Acts, etc—and their replacement by two new enactments which would clearly distinguish between rules of general application and rules for consumer credit transactions, viz:

(*a*) a Lending and Security Act, which would apply across the board, would rationalise the treatment of security interests and conflicts between secured parties, would establish a security register and would facilitate legitimate business transactions;

(*b*) a Consumer Sale and Loan Act, which would harmonise the treatment of all forms of consumer credit, including consumer rental transactions, thus applying a uniform code to sale and loan credit agreements, with strengthened protection for the consumer and proper enforcement through a licensing system operated by a Consumer Credit Commissioner.

## THE GOVERNMENT'S RESPONSE TO THE CROWTHER REPORT

**[1.16]** Despite the overwhelmingly favourable reactions to the Crowther Report, both from the credit industry and from consumer organisations, the government's initial response was muted. This was understandable, since the Department of Trade and Industry wanted time to work out in more detail the implications of the recommendations. Some 15 months elapsed before the government was induced to break its silence as the result of a debate initiated by Baroness Phillips in the House of Lords. In the course of this, it became clear that whilst the government accepted nearly all the recommendations of the Report in relation to *consumer* credit, it was firmly reserving its position on the more fundamental proposals for restructuring of the basic law of lending and security generally.

> "Central to the Committee's proposals in this field is their proposed register of security interests. We can so far find no convincing evidence that, were such a register to be established, it would be sufficiently used to justify its existence . . . If the proposal for a register is in question, the basis of many other of the Committee's suggestions must also be questioned. For example, complex rules to govern third party rights, which the Committee began to draft but did not complete, are predicated on the existence of such a register. It is by no means certain that, when fully elaborated, such rules would be less complex and easier to understand than the present rules, which are based partly on Statute and partly on precedent. If no register were to be established, the Committee's proposals for third party rights would fall and we would either have to leave the law as it now stands or work out a new set of rules using the Committee's principles as a starting point" (Earl of Limerick in *H.L. Debates*, 28th June 1972, cols. 974–975).

[**1.17**] The author's answers to this reasoning have been fully deployed elsewhere (see "Credit Law—The Case for Reform", *Credit*, March 1973, p. 12). Suffice it to say that at the time the above statement was made, there were already no less than seven different registers of security interests in force; and within a matter of weeks the Minister's own Department proceeded with legislation for the creation of an eighth, the Register of Aircraft Mortgages!

## THE WHITE PAPER

[**1.18**] In September 1973, after extensive discussions with interested parties and the dissemination of a number of consultation papers, the government produced a White Paper on the *Reform of the Law on Consumer Credit* (Cmnd. 5427). In this, the government indicated its intention of implementing by legislation virtually the whole of the Crowther Committee's recommendations on consumer credit law, with certain additional safeguards for the consumer that had been shown to be necessary as the result of experiences after the publication of the Report. Two particular deviations from Crowther were the increase in the financial limits for protection from a total purchase price of £2,000 to an *advance* of £5,000—reflecting a substantial drop in the value of money since the Crowther recommendations were formulated—and considerably stronger protection for hirers under hiring contracts. In most other respects, the White Paper closely followed the Crowther Report. The White Paper was a particularly useful document in that it not only depicted in the text the scope of the forthcoming Consumer Credit Bill but also set out in Appendices much of the proposed content of regulations to be made under the Consumer Credit Act, including mathematical formulae for statement of the cost of borrowing in terms of a true percentage rate.

[**1.19**] The White Paper also set out the government's latest thinking in regard to the Committee's proposals for the fundamental restructuring of the general law of credit and security in the Lending and Security Act.

> "The Committee's proposals are for radical reform in a complex field and their implementation would require another major Bill, central to which would be the establishment of a Register of Security Interests and detailed priority provisions depending upon its existence and use. The government accept that there are aspects of the existing law in this field which cause difficulty, but they do not have sufficient evidence either of a need for such major recasting of existing law on new principles or of general support for the particular solution proposed by the Committee. They intend to institute consultations with those most closely concerned in the light of the situation existing after passage of the Consumer Credit Bill" (para. 14).

THE CONSUMER CREDIT ACT

[**1.20**] The government lost no further time in proceeding with the consumer credit legislation, *i.e.* Stage 2 of the Crowther proposals. The White Paper had been published in September 1973. By the beginning of November a Consumer Credit Bill had been presented, running to some 96 pages. The Bill was widely welcomed on both sides of the House for the clarity of its drafting and the comprehensive nature of its provisions. It was accepted as a non-controversial, non-partisan measure, and all parties pledged their support for its speedy enactment. By the beginning of February 1974 it had completed its Committee Stage in the House of Commons and the wind looked fair for a speedy passage through its remaining stages, when, in the light of the prevailing economic crisis and a decision by the members of the National Union of Mineworkers to give their Executive a mandate for a strike, the government called a general election, Parliament was dissolved and the Consumer Credit Bill, with 88 other measures, was lost. However, almost immediately after the election, the new administration re-introduced the Bill in substantially the same form in the House of Lords and it was passed as the Consumer Credit Act on 31st July 1974.

IMPACT ON EXISTING LEGISLATION

[**1.21**] Whilst some parts of the Act came into force on the day of its passing, most of its provisions will become operative in stages by orders made by the Secretary of State, different days being appointed for the commencement of different provisions. When fully operative, the Act will repeal the Hire-Purchase Act 1965, the Advertisements (Hire Purchase) Act 1967, the Moneylenders Acts 1900–1927 and the Pawnbrokers Acts 1872–1960, replacing them with a new and comprehensive structure of regulation covering all forms of consumer credit. Thus has begun the first phase of the reform of English credit law, which has been characterised by an unusual degree of parliamentary bi-partisanship. The Crowther Committee, set up by a Labour Government, reported to a Conservative administration. The latter introduced the Consumer Credit Bill, which was continued and completed by its Labour successor. The Act is influencing developments not only here but abroad. It has been closely studied in America and the Commonwealth and forms the basis of a recent EEC Draft Directive on Consumer Credit. But Phase 1 of Crowther, the reform of the general legal framework underpinning secured transactions in personal property, has yet to come. Meanwhile, the Bills of Sale Acts and all the anomalies created by other statutes in relation to third party rights in secured transactions will continue to cause hardship and injustice and to restrict our ability to influence the adoption in Europe of a modern personal property security law. It is to be hoped that Crowther's Lending and Security Act will not be long delayed.

### THE NEW LEGISLATIVE STRUCTURE

**[1.22]** It may be helpful if we conclude this chapter with a brief picture showing what the structure of legislation affecting credit transactions will look like when the Consumer Credit Act has been brought fully into force.

(*a*) *Licensing and enforcement*
The licensing of those carrying on a consumer credit, consumer hire or ancillary credit business will be regulated by the Consumer Credit Act, which also provides an elaborate enforcement machinery. The relevant provisions are discussed in Chapters 5 and 24.

(*b*) *Seeking business*
Advertisements of credit facilities will now be controlled not by the Advertisements (Hire-Purchase) Act 1967 (which the Consumer Credit Act repeals) but by the Consumer Credit Act itself and regulations under it. This will also regulate canvassing, the issue of quotations and other methods of obtaining business (see Chapter 6, *post*).

(*c*) *Rights of the parties* inter se
The rights of the parties to consumer credit agreements (including pledges to pawnbrokers), consumer hire agreements and linked transactions, and of sureties under contracts of guarantee and indemnity given in relation to such agreements, will be regulated by the Act and regulations, which will also control the taking and enforcement of security. All forms of consumer credit will be covered, and the Moneylenders Acts and Pawnbrokers Acts will be repealed. There is one aspect of the rights of the parties which will continue to be controlled by other legislation. Terms implied in favour of a person acquiring goods under a hire-purchase or instalment sale agreement are prescribed not by the Consumer Credit Act but by the Sale of Goods Act 1893 (in the case of sale) and the Supply of Goods (Implied Terms) Act 1973 (sale and hire-purchase). All that the Consumer Credit Act does is to give the buyer or hirer, in certain circumstances, a right to sue not only the supplier of defective goods but also a connected lender. Moreover, the security provisions of the Consumer Credit Act do not entirely displace other legislation (*e.g.* the Bills of Sale Acts and the property statutes) affecting the rights of the parties to a secured transaction.

(*d*) *Rights of third parties*
The Consumer Credit Act is not, on the whole, concerned with the impact of a hire-purchase or conditional sale agreement or security on the rights of third parties into whose hands the goods or other security

may pass. Thus, conflicts between the owner or conditional seller and one who purchases from the hirer or conditional buyer are governed by common law rules and by s. 9 of the Factors Act 1889, s. 25 (2) of the Sale of Goods Act 1893 and Part III of the Hire-Purchase Act 1964. However the Consumer Credit Act (re-enacting in this respect the provisions of the Hire-Purchase Act 1965) excludes conditional sale agreements within the Act from the scope of the above-mentioned provisions of the Factors Act and Sale of Goods Act (see Fourth Schedule, paras. 2 and 4) and also in certain circumstances excludes hire-purchase agreements and conditional sale agreements within the Act from the scope of certain provisions of the Law of Distress Amendment Act 1908 and the Bankruptcy Act 1914 (Fourth Schedule, paras. 5 and 6). In other respects, the Consumer Credit Act is silent on third party rights in relation to such agreements. Similarly, the efficacy of mortgage and other security interests *vis-á-vis* third parties, and the priority of successive security interests, continues to be governed largely by rules of common law and equity and by the Bills of Sale Acts and property statutes, though the Consumer Credit Act does have some impact in this area through various provisions dealing with ineffective securities (see Chapter 13). However, the definition of "consumer" in s. 137 (2) of the Fair Trading Act 1973 confines consumer transactions within that Act to those on which the recipient of the goods or services does not receive or seek to receive them in the course of a business carried on by him. Thus, whilst a consumer credit agreement entered into by a partnership as debtor is within the Consumer Credit Act if for credit not exceeding £5,000, it would not be a consumer transaction for the purposes of the Fair Trading Act 1973.

(*e*) *Fair trading*

The powers of the Director General of Fair Trading under Parts II and III and Schedule 6 of the Fair Trading Act 1973 remain applicable to consumer credit transactions and practices as much as to other forms of consumer trading. Indeed, in relation to consumer credit business there is a considerable overlap between the powers of the Director under the Fair Trading Act and his powers under the Consumer Credit Act.

(*f*) *Terms control*

In relation to hire-purchase and instalment sale agreements, requirements as to down-payments and maximum payment periods for certain categories of goods are prescribed by the Hire-purchase and Credit Sale Agreements (Control) Order 1973; and the Control of Hiring Order 1973 imposes in relation to hiring agreements covering designated categories of goods requirements as to advance rentals and as to the period of hire and spread of rentals over the hire period. These orders are made under the Emergency Laws (Re-enactments and Repeals) Act 1964, and operate quite independently of the Consumer Credit Act.

# CHAPTER 2

# THE STRUCTURE OF THE ACT

## THE LEGISLATIVE PROCESS

[**2.1**] A major difficulty in grappling with a substantial new enactment is to be able to see the wood for the trees, to get a picture of the structure of the statute, the ground it covers and the objectives it seeks to attain. To a considerable extent this difficulty results from our parliamentary procedure. The general principles of proposed legislation may be embodied in consultation papers distributed for comment to interested parties, but the convention of Parliament precludes publication of a Bill before it has been introduced into one of the Houses of Parliament. The result is that no opportunity for informed comment on the Bill itself is available until it has begun its journey through Parliament, and by this time the structure of the Bill has crystallised and the ability to make sensible changes is correspondingly restricted. What happens is that as the Bill proceeds, more and more weaknesses and practical difficulties come to light as a result of examination by those in business or elsewhere who are going to have to work the legislation, and since the exigencies of the parliamentary timetable do not usually permit the government to scrap the original Bill and start afresh, these deficiencies have to be dealt with by speedy *ad hoc* amendment during the passage of the Bill. All too often the result is that what started as a relatively simple, coherent structure becomes distorted by a mass of detailed drafting, losing much of its original clarity of style and orderliness of arrangement.

[**2.2**] It is a tribute to the skill of the draftsman of the Consumer Credit Act that his creation, widely praised for its lucidity and originality when the Bill was first introduced, managed to withstand the pressures of the parliamentary procedure as well as it did. Nevertheless, the Act in its final form has undoubtedly been affected by the large number of amendments found necessary after it had first been introduced. From a solid 96 pages at its inception it doubled in length, finally embodying a massive 193 sections and five schedules. The purpose of this short chapter is to strip away the foliage and provide a bird's eye view of the framework of the Act, showing its various divisions. Each of these will be examined in more detail in subsequent chapters.

## THE FRAMEWORK OF THE ACT

[**2.3**] The Act is divided into 12 parts, as follows:

Part I—Director General of Fair Trading

Part II—Credit agreements, hire agreements and linked transactions
Part III—Licensing of credit and hire businesses
Part IV—Seeking business
Part V—Entry into credit or hire agreements
Part VI—Matters arising during currency of credit or hire agreements
Part VII—Default and termination
Part VIII—Security
Part IX—Judicial control
Part X—Ancillary credit businesses
Part XI—Enforcement of Act
Part XII—Supplemental

[**2.4**] Even from this bare list of headings, a picture begins to emerge. The Act is designed to provide a comprehensive code regulating the consumer credit and consumer hire industry and almost every aspect of a credit granting operation, from advertising at one end to the consequences of default at the other. All those engaged in the business of granting consumer credit will have to be licensed, as will those carrying on various forms of ancillary credit business, such as credit brokerage and debt collecting. The licensing system will be administered by the Director General of Fair Trading (hereafter referred to as the Director), who is made responsible for overall superintendence of consumer credit and for central enforcement of the Act and regulations made under it. His functions, and those of the Weights and Measures authorities responsible to him, will be discussed more fully in Chapters 5 and 25. Strict controls are imposed on methods of seeking business—advertising, canvassing and the giving of quotations. Detailed provisions are made—and further provisions will be made by regulations—as to the form and content of consumer credit and consumer hire agreements and as to information and documents to be supplied to debtors and hirers. Rights of cancellation are given, broadly along the lines previously prescribed by the Hire-Purchase Act 1965, though with significant changes. The creditor's rights in the event of default are closely circumscribed so as to safeguard the debtor or hirer against unfairness or hardship, and various restrictions are imposed on repossession of goods and on enforcement of securities. Particularly strict are the provisions regulating the enforcement of land mortgages given to secure a regulated agreement. Finally the court is given the widest powers to control enforcement of an agreement, modify the agreement and to re-open extortionate credit bargains.

[**2.5**] In short, what the Consumer Credit Act does is to replace the previous fragmented legislation with a unified code governing all forms of consumer credit and consumer hire, with a battery of provisions for the protection of the consumer backed up by powerful enforcement machinery.

[**2.6**] It is important to remember that detailed though the Act is, it does not represent the whole story. The Act provides for a whole range of subordinate legislation and administrative controls—regulations, orders, directions, general notices and the like—to be made by the Secretary of State or the Director. The statutory instruments alone are likely to run to 70 pages or more and will need to be examined in detail as and when they are published. Fortunately, we are given a reasonably clear advance picture of the intended scope of the regulations by the White Paper previously referred to on *Reform of the Law on Consumer Credit*, the Appendices to which set out the proposed content of the regulations.

## HOW TO READ THE ACT

[**2.7**] The usual approach of a person confronted with new legislation is to begin with section 1 and to go on steadily (or otherwise!) to the end. We shall not employ that method in this book. The draftsman of an Act has reasons of his own for planning the sections in a given sequence, but the adoption of that sequence is not necessarily the best for the reader, particularly since various sections at the end of an Act have an uncomfortable habit of controlling those which appear at the beginning. For this reason, we shall not start with the first section. Instead we shall begin by discussing the scope of the Act, and will then consider a few basic definitions (for the Act creates a whole new legal terminology) before examining the forms of control which the Act imposes on the consumer credit industry and the various ways in which it seeks to protect those entering into a consumer credit or consumer hire transaction.

[**2.8**] As a preliminary we should observe two interesting features of draftsmanship. The first is the collection of definitions in s. 189. This is an extremely useful device. Section 189 not only gives definitions of its own but also indicates all the other sections in which definitions appear. When reading the Act it is essential to refer continually to s. 189, because even words that might be assumed to have a meaning that was self-evident—such as "creditor", "pre-existing arrangements", "security", and the like—are specially defined. The second interesting technique adopted by the parliamentary draftsman is the use of examples to illustrate some of the new terminology adopted in the Act. These examples are contained in the Second Schedule, and reference should be made to see what the draftsman had in mind when coining expressions (and there are several of them) that have not hitherto found place in an English statute.

[**2.9**] We may conclude this short chapter by noting that in terms of function the Consumer Credit Act falls broadly into two halves. One half contains what might be called transactional provisions, that is, provisions which come into effect on the making of an agreement and regulate the rights of the parties to the agreement. The other half is concerned with the general regulation of the consumer credit industry (through licensing, restrictions on seeking business and use of the elaborate enforcement machinery provided by the Act), without having any direct impact on specific contractual relationships. But as we shall see in the next chapter, the definition of a "regulated agreement", which goes to the heart of the Act, not only fixes the transactional boundaries of the Act but is also relevant in determining the applicability of its general regulatory provisions. The principal exceptions are the provisions relating to advertising and extortionate credit bargains, the impact of which is not limited to regulated agreements (see paras. [**6.8**], [**22.42**]).

# CHAPTER 3

# WHEN THE ACT APPLIES

### THE REGULATED AGREEMENT

[**3.1**] A basic definition is that of the **regulated agreement.** The regulated agreement is the key to an understanding of the scope of the Act. We shall discuss the meaning of "regulated agreement" shortly. Its importance lies in the fact that:

(*a*) all regulated agreements are governed by the requirements and restrictions of the Act;

(*b*) transactions linked to regulated agreements—e.g. associated sale, maintenance or insurance contracts—are affected by the Act in various ways;

(*c*) security provided in relation to regulated or linked agreements is controlled by the Act;

(*d*) those wishing to carry on the business of granting credit under regulated agreements must be licensed by the Director;

(*e*) those wishing to carry on an ancillary credit business, the definition of which is in effect tied closely to that of the regulated agreement, must be licensed by the Director.

It will be apparent, as mentioned in paragraph [**2.9**] that the definition of "regulated agreement" is relevant to the overall applicability of the Act, not merely to the operation of its transactional provisions.

[**3.2**] A regulated agreement is a consumer credit agreement or consumer hire agreement which is not an exempt agreement (ss. 189 (1), 8 (3), 15 (2)). A **consumer credit agreement** is an agreement between an individual ("the debtor") and any other person ("the creditor") by which the creditor provides the debtor with credit not exceeding £5,000. In fact, the Act does not lay out the definition of consumer credit agreement in quite this way. It starts by defining a **personal credit agreement** as an agreement between an individual ("the debtor") and any other person ("the creditor") by which the creditor provides the debtor with credit of any amount (s. 8 (1)). It then goes on to say that a consumer credit agreement is a personal credit agreement by which the creditor provides the debtor with credit not exceeding £5,000 (s. 8 (2)). The reason why the term "personal credit agreement" was introduced in the Act was that at certain points in the Act (e.g. ss. 10 and 11) it was desired as a matter of drafting to use a phrase that would denote an agreement having the characteristics of a consumer credit agreement but without the financial limitation. Hence the insertion of "personal credit agreement" is a pure drafting device. The Act is concerned only with those personal credit agreements that lie within the £5,000 ceiling and thus constitute consumer credit agreements. However, this figure may be increased or reduced by statutory instrument laid before and approved by each House of Parliament (s. 181). A **consumer hire agreement** is an agreement made by a person with an individual (the "hirer") for the bailment of goods which (*a*) is not a hire-purchase agreement and (*b*) is capable of subsisting for more than three months and (*c*) does not require the hirer to make payments exceeding £5,000 (s. 15 (1)). Again, the figure of £5,000 may be increased or reduced in the manner above mentioned. The ingredients of a consumer credit agreement and a consumer hire agreement are examined in detail below. It should not be assumed that because the Act uses the phrase "consumer credit" it is confined to domestic transactions. As we shall see, the word "consumer", if taken at face value, is misleading, since a considerable number of commercial transactions are caught by the Act. Moreover the Act is not entirely restricted in its impact to regulated agreements. In particular:

(i) the provisions of the Act also affect linked transactions, as defined by s. 19 (see Chapter 19);

(ii) all credit agreements, of whatever amount, where the debtor is an individual (as defined—see para. [**3.12**]) are subject to the provisions of the Act relating to extortionate credit bargains (see Chapter 22);

(iii) the Secretary of State is empowered to make regulations as to agreements entered into in the course of a business of credit brokerage, debt-adjusting or debt-counselling (s. 156).

[**3.3**] The consumer credit agreement and the consumer hire agreement together encompass every conceivable form of consumer credit—hire-purchase, conditional sale, credit sale, rental, check trading, credit card issuing, budget accounts, unsecured loans and overdrafts, mortgage transactions (if not exempt), pledges and indeed any form of contractual credit that one can conceive. Moreover, it is not confined to the supply of land or goods under credit arrangements; the provision of services on credit is equally within its scope (see para. [**3.9**] and Chapter 18). The term "credit" covers non-instalment as well as instalment credit. But it is intended that regulations shall be made under s. 16 (5) of the Act exempting agreements under which the credit is repayable by fewer than three instalments (see para. [**3.25**]). This will remove from the scope of the Act a large amount of account credit and at the same time render academic some of the more difficult questions arising as to the meaning of "credit" (see, for example, para. [**3.10**]).

## CONSUMER CREDIT AGREEMENT

[**3.4**] The statutory definition of consumer credit agreement embodied in s. 8 (1) of the Act possesses various ingredients each of which needs separate examination. In particular, it is necessary to determine:

(*a*) what constitutes an agreement for the provision of credit;

(*b*) what type of debtor constitutes an "individual" so as to qualify for protection under the Act;

(*c*) what categories of creditor are embodied in the phrase "any other person";
(*d*) the meaning of the phrase "credit not exceeding £5,000";
(*e*) the classes of agreement within the category of exempt agreements.

AGREEMENTS FOR THE PROVISION OF CREDIT

**[3.5]** The Act speaks of "an agreement by which the creditor provides the debtor with credit". The word "provides" is not the happiest choice, since it suggests that the financial accommodation is to be furnished at the time of the agreement, whereas it is clear that what the Act means is an agreement for the provision of credit, whether the credit is to be provided at the time of the agreement or at a later date. For the meaning of "creditor" and "debtor", see para. **[3.44]**.

**[3.6]** The word "agreement", picturesquely defined in an old case as a copulation of two or more minds, means not merely a mutual understanding but a contract, that is, an agreement which produces a legal relationship. To be within the Act, the contract need not be formal. It may be made by an exchange of letters, by word of mouth or even by implication from conduct. It need not be an enforceable contract (for example, the fact that one of the parties may not enforce it for want of a written memorandum prescribed by other legislation does not negate the existence of the contract); but it must be valid in the sense of possessing the minimum attributes required to produce a legal relationship, namely *consensus ad idem* and consideration, i.e. a *quid pro quo* for a promise, the *quid pro quo* taking the form either of a counter promise or of performance of some act.

**[3.7]** In most cases, the need to determine whether a particular form of arrangement constitutes a contract arises not so much from the Consumer Credit Act as from the desire of the parties to know where they stand as a matter of general contract law. If there is no contract the provisions of the Act as to formalities of a contract, for example, do not come into operation, but immunity from these provisions in such a case is of no importance, since *ex hypothesi* there is no enforceable agreement in any event. Unless at least one of the parties seeks to assert the existence of a contract (an issue to be resolved not by the Consumer Credit Act but by the general law of contract) the question whether there is indeed a contract on which the Consumer Credit Act can bite is largely academic. Nevertheless, for certain purposes it may be important to determine whether a particular arrangement generates a contract so as to give rise to a regulated agreement. For example, if a bank agrees to give a customer an overdraft facility up to a stated figure and the customer subsequently draws a cheque which takes his overdraft over the agreed limit, does the bank's decision to honour the cheque constitute a separate agreement which requires compliance with the formalities of the Act in order to be enforceable or is it merely a voluntary waiver (as regards that particular cheque) of the credit limit fixed when the facility was opened? The answer to this particular question is to be found partly in banking law and partly in the Consumer Credit Act itself and is given in paragraph **[3.22]**; but the question suffices to make the point that it may be necessary for the purposes of the Consumer Credit Act, as well as of general contract law, to determine whether a particular act or series of acts constitutes a contract. What is regulated by the transactional provisions of the Act is not the provision of credit as such but the provision of credit *under an agreement*. The question is whether the prospective creditor has bound himself to give credit, not whether the prospective debtor has bound himself to take it. Indeed, an agreement by a prospective debtor to enter into a regulated agreement is void (s. 59 (1)), though a mere option to him to take credit is outside s. 59, even though binding the prospective creditor. The provision of a line of credit constitutes a credit agreement if the lender has committed himself to giving this facility, whether or not the borrower chooses to use it (but see para. [**7.3**] as to the problem of rate disclosure in such a case). On the other hand, a mere letter of intent indicating a willingness to provide a line of credit or other facility without commitment is not a credit agreement.

[**3.8**] We must now turn to the word "credit". Section 9 (1) provides that "credit" includes a cash loan and any other form of financial accommodation. "Cash" includes money in any form (s. 189 (1)). Section 9 (3) makes it clear that without prejudice to the generality of s. 9 (1) a person letting goods on hire-purchase is to be taken to provide the hirer with credit. The purpose of s. 9 (3), which is set out in full a little later, is to avoid a possible argument that hire-purchase is not credit since the hirer is merely hiring goods, with an option to buy, and is paying the hire-rent as he goes along, so that there is no deferred indebtedness generating credit. Section 9 (3) effectively shuts out an argument along these lines.

[**3.9**] The words "any other form of financial accommodation" are extremely wide. They cover all the forms of credit described in paragraph [**3.3**] except the pure rental (or leasing or hiring) agreement, which falls within the separate definition of "consumer hire agreement" and does not involve (in law, at any rate) the extension of credit. But extensive though the connotation of the term "credit" may be, it is not without limit. The facility must be *financial*; it must be in the nature of "accommodation"; and, for the Act to apply to the transaction, it must be provided under an agreement. A provision to make a gift is not within the Act, nor is the gift itself. Neither of these constitutes a contract (since there is no consideration) and in any event the words "financial accommodation" imply financial assistance on terms of repayment, either in cash or in kind. An agreement for exchange, or barter, is not a credit agreement since no *financial* accommodation is involved. On the other hand, an instalment sale in which there is a part exchange does create a financial accommodation, for the primary obligation of the buyer is to pay a money price, and even though part of this is satisfied by delivery of the part exchange goods, there remains a money balance in respect of which the seller's agreement to defer payment constitutes an extension of credit. An agreement for the provision of services to be provided on a single occasion and paid for in arrear is a credit agreement. An agreement to provide continuing services which the debtor pays for at periodic intervals (for example, car hire or television rental) is a credit agreement if the charge for the services for each payment period is payable in arrear, but not if payable in advance. But even agreements for services to be paid for in arrear will be made exempt if payment is to be by fewer than three instalments (see para. [**3.25**]).

[**3.10**] The offer of a line of credit has been dealt with earlier (para. [**3.7**]). More difficult is the question whether accommodation by way of guarantee constitutes credit. If, for example, a bank agrees to lend its name to a bill for the accommodation of its customer, or to honour a cheque under a cheque guarantee card or to enter into some other form of guarantee at the customer's request, is this a form of financial accommodation for the purpose of the Consumer Credit Act? It is thought that the answer is no. The Act deals separately with suretyship agreements, which are embraced in the term "security instrument" and constitute a "security" as defined by s. 189 (1). It is scarcely likely that the Act intended that one and the same obligation should constitute at the same time a granting of credit and a security for repayment of such credit, particularly since consumer credit agreements and security instruments are separately regulated by the Act (see further para. [**3.11**]). In any event, the intended exemption of non-instalment credit agreements by regulations under s. 16 (5) of the Act (see para. [**3.25**]) will for the most part make the question academic.

[**3.11**] It is necessary to distinguish an agreement for the provision of credit from an agreement securing the debtor's obligations under a separate credit agreement. Frequently the agreement to extend credit and the security for repayment are embodied in the same document, but this will not necessarily be the case, a fact recognised in s. 105 of the Act. Unless it is the security instrument itself which provides for the extension of credit, such instrument will not be governed by the provisions of the Act applicable to regulated agreements, though it will, of course, be subject to those parts of the Act relating to security instruments. Let us take the case of a bank loan to an individual customer secured by deposit of the title deeds of the customer's house, on terms embodied in a memorandum of deposit. Under normal banking practice prior to the Consumer Credit Act, the credit agreement would have been made orally (though no doubt confirmed by letter), and the memorandum of deposit would simply have recorded a deposit by the customer of his title deeds, by way of equitable mortgage to secure sums due and owing to the bank, incorporating various obligations, including an undertaking to execute a legal charge if so required. Such a memorandum of deposit would not, under the Act, be a regulated agreement, nor would a legal charge executed pursuant to the undertaking in the memorandum of deposit. The reason is that neither of these instruments represents the agreement by which the credit was provided. As a result of the Act, it will no longer be possible for the credit facility in a regulated transaction to remain oral. If the terms of the credit facility are embodied in some document separate from the memorandum of deposit, then as before the memorandum of deposit will be a security instrument and not a credit agreement for the purpose of the Act. If however the memorandum of deposit were to incorporate the terms of the advance it would constitute both a regulated agreement and a security instrument under the Act; but a legal charge subsequently executed pursuant to an undertaking in the memorandum of deposit would, as before, be a security instrument only, not a regulated agreement, and would thus not be subject to the provisions of the Act relating to regulated agreements. The point is of importance not only on this count but also because of the provisions of s. 59 rendering an agreement void if and to the extent that it purports to bind a person as debtor or hirer to enter into a prospective regulated agreement. An agreement to execute a legal charge securing obligations under that or some prior consumer credit agreement is not caught by s. 59, since the legal charge is not a regulated agreement.

"INDIVIDUAL"; "PERSON"

**[3.12]** "Individual" is defined in s. 189 (1) as including a partnership or other unincorporated body of persons not consisting entirely of bodies corporate. Hence the only type of debtor excluded from the protection of the Act is a body corporate, that is, an association or body constituting a distinct legal entity and having perpetual succession and a common seal. Companies registered under the Companies Acts are bodies corporate, as are corporations created by royal charter or by special Act of Parliament (including public corporations like the B.B.C. and London Transport) and corporations sole, such as bishops and certain Ministers of the Crown. A registered industrial or provident society is by virtue of its registration a body corporate (Industrial and Provident Societies Act 1965, s. 3) and is thus not protected by the Consumer Credit Act. On the other hand, friendly societies and trade unions (whether registered or not) are not bodies corporate and each of these qualifies as an "individual" for the purpose of the Act. The word "individual" likewise covers an unincorporated club and an unincorporated charity. Except where s. 16 of the Act (relating to exempted agreements) applies, it is only the status of the *debtor* that is relevant in determining whether the Act is applicable. The Act bites on credit agreements between "an individual" as debtor and "any other person" as creditor; and by s. 19 of the Interpretation Act 1889 "person", unless a contrary intention appears, includes any body of persons corporate or unincorporate, and thus embraces individuals, partnerships and other unincorporated associations, bodies corporate and indeed every form of entity known to the law. Even a debtor which is a body corporate is protected by the Consumer Credit Act if joined as debtor with an individual in a consumer credit agreement (s. 185 (5)).

"CREDIT NOT EXCEEDING £5,000"

**[3.13]** The Act is restricted to agreements under which the credit to be provided does not exceed £5,000. The meaning of the phrase "credit not exceeding £5,000" is by no means as simple as it appears, and indeed may cover some transactions where there is no credit limit at all (see para. **[3.19]** *et seq.*). Where credit is provided otherwise than in sterling it is to be treated for the purposes of the Act as provided in sterling of equivalent amount (s. 9 (2)).

**[3.14]** The word "credit" denotes the amount of the loan or other financial accommodation extended, not the amount which the debtor has to repay. Hence interest and credit charges do not form part of the credit. The amount of fixed-sum credit (as opposed to revolving credit) is relatively easy to calculate. In the case of a loan, the credit will be the amount of the loan. In the case of a hire-purchase agreement, s. 9 (3) provides that the amount of the credit shall be taken as the total price of the goods less the aggregate of the deposit (if any) and the total charge for credit. This would also be the case (though the Act does not say so in terms) as regards conditional sale and credit sale agreements.

"Deposit" means any sum payable by a debtor or hirer by way of deposit or down-payment, or credited or to be credited to him on account of any deposit or down-payment, whether the sum is to be or has been paid to the creditor or owner or any other person, or is to be or has been discharged by a payment of money or a transfer or delivery of goods or by any other means (s. 189 (1)). A check trading transaction involves credit to an amount equal to the total value of the trading checks supplied under the agreement made between the check trader and the debtor, less any down-payment required by the check trader.

[**3.15**] It will have been seen from the preceding paragraph that whereas under the Hire-Purchase Act 1965 the ceiling figure of £2,000 was fixed by reference to the hire-purchase price or total purchase price, the relevant figure for the purpose of the Consumer Credit Act is the amount of the advance. Thus in determining whether a hire-purchase or credit sale agreement is within the Act one must exclude the down-payment and charges and look only at the amount by which the total purchase price exceeds the aggregate of the deposit and the total charge for credit. If this difference does not exceed £5,000, the transaction is within the statutory ceiling. Hence the increase in scope of the legislation is much greater than a mere jump from £2,000 to £5,000.

[**3.16**] The rule that the credit charge is excluded in computing the amount of the credit applies whether the charge is an add-on charge or is a discount deducted at the outset from the agreed amount of the loan. Thus, on a loan of £500 repayable with interest of £100 by 12 instalments of £50, the credit is £500. The interest of £100 is not part of the credit. If a lender makes an advance of £500 for a year at a discount of 10 per cent. deductible at the outset, the real amount of the loan, representing the amount of the credit for the purpose of the Consumer Credit Act, is £450, and the remaining £50 is the credit charge. Hence if in this case the borrower gives a post-dated cheque for £500, care must be taken not to treat the face value of the cheque as the amount of the credit since it includes a £50 interest charge which must be excluded in computing the credit. (Instruments other than a cheque are prohibited— see s. 123 and para. [**13.33**].)

[**3.17**] Section 9 (4) of the Act provides that for the purpose of the Act an item entering into the total charge for credit shall not be treated as credit even though time is allowed for its payment. Hence where the debtor's total commitment under the loan contract exceeds £5,000, it is important to know what part of this constitutes the credit charge, since this must be excluded in computing the credit (the total charge for credit is also relevant to the calculation of the cost of borrowing as a percentage rate—see Appendix A). By "total charge for credit" is meant a sum calculated in accordance with regulations made under s. 20 (1) of the Act (s. 189 (1)). Such regulations will prescribe (*inter alia*) what items are to be treated as entering into the total charge for credit and how their amount is to be ascertained. Paragraph 28 of the White Paper, as expanded by paragraphs 10.1–10.3 of Appendix II to the White Paper, indicates the manner in which the regulations will define the total charge for credit. Included in this sum will be not only the element stated as interest but all other compulsory charges imposed by the lender as a condition of granting the credit. These will include even charges for ancillary services under separate contracts (*e.g.* of maintenance or insurance), whether with the creditor himself or with a third party, if entry into these contracts is compulsory and the debtor is not allowed to choose his own supplier of the services in question. However, charges that would also be imposed on cash customers would not qualify as part of the charge for credit (see White Paper, Appendix II, para. 10.2.1), since obviously in such a case the charge arises independently of the credit facility. Thus, value added tax is not part of the total charge for credit. Indeed, it would be outside the charge quite independently of the above exemption, since it forms part of the consideration for the supply (Finance Act 1972, s. 10 (2)) and is thus part of the cash price. But value added tax on charges is part of the charge for credit.

[**3.18**] The effect of s. 9 (4), and of the intended definition of "total charge for credit", on the computation of the credit is illustrated by the following example.

A finance house lets goods on hire-purchase at a hire-purchase price of £8,650 made up as follows:

| | |
|---|---|
| Cash price, including VAT | £7,500 |
| Insurance premium under compulsory insurance with company nominated by finance house | £150 |
| Charges | £1,000 |
| Total | £8,650 |

The required down payment is £2,500.

The credit is £5,000, *i.e.* £8,650 — (£2,500 + £1,150). The agreement is therefore a regulated consumer credit agreement within the Consumer Credit Act since the credit does not exceed £5,0000. The total charge for credit is £1,150, *i.e.* £1,000 plus the insurance premium of £150. The insurance premium is part of the *charge* for credit and does not form part of the credit itself (even if not paid direct to the insurance company but given the debtor to enable him to pay the insurance company himself), despite the fact that it represents an amount laid out in the first instance by the finance house and included in the total figure repayable by instalments. The position would be otherwise if entry into the insurance contract were voluntary or if, though the insurance were compulsory, the buyer were left free to choose his own insurer. In either such case, the premium would then form part of the credit, making the amount of the credit £5,150 and thereby placing the agreement outside the Consumer Credit Act.

[**3.19**] So far, we have confined ourselves to *fixed-sum credit*. Special provisions apply to *running-account credit*. This is defined in s. 10 (1) and illustrated in examples 15, 16, 18 and 23 in the Second Schedule to the Act. In essence it means a revolving credit, that is a credit which entitles the debtor to make drawings up to an agreed credit limit on the basis that, whilst each drawing on the account reduces the credit available, the credit is *pro tanto* restored by payments which the debtor makes in reduction of the debt. Within this category are revolving loan accounts (such as overdrafts), credit card arrangements and store budget accounts. It is necessary for the Act to deal separately with running-account credit because, in contrast to fixed-sum credit, the amount of the credit which will actually be utilised is not known at the outset, since this depends on the extent to which the debtor chooses to draw on his account. Section 10 (3) of the Act provides that these running-account credit transactions will be deemed within the £5,000 ceiling if:

(*a*) the credit limit does not exceed £5,000 (for the definition of "credit limit", see para. [**3.22**], below); or

(*b*) whether or not there is a credit limit, and if there is, notwithstanding that it exceeds £5,000

(i) the debtor is not enabled to draw at any one time an amount, which, so far as (having regard to s. 9 (3)) it represents credit, exceeds £5,000, or

(ii) the agreement provides that, if the debit balance rises above a given amount (not exceeding £5,000), the rate of the total charge for credit increases or any other condition favouring the creditor or his associate comes into operation, or

(iii) at the time the agreement is made it is probable, having regard to the terms of the agreement and any other relevant considerations, that the debit balance will not at any time rise above £5,000.

But if an agreement contains a term signifying that in the opinion of the parties section 10 (3) (*b*) (iii) does not apply to the agreement, it is to be taken not to apply unless the contrary is proved (s. 171 (1)).

[**3.20**] The three categories listed in (*b*) above require some explanation. Category (i) is reasonably clear. If at any time the debtor cannot draw more than £5,000, the agreement is within the Act, however high the credit limit. In deciding whether the debtor can draw more than £5,000 at any one time, one must exclude such part of the permitted drawing as represents an item in the total charge for credit, *e.g.* sums payable under compulsory maintenance or insurance contracts as described in paragraphs [**3.17**]–[**3.18**]. In many cases, this point will not arise in relation to drawings by the debtor, since the sums payable under the contract in question will be paid direct by the lender to the supplier of the maintenance service or the insurance company, and category (i) is concerned with the character of drawings by the debtor, not payments by the lender. Even if the lender is to pay such amounts direct to the borrower himself, leaving him to pay the servicing or insurance company, it is unlikely that a stipulation as to the amount of the drawing at any one time will distinguish between the loan element and the credit charge element. Categories (ii) and (iii) are designed to prevent evasion and to ensure that a stated credit limit in excess of £5,000 is not illusory. Where the agreement provides for the rate of the credit charge to increase, or for any other condition favouring the creditor or his associate (as defined by s. 184) to come into operation, if the debit balance rises above £5,000 or any lower figure, the credit will be deemed not to exceed £5,000. Notice that an agreement providing for an increase in interest if drawings exceed £5,000 is still within the financial ceiling of the Act. It is not sufficient to allow the debtor to draw up to £5,000 without an increase in interest rate. If application of the Act is to be avoided, he must be allowed to draw at least some amount (however small) in excess of £5,000 without alteration of the terms in favour of the creditor. If the increase in interest rate does not become operative until the overdraft exceeds £5,001 then the agreement is taken outside category (ii). If the boundary is fixed at exactly £5,000, the agreement remains governed by the Act. Category (iii) (which *prima facie* does not apply if the agreement includes a term signifying that in the opinion of the parties it is inapplicable—s. 171 (1)) is illustrated by example 7 in the Second Schedule to the Act.

*Example 7*

*Facts:* J is an individual who owns a small shop which usually carries a stock worth about £1,000. K makes a stocking agreement under which he undertakes to provide on short-term credit the stock needed from time to time by J without any specified limit.

*Analysis:* Although the agreement appears to provide unlimited credit it is probable, having regard to the stock usually carried by J, that his indebtedness to K will not at any time rise above £5,000. Accordingly the agreement falls within s. 10 (3) (b) (iii) and is a consumer credit agreement.

[**3.21**] In many cases, no difficulty will arise in relation to category (iii) The problem area is in the provision of running-account credit for a debtor whose drawings are likely to be near the £5,000 boundary. The wording of s. 10 (3) indicates that the presumption is in favour of the creditor—i.e. the onus is on the debtor to show that, though the credit limit exceeds £5,000, the agreement falls within category (iii) because of the probability that the debit balance would not at any time rise above £5,000. For this purpose, the probability has to be tested as at the time the agreement is made, not in the light of subsequent events. In so providing s. 10 (3) (*b*) (iii) avoids the inconvenient result that a single running-account credit agreement (and for the purpose of the Act there is a single agreement when the facility is first opened, not a series of agreements constituted by the separate drawings) would be within the Act one day, outside it the next and back within it a few days later, depending on the probability from day to day of the future debit balance. Hence the section provides in effect that if, at the time the facility was opened with a credit limit in excess of £5,000, there was no probability that the debit balance would be restricted to £5,000, the agreement will be outside the Act regardless of the fact that the debtor's regular utilisation of the facility subsequently drops down to or below the £5,000 ceiling. Such a situation is not within the mischief against which s. 10 (3) of the Act is aimed.

[**3.22**] By s. 10 (2), "credit limit" means, as respects any period, the maximum debit balance which, under the credit agreement, is allowed to stand on the account during that period, disregarding any term of the agreement allowing that maximum to be exceeded merely temporarily. The words referring to the maximum debit balance being temporarily exceeded were apparently inserted to meet the wish of the banks to clarify the effect of a bank deciding to honour a cheque drawn by its customer in excess of the previously agreed credit limit. If, when the account is first opened providing for a limit of £5,000, there is a term of the agreement permitting this limit to be temporarily exceeded, such provision will not take the agreement outside the Consumer Credit Act. In practice, this situation will rarely arise, since the typical case—and that to which the banks were drawing attention—is the temporary excess drawing which has not previously been arranged but which the bank, to protect its customer's credit, decides to honour, on the basis that it will then ask its customer to take prompt steps to bring his overdraft down to the agreed limit. However, as the result of other provisions of the Act, s. 10 (2) also applies to this latter situation. It is generally accepted as a matter of banking law that the drawing of a cheque by a customer in excess of an agreed limit constitutes a request to the bank to honour the cheque, in consideration of payment of normal overdraft charges. This request represents an offer which the bank accepts by payment of the cheque, thus giving rise to a new agreement varying the original overdraft agreement. Under s. 82 (2) this latter agreement has the effect of revoking the original agreement and combining its provisions with those of the new agreement, so that in effect there is a single new agreement providing for an overdraft limit, with a temporary excess above that limit. Although this excess is for a fixed amount, s. 18 (5) provides that the term permitting the temporary excess is not to be treated as a separate agreement or as providing fixed-sum credit in respect of the excess. The result is that s. 10 (2) operates in relation to the new agreement as a single agreement for running-account credit, and despite payment of a cheque which takes the customer's overdraft above £5,000, the credit limit is deemed to remain at £5,000 and the entire overdraft agreement (as notionally reconstituted under s. 82 (2)) is within the Act, though it does not again attract the provisions of Part V, other than s. 56 (see s. 82 (4) and para. [**4.19**]

EXEMPT CONSUMER CREDIT AGREEMENTS

[**3.23**] Certain agreements that would otherwise fall within the definition of regulated agreement are designated as exempt agreements. The following paragraphs deal with exempt consumer credit agreements. Exempt consumer hire agreements are dealt with in paragraph [**3.28**]. An exempt agreement is defined by s. 189 (1) as an agreement specified in or under s. 16. Such agreements are not regulated by the Act, except for the provisions of ss. 137–140 relating to extortionate credit bargains, which apply even to exempt agreements (s. 16 (6)). There are other categories of agreement which, though regulated and not exempt, are excluded from certain Parts or provisions of the Act. These are mentioned in paragraph [**3.29**].

[**3.24**] The first category of exempt consumer credit agreement embraces agreements secured by a land mortgage in favour of a local authority or building society (as defined in s. 189 (1)) or in favour of such other class of creditor listed in s. 16 (1) of the Act as may be specified by an order made by the Secretary of State. "Land mortgage" includes any security charged on land (s. 189 (1)) and thus embraces a rent charge. The classes listed in s. 16 (1), in relation to which the Secretary of State may make an order, are insurance companies, friendly societies, organisations of employers or of workers, charities and land improvement companies (each, except for organisations of employers or workers, is defined in s. 189 (1)), and bodies corporate named or specifically referred to in any public general Act, *e.g.* the Commission for the New Towns, the Agricultural Mortgage Corporation and the White Fish Authority. The public utilities, such as the Gas and Electricity Boards, would also come within this last group, but those that do not extend credit on the security of land are unlikely to be included in any order made under s. 16 (1). See further paragraph [**5.5**]. If the mortgage is taken to secure an advance for the purchase of land or provision of dwellings on land which is extended by the vendor or provider or by another pursuant to, or in contemplation of, arrangements, with the vendor or provider, then in order for the agreement to be exempt it must be secured on that land, not on some other land (s. 16 (2) (*a*)). Similarly, if it is to finance a linked transaction geared to the purchase of land in the manner provided by s. 16 (2) (*c*), it must be secured on the land purchased. Section 16 (2) (*c*) is obscure to the point of unintelligibility and was evidently inserted to cover the situation of an additional building society purchase-money advance on the security of an insurance company bond. In any case other than those above mentioned, the mortgage be secured on any land, may whether or not it is land that was purchased with the mortgage money and indeed even if the mortgage money was not utilised for the purchase of land at all. In practice, almost all local authority or building society mortgage transactions within the £5,000 ceiling will be exempt agreements for the purpose of s. 16 (1).

[**3.25**] By s. 16 (5) the Secretary of State may also provide by order that the Act shall not regulate other consumer credit agreements where:

(*a*) the number of payments to be made by the debtor does not exceed the number specified for that purpose in the order, or

(*b*) the rate of the total charge for credit does not exceed the rate so specified, or

(*c*) an agreement has a connection with a country outside the United Kingdom.

The proposed scope of the exemptions is dealt with in paragraph 21 of the White Paper. Exemptions under category (*a*) will be given where the credit is linked to the sale of goods or services and payment is to be made in less than three instalments, excluding any down-payment. This will exclude (*inter alia*) ordinary account credit given by a supplier. So the monthly account for milk or newspapers will be taken out of the Act, as will ordinary trade credit. Exemptions under category (*b*) will be given where the credit charge is 10 per cent. or less and the credit is not linked to the purchase of goods or services from a seller having a business connection with the lender. Category (*c*) was added to cover cases of difficulty arising from the possible application of the Act to international transactions *e.g.* a purchase abroad with a credit card issued by a United Kingdom bank.

## CONSUMER HIRE AGREEMENTS

[**3.26**] The statutory definition of a consumer hire agreement was set out in paragraph [**3.2**]. It possesses four essential ingredients. First, it must relate to goods let as such. A lease of land together with goods in consideration of a single rental issuing out of the land (as in the case of a furnished letting) is not a consumer hire agreement (see para. [**4.19**]). Secondly the agreement must not be a hire-purchase agreement. This means that it must not confer on the hirer an option to buy the goods (see the definition of "hire-purchase agreement" in s. 189 (1)). Thirdly, it must be capable of subsisting for more than three months. This characteristic is fulfilled by any hiring agreement other than a hiring agreement for a fixed term not exceeding three months with no option to either party to renew beyond the three month period. If the agreement is for an indeterminate period (*e.g.* is a periodic hiring such as from week to week or month to month until terminated by a prescribed period of notice) or if it is for a fixed period not exceeding three months but an option to renew beyond the three months is given to one party or the other, the hiring is capable of subsisting for more than three months for the purpose of s. 15. Fourthly, to be a consumer hire agreement within the Act the agreement must not require the hirer to make payments exceeding £5,000. To see whether this condition is fulfilled one looks at the hirer's minimum legal commitment, taking account of any contractual right given to the hirer to terminate the agreement. If the hirer can limit his commitment to £5,000 (e.g. by exercising a power of termination before more than £5,000 rentals have accrued due) the agreement is a regulated agreement (given fulfilment of the other two conditions) even if the hirer has power to incur a total rental liability exceeding £5,000 by exercising a right to renew the agreement or by declining to exercise a contractual right of termination that would restrict his liability to £5,000.

[**3.27**] In computing the hirer's minimum rental liability, the statutory right of termination conferred by s. 101 must be ignored, since that section does not come into operation until it has first been established that the hiring agreement is a consumer hire agreement within the statutory definition. This point is brought out by the parliamentary draftsman in example 20 in the Second Schedule.

EXEMPT CONSUMER HIRE AGREEMENTS

[**3.28**] By s. 16 (6) of the Act the Secretary of State is empowered to provide by order that the Act shall not apply to consumer hire agreements of a description specified in the order where:

(*a*) the owner is a body corporate authorised by or under any enactment to supply electricity, gas or water; and

(*b*) the subject of the agreement is a meter or metering equipment or where the owner is the Post Office or the Kingston-upon-Hull City Council.

The reference to the Kingston-upon-Hull Council arises because the Council operates its own telephone system.

PARTIALLY REGULATED AGREEMENTS

[**3.29**] A consumer credit or consumer hire agreement which is not an exempt agreement under s. 16 is regulated by the Act; but certain classes of regulated agreement are exempt from certain specific provisions of the Act. Into this category fall small agreements (para. [**3.30**]); non-commercial agreements (para. [**3.33**]); multiple agreements (para. [**3.35**]); certain purchase-money land mortgages (see Chapter 8); agreements for overdrafts (para. [**3.37**]); and pledges of documents of title (para. [**3.38**]). A separate chapter is devoted to the important topic of linked transactions (Chapter 19).

SMALL AGREEMENTS

[**3.30**] There are special provisions as to small agreements. As defined by s. 17, these are regulated consumer credit agreements where the credit does not exceed £30 and regulated consumer hire agreements which do not require the hirer to make payments exceeding £30. There are three qualifications. The definition does not embrace conditional sale or hire-purchase agreements. These do not qualify as small agreements, however small the credit. Secured transactions are likewise outside the definition, except where the security is limited to a guarantee or indemnity. In this connection, the wide definition of "security" in s. 189 (1) should be noted. Finally, the provisions of the Act cannot be evaded by the device of breaking up a transaction involving credit over £30 into two or more small agreements between the same parties at or about the same time, or by arranging that part of the transaction is split off into a separate agreement which, though not between the same parties, substitutes for either party an associate of that party, as defined by clause 184 (see s. 17 (3), (4)).

[**3.31**] In determining whether an agreement is a small agreement within s. 17 the figure to be taken (except in the case of consumer hire agreements) is the amount of the credit. This has been dealt with in detail earlier in this chapter, but may be tabulated as follows:

| *Nature of Agreement* | *Figure to be Taken* |
|---|---|
| Credit sale | Total price less deposit and charges |
| Credit card | Credit limit |
| Check trading | Face value of checks less down-payment |
| Unsecured loan | Amount of loan, excluding components of credit charge |

In the case of consumer hire agreements, the total amount to be paid by the hirer must not exceed £30. This would appear to exclude from the small agreement category consumer hire agreements for an indefinite period (*e.g.* weekly or monthly), however low the periodic rental, and consumer hire agreements for a fixed period under which, though the total rent for the period cannot exceed £30, one party has an option to renew for a further period or periods which may take the total rental above £30.

[**3.32**] Small agreements (of which illustrations are given in examples 16, 17 and 22 in the Second Schedule to the Act) enjoy exemption from the whole of Part V of the Act, except ss. 55 and 56, where the agreements are debtor-creditor-supplier agreements for restricted-use credit (s. 74 (2)). These terms are explained in paragraphs [**4.7**] *et seq.* Suffice it to say at this stage that within this exemption fall, for example, small credit sale, check trading and credit card transactions. All these are exempt from the formalities of contract (other than disclosure requirements prescribed by regulations under s. 55) and from the cooling off provisions. In addition, the duty to supply a copy of the executed agreement and any document referred to in it on issue of a new credit token (s. 85 (1)) does not apply in relation to a small agreement of any kind (s. 85 (3)). Further, a creditor under a small agreement is not affected by ss. 78 (4) and (5) relating to the automatic duty to supply periodic statements of account (see s. 78 (7)). On the other hand, small agreements remain controlled by the provisions of Part IV of the Act regulating the seeking of business (see Chapter 6) and by the provisions requiring the creditor or owner to supply information to the debtor or hirer on request (ss. 77, 78). Moreover, the restrictions on remedies for default, including termination, apply to small agreements, which are likewise governed by the whole of Part IX of the Act, relating to judicial control and the re-opening of extortionate credit bargains.

### NON-COMMERCIAL AGREEMENTS

[**3.33**] The transactional provisions of the Consumer Credit Act are primarily aimed at the trader or other professional credit grantor. Accordingly many of the statutory provisions are made inapplicable to a non-commercial agreement, that is, a consumer credit or consumer hire agreement not made by the creditor or owner in the course of a business carried on by him (s. 189 (1)). A person is not to be treated as carrying on a particular type of business merely because occasionally he enters into transactions belonging to a business of that type (s. 189 (2)). It would appear that the onus of proof that an agreement is a non-commercial agreement lies on the party asserting it.

[**3.34**] Non-commercial agreements are exempt from Part V of the Act, other than s. 56 (see s. 74 (1)) and thus are not governed by any formal requirements or by the cooling off provisions. The creditor under a non-commercial agreement cannot incur any liability under s. 75 (1) (see s. 75 (3)). In other words, he does not, in Crowther terms, incur the liability of a connected lender. He is also exempt from the duty to supply information to the debtor or a surety under ss. 77–79 and 107–110 of the Act. Normally the debtor under a regulated agreement which requires him to keep goods to which the agreement relates in his possession or control must supply the creditor with information as to their whereabouts after receipt of a written request (s. 80 (1)); but this duty is excluded in the case of a non-commercial agreement. Other provisions of the Act inapplicable to non-commercial agreements are ss. 40 (1), 82, 103, 112 and 114. Moreover, although the Act does not say so directly, a creditor whose activity is restricted to granting credit under non-commercial agreements need not be licensed, since it follows from the definition of a non-commercial agreement (see para. [**3.33**]) that he is not carrying on a consumer credit or consumer hire business.

### MULTIPLE AGREEMENTS

[**3.35**] These are agreements which for one reason or another fall into more than one category under the Act. So far, we have examined regulated consumer credit and consumer hire agreements, exempt agreements, small agreements and non-commercial agreements, and have briefly commented on the distinction between fixed-sum and running-account credit. But this by no means exhausts the statutory classification, our survey of which is completed in the next chapter, where we shall be better placed to understand the effect of the provisions of s. 18 relating to multiple agreements.

PURCHASE-MONEY LAND MORTGAGES

**[3.36]** Certain types of purchase-money land mortgage are exempted from some of the statutory provisions. These are dealt with in Chapter 8.

OVERDRAFTS

**[3.37]** Debtor-creditor agreements for overdrafts are exempted from Part V of the Act (except s. 56) where the Director so determines (s. 74 (1) (*b*), (3)). Such determination may be made subject to such conditions as the Director thinks fit, but may not be made unless the Director is of opinion that it is not against the interests of debtors (s. 74 (3)). Any determination made under this provision may be revoked or varied by the Director if he thinks fit (s. 183). See further paragraph [**25.6**].

PLEDGES OF DOCUMENTS OF TITLE

**[3.38]** Sections 114–122, relating to pledges, do not apply to pledges of documents of title (s. 114 (3)). The phrase "documents of title" is not defined but in this context denotes documents of title to goods (see para. [**13.22**]). Whereas documents of title to land are documents indicative of ownership, this is not necessarily so in the case of a document of title to goods. It suffices that it is a document used in the ordinary course of business as proof of the possession or control of goods or as authorising (by delivery with any necessary indorsement) the holder of the document to transfer or receive the goods represented by it (see *Ramdas Vithaldas Durbur* v. *S. Amerchand & Co.* (1916), 85 L.J.P.C. 244, at p. 216; and *cf.* Factors Act 1889, s. 1 (4)). A bill of lading is a document of title to the goods represented by it, so long as the goods remain under the shipowner's control, even though the goods have arrived at the port of destination and have been received from the ship into a warehouse (*Barclays Bank Ltd.* v. *Customs and Excise Commissioners*, [1963] 1 Lloyd's Rep. 81). A letter of trust, or trust receipt, taken by a bank as a condition of releasing pledged documents of title is indicative of the bank's continued control of the goods but is not, it is thought, a document of title since it is not ordinarily transferred by indorsement or delivery and the goods remain represented by the bill of lading released against the trust receipt. A delivery order has in one case been held a document of title (*Ant. Jurgens Margarinefabrieken* v. *Louis Dreyfus & Co.*, [1914] 3 K.B. 40) but the reasoning is untenable and the decision can be justified only on the basis that the delivery order in question was indorsed by the warehouse and handed to the intended transferee, so that it became analogous to a warrant by the warehouse itself (see, for example, *Laurie and Morewood* v. *John Dudin & Sons*, [1925] 2 K.B. 383). Even a warehouse or dock warrant or receipt will not usually be considered a document of title unless the warehouse or dock company is created by special Act of Parliament which provides that its warrants are to constitute documents of title, as in the case of the Port of London and the Mersey Docks. A car registration book is not a document of title (*Joblin* v. *Watkin and Roseveare (Motors) Ltd*, [1949] 1 All E.R. 47; *Pearson* v. *Rose & Young, Ltd.*, [1951] 1 K.B. 275; [1950] 2 All E.R. 1027, nor is an invoice or a certificate of completion of a hire-purchase agreement.

HIRE-PURCHASE AND CONDITIONAL SALE AGREEMENTS

**[3.39]** Within the classification previously discussed, and elaborated in the next chapter, the statutory provisions apply across the whole field of consumer credit, so that in the main no distinctive significance attaches to hire-purchase and conditional sale agreements as such, and in the greater part of the Act these forms of contract do not receive specific mention. There are, however, provisions which apply exclusively to hire-purchase and conditional sale agreements. Thus (i) they are excluded from the definition of "small agreement" (s. 17 (1)); (ii) only goods comprised in a hire-purchase or conditional sale agreement can become protected goods so as to attract the prohibition in s. 90 (re-enacting the Hire-Purchase Act 1965, s. 34) against repossession without a court order; (iii) prohibition of entry into premises for the purpose of repossessing goods is confined to goods comprised in a hire-purchase or conditional sale agreement (s. 92 (1)); (iv) special provisions (re-enacting those of the Hire-Purchase Act 1965) give a hirer on hire-purchase and a buyer on conditional sale a right to terminate the agreement (s. 99), restrict his liability on termination (s. 100), regulate the powers of the court (s. 133) and deal with proof of adverse detention (s. 134).

[**3.40**] "Hire-purchase agreement" is defined in s. 189 (1) in terms rather wider than those of s. 1 (1) of the Hire-Purchase Act 1965, fully analysed in the author's work *Hire-Purchase Law and Practice* (2nd edn.), pp. 54–60. In particular, a provision in the agreement for the passing of the property to the hirer suffices to make the agreement a hire-purchase agreement even if the event stipulated as causing the property to pass is not the voluntary act of the owner or hirer but the happening of some other specified event. Hence the type of agreement which the court in *R.* v. *R. W. Proffitt Ltd.*, [1954] 2 Q.B. 35; [1954] 2 All E.R. 798 declined to hold a hire-purchase agreement would fall within the new statutory definition. The meaning of "conditional sale agreement" is the same as in s. 1 (1) of the Hire-Purchase Act 1965, except that it is no longer confined to goods but extends to land.

CONTRACTS WITH A FOREIGN ELEMENT

[**3.41**] As a rule, United Kingdom legislation is construed so as to avoid giving it extra-territorial effect. One might, therefore, expect that the Consumer Credit Act would be held inapplicable to transactions concluded abroad. However, the width of the Act, and the provisions relating to linked transactions, make it impossible to say that a transaction concluded abroad cannot attract the statutory provisions in some way. A good example is the credit card issued by a United Kingdom bank under a credit-token agreement and usable abroad. The debtor might utilise the card to make a foreign purchase. That purchase would no doubt be governed by the law of the country where it was made, but it does not follow that the United Kingdom bank would on that account avoid the liability under s. 75 that would ordinarily arise if the supplier's performance was defective. Indeed, the court would very probably take the view that since (by definition) the debtor-creditor-supplier agreement involved an existing or prospective arrangement between the bank and the foreign supplier who had agreed to accept the card, there was no reason why the bank should not accept the ordinary liability of a connected lender, particularly as the cardholder might have great difficulty in securing redress from the foreign supplier.

[**3.42**] With a view to resolving problems that may arise with transactions involving a foreign element, the Secretary of State is empowered by s. 16 (5) (*c*) to exclude from the scope of the Act agreements "having a connection with a country outside the United Kingdom". This rather vague phrase seems sufficiently wide to enable the Secretary of State to cover most eventualities for which provision needs to be made.

[**3.43**] However, advertisements by an advertiser whose business comprises or relates to unregulated agreements that would be regulated but for the fact that their proper law is that of a country outside the United Kingdom are governed by Part IV of the Act (s. 43 (2)—and see para. [**6.8**]). Such agreements are also relevant to the definition of credit brokerage (s. 145 (2), (3)).

"CREDITOR"; "DEBTOR"

[**3.44**] As has been mentioned earlier in this chapter, the term "credit" in the Consumer Credit Act covers not merely loan credit but every other form of financial accommodation. "Creditor" and "debtor" are given correspondingly extended meanings. "Creditor", as defined by s. 189 (1), "means the person providing credit under a consumer credit agreement or the person to whom his rights and duties under the contract have passed by assignment or operation of law, and in relation to a prospective consumer credit agreement, includes the prospective creditor." "Debtor", under the same provision, "means the individual receiving credit under a consumer credit agreement or the person to whom his rights and duties under the agreement have passed by assignment or by operation of law, and in relation to a prospective consumer credit agreement includes the prospective debtor." Thus "creditor" and "debtor" now embrace the seller and buyer of goods disposed of under an instalment sale agreement and the owner and hirer of goods let on hire-purchase. Included in the definition are assignees and also transferees by operation of law, *e.g.* the trustee in bankruptcy or personal representative of the creditor or debtor. By a drafting slip s. 189 (1), when referring to assignees, speaks of the person to whom rights *and* duties have passed by assignment. Literally construed, this part of the definition would be largely nugatory, since as a matter of contract law an assignment transfers rights but does not relieve the assignor of his duties to the other contracting party or entitle that party to enforce such duties against the assignee. It is thought that this is a case where the court would construe "and" as "or", thus maintaining the sense of the definition as more accurately provided in s. 58 (1) of the Hire-Purchase Act 1965.

"OWNER"; "HIRER"

[**3.45**] The words "owner" and "hirer", hitherto used in the Hire-Purchase Acts to denote the parties to a hire-purchase agreement, are now confined to simple hiring agreements. "Owner", under s. 189 (1), "means a person who bails or (in Scotland) hires out goods under a consumer hire agreement or the person to whom his rights and duties under the agreement have passed by assignment or operation of law, and in relation to a prospective consumer hire agreement, includes the prospective bailor or person from whom the goods are to be hired." "Hirer", by the same section, "means the individual to whom goods are bailed or (in Scotland) hired under a consumer hire agreement, or the person to whom his rights and duties under the agreement have passed by assignment or operation of law, and in relation to a prospective consumer hire agreement includes the prospective hirer." The comments made in para. [**3.44**] are equally applicable here.

# CHAPTER 4

# THE CLASSIFICATION OF AGREEMENTS UNDER THE ACT

## THE PURPOSE OF CLASSIFICATION

[**4.1**] The Consumer Credit Act has many interesting and original features. Not the least of these is the new terminology coined by the draftsman in a highly successful endeavour to encompass not only the extraordinary diversity of forms of consumer credit currently used but also forms not yet conceived which may one day appear on the English financial scene. To a great degree, the classification of agreements made by the Act is modelled on that put forward in the Crowther Report. The language has changed (sometimes for the worse!), the Crowther concepts have been crystallised and refined and the classification has been fuller and more complex in the light of practical problems thrown up by detailed drafting and by consultation with interested parties. But in essence, the framework of regulation is modelled closely on Crowther; and if at first sight the structure created by the Act seems confusing, a perusal of the relevant paragraphs of the Crowther Report will throw light on the policy underlying the new classification of agreements and the reason why it was found necessary to draw distinctions that may on first impression appear to serve no useful purpose. An explanation of these matters will be given in the ensuing paragraphs.

[**4.2**] We have previously discussed the regulated agreement—meaning broadly an agreement which is regulated by the Act—and have seen that this divides into two primary groups, the consumer credit agreement and the consumer hire agreement. It was not found necessary to make any further subdivision of consumer hire agreements in definitional terms and we can accordingly leave this on one side, and concentrate on the consumer credit agreement. Here the position is more complex. Whilst hiring has only one legal form, the rest of consumer credit covers a very wide range of different instruments. Some are concerned exclusively with loans of money unconnected to the purchase of specific goods or services. Others do not, as a matter of law take a loan form at all but involve the deferment of the price of goods under a hire-purchase or instalment sale contract or the deferment of the price of services. Yet others are of a hybrid character, being neither loans in the traditional sense nor ordinary sales or hire-purchase agreements. Into this category fall check trading and credit card arrangements. Some forms of credit involve a loan of an amount fixed at the outset, creating an indebtedness which is reduced by successive payments until it is altogether extinguished, as in the case of the fixed loan, the hire-purchase agreement and the credit sale agreement. Other forms of financial accommodation contemplate a continuing relationship between creditor and debtor through a revolving credit of indefinite duration by which, instead of the credit being used once for all, it is utilised at the pleasure of the borrower up to the agreed limit, and is *pro tanto* restored by payments made in reduction of the debt. Into this category fall bank overdrafts and credit card arrangements. Some forms of purchase-money credit are made by independent lenders having no contact with the supplier, as where a clearing bank lends a customer money to buy a motor car. Others are made by financiers pursuant to a regular business relationship with the supplier, from whom they may get much of their business. An example of this type of agreement is the hire-purchase agreement for a motor vehicle concluded between a finance house and a hirer through the medium of a motor dealer.

**[4.3]** All these distinctions are functional. They reflect differences in the way a transaction is carried out and in the nature and extent of contact between the three parties involved, the debtor, the creditor and the supplier. Problems and policies applicable to one type of credit have little or no relevance to another. It is to reflect these functional differences that the Consumer Credit Act, building on the Crowther Report, has enacted what may at first sight appear to be an over-elaborate structure and classification of agreements. The Credit strength of the Consumer Credit Act is that for the first time in the history of English credit law, Parliament has abandoned a legal structure based on differences in legal form and has instead produced a pattern of regulation which classifies transactions according to their function and effect.

**[4.4]** The classification that we are about to tackle is contained in Part II of the Act. This should be read in conjunction with:

(*a*) the illustrative examples in Schedule 2 to the Act;
(*b*) the list of definitions in s. 189, some of which refer back to definitions in Part II whilst others are provided by s. 189 itself;
(*c*) the White Paper, and in particular the Introduction to the Appendices, including, in paragraph 4 of that Introduction, the tabulation of consumer credit agreements under the new nomenclature.

### FIXED-SUM CREDIT AND RUNNING-ACCOUNT CREDIT

**[4.5]** This is quite simple. Running-account credit is synonymous with revolving credit. The essential ingredient of running-account credit is that whilst drawings reduce the credit, payments made by the debtor top it up again to the original credit limit. The most common examples are the bank overdraft, the credit card and the budget account. All credit other than running-account credit is fixed-sum credit. Into this category fall hire-purchase, conditional sale and credit sale agreements, check and voucher trading transactions, fixed loans (as opposed to overdrafts) and the like. Full definitions of running-account credit and fixed-sum credit are given in s. 10 (1) of the Act and illustrated in Schedule 2, but in essence they are as described above, subject only to the addition that to be within running-account credit or fixed-sum credit, the credit must be one which is provided by a personal credit agreement as defined by s. 8 (1). This has already been discussed in paragraph [**3.2**].

[**4.6**] Why does the Act find it necessary to distinguish running-account credit from fixed-sum credit? There are various reasons. First, as has already been mentioned, running-account credit is subject to special rules for the purpose of determining whether a transaction is within the £5,000 ceiling (see paras. [**3.20**] *et seq.*). Secondly, the debtor in a running-account credit provided under a regulated agreement has an *automatic* right to receive statements of account at least once a year and, where the agreement provides for periodic payments by the debtor, a statement of the state of the account at the end of every period in which there has been a movement in the account (s. 78 (4)). This is in addition to the right to a statement on request which is conferred in relation both to running-account and fixed-sum credit (ss. 77, 78 (1)–(3)), though the information that can be called for by the debtor under these sections and by a surety under ss. 107 and 108 is somewhat different for running-account credit than for fixed-sum credit. Thirdly, where an actual or prospective regulated agreement has two or more debtors, the duty under s. 185 (1) to supply each of them with periodic statements of account under s. 78 (4) can, as regards any of them, be dispensed with by him by a dispensing notice given under s. 185 (2). Finally—and for this we have to refer not to the Act but to the Appendices in the White Paper—information to be provided by the creditor in advertisements, quotations and agreements differs according to whether the document in question deals with fixed-sum credit or running-account credit. For example, the cost of borrowing expressed as a percentage rate cannot be given in the same way for running-account credit as for fixed-sum credit, since the effective rate will depend on the manner in which the debtor uses the facility. Accordingly in the case of running-account credit, what will be required is not the actual rate that the debtor will pay (which will not be known at the outset) but the basis of calculation of the period rate and the effective annual equivalent of the period rate on the basis of annual compounding. Rate disclosure is discussed separately in Appendix A of this book.

### RESTRICTED-USE CREDIT AND UNRESTRICTED-USE CREDIT

[**4.7**] Section 11 (1) of the Act defines a restricted-use credit agreement as a regulated consumer credit agreement:

(*a*) to finance a transaction between the debtor and the creditor, whether forming part of that agreement or not, or

(*b*) to finance a transaction between the debtor and a person (the "supplier") other than the creditor, or

(*c*) to refinance any existing indebtedness of the debtor's, whether to the creditor or another person.

[**4.8**] An unrestricted-use credit agreement is any other class of regulated consumer credit agreement (s. 11 (2)). By s. 11 (3) an agreement is not a restricted-use agreement if the credit is in fact provided in such a way as to leave the debtor free to use it as he chooses, even though certain uses would contravene that or any other agreement. On the other hand, by s. 11 (4) an agreement may fall within s. 11 (1) (*b*) although the identity of the supplier is unknown at the time the agreement is made. In essence, then, restricted-use credit is credit extended to finance a particular purchase or transaction and provided in such a way that the creditor can ensure its application to the purchase or transaction in question. This will be the case where the creditor is himself the supplier—e.g. under a hire-purchase or credit sale agreement—or where the creditor, in advancing money for a purchase by the debtor, pays the price direct to the supplier instead of to the debtor, or where the creditor, instead of paying money to the debtor, furnishes him with a token such as a credit card or voucher which restricts use of the token to a specified supplier or suppliers. If control of one of these kinds is not exercised, as where the advance is paid to the debtor himself in money, the credit is unrestricted-use credit even though the debtor may have contracted to utilise the loan only for a designated purchase. The restricted-use/unrestricted-use classification may be relevant in determining whether a transaction is a linked transaction (see s. 19 (1) (*c*) (iii)), and is material for various other reasons. The advertising of restricted-use credit facilities where the goods or services are not at that time offered for cash by the person advertised as the supplier is an offence (s. 45). Restricted-use credit agreements to finance the purchase of land and to be secured by a mortgage on that land are exempt from the special procedure prescribed for land mortgage transactions which is designed to give the debtor an opportunity to withdraw (see para. [**8.16**]). The cancellation provisions are modified in some respects as regards debtor-creditor-supplier agreements for restricted-use credit; and again, the disclosure requirements depicted in the Appendices to the White Paper vary according to whether the credit is restricted-use credit or unrestricted-use credit.

### DEBTOR-CREDITOR-SUPPLIER AGREEMENT AND DEBTOR-CREDITOR AGREEMENT

[**4.9**] We come now to what is perhaps the most important, and certainly the most difficult, pair of labels in the classification, namely debtor-creditor-supplier agreements and debtor-creditor agreements. Actually, the difficulty is visual rather than conceptual. Debtor-creditor-supplier credit is simply another, and less elegant, name for what the Crowther Committee termed a connected loan, that is to say, a loan extended by the supplier himself (e.g. by deferment of the price under a hire-purchase or instalment sale agreement) or by a connected lender in the sense of a lender having a pre-existing arrangement or contemplating a future arrangement with the supplier. The Crowther Report advanced compelling reasons for distinguishing connected from unconnected loans.

> "Where goods are bought for cash provided by an independent lender there is no reason to regard the sale as any different from a normal cash sale, or to treat the loan as other than a normal loan. Where, however, the price is advanced by the seller or a connected lender the sale and loan aspects of the transaction are closely entwined. The connected lender and the seller, where not the same person, are in effect engaged in a joint venture to their mutual advantage, and their respective roles cannot be treated in isolation" (para. 6.2.24).

The Crowther Report set out three areas in which the distinction was significant.

First, unconnected loans at interest not exceeding 2½ per cent. above Bank Rate were to be exempt from the proposed consumer credit legislation. This exemption will feature, in slightly modified form, in regulations to be made under s. 16 (4) of the Consumer Credit Act, which will exempt unconnected loans at interest of 10 per cent. *per annum* or less (see White Paper, para. 21 (iii)). Secondly, restrictions against contracting out of terms implied in favour of the buyer in an instalment sale were to apply equally to a sale for cash advanced by a loan from a connected lender. This has disappeared as a relevant factor, since all consumer sales, even if for cash, are now within the ambit of the Supply of Goods (Implied Terms) Act 1973, which renders void provisions purporting to exclude or restrict such implied terms. Thirdly, the connected lender was to be liable for misrepresentations made by the supplier in antecedent negotiations and for defects in goods or services purchased by the buyer with the aid of the connected loan. This idea is retained in s. 75 of the Consumer Credit Act, discussed in Chapter 9.

[**4.10**] In essence, therefore, a debtor-creditor-supplier agreement (defined in s. 12 of the Act—and see para. [**4.11**] is an agreement under which credit is extended by the supplier himself (by deferment of the price) or by a third party pursuant to pre-existing arrangements, or in contemplation of future arrangements, with the supplier. Into this category fall hire-purchase, conditional sale and credit sale agreements, check trading and credit card transactions (but not bank cheque guarantee cards—see para. [**4.12**], shop budget accounts and personal loans by finance houses for the purchase of motor cars by customers of a motor dealer who introduces such customers to the finance house pursuant to an arrangement with the finance house. By contrast, a debtor-creditor agreement (defined in s. 13) is what Crowther termed an unconnected loan, that is, a loan not made by the supplier or by any third party under pre-existing arrangements, or in contemplation of future arrangements, with the supplier. Typical examples are the normal bank loan and overdraft, loans by moneylenders and pawnbrokers and personal loans not geared to purchases from specific suppliers.

[**4.11**] Where goods are let on hire-purchase by a finance house, it is the finance house, not the dealer, who is the supplier, so that creditor and supplier are the same and the case falls within s. 12 (*a*), not s. 12 (*b*) or (*e*). As to the latter, regard must be had to s. 187:

> "(1) A consumer credit agreement shall be treated as entered into under pre-existing arrangements between a creditor and a supplier if it is entered into in accordance with, or in furtherance of, arrangements previously made between persons mentioned in subsection 4 (*a*), (*b*) or (*c*).
>
> (2) A consumer credit agreement shall be treated as entered into in contemplation of future arrangements between a creditor and a supplier if it is entered into in the expectation that arrangements will subsequently be made between persons mentioned in subsection (4) (*a*), (*b*) or (*c*) for the supply of cash, goods and services (or any of them) to be financed by the consumer credit agreement.
>
> (3) Arrangements shall be disregarded for the purposes of subsection (1) or (2) if—
>
> (*a*) they are arrangements for the making, in specified circumstances, of payments to the supplier by the creditor, and

(*b*) the creditor holds himself out as willing to make, in such circumstances, payments of the kind to suppliers generally.

(4) The persons referred to in subsections (1) and (2) are—

(*a*) the creditor and the supplier;
(*b*) one of them and an associate of the other's;
(*c*) an associate of one and an associate of the other's.

(5) Where the creditor is an associate of the supplier's, the consumer credit agreement shall be treated, unless the contrary is proved, as entered into under pre-existing arrangements between the creditor and the supplier."

Section 187 (3) makes it clear that cheque guarantee cards issued by a bank do not generate a debtor-creditor-supplier agreement merely because the bank undertakes to suppliers at large that it will honour cheques drawn by the card-holder up to the limit stated on the card.

[**4.12**] It is not possible, in the compass of this introductory Guide, to refer to all the provisions of the Consumer Credit Act in which the distinction between a debtor-creditor-supplier agreement and a debtor-creditor agreement is relevant. Suffice it to mention the five most important.

(*a*) It is an offence to canvass debtor-creditor agreements off trade premises (s. 49 (1)). Hence the canvassing of a loan application at the house of the prospective debtor is prohibited, but the canvassing of entry into a check trading agreement is permitted (see generally Chapter 6).

(*b*) The disclosure requirements to be made by regulations will vary according to whether the agreement is a debtor-creditor-supplier agreement or a debtor-creditor agreement (see White Paper, Appendices I and II).

(*c*) The debtor's exercise of a right to cancel a regulated agreement also automatically cancels a linked transaction (s. 69 (1)); and in the case of a debtor-creditor-supplier agreement the purchase or other transaction financed by the creditor is a linked transaction (s. 19 (1) (*b*)). Thus, if a finance house, pursuant to an arrangement with a motor dealer, advances to the dealer's customer the purchase price of the car being bought by the customer from the dealer, cancellation of the loan agreement with the finance house under the provisions of the Act will automatically rescind the contract of sale between the motor dealer and the customer. In such a case, the finance house is jointly and severally liable with the dealer to repay sums paid by the debtor (s. 70 (3)).

(*d*) The provisions of s. 72 relating to the return of goods on cancellation do not apply to goods purchased with a loan under a debtor-creditor agreement; and on cancellation of a debtor-creditor agreement or indeed any regulated agreement other than a debtor-creditor-supplier agreement for restricted-use credit, the agreement continues in force so far as it relates to repayment of credit and payment of interest (s. 71 (1)).

(*e*) If the debtor in a debtor-creditor-supplier transaction has a claim against the supplier in respect of misrepresentation or breach of contract, the creditor is liable jointly and severally with the supplier (s. 75 (1)), with a right of indemnity against the supplier (s. 75 (2)—and see Chapter 9).

CREDIT-TOKEN AGREEMENTS

[**4.13**] The next type of agreement requiring mention is the credit-token agreement. This is defined by s. 14 (2) of the Act as a regulated agreement for the provision of credit in connection with the use of a credit-token. A credit-token, as defined by s. 14 (1), is a card, check, voucher, coupon, stamp, form, booklet or other document or thing given to an individual by a person carrying on a consumer credit business, who undertakes—

(*a*) that on the production of it (whether or not some other action is also required) he will supply cash, goods and services (or any of them) on credit, or

(b) that where, on the production of it to a third party (whether or not any other action is also required), the third party supplies cash, goods and services (or any of them), he will pay the third party for them (whether or not deducting any discount or commission), in return for payment to him by the individual.

Examples of credit-tokens are bank credit cards enabling the holder to draw cash from a bank or to buy goods or services from a third party such as a shop having an arrangement with the bank to accept the card; cards which enable the card holder to draw money from a cash dispenser (see s. 14 (4)); checks issued by check trading companies; trading vouchers; and credit cards issued by a shop or store authorising the holder to purchase goods from the shop or store in question and have his account debited with the price on credit terms. But a cheque card, by which a bank undertakes to suppliers generally to whom the card is produced to honour cheques drawn by its customers up to the limit stated on the card is not a credit-token, since the bank, in paying the supplier, is not paying for the goods or services but is merely honouring its guarantee of payment of the cheque. This is made clear in example 21 in the Second Schedule to the Act.

[**4.14**] Almost invariably, agreements relating to credit-tokens will be within the £5,000 ceiling so as to constitute regulated agreements and thus credit-token agreements. Special provisions apply in relation to credit-tokens and credit token agreements. The giving of unsolicited credit-tokens is prohibited (s. 51 (1)). This effectively prevents any new mass mailing of credit cards, though it does not inhibit the mass mailing of credit card agreements incorporating a request by the recipients to have a card. The requirements imposed by ss. 63 (1) and 64 (1) for the timing of service of a copy of the executed agreement and of a notice setting out the debtor's cancellation rights are somewhat relaxed by ss. 63 (4) and 64 (2) for credit-token agreements (see paras. [**7.24**], [**7.27**]). The debtor's right to recover, on cancellation, a sum paid, or to be released from liability for a sum payable, for the issue of a credit-token is conditional on his returning the credit-tokens or surrendering them to a supplier (s. 70 (5)). The debtor's liability for unauthorised use of a credit-token by a third party cannot be made to exceed £30 and ceases on notification to the creditor that the card has been lost or is liable to be misused (s. 84 (1), (3), (5)—and see Chapter 16).

MULTIPLE AGREEMENTS

**[4.15]** The neat compartmentalisation of agreements in accordance with the above classifications seems exhaustive enough, without further elaboration. Unhappily, it is still not sufficient to accommodate the diversity of credit transactions. There are various types of agreement which fall into more than one category, either because the agreement is divided up into different parts belonging to different categories (one of which may indeed be outside the Act altogether) or because the agreement, though indivisible, contains terms which place it in two or more categories. Such agreements are known as multiple agreements, and these are treated as follows:

(*a*) As regards parts of an agreement falling into different categories, each part is to be treated as a separate agreement (s. 18 (2)) and to be construed accordingly, with appropriate apportionment of any sums payable thereunder (s. 18 (4)).

(*b*) As regards an agreement falling into two or more categories, the agreement is to be treated as in each category (s. 18 (3)).

**[4.16]** Two illustrations should suffice to show what a multiple agreement is and how the statutory provisions operate on it.

*Example 1*

A opens an account with his bank which agrees to give him overdraft facilities of £500. A is told that so long as his account is kept in credit he will not have to pay any bank charges, but that if he has overdrawn he will have to pay charges of 7½p for each cheque drawn, in addition to interest at the bank's normal prevailing rate.

This is a multiple agreement. That part which relates to the operating of the account while it is in credit is not a credit agreement at all and is outside the Act. That part which deals with the terms of the overdraft is a regulated agreement.

(A fuller illustration of this form of multiple agreement is given in example 18 in the Second Schedule to the Act.)

*Example 2*

B is issued by his bank with a credit card under the terms of an agreement which entitle him to use the card to draw cash from the bank and to obtain goods and services from named suppliers and cash from other named banks who have an arrangement with B's bank to accept the card. In so far as the agreement between B and his bank deals with use of the card to draw cash from that bank, it is a debtor-creditor agreement. In so far as it relates to use of the card to obtain cash from other banks, or goods or services from the named suppliers, it is a debtor-creditor-supplier agreement. The agreement thus falls into both categories and is governed by the provisions of the Act relating to both categories.

(A fuller illustration is given in example 16 in the Second Schedule to the Act).

**[4.17]** If in the second of the above examples the credit card agreement permitted repayment by instalments and the debtor, after drawing cash from his bank and using the card to buy goods from a supplier, were to exercise a right of cancellation after making certain payments to the bank, it might be necessary to determine what instalments had accrued due to the bank as regards the cash drawn and where instalments had accrued due as regards the goods purchased, in order to apply the provisions of s. 71 (3) (see para. [**8.51**]); and for this purpose the court would have to exercise its power of apportionment under s. 18 (4).

[**4.18**] A consequence of s. 18 (2)—whereby a part of an agreement in a different category from the remaining parts is to be treated as a separate agreement—may be to attract the operation of the Act to both parts of the agreement even though, if taken as a whole, the agreement would have provided a credit in excess of £5,000 so as to be outside the Act altogether. If, for example, a creditor agrees to advance £9,000, of which £5,000 is to refinance the indebtedness of the debtor to third parties whilst the remaining £4,000 is for the debtor to use as he chooses, the £5,000 part of the loan is restricted-use credit and the £4,000 is unrestricted-use credit, so that each of these parts is deemed a separate agreement under s. 18 (2) and each is thus controlled by the Act, being within the £5,000 ceiling.

[**4.19**] However, by s. 18 (5) an agreement for temporary excess of an overdraft over the credit limit does not constitute a separate agreement, nor is it to be treated as providing fixed-sum credit for the excess. It thus does not create a distinct fixed-sum category separate from the running-account facility created by the original overdraft arrangement. See also para. [**3.22**].

[**4.20**] Finally, s. 18 (6) provides that the Act is not to apply to a multiple agreement so far as the agreement relates to goods if under the agreement payments are to be made in respect of the goods in the form of rent (other than a rent charge) issuing out of land. It follows that if goods are included in a lease or tenancy agreement relating to land—as in the case of a furnished letting—the lease or tenancy agreement is outside the Act in relation to the goods as well as to the land, provided that the rent attributable to the goods issues out of the land. This will be the case if there is a single rent which does not distinguish between land and goods. It is otherwise, however, if a separate sum is fixed as the rental of the goods.

### LINKED TRANSACTIONS

[**4.21**] These are discussed in detail in Chapter 9.

### OTHER DEFINITIONS

[**4.22**] The above definitions all relate to the classifications of agreements under the Act. There are a number of other important definitions, scattered throughout the Act and gathered together in s. 189 (1). These will be referred to at appropriate points in the chapters which follow.

# CHAPTER 5

# LICENSING

## THE PURPOSE AND IMPACT OF A LICENSING SYSTEM

[**5.1**] No consumer legislation, however sophisticated, is likely to have more than a marginal impact if not underpinned by effective enforcement machinery. The Hire-Purchase Acts provided no mechanism whatever for systematic enforcement. The onus was placed on the individual consumer to take the initiative in invoking the Acts. In many cases he was not equipped to do so, through ignorance of his rights, timidity or inability to incur the legal costs that might be involved. The reputable trader or finance house would endeavour to comply with the law. The less scrupulous creditor, against whose activities the legislation was primarily aimed, could afford to cock a snook—provided that he stood clear of the small number of criminal offences provided by the statutes—since at worst he would lose the occasional case, and this loss was far outweighed by the benefits to be derived from diligent and persistent flouting of the statutory requirements and the recovery from uninformed debtors of sums which they could not legally have been compelled to pay. So far as moneylending was concerned, the law was theoretically stronger because of a licensing system and a battery of criminal sanctions for different types of offence. But as a method of control this also was largely ineffective, partly because the licensing system was decentralised, partly because the Acts failed to impose any duty of enforcement on any specific authority. In the result, prosecutions were infrequent and were left to the occasional initiative of a police officer; and revocation and suspension of licences was almost unknown. A survey conducted by the author in 1968 showed that of the 170 licensing authorities from whom figures were received, only one had a record of any court order in the last ten years forfeiting a certificate issued to a moneylender, while in the same period there was only one recorded instance of suspension of a licence being notified to a licensing authority.

[**5.2**] The Consumer Credit Act has remedied these serious weaknesses of previous legislation by entrusting the overall administration and enforcement of the Act, and of regulations under it, to the Director General of Fair Trading, and by making enforcement at local level the responsibility of Weights and Measures Authorities, who have already developed considerable expertise in this type of control under the Weights and Measures Acts, the Trade Descriptions Acts and other legislation in the public law sector. A linchpin of the enforcement machinery is the licensing system, which will be operated centrally by the Director. Licensing has many advantages as a method of control. First, it provides an extremely powerful sanction against deliberate law breaking. The offender risks not merely the loss of an occasional civil suit or even the occasional fine but the more drastic penalty of being put out of business altogether. It is rarely necessary for enforcement agencies to exercise a sanction of this kind. The mere threat suffices to discourage the licensee from sailing too close to the wind. On the other hand, a licensee who infringes a legal right through inadvertence can be cautioned without the need for the full rigour of the law to be applied to him. The most valuable enforcement work of trading standards inspectors is achieved by friendly caution rather than by prosecution. These are not the only advantages of a licensing system. The value judgment which is inevitably involved in determining the suitability of an applicant for the grant or renewal of a licence gives a measure of flexibility and allows the licensing authority to take into account facts known about the applicant which might be difficult to establish by formal evidence (it has to be said, on the other side, that this same fact also carries a risk of injustice). Through a central licensing system, consistency can be secured in standards of conduct imposed on licensees and in the approach to enforcement. In addition, requirements imposed as to the supply of documents and information by existing and prospective licensees can be expected to produce much needed information concerning the areas of business to which the licensing requirements relate.

[**5.3**] It is for these reasons that licensing has become increasingly popular with successive governments as a method of regulating spheres of business activity. This trend may be expected to accelerate in the light of our entry into the Common Market, since our partners in Europe have long leaned heavily on licensing and in certain fields (*e.g.* banking) the introduction of new licensing systems may become mandatory as a result of EEC directives.

[**5.4**] Yet the manifest advantages of licensing should not blind one to certain dangers endemic in this method of control. The use of administrative procedures, and the exercise of judicial functions by administrative organs, can lead to unfair or unjust decisions which are not easily put right. The very flexibility of the system makes it difficult for a party aggrieved by refusal or revocation of a licence to make a successful challenge on the basis of improper exercise of discretion by the licensing authority. In other countries on the Continent, the power of administrative agencies is counter-balanced by highly developed systems of administrative law, usually applied by separate administrative courts, which are much readier than our own courts have been hitherto to enquire into the manner of exercise of a discretion. As licensing develops in this country, we may expect to see a corresponding development in our administrative law, which, despite its considerable growth in recent years, remains fragmented and undeveloped and has a long way to go before it reaches its potential power. In this chapter, after looking at the mechanism of the licensing system created by the Consumer Credit Act, we shall examine some of the problems that this may create in the administrative law field and the approach that the courts are likely to adopt when asked to review the exercise of discretion by the Director and by the Secretary of State on appeal. It is not possible, in an introductory Guide of this kind, to give more than the broadest outline of the court's power in the licensing field. For a comprehensive analysis of the principles involved in this most difficult aspect of administrative law, the reader should turn to the late Professor de Smith's brilliant book, *The Judicial Review of Administrative Action*, the third edition of which was published in 1973.

THE NEED FOR A LICENCE

[**5.5**] A licence is required to carry on a consumer credit or consumer hire business (s. 21 (1)). The only types of credit grantor not requiring a licence are (i) a local authority and (ii) a body corporate empowered by a public general Act naming it to carry on a business. Into this latter category fall, for example, the Commission for the New Towns, the Agriculture Mortgage Corporation, the White Fish Authority and the public utilities such as gas and electricity boards. These were excluded from the licensing requirement on the ground that where parliament has conferred powers on a body corporate under a public general Act, it would be inappropriate for an independent statutory officer (in this case, the Director General of Fair Trading) to be able to take those powers away. But such bodies remain subject to the other provisions of the Act, except in so far as their agreements are exempted under s. 16 (see para. [**3.24**], [**3.28**]).

[**5.6**] By s. 189 (1) of the Act, "consumer credit business" means any business so far as it comprises or relates to the provision of credit under regulated consumer credit agreements; and "consumer hire business" means any business so far as it comprises or relates to the bailment of goods under regulated consumer hire agreements. A person is not to be treated as carrying on a particular type of business merely because occasionally he enters into transactions belonging to a business of that type (s. 189 (2)). Hence regularity of activity is necessary before that activity can be regarded as a business activity so as to attract the licensing provisions. Thus, a solicitor making *occasional* bridging loans for clients would not on that account alone be carrying on a consumer credit business. It would seem that the onus of showing that a person carries on a consumer credit or consumer hire business lies on the party asserting it.

[**5.7**] A licence is also required to carry on an ancillary credit business (s. 147 (1)), that is, any business so far as it comprises or relates to credit brokerage, debt-adjusting, debt-counselling, debt-collecting or the operation of a credit reference agency (s. 145 (1)). These are fully discussed in Chapter 23.

TYPES OF LICENCE

[**5.8**] By s. 22 (1) a licence may be—

(*a*) a standard licence, that is a licence, issued by the Director to a person named in the licence on an application made by him, which, during the prescribed period, covers such activities as are described in the licence, or

(*b*) a group licence, that is a licence, issued by the Director (whether on the application of any person or of his own motion), which, during such period as the Director thinks fit or, if he thinks fit, indefinitely, covers such persons and activities as are described in the licence.

[**5.9**] The standard licence is issued to a named person (s. 22 (1)) and authorises him to carry on business under the name or names specified in the licence but not under any other name (s. 24). This latter requirement is discussed in detail in paragraphs [**5.17**] *et seq.* Except in the case of a partnership or an unincorporated body of persons, a standard licence must not be issued to more than one person (s. 22 (3)). A standard licence issued to a partnership or unincorporated body is issued in the name of the partnership or body (s. 22 (4)). The effect is that each partner or member of the body for the time being is deemed to hold the licence, and changes in the partnership or in members of the body do not affect the continuance of the licence so long as (in the case of a partnership) the name of the partnership remains unchanged (see para. [**5.17**]).

[**5.10**] A standard licence differs from a group licence in that it requires an individual application, which in the normal course of events will be carefully examined to ensure that the applicant is a proper person to hold a licence (see paras. [**5.29**] *et seq.*). Group licences, on the other hand, do not involve the screening of individual applications. However, the fact that a person is covered by a group licence in respect of certain activities does not prevent a standard licence being issued to him in respect of those activities or any of them (s. 22 (7)).

[**5.11**] The initial number of standard licences to be applied for is likely to be large, and it would be difficult, if not impossible, for all applications to be processed before the day appointed for the commencement of the licensing requirements. This problem is dealt with in paragraph 5 (2) of the Third Schedule (see para. [**5.63**], *post*).

GROUP LICENCES

[**5.12**] Group licences are intended for those categories of creditor or credit business where individual examination is not considered necessary in the public interest. Into this category might fall solicitors regularly making bridging loans to clients; retailers acting without payment as intermediaries in introducing customers to finance houses for the purpose of acquiring goods on hire-purchase or credit sale; and the like. Group licences may be issued by the Director only if it appears to him that the public interest is better served by doing so than by obliging the persons concerned to apply separately for standard licences (s. 22 (5)). The group licence procedure is a useful device for cutting down what would otherwise be a very large number of obligatory individual licences. The estimate of the Crowther Committee was that some 50,000 licences would be in issue; later government enquiries have indicated that the number is likely to be above 70,000. The Director has power to exclude named persons from any group licence (s. 22 (6)). This is a necessary safeguard to allow the Director to exercise more immediate supervision over creditors whose activities are under suspicion, whilst leaving the group licence procedure available for the remaining members of the class.

[**5.13**] A group licence may be issued on the application of any person or by the Director of his own motion (s. 22 (1) (*b*)). When issued on application, it is issued to the applicant (s. 22 (8)). The Director must give general notice of a group licence, whether issued on application or by the Director of his own motion (*ibid.*). A general notice means a notice published by the Director at a time and in a manner appearing to him suitable for securing that the notice is seen within a reasonable time by persons likely to be affected by it (s. 189 (1)).

ACTIVITIES AUTHORISED BY THE LICENCE

[**5.14**] A licence covers all such activities as are described in the licence (s. 22 (1)). Where the licence is to carry on a particular type of business, it covers all lawful activities done in the course of that business, whether by the licensee or other persons on his behalf (s. 23 (1)). This means that the licensee does not as a rule have to procure separate licences for his agents or to satisfy himself that those acting on his behalf in the course of some licensable activity of their own hold a licence. However, an exception to this is made by s. 149 (1) which provides that a regulated agreement made by a debtor or hirer introduced to the creditor or owner by an unlicensed credit-broker is enforceable only on an order made by the Director under s. 148 (2) or s. 149 (2).

[**5.15**] A licence may limit the activities it covers, whether by authorising the licensee to enter into certain types of agreement only, or in any other way (s. 23 (2)). The Act specifies seven different forms of business requiring a licence, namely consumer credit, consumer hire, credit brokerage, debt-adjusting, debt-counselling, debt-collecting and the operation of a credit reference agency. It is anticipated that whilst each licensee will hold a single standard licence, the licence will specify which of these forms of business are covered by the licence, in much the same way as a driving licence specifies the groups of motor vehicles which the licence holder is authorised to drive.

[**5.16**] The canvassing off trade premises of debtor-creditor-supplier agreements or regulated consumer hire agreements is covered by a licence only if, and to the extent that, the licence specifically so provides; and such provision cannot be included in a group licence (s. 23 (3)). In addition, regulations may be made specifying other activities which, if engaged in by or on behalf of the person carrying on a business, require to be covered by an express term in his licence (s. 23 (4)).

BUSINESS TO BE CONDUCTED UNDER AUTHORISED NAME

[**5.17**] As previously mentioned, a standard licence restricts the licensee to carrying on a business under the name or names specified in the licence. This follows a provision to similar effect in s. 1 of the Moneylenders Act 1927. A licensee under a standard licence who carries on business under a name not specified in the licence commits an offence (s. 39 (2); but this would not appear to invalidate an agreement entered into by him, whether in his licensed name or otherwise (see s. 170 (1)). It should, however, be noted, as regards a licence to a partnership, that whilst changes in the partners do not appear to affect the licence so long as the business continues to be carried on under the partnership name or names specified in the licence, if as a result of a change in a partnership the business ceases to be carried on under such name or names, the licence ceases to have effect (s. 36 (5)). In that event the provisions relating to the enforcement of agreements made by unlicensed traders would come into operation (see para. [**5.23**).

[**5.18**] In deciding whether a licensee has committed an offence by carrying on business under a name not specified in the licence, it may be necessary to determine (1) what deviations from the licensed name are to be regarded as legally significant, and (2) whether acts done under such name are to be regarded as constituting the carrying on of a business. On this point, assistance may be derived from cases on the Moneylenders Acts, and in particular from the decisions in *Peizer* v. *Lefkowitz,* [1912] 2 K.B. 275, *Kirkwood* v. *Gadd,* [1910] A.C. 422 and *Cornelius* v. *Phillips,* [1918] A.C. 199, in which the following principles were enunciated—

(i) Slight discrepancies between the name used and the licensed name (*e.g.* discrepancies arising from a slight mis-spelling of the name) will not be considered to contravene the statutory requirements if they are not such as to mislead. On this basis, the court felt able, in *Peizer* v. *Lefkowitz,* to overlook a description of the lender in a promissory note as "Westminster Loan and Discount Company" when the registered name was "Westminster Loan and Discount Office". The same case decided that the materiality of a discrepancy for this purpose is a question of law, not a question of fact.

(ii) Not every act done in furtherance of a business transaction constitutes the carrying on of a business. There is a distinction between the carrying on of the business and the carrying out of transactions which make up the business (*per* Lord Mersey in *Kirkwood* v. *Gadd*). If the business as a whole is carried on in the licensed name (*Kirkwood* v. *Gadd* was in fact concerned with the authorised address, but the principle would seem to be the same), the mere fact that, for example, a different name was used in a visit to the debtor in the course of completing a transaction would not contravene the statutory provisions. As Lord Atkinson put it in *Kirkwood* v. *Gadd*: "It will, I think, suffice if such important portions, or such an important portion, of the dealing are or is transacted there [*i.e.* the authorised address] by communications, verbal or written, as will necessarily reveal to the borrower the identity of the money-lender . . ."

PERIOD OF LICENCE

[**5.19**] The normal period of a licence, and of renewal of a licence is expected to be three years. A shorter period may, however, be prescribed for licences granted pursuant to applications made before the appointed day, since these licences will probably be granted as a matter of course (in extension of the deemed licences arising by virtue of paragraph 4 (2) of the Third Schedule—see para. [**5.62**]), unless anything adverse is known about the applicant, and in the absence of the screening process that will be utilised for applications made after the appointed day it may be thought desirable to restrict the initial period of these licences. Renewal of a licence is dealt with in paras. [**5.42**]–[**5.44**].

CONDUCT OF LICENSED BUSINESS

[**5.20**] Regulations may be made as to the conduct by a licensee of his business, and may in particular specify—

(*a*) the books and other records to be kept by him, and

(*b*) the information to be furnished by him to persons with whom he does business or seeks to do business, and the way it is to be furnished (s. 26).

Such regulations may include provisions further regulating the seeking of business by a licensee who carries on a consumer credit business or a consumer hire business (s. 54).

### ASSIGNABILITY OF LICENCE

[**5.21**] A licence is not assignable; nor, with certain exceptions considered in the next paragraph, is it transmissible on death or in any other way (s. 22 (2)). In general, a standard licence held by an individual terminates if he dies or is adjudged bankrupt or becomes a patient within the meaning of Part VIII of the Mental Health Act 1959 (s. 37 (1), (4)). In relation to a licence held by one individual, or a partnership or other unincorporated body of persons, or a body corporate, regulations may specify other events relating to the licensee on the occurrence of which the licence is to terminate (s. 37 (2)). One such event might be the winding up of a company. This would leave the licence in the company since the property of a company in liquidation, unlike the property of a debtor on bankruptcy (which devolves on the bankrupt's trustee) does not pass to the liquidator. In the case of a group licence, the question of assignability or transmissibility will not usually arise, since any member of the designated group not specifically excluded automatically qualifies as a licensee under a group licence. Similarly, a change in the composition of a partnership firm does not affect continuance of the firm's licence—this being held in the name of the firm—unless the firm's name changes, in which event the licence comes to an end (see para. [**5.17**]).

[**5.22**] The automatic termination of a standard licence under s. 37 (1) could have a disastrous effect on the business of the licensee, since the licensee's trustee or other representative would be disabled from continuing the business, except after obtaining a licence himself. The inevitable interval between cessation of the original licence and grant of a new licence would cause immense difficulties and seriously reduce the ability of the trustee or representative to manage or dispose of the business to the best advantage of the estate and of creditors. Accordingly, s. 37 (3) enables regulations to be made which may—

(*a*) provide for the termination of a licence by s. 37 (1), or under s. 37 (2) to be deferred for a period not exceeding 12 months, and

(*b*) authorise the business of the licensee to be carried on under the licence by some other person during the period of deferment, subject to such conditions as may be prescribed.

### CONSEQUENCES OF CARRYING ON UNLICENSED ACTIVITIES

[**5.23**] A person who engages in any activities for which a licence is required when he is not a licensee under a licence covering those activities commits an offence (ss. 39 (1), 147 (1)). In addition, a regulated agreement (other than a non-commercial agreement) made when the creditor or owner was unlicensed is enforceable against the debtor or hirer only where the Director has made an order under s. 40 which applies to the agreement (s. 40 (1)). The provisions applicable to such an order are contained in s. 40 (2)–(5), which reads as follows:

"(2) Where during any period an unlicensed person (the 'trader') was carrying on a consumer credit business or consumer hire business, he or his successor in title may apply to the Director for an order that regulated agreements made by the trader during that period are to be treated as if he had been licensed.

(3) Unless the Director determines to make an order under subsection (2) in accordance with the application, he shall, before determining the application, by notice—

(*a*) inform the applicant, giving his reasons, that, as the case may be, he is minded to refuse the application, or to grant it in terms different from those applied for, describing them, and

(*b*) invite the applicant to submit to the Director representations in support of his application in accordance with section 34.

(4) In determining whether or not to make an order under subsection (2) in respect of any period the Director shall consider, in addition to any other relevant factors—

(*a*) how far, if at all, debtors or hirers under regulated agreements made by the trader during that period were prejudiced by the trader's conduct,

(*b*) whether or not the Director would have been likely to grant a licence covering that period on an application by the trader, and

(*c*) the degree of culpability for the failure to obtain a licence.

(5) If the Director thinks fit, he may in an order under subsection (2)—

(*a*) limit the order to specified agreements, or agreements of a specified description or made at a specified time;

(*b*) make the order conditional on the doing of specified acts by the applicant."

An appeal lies to the Secretary of State against the Director's refusal to make an order under s. 40 in accordance with the terms of the application (see s. 41 and paras. [**5.51**] *et seq.*).

THE LICENSING SYSTEM—ADMINISTRATION AND PUBLICITY

[**5.24**] The issue, variation, renewal, suspension and revocation of licences is within the exclusive domain of the Director, subject to the rights of appeal mentioned later in this chapter. Hence for the system of local licensing hitherto operated under the Moneylenders Acts there is substituted a central licensing machinery, controlled by the Director. As originally drafted, the functions now allocated to the Director by the Act were to be performed by a separate official, the Consumer Credit Commissioner. But when the Bill was reintroduced, it was decided to merge these functions into those of the Director General of Fair Trading, and there can be little doubt that the decision to do this was sensible. It is to be supposed that to assist him in evaluating applications the Director will be able to call for information from various agencies, including local Weights and Measures authorities, Citizens' Advice Bureaux and the like. This process of channelling information to the Director is already under way in connection with his consumer protection activities under the Fair Trading Act 1973.

**[5.25]** To ensure adequate publicity of matters concerning licensing applications and decisions, the Director is required by s. 35 to establish and maintain a register containing particulars of—

(*a*) applications not yet determined for the issue, variation or renewal of licences, or for ending the suspension of a licence;

(*b*) licences which are in force, or have at any time been suspended or revoked, with details of any variation of the terms of a licence;

(*c*) decisions given by him under the Act, and any appeal from those decisions; and

(*d*) such other matters (if any) as he thinks fit.

The Director is further required to give general notice of the various matters required to be entered in the register, and of any changes in these made under s. 35 (1) (*d*). The provisions of the Act relating to the register enable the Director to establish local registers, or copies of registers, if he thinks it desirable, and to allow local search facilitities (see s. 35 (4), (5)).

**[5.26]** A duty is imposed on the licensee under a standard licence to notify the Director of various changes. As will be seen, the duty will not always be easily performed. A standard (but not group) licensee must give notice to the Director, within 21 working days, of any change:

(i) in any particulars entered in the register in respect of a standard licence or the licensee under s. 35 (1) (*d*) (not being a change resulting from action taken by the Director) (s. 36 (1));

(ii) in the officers of a body corporate licensee or in the officers of a body corporate which is a controller of the licensee (s. 36 (2) (*a*)—and see below as to the definition of "controller");

(iii) in the officers of a licensee which is an unincorporated body of persons (*ibid.*);

(iv) in the members of a partnership licensee, including a change on the amalgamation of the partnership with another firm, or a change whereby the number of partners is reduced to one (s. 36 (2) (*c*)).

In addition, where a body corporate licensee becomes aware that a person has become or ceased to be a controller of the licensee, then the licensee must notify the Director of that fact within 21 working days after becoming aware of it (s. 36 (2) (*b*)). To ensure as far as possible that a body corporate licensee will become aware of changes in the control or officers of its controlling company, the Act provides that the controlling company shall notify the licensee of such changes within 14 working days (s. 36 (3), (4)). "Working day" means any day other than Saturday, Sunday, Christmas Day or Good Friday and a bank holiday within s. 1 of the Banking and Financial Dealings Act 1971 (s. 189 (1)).

**[5.27]** For the purpose of the Act "controller", in relation to a body corporate, is defined by s. 189 (1) as a person—

(*a*) in accordance with whose directions or instructions the directors of the body corporate or of another body corporate which is its controller (or any of them) are accustomed to act, or

(*b*) who, either alone or with any associate or associates, is entitled to exercise or control the exercise of, one third or more of the voting power at any general meeting of the body corporate or of another body corporate which is its controller.

[**5.28**] Any person is entitled, on payment of the specified fee—

(*a*) to inspect the register (or, if so determined by the Director, a copy of the register) during ordinary office hours and to take copies of any entry, or

(*b*) to obtain from the Director a copy, certified by the Director to be correct, of any entry in the register (s. 35 (3), (4)).

THE RIGHT TO A LICENCE

[**5.29**] In the early versions of the Consumer Credit Bill there was no right to a licence. The Director was not obliged to issue a licence to those fulfilling stated requirements; he was merely precluded from granting a licence unless certain conditions were satisfied, but apparently retained an overall discretion to refuse a licence even where such conditions were fulfilled. This was changed by amendment as the Bill proceeded through Parliament; and the effect of s. 25 (1) of the Act is that a standard licence *must* be granted on the application of any person if he satisfies the Director that—

(*a*) he is a fit person to engage in activities covered by the licence, and

(*b*) the name or names under which he applies to be licensed is or are not misleading or otherwise undesirable.

Accordingly, the issue of a licence is in theory a matter of right, not of discretion. In practice, this apparently clear-cut distinction is blurred by the fact that the Director has to be "satisfied" that the two conditions are fulfilled, and in determining whether condition (*a*) is satisfied he may have regard to any circumstances appearing to him to be relevant (see paras. [**5.32**]–[**5.36**]). Hence the "right" to a licence, involving as it does a value judgment on the part of the Director, is in reality much more akin to an administrative discretion. Nevertheless, it is not a discretion in the full sense; the Director cannot refuse a licence on any ground other than a failure to be satisfied as to one or both of the conditions set out in s. 25 (1). Thus, he is not entitled to refuse a licence to a prospective consumer credit grantor on the ground that there are already enough consumer credit businesses in the locality to meet the needs of the local populace. This is an additional test commonly applied in the United States, but it is not a relevant issue in the treatment of applications for licences under the Consumer Credit Act. Again, while the test of the Director's "satisfaction" is plainly subjective, this does not mean that the courts are powerless to intervene where the Director's approach to the assessment of evidence is manifestly unreasonable. This point is adverted to in paragraphs [**5.59**] *et seq*.

[**5.30**] Whilst the Director *must* grant a licence if he is satisfied that the two conditions set out in s. 25 (1) have been met, it is not entirely clear that the Director is precluded from granting a licence without being so satisfied. It certainly seems to have been the intention of Parliament that the Director should not be allowed to issue licences except on compliance with the two specified conditions; and it is thought that the courts would construe the words "if he satisfies . . ." as meaning "if, and only if . . .". Any other conclusion would make it extremely difficult for a third party to upset the issue of a licence on the ground of want of *vires*.

## APPLICATION FOR A LICENCE

[**5.31**] Under s. 6 (2) of the Act, an application for a licence, like any other application to the Director under the Act, must—

- (i) be in writing;
- (ii) be in such form, and accompanied by such particulars, as the Director may specify by general notice; and
- (iii) be accompanied by the specified fee, that is, the fee (or reduced fee) charged by the Director with the approval of the Secretary of State and the Treasury (ss. 189 (1), 2 (4), (5)).

Strict compliance with these requirements is imperative, since otherwise the application is of no effect (s. 6 (1)). No power is conferred on the Director to waive any of these requirements; and since a standard licence can only be issued on application by the intended licensee (ss. 22 (1) (*a*), 25 (1)), it would seem that a licence granted on an invalid application is itself invalid. However, it is within the power of the Director to alleviate the consequences of this situation by making a direction under s. 40 (2) (see para. [**5.23**]) or an order under s. 148 (2) or s. 149 (2) (see para. [**23.12**]) that regulated agreements made by the trader whilst he or the credit broker was unlicensed shall be treated as if he or the credit broker, as the case may be, had been licensed during the relevant period—always assuming that the application for such a direction or order was itself valid under s. 6 (2)!

[**5.32**] The matters that must be taken into account by the Director in deciding whether the applicant for a licence is a fit person to carry on the licensed activity are set out in s. 25 (2), (3), as follows:

> "(2) In determining whether an applicant for a standard licence is a fit person to engage in any activities, the Director shall have regard to any circumstances appearing to him to be relevant, and in particular any evidence tending to show that the applicant, or any of the applicant's employees, agents or associates (whether past or present) or, where the applicant is a body corporate, any person appearing to the Director to be the controller of the body corporate or an associate of any such person, has—
>
> (*a*) committed any offence involving fraud or other dishonesty or violence,
>
> (*b*) contravened any provision made by or under this Act, or by or under any other enactment regulating the provision of credit to individuals or other transactions with individuals,
>
> (*c*) practised discrimination on grounds of sex, colour, race or ethnic or national origins in, or in connection with, the carrying on of any business, or
>
> (*d*) engaged in business practices appearing to the Director to be deceitful or oppressive, or otherwise unfair or improper (whether unlawful or not).
>
> (3) In subsection (2), 'associate', in addition to the persons specified in section 184, includes a business associate."

The above provision needs to be read in conjunction with s. 170 (2):

> "(2) In exercising his functions under this Act the Director may take account of any matter appearing to him to constitute a breach of a requirement made by or under this Act, whether or not any sanction for that breach is provided by or under this Act and, if it is so provided, whether or not proceedings have been brought in respect of the breach."

[**5.33**] The word "associate" is elaborately defined in s. 184, in a definition which embraces certain forms of business association and relatives. To ensure that for licensing purposes forms of business association not mentioned in s. 184 may be brought within the purview of the Director's scrutiny, s. 25 (3) expands the meaning of the word "associate" to include a business associate. This term is not defined (though by s. 189 (1) "business" includes a trade or profession), but presumably covers any person in collaboration with whom business of any kind is transacted. "Relative" is itself widely defined, and includes, for example, not merely a husband or wife but a *former* husband or wife and even a *reputed* husband or wife. To convey the full flavour of "associate" it is necessary to set out s. 184 in full:

> "(1) A person is an associate of an individual if that person is the individual's husband or wife, or is a relative, or the husband or wife of a relative, of the individual or of the individual's husband or wife.
>
> (2) A person is an associate of any person with whom he is in partnership, and of the husband or wife or a relative of the individual with whom he is in partnership.
>
> (3) A body corporate is an associate of another body corporate—
>
> (*a*) if the same person is a controller of both, or a person is a controller of one and persons who are his associates, or he and persons who are his associates, are the controllers of the other; or
>
> (*b*) if a group of two or more persons is a controller of each company, and the groups either consist of the same persons or could be regarded as consisting of the same persons by treating (in one or more cases) a member of either group as replaced by a person of whom he is an associate.
>
> (4) A body corporate is an associate of another person if that person is a controller of it or if that person and persons who are his associates together are controllers of it.
>
> (5) In this section 'relative' means brother, sister, uncle, aunt, nephew, niece, lineal ancestor or lineal descendant, and references to a husband or wife include a former husband or wife and a reputed husband or wife; and for the purposes of this subsection a relationship shall be established as if any illegitimate child, step-child or adopted child of a person had been a child born to him in wedlock."

[**5.34**] Section 25 not only requires the Director to have regard to any circumstances appearing to him to be relevant in determining the fitness of an applicant but virtually gives him *carte blanche* as to the nature of the evidence on which he can act. Even if the applicant is himself guiltless of any offence, his association in business with undesirable characters or his family ties with persons of doubtful repute are sufficient grounds for refusing him a licence. Unfair or improper business practices may be taken into account even if not unlawful. Examples given during the Debates on the Bill were (1) persistently selling credit to those unable to afford it; (2) persistently driving extortionate credit bargains; (3) incompetence in the management of the business; (4) deliberate use of salesmen employing high-pressure techniques to sell credit.

[**5.35**] The second limb of s. 25 (1), namely that "the name or names under which he applies to be licensed is or are not misleading or otherwise undesirable" is not elaborated by the Act, but is obviously capable of covering a wide variety of situations. A name may be misleading or undesirable because it conveys a false impression as to the nature of the business to be carried on (as by improper use of the word "bank" or "insurance") or its size or standing (*e.g.* through use of the word "national", "international" or "British" for a purely local business) or because it too closely resembles the trading name of a third party. The discretion given to the Director in regard to a licensed name corresponds to controls on the use of business names which already exist under other legislation and at common law. Thus, by s. 17 of the Companies Act 1948, no company may be registered by a name which in the opinion of the Board of Trade (now the Department of Trade) is undesirable; and a Practice Direction issued by the Companies Registrar on the 7th September 1972 indicates that a name will be refused if (*inter alia*) it is too like the name of an existing company or other body corporate or if it is misleading, *e.g.* in suggesting that a company with small resources is trading on a great scale or over a wide field. The Registrar of Business Names may refuse registration of any name which in his opinion is undesirable (Registration of Business Names Act 1916, s. 14; Companies Act 1947, s. 116 (1)). Any trader, whether an individual, a partnership or a company, may be restrained at common law from using a name (even the trader's own name) with intent to deceive the public into thinking that the business is that of another trader, and in such case an action for damages will also lie.

[**5.36**] Those proposing to form a company to carry on an activity requiring a licence under the Consumer Credit Act face a potential difficulty in that after overcoming their initial hurdle of securing Department of Trade approval to the intended corporate name they may find after registration that the name is not acceptable to the Director as a licensed name. If it appears that difficulties arise from this in practice, then it is to be hoped that the Director will provide facilities for submission of names for approval in advance.

### OPPOSING AN APPLICATION

[**5.37**] The Act makes no express provision for a third party to oppose an application for a licence. The register which the Director is required to maintain under s. 35 will record applications for a licence that have not yet been determined, and general notice of such applications is required to be given by the Director (s. 35 (2)). Armed with these sources of information as to pending applications, an objector can, of course, write to the Director setting out the grounds of his objection to the proposed licence, and the Director is entitled, though not bound, to take such objections into account in reaching his decision. The Act does not confer on an objector a right to make representations, whether written or oral; indeed it says nothing about objectors at all. Whether a person opposing the grant of a licence has a *locus standi* to challenge by *certiorari* the decision of the Director, or the decision of the Secretary of State on appeal from the Director, on the ground of want of *vires* or of improper exercise of discretion depends on his ability to establish that he is a party aggrieved in the sense of one who has a legitimate interest in the outcome of the licensing application. If he has not, then it is entirely within the discretion of the court whether it will listen to him (see para. [**5.61**]).

REPRESENTATIONS BY THE APPLICANT

[**5.38**] The Director cannot refuse or restrict a licence out of hand. Section 27 (1) provides that unless he determines to issue a licence *in accordance with the application,* he must by notice (that is, by a specific notice in writing to the applicant, as opposed to a general notice)—

"(*a*) inform the applicant, giving his reasons, that as the case may be, he is minded to refuse the application, or to grant it in terms different from those applied for, describing them, and

(*b*) invite the applicant to submit to the Director representations in support of his application in accordance with section 34."

These requirements apply not only where the Director is not proposing to issue a licence at all but where he proposes to issue it in terms different from that applied for. Section 34 prescribes the manner in which the Director's invitation to the applicant to make representations is to be given. The Director must invite the applicant, within 21 days after the notice containing the invitation is given to him or published or such longer period as the Director may allow—

(*a*) to submit his representations in writing to the Director, and

(*b*) to give notice to the Director, if he thinks fit, that he wishes to make representations orally.

Where the applicant notifies the Director that he wishes to make oral representations, the Director must arrange a hearing (s. 34 (1)). There is no requirement that the Director himself shall preside at or participate in the hearing. He may appoint a deputy or indeed outside assessors. The tribunal is required to receive oral representation from the applicant. It is submitted that this requirement, as well as general principles of administrative law, obliges the court to hear not only the applicant himself but also any witnesses he may wish to call on his behalf whose evidence may be relevant. In reaching his determination, the Director must take into account any representations submitted or made by the applicant under s. 34 (s. 34 (2)).

[**5.39**] The Director is not obliged to invite or receive representations made by parties other than the applicant (*e.g.* objectors to a licence), though he is entitled to do so if he wishes. If he does entertain representations from third parties, it is for him to decide whether, and to what extent, to take them into account. It would seem that neither the director nor the tribunal is obliged to inform the applicant of the Director's sources of information (see *R.* v. *Gaming Board for Great Britain, ex parte Benaim,* [1970] 2 Q.B. 417; [1970] 2 All E.R. 528), though the applicant must be told the case he has to meet (*ibid.*).

[**5.40**] The Director may grant the application in terms different from those applied for, *e.g.* by exercising his power under s. 23 (2) to limit the activities covered by the licence (whether by authorising the licensee to enter into certain types of agreement only or in any other way) or by refusing or restricting the canvassing of regulated agreements off trade premises. In such a case, s. 27 (2) provides that the Director shall issue the licence in the terms approved by him unless the applicant by notice informs him that he does not desire a licence in those terms.

[**5.41**] By s. 28, where the Director is minded to issue a group licence (whether on the application of any person or not), and in doing so to exclude any person from the group by name, he shall, before determining the matter—

(*a*) give notice of that fact to the person proposed to be excluded, giving his reasons, and

(*b*) invite that person to submit to the Director representations against his exclusion in accordance with section 34.

RENEWAL OF LICENCE

[**5.42**] If the licensee under a standard licence, or the original applicant for, or any licensee under, a group licence of limited duration, wishes the Director to renew the licence, whether on the same terms (except as to expiry) or on varied terms, he must, during the period specified by the Director by general notice or such longer period as the Director may allow, make an application to the Director for its renewal (s. 29 (1)). Such application, to be valid, must comply with the requirements of s. 6 (see para. [**5.31**]). The Director may of his own motion renew any group licence (s. 29 (2)). The provisions previously discussed regulating the grant of licences apply equally to renewals, except that persons originally excluded from a group licence are not entitled to be given notice of the Director's intention to continue the exclusion in respect of the renewed licence (s. 29 (3)). The Director is required to give general notice of renewal of a group licence (s. 29 (6)).

[**5.43**] Until the determination of an application under s. 29 (1) and, where an appeal lies from the determination, until the end of the appeal period, the licence continues in force, notwithstanding that it would otherwise expire earlier (s. 29 (4)). "Appeal period" means the period beginning on the first day on which an appeal to the Secretary of State may be brought and ending on the last day on which it may be brought or, if it is brought, ending on its final determination, or abandonment (s. 189 (1)).

[**5.44**] On the refusal of a renewal application, the Director may give directions authorising the licensee to carry into effect agreements made by him before the expiry of the licence (s. 29 (5)).

VARIATION OF LICENCE BY REQUEST

[**5.45**] On an application made by the licensee, the Director may, if he thinks fit, by notice to the licensee vary a standard licence in accordance with the application (s. 30 (1)). In the case of a group licence issued on the application of any person, the Director, on an application made by that person, may if he thinks fit by notice to that person vary the terms of the licence in accordance with the application; but the Director must not vary a group licence under this subsection by excluding a named person, other than the person making the request, unless that named person consents in writing to his exclusion (s. 30 (2)). In the case of a group licence from which (whether by name or description) a person is excluded, the Director, on an application made by that person, may if he thinks fit, by notice to that person, vary the terms of the licence so as to remove the exclusion (s. 30 (3)). In all these cases the Director has power to act only if the application conforms to the requirements of s. 6 (see para. [**5.31**]).

## COMPULSORY VARIATION, SUSPENSION AND REVOCATION OF LICENCES

[**5.46**] Sections 31 to 33 of the Act deal with compulsory variation of licences by the Director, and with suspension and revocation of licences by him. The Director's power to vary a licence arises where, at a time during the currency of the licence, he is of opinion that if the licence had expired at that time he would, on an application for its renewal or further renewal on the same terms (except as to expiry), have been minded to grant the application but on different terms (s. 31 (1)). His power to suspend or revoke a licence arises where, at any time during the currency of a licence, the Director is of the opinion that if the licence had expired at that time he would have been minded not to renew it (s. 32 (1)). Suspension or revocation of a licence has more serious consequences for the licensee than refusal of an application for a licence in the first instance, since the latter merely prevents a man starting up a business in which he is not yet engaged, whilst the former deprives a man, temporarily at least, of his livelihood. Hence such a power ought not to be exercised without the fullest enquiry and the most careful sifting of the evidence.

[**5.47**] The procedure to be adopted by the Director is broadly the same for compulsory variation, suspension and revocation.

(1) In the case of a standard licence, the Director must by notice inform the licensee of the variation he is minded to make, or of the fact that he is minded to revoke the licence, or suspend it until a specified date or indefinitely, and must invite the licensee to submit representations in accordance with s. 34 (see para. [**5.38**]).

(2) In the case of a group licence, the Director must give general notice of his intention, as above, and invite any licensee to make representations in accordance with s. 34, and in addition, if the group licence was issued on application, must inform the original applicant of such intention and invite him to submit representations under s. 34.

(3) The Director must give general notice of a variation suspension or revocation of a group licence.

(4) A variation, revocation or suspension of a licence does not take effect before the end of the appeal period.

[**5.48**] By s. 31 (5), if the Director is minded to vary a group licence by excluding any person (other than the original applicant) from the group by name the Director must, in addition, take the like steps under s. 28 as are required in the case mentioned in that section (see para. [**5.41**]).

[**5.49**] If the Director revokes or suspends a licence, he may give directions authorising a licensee to carry into effect agreements made by him before the revocation or suspension (s. 32 (5)). For reasons which are not clear, no such power is conferred in relation to the variation of a licence.

[**5.50**] Section 33 provides for the ending of suspension as follows:

"33. (1) On an application made by a licensee the Director may, if he thinks fit, by notice to the licensee end the suspension of a licence, whether the suspension was for a fixed or indefinite period.

(2) Unless the Director determines to end the suspension in accordance with the application he shall, before determining the application, by notice—

(*a*) inform the applicant, giving his reasons, that he is minded to refuse the application, and

(*b*) invite the applicant to submit to the Director representations in support of his application in accordance with section 34.

(3) General notice shall be given that a suspension of a group licence has been ended under this section.

(4) In the case of a group licence issued on application—

(*a*) the references in subsection (1) to a licensee include the original applicant;

(*b*) the Director shall inform the original applicant that a suspension of a group licence has been ended under this section."

### CHALLENGING A DETERMINATION OF THE DIRECTOR

[**5.51**] A person aggrieved by a determination of the Director has two possible avenues for challenging such determination:

(*a*) by appeal to the Secretary of State, and thence on a point of law to the High Court, pursuant to the provisions of ss. 41 and 42 of the Act (see paras. [**5.52**]–[**5.57**]);

(*b*) by application to the court to exercise its inherent jurisdiction over administrative tribunals by orders of mandamus, prohibition or certiorari (see paras. [**5.59**]–[**5.61**].

[**5.52**] The procedure for appeals to the Secretary of State will be provided by regulations. The intention is that such appeals shall be heard by assessors, who will recommend the order to be made, though the decision whether to make the recommended order will rest with the Secretary of State, who will not be bound by the views of the assessors. In any such order, the Secretary of State may direct payment of costs by any party to the appeal (s. 41 (3)), and such a direction may be made a rule of the High Court (i.e. may be embodied in an order of the court so as to be enforceable as a court order) on application by the party in whose favour the direction was given (s. 41 (4)).

[**5.53**] The appellate functions of the Secretary of State cover all matters relevant to the determination appealed against, whether of fact, law (so long as the Director acted within his jurisdiction—see para. [**5.60**] or the Director's exercise of his discretion.

[**5.54**] Any person who had a right to the appeal to the Secretary of State (whether or not he has exercised that right) may, if dissatisfied in point of law with the decision of the Secretary of State, appeal from him to the High Court or require him to state a case for the opinion of the High Court (Tribunals and Inquiries Act 1971, s. 13 (1), (5A), as added by Consumer Credit Act, s. 42 (1)). The right to appeal, or to require a case to be stated, is thus given to any person (whether or not in fact aggrieved by the decision of the Secretary of State) who falls within the designated category of appellant in column 2 at the end of s. 41 of the Consumer Credit Act (see para. [**5.56**]), even if he had not himself appealed from the original determination of the Director. The matter cannot, of course, come before the High Court at all unless at least one person within the designated category makes an appeal from the Director which results in a decision of the Secretary of State. Hence if there is only one member of the class—as where a standard licence is applied for by and refused to a single individual—the unsuccessful applicant for the licence is the only person who can appeal to the Secretary of State, and he cannot come before the High Court *under the Act* without first obtaining a decision of the Secretary of State on appeal from the Director. If, however, more than one person within the designated categories is aggrieved, as where the Director excludes several persons or a class of persons from a group licence, then if one such person or member of the class exercises his right of appeal to the Secretary of State, the others may appeal to the High Court on a point of law from the decision of the Secretary of State, or require him to state a case, even if they did not themselves appeal against the original determination of the Director.

[**5.55**] The Director himself does not, of course, have any right of appeal from a decision of the Secretary of State varying his original determination, nor is he entitled to require the Secretary of State to state a case.

[**5.56**] The categories of aggrieved party entitled to appeal to the Secretary of State from a determination of the Director are as follows:

TABLE

| *Determination* | *Appellant* |
|---|---|
| Refusal to issue, renew or vary licence in accordance with terms of application | The applicant |
| Exclusion of person from group licence | The person excluded |
| Refusal to give directions in respect of a licensee under section 29 (5) or 32 (5) | The licensee |
| Compulsory variation, or suspension or revocation, of standard licence | The licensee |
| Compulsory variation, or suspension or revocation, of group licence | The original applicant or any licensee |
| Refusal to end suspension of licence in accordance with terms of application | The applicant |
| Refusal to make order under section 40 (2) in accordance with terms of application | The applicant |

[**5.57**] It will be observed that s. 41 is confined to appeals against a "determination" of the Director. What is the position if a party wishes to complain of inaction by the Director—for example, that the Director, whilst not expressly refusing an application for a licence, has simply failed to deal with the application? An inordinate delay could well be held to constitute an implied refusal so as to ground an appeal to the Secretary of State; but the uncertainty of the applicant's position in such a case might well incline the court to entertain sympathetically an application for mandamus to compel an express determination of the application.

STATEMENT OF REASONS FOR DETERMINATION OR DECISION

**[5.58]** Being a tribunal under the direct supervision of the Council on Tribunals (see para. [**25.6**]), the Director is under a duty to furnish a statement, either written or oral, of the reasons for any decision he makes, if requested, on or before the giving or notification of the decision, to state the reasons (Tribunals and Inquiries Act 1971, s. 12 (1)). A similar obligation is imposed on the Secretary of State as regards any decision made by him on appeal from the Director (*ibid.*). Any such statement of reasons is to be taken to form part of the decision and accordingly to be incorporated in the record (*ibid.*, s. 12 (5)). The Director or Secretary of State, as the case may be, may refuse to give a statement of reasons, or may restrict the specification of the reasons, on grounds of national security, and may also refuse to furnish the statement to a person not primarily concerned with the decision if of opinion that to furnish it would be contrary to the interests of any person primarily concerned (*ibid.*, s. 12 (2)). The duty to give reasons may also be excluded by order of the Lord Chancellor and Secretary of State, after consultation with the Council on Tribunals (*ibid.*, s. 12 (6)).

JUDICIAL REVIEW

**[5.59]** If the Director acts in excess of jurisdiction or if, whether or not asked to do so, he gives reasons for a determination which indicate that he has erred in law or has for some reason improperly exercised or failed or refused to exercise his discretion or has adopted an approach which is manifestly unreasonable, the court may intervene by orders of certiorari and mandamus quashing the invalid determination and requiring the Director to hear and determine the application afresh according to law.

**[5.60]** Whether the court will decline to exercise its jurisdiction to grant certiorari or mandamus by reason of the alternative remedy available to the applicant in the form of an appeal to the Secretary of State under s. 41 depends on the circumstances. The court will not refrain from interfering if the defect in relation to the Director's determination goes to jurisdiction, for in that situation there is no valid determination against which an appeal under the statutory machinery can be made; and in any event the court will always be willing to intervene to quash a decision which the tribunal in question had no jurisdiction to make (see *Barnard* v. *National Dock Labour Board* [1953] 2 Q.B. 18; [1953] 1 All E.R. 1113; *R.* v. *Paddington Valuation Officer, Ex parte Peachey Property Corporation, Ltd.*, [1966] 1 Q.B. 380; [1965] 2 All E.R. 836). Even if the complaint is not want of jurisdiction but, *e.g.*, the taking into account of factors not specified in the Act, or the adoption of a manifestly unreasonable approach, the court will not necessarily refuse *certiorari* because of the alternative remedy, particularly where it takes the view that *certiorari* is the most efficacious method of dealing with the matter. See generally de Smith, *op. cit.*, pp. 131–133, 374–376.

[**5.61**] The jurisdiction of the court can be invoked not only by the applicant for a licence, or other party set out in the Table at the end of s. 41 (see para. [**5.56**], but by anyone having a substantial interest (over and above that of the general public) in raising the matter before the court. This would appear to include a competitor, even though he had no statutory right to make representations to the Director or to appear to make representations in connection with an appeal to the Secretary of State (see *R.* v. *Thames Magistrates Court, ex parte Greenbaum* (1957), 55 L.G.R. 129). Exceptionally, the court might, in its discretion, accede to an application by a member of the public not having a distinct interest as an aggrieved party.

### APPLICATION FOR A LICENCE BEFORE THE APPOINTED DAY

[**5.63**] The licensing provisions come into operation on a day to be appointed (Third Schedule, para. 4 (1)). It will obviously be impossible for the Director and his staff to process all applications for licences made prior to the appointed day in time for them to be dealt with by that day. Accordingly the Act provides that where the person carrying on any description of consumer credit business or consumer hire business applies for a licence before the appointed day in relation to a business of that description, he is deemed to have been granted on the appointed day a licence covering that business and continuing in force until the licence applied for is granted or, if the application is refused, until the end of the appeal period (Third Schedule, para. 4 (2)).

### INVESTIGATION BY OMBUDSMAN

[**5.62**] The investigatory powers of the Parliamentary Commissioner for Administration (popularly known as the Ombudsman) under the Parliamentary Commissioner Act 1967 are intended to be extended by Order to the Director pursuant to s. 4 (2) of that Act. But the Commissioner will not usually exercise his powers as regards those determinations of the Director which are subject to appeal to the Secretary of State or acts or omissions of the Director within the scope of judicial review (see *ibid.*, s. 5 (2)).

# CHAPTER 6

# SEEKING BUSINESS

## THE NEED FOR PRE-CONTRACT CONTROL

**[6.1]** Whilst the regulation of the form and content of consumer credit agreements, and of the rights of the parties thereunder, is obviously of great importance, the consumer has need of protection at an earlier stage. Experience has shown that in the field of consumer credit the prospective debtor is peculiarly vulnerable to over-commitment of his resources, through a variety of factors. The first, and most obvious, is the innate attraction of being able to acquire goods or services now without having to put down the whole of the price at the outset. The second is the lack of adequate information to enable him to make an informed choice, to compare one form of credit with another, to evaluate the cost and to judge whether cheaper and better alternatives might not be available. The third is his reliance on information which in many cases is either false or, at best, misleading. The fourth is the immense pressure, both overt and covert, put upon him to buy in general and to utilise credit in particular. This pressure is exerted partly through the mass media, partly by face to face contact with salesmen and canvassers. Particularly prone to abuse are the activities of doorstep purveyors of goods and services on credit. The stories concerning some of these are legion: misrepresenting the organisations on whose behalf they are calling (a common technique used by encyclopedia salesmen to secure entry into a house was to represent themselves as calling to carry out a survey for educational purposes); misrepresentation of the nature of the proposed transaction (as by saying it was a hire-purchase agreement whereas it was a mere hiring, giving the customer no right to become the owner of the goods); foisting inferior or defective goods on the unsuspecting housewife; pressuring the housewife into signing contracts against her better judgment; and, finally, disappearing in a cloud of dust, leaving the consumer to find out at a later date that the company by whom the salesman employed was not to be traced or was impervious to demands for redress of the customer's grievances.

**[6.2]** The legislature has been concerned about these problems, but hitherto has dealt with them only in a fragmentary manner. Pre-contract activity by moneylenders has been closely controlled since 1927. The moneylender is not permitted to employ agents or canvassers to drum up business (Moneylenders Act 1927, s. 5 (3)); he is required to conduct all business in his authorised name from his authorised address (*ibid.*, s. 1 (3)); he is prohibited from despatching unsolicited circulars inviting applications for loans (*ibid.*, s. 5 (1)); and even the permitted content of newspaper advertisements he makes is tightly circumscribed (*ibid.*, s. 5 (2)). These restrictions have stemmed from a well justified concern for the consequences of uncontrolled peddling of loan credit. However, it is only the moneylender that has hitherto been caught in this way. Those exempt from the Moneylenders Acts—banks in particular—have been free to conduct business as they chose; and whilst this may have seemed reasonable enough as regards the clearing banks, the development of the secondary banks, some of whose activities were far from desirable, has shown that such an exemption is no longer acceptable. In the sphere of sale credit, control has been much less stringent. The Advertisements (Hire-Purchase) Act 1967 controlled to some extent the content of advertisements for credit, by requiring certain essential information to appear in such advertisements; and the Hire-Purchase Act 1965 required the pre-contract disclosure of the cash price of goods offered for disposal on hire-purchase or instalment sale terms. That was the limit of statutory intervention, apart from the supply of copies of the intended contract document after signature by the hirer or buyer.

### THE IMPACT OF THE CONSUMER CREDIT ACT

[**6.3**] The Consumer Credit Act for the first time provides for a coherent pattern of control over methods of seeking business in the consumer credit sphere. The thrust of the Act is directed at three main areas of activity, namely:

(i) advertising;
(ii) canvassing;
(iii) quotations and the display of information.

The control will be exercised partly under the provisions of the Act itself, partly under regulations made pursuant to its provisions. In addition to the three specific fields of activity mentioned above, a general power is conferred by s. 54 to include in regulations under s. 26 (see para. [**5.20**]) provisions further regulating the seeking of business by a licensee who carries on a consumer credit business or a consumer hire business.

### ADVERTISING—THE SCOPE OF CONTROL

[**6.4**] Subject to the exceptions mentioned below, Part IV of the Act, regulating the seeking of business, applies to any advertisement, published for the purposes of a business carried on by the advertiser, indicating that he is willing—

(*a*) to provide credit, or
(*b*) to enter into an agreement for the bailment of goods by him (s. 43 (1)).

This subsection involves an analysis of the words "advertisement", "published" and "advertiser".

[**6.5**] By s. 189 (1), "advertisement" includes every form of advertising, whether in a publication, by television or radio, by display of notices, signs, labels, showcards or goods, by distribution of samples, circulars, catalogues, price lists or other material, by exhibition of pictures, models or films, or in any other way, and references to the publishing of advertisements are to be construed accordingly. It should be noted that under this section, unlike the definition section in the Advertisements (Hire-Purchase) Act 1967, the word "advertisement" is not confined to visual advertisements but extends to any form of advertising, visual or oral, including advertising on the radio or through loudspeaker vans or even by sales patter in a shop or showroom. This does not, of course, mean that all types of oral communication by a prospective creditor to a prospective debtor constitute advertisements. The test would seem to be whether the statement is made with the object of drawing attention to the facilities offered by the creditor or whether it is for the sole purpose of answering a specific enquiry without actively trying to promote business. But even a reply to an enquiry will amount to an advertisement if couched in terms calculated to attract business. See, for example, *R.* v. *Delmayne*, [1970] 2 Q.B. 170; [1969] 3 All E.R. 980.

[**6.6**] Whilst the definition of "advertisement" does not in terms require that it be an advertisement to the public, Part IV applies only to advertisements *published* for the purpose of a business carried on by the advertiser (s. 43 (1)). Hence to be within Part IV the advertisement must be issued or displayed either to the public at large or to an individual or individuals as a member or members of the public, not in some other capacity. A letter or circular to employees advising them of preferential credit terms available from the employer would thus not constitute an advertisement published within the Act. On the other hand, an advertisement can be published even if it is merely a letter or circular sent to a single individual, if it is sent to him as a member of the public for the purpose of attracting business. See *R.* v. *Delmayne*, above.

[**6.7**] An advertisement is not within the Act unless it is published for the purpose of the advertiser's business. It should, however, be borne in mind that "advertiser" is not necessarily the person who actually places the advertisement but denotes "any person indicated in the advertisement as willing to enter into transactions to which the advertisement relates" (s. 189 (1)). Accordingly if an advertisement is published by S, the seller of goods, announcing that credit facilities to buy the goods are available from F, a finance house, F is the advertiser for the purpose of the Act and the advertisement, though placed by S, is accordingly an advertisement published by F for the purpose of its business and indicating F's willingness to provide credit. This appears to be so even if the advertisement was placed without F's prior knowledge or authority, though F's responsibility for it may then be negated by s. 168 (see para. [**24.2**]).

### EXEMPTED ADVERTISEMENTS

[**6.8**] By s. 43 (2), an advertisement does not fall within subsection (1) if the advertiser does not carry on—

(*a*) a consumer credit business or consumer hire business, or

(*b*) a business in the course of which he provides credit to individuals secured on land, or

(*c*) a business which comprises or relates to unregulated agreements where—

(i) the proper law of the agreement is the law of a country outside the United Kingdom, and

(ii) if the proper law of the agreement were the law of a part of the United Kingdom it would be a regulated agreement.

By s. 43 (3), an advertisement does not fall within subsection (1) (*a*) if it indicates—

(*a*) that the credit must exceed £5,000, and that no security is required, or the security is to consist of property other than land, or

(*b*) that the credit is available only to a body corporate.

It should be noted that one who carries on a business in the course of which he provides credit to individuals secured on land is caught by the provisions of the Act relating to advertising, even if his business is limited to transactions that are above the £5,000 ceiling and therefore outside the Act and even if the advertisement is expressed to be limited to transactions above £5,000, unless the advertisement makes it clear that security on land is not required. On the other hand, an advertisement is not within the Act if the advertiser's business is restricted to credit to bodies corporate or if the advertisement states that the credit is available only to a body corporate. An advertisement of hire facilities is outside Part IV if it indicates that the advertiser is not willing to enter into a consumer hire agreement (s. 43 (4)). Finally, the Secretary of State may by order provide that Part IV shall not apply to other advertisements of a description specified in the order (s. 43 (5)).

[**6.9**] Whilst agreements entered into by building societies, local authorities and other bodies specified in s. 16 of the Act are exempt from the Act, if secured on land, in the conditions previously discussed (para. [**3.24**]), such creditors are nevertheless subject to the restrictions imposed by Part IV on seeking business. Thus, advertisements by local authorities and building societies offering mortgage facilities for the purchase of dwelling-houses are no more exempt than advertisements by other creditors, unless an exempting order is made by the Secretary of State under s. 43 (5).

FORM AND CONTENT OF ADVERTISEMENTS

[**6.10**] The Secretary of State is empowered by s. 44 of the Act to make regulations as to the form and content of advertisements within Part IV. Such regulations are required to contain such provisions as appear to the Secretary of State appropriate with a view to ensuring that, having regard to its subject matter and the amount of detail included in it, an advertisement conveys a fair and reasonably comprehensive indication of the nature of the credit or hire facilities offered by the advertiser and of their true cost to persons using them (s. 44 (1)). In addition such regulations may, under s. 44 (2)—

(*a*) require specified information to be included in the prescribed manner in advertisements, and other specified material to be excluded;

(*b*) contain requirements to ensure that specified information is clearly brought to the attention of persons to whom advertisements are directed, and that one part of an advertisement is not given insufficient or excessive prominence compared with another.

[**6.11**] Appendix I to the White Paper sets out in detail the contemplated requirements of regulations concerning advertisements. The requirements cover matters such as the deposit, cash price, cost of credit, rate of charge, etc., but will vary in detail according to the nature of the advertisement.

Appendix I (apart from dealing with debt-counselling advertisements) distinguishes advertisements according to a twofold classification:

(1) *Credit advertisements and hire advertisements*
This is self-explanatory. A credit advertisement is an advertisement of facilities for loans or other form of financial accommodation, including instalment sale and hire-purchase. A hire advertisement is an advertisement of hire facilities.

(2) *Specific and unspecific advertisements*
An unspecific advertisement is defined in paragraph 5.1 of Appendix I of the White Paper as a general advertisement merely indicating that credit or hire is available but giving no indication of—

In credit advertisements

(i) the size of the credit advertised (*e.g.* '£500 loan') or the size of any advance allowed (*e.g.* credit up to 20 times your monthly payments), although it would be permitted to show the maximum or minimum amount of credit granted (*e.g.* 'on items in this catalogue' or 'loans up to £500' or 'credit extended up to a maximum of £500') or
(ii) where applicable, the cash price of goods which may be purchased; or
(iii) the cost of the credit in quantitative (*e.g.* 10 per cent per annum) or qualitative (*e.g.* cheap) terms; or
(iv) the size of any deposit or advance payments; or
(v) any of the repayment terms; or
(vi) the total credit price or repayment figure; or
(vii) the period of the credit, number of instalments or amount of any instalment;

In hire advertisements

(viii) any financial details of the hire in actual, quantitative or qualitative terms.

A specific advertisement is any advertisement of credit or hire which does give any of the information listed above (*ibid.*, para. 5.2).

The main consequence of the distinction between specific and unspecific advertisements is that specific credit or hire advertisements will have to set out the detailed information prescribed by the regulations, whilst unspecific advertisements (other than ones not primarily intended to attract trade) would have to indicate that further details were available on request without charge, and upon receipt of such request the advertiser would then have to supply prescribed information. Both specific and unspecific advertisements in which the advertiser was not the creditor himself but an intermediary would have to indicate that fact clearly.

[**6.12**] The content of advertisements would also vary according to whether the credit was fixed-sum or running-account credit, and whether restricted-use or unrestricted-use credit. For the final details, it will be necessary to await the regulations. The only point of which specific mention need be made here is the set of proposals dealing with disclosure of the credit cost as a percentage rate and, as a necessary step in this, the computation of the total charge for credit. The latter has been discussed in connection with the scope of the Act (paras. [**3.14**] *et seq.*), and the principles applicable to rate disclosure generally are set out in Appendix I.

AVAILABILITY OF CASH TERMS

[**6.13**] Section 45 of the Act provides as follows:

"If an advertisement to which this Part applies indicates that the advertiser is willing to provide credit under a restricted-use credit agreement relating to goods or services to be supplied by any person, but at the time when the advertisement is published that person is not holding himself out as prepared to sell the goods or provide the services (as the case may be) for cash, the advertiser commits an offence."

[**6.14**] The object of the above provisions is to outlaw advertisements purporting to show no credit charge, or an attractively modest credit charge, when the advertised supplier does not sell for cash, so that there is no method of determining the cash price and thus of verifying the stated rate or amount of the credit charge. In the absence of an exemption order under s. 43 (5), the prohibition imposed by s. 45 may seriously affect certain mail order companies whose practice is not to sell for cash but only to offer credit terms. Evidence was given to the Crowther Committee that the organisation of some mail order firms was geared exclusively to credit transactions and that the customer who insisted on paying cash was regarded as a considerable nuisance!

[**6.15**] Section 45, as originally drafted, aroused some anxiety in trade circles owing to the width of its provisions, and in particular the requirement that the advertised supplier must at the time of publication of the advertisement not only offer the goods or services for cash but offer them *on the same terms* except as to payment. The requirement created a difficulty due to the fact that because a supply on credit raises problems which do not occur in a cash transaction, the normal form of credit agreement will inevitably include terms (other than as to payment) that would have no place in a cash sale. In view of this, the requirement was dropped by amendment. It is now sufficient that the goods are available for cash from the designated supplier.

FALSE OR MISLEADING ADVERTISEMENTS

[**6.16**] If an advertisement within Part IV conveys information which in a material respect is false or misleading, the advertiser commits an offence (s. 46 (1)). Information stating or implying an intention on the advertiser's part which he has not got is false (s. 46 (2)).

ADVERTISING INFRINGEMENTS

[**6.17**] Section 47 (1) provides as follows:

"Where an advertiser commits an offence against regulations made under section 44 or against section 45 or 46 or would be taken to commit such an offence but for the defence provided by section 168, a like offence is committed by—

(*a*) the publisher of the advertisement, and
(*b*) any person who, in the course of a business carried on by him devised the advertisement, or a part of it relevant to the first-mentioned offence, and
(*c*) where the advertiser did not procure the publication of the advertisement, the person who did procure it."

Case (*b*) would include an advertising agency devising an advertisement for a client. Case (*c*), which at first sight may appear somewhat odd, can arise where, for example, a person is the advertiser not because he placed the advertisement but because he is named in it as the person willing to enter into the transaction to which the advertisement relates (see s. 189 (1) and para. [**6.7**]).

[**6.18**] Section 47 (2) provides an innocent publisher with a defence as follows:

"In proceedings for an offence under subsection (1) (*a*) it is a defence for the person charged to prove that—

(*a*) the advertisement was published in the course of a business carried on by him, and
(*b*) he received the advertisement in the course of that business, and did not know and had no reason to suspect that its publication would be an offence under this Part."

A quite independent defence, available to the publisher as well as the advertiser. is provided by s. 168 of the Act, which is discussed in paragraphs **[24.2]** *et seq*,

[**6.19**] Infringement of provisions in the Act or regulations results merely in the commission of a criminal offence and does not, under the Act, invalidate any agreement which the consumer is induced to enter into as the result of the offending advertisement (s. 170 (1)), though he may, of course, have a right to rescind the agreement at common law for misrepresentation.

CANVASSING

[**6.20**] The Crowther Committee, while recommending the repeal of the Moneylenders Acts, was strongly against the peddling of loan credit at the doorstep, and recommended that the prohibition against canvassing of loan credit imposed by the Moneylenders Acts should be maintained in the new legislation. Sections 48–51 are concerned with the canvassing and solicitation of applications for credit. As originally drawn, these provisions were extremely stringent, and might seriously have impaired check trading, as well as making it illegal to telephone a prospective debtor except in response to his prior request. The provisions finally enacted have avoided these problems and are restricted to the mischief against which the legislation was aimed.

[**6.21**] In essence, canvassing consists of oral representations to the prospective debtor or hirer, or to any other individual, during an unsolicited visit for that purpose to any place other than the *business* premises of the creditor or owner, a supplier, the canvasser himself or his employer or principal or the prospective debtor or hirer. The full definition is contained in s. 48, which provides as follows:

"(1) An individual (the 'canvasser') canvasses a regulated agreement off trade premises if he solicits the entry (as debtor or hirer) of another individual (the 'consumer') into the agreement by making oral representations to the consumer, or any other individual, during a visit by the canvasser to any place (not excluded by subsection (2)) where the consumer, or that other individual, as the case may be, is, being a visit—

(*a*) carried out for the purpose of making such oral representations to individuals who are at that place, but

(*b*) not carried out in response to a request made on a previous occasion.

(2) A place is excluded from subsection (1) if it is a place where a business is carried on (whether on a permanent or temporary basis) by—

(*a*) the creditor or owner, or

(*b*) a supplier, or

(*c*) the canvasser, or the person whose employee or agent the canvasser is, or

(*d*) the consumer."

**[6.22]** The following points should be noted in connection with the above provisions:

(1) If the solicitation occurs at a place where a business is carried on by one of the four categories of person listed in s. 48 (2), it is at (and not off) trade premises, even if the business is conducted there only on a temporary basis. Hence solicitation of the consumer (*i.e.* the prospective debtor or hirer) from a stall at a trade fair or in a tent at an agricultural show used for the purpose of the creditor's business for the duration of the fair or show is not canvassing.

(2) To solicit the consumer at his own premises is not canvassing if he carries on a business at those premises. Thus, a finance house can lawfully solicit stocking or other loan application from its dealers, even if they are not incorporated. But the position is otherwise if the debtor uses the premises exclusively for other purposes, e.g. as a residence.

(3) It is not essential to the definition of canvassing that oral representations should have been made to the consumer himself. Representations to any other individual suffice, so long as they take place during a visit by the canvasser to the non-business address where the representee is. On the other hand, it is the *consumer's* entry into the agreement that has to be canvassed, so that representations to his wife to induce *her* to enter into an agreement will be canvassing of the wife, for example, not of the consumer himself.

(4) To give rise to canvassing within the statutory definition, the visit must be unsolicited and must be carried out for the purpose of making the oral representations to any individual (not necessarily the consumer himself) who may be at the place in question. A visit made to service an existing loan does not give rise to canvassing if, without having called for that purpose, the caller solicits a new loan application.

(5) The term "representation" includes any condition or warranty, and any other statement or undertaking, whether oral or in writing (s. 189 (1)).

## CANVASSING AND OTHER SOLICITATION OF DEBTOR-CREDITOR AGREEMENTS

[**6.23**] It is an offence to canvass debtor-creditor agreements off trade premises (s. 49 (1)). The meaning of "debtor-creditor agreement" has been discussed earlier (paras. [**4.9**] *et seq.*). The effect of s. 49 (1) is to prohibit the canvassing of what Crowther termed unconnected loans, whilst permitting canvassing by check traders, credit traders, credit card issuers (but see para. [**6.27**] as to unsolicited credit-tokens) and persons offering hire-purchase, conditional sale, credit sale and rental facilities.

[**6.24**] Canvassing involves calling "otherwise than in response to a request made on a previous occasion". The request does not for this purpose have to be in any particular form. Any request, whether oral or written, which initiates the visit prevents that visit from giving rise to canvassing in breach of s. 49 (1). However, a separate offence is committed under s. 49 (2) if the request was not in writing signed by or on behalf of the person making it. It is not clear why the draftsman used this cumbersome approach. The requirement of writing and signature was dealt with in this way, and not as an ingredient of the definition of canvassing, because of the relevance of that definition in other sections, *e.g.* s. 23 (3).

[**6.25**] The soliciting of agreements for overdrafts on current accounts of any description is exempt from the provisions of s. 49 (1) and (2) where:

(*a*) the Director has determined that current accounts of that description kept with the creditor are excluded from subsections (1) and (2), and
(*b*) the debtor already keeps an account with the creditor (whether a current account or not) (s. 49 (3)).

Such a determination may be made subject to such conditions as the Director thinks fit, must be made only where the Director is of opinion that it is not against the interests of debtors, and may be revoked or varied by the Director if he thinks fit (ss. 49 (4), 183). If soliciting is done in breach of a condition imposed under s. 49 (4) (*a*), the determination under s. 49 (3) (*a*) does not apply to it (s. 49 (5)).

## CIRCULARS TO MINORS

[**6.26**] By s. 50 (1) a person commits an offence who, with a view to financial gain, sends to a minor (*i.e.* a person under the age of 18 years) any document inviting him to—

(*a*) borrow money, or
(*b*) obtain goods on credit or hire, or
(*c*) obtain services on credit, or
(*d*) apply for information or advice on borrowing money or otherwise obtaining credit, or hiring goods.

In proceedings under s. 50 (1) in respect of the sending of a document to a minor, it is a defence for the person charged to prove that he did not know, and had no reasonable cause to suspect, that he was a minor (s. 50 (2)). Where a document is received by a minor at any school or educational establishment for minors, the person sending it to him at that establishment knowing or suspecting it to be such an establishment is to be taken to have reasonable cause to suspect that he is a minor (s. 50 (3)). The onus lies on the sender to prove that he did not know or suspect the establishment to be a school or other establishment for minors (s. 171 (5)). These provisions are modelled on ss. 2 and 3 of the Betting and Loans (Infants) Act 1892. If a finance house, not knowing that a person is a minor, sends to him at home a circular inviting him to borrow money and the minor's parent forwards the circular to the minor at his school, no offence is committed. The finance house does not contravene s. 50 because it is within s. 50 (2) and is not the person who sent the circular to the school. The parent who is the sender of the circular, commits no offence because his despatch of the circular to the minor is not effected with a view to financial gain. Section 50 does not prohibit the *giving* of a documents to a minor inviting him to borrow, merely the *sending* of such a document, *i.e.*, its transmission through the post or by some other agency, as opposed to delivering to the minor by the creditor in person. If, however, the document is sent to a minor, an offence is committed whether or not the document arrives.

### PROHIBITION OF UNSOLICITED CREDIT-TOKENS

[**6.27**] It is an offence to give a person a credit-token if he has not asked for it (s. 51 (1)). "Give" means deliver or send by post (s. 189 (1)). Except where the credit-token agreement is a small debtor-creditor-supplier agreement (*e.g.* a check trading agreement where the credit does not exceed £30—see para. [**3.30**]–[**3.31**]), the request does not fulfil the requirements of s. 51 (1) unless it is contained in a document signed by the person making the request (s. 51 (2)). But the unsolicited provision of a credit-token is permitted:

(*a*) for use under a credit-token agreement already made, or
(*b*) in renewal or replacement of a credit-token previously accepted by the debtor under a credit-token agreement which continues in force, whether varied or not (s. 51 (3)).

### QUOTATIONS

[**6.28**] Regulations may be made imposing on persons carrying on a consumer credit business or consumer hire business a duty to provide quotations and regulating the form and content of quotations to customers (s. 52). Regulations may likewise be made requiring persons carrying on such a business to display prescribed information about the business in the prescribed manner at any premises where the business is carried on to which the public have access (s. 53).

# CHAPTER 7

# THE FORMALITIES OF AGREEMENT

## INTRODUCTION

**[7.1]** Part V of the Act (which is inapplicable in the cases mentioned in s. 74—see para. [**8.27**]) deals with four principal matters in the following order:

(*a*) Pre-contract disclosure.
(*b*) Withdrawal from a prospective regulated agreement, and the consequences of such withdrawal on that and linked transactions.
(*c*) The formalities for entry into a regulated agreement.
(*d*) Cancellation by the debtor or hirer of a cancellable regulated agreement, and the consequences of cancellation on that and linked transactions.

Since (*b*) and (*d*) are closely related, they are dealt with in Chapter 8. The present chapter discusses the provisions of the Act relating to pre-contract disclosure and formal requirements for regulated agreements, and outlines the intended content of regulations which will fill in the detail of some of the statutory provisions and the consequences of non-compliance by the creditor or owner.

## PRE-CONTRACT DISCLOSURE

**[7.2]** Regulations may require specified information to be disclosed in the prescribed manner to the debtor or hirer before a regulated agreement is made (s. 55 (1)). Thus, in a hire-purchase or instalment sale transaction, regulations may require advance disclosure of the cash price. Failure to comply with the regulations means that the regulated agreement is not properly executed (s. 55 (2)) and is thus enforceable only on an order of the court (s. 65 (1)).

## FORM AND CONTENT OF AGREEMENTS

**[7.3]** The provisions of the Act relating to the form and content of agreements broadly follow the pattern that was laid down in the Hire-Purchase Act 1965. The duty is imposed on the Secretary of State to make regulations as to the form and content of documents embodying regulated agreements (s. 60 (1)); and the Act itself prescribes the procedure for execution of regulated agreements and for supply of copies of contract documents to the debtor or hirer. The regulations to be made by the Secretary of State must contain such provisions as appear to him appropriate with a view to ensuring that the debtor or hirer is made aware of—

(*a*) the rights and duties conferred or imposed on him by the agreement,
(*b*) the amount and rate of the total charge for credit (in the case of a consumer credit agreement),
(*c*) the protection and remedies available to him under the Act, and
(*d*) any other matters which, in the opinion of the Secretary of State, it is desirable for him to know about in connection with the agreement (s. 60 (1)).

Such regulations may in particular—

(*a*) require specified information to be included in the prescribed manner in documents, and other specified material to be excluded;
(*b*) contain requirements to ensure that specified information is clearly brought to the attention of the debtor or hirer, and that one part of a document is not given insufficient or excessive prominence compared with another (s. 60 (2)).

However, a welcome flexibility is introduced into the Act—as recommended by the Crowther Report—by a provision that if, on an application made to the Director by a person carrying on a consumer credit business or consumer hire business, it appears to the Director impracticable for the applicant to comply with any requirement of regulations under s. 60 (1) in a particular case, he may, by notice to the applicant, waive or vary the requirement in relation to such agreements, and subject to such conditions (if any), as he may specify, and the Act and regulations shall have effect accordingly (s. 60 (3)). Thus, if a prospective creditor binds himself to grant a line of credit and charges a commitment fee, the Director might consider that this was a suitable case for waiving the requirement of disclosure of a rate of charge, since this is impossible to calculate until it is known how much credit will be utilised by the debtor. But a notice under s. 60 (3) may be given by the Director only if he is satisfied that to do so would not prejudice the interests of debtors or hirers (s. 60 (4)). The projected content of the regulations is indicated in some detail in Appendix II of the White Paper and is discussed below in paras. [**7.7**] *et seq.*

### DOCUMENTATION OF THE AGREEMENT

[**7.4**] Section 61 of the Act lays down what has to be done in order for a regulated agreement to be properly executed. Compliance with these provisions is important because a regulated agreement that is not properly executed cannot be enforced except on an order of the court (s. 65 (1)); and for this purpose a retaking of goods or land to which a regulated agreement relates is an enforcement of the agreement (s. 65 (2)). Further, a security provided in relation to the improperly executed agreement is itself enforceable only if the court has made an order enforcing the agreement (s. 113 (2)), and if the court dismisses an application for such an order except on technical ground the security is rendered void *ab initio* (ss. 113 (3) (*b*), 106). The rules to be followed by the court when application is made to enforce an agreement which is enforceable only on an order of the court are set out in ss. 127–128, discussed in paragraphs [**22.6**] *et seq.*

[**7.5**] For all transactions except land mortgages (which are subject to special provisions discussed in paragraphs [**8.12**] *et seq.*), the Act requires a regulated agreement to satisfy certain tests in order to qualify as a properly executed agreement:

(*a*) The terms must be embodied in a signed and legible document complying with the requirements of s. 61.

(*b*) A copy of the unexecuted agreement (*i.e.* of the document before it has crystallised into a contract) must be supplied to the debtor or hirer in accordance with s. 62, unless the unexecuted agreement is presented to the debtor or hirer personally for his signature and on the occasion when he signs the document becomes an executed agreement, in which case compliance with requirement (*c*) suffices.

(*c*) A copy of the executed agreement must be supplied to the debtor or hirer in accordance with s. 63, except where the unexecuted agreement was sent to the debtor or hirer for signature and became an executed agreement upon the occasion of such signature.

(*d*) A notice in prescribed form advising the debtor or hirer of his rights of cancellation must be included in the above copies, and where requirement (*b*) is inapplicable the notice must also be sent by post to the debtor or hirer, in accordance with s. 64.

Each of the above requirements will now be considered in turn.

A SIGNED DOCUMENT

[**7.6**] Section 61 (1) provides that a regulated agreement is not properly executed unless—

(*a*) a document in the prescribed form itself containing all the prescribed terms and conforming to regulations under s. 60 (1) is signed in the prescribed manner both by the debtor or hirer and by or on behalf of the creditor or owner, and

(*b*) the document embodies all the terms of the agreement, other than implied terms, and

(*c*) the document is, when presented or sent to the debtor or hirer for signature, in such a state that all its terms are readily legible.

Each of these paragraphs contains various ingredients which require separate examination.

PARAGRAPH (A)

[**7.7**] The first requirement of paragraph (*a*) is that there is a document in the prescribed form, that is, in the form prescribed by regulations. Such regulations will prescribe general legibility requirements similar to those currently contained in the Hire-Purchase (Documents) (Legibility and Statutory Statements) Regulations 1965. They will thus provide for the colouring of the paper used, the size and style of lettering and the prohibition of handwriting except for particulars of parties, goods and finance and any signature and date. The regulations will also prescribe the form and content of statutory notices informing the debtor of certain essential rights, such as the rights of cancellation and termination. In addition, the document must conform to regulations under s. 60 (1). Such regulations (which may either be separate or combined with the legibility, etc., regulations above referred to) will impose detailed disclosure requirements covering a wide range of information varying according to the type of credit agreement. Thus, in a debtor-creditor-supplier agreement details would have to be given of the goods, the cash price, the deposit, any advance payments, the total charge for credit expressed as a percentage rate and other information. Full details will be found in Appendix II of the White Paper.

**[7.8]** The document, in addition to conforming to the above legibility and information requirements, would have to contain "all the prescribed terms". This is a reference not to terms which the parties would have negotiated between themselves independently of the Act (since these are covered by s. 61 (1) (*b*)) but to contract terms which the creditor or owner will be required by regulations to include for the benefit of the debtor or hirer. The White Paper does not give any indication of what these might be, but merely a reference to "certain provisions" (White Paper, para. 46).

**[7.9]** Section 61 (1) (*a*) says that the document "itself" must contain all the prescribed terms. This would seem to mean that incorporation by reference to another document containing the prescribed terms is not sufficient.

**[7.10]** The document must be signed "in the prescribed manner" both by the debtor or hirer and by or on behalf of the creditor or owner. "The prescribed manner" will presumably embrace a prescribed signature block with wording informing the debtor or hirer of the nature of the agreement, as in the present regulations. In the case of a body corporate, it is sufficient if the document is sealed by that body (s. 189 (3)). Whilst the creditor or owner will be permitted to sign by an agent, a debtor or hirer will have to sign personally. The only exception is where the debtor or hirer is a partnership or unincorporated body. In that case it is not necessary for all the partners or members of the body to sign; one can sign on behalf of the others. Indeed there is nothing to prevent a signature on behalf of the partners or unincorporated body by a duly authorised agent who is not himself a partner or member of the body at all.

**[7.11]** What has to be signed is a document in the prescribed form and containing the prescribed terms and information. Accordingly a document conforming fully to the regulations must be completed before signature. Signature of a document in blank or omitting some of the prescribed details does not suffice, even if these are inserted subsequently (cf., on this point, *Eastern Distributors, Ltd.* v. *Goldring*, [1957] 2 Q.B. 600; [1957] 2 All E.R. 525).

PARAGRAPH (B)

**[7.12]** The document must embody all the terms of the agreement, other than implied terms. Terms may be implied in fact—*i.e.* by inferences from the conduct of the parties—or in law, as in the case of terms implied under the Sale of Goods Act 1893 and the Supply of Goods (Implied Terms) Act 1973 relating to title to and quality of the goods. Terms of this kind need not be spelled out in the agreement unless they were the subject of express oral agreement between the parties. No time limit is prescribed for reduction of orally agreed terms to writing; and it would appear sufficient if this is done at any time before the creditor or owner has commenced proceedings or has otherwise taken steps to enforce the agreement or any security.

[**7.13**] Whereas terms prescribed by regulations under paragraph (*a*) must be set out in the contract document itself, the terms required by paragraph (*b*) to be embodied in the document may be so embodied by reference to another document containing those terms. This is the effect of s. 189 (4) which states that a document embodies a provision if the provision is set out either in the document itself or in another document referred to in it.

[**7.14**] The requirement that the document should "embody all the terms of the agreement" appears to create, by statute, a further exception to the parol evidence rule, *i.e.* the rule that extrinsic evidence is not admissible to alter, vary or contradict the terms of a written document. This rule, which is logically indefensible, has in any event been so cut down by exceptions and qualifications that it is now honoured more in the breach than in the observance. If, pursuant to the parol evidence rule, the creditor relying on a written document were to be entitled to shut out evidence from the debtor as to an orally agreed term allegedly omitted from the document, this would largely defeat the purpose of s. 61 (1) (*b*).

[**7.15**] It will, of course, remain a matter of evidence whether an oral statement made by the creditor to the debtor was indeed promissory in nature or whether it was a "mere" representation inducing the contract but not forming a term of it. If the statement, though not a term of the contract to which the subsequent document relates, constituted a collateral promise or warranty, the omission of the collateral term from the document would not appear to contravene s. 61 (1) (*b*). Thus, if a dealer were to warrant to its customer the quality of a motor car which the customer contemplated acquiring on hire-purchase and the customer were then to conclude a hire-purchase agreement with the finance house through the agency of the dealer, the warranty by the dealer, even though it would represent a promise not only by him but also by the finance house by virtue of s. 56 (2) (see para. [**8.29**]) might well be held to be not a term of the hire-purchase agreement itself but a collateral warranty by the finance house and the dealer inducing entry into the hire-purchase agreement. In such a case, omission of the promise from the hire-purchase document would not infringe s. 61 (1) (*b*).

PARAGRAPH (C)

[**7.16**] Paragraph (*c*), requiring that the terms of the document be readily legible when presented or sent to the debtor or hirer for signature, is self-explanatory. This provision may overlap the general legibility requirements to be imposed by regulations made under s. 61 (1) (*a*) (see para. [**7.7**]).

SUPPLY OF COPY OF UNEXECUTED AGREEMENT

[**7.17**] Section 62 lays down the duty of the creditor or owner to supply the debtor or hirer with a copy of the unexecuted agreement, that is, the document embodying the terms of a prospective regulated agreement, or such of them as it is intended to reduce to writing (s. 189 (1)). In general, of course, as has been noted, the document itself will have to embody *all* the express terms. The requirements of s. 62 vary according to whether the contract document is presented personally to the debtor or hirer for his signature or whether it is sent to him for his signature. If the document is presented for signature but will not become an executed agreement on the occasion of such signature (*i.e.* where, as will usually be the case, the agreement is not executed by both parties on the spot but will be signed by the creditor or owner at a later date), the debtor or hirer must there and then have delivered to him a copy of the unexecuted agreement and of any other document referred to in it (s. 62 (1)). It will thereafter be necessary to supply the debtor or hirer with a copy of the executed agreement under s. 63 (see para. [**7.23**]). If the document is sent to the debtor or hirer for signature, a copy of the document, and of any other document referred to in it, must be sent at the same time (s. 62 (2)). The documents need not be sent to the debtor or hirer personally. Dispatch to his solicitor or other authorised agent suffices. If, after his signature, the agreement becomes an executed agreement (*i.e.* because the creditor or owner has already signed) no further copy need be sent.

[**7.18**] There may be some situations in which the unexecuted agreement is neither presented personally to the debtor nor sent to him. Such is the case, for example, where a form of agreement is included in a brochure available at a display stand or in a newspaper. In such situations, there is no duty to supply a copy of the unexecuted agreement at all. There is only a duty, after the debtor has returned the agreement for acceptance and this has been effected as described in paragraph [**7.23**], to supply a copy of the executed agreement within seven days thereafter, under s. 63 (2).

[**7.19**] The obligation to supply not only a copy of the contract document but also a copy of any document referred to in it might, if left in this unqualified form, create difficulties. For example, references to the Consumer Credit Act might attract an obligation to supply a copy of the Act, and a reference to an insurance policy might require the creditor to supply a copy of the policy. To avoid cases of difficulty, the Act provides for regulations to be made which may exclude specified classes of document from the supply requirements (s. 180 (3)) and may authorise the omission from a copy of certain material contained in the original, or the inclusion of such material in condensed form (s. 180 (1)).

[**7.20**] The copy supplied must be a true copy, though no doubt the court would disregard purely trivial deviations as *de minimis*. The copy must also comply meticulously with the prescribed form and prescribed requirements. If it does not, the duty of supply is not fulfilled (s. 180 (2)).

[**7.21**] Failure to comply with any of the above requirements prevents the resulting regulated agreement from being properly executed (s. 62 (3)).

### SUPPLY OF COPY OF EXECUTED AGREEMENT

[**7.22**] If the unexecuted agreement is presented personally to the debtor or hirer for his signature, and on the occasion when he signs it the document becomes an executed agreement, a copy of this, and of any other document referred to in it, must be there and then delivered to him (s. 63 (1)). In practice, this situation will be unusual, because the debtor or hirer is almost invariably required to sign first, and in most types of credit transaction the document is not then immediately signed by the creditor or owner but is taken back by his employee, agent or intermediary for consideration or, in the case of a finance house, is sent back to the finance house, either by the debtor or hirer himself or through a dealer or retailer. Hence in the great majority of cases s. 63 (1) will not apply, and the debtor or hirer will be supplied with a copy of the unexecuted agreement under s. 62 (see para. [**7.17**]) *and* a copy of the agreement itself as subsequently executed, under s. 63 (2) (see para. [**7.23**]).

[**7.23**] Where s. 63 (1) does not apply, then unless the document sent to the debtor or hirer for his signature becomes an executed agreement on the occasion of such signature, a copy of the executed agreement, and of any document referred to in it, must be given to the debtor or hirer within the seven days following the making of the agreement (s. 63 (2)). "Give" means deliver or send by post (s. 189 (1)). Again, the document need not be given to the debtor or hirer personally. It suffices if it is given to his solicitor or other authorised agent. If the agreement is a cancellable agreement, the copy *must* be sent by post (s. 63 (3)). Despatch by post within the seven-day period constitutes compliance with s. 63, whether or not the copy reaches the debtor or hirer in the ordinary course of post or at all; but delay or failure of the post will prolong the debtor's right to cancel (see para. [**8.42**]). An agreement concluded by offer and acceptance is "made", *i.e.* becomes a contract, when the acceptance becomes effective. This will normally be when it is communicated to the offeror. Where the post is an authorised means of communication, acceptance takes effect from the time of posting. Hence if, for example, a prospective debtor signs a hire-purchase document which is then transmitted to the finance house for its signature, that signature alone will not (unless the document otherwise indicates) give rise to a contract. It is only when the finance house's acceptance of the debtor's offer has been communicated to the debtor that the contract becomes complete, and it is from that time that the seven days for giving of a copy starts to run. It follows that if the only communication of acceptance is by despatch of the copy of the agreement itself, such despatch will be simultaneous with the formation of the contract, and if the copy complies with regulations it will satisfy s. 63 (2). (The time at which a contract comes into existence is further discussed in paras. [**8.5**]–[**8.9**].)

[**7.24**] There are special rules for credit-token agreements. First, a copy of the executed agreement need not be given within the seven days following the making of the agreement if it is given before or at the time when the credit-token is given to the debtor (s. 63 (4)). In other words, the time allowed for giving of the copy of the executed agreement does not expire until seven days after the making of the agreement *or* upon giving of the credit-token to the debtor, whichever is the later.

Secondly, whenever, in connection with a credit-token agreement, a credit-token (other than the first) is given by the creditor to the debtor, the creditor must give the debtor a copy of the executed agreement (if any) and of any other document referred to in it (s. 85 (1)). If the creditor fails to comply with this requirement, then

(*a*) he is not entitled, while the default continues, to enforce the agreement; and

(*b*) if the default continues for one month he commits an offence (s. 85 (2)).

[**7.25**] Again, non-compliance with the above requirements prevents the regulated agreement from being properly executed (s. 63 (5)).

NOTICE OF RIGHTS OF CANCELLATION

[**7.26**] In the case of a cancellable agreement (that is, a regulated agreement which may be cancelled by the debtor or hirer under the cooling off provisions contained in s. 67—see Chapter 8), a notice in the prescribed form advising the debtor or hirer of his right to cancel must be included in every copy of the unexecuted or executed agreement supplied in accordance with ss. 62 or 63, as previously discussed. In addition, where the agreement is presented or sent to the debtor for signature and becomes an executed agreement on the spot, either because the creditor has already signed or because he does so immediately after signature by the debtor, a separate notice in prescribed form of the debtor's right of cancellation must be sent to him by post within seven days (s. 64 (1) (*b*)). This is subject to dispensation by the Director pursuant to regulations under s. 64 (4). But where the agreement is not concluded on the spot immediately after the debtor's signature, so that s. 63 (2) applies, there is no need to send a separate notice of cancellation rights; the inclusion of the notice in the copy of the agreement required to be sent by post suffices. The object is to ensure that the debtor is supplied with a notice of cancellation rights by post independently of any notice that may be included in a copy of the agreement handed to him when the creditor or his representative is present. Hence the debtor must be provided either with a copy of the executed agreement on the spot followed by a notice of cancellation rights by post or a copy of the executed agreement by post incorporating such notice.

[**7.27**] Again, there is a relaxation of the rules in relation to credit-token agreements. The seven-day time limit need not be complied with if the notice is sent by post to the debtor or hirer either with the credit-token or before the credit-token is given to the hirer (s. 64 (2)). If there is a failure to comply with the requirements of s. 64, the cancellable agreement is not properly executed (s. 64 (5)). In addition, the time limit for exercise of the right of cancellation may in consequence be indefinitely prolonged (see para. [**8.42**]).

# CHAPTER 8

# WITHDRAWAL AND CANCELLATION

## GENERAL EFFECT OF STATUTORY PROVISIONS

[**8.1**] The Act contains various provisions as to withdrawal by an intending debtor or hirer from a prospective regulated agreement and as to cancellation by a debtor or hirer of an agreement that has actually been concluded.

[**8.2**] The debtor is given a right of cancellation in circumstances similar to those provided at present by the Hire-Purchase Act 1965. There are, however, certain extensions and modifications. First, all types of consumer credit and consumer hire agreement are affected other than land mortgages. Secondly, the phrase "appropriate trade premises" has disappeared, though the concept remains. The cooling off provisions will not apply if the debtor signed the agreement at premises at which a business is carried on by the creditor or owner, any party to a linked transaction (other than the debtor or hirer or a relative of his), or the negotiator. Thirdly, the debtor's right of cancellation is restricted to cases in which oral representations are made in his presence by an individual acting as or on behalf of the negotiator. Thus mail order transactions involving no personal contact with the debtor prior to the agreement will be outside the cooling off provisions.

[**8.3**] Regulated agreements secured by a land mortgage (this term includes a rent charge—see s. 189 (1)) are outside the cooling off provisions. This is not because Parliament does not wish to allow the debtor a period of reflection in such transactions but simply because the Land Registry wished to avoid a situation in which a land mortgage could be cancelled after registration, thus necessitating administrative work and other difficulties in vacating the entry in the Register. Accordingly the Act, instead of allowing the debtor in a land mortgage transaction a right of cancellation, provides him with a period of reflection by a different machinery. The creditor must not send the credit agreement for signature without first sending the debtor a copy of the agreement at least seven days in advance. After this period has expired without receipt by the creditor of any notice of withdrawal by the debtor, the agreement itself may be sent to the debtor for signature. If he signs and returns the agreement, it thereupon takes effect in the usual way. During the interval between giving of the advance copy and the debtor's return of the signed agreement or the expiry of seven days after sending of the unexecuted agreement, whichever first occurs, the creditor or owner must refrain from approaching the debtor (whether in person, by telephone or letter or any other manner) except in response to a specific request by the debtor made after the advance copy has been delivered or posted to him. If any of these requirements are infringed, the agreement will be improperly executed and will be enforceable only on a court order. The requirements apply wherever the enforcement was signed and even if no representations were made.

WITHDRAWAL FROM A PROPOSED AGREEMENT

**[8.4]** The right of an intending debtor or hirer to withdraw from a prospective regulated agreement is not conferred by the Act but derives from the common law rule that an unaccepted offer imposes no obligations on the offeree and may be withdrawn by the offeror at any time before acceptance unless the offeror bound himself not to withdraw by a document under seal or alternatively for valuable consideration (see para. [**8.8**]). Even in the case of a land mortgage, it is not the Act which gives the prospective mortgagor a right of withdrawal; all that the Act does is to prescribe the manner and deemed time of withdrawal, the consequences of a valid withdrawal on linked transactions (see para. [**8.20**]) and the special requirements which have to be fulfilled if the regulated agreement secured by the land mortgage is to be considered properly executed. The sanction for non-compliance with the requirements—namely that the agreement is improperly executed and is thus enforceable only on an order of the court—presupposes that a regulated agreement has come into existence despite, perhaps, some earlier notice of withdrawal by the debtor. Whether an agreement has come into existence has to be determined by application of the general law of contract, including rules as to withdrawal of an offer prior to acceptance.

WHEN IS THE CONTRACT CREATED?

**[8.5]** There are several reasons why it may be important to know the exact point of time at which a consumer credit agreement comes into existence. First, there must be a contract in existence before the transactional provisions of the Act can bite. Secondly, until there is a contract, either party is free to withdraw from the proposed transaction. Thirdly, as was seen in the previous chapter, the seven-day period allowed for despatch to the debtor of a copy of the executed agreement and of a notice as to his rights of cancellation runs from the time the contract is made.

**[8.6]** The normal, though by no means the invariable, sequence of events leading up to a consumer credit agreement relating to goods is that the prospective debtor makes an offer to the prospective creditor to buy goods or take them on hire-purchase, as the case may be, and this offer is subsequently accepted by the creditor. In order to produce a binding contract, acceptance must be intimated to the offeror either by express communication of acceptance to him or by some other act equivalent to such communication, *e.g.* delivery of the goods to which the agreement relates. For example, in the case of a hire-purchase agreement with a finance house, the prospective debtor's signature of the hire-purchase document and its delivery to the dealer for transmission to the finance house do not bind the debtor at that stage, nor is he bound even after despatch of the document to the finance house, since he has merely made an offer which has yet to be considered by the finance house. That offer will usually be accepted by signature of the agreement by the finance house, and the acceptance will be considered complete by communication to the debtor when a letter of acceptance, or a copy of the contract showing that it has been signed by the finance house, is put in the post to the debtor or where acceptance is conveyed to him in some other manner, as by telling him face to face or on the telephone or by procuring delivery of the goods to him. Similarly, an applicant for a loan may be asked to sign a form of application and to send this back to the prospective lender. Such an application is merely an offer and it is for the prospective lender to decide whether to accept the offer by notifying the prospective borrower that the loan will be granted.

[**8.7**] An example of the reverse sequence, where the offer comes from the prospective creditor, is the bank overdraft. A bank agrees to allow its customer to overdraw up to a stated amount. This "agreement" by the bank constitutes a continuing offer which remains open until withdrawn prior to acceptance and which the customer accepts each time he overdraws his account. Hence each drawing on the account when it is not in credit constitutes a separate acceptance and thus generates a separate contract, the consideration for the bank's promise to honour the cheque being the customer's express or implied undertaking to repay the advance with interest. If the customer, without authority, overdraws beyond the agreed limit, this is not an acceptance of the bank's offer (since the offer is limited to the agreed credit ceiling) but a request to the bank to honour the further drawing (*i.e.* an offer by the customer to repay the bank with interest if it honours the further cheque), which the bank impliedly accepts by payment. It is at this point that the contract comes into existence as regards the excess overdraft. (However, for the purpose of the Consumer Credit Act such contract is deemed to be part of the original credit agreement and does not constitute a separate agreement attracting the formal requirements of the Act or the cancellation provisions—see paras. [**3.22**], [**4.19**].)

[**8.8**] The contracts referred to above are bilateral or (as they are sometimes called) synallagmatic, meaning that they impose mutual obligations in that both parties undertake a commitment. This ingredient of *bargain* is the essence of a contract, and lawyers call it *consideration*. A person making a promise is not bound by it unless he receives some consideration, or *quid pro quo*, in the shape of a counterpromise by the other party or of performance of an act by the other party. Such consideration is an essential ingredient of every contract, except in rare cases, such as the commitment undertaken by a banker issuing an irrevocable letter of credit. A promise may also be binding where it is contained in a document under seal; but the binding nature of the promise then derives from the seal, not because there is a contract. In the case of bilateral contracts such as those described in paragraphs [**8.6**] and [**8.7**], the prospective debtor makes a promise in return not for immediate performance of an act by the prospective creditor but for the promise of performance. The contract thus comes into existence by acceptance at a time when obligations remain to be performed on both sides. The contract is thus said to be executory since it consists on both sides of promises as yet unfulfilled but is nevertheless binding on the parties.

[**8.9**] To be contrasted with this is the *unilateral* contract, so called because only one party undertakes a future commitment, the consideration being not a counterpromise by the other party but actual performance by that party. The latter therefore never *promises* anything, since the consideration is actual performance, and it is by performance that he accepts the promisor's offer. In other words, in a unilateral contract, the creation of the contract and performance by the offeree are simultaneous. Until the offeree performs, there is no contract at all. After he has performed, nothing remains to be done by him. A common example is a guarantee. The guarantor agrees that in consideration of A making advances to B, the guarantor will guarantee payment. A incurs no liability to the guarantor to make any advance to B; but each advance made by A to B constitutes a distinct acceptance of the continuing offer by the guarantor and imposes on the guarantor in relation to that advance the obligations created by the contract of guarantee brought into existence as the result of the advance. The guarantor is free to withdraw his guarantee at any time by notice to A as regards advances not made at the time of such notice. A consumer credit agreement will itself be a unilateral contract where, as often occurs, the prospective lender does not bind himself to make the loan but accepts the borrower's offer to take a loan at interest by simply advancing the money without a prior promise to do so. In such a case no contract comes into existence until the advance is made. The same situation arises where a bank's customer overdraws without prior arrangement or in excess of the agreed overdraft limit. The bank is not bound to honour the cheque, but if it does so it accepts the customer's offer to repay the loan with interest, so that the contract comes into existence when the cheque is paid.

### MODE OF WITHDRAWAL IN GENERAL

**[8.10]** Unless a party has bound himself not to withdraw an offer (by promising under seal or for valuable consideration to hold the offer open) he can withdraw the offer by notice to the offeree before the offeree's acceptance has been manifested by communication or conduct. In the case of a prospective regulated agreement the Act provides that the giving to a party of a written or oral notice which, however expressed, indicates the intention of the other party to withdraw from the agreement, operates as a withdrawal from it (s. 57 (2)). At common law, withdrawal of an offer is in general ineffective unless communicated to the offeree, and if sent by post takes effect not at the time of posting but at the time of receipt. If before that time there has been a proper acceptance, the withdrawal is too late and the offeror is bound. A provision in the Consumer Credit Bill that the debtor's posted notice of withdrawal should take effect on posting was dropped; and s. 69 (7), which so provides in regard to notices of cancellation, is not made applicable to a notice of withdrawal by s. 57 (1), since that section merely applies the same statutory *consequences* to withdrawal as to cancellation, and does not operate until there has been an effective withdrawal. Hence a posted notice of withdrawal is governed by the common law rule. The debtor or hirer need not necessarily serve the notice of withdrawal on the creditor or owner himself. By s. 57 (3) each of the following is deemed to be the agent of the creditor or owner for the purpose of receiving a notice under subsection (2)—

(*a*) a credit-broker or supplier who is the negotiator in antecedent negotiations, and

(*b*) any person who, in the course of a business carried on by him, acts on behalf of the debtor or hirer in any negotiations for the agreement.

Hence a prospective hirer of a motor car can give notice of intended withdrawal to the finance house which is to let the car on hire-purchase to him or alternatively to the dealer. General provisions as to the mode of service of notices, including notice of withdrawal from a prospective regulated agreement, are contained in s. 176, as to which see para. [**27.8**].

[**8.11**] Whilst as a matter of general contract law a party may bind himself not to withdraw an offer (as where the owner of land grants an option to purchase under seal or in consideration of payment of an option fee), a prospective debtor or hirer cannot usually bind himself to enter into an agreement that is a regulated agreement within the Consumer Credit Act. This is the effect of s. 59 (1) of the Act, which provides that an agreement is void if, and to the extent that, it purports to bind a person to enter as debtor or hirer into a prospective regulated agreement. However, as there may be transactions where this causes difficulty, power is given to make regulations excluding from s. 59 (1) agreements such as are described in the regulations (s. 59 (2)).

WITHDRAWAL FROM PROSPECTIVE LAND MORTGAGE

[**8.12**] It has previously been mentioned that the right conferred on a debtor or hirer, in given conditions described below, to cancel what would otherwise be a binding regulated agreement does not apply to agreements secured on land (s. 67), since this would cause administrative difficulties for the Land Registry. Hence instead of giving the debtor or hirer a post-contract cooling off period, what the Act does is to lay down a procedure designed to ensure that he is granted a minimum period of reflection *before* contract in which he can consider the prospective contract terms without pressure or indeed unsolicited communication of any kind from the prospective mortgagee. The statutory procedure (which will apply wherever the agreement was signed by the debtor—see para. [**8.3**]) involves compliance with three primary requirements:

(1) Despatch to the debtor or hirer of an advance copy of the agreement he will later be asked to sign, and of any other document referred to in it (s. 58 (1)).

(2) Despatch to the debtor or hirer of the contract document itself not less than seven days later, for signature by the debtor (s. 61 (2) (*b*)).

(3) No unsolicited communication with the debtor or hirer during the consideration period (s. 61 (2) (*c*)), that is, the period beginning with supply of the advance copy and ending seven days after despatch or delivery of the contract document itself for signature *or* signature and return of the contract document by the debtor or hirer, whichever is the earlier (s. 61 (3)).

Breach of any of these requirements has the consequence that any resulting regulated agreement is not properly executed (s. 61 (2)), and is accordingly enforceable only on an order of the court (s. 65 (1)). Requirements (1) and (3) call for certain observations. There are also two cases, mentioned in s. 58 (2), where this special three-stage procedure does not have to be complied with (see para. [**8.16**]), though the transactions in question will remain exempt from the cancellation provisions. As to first mortgage transactions, see para. [**8.19**].

DESPATCH OF THE ADVANCE COPY

[**8.13**] The requirement to despatch an advance copy to the prospective debtor or hirer is contained in s. 58 (1), which provides as follows:

> "Before sending to the debtor or hirer, for his signature, an unexecuted agreement in a case where the prospective regulated agreement is to be secured on land (the 'mortgaged land'), the creditor or owner shall give the debtor or hirer a copy of the unexecuted agreement which contains a notice in the prescribed form indicating the right of the debtor or hirer to withdraw from the prospective agreement, and how and when the right is exercisable, together with a copy of any other document referred to in the unexecuted agreement."

[**8.14**] Several points arise in relation to s. 58 (1). First, it applies whether the land mortgage is to be given by the debtor himself or by a third party. Secondly, the test of applicability of s. 58 (1) is whether there is a prospective regulated agreement which is to be secured on land. Hence for s. 58 (1) to apply, the projected agreement must be one which, when made, will be regulated by the Act; and the intention must exist, prior to formation of the agreement, to secure it on land. If, up to the time when the regulated agreement is concluded, the transaction is intended to be unsecured, s. 58 (1) will not apply, even though the creditor may ask for and receive security subsequently—a not uncommon event in the case of loan credit. There may sometimes be a factual dispute between the parties as to whether security taken after execution of the regulated agreement was intended to be given all along (in which case s. 58 (1) would apply) or whether it resulted merely from a subsequent desire by the creditor to protect his position. Thirdly, although what has to be supplied to the prospective debtor is an advance copy of the unexecuted agreement (*i.e.* the *credit* agreement, which is not necessarily the mortgage document—see para. [**3.11**]), the debtor must also be given an advance copy of any other document referred to in the unexecuted agreement. Hence if a finance house proposes to lend money under a loan agreement which requires a mortgage to be executed by way of security, the debtor must be supplied with advance copies of both the loan agreement and the intended mortgage, whether the mortgage is to be given by the debtor himself or by a third party. Since the object of s. 58 (1) is to supply the debtor or hirer with advance details of all the credit terms, it is thought that if a document referred to in the copy of the unexecuted agreement itself incorporates by reference provisions of another document, the two documents should be taken as together constituting the document referred to in the copy of the unexecuted agreement and copies of both such documents should therefore be supplied. Any other conclusion would enable a prospective creditor to frustrate the purpose of s. 58 (1) by including in the unexecuted agreement a reference to the terms of a short document which itself did no more than refer to a third document, and to supply the prospective debtor with merely a copy of the short document, leaving him quite unenlightened as to the precise terms to which that document would commit him.

[**8.15**] The advance copy of the unexecuted agreement must contain a notice in prescribed form indicating the right of the debtor or hirer to withdraw from the prospective agreement, and how and when the right is exercisable (s. 58 (1)). The copy must in addition conform to such other requirements as may be prescribed by regulations under s. 180 (1) of the Act. If the copy fails to meet these conditions, the duty to supply the copy is not considered satisfied (s. 180 (2)), with the consequence that any resulting regulated agreement will not be properly executed (s. 61 (2) (*a*)). The copy need not be served on the debtor personally. Service on an authorised agent, *e.g.* his solicitor, suffices.

### WHEN AN ADVANCE COPY NEED NOT BE SENT

[**8.16**] By s. 58 (2), the duty imposed by s. 58 (1) to supply an advance copy of the unexecuted agreement and of any document referred to in it does not apply to—

(*a*) a restricted-use credit agreement to finance the purchase of the mortgaged land, or

(*b*) an agreement for a bridging loan in connection with the purchase of the mortgaged land or other land.

The reason for these exceptions is that a purchase money loan which is to be secured on the purchased land may need to be provided very quickly if the transaction is not to fall through, and the delays imposed by the s. 58 (1) procedure could therefore cause difficulties. Case (*a*) of s. 58 (2) covers the situation where the link between the loan and the purchase can be readily established because the credit agreement is a restricted-use credit agreement, so that by definition the creditor controls the application of the loan to the intended purchase (see para. [**4.8**]). Case (*b*) of s. 58 (2) is inserted to cover the not uncommon position that arises where, for example, a person selling his house and buying another wants temporary accommodation from his bank to tide him over in connection with his purchase pending sale of his existing home. Such temporary loans will not necessarily involve control by the bank of application of the loan monies so as to give rise to a restricted-use credit agreement satisfying case (*a*) of s. 58 (2). The credit may be provided by overdraft or loan which, though intended for the purchase of the new house, is provided in such a way as to leave the debtor free to utilise it as he chooses (see s. 11 (2) and para. [**4.8**]). It is for this reason that case (*b*) does not import the requirement that the credit agreement shall be a *restricted-use* agreement. But case (*b*) is restricted to bridging loans, a term which is not defined but denotes a temporary advance to bridge a period of time at the end of which the debtor is to raise the required finance from another source and repay the temporary advance.

### THE DEBTOR'S ISOLATION PERIOD

[**8.17**] During the consideration period (see para. [**8.12**]) the creditor or owner must "refrain from approaching the debtor or hirer (whether in person, by telephone or letter, or in any other way) except in response to a specific request made by the debtor or hirer after the beginning of the consideration period" (s. 61 (2) (*c*)). Compliance with this requirement (which does not apply in cases within s. 58 (2)—see para. [**8.16**]) is not as easy as it might appear, and there are many pitfalls for the unwary.

*Example 1*

The advance copy of the proposed credit agreement to be secured on land is sent to the prospective debtor, who writes by return of post to say that he approves the terms. As a matter of office routine, a member of the creditor's staff sends the debtor a printed card acknowledging receipt of his letter and saying that this is receiving attention. The effect is that the credit agreement subsequently signed by the parties is improperly executed.

*Example 2*

The prospective debtor consults his solicitor with instructions to act on his behalf in connection with a projected loan from a finance house on the security of a second mortgage of his house. The solicitor writes to the finance house for particulars and is sent details of the transaction, together with a copy of the proposed credit agreement. As the result of a sudden rise in minimum lending rate, the finance house finds it necessary to revise its quotation and writes to the solicitor with the new figures. The resultant credit agreement is improperly executed. The solicitor is the agent of the debtor and communication to him is equivalent to communication to the debtor, in breach of s. 61 (2) (*c*).

[**8.18**] If a mistake of the kind illustrated in the above examples is discovered in time, there seems no reason why the creditor should not be able to rectify the matter by beginning again and sending the debtor a fresh copy of the unexecuted agreement. This will then become the relevant copy for the purpose of establishing the commencement of the consideration period, and so long as there is no communication with the debtor during this new consideration period (except in response to a specific request made by the debtor after commencement of that period) all will be well.

### MOST FIRST MORTGAGE TRANSACTIONS EXEMPT

[**8.19**] The special procedure described above for agreements secured on land is, of course, confined to *regulated* agreements. It will therefore not apply to the ordinary building society or local authority mortgage, which will be exempt under s. 16 (1) of the Act (see paras. [**3.23**] *et seq.*). Hence most first mortgage transactions will not be affected by this procedure or indeed by the Act as a whole. The main thrust of ss. 58 (1) and 61 (2) will thus be directed at the second mortgage market.

### CONSEQUENCES OF WITHDRAWAL

[**8.20**] Withdrawal of either party from a prospective regulated agreement not only terminates any outstanding offer in relation to the agreement, making this incapable of acceptance, but also operates to cancel any linked transaction (see paras. [**8.44**]–[**8.45**]) and to withdraw any offer by the debtor or hirer to enter into a linked transaction (ss. 57 (1), 69 (1)). A linked transaction cancelled in this way is to be treated as if it had never been entered into (s. 69 (4)), so that it is rescinded *ab initio*. However, regulations may be made excluding linked agreements of the prescribed descriptions from the scope of the above provisions (s. 69 (5)).

**[8.21]** All the provisions relating to the consequences of cancellation of a regulated agreement—the debtor's right to repayment, the return of part-exchange goods or payment of the part-exchange allowance, and the like—apply with equal force to withdrawal from a prospective regulated agreement (s. 57 (1)), whether or not such agreement, if made, would itself have been cancellable (s. 57 (4)). These provisions are examined in detail in relation to cancellation in the following paragraphs. Whatever may have been stipulated between the parties, the creditor is not entitled to retain any sum paid by the debtor, *e.g.* as an earnest of good faith designed to secure that the debtor proceeded with the transaction. Similarly, parties to linked transactions must return all payments received.

*Example*

H signs an agreement to take a car on hire-purchase from a finance house, F, and pays the requisite deposit to the dealer, D. The agreement requires H to keep the car insured throughout the period of the agreement. D arranges insurance on behalf of H, who reimburses D in respect of the premium. Before F signs the hire-purchase agreement, H notifies D that he does not wish to proceed with the transaction. The effect is that H's offer to take the car on hire-purchase from F is withdrawn and F and D are jointly and severally liable to repay to H the amount of the down-payment and the insurance premium paid to D (s. 70 (1), (3)). F is entitled to an indemnity from D in respect of such liability (s. 70 (4)).

**[8.22]** Specific mention needs to be made of the effect of withdrawal on the rights of a debtor who has been credited with an allowance for goods tendered in part-exchange. Section 73 (2)—which applies to withdrawal as well as cancellation by virtue of s. 57 (1)—provides that unless, before the end of the period of 10 days beginning with the date of cancellation, the part-exchange goods are returned to him in a condition substantially as good as when they were delivered to the negotiator, the debtor shall be entitled to recover from the negotiator a sum equal to the part-exchange allowance as defined, that is, the sum agreed as the part-exchange allowance or, if no such sum was agreed, such sum as would have represented a reasonable allowance (s. 73 (7)). The above section—which is not, it would appear, intended to derogate from the rights of the debtor at common law—does not confer on the negotiator the option to retain the part-exchange goods or pay the part-exchange allowance. It merely says that if he fails to return the part-exchange goods in the stipulated time and condition, he incurs an obligation to pay the part-exchange allowance. To comply with the time limit he must return the goods "before the end of the period of 10 days beginning with the date of cancellation", so that if notice of withdrawal is given on a Monday, the part-exchange goods must be returned to the debtor on or before Wednesday of the following week if the obligation to pay the part-exchange allowance is to be avoided. But even after expiry of the 10-day period, the debtor may be entitled to insist upon a return of the part-exchange goods *in specie*, and to sue for damages for detention or conversion if the negotiator fails or refuses to return them, or for conversion if he has sold them. Whether the debtor has the right to do this depends on the terms of the part-exchange agreement, and in particular on whether it was intended that ownership of the part-exchange goods should pass to the negotiator immediately on delivery or whether (as will usually be the case) the transfer of property to the negotiator was expressly or impliedly conditional on the consumer credit agreement coming into operation. For a full discussion of problems concerning part-exchange reference should be made to the author's book *Hire Purchase Law and Practice* (2nd edn.) pp. 185–186 and Chapter 14. Other points concerning s. 72 are discussed in paragraphs [**8.55**] *et seq*.

CANCELLATION

[**8.23**] The right to cancel (*i.e.* rescind) a concluded agreement was first conferred by the Hire-Purchase Act 1964 and re-enacted in the Hire-Purchase Act 1965. It was aimed primarily at the doorstep salesman who, taking advantage of the unsuspecting housewife, would there and then sign her up on the spot to an onerous agreement for goods she might not be able to afford, frequently inducing her entry into the agreement by oral misrepresentations of various kinds, secure in the knowledge that no-one else was present to overhear him and that the organisation he represented would rely on the agreement to disclaim any responsibility for his statements. The Hire-Purchase Act dealt with the matter by providing that any hirer or buyer signing a hire-purchase or instalment sale agreement within the Act at a place other than appropriate trade premises (*i.e.* broadly the premises of a dealer or finance house) should be entitled to cancel the agreement during a period of four days commencing with the day of receipt by post of the requisite copy of the executed agreement.

[**8.24**] How widely the right of cancellation under the Hire Purchase Act was exercised is not known for certain. The indications are that it was infrequently used and that the value of the statutory provisions lay more in the fact that they *might* be used—thus discouraging certain forms of doorstep selling—than in the actual exercise of the statutory rights. The Act certainly appeared to be effective in warning off some of the more unscrupulous door-to-door sales organisations.

[**8.25**] The cancellation provisions of the Hire-Purchase Act were at once too wide and too narrow: too wide in that they applied even if there had been no personal contact between creditor and debtor at all, as in the case of many mail order credit sale transactions; too narrow, in they they were confined to hire-purchase and instalment sale agreements and could not be invoked in relation to other forms of credit, such as rental and loan agreements. These deficiencies have been remedied in the Consumer Credit Act.

[**8.26**] Section 67, which confers the right of cancellation, provides as follows:

> "A regulated agreement may be cancelled by the debtor or hirer in accordance with this Part if the antecedent negotiations included oral representations made when in the presence of the debtor or hirer by an individual acting as, or on behalf of, the negotiator, unless—
>
> (*a*) the agreement is secured on land, or is a restricted-use credit agreement to finance the purchase of land or is an agreement for a bridging loan in connection with the purchase of land, or
>
> (*b*) the unexecuted agreement is signed by the debtor or hirer at premises at which any of the following is carrying on any business (whether on a permanent or temporary basis)—

(i) the creditor or owner;
(ii) any party to a linked transaction (other than the debtor or hirer or a relative of his);
(iii) the negotiator in any antecedent negotiations."

We shall examine, first, the conditions that have to be satisfied in order for the right of cancellation to arise (paras. [**8.27**]–[**8.33**]) and secondly, the two exceptions (para. [**8.35**].

[**8.27**] It is only a regulated agreement that can be cancelled under s. 67. Exempt agreements are not cancellable; nor are agreements excluded by s. 74 from Part V of the Act, that is to say:

(*a*) non-commercial agreements (*i.e.* those not made by the creditor or owner in the course of a business carried on by him—s. 189 (1));
(*b*) debtor-creditor overdraft agreements, if so determined by the Director, but only if he is of opinion that such determination is not against the interests of debtors, and subject to conditions specified by him;
(*c*) small debtor-creditor-supplier agreements for restricted-use credit, *e.g.* check trading and credit sale agreements where the credit does not exceed £30.

Further, a temporary overdraft in excess of the previously agreed limit does not give rise to a separate agreement attracting the cancellation provisions. See paragraphs [**3.22**], [**4.19**], [**8.7**].

[**8.28**] Even if the agreement is a regulated agreement and is not excluded from Part V, it will not be a cancellable agreement unless:

(*a*) the antecedent negotiations included oral representations;
(*b*) the oral representations were made in the presence of the debtor or hirer;
(*c*) they were made by an individual acting as, or on behalf of, the negotiator.

The onus of establishing the above facts lies on the debtor or hirer. Even if all these facts are proved, the debtor or hirer will have no right to cancel if the case falls within one of the two exceptions provided by s. 67 itself (see para. [**8.35**]). The onus of establishing these exceptions however lies on the creditor.

[**8.29**] The term "antecedent negotiations" is elaborately defined in s. 56 of the Act, which is of sufficient importance to set out in full:

"(1) In this Act 'antecedent negotiations' means any negotiations with the debtor or hirer—

(*a*) conducted by the creditor or owner in relation to the making of any regulated agreement, or
(*b*) conducted by a credit-broker in relation to goods sold or proposed to be sold by the credit-broker to the creditor before forming the subject-matter of a debtor-creditor-supplier agreement within section 12 (*a*), or
(*c*) conducted by the supplier in relation to a transaction financed or proposed to be financed by a debtor-creditor-supplier agreement within section 12 (*b*) or (*c*),

and 'negotiator' means the person by whom negotiations are so conducted with the debtor or hirer.

(2) Negotiations with the debtor in a case falling within subsection 1 (*b*) or (*c*) shall be deemed to be conducted by the negotiator in the capacity of agent of the creditor as well as in his actual capacity.

(3) An agreement is void if, and to the extent that, it purports in relation to an actual or prospective regulated agreement—

(*a*) to provide that a person acting as, or on behalf of, a negotiator is to be treated as the agent of the debtor or hirer, or

(*b*) to relieve a person from liability for acts or omissions of any person acting as, or on behalf of, a negotiator.

(4) For the purposes of this Act, antecedent negotiations shall be taken to begin when the negotiator and the debtor or hirer first enter into communication (including communication by advertisement), and to include any representations made by the negotiator to the debtor or hirer and any other dealings between them."

[**8.30**] It will be apparent from s. 56 (4) that all regulated agreements within Part V must inevitably be preceded by antecedent negotiations. It is manifestly impossible for a regulated agreement to come into existence without some prior communication between creditor/owner and debtor/hirer. Hence s. 56 (4) somewhat expands the normal meaning of the word "negotiate". Moreover, since "communication" in s. 56 (4) is expressed to include communication by advertisement, antecedent negotiations will in many cases begin before the creditor is even aware of the debtor's existence! It may be wondered why the draftsman thought it necessary to include advertisements as a form of communication. Section 67 only comes into operation if oral representations are made in the course of antecedent negotiations, and the commencement of an oral representation must inevitably constitute a communication sufficient to start "antecedent negotiations" for the purpose of the Act, even if there had been no prior contact between the parties. The reason why advertisements are included as a communication is that the definition of "antecedent negotiations" is relevant not only to the cancellation provisions of the Act but also to the provisions of s. 56 (3), which render void an agreement purporting to make a negotiator the agent of the debtor or hirer or to relieve any person from liability for the acts of a negotiator. Hence the creditor under a regulated agreement will, for example, be liable for the misrepresentations contained in a poster or advertisement put out on his behalf by the dealer through whom the agreement was concluded and which induced the debtor's entry into the agreement, whether or not any oral representations were made.

[**8.31**] Negotiations are "antecedent negotiations" only if conducted by a person within categories (*a*), (*b*) or (*c*) in s. 56 (1). Category (*a*) covers the creditor or owner (which for this purpose includes a prospective creditor or owner—see s. 189 (1)); and as a matter of agency law negotiations conducted by an agent or employee of the creditor or owner acting in the course of his agency or employment will be treated as conducted by the creditor or owner himself within category (*a*). Category (*b*) will typically cover a dealer selling goods to a finance house to be let on hire-purchase or sold on conditional sale or credit sale to the hirer or buyer introduced by the dealer to the finance house.

Category (*c*) will embrace a supplier selling goods against a credit card or trading check and a motor dealer selling a car for cash advanced to the buyer by a finance house to whom the buyer was introduced by the dealer. Any person within the above categories who conducts negotiations is a negotiator within s. 56 (1), and the negotiations he conducts are antecedent negotiations for the purpose of the cancellation provisions.

[**8.32**] It will be observed that category (*b*) of s. 56 (1) does not include a credit broker engaged in negotiations for debtor-creditor credit. The reason is that such a broker is almost invariably the agent of the creditor so as to come within category (*a*) (see para. [**8.31**]), whereas a person selling goods to a finance house to be let on hire-purchase or sold on instalment sale is not usually considered the agent of the finance house in law but is carrying out the transaction in furtherance of his own business (see *Branwhite* v. *Worcester Works Finance, Ltd.* [1969] 1 A.C. 552; [1968] 3 All E.R. 104), so that it was necessary to create category (*b*) in s. 56 (1) in order to bring him within the definition of a negotiator and make him a deemed agent under s. 56 (2).

ORAL REPRESENTATIONS

[**8.33**] Once the activities constituting antecedent negotiations have been established—by demonstrating that negotiations (including communication by advertisement) have been conducted by a person who is a negotiator within s. 56 (1)—we have then to see whether such negotiations included oral representations made when in the presence of the debtor or hirer by an individual acting as, or on behalf of, the negotiator. In the absence of such face-to-face oral representations, the cancellation provisions do not apply. This is one of the respects in which the provisions differ from those of the previous legislation.

[**8.34**] "Representation" is defined as including any condition or warranty, and any other statement or undertaking, whether oral or in writing (s. 189 (1)). However, the cancellation provisions operate only where the representation is oral, and even then only if made when in the presence of the debtor or hirer. A telephone discussion with the debtor is thus outside s. 67. The words "in the presence of the debtor or hirer" do not require that the representation shall actually have been addressed to the debtor or hirer himself. Remarks made in his presence to a third party—*e.g.* his wife or a friend—designed to further his entry into the prospective agreement will be within the section. On the other hand, it would seem that the debtor must be present personally. Presence by an agent would not, it is thought, suffice. The object of the statutory provisions is to protect a prospective debtor who is subjected to sales talk in person, not by proxy. The oral representations must be made by an individual, a somewhat superfluous provision, since a body corporate has no physical voice and cannot make statements orally save through an individual. The representor may be the negotiator himself or his agent or employee acting in the course of his agency or employment. The negotiator as such need not, of course, be an individual.

EXCEPTIONS

[**8.35**] Apart from the general exemptions from Part V (see para. [**8.27**] section 67 itself lays down two categories of case in which the cooling off provisions are not to apply, even if all the other requirements of the section are satisfied. The first is where the agreement is secured on land or is a restricted-use credit agreement to finance the purchase of land or is an agreement for a bridging loan in connection with the purchase of land. The onus of establishing that the agreement is within this category lies on the creditor asserting it. Agreements secured on land have been discussed earlier in this chapter. They are governed by the special advance copy procedure described in paragraphs [**8.12**] *et seq.* Restricted-use agreements to finance the purchase of land and agreements for a bridging loan in connection with the purchase of land are excluded both from the cooling off provisions and from the advance copy requirement. They have been discussed in paragraph [**8.16**]. The second category of excluded agreement depends not on the character of the agreement but on the place where it is signed by the debtor or hirer. If it is signed at business premises (whether permanent or temporary) of the creditor or owner, any party to a linked transaction (see para. [**8.45**]) or the negotiator in any antecedent negotiations, the cooling off provisions do not apply. Thus, if a prospective hirer signs a hire-purchase agreement at the premises of the dealer or finance house, he has no statutory right of cancellation. Note, however, that (in contrast to the position under the Hire-Purchase Act 1965) this is so only where signature takes place at the business address of the finance house or dealer concerned in the transaction. Signature at the business premises of some other dealer dealing in goods of a similar description does not suffice. In such a case, the hirer will have a right to cancel, as he will also if he signs the agreement at his home, his own business premises or at the offices of his solicitor. Again, the onus is on the creditor to show that because of the place of signature the cooling off provisions do not apply; for it is the creditor who is relying on the exception. It is not for the debtor or hirer to prove where he signed the agreement.

MODE OF CANCELLATION

[**8.36**] By s. 69 (1) the right of cancellation is exercised by notice (*i.e.* notice in writing—s. 189 (1)) served by the debtor or hirer within the prescribed time (see para. [**8.39**]) on:

(*a*) the creditor or owner; or
(*b*) the person specified in the notice under s. 64 (1) as the person to whom notice of cancellation may be given; or
(*c*) a person who (whether by virtue of s. 69 (6) or otherwise) is the agent of the creditor or owner.

[**8.37**] "Creditor" means the person providing credit under the consumer credit agreement or his assignee; "owner" means the person who bails goods under the consumer hire agreement or his assignee (s. 189 (1)). Section 69 (6) provides that each of the following shall be deemed to be the agent of the creditor or owner for the purpose of receiving a notice of cancellation—

(*a*) a credit broker or supplier who is the negotiator in antecedent negotiations, and
(*b*) any person who, in the course of a business carried on by him, acts on behalf of the debtor or hirer in any negotiations for the agreement.

Thus, in a normal hire-purchase or instalment sale transaction with a finance house, the hirer or buyer can serve his notice of cancellation on the finance house or on the dealer. In a check trading transaction, the notice would normally have to be served on the check trader. A supplier would not as a rule fall within s. 69 (6) (*a*) as a negotiator since in general the initiative for entry into a check trading agreement is taken by the check trader, and the debtor's contact with the various suppliers in connection with the credit does not take place until afterwards. If, however, a particular supplier did in fact act as a negotiator within the definition of s. 56 (1), the debtor would be entitled to serve his notice of cancellation on that supplier.

[**8.38**] Paragraph (*b*) of s. 69 (6), by which the debtor's agent is deemed to be the creditor's agent, appears startling at first sight, but is necessary in view of the fact that there are various types of broker (particularly in the insurance world) who, though not in law the agent of the creditor, are often taken to be such by the consumer, who might thus assume that communication to them was equivalent to communication to the other party. The Act gives statutory effect to that assumption for the purpose of service of a notice of cancellation.

## TIME LIMIT WITHIN WHICH NOTICE MUST BE SERVED

[**8.39**] The Hire-Purchase Act 1965 allowed a hirer or buyer a period of four days, beginning with the day of receipt of the copy of the executed agreement, within which to exercise a right of cancellation. The Consumer Credit Act effectively extends this by two days in the normal case, but introduces some variations. The time limit is laid down by s. 68. The commencement of the period in which the debtor can cancel is the date of his signature of the unexecuted agreement. The date of expiry of the period depends on whether the agreement is concluded on the spot after the debtor's signature or whether, as is the usual case, it is not concluded until later.

[**8.40**] If the agreement is concluded on the spot, the debtor (in addition to being supplied with a copy there and then) must be sent by post within seven days a notice advising him of his right of cancellation. The debtor then has until the end of the fifth day *following* the date of receipt of such notice within which to serve a notice of cancellation. Thus, if the debtor received the s. 64 (1) (*b*) notice on a Monday, he has until midnight on the ensuing Saturday within which to serve a cancellation notice. If, however, a s. 64 (1) (*b*) notice is not served on the debtor, because the Director has dispensed with this requirement pursuant to regulations under s. 64 (4) (see para. [**7.26**]), then the debtor has until the end of the fourteenth day following the day on which he signed the unexecuted agreement (s. 68 (*b*)).

[**8.41**] If the agreement is not concluded on the spot after signature by the debtor—*e.g.* because it then has to be sent or taken for signature by the creditor—the duty of the creditor is to send not a separate notice advising the debtor of his cancellation rights but a copy of the executed agreement incorporating such a notice. The debtor then has until the end of the fifth day following receipt of such copy within which to serve his cancellation notice (s. 68 (*a*)).

[**8.42**] Except where s. 68 (*b*) applies (as the result of the Director's dispensing with service of a notice under s. 64 (1) (*b*)), the debtor's period of cancellation is geared to the date of his receipt of the notice under s. 64 (1) (*b*) or of the copy of the executed agreement, as the case may be. If the notice or copy goes astray in the post and does not reach him, his time for cancellation is indefinitely prolonged. If the creditor discovers the postal failure in time to serve a fresh notice or copy within the permitted seven days from the making of the agreement, he can rectify the situation in this way. If, however, he does not discover it until after the seven-day period has expired, it would seem that he is powerless to start the cancellation period running by service of a fresh notice or copy, since this, being served outside the time laid down by ss. 64 (1) (*b*) and 63 (2), could not be said to be a notice "under s. 64 (1) (*b*)" or a copy "under s. 63 (2)", and the receipt of such a notice by the debtor is essential to start time running against him. In such a case, all the creditor could do, if he came to enforce the agreement, would be to hope that the debtor would not exercise his right to cancel. Subject to such right, the agreement is fully enforceable as a properly executed agreement, since service by post is compliance with ss. 63 and 64 whether or not the copy or notice reaches its destination.

[**8.43**] If the debtor serves his cancellation notice by post, this is deemed to be served at the time of posting (s. 69 (7)), irrespective whether or when the notice arrives.

### EFFECT OF CANCELLATION

[**8.44**] By s. 69 (1) service of a notice of cancellation by the debtor operates:

(i) to cancel the agreement, and any linked transaction; and

(ii) to withdraw any offer by the debtor, or his relative, to enter into a linked transaction.

Subject to s. 71 (see para. [**8.49**]), an agreement or transaction cancelled as above is to be treated as if it had never been entered into (s. 69 (4)). On cancellation the debtor, except in cases within s. 70 (5) (see para. [**8.48**]), is released from liability for any payment, whether accrued due or payable in the future, and is entitled to:

(*a*) repayment of sums paid under or in contemplation of the consumer credit or consumer hire agreement or linked transaction;

(*b*) recovery of any goods tendered in part exchange or, if not recovered within ten days in substantially the same condition as when delivered, a sum equal to the part-exchange allowance;

(*c*) a lien on goods received by him under the consumer credit or consumer hire agreement, pending fulfilment of (*a*) and (*b*) (ss. 70 (1), (2), 73 (2), (5)).

Further, the effect of cancellation is that any security given is to be treated as never having effect and any property lodged with the creditor or owner solely for the purposes of the security must be returned by him forthwith (s. 106, as applied by s. 113 (3)). For his part, the debtor (except in cases within s. 72 (9)—see para. [**8.63**]) is obliged to surrender goods received by him under the agreement, and meanwhile to retain possession of the goods and take reasonable care of them (s. 72 (4)). But where the creditor has taken security, these duties cannot be enforced against the debtor until the creditor has complied with his obligations under s. 106 (see para. [**13.13**]) in relation to the security (s. 113 (5)). A debtor or hirer who has cancelled an agreement pursuant to s. 69 is entitled to apply to the court for a declaration that the agreement was so cancelled (s. 142 (2)).

## LINKED TRANSACTIONS

[**8.45**] Linked transactions are defined in s. 19, which is examined in detail in Chapter 19. Suffice it at this stage to give a few illustrations of the types of agreement that will automatically be cancelled as the result of cancellation of the consumer credit or consumer hire agreement.

*Example 1*

Pursuant to a provision in a regulated hire-purchase agreement, the hirer insures the goods. Cancellation of the hire-purchase agreement automatically rescinds the insurance contract and entitles the hirer to be repaid the premium by the insurer. This is so whether or not there was any arrangement between the insurer and the owner, and indeed even though the insurer was unaware that the insurance was taken out pursuant to a requirement of the hire-purchase agreement. The same would apply to an associated contract of maintenance entered into pursuant to a provision of the hire-purchase agreement.

*Example 2*

A car is bought from a motor dealer for cash paid with the aid of an advance from a finance house under a regulated loan agreement, the purchaser having been introduced to the finance house by the dealer pursuant to arrangements between them for the provision of finance for customers of the dealer. The borrower exercises his right to cancel the loan agreement. The cash sale by the dealer to the buyer, being a linked transaction, is thereby rescinded, and the buyer is entitled to recover any payment made to the dealer.

*Example 3*

The holder of a credit card exercises a right to cancel the credit-token agreement under which the card was issued. All purchases made with the card (otherwise than to meet an emergency) are thereby automatically cancelled and the debtor is entitled to recover his payments from the creditor (*i.e.* the issuer of the card), except that a payment made for the issue of the card is recoverable only on surrender of the card to the issuer or a supplier (s. 70 (5)).

Section 69 (5) enables regulation to be made preserving linked transactions of the prescribed description from retrospective obliteration under s. 69 (1), (4). This saving was introduced primarily to cover situations where cancellation of a deemed withdrawal from the linked transaction might unfairly affect the debtor, *e.g.* by retrospectively invalidating insurance taken out on a motor vehicle comprised in a regulated or prospective agreement. For the same reason, the operation of s. 19 (3) (which provides that a linked transaction entered into before the making of the principal agreement has no effect until such time (if any) as the principal agreement is made) may be excluded by regulations (s. 19 (4)).

REPAYMENT TO AND RELEASE OF THE DEBTOR

[**8.46**] On cancellation, the debtor is entitled to recover all payments made under or in contemplation of the cancelled agreement or any linked agreement (s. 70 (1)), except that if the total charge for credit includes an item in respect of a fee or commission charged by a credit broker, the amount repayable in respect of that item is the excess over £1 of the fee or commission (s. 70 (6)). Usually, the debtor's claim for repayment must be made against the person to whom he made the payment (s. 70 (3)). But where the credit agreement is a debtor-creditor-supplier agreement and the creditor is not the supplier himself, the creditor and the supplier are jointly and severally liable for the repayment (*ibid.*). Thus, a debtor cancelling a purchase-loan agreement with a finance house concluded through the dealer supplying the goods will be entitled to recover a deposit paid to the dealer either from the dealer or from the finance house or from both together. In such a case, the finance house is entitled (subject to any agreement with the dealer) to be indemnified by the dealer for the loss it suffers in consequence of this liability, including costs reasonably incurred by the finance house in defending the hirer's claim (s. 70 (4)). Such a defence might be made, for example, where the finance house had been misled by the dealer into thinking that the agreement was signed at the dealer's premises and was thus not a cancellable agreement. Where a finance house supplies goods on hire-purchase or instalment sale, the second limb of s. 70 (3) does not apply, since the finance house is both creditor and supplier; but whilst under the first limb a deposit paid to the dealer is recoverable only from the dealer, there is also a common law right of recovery from the finance house, as deemed recipient (*Branwhite* v. *Worcester Works Finance, Ltd.*, [1968] 3 All E.R. 104).

[**8.47**] In addition to being entitled to repayment of sums paid, the debtor is released from liability for sums (including credit charges) payable under the cancelled agreement or any linked agreement (s. 70 (1) (*b*)).

[**8.48**] In the case of a debtor-creditor-supplier agreement for restricted-use credit financing the doing of work or supply of services to meet an emergency or the supply of goods which become incorporated by the debtor into land or other goods prior to the notice of cancellation, the service of such notice retrospectively extinguishes the credit obligations of the debtor under the credit agreement or any linked transaction but leaves him liable to the supplier for the cash price of the goods or services (s. 69 (2), (3)). For the debtor's right to repayment of a sum paid for issue of a credit-token, see para. [**16.7**]. By virtue of s. 70 (5), the debtor is not released from liability for repayment of a loan made under an unrestricted-use loan agreement which continues under s. 71 (1) and is not repaid under s. 71 (2) (see para. [**8.49**]).

CONTINUANCE OF UNRESTRICTED-USE LOAN AGREEMENTS

[**8.49**] Section 71 of the Act contains provisions which are deliberately designed to discourage a lender from making a cash loan under a cancellable credit agreement before expiry of the period allowed to the debtor for cancellation. The debtor who during the period allowed for cancellation receives a loan is likely to spend it immediately; and if his exercise of the right to cancel were then to involve him in immediate repayment of the loan, with interest, he could be placed in acute financial difficulty. Section 71 (1) accordingly provides that notwithstanding the cancellation of a regulated agreement, other than a debtor-creditor-supplier agreement for restricted-use credit, the agreement shall continue in force so far as it relates to repayment of credit and payment of interest.

**[8.50]** Section 71 (1) is in effect confined to loan agreements under which the loan is paid direct to the debtor in a form which (even though the loan may have been advanced for a specific purpose) leaves the debtor free to use it as he wishes —in other words, a loan paid direct to the debtor in money, as opposed to a credit-token. Where the debtor exercises a right to cancel such an agreement, it nevertheless continues in force "so far as it relates to the repayment of credit and payment of interest". The meaning of this phrase is not entirely clear. It is reasonable to assume that it is confined to repayment of a loan already made (wholly or in part) at the date of cancellation. Taken by themselves, the words "repayment of credit" are capable of referring to a contractual provision for repayment of a loan to be made in the future; but if the agreement as to future advances goes by the board, a provision for repayment obviously cannot operate on such future advances. Moreover, subsections (2) and (3) make it fairly clear that the section as a whole is concerned with cash already paid to the debtor at the time of cancellation. Hence that part of the agreement which relates to advances that have not been made at the date of cancellation, and the repayment of such advances, is retrospectively extinguished. The creditor ceases to be bound to provide such advances and the debtor to take them. But what of other covenants by the debtor, *e.g.* for the provision of security or for maintenance and insurance of an asset purchased with the loan? It would seem that all such undertakings are extinguished—even guarantees and indemnities given in connection with the loan. Any security given (and this would cover an agreement for security) is extinguished by s. 113 (3), which in the case of cancellation brings s. 106 into effect in relation to the security. The other undertakings, such as maintenance and insurance, would also appear to become inoperative. Section 71 (1) obviously contemplates that the debtor will not incur any future liability beyond repayment of the loan with interest, so that executory obligations of insurance and maintenance—whether contained in the credit agreement itself or in associated contracts—will, it seems, be extinguished. This may seem hard on the creditor, but helps to achieve the desired objective of giving the debtor a period for reflection *before* he receives his loan.

**[8.51]** Further protection for the debtor, and discouragement of the creditor from making the loan during the period allowed for cancellation, is provided by the remaining provisions of s. 71:

> "(2) If, following the cancellation of a regulated consumer credit agreement, the debtor repays the whole or a portion of a credit—
>
> (*a*) before the expiry of one month following service of the notice of cancellation, or
>
> (*b*) in the case of a credit repayable by instalments, before the date on which the first instalment is due,
>
> no interest shall be payable on the amount repaid.

(3) If the whole of a credit repayable by instalments is not repaid on or before the date specified in subsection (2) (*b*), the debtor shall not be liable to repay any of the credit except on receipt of a request in writing in the prescribed form, signed by or on behalf of the creditor, stating the amounts of the remaining instalments (recalculated by the creditor as nearly as may be in accordance with the agreement and without extending the repayment period), but excluding any sum other than principal and interest.

(4) Repayment of a credit, or payment of interest, under a cancelled agreement shall be treated as duly made if it is made to any person on whom, under section 69, a notice of cancellation could have been served, other than a person referred to in section 69 (6) (*b*)."

The effect of s. 71 as a whole is thus to give the debtor who cancels a cash loan agreement three choices:

(*a*) to repay the loan in full without interest within the time prescribed by s. 71 (2);

(*b*) to repay part of the advance without interest within that time, and repay the balance with pro-rated interest, after receipt of a written request, over the contractual period for repayment then remaining (see para. [**8.52**]);

(*c*) to make no repayment at all within the time prescribed by s. 71 (2), but to repay the advance, with the stipulated interest, after receipt of a written request, over the contractual period for repayment then remaining (see para. [**8.52**]).

But where the creditor has taken security, the debtor's duty of repayment cannot be enforced against him until the creditor has complied with his obligations under s. 106 (see para. [**13.13**]) in relation to the security (s. 113 (5)).

[**8.52**] Thus the debtor who cancels can obtain a loan free of interest for at least a month, and possibly much longer, depending on how long before expiry of the cancellation period he received the loan and the time allowed for payment of the first instalment. As is apparent from the opening lines of s. 71 (3), the time limit in s. 71 (2) (*a*) is confined to loans repayable by instalments. Section 71 (3) would seem to mean that a loan not repaid in full within the time specified in s. 71 (2) becomes repayable over the period between receipt of the request for repayment under s. 71 (3) and the contractual date for payment of the last instalment, by instalments of the frequency stipulated in the contract at interest pro-rated on an even-spread basis. A consequence of this statutory re-arrangement is, of course, that the payment period is shortened (since it does not begin until the creditor's written request for repayment has been received) so that the instalments will be larger than the amount (or in the case of a partially repaid loan, than a due proportion of the amount) stipulated in the contract.

*Example 1*

On 1st January 1976, pursuant to a cancellable agreement, a cash advance of £1,000 is made to A, repayable with interest of £200 over a period of 12 months by equal instalments of £100 a month commencing on 31st January 1976. On 15th January, A cancels the loan agreement but does not make any repayment by the end of that month. On 1st April A receives from the lender notice in writing under s. 71 (3) requiring repayment, on rescheduled terms set out in the notice. This will show that the total of £1,200, representing the principal and agreed interest, is now repayable over a period of 10 months ending on 31st January 1977, so that the monthly instalments become £120 instead of £100.

*Example 2*
The facts are as above except that A repays £400 on 28th January 1976, thus reducing the principal indebtedness to £600. For the purpose of working out the revised terms to be stated in his request of 1st April, the lender will take the period 1st April 1976 to 31st January 1977, *i.e.* 10 months, adjust the interest—to reflect reduction in the principal to £600 and in the payment period from 12 to 10 months—to the sum of £100 (*i.e.* £200 × 6/10 × 10/12) and spread the total sum of £700 (*i.e.* revised principal of £600 plus revised interest of £100) over the 10 months to 31st January 1977, producing revised monthly instalments of £70.

[**8.53**] The adjustment of interest on a partially repaid loan operates to the detriment of the creditor, since his fixed administration and overhead expenses remain constant despite what amounts to a reduction in the loan, and he might well have stipulated a higher rate of interest if at the outset the loan had been for the lower figure. In effect, the debtor who exercises a right to make a partial repayment under s. 71 (2) secures not only the benefit of freedom from interest on the part repaid but also the benefit of an interest rate originally fixed on the basis of the full amount of the loan, not on the basis of the reduced amount.

RECOVERY OF PART-EXCHANGE GOODS OR ALLOWANCE

[**8.54**] We have seen that on cancellation, the debtor is entitled by s. 70 (1) to repayment of any sum paid by him, or his relative, under or in contemplation of the cancelled agreement. However, there are many transactions in which an initial payment by the debtor is made wholly or partly by the crediting to him of an allowance for goods tendered in part-exchange. Section 73 (2) accordingly confers on the debtor the right to recover a sum equal to the part-exchange allowance in the circumstances previously mentioned (para. [**8.22**]). In the case of a debtor-creditor-supplier agreement within s. 12 (*b*)—*e.g.* a personal loan agreement with a finance house providing for a loan to buy a car from a motor dealer who had introduced the buyer to the finance house pursuant to an arrangement with the finance house—the negotiator and the creditor (*i.e.* in our example the dealer and the finance house) are jointly and severally liable for payment to the debtor of the part-exchange allowance (s. 73 (3)). But the creditor is entitled to be indemnified against this liability (s. 73 (4)) in the same way as on a liability for repayment of money paid by the debtor (see para. [**8.46**]).

DEBTOR'S LIEN

[**8.55**] If the debtor or his relative is in possession of the goods comprised in the cancelled agreement, he has a lien on the goods for any sums repayable to him under s. 70 (1) of the Act (s. 70 (2)). In addition, during the ten days allowed to the negotiator for return of the part-exchange goods, the debtor has a lien on the goods in his possession to secure return of the part-exchange goods or payment of the part-exchange allowance (s. 73 (5)). The negotiator can thus secure release of the goods from the lien either by returning the part-exchange goods or, at his option, by paying the debtor the part-exchange allowance, but after the ten-day period has expired the negotiator cannot force the debtor to accept return of the part-exchange goods and must tender a sum equal to the part-exchange allowance if he wishes to terminate the lien.

RETURN OF GOODS BY DEBTOR OR RELATIVE

**[8.56]** Section 72 provides for the return to the creditor or other authorised person of goods comprised in a cancelled agreement and for exercise of reasonable care in relation to the goods pending their return. The section applies where any agreement or transaction relating to goods, being—

(*a*) a restricted-use debtor-creditor-supplier agreement, a consumer hire agreement, or a linked transaction to which the debtor or hirer under any regulated agreement is a party, or

(*b*) a linked transaction to which a relative of the debtor or hirer under any regulated agreement is a party,

is cancelled after the debtor or hirer (in a case within paragraph (*a*)) or the relative (in a case within paragraph (*b*)) has acquired possession of the goods by virtue of the agreement or transaction (s. 72 (1)). A typical case is that of a hirer or buyer acquiring possession under a hire-purchase, conditional sale or credit sale agreement (other than a small agreement—see s. 74 (2)). Also within the provision is one who buys goods with the aid of a credit card or trading check, assuming that the credit agreement is not a small agreement. These are cases of possession by the debtor himself. Possession by a relative under a linked transaction is less likely. An example is delivery of goods to a minor on a cash sale where the price was advanced by a personal loan to the minor's parent under a regulated agreement pursuant to arrangements between the lender and the supplier.

**[8.57]** The Act provides that on cancellation the possessor (*i.e.* the debtor or relative acquiring possession under the regulated agreement or linked transaction) shall:

(1) be under a duty, subject to any lien (see para. [**8.55**]), to return the goods to the other party (*i.e.* the person from whom he acquired possession) in accordance with s. 72, and meanwhile to retain possession of the goods and take reasonable care of them (s. 72 (4)); and

(2) be treated as having been under a duty throughout the pre-cancellation period (*i.e.* the period beginning with the acquiring of possession and ending with cancellation—s. 72 (2)) to retain possession of the goods and to take reasonable care of them (s. 72 (3)).

Each of these duties requires separate examination. The exceptional cases in which such duties do not arise are discussed in paragraph [**8.63**]. Where security has been taken by the creditor, none of the duties is enforceable until the creditor has complied with his obligations under s. 106 (see para. [**13.13**]) in relation to the security (s. 113 (5)).

THE DUTY TO RESTORE

[**8.58**] The obligation is to restore the goods to the person from whom the possessor acquired possession. It would seem that this refers to the *legal* supplier, not the physical supplier, so that, for example, if a person enters into a hire-purchase agreement with a finance house, he acquires possession of the goods from the finance house, not from the dealer who delivered them. The point will normally be academic, since the possessor's duty is discharged by delivering the goods (whether at his own premises or elsewhere), or by sending them, to any person on whom a notice of cancellation could have been served under s. 69, other than a person who acted for the debtor himself in negotiations for the agreement (s. 72 (6)). Thus delivery may be made:

(i) to the creditor, that is, the person providing credit or his assignee (s. 189 (1)); or

(ii) to any person specified in a notice of cancellation served, or incorporated in a copy of a document served, on the debtor in conformity with s. 64 (1); or

(iii) a credit broker or supplier who was the negotiator in antecedent negotiations; or

(iv) any agent of the creditor.

[**8.59**] The possessor need not return the goods to the other party's premises. It suffices if he holds them available for collection at his own premises; and he is under no duty to surrender them except pursuant to a written request signed by or on behalf of the other party and served on him either before or at the time when the goods are collected from his premises (s. 72 (5)). If the address of the possessor is specified in the cancelled agreement (as it almost invariably will be) then for the purpose of the above provisions he is only entitled, and obliged, to treat that address as his own premises (s. 72 (10)). On delivery in accordance with s. 72 (6) (*a*), the debtor's obligation to take care of the goods ceases (s. 72 (7)), and provided that he delivers to a person who is within one of the four categories mentioned in paragraph [**8.58**] the debtor is not concerned to see that the goods actually reach the person entitled to possession of them. If, instead of delivering the goods, he sends them to a person within such a category, he is under a duty to take reasonable care to see that they are received by the other party and not damaged in transit (*e.g.* he must ensure that they are properly packed and sent by an apparently competent carrier), but in other respects his duty to take care of the goods then ceases (s. 72 (7)).

[**8.60**] Failure by the debtor to surrender the goods in accordance with the statutory provisions exposes him to an action for damages for breach of statutory duty (s. 72 (11)).

THE DUTY OF CARE

[**8.61**] After cancellation, the possessor has a duty to take reasonable care of the goods until he has delivered or sent them pursuant to the above provisions; but his duty of care in any event comes to an end on the expiration of 21 days following the cancellation unless he has by then received a written and signed request for delivery under s. 72 (5) and has unreasonably refused or failed to comply with it (s. 72 (8)). This provision is designed to ensure that a debtor exercising a right of cancellation is not inconvenienced by having to house the goods indefinitely as the result of the other party's failure to collect. If the latter does not serve such a request within 21 days, or if having served it he does not call to collect the goods within such period, the debtor's duty to take reasonable care ceases, and his obligation in relation to the goods becomes limited to that of an involuntary bailee, viz. to refrain from causing wilful damage.

**[8.62]** Not only is the possessor under a duty of care after the cancellation; he is deemed to have been under a duty to retain possession of the goods and take reasonable care of them throughout the cancellation period (s. 72 (3)). This provision ensures that a debtor who cancels an agreement does not escape liability merely because restoration of the goods in proper condition had already become impossible prior to cancellation as the result of damage to or disposal of the goods. If, therefore, the debtor or other person parted with possession prior to cancellation, then whilst this might at the time have been perfectly lawful (as where the buyer under a credit sale agreement resells the goods immediately and delivers possession to his purchaser) the subsequent cancellation retrospectively places him in breach of his deemed statutory duty to retain possession, and he is liable to the other party in damages for the value of the goods. Similarly, if he damages the goods before cancellation, then even if at the time of such damage the goods were his own property (as under a credit sale agreement) he is liable under s. 72 (7) for the damage so caused.

EXEMPTIONS

**[8.63]** Section 72 (9) provides as follows:

"The preceding provisions of this section do not apply to—

(*a*) perishable goods, or

(*b*) goods which by their nature are consumed by use and which, before the cancellation, were so consumed, or

(*c*) goods supplied to meet an emergency, or

(*d*) goods which, before the cancellation, had become incorporated in any land or thing not comprised in the cancelled agreement or a linked transaction."

These provisions require some explanation, as their effect is more striking than may at first sight be apparent.

**[8.64]** The effect of paragraph (*a*) is that the possessor of perishables has no duty to retain possession or to restore them. He may consume them or dispose of them as he thinks fit. Indeed, he will usually have little choice, since by their nature perishables are unlikely to be returnable to the supplier in suitable condition. On the other hand, consumer credit agreements relating to perishables are not excluded from the cancellation provisions, so that the debtor, having consumed the perishables, is none the less entitled to recover under s. 70 (1) the sums paid in respect of them and to obtain release from liability for sums remaining payable. In short, he can have his cake without paying for it! This may appear startling, but reflects a deliberate policy to ensure that a debtor having a right of cancellation is not inhibited from exercising that right by the prospect of incurring some financial liability. One of the typical transactions against which the provision is aimed is an agreement under which a freezer is supplied on credit together with food to stock the freezer, the food itself being supplied on credit terms. There have been many complaints concerning such transactions, and the fear was that if the consumer cancelling the freezer agreement were thereby to incur a liability to pay for the food, he might be inhibited from exercising his right of cancellation. The statutory provision is not, indeed, limited to cases of this kind but applies even where the supply of food on credit is the sole transaction. In practice, however, such agreements are uncommon, and the supplier can in any event avoid difficulty by deferring delivery until after expiration of the cancellation period or alternatively (if the circumstances warrant) by relying on the provisions of s. 69 (2) (*a*) relating to goods supplied to meet an emergency.

[**8.65**] A similar reasoning applies under s. 70 (9) (*b*) to other consumables, *e.g.* fuel, though in this case, since the goods do not automatically perish with the passing of time but are merely consumed through use, the debtor is only absolved of his duty to return the goods if they were in fact consumed prior to cancellation.

[**8.66**] The position is somewhat different in the case of goods supplied in the circumstances described in s. 70 (9) (*c*) and (*d*). Despite cancellation, the debtor to whom goods are supplied for an emergency or by whom goods are incorporated into land or other goods remains obliged to pay the cash price to the supplier (see para. [**8.48**]). Hence in these cases, exemption of the debtor from a duty to return the goods after cancellation is given simply because restoration of the goods would usually be impracticable. Goods supplied for an emergency will normally have been employed to cope with that emergency, and may continue to be needed for that purpose. Goods which become incorporated into land lose their identity as chattels and usually pass into the ownership of the owner of the land. Similarly, goods which become annexed as accessions to other chattels, and thus cannot be detached without material damage to those chattels, will in general pass to the owner of the chattels (see generally R. M. Goode, *op. cit.*, Chapter 33).

LOSS OF RIGHT TO CANCEL

[**8.67**] The only circumstance in which the statutory right to cancel is lost is where the debtor fails to serve a cancellation notice within the time prescribed by s. 68 (see para. [**8.39**]). Factors which would at common law preclude rescission, such as inability to restore the goods through loss, consumption or disposition to a third party, do not appear to affect the statutory right of cancellation. This, indeed, is apparent from s. 72 (3) and (9). The sanction for a debtor who damages or disposes of the goods in the pre-cancellation period is not loss of the right to cancel but damages for breach of statutory duty (see para. [**8.62**]). The debtor who before cancellation consumes goods or has them incorporated in land or other goods may still cancel but is exempted from the usual consequential obligation to return the goods. Even destruction of the goods otherwise than by consumption does not affect the right of cancellation under the Act. Moreover, the right to cancel would appear to be unaffected even by the fact that at the time when notice of cancellation is given the agreement has already come to an end, *e.g.* through exercise by one party of a right to terminate or through frustration. It may seem odd to speak of rescinding an agreement which has ceased to exist, but there is nothing illogical in this, since the remedy of rescission operates retrospectively, cancelling the contract from the beginning and thus overriding a purported termination of the agreement by the other party. This result is reasonable, since destruction of the right of cancellation by exercise by the creditor of a power of termination would deprive the debtor of the protection which the Act intends to give him. If, for example, the owner of goods let on hire-purchase were to fail to send the debtor a notice or copy of an agreement informing the debtor of his right to cancel, and after collecting payments from the debtor were then to terminate the agreement for default, it is unlikely that the court would regard the debtor's remedy as restricted to reliance on unforceability of the agreement. Almost certainly, he would be held entitled to exercise a right to cancel, despite the owner's termination, on the ground that the time for cancellation had not begun to run against him. On the other hand, if the hirer, being aware of his right to cancel, deliberately chooses an alternative remedy by electing to terminate the agreement himself he would, it is thought, be precluded from invoking the statutory right of cancellation.

RESCISSION AT COMMON LAW

[**8.68**] The cancellation provisions do not in any way affect the debtor's right of rescission for misrepresentation at common law and under the Misrepresentation Act 1967. However, s. 102 (1) of the Act (re-enacting in this respect s. 31 (2) of the Hire-Purchase Act 1965) facilitates exercise of such right by providing that the following are to be deemed the agent of the creditor or owner for the purpose of receiving any notice rescinding the agreement which is served by the debtor or hirer—

(*a*) a credit broker or supplier who was the negotiator in antecedent negotiations, and

(*b*) any person who, in the course of a business carried on by him, acted on behalf of the debtor or hirer in any negotiations for the agreement.

By s. 102 (2), it is provided that in s. 102 (1) "rescind" does not include—

(*a*) service of a notice of cancellation, or

(*b*) termination of an agreement under s. 99 or 101, or by the exercise of a right or power in that behalf expressly conferred by the agreement.

# CHAPTER 9

# MISREPRESENTATION AND BREACH OF CONTRACT BY SUPPLIER

## THE DUTY OWED BY THE SUPPLIER

[**9.1**] The Consumer Credit Act says nothing about the duties owed by the supplier of goods or services to the person to whom these are supplied, nor does it deal directly with the supplier's liability for misrepresentation. What the Act does provide is that if the debtor under a debtor-creditor-supplier agreement in which the creditor is not the supplier himself has a claim against the supplier for misrepresentation or breach of contract, he is to have a like claim against the creditor, who accordingly is made jointly and severally liable with the supplier (s. 75 (1)). Whether the debtor has a claim against the supplier for misrepresentation or breach of contract has to be determined by reference to the general law of contract and relevant provisions of other statutes, notably the Misrepresentation Act 1967, the Sale of Goods Act 1893, the Supply of Goods (Implied Terms) Act 1973 and the Consumer Protection Act 1961. Space does not permit more than a brief summary here, and for further detail the reader should refer to standard works on contract and sales law. In this chapter we shall consider first the circumstances in which the supplier himself incurs a liability to the debtor and secondly the provisions of s. 75 by which the creditor is in these circumstances made jointly and severally liable with the supplier.

## SUPPLIER'S LIABILITY FOR MISREPRESENTATION

[**9.2**] An actionable misrepresentation is a false statement of fact (including a statement of belief or intention when this is not held by the maker of the statement) which induces the representee to enter into a contract with the representor in reliance on the truth of the statement. The misrepresentation necessarily precedes the contract which it induces and does not constitute a breach of the contract unless it becomes incorporated as a term of the contract. The distinction between a "mere" representation inducing, but not forming part of, the contract and a statement constituting a term of the contract is more easily expressed than applied. At common law, the issue was whether a reasonable onlooker would assume that the maker of the statement intended to warrant its truth or make it as a promise (in which case the statement would have contractual force) or whether, in the eyes of the reasonable onlooker, the maker of the statement was simply asserting a fact without intending to be bound by the statement. The distinction between a "mere" representation and a contract term was formerly of great importance in that while a fraudulent misrepresentation always gave rise to a claim for damages in tort for deceit, a misrepresentation made in good faith merely entitled the representee to rescind the contract, but conferred no remedy in damages, even if the statement were negligently made, except in very restricted categories of case, *e.g.* where reliance on the negligent statement led to the representee suffering physical injury to his person or damage to his property, or where there was some kind of special relationship within the principle enunciated by the House of Lords in *Hedley Byrne & Co., Ltd.*, v. *Heller & Partners, Ltd.*, [1964] A.C. 465; [1963] 2 All E.R. 575. The distinction has, however, lost much of its importance since the passing of the Misrepresentation Act 1967, which in given conditions entitles the representee to damages even for a non-fraudulent misrepresentation, unless the representor can show that this was not made negligently (see para. [**9.6**]).

[**9.3**] Sometimes the courts experienced a difficulty in that a false statement made prior to a written contract, and plainly intended to have the character of a promise or warranty, was not incorporated into the written document, so that the representee might be barred by the parol evidence rule (see para. [**7.14**]) from asserting that the statement formed part of the contract embodied in the document. How was the court to give effect to the promise or warranty in such a case? The judicial solution was to treat the statement as a collateral promise or warranty generating a distinct contract, the maker of the statement promising to perform, or warranting the truth of the statement, in consideration of the representee entering into the main contract. Since the promise or warranty thus formed the essential obligation of a contract entirely distinct from that embodied in the document, it was not caught by the parol evidence rule and could be proved by extrinsic evidence in the usual way. The device of the collateral contract, or collateral warranty, was also useful to give a remedy where the false statement induced the representee to enter into a contract not with the representor but with a third party. For example, if a motor dealer were to make a false statement about the quality of a car for the purpose of inducing a prospective customer to acquire it on hire-purchase from a finance house introduced by the dealer, the dealer's warranty could not be treated at common law as a term of the hire-purchase agreement, since the dealer was not a party to that agreement, but it could be accorded force as a collateral warranty generating a separate contract for the breach of which the customer would have a remedy in damages. See, for example, *Andrews* v. *Hopkinson*, [1957] 1 Q.B. 229; [1956] 3 All E.R. 422.

[**9.4**] Even a wholly innocent misrepresentation (i.e. a misrepresentation made in good faith and without negligence) entitled the innocent party at common law to rescind the contract. Rescission is not the same as termination. A contract terminated for breach puts an end to future obligations without disturbing accrued rights and liabilities (though in the case of a total failure of consideration the innocent party has a right to recover all his payments), and the innocent party's remedy consequent upon such termination is usually damages. Rescission of a contract, on the other hand, cancels it from the beginning, so that it is treated as if it had never existed. The consequence is that both parties must as nearly as possible be restored to their *status quo*, so that each is entitled to recover payments made and property transferred under the rescinded contract. If for some reason restitution is not possible—*e.g.* because a third party has acquired an interest in the subject matter of the contract—then the innocent party usually loses the right to rescind. It should be noted that the innocent party's right after rescission to recover payments made is a right not to damages but to restitution. What is involved is not compensation to the innocent party for loss he has suffered through the contract not proceeding but return by the guilty party of benefits conferred on him by the contract, which the law will not allow him to retain once the contract has become ineffective through rescission. The distinction between restitution and damages is not always appreciated, and indeed was overlooked in the original version of what is now s. 75 (1) of the Consumer Credit Act (see para. [**9.23**]).

[**9.5**] We have mentioned one barrier to rescission, namely the inability of a party to give restitution. There were other barriers at common law, *e.g.* election by the innocent party to affirm the contract, completion of performance of the contract by one party (so that it became an executed contract), and incorporation of the misrepresentation as a term of the contract, in which case the better view was that the innocent party was restricted to his common law remedy and lost his equitable right to rescind.

## THE MISREPRESENTATION ACT 1967

[**9.6**] The Misrepresentation Act 1967 has made a number of changes to the common law rules. First, it removes two of the bars to rescission, by providing that the innocent party retains the right to rescind even if the misrepresentation has become a term of the contract and even if the contract has been performed (s. 1). Secondly, the Act confers on the innocent party a right to damages (either in addition to or in lieu of rescission) for negligent misrepresentation, the onus being placed on the representor to show that he had reasonable ground to believe and did believe up to the time that the contract was made that the facts represented were true (s. 2 (1)). Thirdly, it confers on the court (except in the case of a fraudulent misrepresentation) the power to require the innocent party to accept damages in lieu of rescission, even if the innocent party has already exercised a right to rescind (s. 2 (2)). Finally, the Act renders void any provision in *any* agreement (*i.e.*, whether it be the contract to which the misrepresentation relates or an entirely separate contract) purporting to exclude or restrict liability for misrepresentation or remedies available to the innocent party by reason of the misrepresentation, except so far as the court or an arbitrator allows reliance on the provision as being in all the circumstances fair and reasonable (s. 3).

## TERMS IMPLIED IN FAVOUR OF BUYER

[**9.7**] The Sale of Goods Act 1893, as amended by the Supply of Goods (Implied Terms) Act 1973, imports into a contract of sale a set of implied terms in favour of the buyer in relation to the goods. These are:

(*a*) an implied condition that the seller has a right to sell or will have a right to sell at the time the property is to pass (Sale of Goods Act 1893, s. 12 (1));

(*b*) an implied warranty that the goods are free, and will remain free until the time when the property is to pass, from any charge or encumbrance not disclosed or known to the buyer before the contract is made and that the buyer will enjoy quiet possession (*ibid.*);

(*c*) in the case of a sale by description or sample, an implied condition that the goods shall correspond with the description or sample (ss. 13, 15);

(*d*) where the seller sells goods in the course of a business, an implied condition that the goods are of merchantable quality, except as regards defects specifically drawn to the buyer's attention before the contract is made or, if the buyer examines the goods before the contract is made, defects which that examination ought to reveal (s. 14 (2));

(*e*) where the seller sells goods in the course of a business and the buyer, expressly or by implication, makes known to the seller any particular purpose for which the goods are being bought, an implied condition that the goods supplied under the contract are reasonably fit for that purpose, whether or not that is a purpose for which such goods are commonly supplied, except where the circumstances show that the buyer does not rely, or that it is unreasonable for him to rely, on the seller's skill or judgment (s. 14 (3)).

**[9.8]** The seller cannot contract out of the implied condition of title (s. 55 (3)), though he can limit his implied obligation by contracting to transfer only such title as he or a third party may have (s. 12 (2)). In the case of a consumer sale any provision exempting from the implied terms of correspondence with description and sample, merchantable quality or fitness is void (s. 55 (4)). For this purpose "consumer sale" means a sale of goods (other than a sale by auction or by competitive tender) by a seller in the course of a business where the goods are of a type ordinarily bought for private use or consumption and are sold to a person who does not buy or hold himself out as buying them in the course of a business (s. 55 (7)). There is no requirement that goods should be bought exclusively for business use in order for the sale to be excluded from the definition of "consumer sale". Hence a sale of goods for both business and personal use (*e.g.* a car) is not a consumer sale. The onus of proving that a sale falls to be treated as not being a consumer sale lies on the party so contending (s. 55 (8)). It is not merely an outright exemption which is avoided in the case of a consumer sale. Section 55 (9) provides that any reference in s. 55 to a term exempting from all or any of the provisions of any section of the Act is a reference to a term which purports to exclude or restrict, or has the effect of excluding or restricting, the operation of all or any of the provisions of that section, or the exercise of a right conferred by any provision of that section, or any liability of the seller for breach of a condition or warranty implied by any provision of that section. Further, any reference in s. 55 to a term of a contract includes a reference to a term which although not contained in the contract is incorporated in the contract by another term of the contract (s. 55 (1)).

**[9.9]** In the case of a sale other than a consumer sale, a provision excluding the implied terms is not void but is not enforceable to the extent that it is shown that it would not be fair or reasonable to allow reliance on the term (s. 55 (4)). The onus of proving that reliance on the term is not fair or reasonable is on the buyer. The question is not whether the provision itself is *per se* fair or reasonable as seen at the date of the contract but whether *reliance* on it would be fair or reasonable. This requires the court to look at all the circumstances, including events up to the time of the hearing. Thus a clause in a commercial sale requiring the buyer to notify the seller of defects within 14 days might *per se* be entirely reasonable; but if it emerged that at the time of the delivery the seller was aware, for example, that the buyer would be abroad during the whole of that time, reliance on the clause might be held unfair to the buyer in the circumstances. Section 55 (5) of the Sale of Goods Act gives further guidance by providing that in determining whether or not reliance on any term would be fair or reasonable regard is to be had to all the circumstances of the case and in particular to the following matters:

(*a*) the strength of the bargaining positions of the seller and buyer relative to each other, taking into account, among other things, the availability of suitable alternative products and sources of supply;

(*b*) whether the buyer received an inducement to agree to the term or in accepting it had an opportunity of buying the goods or suitable alternatives without it from any source of supply;

(*c*) whether the buyer knew or ought reasonably to have known of the existence and extent of the term (having regard, among other things, to any custom of the trade and any previous course of dealing between the parties);

(*d*) where the term exempts from all or any of the provisions of ss. 13–15 of the Act if some condition is not complied with, whether it was reasonable at the time of the contract to expect that compliance with that condition would be practicable;

(*e*) whether the goods were manufactured, processed or adapted to the special order of the buyer.

[**9.10**] Quite apart from s. 55 (4), exemption clauses in a non-consumer sale will not normally avail the seller if he has committed a fundamental breach of the contract, as by delivering goods fundamentally different from those contracted for. The relevant authorities, from *Suisse Atlantique Société d'Armement Maritime S.A.* v. *N.V. Rotterdamsche Kolen Centrale,* [1967] 1 A.C. 361; [1966] 2 All E.R. 61, to *Farnworth Finance Facilities, Ltd.* v. *Attryde,* [1970] 2 All E.R. 774; [1970] 1 W.L.R. 1053, are summarised in the judgment of Donaldson, J., in *Kenyon, Son and Craven, Ltd.* v. *Baxter, Hoare and Co., Ltd.,* [1971] 2 All E.R. 708; [1971] 1 W.L.R. 519.

[**9.11**] It is only the exclusion of *contractual* liability that is restricted by s. 55 of the Sale of Goods Act. The seller remains free to exclude liability in tort, *e.g.* for negligence. Moreover, not all forms of contractual liability are within the section. An exemption clause in a consumer sale agreement cannot exclude the implied terms set out in ss. 12–15 of the Act, but it may validly exclude or modify the seller's duty of delivery.

[**9.12**] The efficacy of exemption clauses is preserved in relation to contracts for the international sale of goods (s. 61 (6)). By s. 62 (1) a contract for the international sale of goods means a contract of sale of goods made by parties whose places of business (or, if they have none, habitual residences) are in the territories of different States (the Channel Islands and the Isle of Man being treated for this purpose as different States from the United Kingdom) and in the case of which one of the following conditions is satisfied, that is to say:

(*a*) the contract involves the sale of goods which are at the time of the conclusion of the contract in the course of carriage or will be carried from the territory of one State to the territory of another; or

(*b*) the acts constituting the offer and acceptance have been effected in the territories of different States; or

(*c*) delivery of the goods is to be made in the territory of a State other than that within whose territory the acts constituting the offer and the acceptance have been effected.

[**9.13**] Save in the case of international sales, the use of a choice of law clause to select a foreign law for a contract of sale that would otherwise be governed by English law is ineffective to displace the operation of ss. 12–15 and 55 of the Act (s. 55A).

### BUYER'S REMEDIES AGAINST SELLER FOR BREACH

[**9.14**] Where the implied term broken by the seller is a warranty, the buyer can sue for damages, the normal measure of damages being the amount by which the value of the goods as warranted exceeds their value as delivered (Sale of Goods Act 1893, s. 53 (3)). Alternatively, the buyer can set up a breach of warranty in diminution or extinction of the price (s. 53 (1)) and, if his loss exceeds the price, can sue for the balance as damages (s. 53 (4)). Where the term broken is a condition, the buyer can either affirm the contract, treat the breach of condition as a breach of warranty and claim damages or reject the goods as not tendered in conformity with the contract. If he exercises a right to reject, the effect is that the seller has not made delivery in accordance with the contract. If the seller still has time to deliver, he can perform by a fresh tender of goods that do conform to the contract. If it is too late for the seller to put the matter right (either because the contract time of delivery was of the essence and has expired or because a reasonable time for delivery has already elapsed), or if the seller is unwilling or unable to make a fresh tender, the buyer can treat the contract as repudiated, and either sue for damages for non-delivery (s. 51 (1)) or bring a quasi-contractual claim for recovery of the price (to the extent he has paid it) on the basis of a total failure of consideration. The buyer is not obliged to accept a credit note; he is entitled to the return of his money or to damages, whichever of the above two remedies he prefers. The normal measure of damages is the amount by which the market price at the contract date for delivery (or if none, at the time of refusal to deliver) exceeds the contract price (s. 51 (3)).

[**9.15**] As a rule, the buyer loses his right to reject (and is accordingly limited to damages) if the contract of sale is not severable and he has accepted the goods or a part of them (s. 11 (1) (*c*)). He is deemed to have accepted where he intimates to the seller that he has accepted them or where (having had a reasonable opportunity to examine the goods) he takes delivery and does any act in relation to the goods which is inconsistent with the ownership of the seller or, after the lapse of a reasonable time, retains the goods without intimating to the seller that he has rejected them (ss. 35, 34). But s. 11 (1) (*c*) does not apply to conditional sale agreements which are agreements for consumer sales (Supply of Goods (Implied Terms) Act, s. 14 (1)). Moreover, a breach of condition of a consumer conditional sale agreement is to be treated as a breach of warranty (so as to bar the right to reject and treat the contract as repudiated) only if it would have fallen to be so treated had the condition been contained or implied in a corresponding hire-purchase agreement as a condition to be fulfilled by the owner (s. 14 (2)). "Corresponding hire-purchase agreement" means, in relation to a conditional sale agreement, a hire-purchase agreement relating to the same goods as the conditional sale agreement and made between the same parties and at the same time and in the same circumstances and, as nearly as may be, in the same terms as the conditional sale agreement (s. 15 (4)). The effect of s. 14 (2) of the Supply of Goods (Implied Terms) Act is that technical rules in the Sale of Goods Act as to deemed acceptance do not apply, and the question whether the buyer has accepted the goods is to be determined by reference to the more liberal common law principles applicable to hire-purchase agreements.

## TERMS IMPLIED IN FAVOUR OF HIRER UNDER HIRE-PURCHASE AGREEMENT

[**9.16**] These are set out in ss. 8–11 of the Supply of Goods (Implied Terms) Act 1973 and correspond to the terms implied under the Sale of Goods Act in favour of the buyer under a contract of sale. But the hirer remains entitled to the benefit of any wider common law terms (other than as to quality or fitness), so far as not excluded by the contract (see s. 15 (5)). Thus, although under s. 8 (1) the owner is not required to have a right of disposal until the time when the property is to pass to the hirer, the duty at common law is to have a right to dispose at the time of delivery to the hirer under the hire-purchase agreement (*Mercantile Union Guarantee Corporation, Ltd.* v. *Wheatley*, [1938] 1 K.B. 490; [1937] 4 All E.R. 713). The hirer can invoke this wider common law rule unless the agreement otherwise provides.

[**9.17**] In the case of a contract of sale, the implied condition of fitness for purpose arises only where the buyer has expressly or by implication made known to the seller the purpose for which the goods are being bought (s. 14 (3)). In the case of a hire-purchase agreement, however, the required purpose need not be communicated to the owner himself; communication, expressly or by implication, to a credit-broker in the course of pre-contract negotiations suffices to attract the implied condition of fitness (Supply of Goods (Implied Terms) Act 1973, s. 10 (3), as amended by Consumer Credit Act, Fourth Schedule, para. 35). Thus, where goods are let on hire-purchase by a finance house, communication of the required purpose to the dealer is sufficient.

[**9.18**] The same restrictions on exemption clauses apply to a consumer hire-purchase agreement as to a consumer sale agreement (see Supply of Goods (Implied Terms) Act, ss. 12, 13).

### REMEDIES OF HIRER FOR BREACH BY OWNER

[**9.19**] The remedies of the hirer where the owner commits a breach of the implied terms relating to the goods comprised in the hire-purchase agreement are broadly the same as those of the buyer under a conditional sale agreement. For a comprehensive treatment, see R. M. Goode, *Hire-Purchase Law and Practice* (2nd edn.), Chapter 20.

### HIRING AGREEMENTS

[**9.20**] On a contract of simple hire, the terms implied in favour of the hirer are similar to those implied in favour of the hirer under a hire-purchase agreement, except that there is no implied condition that the owner has a right to let the goods on hire. Indeed, the hirer is usually estopped from disputing his bailor's title (*Biddle* v. *Bond* (1865), 6 B. & S. 225; [1861–73] All E.R. Rep. 477). There appears little justification for retention of this old common law rule precluding the hirer under a simple hiring agreement from disputing his bailor's title or from complaining of a defect in title. It is true that if the hirer is dispossessed by the true owner while in possession, he can sue the bailor for damages for breach of the implied warranty of quiet possession. But such a remedy is of no use to a hirer who, after returning the hired goods to the bailor on termination of the hiring, is sued by the owner for damages for conversion. The hirer has instead to fall back on the indirect, and less certain, remedy of seeking an indemnity from the bailor as a co-tortfeasor under s. 6 (1) (*c*) of the Law Reform Married Women and Tortfeasors) Act 1935. Moreover, the Sale of Goods Act and the Supply of Goods (Implied Terms) Act do not apply to contracts of simple hire, so that the owner remains free to exclude all or any of the implied terms, and to exempt himself from liability for breach, within the limits marked out at common law by principles such as the doctrine of fundamental breach.

### CONTRACTS FOR SERVICES

[**9.21**] Similarly, there is no legislation prescribing the contractual duties of the supplier of services. In general, and subject to the express or implied terms of the agreement, the supplier's duty is to perform the services with reasonable care and skill; but he may exclude or restrict this duty, or his liability for breach of it, by a suitably worded exemption clause, subject, again, to the limitations imposed by the doctrine of fundamental breach and other common law rules, and to any special statutes (see also para. [**18.8**]).

### LIABILITY OF CREDITOR FOR MISREPRESENTATION OR BREACH OF CONTRACT BY SUPPLIER

[**9.22**] In considering the creditor's liability for misrepresentations or breaches of contract by the supplier, it is necessary to distinguish the case where the creditor is himself the legal supplier—as where a finance house buys goods from a dealer and lets them on hire-purchase, or agrees to sell them on instalment sale, to the dealer's customer—from the case where the sale is by the dealer himself, the purchase price being advanced by the finance house or other creditor by way of loan. Where a finance house disposes of goods under a regulated hire-purchase or instalment sale agreement, it is liable for misrepresentations made by the dealer in the course of antecedent negotiations, since the dealer is the negotiator by virtue of s. 56 (1) (*b*) (see para. [**8.29**]), and the negotiations are accordingly deemed to have been conducted by him as agent for the finance house as well as in his actual capacity (s. 56 (2)). The meaning of "negotiator" and "antecedent negotiations" has been fully discussed earlier (para. [**8.29**]). Section 56 (2) applies also where a finance house, pursuant to a pre-existing arrangement or in contemplation of a future arrangement with the dealer, lends money under a regulated agreement to enable the borrower to buy the goods from the dealer, who is then a negotiator under s. 56 (1) (*c*). But in this case s. 56 (2) is reinforced by s. 75 (1), which provides as follows:

> "If the debtor under a debtor-creditor-supplier agreement falling within section 12 (*b*) or (*c*) has, in relation to a transaction financed by the agreement, any claim against the supplier in respect of a misrepresentation or breach of contract, he shall have a like claim against the creditor, who, with the supplier, shall accordingly be jointly and severally liable to the debtor".

Hence even where the finance house is not a party to the contract of supply, it can be sued as a person jointly and severally liable to the debtor under s. 75 (1). The finance house will, of course, be entitled to avail itself of any defences that would be open to the supplier. Thus it can invoke an exemption clause, subject to the statutory provisions and common law rules previously mentioned.

[**9.23**] It should be noted that the liability of the creditor is not (as it was in an earlier version of the Consumer Credit Bill) limited to cases where the debtor's claim against the supplier is in the form of damages. Thus, if the debtor exercises a right to rescind the sale agreement for misrepresentation and pursues a restitutionary remedy for recovery of payments he has made, then whilst the finance house would not be a proper party to a claim for rescission (which can only be made against the other contracting party) it is jointly and severally liable to give restitution by paying back to the debtor sums paid by him under the rescinded agreement, whether those sums were paid to the finance house or to the supplier.

[**9.24**] The creditor's liability under s. 75 (1) arises even if the debtor, in entering into the supply transaction, exceeded the credit limit or otherwise contravened any term of the agreement (s. 75 (4)).

[**9.25**] The debtor can pursue his claim under s. 75 (1) against the supplier, the creditor or both. An unsatisfied judgment against one does not bar proceedings against the other (see *Blyth* v. *Fladgate*, [1891] 1 Ch. 337).

[**9.26**] Section 75 (3) exempts the creditor from the liability he would ordinarily incur under s. 75 (1):

(*a*) where the claim is under a non-commercial agreement, or

(*b*) so far as the claim relates to any single item to which the supplier has attached a cash price not exceeding £30 or more than £10,000.

The wording of s. 75 (3) (*a*) is a little curious, since one would have thought that the agreement under which the claim arose was the supply agreement, not the credit agreement. But the definition of "non-commercial agreement" in s. 189 (1) makes it clear that what is being referred to in s. 75 (3) (*a*) is not the supply agreement but the credit agreement. Hence the creditor can invoke s. 75 (3) (*a*) if, but only if, the loan was not made in the course of a business carried on by him.

As regards s. 75 (3) (*b*), the purpose of the £10,000 ceiling is to avoid a situation in which a lender financing, say, a purchase of goods at a price of £100,000 would become jointly and severally liable for defects because he advanced no more than £5,000 towards the price.

### CREDITOR'S RIGHT OF INDEMNITY

[9.27] Subject to any agreement between them, the creditor is entitled to be indemnified by the supplier for loss suffered by the creditor in satisfying his liability under s. 75 (1), including costs reasonably incurred by him in defending proceedings instituted by the debtor (s. 75 (2)). For this purpose, the creditor is entitled, when sued by the debtor, to have the supplier made a party to proceedings in accordance with rules of court (s. 75 (5)), *i.e.*, by third-party notice under R.S.C. Order 16 or C.C.R. Order 12.

# CHAPTER 10

# THE SUPPLY OF INFORMATION

## THE NEED TO KNOW

[**10.1**] A key feature of protection for the consumer in credit transactions is the supply of information before, upon and after entering into the contract, which will make him aware of his essential statutory rights and keep him informed as to the state of his account with the creditor. The Consumer Credit Act thus contains numerous provisions designed to ensure that the debtor or hirer is suitably informed. Similar protection is given to a surety. There is also one case in which the duty goes the other way, and the obligation is imposed on the debtor or hirer to supply information to the creditor or owner.

## PRE-CONTRACT DISCLOSURE

[**10.2**] We have already discussed the provisions of Part IV relating to advertisements, quotations and the display of information (see Chapter 6) and the provisions of Part V as to the disclosure of information before the making of a regulated agreement and in documents embodying a regulated agreement (see Chapter 7). The duty to supply copies of the contract document, and of documents referred to in it, has also been noted (Chapter 7). In addition the Act provides for the supply of information to the debtor or hirer during the currency of the agreement. Under some provisions, the duty is to provide information on request; under others, it is automatic. The nature of the information to be provided depends upon whether the agreement is a consumer credit or consumer hire agreement, and in the former case whether it is for fixed-sum credit or running-account credit. Regard should also be had to the entirely distinct duty imposed by s. 97 to supply a settlement figure on request (see para. [**10.8**]) and by s. 110 to supply the debtor or hirer with a copy of any security instrument (para. [**10.10**]).

## FIXED-SUM CREDIT

[**10.3**] Section 77 provides as follows:

"(1) The creditor under a regulated agreement for fixed-sum credit, within the prescribed period after receiving a request in writing to that effect from the debtor and payment of a fee of 15 new pence, shall give the debtor a copy of the executed agreement (if any) and of any other document referred to in it, together with a statement signed by or on behalf of the creditor showing, according to the information to which it is practicable for him to refer—

(*a*) the total sum paid under the agreement by the debtor;
(*b*) the total sum which has become payable under the agreement by the debtor but remains unpaid, and the various amounts comprised in that total sum, with the date when each became due; and
(*c*) the total sum which is to become payable under the agreement by the debtor, and the various amounts comprised in that total sum, with the date, or mode of determining the date, when each becomes due.

(2) If the creditor possesses insufficient information to enable him to ascertain the amounts and dates mentioned in subsection (1) (*c*), he shall be taken to comply with that paragraph if his statement under subsection (1) gives the basis on which, under the regulated agreement, they would fall to be ascertained.

(3) Subsection (1) does not apply to—

(*a*) an agreement under which no sum is, or will or may become, payable by the debtor, or
(*b*) a request made less than one month after a previous request under that subsection relating to the same agreement was complied with.

(4) If the creditor under an agreement fails to comply with subsection (1)—

(*a*) he is not entitled, while the default continues, to enforce the agreement; and
(*b*) if the default continues for one month he commits an offence.

(5) This section does not apply to a non-commercial agreement."

It is in the creditor's own interest to ensure that the information supplied in a statement under s. 77 (1) is correct, since the statement is binding on him (s. 172 (1)). If, therefore, the creditor informs the debtor that the outstanding balance is £100 when it is in fact £500, the debtor is entitled to a termination statement (see para. [**10.12**]) on tendering £100. This is subject, however, to the powers of the court under s. 172 (3) to direct such relief (if any) to be given to the creditor, or owner as appears to the court to be just (see para. [**27.3**]).

RUNNING ACCOUNT CREDIT

[**10.4**] In the case of running-account credit, s. 78 (1) imposes a similar duty to supply information on request, save that the information to be supplied is:

(*a*) the state of the account, and
(*b*) the amount, if any, currently payable under the agreement by the debtor to the creditor, and
(*c*) the amounts and due dates of any payments which, if the debtor does not draw further on the account, will later become payable under the agreement by the debtor to the creditor.

The same qualifications and exceptions are provided by s. 78 (2) and (3) as are furnished by s. 77 (2) and (3) in relation to fixed-sum credit; and a statement under s. 78 (1) is binding under s. 172 (1) in the same way as a statement under s. 77 (1), and subject to the same relief.

[**10.5**] In addition, where running-account credit is provided there is a duty to furnish periodic statements of account automatically, whether or not requested by the debtor. Section 78 of the Act further provides—

"(4) Where running-account credit is provided under a regulated agreement, the creditor shall give the debtor statements in the prescribed form, and with the prescribed contents—

(*a*) showing according to the information to which it is practicable for him to refer, the state of the account at regular intervals of not more than twelve months, and

(*b*) where the agreement provides, in relation to specified periods, for the making of payments by the debtor, or the charging against him of interest or any other sum, showing according to the information to which it is practicable for him to refer the state of the account at the end of each of those periods during which there is any movement in the account.

(5) A statement under subsection (4) shall be given within the prescribed period after the end of the period to which the statement relates.

(6) If the creditor under an agreement fails to comply with subsection (1)—

(*a*) he is not entitled, while the default continues, to enforce the agreement; and

(*b*) if the default continues for one month he commits an offence."

But apart from the general exception in respect of non-commercial agreements (s. 78 (7)), the duty to supply information automatically is also excluded in the case of small agreements (*ibid.*). Moreover, a statement under s. 78 (4) is not caught by s. 172 (1) and is therefore not binding on the creditor under that section, though it may in certain cases bind the creditor as a matter of general law.

## CONSUMER HIRE

[**10.6**] Section 79 (1) provides:

"The owner under a regulated consumer hire agreement, within the prescribed period after receiving a request in writing to that effect from the hirer and payment of a fee of 15 new pence, shall give to the hirer a copy of the executed agreement and of any other document referred to in it, toether with a statement signed by or on behalf of the owner showing, according to the information to which it is practicable for him to refer, the total sum which has become payable under the agreement by the hirer but remains unpaid and the various amounts comprised in that total sum, with the date when each became due."

The same exemptions from this duty are given as in s. 77 (3) and (5), and the same sanctions for infringement are imposed as in ss. 77 (4) and 172 (1) (see para. [**10.3**]).

## WHEREABOUTS OF GOODS

[**10.7**] Where a regulated agreement, other than a non-commercial agreement, requires the debtor or hirer to keep goods to which the agreement relates in his possession or control, he must, within seven working days after he has received a request in writing to that effect from the creditor or owner, tell the creditor or owner where the goods are (s. 80 (1)). "Working day" is defined in s. 189 (1) (see para. [**5.27**]). If the debtor or hirer fails to comply with s. 80 (1) and the default continues for 14 days, he commits an offence (s. 80 (2)).

INFORMATION AS TO SETTLEMENT FIGURE

[**10.8**] Section 97 provides as follows:

"(1) The creditor under a regulated consumer credit agreement, within the prescribed period after he has received a request in writing to that effect from the debtor, shall give the debtor a statement in the prescribed form indicating, according to the information to which it is practicable for him to refer, the amount of the payment required to discharge the debtor's indebtedness under the agreement, together with the prescribed particulars showing how the amount is arrived at.

(2) Subsection (1) does not apply to a request made less then one month after a previous request under that subsection relating to the same agreement was complied with.

(3) If the creditor fails to comply with subsection (1)—

(*a*) he is not entitled, while the default continues, to enforce the agreement; and

(*b*) if the default continues for one month he commits an offence."

At first sight, this section would appear to overlap completely with ss. 77 and 78, which require the creditor to supply the debtor on request with (*inter alia*) a statement of the total sum remaining payable under the agreement. It must, however, be remembered that this is not necessarily the same as the settlement figure called for by s. 97, which must be calculated so as to take into account any statutory rebate to which the debtor will be entitled by virtue of regulations under s. 95 (see para. [**12.5**]. Such regulations can only provide for a rebate in relation to a consumer credit agreement, not a consumer hire agreement. It is for this reason that s. 97 is itself confined to consumer credit agreements.

[**10.9**] A statement under s. 97 (1) binds the creditor under s. 172 (1) in the same way as under s. 77 (1) (see para. [**10.3**]).

SECURITY INSTRUMENT

[**10.10**] Section 110 provides as follows:

"(1) The creditor or owner under a regulated agreement, within the prescribed period after receiving a request in writing to that effect from the debtor or hirer and payment of a fee of 15 new pence, shall give the debtor or hirer a copy of any security instrument executed in relation to the agreement after the making of the agreement.

(2) Subsection (1) does not apply to—

(*a*) a non-commercial agreement, or

(*b*) an agreement under which no sum is, or will or may become, payable by the debtor or hirer, or

(*c*) a request made less than one month after a previous request under subsection (1) relating to the same agreement was complied with.

(3) If the creditor or owner under an agreement fails to comply with subsection (1)—

(*a*) he is not entitled, while the default continues, to enforce the security (so far as provided in relation to the agreement); and

(*b*) if the default continues for one month he commits an offence."

SURETIES

[**10.11**] Sections 107–109 require the creditor, within the prescribed period after receiving a request in writing to that effect from a surety and payment of a fee of 15 new pence, to provide the surety with the same statement as could have been called for by the debtor under ss. 77–79, and in addition to supply a copy of the executed agreement (if any) and of any other document referred to in it, together with a copy of the security instrument (if any). "Security instrument" will normally denote the contract of guarantee itself (see the definition of "security instrument" in s. 105 (2) and of "security" in s. 189 (1), discussed in para. [**13.4**]–[**13.5**]), but would also embrace any other form of security document taken by the creditor, whether from the surety, the debtor or another surety. The same exceptions apply, and the same sanctions are imposed, *i.e.* unforceability of the security (so far as provided in relation to the agreement) while the default continues and the commission of an offence if the default continues for one month. A statement given to the surety under s. 107 (1) (*c*), 108 (1) (*c*) or 109 (1) (*c*) is binding under s. 172 in the same circumstances as described for a statement under s. 77 (1) (see para. [**10.3**]).

TERMINATION STATEMENT

[**10.12**] From time to time a debtor under a completed credit agreement may have need of written evidence to show that he has completed his payments. Some creditors automatically provide this; other do not unless requested; whilst some even decline altogether to furnish completion certificates. To remedy this difficulty, s. 103 of the Consumer Credit Act provides as follows:

"(1) If an individual (the 'customer') serves on any person (the 'trader') a notice—

(*a*) stating that—

(i) the customer was the debtor or hirer under a regulated agreement described in the notice, and the trader was the creditor or owner under the agreement, and

(ii) the customer has discharged his indebtedness to the trader under the agreement; and

(iii) the agreement has ceased to have any operation; and

(*b*) requiring the trader to give the customer a notice, signed by or on behalf of the trader, confirming that those statements are correct,

the trader shall, within the prescribed period after receiving the notice, either comply with it or serve on the customer a counter-notice stating that, as the case may be, he disputes the correctness of the notice or asserts that the customer is not indebted to him.

(2) Where the trader disputes the correctness of the notice he shall give particulars of the way in which he alleges it to be wrong.

(3) Subsection (1) does not apply in relation to any agreement if the trader has previously complied with that subsection on the service of a notice under it with respect to that agreement.

(4) Subsection (1) does not apply to a non-commercial agreement.

(5) If the trader fails to comply with subsection (1), and the default continues for one month, he commits an offence."

A notice given by a trader under s. 103 (1) (*b*) is binding on him (s. 172 (2)), subject to the provisions of s. 172 (3) (see para. **27.3**]).

# CHAPTER 11

# VARIATION OF AGREEMENTS

## INTRODUCTION

[**11.1**] In general, the parties to a consumer credit or consumer hire agreement are free to vary it as they think fit, as in the case of other contracts. However, in the consumer credit field special care needs to be exercised by the creditor to ensure:

(*a*) that he does not, by concluding a binding variation, discharge a surety who has guaranteed the debtor's obligations;
(*b*) that the variation does not infringe any applicable hire-purchase or hiring Control Order;
(*c*) that the variation agreement accords with such formalities as may be prescribed by or under the Consumer Credit Act;
(*d*) that he is aware of the effect of the variation under the Act.

[**11.2**] The general principles governing the variation of credit agreements have been analysed in some detail by the author in *Hire-Purchase Law and Practice* (2nd edn.), Chapter 15. The same work deals with the restrictions on variation imposed by the Hire-Purchase and Credit Sale Agreements (Control) Order and the Control of Hiring Order (see *op. cit.*, pp. 968–970, 987–988), and whilst the Orders there referred to are the 1969 Orders, the same reasoning applies to the 1973 Orders which are in almost identical language. As regards the general law, a surety is usually discharged by a variation in the agreement to which his guarantee relates, unless the variation was made with his consent or the contract of guarantee contains provisions preserving his liability. Hence an agreement to substitute goods or to reschedule payments would release the surety (see generally R. M. Goode, *op. cit.*, pp. 494 *et seq*).

## GENERAL EFFECT OF VARIATIONS UNDER THE ACT

[**11.3**] The consequences of a contractual variation of a regulated agreement are dealt with by s. 82 which provides as follows:

"(1) Where, under a power contained in a regulated agreement, the creditor or owner varies the agreement, the variation shall not take effect before notice of it is given to the debtor or hirer in the prescribed manner.

(2) Where an agreement (a "modifying agreement") varies or supplements an earlier agreement, the modifying agreement shall for the purposes of this Act be treated as

(*a*) revoking the earlier agreement, and

(*b*) containing provisions reproducing the combined effect of the two agreements,

and obligations outstanding in relation to the earlier agreement shall accordingly be treated as outstanding instead in relation to modifying agreement.

(3) If the earlier agreement is a regulated agreement but (apart from this subsection) the modifying agreement is not then, unless the modifying agreement is for running-account credit, it shall be treated as a regulated agreement.

(4) If the earlier agreement is a regulated agreement for running-account credit, and by the modifying agreement the creditor allows the credit limit to be exceeded but intends the excess to be merely temporary, Part V (except section 56) shall not apply to the modifying agreement.

(5) If—

(*a*) the earlier agreement is a cancellable agreement, and

(*b*) the modifying agreement is made within the period applicable under section 68 to the earlier agreement,

then, whether or not the modifying agreement would, apart from this subsection, be a cancellable agreement, it shall be treated as a cancellable agreement in respect of which a notice may be served under section 68 not later than the end of the period applicable under that section to the earlier agreement.

(6) Except under subsection (5A), a modifying agreement shall not be treated as a cancellable agreement.

(7) This section does not apply to a non-commercial agreement."

The effect of this section is not altogether easy to determine, and we shall consider different aspects in the following paragraphs.

NO VARIATION WITHOUT NOTICE

**[11.4]** Section 82 (1) requires a creditor who exercises a power to vary the agreement to give notice of it in the prescribed manner in order for the variation to take effect. This provision was, it seems, intended to apply not only where under the terms of the contract the variation involves some active step by the creditor, *e.g.* notification to the debtor, but where it arises automatically under the agreement, as where the agreement provides for interest to fluctuate automatically with Finance House Base Rate. It is, however, doubtful whether s. 82 (1) applies to such an automatic variation, since this arises as a term of the original agreement and does not involve the exercise of a "power" by the creditor at all. On the contrary, he is bound by such a variable interest clause to the same extent as the debtor, whether the rate goes up or down. It is therefore submitted that s. 82 (1) applies only to those cases where the creditor has an *option* to vary and proceeds to exercise the option. If this be right, a provision gearing interest to a given Base Rate for the time being would be outside s. 82 (1), whereas, for example, a provision entitling the creditor to increase rentals by notice because of a change in Base Rate or in corporation tax or the inability to recover or retain a regional development grant would be caught and would require notice in the prescribed manner (*i.e.*, as provided by regulations) before it could take effect.

VARIATION REVOKES AND REPRODUCES

[**11.5**] English law has long recognised the distinction between a variation of an agreement and a novation. A variation preserves the original agreement but amends it in one or more particulars; a novation replaces it entirely. The distinction was significant under the Hire-Purchase Act 1965 (see R. M. Goode, *op. cit.*, Chapter 15) and remains significant for the purpose of the Control Orders, which differentiate between variation of an agreement and substitution of another agreement (*op. cit.*, Chapter 46). But for the purpose of the Consumer Credit Act, the distinction between variation and novation is obliterated. Where an agreement varies or supplements an earlier agreement, the Act applies as if the modifying agreement revoked the earlier agreement and reproduced the combined effect of the two agreements (s. 82 (2)). Again, it is submitted that s. 82 (2) applies only where there is an entirely distinct variation agreement concluded after the making of the original agreement. A variation of a term taking effect automatically under the provisions of the original agreement is not within s. 82 (2), since it arises independently of any subsequent agreement between the parties and does not require the assent of either of them in order to come into operation. The example previously given of a variable interest rate is a case in point. Section 82 (2) is also inapplicable to an entirely new agreement which does not alter or add to an existing agreement.

[**11.6**] If the earlier agreement is a regulated agreement, the modifying agreement will also be a regulated agreement, even if the effect of the variation would otherwise have been to take the modifying agreement outside the scope of the Act (see s. 82 (3)). Hence in general, the principle is: once a regulated agreement, always a regulated agreement. The only exception is where the modified agreement is for running-account credit (*ibid.*). In that case, it will be regulated only if it meets the ordinary definition of a regulated agreement. Conversely, if the earlier agreement was not a regulated agreement but the effect of the variation is to bring the modifying agreement within the definition of a regulated agreement, it will constitute a regulated agreement for the purpose of the Act.

[**11.7**] As a rule, a modifying agreement is not cancellable, wherever it may have been signed (see s. 82 (6)). If, however, the earlier agreement was a cancellable agreement and the modifying agreement is made within the time allowed by s. 68 for cancellation of the earlier agreement, the modifying agreement (even if it would not otherwise have been a cancellable agreement) becomes cancellable within the original time for cancellation (s. 82 (5)). In other words, on modification of the cancellable agreement before the time for cancellation of that agreement has expired the right of cancellation continues in relation to the modified agreement but the time for cancellation does not begin again and remains that prescribed for the original agreement.

[**11.8**] Since, under s. 82 (2), the modifying agreement is deemed to revoke the original agreement and obligations outstanding under the original agreement are to be treated as outstanding instead under the combined provisions, it would seem to follow that even if the original agreement was made before the coming into force of the Act, the provisions of the Act apply to the original unvaried terms carried over into the modifying agreement as well as to the new terms, if the modifying agreement was made on or after the day appointed for the coming into operation of s. 82.

FORMALITIES GOVERNING MODIFYING AGREEMENT

**[11.9]** The broad intention of s. 82 is that the provisions of the Act shall apply as if the combined terms (both the unvaried terms of the original agreement and the new terms) had been agreed at the time and in the manner of making of the new agreement. Hence, subject to s. 82 (4), (5) and (6) and to any special provisions that may be made for modifying agreements by regulations made under ss. 60 and 61, the formalities prescribed by Part V will apply in relation to all the terms, and not merely the new terms. Whether this will mean that the whole of the combined terms will have to be set out in a new document, instead of simply having the unvaried terms of the original agreement incorporated by reference to the document embodying that agreement, remains to be seen.

APPROVAL OF TEMPORARY EXCESS OVERDRAFT

**[11.10]** By s. 82 (4), if the earlier agreement is a regulated agreement for running-account credit, and by the modifying agreement the creditor allows the credit limit to be exceeded but intends the excess to be merely temporary, Part V of the Act (except s. 56) is not to apply to the modifying agreement. This provision has been discussed in paragraph [**3.22**].

VARIATION OF AGREEMENT BY COURT

**[11.11]** Part IX of the Act confers on the court wide powers to modify and adjust regulated agreements. These are discussed in Chapter 22.

# CHAPTER 12

# EARLY SETTLEMENT AND VOLUNTARY TERMINATION BY DEBTOR OR HIRER

## EARLY SETTLEMENT

[**12.1**] The debtor under a regulated consumer credit agreement is entitled at any time, by notice to the creditor and the payment to the creditor of all amounts payable by the debtor to him under the agreement (less any rebate allowable to him under s. 96), to discharge the debtor's indebtedness under the agreement (s. 95 (1)). It should be noted that this provision is confined to consumer credit agreements and does not extend to consumer hire agreements, where early settlement (as opposed to early termination—see para. [**12.20**]) does not arise. The notice must be in writing (see definition of "notice" in s. 189 (1)) but need not be signed or be of any minimum length (see para. [**12.3**]). Although in general payment includes tender (s. 189 (1))—a fact relevant, for example, to the question whether goods have become protected goods under s. 90 (7)—the opening words of s. 189 (1) show that this is only the case "unless the context otherwise requires", and it is obvious that an unaccepted tender will not discharge the debtor's indebtedness so as to allow him to claim a release from payment of the balance outstanding under the agreement. If the agreement under which tender of the outstanding balance is made is a hire-purchase or conditional sale agreement, it would seem that the property in the goods passes to the hirer or buyer upon the tender being made even if it is not accepted (see *City Motors, Ltd.* v. *Southern Aerial Super Service Pty., Ltd.* (1961), 35 A.L.J.R. 206; *Motor Mart, Ltd.* v. *Webb,* [1958] N.Z.L.R. 773) and that the hirer or buyer remains liable for payment of the amount tendered but can, if sued, make a payment into court with a plea of tender, under R.S.C. Order 18, r. 16 (High Court) or C.C.R. Order 9, r. 4 (9) (County Court). See generally R. M. Goode, *Hire-Purchase Law and Practice* (2nd edn.) pp. 242–243.

[**12.2**] A notice under s. 94 (1) may embody the exercise by the debtor of any option to purchase goods conferred on him by the agreement, and deal with any other matter arising on, or in relation to, the termination of the agreement (s. 94 (2)).

[**12.3**] The notice can be given at any time. It does not have to be of any minimum length and can be given to take effect immediately, if accompanied by payment of the outstanding balance less the statutory rebate. Equally, the debtor appears to be entitled to specify any future settlement date he chooses, provided that it is not later than the contractual date for completion of payment.

[**12.4**] On settlement, the debtor is entitled to a termination statement under s. 103 as previously described (para. [**10.12**]).

REBATE FOR EARLY SETTLEMENT

[**12.5**] Regulations may provide for the allowance of a rebate of credit charges under a regulated consumer credit agreement where the debtor's indebtedness is settled ahead of time, whether this is by payment under s. 94 or on refinancing, on breach of the agreement (*e.g.* under an acceleration clause) or for any other reason (s. 95 (1)). Indeed, regulations under s. 95 (1) need not be confined to early settlement of the agreement as a whole but may prescribe a rebate where *any sum* becomes payable by the debtor before the time fixed by the agreement.

[**12.6**] Full details of the proposed regulations on rebates are set out in Appendix III of the White Paper, reproduced in Appendix B of this book. The intention is that the rebate shall be calculated according to the rule of 78 but (except in the case of settlement through refinancing) on the basis that settlement was made three months after the deemed quotation date. For this purpose, the quotation date would be the instalment due date nearest the date when the request for a quotation was received, so that in a monthly instalment contract a request received on or before the fifteenth day following an instalment date would be treated as made on that instalment date, and a request received on or after the sixteenth day following an instalment date would be treated as made on the next instalment date (White Paper, Appendix III, paras. 14, 15). Since a quotation would be binding for 21 days (*ibid.*, para. 17), the creditor quoting immediately could lose a maximum of three weeks' interest if the request for a settlement figure was made nearer the next instalment date or five weeks' interest if made nearer the previous instalment date. The creditor is under a statutory duty to quote a settlement figure within the prescribed time (*i.e.* prescribed by regulations) after receipt of a written request by the debtor (s. 97 (1)—see para. [**10.8**]).

[**12.7**] The following explanation of the rule of 78, taken from Appendix A to the author's work *Hire-Purchase Law and Practice* (2nd edn.), indicates its impact on the rebate calculation:

> "*The Direct Ratio Method or Rule of* 78
>
> This method of spreading charges is widely used owing to its simplicity and the fact that it gives a close approximation to an actuarial rate. The rule of 78 assumes that charges are spread in the ratio which the number of instalments remaining to be paid bears to the total number of instalments in the contract. Thus on a twelve-month contract where payment is to be made by equal monthly instalments $\frac{12}{78}$ of the charge is treated as earned in the first month, $\frac{11}{78}$ in the second month, $\frac{10}{78}$ in the third month, and so on. This method is known as the rule of 78 because the sum of the numbers one to twelve is 78. Looked at another way the rule of 78 assumes that on a twelve-month contract where payment is to be made by equal monthly instalments the number of instalments remaining to be paid is constantly diminishing, so that the principal outstanding in the first month is twelve times as large as that outstanding in the last; in the second month is eleven times as large as that in the last month; and so on; and the charges are treated as spread in the same way.

The rule of 78 is also used as a convenient method of calculating rebates for early settlement. Thus if on a twelve-month contract providing for blended payments of principal and charges in twelve equal monthly instalments the debtor pays in full at the end of the ninth month he would, under the rule of 78, be given a rebate equivalent to the charges that would have been earned during the remaining three months, *i.e.* $\frac{3 + 2 + 1}{78} = \frac{1}{13}$ of the total charge. The term 'rule of 78' is applied to all cases where this method of spread is adopted, whatever the contract length, but the figure 78 is, of course, applicable only to a twelve-month contract. For a 24-month contract the series is 24 + 23 + 22 . . . 1 and the sum of the series is 300. For a 36-month contract the series is 36 + 35 + 34 . . . 1 and the sum of the series is 666. The formula for calculating the sum of the series is $\frac{n}{2}(n + 1)$ where $n$ is the number of terms in the series."

[**12.8**] The reason why the creditor is allowed a loading factor—by taking the settlement date as three months after the deemed quotation date—is that the rule of 78 does not adequately compensate the creditor for the heavy initial costs of setting up a transaction. The loading factor is intended to provide for this, and three months has in fact been a conventional period in the trade for many years. The loading factor will not be permitted in the case of early settlement through refinancing.

[**12.9**] Regulations under s. 95 (1) may provide for calculation of the rebate by reference to any sums paid or payable by the debtor or his relative under or in connection with the agreement (whether to the creditor or some other person), including sums under linked transactions and other items in the total charge for credit (s. 95 (2)).

[**12.10**] Paragraph 4 of Appendix III to the White Paper sets out various cases in which no rebate can be claimed. These include fixed-sum credit for less than £30 or for not more than 26 weeks. Presumably regulations will so provide.

### EFFECT OF EARLY SETTLEMENT ON LINKED TRANSACTIONS

[**12.11**] The early settlement of a regulated consumer credit agreement automatically discharges the liability of the debtor, and any relative of his, under a linked transaction, except as regards a debt which has already become payable (s. 96 (1)). But this does not apply to a linked transaction which is itself an agreement providing the debtor or his relative with credit (s. 96 (2)).

### VOLUNTARY TERMINATION BY DEBTOR

[**12.12**] The provisions discussed in the preceding paragraphs deal with the debtor's right to discharge his indebtedness by completing payments ahead of time. But the hirer or buyer under a regulated hire-purchase or conditional sale agreement has an alternative right to terminate the agreement without completing payments under it. This right, and the liability of the debtor who exercises it, are governed by ss. 99 and 100 of the Act, re-enacting provisions formerly contained in ss. 27 and 28 of the Hire-Purchase Act 1965.

[**12.13**] At any time before the final payment by the debtor under a regulated hire-purchase or regulated conditional sale agreement falls due, the debtor is entitled to terminate the agreement by giving notice to any person entitled or authorised to receive the sums payable under the agreement (s. 99 (1)). It will be remembered that "conditional sale agreement" is not confined to the conditional sale of goods but covers the conditional sale of land as well (s. 189 (1)). However, by s. 99 (3) the debtor ceases to be entitled to terminate a conditional sale agreement relating to land after title to the land has passed to the debtor.

The debtor's right to terminate a conditional sale agreement relating to goods is lost if the property in the goods is transferred to a person who does not become the debtor under the agreement (s. 99 (4)). This provision, re-enacting s. 27 (2) of the Hire-Purchase Act 1965, is designed to cover the eventuality of a conditional sale agreement which provides for the debtor to acquire title before he has made all the payments called for by the agreement, *e.g.* after payment of 50 per cent. Such an agreement would be unusual, but if the buyer, having acquired ownership, were then to resell he would lose his right of termination. The right to terminate would equally be lost where title had passed from the conditional buyer to a third party by virtue of some exception to the *nemo dat* rule, *e.g.* under Part III of the Hire-Purchase Act 1965. But s. 99 (4) does not cover the case of a debtor who assigns his rights under the conditional sale agreement; for the assignee then becomes the debtor (see definition of "debtor" in s. 189 (1)).

[**12.14**] Section 99 (5), re-enacting s. 27 (3) of the Hire-Purchase Act 1965, provides as follows:

> "Subject to subsection (4), where a debtor under a conditional sale agreement relating to goods terminates the agreement under this section after the property in the goods has become vested in him, the property in the goods shall thereupon vest in the person (the "previous owner") in whom it was vested immediately before it became vested in the debtor;
>
> Provided that if the previous owner has died, or any other event has occurred whereby that property, if vested in him immediately before that event, would thereupon have vested in some other person, the property shall be treated as having devolved as if it had been vested in the previous owner immediately before his death or immediately before that event, as the case may be."

The effect of this provision is that exercise of a power of termination by a debtor who has acquired title and still owns the goods at the time of his notice to terminate revests ownership in the conditional seller or his successor in interest. Thus, if by the time of termination by the debtor, the conditional seller has transferred the property in the goods to another, they will vest in the transferee; if he has become bankrupt, they will pass to his trustee in bankruptcy; and if he has died they will vest in his personal representative. If the conditional seller is a company which has gone into liquidation, property revests in the company itself, since liquidation does not of itself divest a company of its property or transmit it to the liquidator.

LIABILITY OF DEBTOR ON VOLUNTARY TERMINATION

[**12.15**] Termination of an agreement under s. 99 (1) does not affect any liability accrued due before the termination (s. 99 (2)). Hence the creditor is entitled to recover arrears of instalments and damages for any other breach of the agreement (the failure to take reasonable care of the goods is, in addition, covered expressly by s. 100 (4)—see below). Apart from his accrued liability the debtor is liable, unless the agreement provides for a smaller payment, or does not provide for any payment, to pay to the creditor the amount (if any) by which one-half of the total price exceeds the aggregate of the sums paid and the sums due in respect of the total price immediately before the termination (s. 100 (1)). Where the creditor was required under the agreement to carry out any installation and the agreement specifies an installation charge as part of the total price, the reference in s. 100 (1) to one-half of the total price is to be construed as a reference to the aggregate of the installation charge and one-half of the remainder of the total price (s. 100 (2)). Thus, if the total price is £850 of which £30 is specifically identified in the agreement as the installation charge, the sum to which the debtor can be required to make up his payments (subject to s. 100 (3)—see para. [**12.16**]) is $£30 + \frac{£850 - 30}{2} = £440$.

[**12.16**] If in any action the court is satisfied that a sum less than the amount specified in s. 100 (1) would be equal to the loss sustained by the creditor in consequence of the termination of the agreement by the debtor, the court may make an order for payment of that lower sum (s. 100 (3)). The word "loss" appears to mean loss calculated on the footing that but for the termination by the debtor the creditor would have received the total price (see R. M. Goode, *op. cit.*, pp. 406–407). But, for a different view, see A. G. Guest, *Law of Hire-Purchase*, para. 609.

[**12.17**] If the debtor has contravened an obligation to take reasonable care of the goods or land, the amount payable by him must be increased by the sum required to recompense the creditor for that contravention (s. 100 (4)).

[**12.18**] If the agreement itself confers an express power of termination, it may not be easy to decide whether the notice given by the debtor is to be construed as an exercise of his contractual right (which would not attract the liability under s. 100) or his statutory rights under s. 99 (which would attract such liability). The court would probably construe the notice as evincing an intention to select the alternative least burdensome to the debtor, in accordance with the principle enunciated in *Withers* v. *General Theatre Corporation, Ltd.*, [1933] 2 K.B. 536.

RETURN OF GOODS

[**12.19**] Where the debtor, on the termination of the agreement, wrongfully retains possession of goods to which the agreement relates, then in any action brought by the creditor to recover possession of the goods from the debtor, the court, unless it is satisfied that having regard to the circumstances it would not be just to do so, must order the goods to be delivered to the creditor without giving the debtor an option to pay the value of the goods (s. 100 (5)). The word "wrongfully" in this context presumably means without the consent of the creditor. Section 100 (5), though part of a section which in all other respects is confined to termination by the debtor is not by itself expressly so confined, but would almost certainly be construed as inapplicable to termination by the creditor (see para. [**12.19**]).

### TERMINATION OF HIRING AGREEMENT

[**12.20**] Sections 99 and 100 are confined to termination by a hirer or buyer under a hire-purchase or conditional sale agreement. The position of a hirer under a hiring agreement who wishes to terminate is governed by s. 101, which (subject to exceptions designed to exclude equipment leasing—see para. [**12.22**]) gives the hirer under a consumer hire agreement a cut-off point at 18 months. The object is to prevent hirers from being locked into burdensome contracts for long periods, possibly committing themselves to a total rental amounting to many times the value of the goods. Section 101 (1) therefore provides that the hirer under a regulated consumer hire agreement is entitled to terminate the agreement by giving notice (*i.e.*, written notice) to any person entitled or authorised to receive the sums payable under the agreement. By s. 101 (3) the notice cannot be given to expire earlier than 18 months after the making of the agreement (this is not necessarily 18 months from commencement of the period of hire). Subject to this the minimum period of notice, unless the agreement provides for a shorter period, is as follows:

(1) If the agreement provides for the making of payments by the hirer to the owner at equal intervals, the minimum period of notice is the length of one interval or three months, whichever is less (s. 101 (4)).
(2) If the agreement provides for the making of such payments at differing intervals, the minimum period of notice is the length of the shortest interval or three months, whichever is less (s. 101 (5)).
(3) In any other case, the minimum period of notice is three months (s. 101 (6)).

The consumer hirer appears to be entitled to fix any termination date he wishes, provided that it allows the minimum 18 months period specified above, is of the requisite minimum length and has an expiry date not later than the date fixed by the agreement for expiry of the period of hire.

### LIABILITY OF HIRER ON TERMINATION

[**12.21**] Termination of an agreement under s. 101 (1) does not affect any liability accrued due under the agreement before the termination (s. 101 (2)). It would seem that any provision in the agreement purporting to impose an additional liability on the hirer (*e.g.* by way of compensation for loss of future rentals) is void (s. 173 (1), (2)).

### EXCLUSION OF RIGHT TO TERMINATE

[**12.22**] The proposal to give the hirer under a regulated consumer hire agreement the right to bring the agreement to an end after 18 months caused considerable anxiety to equipment leasing companies, whose rental terms were customarily tailored to leases of four years and upwards. From the viewpoint of a leasing company, an equipment lease is essentially a financial operation, in which the rentals are so structured as to secure the payment to the company, over the minimum period of the lease, of sums equal to the capital cost of the equipment plus the desired return on capital, after taking due account of corporation tax, capital allowances and regional development grant. In order for equipment leasing to be viable, it is essential that the lessor shall be committed to a minimum leasing period sufficient to generate enough rentals for the above purpose. Theoretically, rentals *could* be spread over a period as short as 18 months, but no lessee would be willing to do business on this basis, since the ability to spread what is in essence the capital cost of the equipment with charges over at least a four- to five-year period is a *raison d'être* of the transaction from the lessee's point of view, and payment of the total rent over 18 months would in many cases be impossible for him. The 18 month cut-off point thus placed seriously at risk leasing to unincorporated bodies—in particular sole traders and partnerships—where the rentals did not exceed £5,000. The industry wanted the government to grant leasing of goods for business purposes a blanket exemption from the Act, but this the government, like its predecessor, steadfastly refused to do, in the light of many complaints received showing that the small trader was just as much in need of protection as the private individual.

[**12.23**] The solution was therefore to select the characteristics of that part of the leasing business that had not been found to generate abuse, and to use these characteristics as the criteria for exemption from s. 101. It is on this basis that s. 101 (7) exempts from the termination provisions:

> "(*a*) any agreement which provides for the making by the hirer of payments which in total (and without breach of the agreement) exceed £300 in any year, or
>
> (*b*) any agreement where—
>
> (i) goods are bailed or (in Scotland) hired to the hirer for the purposes of a business carried on by him, or the hirer holds himself out as requiring the goods for those purposes, and
>
> (ii) the goods are selected by the hirer, and acquired by the owner for the purposes of the agreement at the request of the hirer from any person other than the owner's associate, or
>
> (*c*) any agreement where the hirer requires, or holds himself out as requiring, the goods for the purpose of bailing or hiring them to other persons in the course of a business carried on by him."

Category (*a*) is effective to exclude a large number of equipment leases. Category (*b*) covers the traditional equipment lease under which the intended lessee conducts negotiations direct with the manufacturer or other supplier, selects the equipment and then asks the leasing company to buy the equipment and let it to him on lease. Category (*c*) exempts leases to a lessee whose business involves sub-leasing, *e.g.* a lease of a fleet of motor vehicles to a car hire firm with permission to sub-hire to the end user.

[**12.24**] To cover the possibility of other types of leasing contract for which the termination provisions would cause unintended difficulties, s. 101 (8) provides that if, on an application made to the Director by a person carrying on a consumer hire business, it appears to the Director that it would be in the interest of hirers to do so, he may by notice to the applicant direct that s. 101 shall not apply to consumer hire agreements made by the applicant, and subject to such conditions (if any) as the Director may specify, the Act is to have effect accordingly.

# CHAPTER 13

# SECURITY

## INTRODUCTION

**[13.1]** The Consumer Credit Act embodies the first attempt to provide a coherent pattern of rules governing the taking and enforcement of security given in connection with a consumer credit or consumer hire transaction. Hitherto, apart from the Bills of Sale Acts (see Chapter 1) there have been merely a few scattered provisions in the Moneylenders Acts and Hire-Purchase Acts relating to security. Part VIII of the Consumer Credit Act is devoted exclusively to security; and there are various other provisions which also bear on the rights of the secured party *vis-à-vis* the debtor and sureties.

**[13.2]** The security provisions of the Act are for the most part confined to relations between the creditor on the one hand and the debtor and sureties on the other. Third party rights are affected only to a minor degree, and these must largely be determined by reference to rules of common law and equity and to other legislation affecting security by individuals, *e.g.* the Bills of Sale Acts (for written chattel mortgages generally), the Mortgaging of Aircraft Order (for aircraft mortgages) and the Law of Property Acts, Land Charges Acts and Land Registration Acts (for mortgages of land).

**[13.3]** The Consumer Credit Act seeks to control security taken in relation to a regulated agreement by:

(*a*) providing for the form and content of securities;
(*b*) requiring specified information and documents to be supplied to sureties;
(*c*) controlling the realisation or other enforcement of securities;
(*d*) preventing evasion of the Act through use of a security;
(*e*) providing that in various circumstances securities shall become ineffective, *i.e.*, void *ab initio*;
(*f*) making special provision for pledges, in replacement of the Pawnbrokers Acts 1872–1960.

Each of these will be considered in turn.

## "SECURITY"; "SECURITY INSTRUMENT"; "SURETY"

**[13.4]** The term "security", in relation to an actual or prospective consumer credit agreement or consumer hire agreement, or any linked transaction, means a mortgage, charge, pledge, bond, debenture, indemnity, guarantee, bill, note or other right provided by the debtor or hirer, or at his request (express or implied), to secure the carrying out of the obligations of the debtor or hirer under the agreement (s. 189 (1)). It will be seen that the term is thus given the widest connotation, embracing not only real security (mortgage, charge, pledge) but personal security (bond, guarantee, indemnity, bill, note). The only qualification is that to fall within the statutory definition the security must be provided by or at the request of the debtor or hirer. Thus, a guarantee of the hirer's obligations under a hire-purchase agreement with a finance house is a security if given, for example, by the hirer's friend at the hirer's request but not if given by a dealer as part and parcel of a master agreement with a finance house or pursuant to a request by the finance house.

[**13.5**] A document which, in conformity with the requirements of s. 105 (1) (see para. [**13.6**]) expresses the terms of a security provided in relation to a regulated agreement is termed by the Act a "security instrument". Since those requirements do not apply to a security provided by the debtor or hirer himself (see para. [**13.6**]), it follows that "security instrument" is limited to documents embodying a security given by a third party at the request of the debtor or hirer. The term "surety", which in ordinary legal usage denotes a guarantee, has a much wider meaning under the Act, being defined as "the person by whom any security is provided, or the person to whom his rights and duties in relation to the security have passed by assignment or operation of law" (s. 189 (1)). Hence except where the Act otherwise indicates, "surety" covers not only a guarantor but the principal debtor if he provides a security.

[**13.6**] Any security provided in relation to a regulated agreement is required by s. 105 (1) to be expressed in writing. This provision does not apply to security provided by the debtor or hirer himself (s. 105 (6)), but a similar effect will be achieved by regulations under s. 105 (9) (see para. [**13.7**]). In some cases, a security provided by a third party will be part and parcel of the consumer credit or consumer hire agreement, as where the agreement incorporates a guarantee or indemnity or where a third party joins in the credit agreement to give a mortgage or charge. In other cases, the third party's security is distinct. Either way, it will have to be expressed in writing. This is a departure from the previous law, which required contracts of guarantee and certain types of mortgage to be *evidenced* by a note or memorandum in writing but permitted them to be *made* orally.

[**13.7**] The requirement of writing applies only to a security provided in relation to a regulated agreement, as opposed to an exempt agreement or an agreement which is not a consumer credit or consumer hire agreement at all; and, as we have seen, even a security provided in relation to a regulated agreement is not within s. 105 (1) if provided by the debtor or hirer himself. Regulations under s. 60 (1) are required to include provision requiring documents embodying regulated agreements also to embody any security provided in relation to a regulated agreement by the debtor or hirer (s. 105 (9)). (This does not mean that the regulations must necessarily require the security to be set out in the credit agreement itself. Section 105 (9) will be sufficiently complied with if the regulations provide for the credit agreement to refer to some other document containing the terms of the security—see s. 189 (4)). The effect of such regulations will be that even security provided by the debtor or hirer himself will have to be in writing—whether in the credit or hire agreement or in a separate document—if provided in relation to a regulated agreement. There is no exemption from this requirement. Even security given by way of deposit of documents of title will have to be embodied in a document, since whilst pledges of documents of title are exempt from the provisions of ss. 114–122 relating to pledges (see s. 114 (3) and para. [**13.21**]), they are not excluded from the scope of s. 105 (9). Where security is provided in connection with a *prospective* regulated agreement, the security does not become subject to Part VIII (other than s. 113 (6)) until the regulated agreement is actually made. In such a case, the security is not enforceable until after the making of the regulated agreement (s. 113 (6)); and until that time the person providing the security is entitled, by notice to the creditor or owner, to require that s. 106 shall apply to the security (*ibid.*; and see para. [**13.15**]).

[**13.8**] By s. 105 (2) regulations may prescribe the form and content of security instruments (*i.e.*, third party security documents—see para. [**13.5**]) to be made in compliance with s. 105, (1) and by s. 105 (3) may in particular—

(*a*) require specified information to be included in the prescribed manner in documents, and other specified material to be excluded;

(*b*) contain requirements to ensure that specified information is clearly brought to the attention of the surety and that one part of a document is not given insufficient or excessive prominence compared with another.

## OTHER FORMALITIES

[**13.9**] By s. 105 (4), (5) a security instrument is not properly executed (and is therefore enforceable only on an order of the court—s. 105 (7) unless—

(*a*) a document in the prescribed form, itself containing all the prescribed terms and conforming to regulations under sub-section (2), is signed in the prescribed manner by or on behalf of the surety, and

(*b*) the document embodies all the terms of the security, other than implied terms, and

(*c*) the document, when presented or sent for the purpose of being signed by or on behalf of the surety, is in such a state that its terms are readily legible, and

(*d*) when the document is presented or sent for the purpose of being signed by or on behalf of the surety there is also presented or sent a copy of the document, and

(*e*) where the security is provided after, or at the time when, the regulated agreement is made, a copy of the executed agreement, together with a copy of any other document referred to in it, is given to the surety at the time the security is provided, and

(*f*) where the security is provided before the regulated agreement is made, a copy of the executed agreement, together with a copy of any other document referred to in it, is given to the surety within seven days after the regulated agreement is made.

It will be seen that the surety need not sign the guarantee personally. Signature on his behalf suffices.

[**13.10**] It will be recalled that the requirements of s. 105 (4) and (5) apply only to a security instrument as defined in s. 105 (2) (see paras. [**13.5**]–[**13.6**]). Security provided by the debtor or hirer will, by virtue of s. 105 (9), be governed by regulations under s. 60 (1).

CONSEQUENCES OF NON-COMPLIANCE

[**13.11**] The consequences of non-compliance with the statutory provisions are potentially severe. Subsections (7) and (8) of s. 105 provide as follows:

"(7) If—

(*a*) in contravention of subsection (1) a security is not expressed in writing, or

(*b*) a security instrument is improperly executed,

the security (so far as provided in relation to a regulated agreement) is enforceable against the surety on an order of the court only.

(8) If an application for an order under subsection (7) is dismissed (except on technical grounds only) section 106 (ineffective securities) shall apply to the security."

It is to be observed that the sanctions prescribed by the above subsections will apply not only to non-compliance with s. 105 (1), (4) but also to a failure to comply with regulations under s. 60 (1) as to embodying of security by the debtor or hirer in the executed agreement; for non-compliance with such regulations will render the regulated agreement (including the security it embodies) improperly executed (s. 61 (1) (*a*)).

[**13.12**] In all these cases, the security will be enforceable only on an order of the court. The principles to be applied by the court in dealing with an application for an enforcement order in the above circumstances are set out in s. 127 (see para. [**22.7**]). If an application for an order is dismissed otherwise than on technical grounds, the security becomes retrospectively invalidated and all the other consequences prescribed by s. 106 (see para. [**13.13**]) will apply. An application is to be taken to be dismissed on technical grounds if the court so certifies (s. 189 (5)). This provision, if construed as requiring the court to determine whether in ordinary parlance the defect was to be considered technical, could occasion the court considerable difficulty. A procedural defect in making the application—as by inadvertent failure to comply with a rule of court or by defect in a pleading—could readily be treated as a mere technical defect. But what if the action in which the application to enforce the security is made is dismissed because, for example, the creditor had omitted to serve a notice of default, or had served an invalid notice or had begun his action prematurely, by miscalculating the date of expiry of the requisite default notice? In a popular sense, these might well be considered mere technical defects, yet they are all matters which prevent the creditor from establishing his cause of action. It is thought that s. 189 (5) is intended to give the court a wide discretion to overlook irregularities that do not furnish a meritorious defence for the debtor or hirer, and that accordingly the court is not obliged to apply the dictionary meaning of "technical grounds" but can treat any ground of dismissal of an application as if it were technical and certify accordingly. On the other hand, the spirit of s. 189 (5) would seem to require that the court should not give a certificate where the ground of dismissal is a substantial and meritorious ground of defence to the application. Moreover, even if the court has certified a ground for dismissal as technical, the debtor or hirer is entitled to apply for a declaration that the creditor or owner is not entitled to do the thing for which he requires the enforcement order; and if the court makes such a declaration as respects any regulated agreement, no application for an enforcement order in respect of that thing can thereafter be entertained (s. 142 (1)), and s. 106 becomes applicable to any security provided in relation to that agreement (s. 113 (3) (*d*)).

## INVALIDATION OF SECURITIES

**[13.13]** Section 106 provides that where, under any provision of the Act, that section is applied to any security provided in relation to a regulated agreement (see para. **[13.15]**), then subject to s. 177—

"(*a*) the security, so far as it is so provided, shall be treated as never having effect;

(*b*) any property lodged with the creditor or owner solely for the purposes of the security as so provided shall be returned by him forthwith;

(*c*) the creditor or owner shall take any necessary action to remove or cancel an entry in any register, so far as the entry relates to the security as so provided; and

(*d*) any amount received by the creditor or owner on realisation of the security shall, so far as it is referable to the agreement, be repaid to the surety."

**[13.14]** Section 177 provides two exceptions from s. 106. By s. 177 (1) nothing in the Act affects the right of a proprietor of a registered charge (within the meaning of the Land Registration Act 1925), who—

(*a*) became the proprietor under a transfer for valuable consideration without notice of any defect in the title arising (apart from s. 177) by virtue of the Act, or

(*b*) derives title from such a proprietor.

But a transferee of the security carrying on a business of debt-collecting is not within this exemption (s. 177 (3)). Hence one whose business consists, for example, of taking assignments of mortgages is caught by the full rigours of s. 106. Where, by virtue of the exemption under s. 177 (1), a land mortgage is enforced which would otherwise be treated as never having effect, the original creditor or owner is liable to indemnify the debtor or hirer against any loss thereby suffered by him (s. 177 (4)). The second exception is furnished by s. 177 (2), which provides that nothing in the Act is to affect the operation of s. 104 of the Law of Property Act 1925. The effect of s. 104 is that a purchaser from a mortgagee exercising a power of sale under that Act is not, either before or on conveyance, concerned to see or inquire whether the power of sale has been properly and regularly exercised (s. 104 (2)), provided that such purchaser did not take with notice of the irregularity (*Bailey* v. *Barnes*, [1894] 1 Ch. 25) or collude with the mortgagee to obtain the property at an undervalue (*Haddington Island Quarry Co., Ltd.* v. *Huson*, [1911] A.C. 727). Any person damnified by an unauthorised or improper or irregular exercise of the power can recover damages from the person exercising the power (s. 104 (2)). Hence if a mortgagee under a mortgage caught by s. 106 of the Consumer Credit Act nevertheless enforces the mortgage by exercising a power of sale conferred by s. 101 of the Law of Property Act 1925, the purchaser gets a good title, but the debtor can recover damages, if he can show that he has suffered loss.

[**13.15**] Section 106 applies in the following cases to a security provided in relation to a regulated agreement:

(*a*) Where an application to the court to enforce the security where it is not expressed in writing or is improperly executed is dismissed by the court otherwise than on technical grounds (s. 105 (8)).

(*b*) Where the regulated agreement is cancelled under s. 69 (1) or becomes subject to s. 69 (2) or is terminated under s. 91 (s. 113 (*a*), (*b*)).

(*c*) Where the Director dismisses otherwise than on technical grounds an application under s. 40 (2) for an order that the regulated agreement made by a trader when unlicensed should be treated as if he had been licensed (s. 113 (3) (*c*)).

(*d*) Where the Director dismisses otherwise than on technical grounds an application for an order under s. 149 (2) that the regulated agreement made with a debtor introduced by an unlicensed credit-broker should be treated as if the credit-broker had been licensed (*ibid.*);

(*e*) Where the court dismisses otherwise than on technical grounds an application under s. 65 (1) to enforce the regulated agreement when improperly executed (*ibid.*).

(*f*) Where the court dismisses an application under s. 124 (1) or (2) to enforce the regulated agreement or security, being an agreement or security in respect of which a negotiable instrument has been taken or negotiated in breach of s. 123 of the Act (ss. 113 (3) (*c*), 124 (3)).

(*g*) Where the court, on application by the debtor or hirer, makes a declaration under s. 142 (1) that the creditor or owner is not entitled to enforce the regulated agreement (s. 113 (3) (*d*)). But in this case, if the declaration relates to a part only of the regulated agreement, s. 106 applies to the security only so far as it concerns that part (s. 113 (4)).

(*h*) Where the security is provided in relation to a prospective agreement and before the agreement is made the person providing the security gives notice to the creditor or owner requiring that s. 106 shall apply to the security (s. 113 (6)).

[**13.16**] Where a security is provided in relation to an actual or prospective linked transaction, the above provisions apply as if references to the agreement were references to the linked transaction and as if references to the creditor or owner were references to the person (other than the debtor or hirer or his relative) who is a party, or prospective party, to the linked transaction (s. 113 (8)).

PROVISION OF INFORMATION TO SURETY

**[13.17]** The provisions of ss. 107–109 relating to information to be provided to a surety have already been discussed (para. [**10.11**]).

DEFAULT NOTICES

**[13.18]** The requirement to serve on the surety a copy of a default notice served on a debtor or hirer is discussed in paragraph [**14.6**].

ENFORCEMENT AND REALISATION OF SECURITIES

**[13.19]** A land mortgage securing a regulated agreement is enforceable on an order of the court only (s. 126). The creditor's right to enforce and realise other valid and properly executed securities will be governed by regulations under s. 112 of the Act and by the general law and such other legislation as may be relevant, *e.g.* the Bills of Sale Acts. However, paragraph 1 of s. 7 of the Bills of Sale Act (1878) Amendment Act 1882 (which entitles the grantee of a security bill of sale to seize the goods on default of payment) is, by s. 7A of that Act, as added by paragraph 1 of the Fourth Schedule to the Consumer Credit Act, made inapplicable to a default relating to a bill of sale by way of security for the payment of money under a regulated agreement within s. 87 (1) of the Consumer Credit Act—

(*a*) unless the restriction imposed by s. 88 (2) of that Act (expiry of default notice) has ceased to apply to the bill of sale; or

(*b*) if, by virtue of s. 89 of that Act (remedying of breach by debtor), the default is to be treated as not having occurred.

Where paragraph 1 of s. 7 does apply, application by the debtor for relief under the proviso to s. 7 of the Act of 1882 must be made to the County Court, not the High Court (Bills of Sale Act (1878) Amendment Act 1882, s. 7A, as added by Consumer Credit Act Fourth Schedule, para. 1).

**[13.20]** The first two subsections of s. 113 provide as follows:

"(1) Where a security is provided in relation to an actual or prospective regulated agreement, the security shall not be enforced so as to benefit the creditor or owner, directly or indirectly, to an extent greater (whether as respects the amount of any payment or the time or manner of its being made) than would be the case if the security were not provided and any obligations of the debtor or hirer, or his relative, under or in relation to the agreement were carried out to the extent (if any) to which they would be enforced under this Act.

(2) In accordance with subsection (1), where a regulated agreement is enforceable on an order of the court or the Director only, any security provided in relation to the agreement is enforceable (so far as provided in relation to the agreement) where such an order has been made in relation to the agreement, but not otherwise."

The effect of this provision is that a creditor cannot, by enforcing a security, recover more than he could have done under the regulated agreement itself. By reason of the definition of "security" (see para. [**13.4**]), this section applies not only to enforcement of a real security such as a mortgage but also enforcement of a guarantee or indemnity. However, where an indemnity is given in a case where the debtor or hirer is a minor, or is otherwise not of full capacity, the reference in s. 113 (1) to the extent to which his obligations would be enforced is to be read in relation to the indemnity as a reference to the extent to which they would be enforced if he were of full capacity (s. 113 (7)). Breach of s. 113 attracts no sanction; the debtor's only remedy is to seek an injunction (see para. [**15.7**]).

PLEDGES

[**13.21**] Sections 114–122 of the Act provide a new code for pawnbroking, replacing the Pawnbrokers Acts 1872–1960. Strictly speaking, ss. 114–122 are not limited to pawnbrokers but apply to any creditor who takes an article in pawn under a regulated agreement (s. 114 (1)), other than a non-commercial agreement (s. 114 (3) (*b*)). But pledges taken by creditors who are not pawnbrokers usually take the form of a pledge of documents of title, and since such pledges are excluded from ss. 114–122 (s. 114 (3) (*a*)), it is only pawnbrokers who are likely to be substantially affected by these sections.

[**13.22**] The expression "document of title" is not defined by the Act, but in this context plainly denotes a document of title to goods, as opposed to land, since only goods are susceptible of pledge, and title deeds, if deposited as such for the purpose of security over the land and not merely as pieces of paper and wax "savour of the realty" and are not personal chattels (see *Swanley Coal Co.* v. *Denton*, [1906] 2 K.B. 873). As to what documents are documents of title to goods, see para. [**3.38**].

FORMALITIES OF CONTRACT

[**13.23**] Section 114 (1) requires the creditor to issue a pawn-receipt to the pledgor at the time of receipt of the pledge by the creditor. Sections 62–64 of the Act (discussed in Chapter 7) apply to regulated agreements for a pledge as to any other regulated agreement. But the sanction for non-compliance is still more powerful, since a creditor under a regulated agreement to take an article in pawn who infringes ss. 62–64 or s. 114 (1) commits an offence (s. 115).

PLEDGES FROM MINORS

[**13.24**] A person who takes any article in pawn from an individual whom he knows to be, or who appears to be and is, a minor commits an offence (s. 114 (2)).

REDEMPTION PERIOD

[**13.25**] The combined effect of subsections (1)–(3) of s. 116 appears to be that the pawnor can redeem the pawn until the occurrence of whichever of the following events is the latest, viz.:

(*a*) the expiry of six months from the taking of the pledge; or

(*b*) the expiry or termination of the period fixed by the parties for the duration of the credit secured by the pledge (taking into account, it is assumed, any acceleration clause coming into force under the agreement after expiry of the notice of default served under s. 87); or

(*c*) expiry of such longer period as the parties may agree; or

(*d*) realisation of the pawn by the pawnee under s. 121 (para. [**13.31**]) or forfeiture of the pledge to the pawnee under s. 120 (1) (*a*) (see para. [**13.30**]).

[**13.26**] No special charge may be made for redemption of a pawn after the end of the redemption period, and charges in respect of the safekeeping of the pawn must not be at a higher rate after the end of the redemption period than before (s. 116 (4)).

REDEMPTION PROCEDURE

[**13.27**] On surrender of the pawn-receipt, and payment of the amount owing, at any time when the pawn is redeemable, the pawnee must deliver the pawn to the bearer of the pawn-receipt (s. 117 (1)), except where he knows or has reasonable cause to suspect that the bearer of the pawn-receipt is neither the owner of the pawn nor authorised by the owner to redeem it (s. 117 (2)). The pawnee making delivery under the provisions of s. 117 (1), or refusing to make delivery where the person demanding delivery does not comply with s. 117 (1), incurs no liability in tort to any person (s. 117 (3)).

LOSS OF PAWN-RECEIPT

[**13.28**] As under the Pawnbrokers Acts, the person entitled to redeem the pledge who through loss or other reason is not in possession of the pawn-receipt may redeem the pawn by tendering a prescribed form of statutory declaration or, in the case of a pawn which is security for fixed-sum credit not exceeding £15 or running-account credit on which the credit limit does not exceed £15, a prescribed form of written statement (s. 118).

UNREASONABLE REFUSAL TO DELIVER PAWN

[**13.29**] If a person who has taken a pawn under a regulated agreement refuses without reasonable cause to allow the pawn to be redeemed, he commits an offence (s. 119 (1)). The onus lies on the pawnee to prove that he had reasonable cause to refuse to allow the pawn to be redeemed (s. 171 (6)).

CONSEQUENCES OF FAILURE TO REDEEM

[**13.30**] Where the pawn is security for fixed-sum credit not exceeding £15 or running-account credit on which the credit limit does not exceed £15 and the redemption period is six months, the property in the pawn passes to the pawnee automatically at the end of the six-month period if the pawn has not then been redeemed (s. 120 (1) (*a*)). In any other case, the pawn is realisable by the pawnee (s. 120 (1) (*b*)) by sale in accordance with s. 121 (see para. [**13.31**]). Where the debtor or hirer is entitled to apply to the court for a time order under s. 131, an additional five days following the end of the redemption period must expire before the property in the pawn passes to the pawnee, or the pawn becomes realisable by the pawnee, as the case may be (s. 120 (2)).

*Realisation of Pawn*

[**13.31**] Section 121 provides for realisation of the pawn as follows:

"(1) Where a pawn has become realisable by him, the pawnee may sell it, after giving to the pawnor (except in such cases as may be prescribed) not less than the prescribed period of notice of the intention to sell, indicating in the notice the asking price and such other information as may be prescribed.

(2) Within the prescribed period after the sale takes place, the pawnee shall give the pawnor the prescribed information in writing as to the sale, its proceeds and expenses.

(3) Where the net proceeds of sale are not less than the sum which, if the pawn had been redeemed on the date of the sale, would have been payable for its redemption, the debt secured by the pawn is discharged and any surplus shall be paid by the pawnee to the pawnor.

(4) Where subsection (3) does not apply, the debt shall be treated as from the date of sale as equal to the amount by which the net proceeds of sale fall short of the sum which would have been payable for the redemption of the pawn on that date.

(5) In this section the "net proceeds of sale" is the amount realised (the "gross amount") less the expenses (if any) of the sale.

(6) If the pawnor alleges that the gross amount is less than the true market value of the pawn on the date of sale, it is for the pawnee to prove that he and any agents employed by him in the sale used reasonable care to ensure that the true market value was obtained, and if he fails to do so subsections (3) and (4) shall have effect as if the reference in subsection (5) to the gross amount were a reference to the true market value.

(7) If the pawnor alleges that the expenses of the sale were unreasonably high, it is for the pawnee to prove that they were reasonable, and if he fails to do so subsections (3) and (4) shall have effect as if the reference in subsection (5) to expenses were a reference to reasonable expenses."

NEGOTIABLE INSTRUMENTS

[**13.32**] The use of bills of exchange in connection with consumer credit transactions has long been a source of concern and was the subject of evidence to the Crowther Committee. Typically, the problem arose where a consumer wishing to have central heating or double glazing installed in his home gave the supplier, prior to the work being put in hand, a promissory note or bill of exchange in favour of the supplier providing for payment of the price with interest or charges by stated instalments, the whole to become due on default in payment of any instalment. The note or bill would then be discounted by the supplier to a finance house, so that the burden of the credit extension did not fall on the supplier. If, as not uncommonly occurred, the installation proved defective or if it was never provided at all—which sometimes happened because the supplier became insolvent—the consumer seeking to withhold payment of the note or bill would find himself legally bound to pay the finance house, despite the supplier's breach, because the finance house was a holder in due course and therefore took the note or bill free of defences, pursuant to s. 38 (2) of the Bills of Exchange Act 1882. In such cases the consumer, having temporarily withheld payment, might then find himself liable to pay the full outstanding balance immediately as a result of the provision in the bill or note for acceleration of payment in the event of failure to pay an instalment.

[**13.33**] The Consumer Credit Act does not attempt to disturb the privileged position of a holder in due course. What it does is to restrict the taking and negotiation of negotiable instruments in connection with a regulated agreement in such a way as to make it difficult for these to come into the possession of a holder in due course (or indeed any holder) other than a bank; and usually the bank would be acting as agent for collection of the instrument on behalf of the original creditor. The Act achieves the desired result in three ways. First, it provides that the creditor or owner shall not take a negotiable instrument, other than a bank note or cheque, in discharge of any sum payable by the debtor or hirer under a regulated agreement or by any person as surety in relation to the agreement (s. 123 (1)). The exemption of cheques is not confined to currently dated cheques but covers post-dated cheques. The prohibition does not apply to a postal order, which is not a negotiable instrument. Secondly, the Act precludes a creditor who has taken a cheque as payment (which is permitted by s. 123 (1)) from negotiating this except to a bank within the meaning of the Bills of Exchange Act 1882, *i.e.*, a person or body of persons carrying on the business of banking. This is effective to prevent any person, other than a bank, from becoming a holder in due course, since the definition of "holder in due course" in s. 29 (1) of the Bills of Exchange Act requires that he be a person to whom the bill has been negotiated. A bill is negotiated when transferred from one person to another in such a manner as to constitute the transferee the holder of the bill (Bills of Exchange Act s. 31 (1)). A bearer bill is negotiated by delivery, an order bill, by indorsement of the holder completed by delivery (*ibid.*, s. 31 (2), (3)). Transfer of a bill otherwise than by negotiation (*e.g.* by assignment or charge, as where a factoring agreement or floating charge embodies an equitable assignment sweeping up bills and notes of the supplier or chargor) is not prohibited, since the transferee cannot then be a holder in due course (indeed he cannot be a holder at all) and thus cannot bring an action on the bill unless he takes a statutory assignment of the holder's rights in conformity with s. 136 of the Law of Property Act 1925. He can then sue as assignee, but takes subject to all equities and defences of which the debtor could have availed himself against the original payee, so that the mischief against which the Act is aimed is thus prevented. Thirdly the creditor or owner cannot take a negotiable instrument as security, but only as conditional payment (s. 123 (3)). He will be regarded as taking the negotiable instrument as security for discharge of a sum if the sum is intended to be paid in some other way, and the negotiable instrument is to be presented for payment only if the sum is not paid in that way (s. 123 (4)).

EXEMPTION FROM S. 124

**[13.34]** The Secretary of State may, by order, provide that s. 123 shall not apply where the regulated agreement has a connection with a country outside the United Kingdom (s. 123 (6)).

CONSEQUENCES OF BREACH

**[13.35]** After any contravention of s. 123 has occurred in relation to a sum payable as mentioned in s. 123 (1) (*a*), the agreement under which the sum is payable is enforceable against the debtor or hirer on an order of the court only (s. 124 (1)). If the application is dismissed by the court otherwise than on technical grounds, a security taken in relation to the agreement becomes void *ab initio* under s. 106 of the Act (see s. 113 (3) (*b*), and para. [**13.13**]). Similarly, after contravention of s. 123 in relation to a sum payable by any surety, the security is enforceable on an order of the court only (s. 124 (2)); and if an application to enforce the security is dismissed otherwise than on technical grounds, s. 106 becomes applicable to the security (s. 124 (2)).

**[13.36]** Section 125 (1) provides that a person who takes a negotiable instrument in contravention of s. 123 (1) or (3) is not a holder in due course, and is not entitled to enforce the instrument. But this disability is restricted to the creditor or owner himself, since it is only a taking of the negotiable instrument by the creditor or owner that contravenes s. 123 (1) or (3). If the creditor or owner negotiates a cheque in contravention of s. 123 (2), his doing so constitutes a defect in title within the meaning of the Bills of Exchange Act (Consumer Credit Act s. 125 (2)), with the result that if he negotiates the instrument to any person taking with notice of the contravention, such person does not become a holder in due course (see Bills of Exchange Act, s. 29 (1) (*b*)). If, however, the creditor negotiates the instrument to a person who takes in good faith and without notice of the creditor's contravention of s. 123 of the Consumer Credit Act, then provided that such person fulfils the other requirements of a holder in due course under s. 29 of the Bills of Exchange Act he takes free from the defect in title generated by the contravention (Bills of Exchange Act s. 38 (2)) and can enforce the instrument as such in the usual way (Consumer Credit Act s. 125 (4)). In that event, the debtor or hirer is entitled to be indemnified by the creditor or owner in respect of the liability incurred to the holder in due course (s. 125 (3)).

# CHAPTER 14

# GUARANTEES AND INDEMNITIES

## INTRODUCTION

[**14.1**] The contract of guarantee has long been the Cinderella of the law. Legislation, apart from requiring such contracts to be evidenced by a note or memorandum in writing (Statute of Frauds 1677, s. 4; Hire-Purchase Act 1965 s. 22 (1)) and conferring a limited measure of protection under the Hire-Purchase Act 1965, has done little for the guarantor, and it has been left to the courts to safeguard his interests by developing various grounds for his release, *e.g.* the variation of the principal agreement without his consent or the impairment of securities taken by the creditor.

[**14.2**] If this is true of guarantors, it is applicable with even greater force to indemnifiers. A guarantor is one whose liability is secondary, *i.e.* dependent on that of the principal debtor. He incurs no liability until the debtor has made default, and unless otherwise provided by the contract of guarantee can repudiate the guarantee if the principal contract to which the guarantee relates is invalid or unenforceable. On the other hand, the liability of an indemnifier under a contract of guarantee (which does not require to be evidenced in writing except where it is governed by the Hire-Purchase Act 1965) is a principal liability and not in any way dependent on default by the principal debtor or on the validity of the contract entered into by the debtor. The classic exposition of the difference is the example given in *Birkmyr* v. *Darnell* (1704), 1 Salkeld 27. A says to B: "Supply goods to C and if he does not pay you I will." That is a contract of guarantee. A says to B: "Supply goods to C and I will see that you are paid." That is a contract of indemnity. The difference between the two contracts produces substantial legal consequences, yet in most cases it is totally unreal. If the obligations of the indemnifier have the same content as those of the principal debtor, it is mere sophistry to say that the indemnifier's liability is not dependent on the principal debtor's default; for performance of their respective obligations falls due at the same time and if the principal debtor meets his obligations, there will be no remaining liability to which the indemnity can attach.

[**14.3**] The Hire-Purchase Act assimilated the treatment of guarantees and indemnities as regards the limited range of safeguards conferred on the guarantor by that Act. The Consumer Credit Act goes much further, and when its various provisions relating to guarantees and indemnities are drawn together they will be found to provide a reasonably comprehensive pattern of protection for guarantors and indemnifiers. The Act does not in fact refer to a "guarantor" or an "indemnifier" but to a "surety", *i.e.*, the person by whom any security is provided, or the person to whom his rights and duties in relation to the security have passed by assignment or operation of law (s. 189) (1)). Moreover, in looking at the statutory provisions the reader should bear in mind that the Act rarely uses the words "guarantee" and "indemnity". Instead it refers to "security". This usage is unfortunate since it confuses the genus with the species. A guarantee or indemnity is a form of security, but the term "security" as defined in s. 189 (1) embraces many other security forms, including mortgages. By using the word "security" when what was meant was "guarantee or indemnity" the Act raises doubts as to the full impact of some of its provisions.

### FORMAL REQUIREMENTS

[**14.4**] The provisions of the Act relating to the form and contents of securities, including guarantees and indemnities, have been discussed in the previous chapter (paras. [**13.6**] *et seq.*).

### SUPPLY OF INFORMATION AND DOCUMENTS TO SURETY

[**14.5**] For the right of a surety to information and documents, see paragraph [**10.11**].

### NOTICE OF DEFAULT

[**14.6**] Service of a notice of default on the debtor or hirer in accordance with s. 88 is necessary before any security (including a guarantee or indemnity) can be enforced (s. 87 (1) (*d*)). Where such a notice of default is served on the debtor or hirer, a copy must be served on any surety (s. 111 (1)), otherwise the security becomes unenforceable against the surety, except on a court order, in respect of the breach or other matter to which the notice relates (s. 111 (2)). But no time limit is laid down for compliance with s. 111 (1), so that the creditor can avoid the disability imposed by s. 111 (2) by serving the copy of the notice of default before starting proceedings, or taking extra-judicial steps, to enforce his claim against the surety. Moreover, it is only the matters specified in the notice of default that cannot be relied on against the surety without service of a copy of the notice of default. Hence if the debtor remedies the breach under s. 89 and subsequently commits a fresh breach in respect of which a new notice of default is served on him, it is only a copy of the new notice that needs to be served on the surety. Section 111 applies also to notices under ss. 76 (1), 98 (1).

### LIMITATION OF LIABILITY TO THAT OF PRINCIPAL DEBTOR

[**14.7**] A consequence of s. 113 (1) (discussed in para. [**13.20**]) is that notwithstanding any provision of the guarantee or indemnity itself, the creditor or owner cannot recover from the guarantor or indemnifier a sum greater than that recoverable from the debtor or hirer himself. This goes much further than the common law rule, which can be excluded by agreement (see para. [**14.8**]).

An exception is provided in relation to contracts of indemnity (but not contracts of guarantee) by s. 113 (7), to which reference has been made earlier (para. [**14.20**]).

UNENFORCEABILITY OF GUARANTEE OR INDEMNITY

[**14.8**] At common law, the liability of a guarantor, unlike that of an indemnifier, is *prima facie* co-terminous with that of the principal debtor, so that if for any reason the contract entered into by the principal debtor is void or unenforceable the guarantee is affected to the same extent. But whereas at common law this principle may be excluded by the terms of the guarantee, s. 113 (1) of the Act prevents the guarantor from incurring a liability which would not fall on the debtor or hirer. If the regulated agreement, though not void, is enforceable only on an order of the court, then until such order has been made the guarantee is likewise unenforceable (s. 113 (2)). This is, of course, entirely distinct from the statutory rule that if the guarantee itself is not properly executed, an order of the court must be obtained to enforce the guarantee, so far as it is provided in relation to the regulated agreement (s. 105 (6)). It should be noted that if the debtor under a regulated debtor–creditor agreement, or a debtor–creditor–supplier agreement for unrestricted-use credit, exercises a right to cancel but elects under s. 71 to leave the whole or part of the credit outstanding, all guarantees, indemnities and other forms of security are extinguished, and the credit agreement continues as an unsecured agreement (see para. [**8.50**]).

NEGOTIABLE INSTRUMENTS

[**14.9**] If the creditor or owner contravenes the provisions of s. 123 relating to the taking or negotiation of a negotiable instrument, the surety is protected in the same way as the debtor, since the security cannot be enforced except on an order of the court (s. 124 (2)—see para. [**13.35**]).

EXTORTIONATE BARGAINS

[**14.10**] The provisions of the Act relating to extortionate credit bargains (see Chapter 22) enure for the protection of the surety as well as of the debtor or hirer in respect of whose obligations the guarantee or indemnity was given.

CONTINUANCE OF COMMON LAW RULES

[**14.11**] Nothing in the Act affects the principles evolved at common law for the protection of guarantors. See generally R. M. Goode, *op. cit.*, Chapter 22.

# CHAPTER 15

# LAND MORTGAGE TRANSACTIONS

APPLICATION OF ACT

[**15.1**] In principle, the Act regulates all forms of consumer credit and consumer hire agreement, and does not cease to apply merely because the agreement is secured on land or the credit is extended for the purchase of land. But land mortgages extended by certain types of creditor (notably local authorities and building societies) are for the most part exempt under s. 16 (1), and the Secretary of State may by order extend the exemption to mortgages entered into as creditor by other classes specified in s. 16 (1) (see para. [**3.24**]). However, whilst total exemption is limited to cases within s. 16, consumer credit agreements which are secured by a land mortgage or under which the credit is extended in connection with the purchase of land are in given conditions exempted from certain specific parts or provisions of the Act (see below). The term "land mortgage" includes any security charged on land (s. 189 (1)), and thus embraces a rent charge.

ADVERTISEMENTS

[**15.2**] Advertisements of credit facilities which would otherwise be outside Part IV of the Act may be brought within it if the advertiser carries on a business of a type mentioned in s. 43 (2) (see paras. [**6.8**], [**3.43**]).

WITHDRAWAL AND CANCELLATION

[**15.3**] The right of cancellation conferred by s. 67 does not apply to (i) a regulated agreement secured on land; or (ii) a restricted-use credit agreement to finance the purchase of land; or (iii) an agreement for a bridging loan in connection with the purchase of land. Instead, the Act provides the debtor (except in cases (ii) and (iii), above) with a period of reflection by prescribing a special documentation procedure and an isolation period in which the debtor must not be disturbed by unsolicited communications (see Chapter 8).

ENTRY ON LAND

[**15.4**] Except under an order of the court, the creditor or owner is not entitled to enter any premises to take possession of goods subject to a regulated hire-purchase agreement, regulated conditional sale agreement or regulated consumer hire agreement (s. 92 (1)). Entry in contravention of this provision is actionable as a breach of statutory duty (s. 92 (3)). It is not, however, a breach to enter with the consent of the debtor or hirer given at the time (s. 173 (3)).

### RECOVERY OF LAND

[**15.5**] At any time when the debtor is in breach of a regulated conditional sale agreement relating to land, the creditor is entitled to recover possession of the land from the debtor, or any person claiming under him, on an order of the court only (s. 92 (2)). The possession in breach of s. 92 (2) is actionable as a breach of statutory duty (s. 92 (3)) unless with the consent of the debtor given at the time of repossession (s. 173 (3)). Section 92 (2) does not cover mortgages of land, which are in any event enforceable only on an order of the court (s. 125—see para. [**15.7**]).

### BUYER'S TERMINATION OF CONDITIONAL SALE AGREEMENT COMPRISING LAND

[**15.6**] The statutory right of a buyer under a conditional sale agreement to terminate it at any time by notice (s. 99 (1)) applies to a conditional sale agreement relating to land (see definition of "conditional sale agreement" in s. 189 (1)). But the right of termination ceases to be exercisable after title to the land has passed to the buyer (s. 99 (2A)). Accordingly, sub-ss. (3) and (4) of s. 99 (see paras. [**12.13**]–[**12.14**]) are restricted to conditional sale agreements relating to goods.

### ENFORCEMENT OF LAND MORTGAGE

[**15.7**] A land mortgage securing a regulated agreement is enforceable (so far as provided in relation to the agreement) on an order of the court only (s. 125). However, by a curious omission no sanction is provided for enforcement without a court order, *e.g.* by repossession or sale; and s. 170 (1) precludes an action for damages for breach of statutory duty where this is not expressly provided. Hence the debtor's only remedy is to apply to the court for an injunction, this being outside the scope of s. 170 (1) (see s. 170 (3)). The court clearly has power to restrain a threatened breach; and even if the debtor's application is not made until after the breach has occurred, the court would seem to have power to grant a mandatory injunction to restore the *status quo*, except where this would affect the rights of an innocent third party, *e.g.* a *bona fide* purchase from the mortgagee.

# CHAPTER 16

# CREDIT-TOKEN AGREEMENTS

## DEFINITION

[**16.1**] A credit-token agreement is defined in s. 14 (1), discussed in paragraph [**4.13**]. As there noted, the term "credit-token" covers bank and other credit cards, trading checks and trading vouchers, but not bank cheque guarantee cards. Special provisions apply to credit-token and credit-token agreements (see para. [**4.14**]) which will now be examined in more detail.

## UNSOLICITED CREDIT-TOKENS PROHIBITED

[**16.2**] The provisions of s. 51 prohibiting unsolicited credit-tokens have been mentioned earlier (para. [**6.27**]).

## SUPPLY OF COPY OF EXECUTED AGREEMENT

[**16.3**] As a rule, a copy of the executed consumer credit or consumer hire agreement must be sent to the debtor or hirer within seven days following the making of the agreement (s. 63 (2)—and see Chapter 7). But in the case of a credit-token agreement, it suffices that the copy is given before or at the time when the credit-token is given to the debtor (s. 63 (4)). The requirements on the issue of new credit-token agreements have been mentioned earlier (para. [**7.24**]).

## NOTICE OF CANCELLATION

[**16.4**] Where, in the case of a cancellable agreement, the agreement is presented or sent to the debtor for signature and becomes an executed agreement on the spot, a separate notice in prescribed form setting out the debtor's right of cancellation must usually be sent to him by post within seven days (s. 64 (1) (*b*)—and see para. [**7.26**]). But in the case of a credit-token agreement, it suffices if the copy is sent by post either before the credit-token is given to him or with the credit-token (s. 64 (2)).

## ACCEPTANCE OF CREDIT-TOKEN

[**16.5**] The debtor incurs no liability under a credit-token agreement for use made of the credit-token by any person unless the debtor had previously accepted the credit-token, or the use constituted an acceptance of it by him (s. 66 (1)). By s. 66 (2), the debtor accepts a credit-token when—

(*a*) it is signed, or
(*b*) a receipt for it is signed, or
(*c*) it is first used,

either by the debtor himself or by a person who, pursuant to the agreement, is authorised by him to use it. The debtor would not, it is thought, be treated as having signed a receipt for a credit-token unless the receipt is given for the credit-token as such, and not merely for the package containing it. Hence a receipt for a registered or special delivery letter containing a credit-token does not thereby constitute signature of receipt for the token itself unless the delivery receipt expressly refers to the token.

## CANCELLATION OF CREDIT-TOKEN AGREEMENT

[**16.6**] The right of cancellation applies to credit-token agreements, in the circumstances set out in s. 67, in the same way as to other regulated agreements. On cancellation, the debtor is entitled (subject to s. 70 (5)—see below) to recover payments made to the creditor either from the creditor himself or from the various suppliers in respect of whose accounts the debtor has made payment to the creditor (s. 70 (3)). For the purpose of determining to which of such accounts payments made by the debtor to the creditor relate, the court will, under common law rules, have regard to any appropriation made by the debtor; but in the absence of such appropriation the court will presumably apply the rule in *Clayton's case* (1816), Mer. 572, and treat each payment as made in reduction of the earliest account first.

[**16.7**] There is, however, a special rule applicable to credit-token agreements. The debtor is not entitled to repayment of a sum payable for the issue of the credit-token, or to release from liability for payment of such sum, until the credit-token has been returned to the creditor or surrendered to a supplier (s. 70 (5)). The limited effect of this provision should be noted. It applies not to sums paid or payable in respect of goods or services acquired with the token but only to a sum paid or payable for the *issue* of the token. It is thus directed at those check trading agreements which require the debtor to pay the check trader a sum of money for the privilege of having the trading checks issued to him.

## MISUSE OF CREDIT-TOKEN

[**16.8**] By s. 83 (1), the debtor under a regulated consumer credit agreement is not liable to the creditor for any loss arising from use of the credit facility by another person not acting, or to be treated as acting, as the debtor's agent. This provision is not confined to misuse of credit-tokens (it could, for example, cover pledge of a debtor's credit by another but it does not apply to forgery of a cheque or any other misuse of an instrument within s. 4 of the Cheques Act 1957 (s. 83 (2)) and is most likely to arise from theft or other unauthorised use of a credit card or other credit-token. But s. 84 sets out various cases in which the debtor can be made liable, within the limits laid down by that section, for loss to the creditor arising from misuse of the credit-token. The rules embodied in s. 84 may be summarised as follows:

(1) Subject to (2) and (3) below, the debtor can be made liable (either by virtue of the credit-token agreement or in tort for negligence):

(i) without limit, for loss to the creditor from use of the credit-token by a person who acquired possession of it with the debtor's consent (s. 84 (2)), even if the particular use was not with the debtor's consent;

(ii) to the extent of £30 (or the credit limit if lower) for loss to the creditor from use of the credit-token during the period when it is not in the possession of an authorised person (s. 84 (1)), i.e. the debtor, the creditor and any person authorised by the debtor to use the token (s. 84 (7)).

(2) No liability for unauthorised use is incurred by the debtor under (1) unless there are contained in the credit-token agreement in the prescribed manner particulars of the name, address and telephone number of a person stated to be the person to whom notice is to be given under s. 84 (3) (s. 84 (4)).

(3) Once the debtor has given notice to the creditor that the token is lost or stolen or is for any other reason liable to be misused, he ceases to incur any further liability in respect of the token (s. 84 (3)), even within the £30 limit. Such notice may be given orally or in writing (s. 84 (3)) and takes effect when received (s. 84 (5)); but where it is given orally, and the agreement so requires, it is to be treated as not taking effect if not confirmed in writing within seven days (*ibid.*). This allows the creditor, by appropriate provision in the agreement, to safeguard himself against false assertions by the debtor that he gave oral notification of loss. If, therefore, the credit-token agreement requires oral notice of loss to be confirmed in writing within seven days and the debtor fails to give any written confirmation at all, his liability continues to accrue up to the maximum of £30 or the credit limit if lower. If, where there is such a requirement, the debtor does give written confirmation but this does not reach the creditor until, say, ten days after the oral notice was given, the debtor is liable, within the above limit, for all unauthorised purchases made up to the date of receipt of the written confirmation, but incurs no liability for purchases made thereafter.

(4) Any sum paid by the debtor for the issue of the credit-token, to the extent (if any) that it has not been previously offset by use made of the credit-token, is to be treated as paid towards satisfaction of any liability under s. 84 (1) or (2) (s. 84 (6)).

(5) Where two or more credit-tokens are given under one credit-token agreement, the provisions of s. 84 apply to each credit-token separately (s. 84 (8)).

# CHAPTER 17

# LEASING, HIRE AND RENTAL AGREEMENTS

## NATURE OF AGREEMENT

[**17.1**] A leasing (or hire or rental) agreement is an agreement for the hire of goods which does not provide for ownership of the goods to pass to the lessee. The terms "leasing", "hire", "contract hire" and "rental" have different business connotations (see R. M. Goode, *Hire-Purchase Law and Practice* (2nd edn.), p. 880) but are legally interchangeable, the distinctions being purely functional and having no legal significance. Nevertheless, as we shall see, there is one provision of the Consumer Credit Act, namely s. 101, in which Parliament has endeavoured to isolate transactions which in the business world would be termed "equipment leasing" and to exclude these from the provisions of that section conferring on the hirer the right to bring the agreement to an end after 18 months. In all other respects, the Act draws no distinction between these different forms of hiring agreement; and in discussing the provisions of the Act we shall employ the statutory term "consumer hire agreement", drawing attention to the fact that except where the hirer is a body corporate this term covers all forms of hiring subsumed under the above labels.

## LEGAL CONTROL OF HIRING AGREEMENTS

[**17.2**] Prior to the Consumer Credit Act, hiring agreements were free from legal controls other than those imposed as a measure of economic regulation by the Control of Hiring Order 1973, which continues in force. The Consumer Credit Act, embodying the recommendations of the Crowther Committee, brings such agreements for the first time within the scope of consumer protection legislation under the description "consumer hire agreement".

## SCOPE OF THE ACT

[**17.3**] The Act applies to all consumer hire agreements as defined by s. 15 (see para. [**3.26**]), other than agreements exempted by order of the Secretary of State under s. 16 (6) (see para. [**3.28**]). Except as indicated below, the provisions relating to consumer credit agreements apply equally to consumer hire agreements. It should be noted that unlike consumer credit agreements, consumer hire agreements are by definition (s. 15) limited to goods and do not extend to the hire of services or the letting of land.

FORMALITIES OF CONTRACT

[**17.4**] No distinction is drawn by the Act between regulated consumer credit agreements and regulated consumer hire agreements in relation to the formalities of contract, though the disclosure requirements to be imposed by regulations will obviously have to reflect differences between the two forms of agreement.

INFORMATION AND DOCUMENTS

[**17.5**] The hirer's right to information and documents under s. 79 of the Act has been previously discussed (para. [**10.6**]), as has the hirer's duty under s. 80 to inform the owner, on request, of the whereabouts of the goods comprised in the agreement which the hirer is required to keep in his possession or control (para. [**10.7**]), and the owner's duty under s. 109 to supply information to a surety (para. [**10.11**]).

MISUSE OF CREDIT FACILITIES

[**17.6**] The provisions of s. 83 (para. [**16.8**]) are not applicable to the misuse of consumer hire facilities.

TERMINATION OF HIRING AGREEMENT

[**17.7**] The provisions of ss. 99 and 100 conferring a right on the hirer or buyer to terminate a hire-purchase or conditional sale agreement by notice in writing, and restricting his liability on such termination, have no application to consumer hire agreements. Instead, a more restricted right of termination, with limitation of liability to that accrued prior to termination, is conferred by s. 101. This has been fully discussed in paras. [**12.20**]–[**12.23**].

RECOVERY OF HIRED GOODS

[**17.8**] The provisions of ss. 90 and 91 relating to protected goods do not apply to goods comprised in a consumer hire agreement. The owner remains free to exercise a contractual right to repossess, subject to—

(i) service of the requisite notice under s. 76 (1) if the period of hire has not expired (s. 76 (2));

(ii) service of the requisite default notice under ss. 87 and 88, and its expiry without the default having been remedied within the specified time;

(iii) exercise by the court of its powers under Part IX of the Act (see Chapter 22);

(iv) exercise by the court of its general equitable jurisdiction to grant relief against forfeiture (see para. [**17.11**]).

It is thought that a default notice complying with s. 88 will *ipso facto* constitute at the same time a notice complying with s. 76 (1).

[**17.9**] Whilst the owner can repossess hired goods in the conditions mentioned in the preceding paragraph, or alternatively can apply to the court for an order for return of the goods (see para. [**17.10**]), he incurs some risk in so doing in that the court's power under s. 132 to order return of payments to the hirer then becomes exercisable (see para. [**22.23**]).

[**17.10**] Instead of exercising a power to repossess, the owner can apply to the court for an order for return of the goods, with or without the option to the hirer to pay their value. Such an order is in common law form (the statutory orders provided by s. 133 are confined to hire-purchase and conditional sale agreements) and it is within the discretion of the court whether to make an order for specific delivery without giving the hirer the option to pay the value of the goods or to give him such option or to make no return order at all but merely order payment of the value of the goods as damages. If the court does make an order for return of the goods, it may do so conditionally on the doing of specified acts by the owner or hirer (s. 135 (1) (*a*)), and may in any event suspend the operation of any term of the order until such time as it subsequently directs or until the occurrence of a specified event or events (s. 135 (1) (*b*)). But the court's power to suspend the operation of an order under s. 135 (1) (*b*) may not be exercised so as to extend the period for which the hirer is entitled to possession under the terms of the consumer hire agreement (s. 135 (3)). It would seem to follow that the court cannot vary the agreement under s. 136 so as to prolong the period of hire beyond that provided by the agreement. See also s. 135 (2).

RELIEF AGAINST FORFEITURE

[**17.11**] The court has an inherent equitable jurisdiction to grant the hirer relief against forfeiture of a hiring agreement in cases where it would be harsh and unconscionable for the owner to refuse the hirer an opportunity to tender late performance, subject, however, to application for relief being made promptly and to the hirer showing he can within a reasonable time discharge arrears and remedy other breaches. See generally *Barton Thompson & Co., Ltd.* v. *Stapling Machine Co., Ltd.*, [1966] Ch. 499; [1966] 2 All E.R. 222 and *Starside Properties, Ltd.* v. *Mustapha*, [1974] 2 All E.R. 567.

EXTORTIONATE CREDIT BARGAINS

[**17.12**] The provisions of ss. 137–140 relating to extortionate credit bargains do not apply to hiring agreements. Hence unless the owner repossesses the goods or obtains an order for their return (in which case the court's power to order return of payments to the hirer under s. 132 becomes exercisable), the court has no power to re-open or modify the terms of the hiring agreement. In most cases, however, the hirer under a consumer hire agreement will be adequately protected, first, by the power of termination given to him by s. 101 and secondly by the court's wide discretion as to time orders under ss. 129 and 130. Whilst an order for return of the goods cannot be suspended so as to allow the debtor a right to remain in possession beyond the contractual period of hire (s. 135 (3)), no such limitation is imposed on the court in relation to the time it can allow the hirer for payment where possession of the goods by the hirer beyond the contract period of hire is not thereby involved.

# CHAPTER 18

# AGREEMENTS FOR SERVICES

## THE NEED FOR CONTROL

[**18.1**] It is a remarkable fact that until the advent of the Trade Descriptions Act 1968, there were no general statutory provisions conferring on the aggrieved consumer redress for non-performance or defective performance of contracts for the supply of services; and even the Trade Descriptions Act is limited to sanctions for false or misleading statements as to services, the making of which constitutes an offence under that Act (s. 14 (1)) and entitles any person who thereby suffers loss to apply for a compensation order under s. 1 of the Criminal Justice Act 1972. The lack of attention devoted to services by the legislature did not pass unnoticed in the Crowther Report:

> "Consumer protection legislation has tended to concentrate on transactions involving the disposition of goods. Agreements for the provision of services have so far received little attention from the legislature, although they give rise to equally serious forms of hardship and abuse. We consider that the extension of legislation to deal with this situation is long overdue" (para. 6.8.2.).

[**18.2**] In accordance with the Crowther Committee's recommendations the Consumer Credit Act takes in agreements for the provisions of services on credit as well as contracts for the supply on credit of goods and land.

## APPLICATION OF THE ACT

[**18.3**] Only those provisions of the Act relating to consumer credit (as opposed to consumer hire) affect the supply of services. The Crowther Report drew a distinction between the sale of services (i.e. the supply of services on a particular occasion only, as in the case of holidays and hotel accommodation) and the hire of services (i.e. the provision of services which are continuous and for which the consumer pays as he goes along). The Report recommended that both forms of contract should be controlled, the sale of services on credit being equated as far as possible with the sale of goods, whilst the hire of services, not being a credit transaction, should be treated in broadly the same way as the hire of goods. The Act does not wholly implement this recommendation. It embraces contracts for the supply of services on credit within the definition of "consumer credit agreement", but does not touch the hire of services at all, except in relation to linked transactions (see para. [**18.4**]) and agreements with a credit-broker, debt-adjuster or debt-counsellor (see s. 156 and para. [**23.17**]). The provisions relating to "consumer hire agreements" are confined to contracts for the hire of goods.

[**18.4**] The distinction between contracts for the provision of services on credit and contracts under which the acquirer of the services pays as he goes along has been exemplified in paragraph [**3.9**]. The former are within the Act; the latter are outside it except insofar as the agreement for services is a linked transaction within s. 19 of the Act (see Chapter 19).

### EXTENT OF CONTROL

[**18.5**] Except for those provisions of the Act which are peculiar to hire-purchase and conditional sale agreements (see para. [**3.39**]) or which otherwise refer exclusively to goods or land, the Act applies to advertisements of services on credit and to regulated consumer credit agreements relating to services in the same way and to the same extent as advertisements of goods on credit and regulated consumer credit agreements relating to goods. Provisions relating exclusively to goods or land, apart from those mentioned in para. [**3.39**], are s. 72 (see para. [**18.6**]), with which must be read s. 57 (1), ss. 114–122 (pledges) and s. 126 (enforcement of land mortgages).

### WITHDRAWAL AND CANCELLATION

[**18.6**] Whilst a debtor who, having received goods prior to entry into a regulated agreement or before expiry of the period allowed for cancellation of a cancellable agreement, must surrender the goods on exercising his right of cancellation, the "return" of services already provided to a debtor who withdraws from a prospective agreement or who cancels a cancellable agreement is obviously not possible. Accordingly the provisions of s. 72 of the Act (discussed in paras. [**8.56**] *et seq.*) are inapplicable to services supplied on credit. The consequence is that if the provider of the services is rash enough to furnish them before contract or before expiry of the time allowed for cancellation, he must accept the fact that the debtor, having had the benefit of the services, can by withdrawal (s. 57 (1)) or cancellation (s. 70 (1)) disclaim liability for payment and recover any payments he has made. The only exceptions are those prescribed by s. 69 (2) (*a*) (see paras. [**8.48**] *et seq.*).

### APPROPRIATION OF PAYMENTS

[**18.7**] The provisions of s. 81 (2), providing for a statutory appropriation of payments where the debtor under two or more regulated agreements with the same person fails to appropriate himself under s. 81 (1), do not apply to a regulated consumer credit agreement for the provision of services unless it or the other agreement is an agreement in relation to which security is provided (see s. 81 (2) (*c*)) or the other agreement is a hire-purchase, conditional sale or consumer hire agreement.

EXEMPTION CLAUSES

[**18.8**] The Supply of Goods (Implied Terms) Act 1973, discussed in Chapter 9, does not apply to contracts for services, whether to be supplied on credit or otherwise, and the supplier's duty is governed by common law principles and by any special statutes that may be applicable. Unless the contract otherwise provides or is of a class which imposes a *prima facie* strict liability (*e.g.* a contract for the carriage of goods by a common carrier) the duty of the supplier of services is limited to the exercise of reasonable care and skill in the performance of the contract. This duty may usually be excluded or restricted by the contract, though the effectiveness of an exemption clause may be limited both at common law (e.g. by the doctrine of fundamental breach) and by special statute, as in the case of contracts of carriage of persons by rail purporting to exclude liability for death or bodily injury (see Transport Act 1962, s. 43 (7) and Carriage by Railway Act 1972).

[**18.9**] Where the supplier of services effectively excludes or restricts his liability by a valid exemption clause, such exclusion or restriction operates also for the benefit of a creditor who would otherwise incur a liability under s. 75 of the Consumer Credit Act (see para. [**9.22**]).

# CHAPTER 19

# LINKED TRANSACTIONS

## INTRODUCTION

[**19.1**] In preceding chapters, we have examined in some detail the rights and duties of one who is the debtor under a consumer credit agreement or the hirer under a consumer hire agreement. So far, we have concentrated attention on such rights and duties as may arise in relation to the credit or hire agreement itself. But if that agreement is a debtor-creditor-supplier agreement, it cannot be divorced from the supply transaction which it financed. Moreover, the debtor may have entered into other, ancillary contracts, e.g. maintenance or insurance, which may be affected by the impact of the Act on the regulated agreement to which they are linked. The draftsman has in fact taken considerable trouble to work out the effect which different events occurring in relation to a regulated agreement are to have on these linked transactions. This is of great importance; for if, for example, a debtor who had taken out insurance or life assurance pursuant to a requirement of a cancellable regulated agreement were to remain bound by his contract with the insurers after cancellation of the regulated agreement, he would be placed in a most unfortunate position, the prospect of which might well discourage him from exercising his right to cancel. The Act deals with this and various other problems arising in relation to linked transactions in the manner described below.

## DEFINITION OF LINKED TRANSACTION

[**19.2**] This is contained in s. 19 (1) and (2), which provide as follows:

"(1) A transaction entered into by the debtor or hirer, or a relative of his, with any other person ("the other party"), except one for the provision of security, is a linked transaction in relation to an actual or prospective regulated agreement of which it does not form part (the 'principal agreement') if—

(*a*) the transaction is entered into in compliance with a term of the principal agreement; or

(*b*) the principal agreement is a debtor-creditor-supplier agreement and the transaction is financed, or to be financed, by the principal agreement; or

(*c*) the other party is a person mentioned in subsection (2), and a person so mentioned initiated the transaction by suggesting it to the debtor or hirer, or his relative, who enters into it—

(i) to induce the creditor or owner to enter into the principal agreement, or

(ii) for another purpose related to the principal agreement, or
(iii) where the principal agreement is a restricted-use credit agreement, for a purpose related to a transaction financed, or to be financed, by the principal agreement.

(2) The persons referred to in subsection (1) (*c*) are—
(*a*) the creditor or owner, or his associate;
(*b*) a person who, in the negotiation of the transaction, is represented by a credit-broker who is also a negotiator in antecedent negotiations for the principal agreement;
(*c*) a person who, at the time the transaction is initiated, knows that the principal agreement has been made or contemplates that it might be made."

[**19.3**] The Act refers to a linked "transaction", not "agreement". The word "transaction" is not defined, but is plainly wider than "agreement". In *Greenberg* v. *Inland Revenue Commissioners*, [1972] A.C. 109; [1971] 3 All E.R. 136, it was said that "the word 'transaction' is normally used to denote some bilateral activity but it can be used to denote an activity in which only a single person is engaged" (*per* Lord Reid, at p. 149) and that "its ordinary meaning is 'proceeding' or 'action' or, in particular, 'business deal'" (*per* Lord Simon, at p. 159). It is thus clear that the phrase "linked transaction" covers not only the ancillary agreement itself but any acts done or to be done (whether by one party or both) by way of implementation of the agreement. However an agreement for the provision of security is expressly excluded by the opening words of s. 19 (1). Accordingly, a mortgage given to secure a regulated agreement is not a linked transaction, nor is a guarantee or indemnity entered into on the insistence of the creditor. Thus, whilst a life policy taken out by the debtor pursuant to a requirement of a regulated agreement is a linked transaction, the charging of such policy to the creditor, being a transaction for the provision of security, is not a linked transaction (see Second Schedule, example 11).

[**19.4**] It should be noted that a transaction may be a linked transaction even though the parties to it were not the same as the parties to the regulated agreement to which the transaction is linked. It suffices if they are parties connected by a relationship which falls within one of the categories mentioned in s. 19 (1) or (2). The purpose of the provisions is to prevent evasion through use of persons associated with one of the parties to the regulated agreement; and in defining the types of association which are to attract the statutory provisions, the Act casts its net far and wide. The reach of the net depends on whether the transaction falls within category (*a*), (*b*) or (*c*) of s. 19 (1). Even where it is the debtor or hirer himself who is a party to the linked transaction, if the other party is not the creditor or owner he may well be unaware of the existence of the principal agreement. The status of a transaction as a linked transaction does not in any way depend on knowledge by the third party that such transaction is entered into with him by the debtor or hirer for the purposes of or in compliance with the regulated agreement. See further paragraph [**19.11**].

### CATEGORY (*a*)

[**19.5**] Into category (*a*) fall transactions entered into by the debtor or hirer, or a relative of his, with any other person in compliance with a term of the regulated agreement. Thus if, in compliance with a hire-purchase agreement, the hirer insures the goods, the contract of insurance is a linked transaction. Similarly, a maintenance agreement entered into by the hirer pursuant to the hire-purchase agreement is a linked transaction, whether entered into with the owner or with a third party. The fact that no arrangement or business relationship between the creditor and the third party exists or is contemplated is irrelevant to the application of category (*a*). The position would be the same if the insurance or maintenance contract were taken out not by the debtor but by a relative of his, that is, an associate as defined in s. 184 (1) (see s. 189 (1) and para. [**5.33**]).

[**19.6**] Category (*a*) obviously applies only where the regulated agreement is made first. A transaction made prior to the regulated agreement cannot be a linked transaction in category (*a*), though it may fall within category (*b*) or category (*c*).

### CATEGORY (*b*)

[**19.7**] This category brings in the definition of "debtor-creditor-supplier agreement" in s. 12, and thus entails a regulated agreement to finance a transaction with a supplier and entered into by the creditor under pre-existing arrangements, or in contemplation of future arrangements, with the supplier. The following are illustrations of linked transactions within category (*b*).

(1) A finance house, pursuant to an arrangement with a motor dealer, grants a personal loan to the dealer's customer to enable that customer to buy a motor vehicle from the dealer. The loan is applied for that purpose. The sale by the dealer to the customer is a linked transaction.

(2) The debtor under a check-trading agreement uses checks to buy goods from a supplier who has an arrangement with the check-trader to accept as payment checks issued by the check-trader. The purchase made by the debtor from the supplier is a linked transaction.

(3) The holder of a bank credit card uses it to pay for the cost of a flight on an airline which recognises the card, pursuant to arrangements between the bank and the airline. The contract of carriage by air between the cardholder and the airline is a linked transaction.

Section 19 (1), when defining a linked transaction, excludes a transaction which forms part of the regulated agreement itself. Hence an agreement in which the creditor is himself the supplier of the goods or services—*e.g.* a hire-purchase agreement—is not a linked transaction, even though it would otherwise fall within category (*b*) of that subsection.

### CATEGORY (*c*)

[**19.8**] This category subdivides into three. In each case, the other party is a person within s. 19 (2) and initiates the transaction by suggesting it to the debtor or hirer, or his relative.

*Category* (*c*) (*i*)

The debtor or hirer, or his relative, on the suggestion of the creditor or owner or other person of a kind mentioned in s. 19 (2), enters into the transaction to induce the creditor or owner to enter into the principal agreement. Into this category would fall, for example, insurance and maintenance contracts which, though not made compulsory under a term of the regulated agreement itself, are orally stipulated by the creditor as a prerequisite of his entry into the agreement.

*Category* (*c*) (*ii*)

This is a somewhat wider category, where the debtor or hirer, or his relative, on the suggestion of the creditor or owner, or of another person of a kind mentioned in s. 19 (2), enters into the transaction for another purpose linked to the principal agreement. If a person enters into an agreement with a tour operator for a holiday on credit and at the tour operator's suggestion takes out a policy of assurance covering death or disability whilst travelling or insures against the risk of a wasted payment as a result of his having to cancel the holiday through illness, such insurance transactions are linked transactions within category (*c*) (ii).

*Category* (*c*) (*iii*)

This category is confined to cases where the principal agreement is a restricted-use credit agreement. Category (*c*) (iii) is somewhat difficult to envisage at first sight, involving (*a*) a transaction entered into on the suggestion of the creditor etc., which is (*b*) entered into for a purpose related to another transaction, which in turn is (*c*) financed or to be financed by the restricted-use credit agreement. However category (*c*) (iii) is less formidable than it seems. It is primarily concerned with an ancillary contract for the provision of goods or services not as a condition of the creditor's entry into the regulated agreement nor as a term of that agreement or for the purposes of the agreement but in order to provide or facilitate a use of the goods or services acquired with the finance provided under the principal agreement. An example is a maintenance agreement entered into with the supplier of a television set from whom the debtor has bought it on credit sale (this is within (*c*) (iii) rather than (*c*) (ii) because its purpose is related to the use of the television set, not to the credit by which the purchase of this was financed). Another case is where the debtor, on the suggestion of the creditor, buys food to stock a deep-freeze which he is acquiring on credit from the creditor. The contract for the purchase of the food (whether or not itself a credit agreement) is a linked transaction within (*c*) (iii).

## IMPACT OF THE ACT ON LINKED TRANSACTIONS

**[19.9]** The definition of "linked transaction" is relevant for the following reasons.

(1) A linked transaction entered into before the making of the regulated agreement to which it relates has no effect until such time (if any) as

that agreement is made (s. 19 (3)), unless the linked transaction is of a description exempted by regulations from this provision (s. 19 (4)). Some insurance contracts are likely to be excluded under s. 19 (4), for much the same reason as in the case of cancellation (see para. [**8.45**]).

(2) Withdrawal of a party from a prospective regulated agreement operates as a withdrawal from a linked transaction (ss. 57 (1), 69 (1)); and cancellation of a cancellable agreement by the debtor or hirer operates to cancel any linked transaction and to withdraw any offer by him, or his relative, to enter into a linked transaction (s. 69 (1)). But regulations may exclude linked transactions of the prescribed description from the above provisions (s. 69 (3)). Again, certain insurance contracts are likely to qualify for such exclusion (see para. [**8.45**]).

(3) On cancellation of any linked transaction, any sum paid by the debtor or hirer or his relative is repayable, and any sum which but for the cancellation would have become payable by the debtor or hirer or his relative ceases to be payable, under the provisions of s. 70, and subject to the exemption in s. 70 (5), previously discussed (para. [**8.45**] *et seq.*). If the linked transaction relates to goods, the debtor or hirer or relative has a duty, under the provisions of s. 72 and subject to the exceptions in s. 72 (9), to surrender the goods to the other party to the linked transaction and meanwhile to retain possession of them and take reasonable care of them (see paras. [**8.56**] *et seq.*).

(4) Regulations under s. 95 (1) prescribing rebates for early settlement of a regulated consumer credit agreement (paras. [**12.5**] *et seq.*) may provide for calculation of the rebate by reference to any sums paid by the debtor or his relative under or in connection with the agreement (whether to the creditor or some other person) including sums under linked transactions (s. 95 (2)).

(5) Where for any reason the indebtedness of the debtor under a regulated consumer credit agreement is discharged before the time fixed by the agreement, he, and any relative of his, is at the same time discharged from any liability under a linked transaction, other than a debt which has already become payable (s. 96 (1)). But this does not apply to a linked transaction which is itself an agreement providing the debtor or his relative with credit (s. 96 (2)), or to linked transactions excluded by regulations (s. 96 (3)). It should be noted that s. 97 (1) applies only to early settlement and not, for example, to termination by the debtor under s. 99 or by the creditor for breach.

(6) The provisions of s. 113—preventing evasion of the Act through use of security (see para. [**13.2**] *et seq.*)—apply to security provided in relation to an actual or prospective linked transaction as they do to security provided in relation to the actual or prospective regulated agreement (s. 113 (8)—and see para. [**13.20**].

(7) The provisions of s. 173, dealing with attempted contracting out of the statutory provisions for the protection of the debtor or hirer or his relative (para. [**27.4**]) apply to a linked transaction as well as to the regulated agreement.

(8) The power under s. 179 (1) to make regulations as to the form of

secondary documents (para. [**27.9**]) applies to documents or things issued in connection with linked transactions.

[**19.10**] Mention should also be made of certain other provisions of the Act which, though not confined to linked transactions, will almost invariably affect them. These are s. 75 (relating to the creditor's liability for misrepresentations and breaches of contract by the supplier—see paras. [**9.22**] *et seq.*) and s. 139 (relating to the re-opening of extortionate agreements—see paras. [**22.37**] *et seq.*).

[**19.11**] A significant feature of the provisions discussed above is that if the other party to the linked transaction is not the creditor himself but a third party, the linked transaction may suddenly become inoperative without the third party being aware of the fact. Indeed, it is quite possible for a person to be a party to a linked transaction with a debtor without knowing of the principal agreement to which the transaction is linked (see para. [**19.4**]). This may well cause considerable complications in the unscrambling of linked transactions, particularly where there is a dispute between the debtor and creditor as to whether the regulated agreement has been effectively terminated, cancelled or affected in some way having a bearing on the linked transaction.

IMPROPERLY EXECUTED AGREEMENTS AND SECURITIES

[**19.12**] The fact that an agreement or security has been, or is to be deemed, improperly executed so as to be enforceable only on an order of the court appears to have no impact on the enforceability of a linked transaction. Indeed, apart from s. 139 relating to extortionate credit bargains (see paras. [**22.37**] *et seq.*), there is no provision of the Act which gives the court special powers over the linked transactions which are not themselves regulated agreements. In particular, the provisions of Part IX (other than ss. 139–142) are restricted to the making of orders in relation to regulated agreements and securities.

EXTORTIONATE CREDIT BARGAINS

[**19.13**] The powers of the court to re-open a credit agreement under ss. 137–140) arise where the court finds a credit bargain extortionate. "Credit bargain" means not only the credit agreement itself but also, where one or more other transactions are to be taken into account in computing the total charge for credit, those other transactions taken together with the credit agreement (s. 137 (2) (*b*) (ii)). In re-opening the agreement the court may, for the purpose of relieving the debtor or a surety from payment of any sum in excess of that fairly due and reasonable, make various orders under s. 139 (2) and may in particular—

(*a*) direct accounts to be taken between any persons,

(*b*) set aside the whole or part of any obligation imposed on the debtor or a surety by the credit bargain or any related agreement,

(*c*) require the creditor to repay the whole or part of any sum paid under the credit bargain or any related agreement by the debtor or a surety, whether paid to the creditor or any other person.

[**19.14**] An order may be made under s. 139 (2) notwithstanding that its effect is to place a burden on the creditor in respect of an advantage unfairly enjoyed by another person who is a party to a linked transaction (s. 139 (3)). Hence if, for example, the total charge for credit imposed by a credit agreement relating to goods includes as a component the cost to the creditor of procuring servicing of the goods under a maintenance contract with a third party, and the court takes the view that the maintenance charge is extortionate, the court may require the creditor to repay the whole or any part of the sum paid under the credit agreement even though the effect may be that the creditor has to carry the burden of having paid, or incurred a liability to pay, sums due to the third party under the extortionate maintenance agreement.

# CHAPTER 20

# AGREEMENTS WITH MORE THAN ONE DEBTOR/HIRER OR CREDITOR/OWNER

## THE PROBLEM STATED

[**20.1**] In the preceding analysis of the Consumer Credit Act, it has been assumed that each regulated agreement involves one person as debtor or hirer, another as creditor or owner. In practice, it not infrequently happens that there are two or more debtors or hirers (either specifically named or constituting members of a partnership that is a debtor or hirer) or two or more creditors as owners. In situations such as these, complex questions may arise, *e.g.* as to the liability of the co-debtors or co-hirers *inter se* and *vis-a-vis* the creditor or owner, and as to the procedure to be adopted where the creditor or owner wishes to terminate the agreement against all the debtors or hirers. These problems, discussed by the author elsewhere in relation to co-hirers under hire-purchase agreements (see R. M. Goode, *Hire-Purchase Law and Practice* (2nd edn.), Chapter 21) were not touched on in the Hire-Purchase Act 1965. The Consumer Credit Act, however, has two provisions dealing with the matter, s. 185 (concerning an agreement with more than one debtor or hirer) and s. 186 (concerning an agreement with more than one creditor or owner). The effect of the statutory provisions is in some respects obscure, partly because the provisions are very general in character and do not link up with any specific requirements of the Act. It is therefore necessary to examine the various stages of a typical transaction and see what needs to be done to meet the requirements of the Act where two or more parties are involved on one side or the other.

## AGREEMENTS WITH MORE THAN ONE DEBTOR OR HIRER

[**20.2**] Section 185 provides as follows:

"(1) Where an actual or prospective regulated agreement has two or more debtors or hirers (not being a partnership or an unincorporated body of persons)—

(*a*) anything required by or under this Act to be done to or in relation to the debtor or hirer shall be done to or in relation to each of them; and

(*b*) anything done under this Act by or on behalf of one of them shall have effect as if done by or on behalf of all of them.

(2) Notwithstanding subsection (1) (*a*), where running-account credit is

provided to two or more debtors jointly, any of them may by a notice signed by him (a "dispensing notice") authorise the creditor not to comply in his case with section 78 (4) (giving of periodical statement of account); and the dispensing notice shall have effect accordingly until revoked by a further notice given by the debtor to the creditor:

Provided that:

(*a*) a dispensing notice shall not take effect if previous dispensing notices are operative in the case of the other debtor, or each of the other debtors, as the case may be;

(*b*) any dispensing notices operative in relation to an agreement shall cease to have effect if any of the debtors dies.

(3) Subsection (1) (*b*) does not apply for the purposes of section 61 (1) (*a*) or 127 (3).

(4) Where a regulated agreement has two or more debtors or hirers (not being a partnership or unincorporated body of persons) s. 86 applies to the death of any of them.

(5) An agreement for the provisions of credit, or the bailment or (in Scotland) the hiring of goods, to two or more persons jointly where—

(*a*) one or more of those persons is an individual, and

(*b*) one or more of them is a body corporate,

is a consumer credit agreement or consumer hire agreement if it would have been one had they all been individuals; and the body corporate or bodies corporate shall accordingly be included among the debtors or hirers under the agreement.

(6) Where subsection (4) applies, references in this Act to the signing of any document by the debtor or hirer shall be construed in relation to a body corporate as referring to a signing on behalf of the body corporate."

ACTS TO BE DONE TO OR IN RELATION TO DEBTOR OR HIRER

**[20.3]** Leaving on one side partnerships and unincorporated bodies (discussed in paras. [**20.10**]–[**20.11**]), the general effect of s. 185 (1) (*a*) is that where there are two or more debtors or hirers:

(*a*) pre-contract disclosure prescribed by regulations under s. 55 (1) must be given to all the debtors or hirers, unless otherwise provided by such regulations;

(*b*) the regulated agreement must be signed by each debtor or hirer personally;

(*c*) the copies prescribed by ss. 62 and 63, and the notice prescribed by s. 64, must be supplied to each debtor or hirer in accordance with those sections;

(*d*) sums repayable under ss. 57 (1), 70 and 73 in respect of a transaction from which the debtors or hirers have withdrawn or which they have exercised their right to cancel (see para. [**20.4**]) are repayable to all of them;

(*e*) information and documents to be provided to a debtor or hirer under ss. 77–79 must be supplied to all;

(*f*) a notice under s. 76 or notice of default under s. 87 or of termination under s. 98 must be served on all the debtors or hirers;

(*g*) a statutory rebate allowable by regulations under s. 95 must be allowed to all the debtors or hirers.

It seems clear that failure to comply with the above statutory provisions as regards all the debtors or hirers involves a contravention of those provisions, even if they have been complied with as regards some of the debtors or hirers.

[**20.4**] When examined more closely, some of the effects listed above are much more difficult to apply than the simplistic wording of s. 185 (1) (*a*) would suggest. Consider first the documentation requirements of ss. 62 and 63. If the unexecuted agreement is sent to one debtor for signature but presented to the other, which of the alternative procedures laid down in these sections applies? Common sense would suggest that for the former debtor, the procedure laid down for documents sent for signature applies, and for the latter debtor the procedure prescribed for documents presented for signature operates. But s. 185 (1) (*a*) appears to preclude such a simple solution. Next, let us consider the question of cancellation, which also raises difficulties under s. 185 (1) (*b*) (see para. [**20.7**]). If one of the debtors serves a notice of cancellation (and this would seem to be effective as a notice by all), are repayments under ss. 57 (1) or 70 to be made to the debtor by whom the payment was made in the first instance or are they to be made to all the debtors by way of a joint remittance? Apparently the latter. Again, a sum equal to the part-exchange allowance and payable under s. 73 must, it seems, be paid to all the debtors, not merely to the debtor who tendered the part-exchange goods to which the allowance relates. The assumption apparently is that the debtors must sort out these matters among themselves afterwards.

[**20.5**] The only relief provided in respect of s. 185 (1) (*a*)—except in the case of a partnership or unincorporated body—is that where there are joint debtors on a running-account, any of them may by dispensing notice under s. 185 (2) waive the requirement that he be supplied automatically with the periodic statements of account prescribed by s. 78 (4). But the obligation must remain to supply such accounts to at least one joint debtor. Accordingly if all the joint debtors give dispensing notices, the last of these is ineffective (s. 185 (2), proviso).

ACTS TO BE DONE BY OR ON BEHALF OF THE DEBTOR OR HIRER

[**20.6**] The effect of s. 185 (1) (*b*) is that:

(*a*) service by one debtor or hirer of a notice of cancellation under s. 69 or a notice of termination under s. 99 or 101 operates as cancellation or termination by all the debtors or hirers;

(*b*) early settlement by one debtor under s. 94 constitutes settlement on behalf of all;

(*c*) a request for information and documents by a debtor or hirer under ss. 77–79 constitutes a request by all, which must accordingly be complied with in regard to all;

(*d*) supply of information by one debtor or hirer as to the whereabouts of goods, pursuant to s. 80, constitutes compliance with that section by the other debtors or hirers as well;

(*e*) an application by one debtor or hirer to the court under s. 129, or by one hirer under s. 132, operates as an application by all.

On the other hand, a breach by one debtor or hirer of his statutory obligations is not a breach by all by virtue of s. 185 (1) (*b*), since a breach is not a thing done "under" the Act for the purpose of s. 185 (1) (*b*) but is a contravention of the Act. It may, however, constitute a breach by all the debtors as a matter of general law.

[**20.7**] Just as difficulties arise in applying s. 185 (1) (*a*), so also they arise in connection with s. 185 (1) (*b*). If one debtor signs a regulated agreement at his own home, while another signs at the creditor's premises, is the agreement (if otherwise fulfilling the requirements of a cancellable agreement) cancellable under s. 67? Apparently it is, since the debtor who signed at home fulfils the requirements of s. 67 and by virtue of s. 185 (1) (*b*) service of a notice of cancellation by him is service for all. What if one debtor wishes to cancel and the other does not? Seemingly, the former's notice of cancellation is effective despite the opposition of the latter. Nice questions arise where one debtor serves a termination notice under s. 99 whilst at the same time the other applies under s. 129 for further time to remedy a breach of the agreement!

[**20.8**] What emerges from this analysis is the undesirability of trying to regulate a number of diverse situations by a general catch-all provision not worked out in relation to each situation individually. It would have been very much better if Parliament in its wisdom had left the subject matter of s. 182 (and of s. 183) to be dealt with by regulations.

[**20.9**] There are in fact two cases, set out in s. 185 (3), in which the draftsman has addressed his mind to specific sections that might otherwise have been caught by s. 185 (1) (*b*). That subsection does not apply for the purpose of s. 61 (1) (*a*), so that signature of the regulated agreement by one debtor or hirer does not constitute signature for all, and each of the debtors or hirers must sign individually. As a corollary, the court cannot make an enforcement order in respect of a regulated agreement not signed by all the debtors or hirers, since s. 185 (1) (*b*) is made inapplicable for the purpose of s. 127 (3).

### PARTNERSHIPS

[**20.10**] Section 185 does not apply where the debtor is a partnership. Section 61 (4) establishes that the regulated agreement need not be signed by all (or indeed any) of the partners. It suffices if it is signed on behalf of the firm by a partner or by any other person authorised for that purpose. The effect on the partnership of other acts done by or to a partner has to be determined by general agency principles and by the Partnership Act 1890. By s. 6 of the Partnership Act, the firm and all the partners are bound by any act or instrument relating to the firm's business done or executed in the firm's name, or in any other way showing an intention to bind the firm, by any person thereto authorised, whether a partner or not. Moreover, as a matter of agency law the acts of a partner within the scope of his actual, apparent or usual authority bind the partnership. If, therefore, a partner signs a regulated agreement on behalf of the firm and the agreement is one which is on the face of it entered into for the purposes of the partnership business and is the type of agreement which it would be usual for a firm engaged in that type of business to make, the agreement will bind the firm. But in the case of a non-commercial firm, a partner has no implied authority to borrow money, to accept, make or indorse negotiable instruments other than cheques, or to mortgage or pledge partnership property; and even in a commercial partnership, a partner has no implied authority to give a guarantee on behalf of the firm. It follows that in these cases the mere fact that a person is a partner does not give him ostensible authority to do any of these acts on behalf of the firm, though the firm will be bound if the partner in question has been held out as having authority. If a partner has, or is held out as having, authority to enter into a regulated agreement or linked transaction, then no doubt the court will readily infer authority, or ostensible authority, on his part to cancel or terminate the agreement or transaction, or to give or receive notices in respect of it, on behalf of the firm. The firm will similarly be bound by such acts when within the usual authority of the partner concerned.

### UNINCORPORATED BODIES

[**20.11**] Similarly the ability of a member of an unincorporated body to bind the body as a whole depends on agency principles. There is however the added complication that whilst a partnership, though juridically not a legal *persona*, is for certain purposes recognised by the law as a distinct legal entity, an unincorporated association has no status distinct from that of its members, so that the membership as a whole can only be bound by acts which they have collectively authorised, or ostensibly authorised, one of their number to carry out. In the case of a members' club, authority to act would normally be conferred by rules of the club adopted by the members and by decisions taken at meetings held in conformity with the rules. Ostensible authority to manage the affairs of an association generally (as opposed to ostensible authority to conclude a specific transaction) is not easy to establish in the case of an unincorporated association, so that if the committee of a club contracts without authority, the remedy of the other party to the contract will usually be an action against the committee members personally. See further J. F. Keeler (1971), 34 M.L.R. 615.

### BODY CORPORATE AS ONE OF JOINT DEBTORS OR HIRERS

[**20.12**] The provisions of s. 185 (5) (see para. [**20.2**]) are limited to joint debtors and joint hirers and thus appear to exclude transactions in which the liability of the debtors or hirers is joint and several. In the latter case, the agreement will be a consumer credit or consumer hire agreement as regards the individuals but not as regards the bodies corporate. The distinction may appear surprising but has a certain logic. A joint liability is indivisible, and therefore could scarcely be regulated by the Act as regards some parties but not others. Hence all parties are brought within the Act by s. 185 (5). A joint and several liability creates both a joint obligation and several obligations on the part of the various co-contractors, so that there is no difficulty in limiting the application of the Act to those debtors or hirers who are individuals. Whether in a given case the liability is joint only or joint and several depends on the absence or presence of words of severance. See R. M. Goode, *op. cit.*, p. 471.

AGREEMENTS WITH MORE THAN ONE CREDITOR OR OWNER

[**20.13**] The case of several creditors or owners is dealt with summarily by s. 186 as follows:

> "Where an actual or prospective regulated agreement has two or more creditors or owners, anything required by or under this Act to be done to, or in relation to, or by, the creditor or owner shall be effective if done to, or in relation to, or by, any one of them."

Hence one of several creditors or owners can perform all or any of the following acts on behalf of the other or others:

(*a*) supply pre-contract information to a prospective debtor or hirer pursuant to regulations under s. 55 (1);
(*b*) sign a regulated agreement;
(*c*) supply documents to the debtor or hirer in accordance with ss. 62–64 and s. 110 of the Act;
(*d*) repay sums payable under ss. 70 and 57 to a debtor or hirer who has exercised his right of cancellation or has withdrawn from a proposed transaction;
(*e*) supply information and documents to the debtor or hirer in accordance with ss. 77–79 and to a surety in accordance with ss. 107–109;
(*f*) serve a notice under s. 76 or a default notice under s. 87 or notice of termination under s. 98;
(*g*) institute proceedings for the recovery of protected goods in conformity with the requirements of s. 90.

These powers are exercisable by such creditor or owner whether or not he has actual or ostensible authority from his co-creditors or co-owners, though if he exercises the powers in excess of authority he may incur a liability to such co-creditors or co-owners. But it is only those acts *required by the Act* that fall within s. 186. Hence this section cannot be invoked to support, for example, a variation of the regulated agreement made by one creditor or owner without the consent of the others. Whether such variation is effective depends on the ordinary principles of agency previously mentioned.

[**20.14**] Just as s. 186 empowers an actual or prospective creditor or owner to perform acts on behalf of the other or others, so also it makes acts required by the Act to be done to, or in relation to, the creditor or owner or prospective creditor or owner effective if done to, or in relation to, one such creditor or owner. Such acts would include:

(*a*) service of a notice of withdrawal under s. 57 or of cancellation under s. 69;
(*b*) making of a request for information under ss. 77–79;
(*c*) giving of notice of intended early settlement under s. 94 and payment under that section;
(*d*) giving of notice of termination under s. 99 or s. 101.

# CHAPTER 21

# REMEDIES OF CREDITOR OR OWNER ON DEFAULT

## NATURE AND RANGE OF REMEDIES

[**21.1**] Where a debtor or hirer commits a breach of a regulated agreement, the remedies of the creditor or owner depend partly on the common law, partly on the terms of the regulated agreement itself, and of any security instrument made in connection with it, and partly on the Consumer Credit Act and regulations thereunder.

## REMEDIES CONFERRED OR IMPLIED BY LAW

[**21.2**] The remedies for default given by the common law to the creditor or owner, insofar as not provided for by the credit or security agreement itself, vary according to the nature of the transaction. Under all forms of agreement—whether conditional sale, hire-purchase, credit sale, rental or secured or unsecured loan—the creditor is entitled to sue (i) for each sum payable under the agreement as it falls due; (ii) for damages for loss suffered as the result of a breach other than non-payment. Other remedies given or implied by law (as opposed to an express contractual provision) vary according to the nature of the credit agreement.

[**21.3**] In the case of breach of a conditional sale, hire-purchase or hiring agreement, where the term broken is a condition (*i.e.* a major term) or the breach evinces an intention on the part of the debtor or hirer to repudiate the contract or produces consequences so serious as to frustrate the commercial purpose of the contract, the seller or owner has the option to treat the contract as at an end and recover damages on that basis, or to affirm the contract, in which event his claim is limited to damages for such loss (if any) as he can establish. Where the debtor or hirer did not have a right to terminate the agreement himself—as in the case of a conditional sale agreement or a hiring for a fixed term—the damages recoverable by the creditor or owner who elects to treat the contract as terminated will include the loss of profit resulting from premature termination. *i.e.* loss of the profit (duly discounted to allow for any acceleration of payment) that would have been made by him if the contract had run its full course. Where the agreement is a hire-purchase agreement giving the hirer a right to terminate at any time, then logically the owner's damages on accepting the hirer's repudiation should not exceed the amount (if any) for which the hirer would have become liable if he himself had exercised the power of termination conferred on him. But by an anomaly established in *Yeoman Credit, Ltd.* v. *Waragowski*, [1961] 3 All E.R. 145, as modified by *Yeoman Credit Ltd.* v. *Maclean*, [1962] 1 W.L.R. 131 and *Overstone, Ltd.* v. *Shipway*, [1962] 1 All E.R. 52, the owner is in such a case held entitled to recover the unpaid balance of the hire-purchase price less the sum fixed as the fee for exercise of the option to purchase and a discount to allow for acceleration of payment. In addition, the conditional seller or owner who terminates the agreement by acceptance of the other party's repudiation becomes entitled to sue in detinue for return of the goods or payment of their value and damages for their detention or alternatively in conversion for the value of the goods.

**[21.4]** In the event of breach of a credit sale agreement, the seller is usually restricted to an action for the price, and (in the absence of an acceleration clause in the agreement) must wait for each instalment to fall due before he can sue for it. His statutory right of resale under ss. 39 and 48 of the Sale of Goods Act 1893 ceases to be exercisable when both the property in the goods and possession have passed to the buyer, though he may have a right at common law to treat the credit sale agreement as repudiated for breach and on that basis recover the goods and damages for breach of contract (*Commission Car Sales* (*Hastings*), *Ltd.* v. *Saul*, [1957] N.Z.L.R. 144).

**[21.5]** On default in payment of a loan, the lender can recover the instalments in arrear, but must usually wait to sue for each instalment as it falls due, in the absence of an acceleration clause in the loan agreement entitling him to call up the outstanding balance. If he has taken a mortgage as security, he has in addition all the remedies accorded to a mortgagee by the common law and by the Law of Property Act 1925. These include possession, sale, appointment of a receiver and an application to the court for foreclosure. The availability of these remedies depends partly on whether the mortgage is of goods or of land, partly on whether it is legal or equitable and partly on whether it is under seal or under hand only.

## REMEDIES CONFERRED BY THE AGREEMENT

**[21.6]** The credit agreement itself may, and almost invariably does, contain express provisions conferring a range of remedies on the creditor in the event of the debtor's default. Within limits, and subject to statutory provisions of the kind we are about to consider, the law gives effect to the contract. Thus at common law the court will uphold provisions which:

(i) call up the outstanding balance in the event of a breach by the debtor;

(ii) empower the creditor to terminate the agreement in specified events, *e.g.* if the debtor commits a breach of the agreement or allows a judgment to remain outstanding against him for more than a stated period or has execution levied on his goods;

(iii) empower the creditor to remedy breaches himself and charge the debtor with the cost;

(iv) confer on the creditor powers of repossession and sale of goods or property comprised in the agreement or security;

(v) fix in advance the damages to be paid for a breach, if the sum fixed is a reasonable pre-estimate of the loss likely to flow from the breach (see below).

[**21.7**] In fact the common law has always adopted a very liberal attitude towards creditors' rights in general and self-help in particular. Buf even at common law (including for this purpose rules of equity) there are certain limitations on freedom of contract. Thus a mortgagee's right to redeem the mortgaged property cannot be cut off except by sale or foreclosure, whatever the mortgage may provide; and if realisation of the security produces a surplus, this is payable to the debtor (in the absence of any other incumbrances affecting the property) notwithstanding any agreement to the contrary. Again, whilst it is open to the parties to stipulate in the contract a sum to be paid as liquidated damages in the event of a breach, the sum so fixed must, as seen at the date of the contract, be a reasonable pre-estimate of the loss likely to flow from the breach and not a penalty imposed to deter the debtor from breaking the contract or to give the creditor an additional windfall in the event of breach. On this basis, provisions in hire-purchase agreements purporting to give the owner, on termination for breach, a right to recover sums over and above accrued arrears and interest have been repeatedly struck down by the courts as contrary to the rule against penalties, though occasionally they have been upheld where the court was satisfied that the contractual provision was a reasonable attempt to assess in advance loss that might be suffered as the result of the goods depreciating at a faster rate than covered by the instalments. See, for example, *Bridge* v. *Campbell Discount Co., Ltd.*, [1962] A.C. 600; [1962] 1 All E.R. 385; *Anglo-Auto Finance Co., Ltd.* v. *James*, [1963] 3 All E.R. 566; and other cases explored in detail in R. M. Goode, *op. cit.*, Chapter 18.

BROAD EFFECT OF THE CONSUMER CREDIT ACT

[**21.8**] The Consumer Credit Act, adopting and strengthening provisions previously contained in the Hire-Purchase Act, imposes various restrictions on contractual remedies, notably by:

(*a*) requiring at least seven days' notice of an intention by the creditor or owner to invoke (otherwise than on the ground of a breach) an acceleration clause or to recover possession of goods or land or treat any right conferred on the debtor or hirer by the agreement as terminated, restricted or deferred (s. 76 (1)—see paras. [**21.9**] *et seq.*);

(*b*) requiring the creditor or owner to serve at least seven days' notice of default before exercising, by reason of a breach on the part of the debtor or hirer, any of the above rights or enforcing any security, so as to give the debtor an opportunity to remedy the breach if it is remediable (ss. 87–89—see paras. [**21.12**] *et seq.*) or to apply to the court for a time order under s. 129 (see paras. [**22.11**] *et seq.*) or for equitable relief against forfeiture (see para. [**17.11**]);

(*c*) requiring the creditor or owner to give at least seven days' notice before terminating a regulated agreement otherwise than by reason of a breach by the debtor or hirer (s. 98—see paras. [**21.20**–[**21.21**]);

(*d*) prohibiting enforcement of a right to recover possession of protected goods except on an order of the court (s. 90 (1)—see paras. [**21.22**] *et seq.*);

(*e*) restricting the exercise of contractual rights that would otherwise be exercisable by reason of the death of the debtor or hirer (s. 86—see paras. [**21.39**] *et seq.*);

(*f*) nullifying a contractual provision purporting to make the debtor liable to pay default interest at a rate exceeding the contract rate (s. 93—see para. [**21.41**]);

(*g*) limiting the liability of a hirer under a regulated hire-purchase or conditional sale agreement who, pursuant to s. 99, terminates the agreement (s. 100—see paras. [**12.15**] *et seq.*);

(*h*) prohibiting enforcement of an improperly executed agreement or security without an order of the court (ss. 65 (1), 105 (6)—see paras. [**22.6**] *et seq.*);

(*i*) regulating the redemption and realisation of pawns (ss. 116–121—see paras. [**13.25**] *et seq.*);

(*j*) prohibiting, except on an order of the court, enforcement of a regulated agreement or security in respect of which a negotiable instrument has been taken or negotiated in contravention of s. 123 (see paras. [**13.33**] *et seq.*);

(*k*) prohibiting enforcement of a land mortgage otherwise than on an order of the court (s. 126—see para. [**15.7**]);

(*l*) conferring wide powers on the court to give relief to a defaulting debtor or hirer by orders under Part IX of the Act in proceedings brought in respect of a consumer credit or consumer hire agreement or security (see Chapter 22);

(*m*) empowering the court to re-open a credit agreement with an individual (whether a regulated agreement or not and whether a consumer credit agreement or not) where the credit bargain is extortionate (ss. 137–140—see Chapter 22);

(*n*) nullifying contractual provisions inconsistent with a provision for the protection of the debtor or hirer or his relative or any surety contained in the Act or in any regulation made under the Act or imposing on any such party a liability greater than that specified in such a provision (s. 173—see para. [**27.4**]);

The matters referred to in paragraphs (*g*)–(*n*) are dealt with elsewhere in this book, at the paragraph numbers indicated. The present chapter will be devoted to an examination of the provisions referred to in paragraphs (*a*)–(*f*). The provisions of s. 176 of the Act laying down general rules as to the service of notices and other documents are discussed in Chapter 27.

### DUTY TO GIVE NOTICE BEFORE TAKING CERTAIN ACTION

[**21.9**] Section 76 of the Act provides as follows:

"(1) The creditor or owner is not entitled to enforce a term of a regulated agreement by—

(*a*) demanding earlier payment of any sum, or
(*b*) recovering possession of any goods or land, or
(*c*) treating any right conferred on the debtor or hirer by the agreement as terminated, restricted or deferred,

except by or after giving the debtor or hirer not less than seven days' notice of his intention to do so.

(2) Subsection (1) applies only where—

(*a*) a period for the duration of the agreement is specified in the agreement, and
(*b*) that period has not ended when the creditor or owner does an act mentioned in subsection (1),

but so applies notwithstanding that, under the agreement, any party is entitled to terminate it before the end of the period so specified.

(3) A notice under subsection (1) is ineffective if not in the prescribed form.

(4) Subsection (1) does not prevent a creditor from treating the right to draw on any credit as restricted or deferred and taking such steps as may be necessary to make the restriction or deferment effective.

(5) Regulations may provide that subsection (1) is not to apply to agreements described by the regulations.

(6) Subsection (1) does not apply to a right of enforcement arising by reason of any breach by the debtor or hirer of the regulated agreement."

[**21.10**] It will be observed that s. 76 does not apply to a right of enforcement arising by reason of a breach by the debtor or hirer. Where it is desired to exercise a remedy for a breach, s. 87 (relating to default notices) comes into play. But s. 76 is available to control the exercise of remedies conferred by the agreement in events which, though not technically breaches, are for practical purposes equated with breaches by the agreement. For example, a provision that the full balance shall immediately become payable, or that the creditor shall be entitled to terminate the agreement and/or to repossess the goods, if the debtor or hirer becomes bankrupt or has execution levied against his assets or allows a judgment to remain unsatisfied against him for more than a given period, is not within s. 87, since none of the specified events is a breach, but is controlled by s. 76. In the result, seven days' notice, in prescribed form, must be given of the intention of the creditor or owner to invoke the provision. There are, however, three qualifications. First, s. 76 does not apply where at the outset the credit is repayable on demand, as in the case of the traditional bank overdraft. A distinction must, however, be made between a credit repayable on demand because no period is specified for the duration of the credit agreement (such a case is exempt from s. 76) and an agreement to give credit for a specified period with an overriding right to the creditor to make demand for payment at any time (such a case remains governed by s. 76). Secondly, the creditor or owner can, without serving such notice treat the right to draw on a credit as restricted or deferred and take such steps as may be necessary to make the restriction or deferment effective. Accordingly a bank does not have to give notice before terminating or suspending an overdraft facility; and a credit card issuer can without notice exercise a right to terminate a card holder's entitlement to his credit card and can make that termination effective by notifying suppliers that a stop has been placed on the card and that it should not be accepted. Thirdly, regulations under s. 76 (5) may exempt specified agreements from the notice requirements.

[**21.11**] It would seem that s. 76 (1) (*c*) is confined to termination, restriction or deferment of a specific right or rights of the debtor or hirer and is not applicable to termination of the agreement as a whole, this being governed by s. 98. It is apparent from s. 87 (1) (*a*) and (*d*) that the Act does not consider termination of an agreement as a whole to be adequately covered by a provision dealing merely with termination of a right. On the other hand, while s. 98 is the section controlling termination of an agreement otherwise than for breach, enforcement of the contractual consequences of that termination is regulated by s. 76, insofar as the consequences are of a kind specified in s. 76 (1). Hence an owner who wishes to exercise a contractual right to terminate a hire-purchase agreement, and recover possession of the goods by reason of the fact that the hirer has allowed a judgment obtained against him by a third party to remain unsatisfied for more than a given period, must give at least seven days' notice of termination under s. 98 (1) and at least seven days' notice of his intention to repossess under s. 76 (1) (*b*). There seems no reason why the two notices should not be combined in one document or why the two seven-day periods should not run concurrently. If the goods are protected goods, then repossession without the defendant's consent requires a court order (see paras. [**22.22**] *et seq.*). It should be noted that whereas a debtor or hirer can extinguish the operation of a default notice under s. 87 by remedying the breach or paying specified compensation, there is no way in which he can procure the extinguishment of a notice served under s. 76 or s. 98. He can however apply to the court for a time order under s. 129 (see paras. [**22.11**] *et seq.*) or for equitable relief against forfeiture (see para. [**17.11**]).

NOTICE OF DEFAULT

[**21.12**] Sections 76 and 98, referred to earlier, deal with the exercise of contractual rights otherwise than on the ground of default by the debtor or hirer. Section 87 controls the exercise of remedies on a breach. By s. 87 (1), service of a default notice in accordance with s. 88 is necessary before the creditor or owner can become entitled, by reason of a breach by the debtor or hirer, to terminate the agreement, demand earlier payment of any sum, recover possession of any goods or land or treat any right conferred on the debtor or hirer by the agreement as terminated, restricted or deferred. If the debtor or hirer has died, the notice of default can be served on his executor (even before probate) as the "debtor" or "hirer" within s. 189 (1) or, if there is no executor, on the person to whom letters of administration were granted; but it is unnecessary to serve in this way, since service will be validly effected if addressed to the debtor or hirer and sent by post to, or left at, his address last known to the creditor or owner (s. 176 (1)–(6)). This is so even if the creditor or owner was aware at the time that the debtor or hirer had died (s. 176 (6)). Service in this way is necessary where the debtor or hirer died intestate and it is desired to serve a notice of default prior to letters of administration, since it is not permitted to serve a default notice on the Probate Judge, even though the estate is vested in him pending the grant (s. 176 (7)—and see para. [**21.33**]). It is to be observed that

s. 87 is considerably wider than its predecessor, s. 25 of the Hire-Purchase Act 1965. Section 87 applies to all types of breach, whether taking the form of a default in payment or a breach of some other provision. Moreover, s. 87 is not confined to cases where a remedy of the kind described in s. 87 (1) is conferred expressly by the agreement, but also controls the exercise of such a remedy (other than termination, restriction or deferment of a right under s. 87 (1) (*d*)) where given by general contract law, *e.g.* the right to treat the agreement as repudiated by reason of a major breach.

[**21.13**] There are three cases where a notice need not be served:

(1) Section 87 (1) does not prevent the creditor from treating the right to draw upon any credit as restricted or deferred, and taking such steps as may be necessary to make the restriction or deferment effective (s. 87 (2)). This matches a corresponding exception to s. 76, discussed in paragraph [**21.10**].

(2) Regulations may provide that s. 87 (1) is not to apply to agreements described by the regulations (s. 87 (4)).

(3) Where a breach triggers off another provision of the agreement (as where the full outstanding balance is made payable on default in payment of an instalment), non-compliance with such provision does not necessitate (and indeed cannot be the subject of) a distinct default notice; it suffices that a default notice was served, and not complied with, in respect of the breach which makes the provision operative (s. 88 (4)). (For a further illustration of the impact of s. 88 (4), see para. [**21.18**]).

[**21.14**] The doing of an act by which a floating charge becomes fixed is not enforcement of a security (s. 87 (3)). A floating charge becomes fixed on the appointment of a receiver or on commencement of winding up of the chargor company or on the occurrence of any other event which by the terms of the charge causes it to crystallise. Section 87 (3) makes it clear that no notice is required to be given under s. 87 (1) (*e*) of any act which causes the floating charge to crystallise, though notice will, of course, be required if the act falls within one of the other categories listed in s. 87 (1). Section 87 (3) will rarely apply to a floating charge given by the debtor himself, since except where s. 185 (5) applies (see paras. [**20.2**], [**20.12**]) the debtor will be an individual (bodies corporate being outside the protection of the Act) and the Bills of Sale Act (1878) Amendment Act 1882, s. 5, precludes the granting of a security bill of sale over after-acquired chattels. There are certain statutory exceptions, both under the 1882 Act itself and under other legislation (*e.g.* Part II of the Agricultural Credits Act 1928 as regards agricultural charges by farmers) but save in such exceptional cases a floating charge by an individual over future chattels will usually be ineffective, and a floating charge by an individual over after-acquired land, though legally permitted, is of limited practical value, since until the land is acquired there is no machinery for registering the charge so as to give public notice of it. On the other hand, a floating charge might well be given by a body corporate at the request of an individual debtor (*e.g.* for the purpose of securing a guarantee given by the body corporate) and s. 87 (3) would enable a receiver to be appointed without service of a seven-day notice on the debtor under s. 87 (1).

FORM AND CONTENTS OF DEFAULT NOTICE

**[21.15]** By s. 88 (1), the default notice must be in the prescribed form and specify—

(*a*) the nature of the alleged breach;

(*b*) if the breach is capable of remedy, what action is required to remedy it and the date before which that action is to be taken;

(*c*) if the breach is not capable of remedy, the sum (if any) required to be paid as compensation for the breach, and the date before which it is to be paid.

A date specified under s. 88 (1) must be not less than seven days after the date of service of the default notice, and the creditor or owner must not take action such as is mentioned in s. 87 (1) before the date so specified or (if no requirement is made under sub-s. (1) before those seven days have elapsed (s. 88 (2)).

**[21.16]** The above provisions closely follow s. 146 (1) of the Law of Property Act 1925 (prescribing the notice to be served by a landlord before forfeiting a lease otherwise than for non-payment of rent), save that instead of the "reasonable time" allowed to the lessee under s. 146 for remedying the breach, s. 88 (2) allows the debtor or hirer the period specified in the default notice, with a minimum of seven days. With this qualification, and subject to certain fundamental differences between the legal treatment of goods and that of land (see (3) below), cases on s. 146 of the Law of Property Act provide a useful guide to the interpretation of s. 88 of the Consumer Credit Act, the effect of which may accordingly be summarised as follows:

(1) For a breach to be capable of remedy within s. 88 (1) (*b*), it must, by implication, be completely remediable within a reasonable time (see *Rugby School (Governors)* v. *Tannahill*, [1935] 1 K.B. 87; *Egerton* v. *Esplanade Hotels London, Ltd.*, [1947] 2 All E.R. 89). But the fact that a breach is not capable of being remedied within the minimum seven-day period prescribed by s. 88 (2) does not on that account make it irremediable (see para. [**21.16**]).

(2) Bankruptcy, if it is a breach of the agreement at all, is an irremediable breach (*Civil Service Cooperative Society* v. *McGrigor's Trustee*, [1923] 2 Ch. 347, *per* Russell, J., at p. 356) but it is unusual for a credit agreement to provide that the debtor shall not become bankrupt. Bankruptcy is usually specified not as a breach of the agreement but as a ground for exercise of remedies under it (see para. [**21.10**]), and will thus normally be caught by ss. 76 and 98, not by s. 87.

(3) Although it has been held that a covenant against assignment or sub-letting in a lease of land is irremediable (*Scala House and District Property Co., Ltd.* v. *Forbes*, [1973] 3 All E.R. 308), it is submitted that this is not necessarily so in the case of an agreement relating to goods. The grant of a lease of land confers an estate on the lessee and an assignment or sub-letting, even if unlawful, is effective to vest a term of years in the assignee or sub-lessee. But ownership of goods is indivisible, so that no "estate" vests in the hirer or conditional buyer, merely contractual rights accompanied by possession. If the hirer or

buyer wrongfully assigns or sub-lets, the assignment or sub-letting will usually have no impact on the rights of the owner or seller, so that the breach does not affect him and can be remedied by the hirer or buyer regaining possession, if he is able to do so.

(4) The creditor need not claim compensation for an irremediable breach if he does not wish to do so. This is clear from the words "if any" in s. 88 (1) (*c*), and would in any event follow as a matter of general law (see *Rugby School* (*Governors*), v. *Tannahill*, [1935] 1 K.B. 87; *Lock* v. *Pearce*, [1893] 2 Ch. 271.

(5) Even if the breach is irremediable and the creditor does not wish to claim compensation, he must serve a default notice specifying the breach, in order to give the debtor an opportunity of considering his position (see *Civil Service Cooperative Society* v. *McGrigor's Trustee*, [1923] 2 Ch. 347; *Horsey Estate, Ltd.* v. *Steiger*, [1899] 2 Q.B. 79). Such a requirement is by no means otiose, since even though the debtor is *ex hypothesi* unable to comply with the default notice, his attention is thereby directed to the consequences of failure to comply (see para. [**21.19**]) and he is given an opportunity to apply to the court for relief in the form of a time order under s. 129 (1) (see paras. [**22.11**] *et seq.*) or equitable relief against forfeiture (see para. [**17.11**]).

(6) A default notice specifying several breaches is not invalidated by reason of the fact that some of the alleged acts of default have not in fact been committed or, though committed, are not breaches of the agreement. It suffices that at least one of the specified defaults has been committed and constitutes a breach (*Pannell* v. *City of London Brewery Co.*, [1900] 1 Ch. 496, approved by the House of Lords in *Fox* v. *Jolly*, [1916] 1 A.C. 1; *Blewett* v. *Blewett*, [1936] 2 All E.R. 188).

(7) A default notice cannot validly specify a non-continuing breach that has been waived, *e.g.* by acceptance of rent with knowledge of the breach (*Jacob* v. *Down*, [1900] 2 Ch. 156).

[**21.17**] In contrast to a notice under s. 146 (1) of the Law of Property Act 1925, a default notice served in compliance with s. 87 of the Consumer Credit Act must not merely require the debtor or hirer to remedy a remediable breach but must specify what action is required to remedy it and the date by which that action is to be taken (s. 88 (1) (*b*)). It would seem to follow from s. 88 (2) that the creditor or owner need not allow more than seven days for remedying of the breach. But a breach which is incapable of being remedied within that time, or within any other time specified in the section which is less than a reasonable time, is not on that account an irremediable breach so as to be outside s. 88 (1) (*b*); for in determining whether a breach is remediable the court must, it is submitted, consider what would be a reasonable time for remedying it (see point (1) of para. [**21.16**]), not such limited time as the creditor or owner may choose to allow within the restriction imposed by s. 88 (2). It should be borne in mind, when reading these provisions, that the fact that a breach is not remediable does not debar the court from granting relief to the defaulting debtor or hirer (see paras. [**17.11**], [**22.11**] *et seq.*).

[**21.18**] Whereas s. 146 of the Law of Property Act 1925 enables the lessor to specify a sum required as compensation for the breach even if it is a remediable breach, s. 88 (1) only speaks of compensation in the paragraph dealing with irremediable breaches. But s. 88 (1) merely prescribes the minimum content of a default notice. There seems no reason why compensation for loss cannot be claimed in a default notice even in the case of a remediable breach. In such case, no time limit for payment of the compensation need be specified, unless such payment is itself the remedial action required; for it is only in cases of irremediable breach that s. 88 (1) (*c*) requires a date to be specified for payment of compensation. This causes no hardship to the debtor or hirer, for the taking of the remedial action specified under s. 88 (1) (*b*) suffices to extinguish the breach, under s. 89, even if the specified compensation for loss has not then been paid. Such loss is recoverable by action without service of any fresh notice of default (see s. 88 (3)).

[**21.19**] The default notice must contain information in the prescribed terms about the consequences of failure to comply with it (s. 88 (4)). When making a requirement as to remedial action, or as to compensation for an irremediable breach, the default notice may include a provision for the taking of action such as is mentioned in s. 87 (1) at any time after the restriction imposed by s. 88 (2) will cease, together with a statement that the provision will be ineffective if the breach is duly remedied or the compensation duly paid (s. 88 (5)). If before the date specified for that purpose in the default notice the debtor or hirer takes the action specified under s. 88 (1) (*b*) or (*c*) the breach is to be treated as not having occurred (s. 89).

## NOTICE OF TERMINATION OTHERWISE THAN FOR BREACH

[**21.20**] Section 98 (1) provides that the creditor or owner is not entitled to terminate a regulated agreement except by or after giving the debtor or hirer not less than seven days' notice of termination. This provision has been mentioned earlier (para. [**21.11**]). The notice under s. 98 need not be drawn so as to terminate the agreement automatically on expiry of the period specified in the notice. The creditor or owner may, if he wishes, state simply that he reserves the right to give notice of termination at any time after expiry of the s. 98 notice. As mentioned previously (para. [**21.11**]), a notice under s. 98 cannot be rendered ineffective by any action on the part of the debtor or hirer comparable to the remedial action provided by ss. 88 and 89 in relation to a notice of default. The remedy of the debtor or hirer who wishes to avoid the consequences of termination of the agreement is to apply to the court for a time order under s. 129 of the Act (see paras. [**22.11**] *et seq.*) or for equitable relief against forfeiture (see para. [**17.11**]).

[**21.21**] The provisions of s. 98 (2)–(6), limiting the operation of s. 98 (1) and providing for notices to be in the prescribed form, exactly match those of s. 76 (2)–(6), discussed in paras. [**21.9**]–[**21.10**].

## RECOVERY OF PROTECTED GOODS

[**21.22**] Sections 90 and 91 of the Act, re-enacting in somewhat different form the provisions of ss. 33 and 34 of the Hire-Purchase Act 1965, preclude the creditor under a hire-purchase or conditional sale agreement from recovering possession of protected goods from the debtor without the latter's consent, except on an order of the court, and entitle the debtor to recover all his payments, and to be released from further liability, if the creditor infringes this prohibition (see R. M. Goode, *Hire-Purchase Law and Practice* (2nd edn.) pp. 413–421). The restrictions imposed by ss. 90 and 91 are additional to those imposed by other provisions of the Act. Hence the creditor cannot begin proceedings for recovery of possession under s. 90 unless the requisite default notice prescribed by s. 87 has been served and has expired without the debtor remedying the breach. In addition, the creditor must comply with the requirements of s. 134 in order to establish adverse possession so as to ground an action for detinue or on the contract for failure of the debtor to deliver up the goods (see paras. [**21.26**]–[**21.27**]).

MEANING OF "PROTECTED GOODS"

[**21.23**] Goods are "protected goods" if falling within s. 90 (s. 90 (7)). The basic provision is s. 90 (1), which provides as follows:

> "At any time when—
>
> (*a*) the debtor is in breach of a regulated hire-purchase or a regulated conditional sale agreement relating to goods, and
>
> (*b*) the debtor has paid to the creditor one-third or more of the total price of the goods, and
>
> (*c*) the property in the goods remains in the creditor,
>
> the creditor is not entitled to recover possession of the goods from the debtor except on an order of the court."

But s. 90 (1) does not apply, or ceases to apply, to an agreement if the debtor has terminated, or terminates the agreement (s. 90 (5)). Hence exercise by the debtor of a right of termination, whether conferred by the agreement or by the Act, extinguishes his right to rely on s. 90 (1) and removes the barrier created by that section to recovery of possession by the creditor, though it does not preclude the debtor from applying for relief in the form of a time order under s. 129 (1) (see paras. [**22.11**] *et seq.*). To exclude the debtor's protection under s. 90 (1), his act of termination must be a genuinely voluntary and informed act as opposed, for example, to despatch of a letter of termination dictated by the creditor to which the debtor did not really address his mind (*United Dominions Trust* (*Commercial*), *Ltd.* v. *Ennis*, [1968] 1 Q.B. 54; [1967] 2 All E.R. 345). A wrongful repudiation of the agreement by the hirer which is accepted by the creditor would seem to be outside the scope of s. 90 (5), since what brings the agreement to an end in such a case is not the debtor's own repudiatory act but the owner's acceptance of it as discharging the contract. Cf. *F.C. Finance, Ltd.* v. *Francis* (1970), 114 Sol. Jo. 568.

[**21.24**] The provisions of s. 90 (1) are confined to hire-purchase and conditional sale agreements. They cannot be invoked by a hirer under a consumer hire agreement. His protection is given in other ways, notably by application to the court for a time order under s. 129 (see paras. [**22.11**] *et seq.* or for relief against forfeiture in equity (see para. [**17.11**]) or, if the goods are repossessed or are ordered to be returned to the owner, for an order for repayment under s. 132 (see para. [**22.23**]). Moreover, unlike s. 33 of the Hire-Purchase Act 1965, s. 90 (1) of the Consumer Credit Act limits protected goods to those comprised in the regulated hire-purchase or conditional sale agreement at a time when the debtor is in breach of the agreement. It follows that even where the debtor has paid or tendered one-third of the total price, the owner remains entitled to seize goods if the debtor is not then in breach of the agreement but some event other than a breach which is stipulated in the agreement as a ground for re-possession (e.g. levy of execution by a third party against the debtor's assets) has occurred. This is a surprising diminution of the protection previously given under s. 33 of the Hire-Purchase Act 1965 and is probably due to an oversight. In practice, it is unlikely to affect the debtor, since it is extremely unusual for a non-breach ground of possession to arise where the debtor is not already in default of some obligation under the agreement.

[**21.25**] In order for the goods to be protected goods, the debtor must have "paid" one-third or more of the total price (s. 90 (1) (*b*)); but "paid" includes "tendered" (s. 189 (1)). There is a special provision as to successive agreements (see paras. [**21.31**] *et seq.*). Where the agreement requires the creditor to carry out any installation, and specifies an installation charge as part of the total price, the reference to one-third of the total price is to be construed as a reference to the aggregate of the installation charge and one-third of the remainder of the total price (s. 90 (2)). Hence if the total price is £900, of which the installation charge is £60, the one-third requirement is met once the debtor has paid or tendered $£60 + \frac{£900 - £60}{3} = £340$. By s. 189 (1), "installation" means—

(*a*) the installing of any electric line or any gas or water pipe,
(*b*) the fixing of goods to the premises where they are to be used, and the alteration of premises to enable goods to be used on them,
(*c*) where it is reasonably necessary that goods should be constructed or erected on the premises where they are to be used, any work carried out for the purpose of constructing or erecting them on those premises.

"Electric line" has the meaning given by the Electric Lighting Act 1882 (Consumer Credit Act, s. 189 (1)), that is, "a wire or wires, conductor, or other means used for the purpose of conveying, transmitting or distributing electricity with any casing, coating, covering, tube, pipe, or insulator, enclosing, surrounding or supporting the same or any part thereof, or any apparatus connected therewith for the purpose of conveying, transmitting, or distributing electricity or electric currents" (Electric Lighting Act, s. 32). The modification made by s. 90 (2) to the one-third formula applies only where the creditor *is required under the agreement* to carry out the installation. If the agreement imposes no obligation on the creditor to install, but merely fixes an installation charge if he does install, the normal formula applies, so that in our illustration the goods would become protected goods (in the event of a breach by the debtor) after payment or tender of £300.

PROOF OF ADVERSE DETENTION

**[21.26]** A creditor bringing an action in detinue or in contract for return of the goods by the debtor must ordinarily show that the debtor has without lawful justification failed or refused to surrender the goods after demand by the creditor, so that the debtor's continued possession is in defiance of the creditor's right to possess. At common law, there are no special requirements in relation to the creditor's demand for surrender of the goods, other than that the demand must be unconditional and must describe the goods in a manner sufficient to enable them to be identified. The demand may thus be made in writing or orally. But in the case of protected goods, or of any other goods recoverable only on an order of the court, it is necessary to make special provision for establishing adverse detention, for in the absence of such provision the debtor would be entitled to say that in remaining in possession he was not acting in defiance of the creditor's right to possess but was merely invoking the right conferred by the Act to require the creditor to obtain a court order (see *Smart Brothers, Ltd.* v. *Pratt,* [1940] 2 K.B. 498; [1940] 3 All E.R. 432, *per* MacKinnon, L.J., at p. 437). Section 134 (1) of the Act accordingly provides as follows:

> "Where goods are comprised in a regulated hire-purchase agreement, regulated conditional sale agreement or regulated consumer hire agreement, and the creditor or owner—
>
> (*a*) brings an action or makes an application to enforce a right to recover possession of the goods from the debtor or owner, and
>
> (*b*) proves that a demand for the delivery of the goods was included in the default notice under section 88 (5), or that, after the right to recover possession of the goods accrued but before the action was begun or the application was made, he made a request in writing to the debtor or hirer to surrender the goods,
>
> then, for the purposes of the claim of the creditor or owner to recover possession of the goods, the possession of them by the debtor or hirer shall be deemed to be adverse to the creditor or owner."

**[21.27]** Section 134 (1) in effect re-enacts s. 48 of the Hire-Purchase Act 1965 but with a significant modification. Under s. 48, a written request to surrender could not be made until after the right to recover possession of the goods had accrued due but before proceedings for possession. Since the right to possession did not accrue until after expiry of the requisite default notice, it followed that the request to surrender could not be incorporated in the default notice itself but had to be made separately in writing after the default notice had expired. Section 134 (1) allows the creditor the alternative of including the request to surrender in the notice of default. If he omits to do this, he must wait until after expiry of the default notice before making a separate written request. It should be noted that s. 134 is not confined to protected goods but extends to all claims for recovery of goods under a regulated hire-purchase, conditional sale or consumer hire agreement. This extension is necessary to cover other cases where the goods are recoverable only on an order of the court, *e.g.* because the agreement was improperly executed. Where the creditor has a right to repossess without a court order, he has no need to rely on s. 134 and can make his demand in any way permitted at common law, though he must, of course, have a right to possession at the time of demand and must therefore wait for expiry of any requisite notice of default or notice under s. 76 or s. 98.

[**21.28**] Section 134 (2) provides that in sub-s. (1) "the debtor or hirer" includes a person in possession of the goods at any time between the debtor's or hirer's death and the grant of probate or administration. Accordingly a creditor or owner who, after the death of the debtor or hirer, wishes to establish adverse possession on the part of the person in possession prior to the grant of probate or administration may comply with s. 134 (1) by making a written request to surrender to the person in possession.

REPOSSESSION WITH CONSENT PERMITTED

[**21.29**] Section 33 of the Hire-Purchase Act 1965 did not preclude recovery of possession as such, but merely *enforcement* of a right to recover possession. Acceptance of a surrender by the hirer was therefore permissible (*Mercantile Credit Co., Ltd.* v. *Cross*, [1965] 2 Q.B. 205; [1965] 1 All E.R. 577), so long as the debtor's consent to the repossession was truly free and voluntary (*ibid.*). Section 90 (1) of the Consumer Credit Act, on the other hand, provides that "the creditor is not entitled to recover possession of the goods from the debtor except on an order of the court". At first sight, this may appear to preclude even acceptance of a voluntary surrender by the debtor or hirer. However, s. 173 (3) states that a provision of the Act under which a thing may be done in relation to any person on an order of the court or the director only shall not be taken to prevent its being done at any time, with that person's consent given at that time, though the refusal of such consent is not to give rise to any liability. Hence recovery of possession with consent of the debtor *given at the time* is not a contravention of s. 90 (1); but a consent given in advance, *e.g.* in the agreement itself, is not within s. 173 (3) and will not by itself protect the creditor from liability if he repossesses without a court order. What if the debtor simply abandons the goods? The position under s. 33 of the Hire-Purchase Act 1965 was clear. By the act of abandonment, the debtor made it plain that he did not wish to retain possession, so that repossession of the abandoned goods was not "enforcement" of a right to repossess (*Bentinck, Ltd.* v. *Cromwell Engineering Co.*, [1971] 1 Q.B. 324; [1971] 1 All E.R. 33). But s. 90 (1) of the Consumer Credit Act has dropped the word "enforce", so that the creditor has to rely on s. 173 (3). Though not as explicit as it might be, this seems sufficient to protect the creditor who repossesses abandoned goods, since the debtor's abandonment implies a consent to repossession by the creditor and such implied consent would continue to subsist up to the date of repossession, thus fulfilling the requirement of s. 173 (3) that there should be consent at that time.

REPOSSESSION FROM THIRD PARTY

[**21.30**] Where the debtor has not abandoned the protected goods or terminated the agreement, recovery of the goods by the creditor without the debtor's consent is a contravention of s. 90 (1) whether the goods are repossessed from the debtor himself or from some third party to whom the debtor has entrusted them. Thus, repossession of a motor vehicle from a garage where the debtor has deposited the vehicle for repair is equivalent to recovery of possession from the debtor himself (*Bentinck, Ltd.* v. *Cromwell Engineering Co., supra*).

APPLICATION OF SECTION 90 (1) TO SUCCESSIVE AGREEMENTS

[**21.31**] Section 90 (3), re-enacting in somewhat different form provisions previously contained in s. 47 of the Hire-Purchase Act 1965, provides as follows:

"In a case where—

(*a*) subsection (1) (*a*) is satisfied, but not subsection (1) (*b*), and

(*b*) subsection (1) (*b*) was satisfied on a previous occasion in relation to an earlier agreement, being a regulated hire-purchase or regulated conditional sale agreement, between the same parties, and relating to any of the goods comprised in the later agreement (whether or not other goods were also included),

subsection (1) shall apply to the later agreement with the omission of paragraph (*b*)."

The purpose of this provision is to ensure that a debtor who has paid one-third of the total price under a regulated hire-purchase or conditional sale agreement, thereby prospectively (*i.e.* subject to his default—see s. 90 (1) (*a*)) securing protection under s. 90 (1) for all the goods comprised in the agreement, does not lose that protection as regards some of the goods by coming to an agreement with the creditor that those goods shall be transferred to a new agreement (with or without additional goods), payments under the original agreement being attributed to the remaining goods. But for s. 90 (3), the consequence of the transfer would be that to secure protection again for the goods transferred to the new agreement, the debtor would have to pay a sum equal to one-third of the total price fixed by the new agreement. The effect of s. 90 (3) is to ensure that once one-third of the total price has been paid under the original agreement the transferred goods will be automatically protected under the new agreement when the debtor is in breach of that agreement, whether or not one-third of the total price payable under the new agreement has been paid or tendered. It is not necessary for this purpose that condition (*a*) of s. 90 (1) (*i.e.* default by the debtor) should have been satisfied in relation to the original agreement in order for the transferred goods to be protected under the new agreement.

[**21.32**] If the later agreement is a modifying agreement (as defined by s. 82—see para. [**11.15**] and *infra*), s. 90 (3) applies with the substitution, for the second reference to the later agreement, of a reference to the modifying agreement (s. 90 (4)). The effect of this provision is that where an agreement varies or supplements a regulated hire-purchase or conditional sale agreement under which one-third of the total price has been paid, s. 90 (1) applies to the two agreements together (as notionally combined by s. 82 (2)) without the one-third requirement having to be satisfied in relation to the combined agreements. In consequence, if default is made by the debtor under the agreements as combined, then not only will the goods comprised in the original agreement be protected but any goods added by the later agreement will be protected as well, regardless of the sum (if any) paid under the modifying agreement. Any successive agreement will constitute a modifying agreement except where the original agreement, instead of being merely varied or supplemented, is discharged altogether by, or on or before the making of, the later agreement.

APPLICATION OF SECTION 90 (1) ON DEATH OF DEBTOR

**[21.33]** The Third Schedule to the Hire-Purchase Act 1965 contained complicated provisions designed to ensure that where goods had become protected goods before the death of the hirer or buyer, his estate should be protected against repossession of the goods by the owner or seller prior to a grant of probate or letters of administration of the estate (see R. M. Goode, *op. cit.*, pp. 558–574). These extremely intricate provisions have been swept away and replaced by the admirably short and simple provisions of s. 90 (6):

> "Where subsection (1) applies to an agreement at the death of the debtor, it shall continue to apply (in relation to the possessor of the goods) until the grant of probate or administration . . ."

This elegant solution to a problem made unnecessarily complicated by the Hire-Purchase Act 1965 means that goods which are protected goods at the death of the debtor cannot after his death and until a grant of probate or letters of administration be recovered from the person in possession of them without the consent of "the debtor" except on an order of the court. (As to service of the requisite default notice after the death of the debtor or hirer, see para. [**21.12**].) The executor of a debtor who dies testate becomes "the debtor" immediately upon the death, by virtue of the definition of "debtor" in s. 189 (1), since the debtor's rights pass to him by operation of law even before probate, though the court will not usually allow him to enforce such rights prior to a grant. Accordingly if at the death the goods are in possession of some third party, *e.g.* a repairer, the executor as "the debtor" can give his consent to collection of the goods from the third party, but a purported consent by any other person is not effective (see *Peacock* v. *Anglo-Auto Finance Co., Ltd.* (1968), 112 Sol. Jo. 746). Where the debtor dies intestate, his administrator becomes "the debtor" upon the grant of letters of administration. Until then the debtor's rights vest in the Probate Judge (Administration of Justice Act 1925, s. 9), *i.e.* the President of the Family Division of the High Court (*ibid.*, s. 55; Administration of Justice Act 1970, s. 1 (1), (6)). It should be noted that s. 90 (6) of the Consumer Credit Act operates only where the debtor was in breach of the agreement at the date of his death, for it is only during the continuance of a breach that the goods can be protected goods (see s. 90 (1) (*a*)). It follows that if the debtor, having paid or tendered one-third of the total price, dies without being in breach of the agreement at the date of his death, the goods will not become protected goods unless a default occurs after the death in payment of instalments or in performance of other obligations imposed by the agreement. Such a default will make the goods protected goods (assuming that the other requirements necessary for this have been fulfilled); and if the creditor repossesses them before probate or letters of administration have been taken out, he infringes s. 90 (1), as applied to the person in possession by s. 90 (6).

**[21.34]** Even if the goods are not protected goods at the date of death of the debtor or hirer, enforcement of contractual rights arising by reason of the death is restricted by ss. 86 and 128 (see paras. [**21.39**]–[**21.40**], [**22.9**]).

EFFECT OF CONTRAVENTION OF SECTION 90

[**21.35**] Section 91 provides that if goods are recovered by the creditor in contravention of s. 90

(*a*) the regulated agreement, if not previously terminated, shall terminate, and

(*b*) the debtor shall be released from all liability under the agreement, and shall be entitled to recover from the creditor all sums paid by the debtor under the agreement.

[**21.36**] The above consequences ensue whether the creditor repossesses all the goods comprised in the regulated agreement or only some of them. If he repossesses some only, he becomes entitled to take possession of the remaining goods thereafter. The agreement is brought to an end by the first repossession (s. 91 (*a*)), and exercise of the court's power to make a time order under s. 129 or an order under s. 133 does not arise, since the owner is not seeking (and indeed cannot seek) judicial enforcement of the agreement and the debtor's liability under the agreement is extinguished, and he is entitled to recover all his payments. If the debtor wishes to establish beyond doubt that s. 91 has come into operation so as to bring the agreement to an end, he can apply to the court for a declaration to that effect (s. 142 (2)).

[**21.37**] Termination of the agreement under s. 91 attracts the operation of s. 106 to a security provided in relation to the agreement (s. 113 (3)), with the result that (*inter alia*) the security (including any guarantee or any indemnity) is deemed never to have had effect and the surety is entitled to repayment of sums he has paid (see para. [**13.13**]).

[**21.38**] Section 170 (1) makes it clear that the above remedies are exhaustive. Thus the debtor from whom the goods are repossessed in contravention of s. 90 cannot, for example, bring an action in detinue or conversion for breach of statutory duty (and see, on this point, *Carr* v. *James Broderick & Co., Ltd.*, [1942] 2 K.B. 275; [1942] 2 All E.R. 441).

RIGHTS EXERCISABLE BY REASON OF DEATH OF DEBTOR OR HIRER

[**21.39**] The creditor or owner under a regulated agreement is not entitled, by reason of the death of the debtor or hirer, to do an act specified in paragraphs (*a*) to (*e*) of s. 87 (1) if at the death the agreement is fully secured (s. 86 (1)). The term "fully secured" is not defined but apparently means that the value of the security is adequate to cover all the obligations of the debtor or hirer remaining to be performed at the date of his death. The value judgment thus involved in determining whether s. 86 (1) applies may create difficulty, particularly where the security is not real security but personal security in the form of a guarantee or indemnity. Hence the creditor or owner should not launch proceedings under s. 86 (2) (see below) unless he is confident that he can establish the inadequacy of his security. If at the date of the death the agreement is unsecured or partly secured, the creditor or owner must, by s. 86 (2), obtain an order of the court if he wishes to do any of the acts specified in paragraphs (*a*) to (*e*) of s. 87 (1). The court can only make an enforcement order if the conditions specified in s. 128 are fulfilled (see para. [**22.9**]).

[**21.40**] The scope of s. 86 (1) and (2) is in fact fairly limited. It is restricted to cases where the right to do an act of the kind specified in paragraphs (*a*) to (*e*) of s. 87 (1) becomes exercisable *by reason of* the death of the debtor or hirer, that is, where the act is done under a power conferred by the agreement which is exercisable on the death of the debtor or hirer or exercisable at will and exercised at any time after his death (s. 86 (6)). Moreover, three additional limits on the operation of s. 86 (1) and (2) are imposed by sub-ss. (3), (4) and (5), which provide as follows:

> "(3) This section applies in relation to the termination of an agreement only where—
>
> (*a*) a period for its duration is specified in the agreement, and
>
> (*b*) that period has not ended when the creditor or owner purports to terminate the agreement,
>
> but so applies notwithstanding, that, under the agreement, any party is entitled to terminate it before the end of the period so specified.
>
> (4) This section does not prevent the creditor from treating the right to draw on any credit as restricted or deferred and taking such steps as may be necessary to make the restriction or deferment effective.
>
> (5) This section does not affect the operation of any agreement providing for payment of sums—
>
> (*a*) due under the regulated agreement, or
>
> (*b*) becoming due under it on the death of the debtor or hirer,
>
> out of the proceeds of a policy of insurance on his life."

Subsections (3) and (4) follow the wording of s. 26 (2) and (4) and have the same meaning (see paras. [**21.9**]–[**21.10**]).

DEFAULT RATE OF INTEREST NOT TO EXCEED CONTRACT RATE

[**21.41**] Section 93 of the Act provides as follows:

> "The debtor under a regulated consumer credit agreement shall not be obliged to pay interest on sums which, in breach of the agreement, are unpaid by him at a rate—
>
> (*a*) where the total charge for credit includes an item in respect of interest, exceeding the rate of that interest, or
>
> (*b*) in any other case, exceeding what would be the rate of the total charge for credit if any items included in the total charge for credit by virtue of section 20 (2) were disregarded."

# CHAPTER 22

# JUDICIAL CONTROL

## INTRODUCTION

[**22.1**] Part IX of the Act is devoted to judicial control of regulated agreements and securities given in connection with such agreements. It also confers on the court wide powers to re-open extortionate credit bargains; and these powers are exercisable in relation to *any* credit agreement in which the individual is the debtor, even if the credit agreement is outside the scope of the Act. Part IX bears little resemblance to the provisions of the Hire-Purchase Act 1965 (ss. 33–49) which it is designed to replace; and those who have become accustomed to working with the former legislation may initially experience some difficulty in finding in Part IX the equivalents of orders available under the previous legislation. For example, no reference to postponed orders for specific delivery of protected goods will be found in Part IX, but the powers conferred on the court will in fact enable such orders to be made in the same way as under the Hire-Purchase Act 1965 (see para. [**22.14**]). Indeed, the court's powers are very much wider under Part IX, since they are exercisable not only in actions concerning protected goods but in any action or application concerning a regulated agreement or a security given in connection with a regulated agreement.

[**22.2**] For the purpose of the Act, "the court" means the county court (s. 189 (1)). It follows that in addition to any jurisdiction it possesses independently of the Act, the county court has exclusive jurisdiction as regards all the matters listed in paragraph [**22.3**], other than the re-opening of extortionate credit agreements. In respect of these it has exclusive jurisdiction over applications by the debtor or a surety where the agreement is a regulated agreement or an agreement for fixed-sum credit not exceeding £750 or running-account credit with a credit limit not exceeding £750 (s. 139 (5)), but in other cases relating to extortionate credit agreements it has jurisdiction concurrently with the High Court (s. 139 (1)). But an action or application brought in the High Court which by virtue of the Act ought to have been brought in the county court is not to be treated as improperly brought but it is to be transferred to the county court (s. 141 (2)). The effect of the above provisions is to remove (with effect from the relevant appointed day) a sizeable area of jurisdiction from the High Court, which, under the Hire-Purchase Act 1965, has been able to entertain all actions other than actions for recovery of protected goods and actions to recover goods where less than one-third of the hire-purchase price or total purchase price had been paid or tendered. Even a claim for, say, £4,000 arrears under a regulated agreement, where no claim is made for recovery of the goods, will henceforth be within the exclusive jurisdiction of the county court.

SUMMARY OF COURT'S POWERS

[**22.3**] The powers of the court under Part IX, each of which will be examined in detail in this chapter, may be summarised as follows:

(i) To hear and determine any action by the creditor or owner to enforce a regulated agreement or any security relating to it or any action to enforce any linked transaction against the debtor or hirer or his relative.

(ii) To make or refuse orders enforcing agreements and securities which, under the provisions of the Act, are enforceable only on an order of the court (see paras. [**22.6**] *et seq.*).

(iii) To make a time order allowing the debtor or hirer or a surety to pay any sum owed under a regulated agreement or a security by instalments or extending the time for remedying of any other breach (see paras. [**22.11**] *et seq.*).

(iv) To make a protection order preserving any property of the creditor or owner, or property subject to any security, from damage or depreciation pending the determination of proceedings, including an order restricting or prohibiting use of the property or giving directions as to its custody (see para. [**22.22**]).

(v) To order repayment to a hirer under a consumer hire agreement of the whole or any part of any sum paid by him, and his release from liability for any sum payable by him, in respect of the goods where these have been repossessed by the owner or where an order has been made for their delivery to the owner (see para. [**22.23**]).

(vi) Upon an application for a time order or an enforcement order in relation to a regulated hire-purchase or conditional sale agreement, or in proceedings by the creditor to recover possession of the goods comprised in such an agreement, to make an order:

(*a*) directing return of the goods to the creditor (see paras. [**22.7**] *et seq.*); or

(*b*) by way of a transfer (or "split") order, transferring title to certain of the goods to the debtor and directing return to the creditor of the remaining goods (see paras. [**22.31**] *et seq.*).

(vii) To make conditional or suspend the operation of any term of an order made in relation to a regulated agreement (see paras. [**22.7**] *et seq.*).

(viii) To include in any order made under the Act such provision as the court thinks just for amending any agreement or security in consequence of a term of the order (see para. [**22.26**]).

(ix) To re-open a credit agreement where the credit bargain is extortionate and provide various forms of consequential relief to the debtor or a surety (see paras. [**22.42**] *et seq.*).

(x) To make certain types of declaratory order (see para. [**22.56**]).

(xi) To make such orders in relation to agreements for credit brokerage, debt-adjusting or debt-counselling as the court may be empowered to make as the result of regulations made by the Secretary of State under s. 156 of the Act (see para. [**23.17**]).

[**22.4**] In addition, the court retains all the powers it would possess apart from the Act, except to the extent to which those powers are excluded or restricted by the provisions of Part IX.

EXCLUSIVE JURISDICTION OF COUNTY COURT

[**22.5**] The exclusive jurisdiction of the county court, derived partly from s. 141 of the Act, partly from the definition of "court" in s. 189 (1) of the Act, has been noted in paragraph [**22.2**], where it was also pointed out that an action or application within such exclusive jurisdiction but brought or made in the High Court is nevertheless valid, the sole effect being that it must be transferred to the county court (s. 141 (2)). As to the particular county court that must be selected for the commencement of proceedings within the Act, see para. [**22.55**].

ENFORCEMENT ORDERS IN CASES OF INFRINGEMENT

[**22.6**] Section 127 (3) precludes the court from making an enforcement order under s. 65 (1) in the case of non-compliance with s. 61 (1) (*a*) unless a document (whether or not in the prescribed form and complying with regulations under s. 60 (1)) itself containing all the prescribed terms of the agreement was signed by the debtor or hirer (whether or not in the prescribed manner). In other words, failure to set out all the prescribed terms in the contract document, or failure to procure signature by the debtor or hirer of a document containing those prescribed terms, cannot be dispensed with by the court, so that in these cases the agreement is perpetually unenforceable. The court is also precluded by s. 127 (4) of the Act from making an enforcement order in the case of a cancellable agreement if—

(*a*) a provision of s. 62 or 63 was not complied with, and the creditor or owner did not give a copy of the executed agreement, and of any other document referred to in it, to the debtor or hirer before the commencement of the proceedings in which the order is sought, or

(*b*) section 64 (1) was not complied with.

[**22.7**] Save in the three cases mentioned in paragraph [**22.6**], the court, on entertaining an application for which an order is required by reason of infringement (*i.e.* of ss. 61–64, 105 (1) or (4), 111 (1) or 123), is to dismiss the application if, but only if, it considers it just to do so having regard to—

(i) prejudice caused to any person by the contravention in question, and the degree of culpability for it; and

(ii) the powers conferred on the court by ss. 127 (2), 135 and 136 (s. 127 (1)).

The court may consider that it would be unjust to dismiss the application if, for example, the infringement had not seriously affected the debtor or hirer or a surety or if the adverse consequences of the infringement can be substantially eradicated by exercise of the court's powers to give relief under s. 127 (reduction or discharge of sum payable by debtor or hirer to compensate him for prejudice suffered through the contravention) s. 135 (imposition of condition or suspension of order) or 136 (amendment of agreement or security in consequence of a term of the order). If the court makes an enforcement order in cases within s. 127 (3) (as it has power to do if the only contravention of s. 61 (1) (*a*) was failure to ensure that the document was in the prescribed form or complied with regulations under s. 60 (1) or was signed by the debtor or hirer otherwise than in the prescribed manner), the court may direct that the regulated agreement is to have effect as if it did not include a term omitted from the document signed by the debtor or hirer (s. 127 (5)).

### ORDERS WHERE NO INFRINGEMENT INVOLVED

[**22.8**] There are three cases in which an order (which is not technically an "enforcement order" within s. 181 (1)) is necessary under the Act even though the creditor or owner has not infringed any of the statutory requirements. These are:

(i) exercise by an unsecured or partly secured creditor or owner of certain rights arising by reason of the death of the debtor or hirer (s. 86 (2)—see paras. [**21.39**] *et seq.*);
(ii) recovery of protected goods without the consent of the debtor (s. 90 (1)—see paras. [**21.22**] *et seq.*);
(iii) enforcement of a land mortgage (s. 126—see para. [**22.10**]).

[**22.9**] By s. 128, the court is to make an order under s. 86 (2) if, but only if the creditor or owner proves that he has been unable to satisfy himself that the present and future obligations of the debtor or hirer under the agreement are likely to be discharged.

[**22.10**] The Act contains no provisions dealing specifically with the approach to be adopted by the court in dealing with actions for recovery of protected goods or for enforcement of a land mortgage. Sections 129–131 and 133–136 confer the widest discretion on the court as to the orders it can make in entertaining an application involving a regulated agreement or security, and the few restrictions that do exist (*i.e.* in ss. 130 (3), 133 (3) and 135 (3)) are not peculiar to actions for recovery of protected goods or for enforcement of a land mortgage.

### TIME ORDERS

[**22.11**] Section 129 (1) provides as follows:

"If it appears to the court just to do so—

(*a*) on an application for an enforcement order; or
(*b*) on an application made by a debtor or hirer under this paragraph after service on him of—
  (i) a default notice, or
  (ii) a notice under section 76 (1) or 98 (1); or

(*c*) in an action brought by a creditor or owner to enforce a regulated agreement or any security, or recover possession of any goods or land to which a regulated agreement relates,

the court may make an order under this section (a 'time order')."

An "enforcement order" is defined in s. 189 (1) as an order made under ss. 65 (1), 105 (7) (*a*) or (*b*), 111 (2) or 124 (1) or (2). By s. 129 (2) a time order must provide for one or both of the following, as the court considers just—

(*a*) payment by the debtor or hirer or any surety of any sum owed under a regulated agreement or a security by such instalments, payable at such times, as the court, having regard to the means of the debtor or hirer and any surety, considers reasonable;

(*b*) the remedying by the debtor or hirer of any breach of a regulated agreement (other than non-payment of money) within such period as the court may specify.

Where in accordance with rules of court an offer to pay any sum by instalments is made by the debtor or hirer and accepted by the creditor or owner, the court may in accordance with rules of court make a time order under s. 129 (2) (*a*) giving effect to the offer without hearing evidence of means (s. 130 (1)).

[**22.12**] The court's power to make a time order is qualified, in relation to a regulated agreement secured by a pledge, by s. 130 (3), which precludes the court from making a time order in such a case if, by virtue of regulations made under s. 76 (4), 87 (3) or 99 (4), service of a notice is not necessary for enforcement of the pledge.

[**22.13**] It will be seen that the power to make time orders is not confined to actions for the recovery of protected goods but (subject to s. 130 (3)—see para. [**22.12**]) extends to almost every type of action concerning a regulated agreement or goods or land comprised in a regulated agreement or a security given in relation to a regulated agreement. The power to make an instalment order under s. 129 (2) (*a*) goes no further than the court's existing power to make instalment orders under s. 99 of the County Courts Act 1959. However, a time order under s. 129 (2) (*a*) is more powerful in its impact, since it attracts the operation of the supplemental provisions embodied in s. 130, including those of s. 130 (2) empowering the court, in the case of a hire-purchase or conditional sale agreement, to deal with sums not becoming payable until after the date of the order. Moreover, the making of an *application* for a time order suffices to enable the court to exercise its special powers under s. 133 of the Act (see paras. [**22.24**] *et seq.*). Section 129 (2) (*b*) has a still more radical effect, as will be seen below.

[**22.14**] It has been mentioned earlier that the Consumer Credit Act does not in terms provide for the making of a postponed order for specific delivery of the type hitherto available under s. 35 (4) (*b*) of the Hire-Purchase Act 1965. However, the Consumer Credit Act has not abolished the court's power to make a postponed order, but has merely scattered the ingredients of such an order over different sections. The court can produce the effect of the old-style postponed order by combining a time order under s. 129 with a return order under s. 133 (1) (*b*) (i) and a suspension of the operation of that order, under s. 135 (1) (*b*) (ii) (see para. [**22.21**]), for so long as the debtor complies with the requirements of the time order. If the debtor completes payment of the total price in pursuant to the time order and fulfils "any other necessary conditions" (by which is presumably meant conditions specified in the agreement as necessary for ownership to pass to him) the creditor's title to the goods vests in the debtor (s. 133 (5)). In the case of goods comprised in a regulated consumer hire agreement, the court cannot make a return order under s. 133 (1) (*b*) (i) (since the section is confined to hire-purchase and conditional sale agreements) but remains entitled to make an order for specific delivery in common law form and can suspend the operation of that order under s. 135 (1) (*b*).

### EFFECT OF TIME ORDER

[**22.15**] The effect of a time order is spelled out in s. 130 (4) and (5) as follows:

> "(4) Where, following the making of a time order in relation to a regulated hire-purchase or conditional sale agreement or a regulated consumer hire agreement, the debtor or hirer is in possession of the goods, he shall be treated (except in the case of a debtor to whom the creditor's title has passed) as a bailee or (in Scotland) a custodier of the goods under the terms of the agreement, notwithstanding that the agreement has been terminated.
>
> (5) Without prejudice to anything done by the creditor or owner before the commencement of the period specified in a time order made under section 129 (2) (*b*) ("the relevant period")—
>
> (*a*) he shall not while the relevant period subsists take in relation to the agreement any action such as is mentioned in section 87 (1);
>
> (*b*) where—
>
> (i) a provision of the agreement ("the secondary provision") becomes operative only on breach of another provision of the agreement ("the primary provision"), and
>
> (ii) the time order provides for the remedying of such a breach of the primary provision within the relevant period,
>
> he shall not treat the secondary provision as operative before the end of that period;
>
> (*c*) if while the relevant period subsists the breach to which the order relates is remedied it shall be treated as not having occurred."

### STATUTORY BAILMENT

[**22.16**] Section 130 (4)—which broadly corresponds to s. 38 (1) of Hire-Purchase Act 1965 though the scope of s. 130 (4) is much wider—does not, strictly speaking, resuscitate a terminated hire-purchase, conditional sale or consumer hire agreement but makes the debtor or hirer in possession a statutory bailee under the terms of the agreement, as controlled by a time order under s. 129 or consequential amendment under s. 136. This means that subject to such order, the obligations of the debtor or hirer under the terminated agreement are notionally revived, so that from the making of the time order payments again accrue due under the agreement (as controlled by the time order), other obligations (*e.g.* as to maintenance or insurance) are restored, and these continue in force while the debtor remains in possession, even, it seems, if the time order is later revoked. So far as payment obligations are concerned, the notional accrual of payments under the agreement will rarely arise, since each payment will be fixed by the time order itself which, in the case of hire-purchase or conditional sale agreement but not any other type of agreement, can deal with future instalments as well as arrears (s. 130 (2)). If the time order is revoked, then presumably payments accrued under the time order prior to revocation are enforceable by virtue of the order whilst the agreement again become fully operative according to its terms in relation to periods arising after revocation of the time order.

FREEZING OF RIGHTS

[**22.17**] The effect of s. 130 (5) (which is restricted to time orders providing for the remedying of non-monetary breaches and is thus of somewhat limited importance—see para. [**22.19**]) depends on whether the regulated agreement is still in force at the commencement of the period allowed by the time order for remedying of the breach or whether it has already been terminated by that date. If the agreement is still in force, the time order in effect freezes the creditor's remedies for the period specified in the time order (as varied by any variation order made under s. 130 (6)) until the time order is revoked by the court under s. 130 (6). Thus the creditor is, during the specified period, disabled from terminating the agreement or exercising any of the other rights enumerated in s. 87 (1). This restriction operates not only in relation to a breach for the remedying of which time is allowed by the time order but any other breach, including fresh breaches committed during the currency of the time order itself. The creditor's remedy in such a case is to apply for revocation of the time order. In addition, none of the rights listed in s. 87 (1) or any other rights expressed to arise on breach of a contractual provision which the time order allows the debtor time to remedy within a given period can be treated as arising before the end of that period. If the breach in question is remedied within such period, it is to be treated as not having occurred, with the result that in the absence of any other unremedied breach the agreement continues in force as if nothing had happened. If the breach is not remedied within the time stipulated in the time order, or if the time order is revoked, the restraints imposed by s. 130 (5) are removed and subject to the powers of the court to vary the time order under s. 130 (6) or to make a new time order or exercise its other powers under Part IX, the creditor can proceed to enforce his contractual rights in the ordinary way. He is still, of course, obliged to obtain an enforcement order for those rights which, under the provisions of the Act, are enforceable only on an order of the court. Where the creditor has duly terminated the agreement prior to the making of the time order and/or exercised other remedies such as the right to repossess, the position is more complex. Section 130 (5) is expressed to be "without prejudice to anything done by the creditor or owner before the commencement of the period specified in a time order made under s. 129 (2) (*b*)." If the agreement has been terminated prior to the commencement of that period, a time order under s. 129 (2) (*b*) does not disturb the termination but it does prevent the creditor from exercising any consequential right of repossession until expiry of the period in question. If during that period the breach is remedied, it is treated as not having occurred, and the debtor continues in possession as statutory bailee under the terms of the agreement, despite its termination, by virtue of s. 130 (4). Where, however, the creditor has repossessed the goods before the commencement of the period allowed in the time order for remedial action, the time order does not entitle the debtor to have the goods returned to him. Its sole effect in such a case is to freeze remedies not already exercised so as to allow the debtor or hirer to remedy the breach within the period specified in the order. In this situation, no statutory bailment is created under s. 130 (4), which is restricted to cases where the debtor is still in possession after the making of the time order.

[**22.18**] As a result of s. 130 (5), it would seem that during the period for remedial action specified in a time order under s. 129 (2) (*b*) the creditor or owner is precluded even from serving a notice of default under s. 87 in respect of other breaches. On the other hand, a default notice served prior to the commencement of the period continues to run during that period, and can accordingly be relied upon by the creditor or owner on revocation of the time order, and acted upon immediately if the time specified in the default notice has then expired.

[**22.19**] The freeze imposed by s. 130 (5) is limited to time orders under s. 129 (2) (*b*), *i.e.* time orders which provide for the remedying of a breach other than non-payment of money. Since default in payment is by far the most common breach complained of by creditors, s. 130 (5) will only operate in a minority of actions. A time order which is made solely under s. 129 (2) (*a*) and is thus restricted to fixing payment by instalments does not by itself restrict the creditor's remedies for default and, if no other order is made, leaves the creditor free to seize the goods (unless they are protected goods) or to bring an action for recovery of the goods. But on the debtor's application for a time order, or on the creditor's application for recovery of possession of the goods, the court's powers under s. 133 (1) become exercisable, so that the court may, for example, make an order for the return of the goods suspended so long as the payments fixed by the time order continue to be made. The powers under s. 133 (1) are not, however, exercisable in relation to consumer hire agreements, and goods comprised in such agreements cannot be protected goods for the purpose of s. 90. Accordingly where the hirer under a consumer hire agreement defaults in payment and fails to comply with a default notice served on him in accordance with s. 87, the hirer cannot invoke the Act to stop the owner from exercising a right to seize the goods, even if the court has made a time order providing for payment of the arrears by instalments. The only remedies open to the hirer in such a case are (*a*) to invoke the court's equitable jurisdiction to grant relief against forfeiture (see para. [**17.11**]) or (*b*) to apply to the court for an order for repayment of monies under s. 132 (see para. [**22.23**]). This latter provision is in fact a powerful inducement to owners not to act unreasonably in the enforcement of their rights of repossession.

### VARIATION AND REVOCATION OF TIME ORDER

[**22.20**] The court may vary or revoke a time order on the application of any person affected by it (s. 130 (6)). Revocation of a time order removes the restrictions imposed by s. 130 (5) (see para. [**22.16**]), since the "relevant period" referred to in that sub-section (*i.e.* the period allowed the debtor for remedying of a non-monetary breach) ceases to subsist when the time order is revoked. The creditor can thereupon proceed to exercise his remedies in the ordinary way, subject to the other provisions of the Act (see para. [**22.17**]). A default notice served prior to the date of commencement of a period stipulated in a time order under s. 129 (2) (*b*) but not expired before that date nevertheless continues to run so as to be available to the creditor or owner on revocation of the time order (see also para. [**22.18**]).

BREACH OF TIME ORDER

[**22.21**] If a time order for payment of a sum by instalments is made under s. 129 (2) (*a*) and the debtor or hirer defaults in payment of an instalment fixed by the order, the creditor or owner can forthwith issue execution for the whole of such sum then remaining unpaid or for such part as he wishes, not being less than £3 or the amount of one monthly instalment or four weekly instalments, whichever is the greater (C.C.R. Order 25, r. 13 (5)). But the debtor or hirer can prevent such execution by tendering the instalment or instalments in arrear prior to issue of the warrant of execution (*ibid.*, proviso), in which case the time order continues in force. In the case of a hire-purchase or conditional sale agreement where a return order has been made under s. 133 (1) (*b*) (i) but suspended under s. 135 (1) (*b*), default in payment under the time order entitles the creditor to have the return order executed immediately, without further order of the court, if the suspension was made under s. 135 (*b*) (ii) and was expressed to be until default in payment; but if the suspension was expressed to be under s. 135 (*b*) (i), *i.e.* until such time as the court would subsequently direct, the return order cannot be executed until a further order of the court has been made lifting the suspension. The same considerations apply to an order made in common law form for specific delivery of goods comprised in a consumer hire agreement but suspended under s. 135 (1) (*b*). The position is the same where the debtor or hirer fails to remedy a non-monetary breach within the period stipulated in a time order made under s. 129 (2) (*b*).

PROTECTION ORDERS

[**22.22**] The court, on the application of the creditor or owner under a regulated agreement, may make such orders as it thinks just for protecting any property of the creditor or owner, or property subject to any security, from damage or depreciation pending the determination of any proceedings under this Act, including orders restricting or prohibiting use of the property or giving directions as to its custody (s. 131). This re-enacts s. 35 (3) of the Hire-Purchase Act 1965. Quite independently of s. 131, the court has a general power under rules of court to make orders for the sale of perishables, etc. and for the detention, preservation, inspection, surveying, measuring and weighing of any property the subject of an action or as to which any question may arise therein (C.C.R., Order 13, rr. 11, 12—see also *ibid.*, r. 10).

REPAYMENT TO CONSUMER HIRER

**[22.23]** Where the owner under a regulated consumer hire agreement recovers possession of goods comprised in the agreement otherwise than by action or in proceedings relating to such an agreement obtains an order for delivery of the goods, the hirer may apply to the court for repayment of the whole or part of any sum paid by him to the owner in respect of the goods and for cessation of any obligation to pay the whole or part of any sum owed by him to the owner in respect of the goods; and if it appears to the court just to do so, having regard to the extent of the enjoyment of the goods by the hirer, the court must grant the application in full or in part (s. 132). These provisions, which may appear somewhat Draconian, are designed to enable the court to alleviate hardship that may be suffered by a hirer locked into a harsh consumer hire agreement that enables the owner, on repossessing for a default, to receive a windfall at the expense of the hirer. A graphic illustration of this type of case is *Galbraith* v. *Mitchenall Estates, Ltd.*, [1965] 2 Q.B. 473; [1964] 2 All E.R. 653, where the plaintiff, a working gardener and handyman, signed a hiring agreement relating to a caravan which he required as a home for his wife and family, and made a down-payment of £550.10.0, incurring an obligation under the agreement to pay 60 rentals of £12.10.0 every month over a five-year period. After five months, the defendants terminated the agreement owing to the non-payment of any instalments by the plaintiff, and after repossessing the caravan they sold it for £775 and would, indeed, have obtained even more but for the damage caused by mishandling by the repossession agents. The original retail price of the caravan was £1,050. Hence after only five months, the defendants had received, with the down-payment, a total sum of over £250 above the retail price of the caravan, whilst the only benefit that the hirer had received from his initial payment of £550.10.0 was five months' occupation of the caravan. Nevertheless the judge felt constrained by authority to refuse him relief in the absence of unconscionable conduct at the time of the making of the agreement. Section 132 of the Consumer Credit Act would enable the court to grant such relief in a case of this kind. The section is particularly necessary in view of the fact that the provisions of the Act relating to extortionate credit bargains (see paras. **[22.37]** *et seq.*) are not applicable to consumer hire agreements.

SPECIAL POWERS OF THE COURT

**[22.24]** Section 133 of the Act, taken in conjunction with s. 135, enables the court to make the same range of orders as it was empowered to make under s. 35 (4) of the Hire-Purchase Act 1965. There is, however, the striking difference that whereas the powers under s. 35 (4) were exercisable only in proceedings by the owner or seller for recovery of protected goods, the powers under s. 133 of the Consumer Credit Act may be exercised in relation to any goods comprised in a regulated hire-purchase or conditional sale agreement if it appears to the court just to do so—

(*a*) on an application for an enforcement order or a time order; or
(*b*) in an action by the creditor to recover possession of goods to which the agreement relates.

This is the case even where it was the debtor himself who terminated the agreement; in such a case the discretion of the court to refuse an order for specific delivery is restricted by s. 100 (5) of the Act, but this restriction is of somewhat limited impact in view of the provisions of s. 133 (5) (see para. [**22.29**]). It should be noted that the powers under s. 133 are exercisable only in relation to regulated hire-purchase and conditional sale agreements, not in relation to regulated consumer hire agreements.

TYPES OF SPECIAL ORDER THAT MAY BE MADE

[**22.25**] The court may, under the provisions of s. 133 (1) (*b*)—

(i) make an order (a "return order") for the return to the creditor of goods to which the agreement relates;

(ii) make an order (a "transfer order") for the transfer to the debtor of the creditor's title to certain goods to which the agreement relates ("the transferred goods"), and the return to the creditor of the remainder of the goods.

But the court cannot suspend an order requiring the debtor to deliver up goods unless satisfied that the goods are in his possession or control (s. 135 (2)), nor suspend an order against a hirer under a consumer hire agreement so as to entitle him to remain in possession for longer than the contractual period of hire (s. 135 (3)).

AMENDMENT OF AGREEMENT OR SECURITY

[**22.26**] The court may in an order by it under the Act include such provision as it considers just for amending any agreement or security in consequence of a term of the order (s. 136). It would seem that termination of an agreement does not preclude a variation order under s. 136 in cases where the agreement is notionally revived under s. 129 (4).

RETURN ORDER

[**22.27**] The first type of order listed in s. 133 (1) is an order for the return to the creditor of goods to which the agreement relates. The order may be immediate and unqualified or, under s. 135 (1), it may be made subject to a suspension (though only if the goods are in the debtor's possession or control—see paras. [**22.25**], [**22.30**]) or condition. Again, the order may direct return of goods without giving the debtor an option to pay their value (an order described in the Hire-Purchase Act as an order for *specific* delivery) or it may allow the debtor the option of paying the value of the goods if he fails to return them within the time stipulated by the order. However, where a debtor, having exercised his statutory right to terminate the agreement under s. 99, wrongfully retains possession, then in proceedings by the creditor to recover possession the court is obliged to order delivery of the goods to the creditor without giving the debtor an option to pay their value, unless the court is satisfied that having regard to the circumstances it would not be just to do so (s. 100 (5)). But this provision is of limited significance in view of the debtor's rights under s. 133 (4) (see para. [**22.29**]). The effect of contravention of a return order is considered in paragraph [**22.34**].

[**22.28**] It is in relation to return orders that the court is most likely to exercise its discretion to make a conditional or suspended order. Of the two, the conditional order in favour of the creditor is, perhaps, the less likely, though it allows the court great flexibility in arriving at a just result. For example, if the court, though minded to make a return order, considers that the value of the goods exceeds the unpaid balance due under the agreement, so that sale of the returned goods by the creditor would produce a surplus, the court can make it a condition of the order that any such surplus shall be paid to the debtor. The more common form of order is likely to be (as under the Hire-Purchase Act) a suspended order (the equivalent of the postponed order provided by the Hire-Purchase Act), *e.g.* an order for delivery (with or without an option to the debtor to pay the value of the goods), suspended on condition that the debtor pays the arrears and future sums falling due by instalments specified in the order. If the debtor completes the payments due under the agreement and fulfils any other conditions necessary under the agreement for the transfer of ownership to him he acquires title (s. 133 (5)). If he defaults in payment, the creditor can immediately proceed to execute the order if the suspension was expressed to be until non-payment, pursuant to s. 135 (*b*) (ii). If, however, the suspension was in the form provided by s. 135 (*b*) (i), *i.e.* "until such time as the court subsequently directs", the creditor cannot enforce the return order immediately but must apply for the suspension to be lifted.

[**22.29**] Whilst the court can deprive the debtor of an option to pay the value of the goods instead of returning them to the creditor, little is achieved by so doing, since the Act provides that notwithstanding the making of a return order the debtor may at any time before the goods enter the possession of the creditor, on payment of the balance of the total price and the fulfillment of any other necessary conditions, claim the goods ordered to be returned to the creditor (s. 133 (4)).

[**22.30**] The court has no power to suspend the operation of a term requiring the delivery up of goods by the debtor, or indeed by any other person, unless satisfied that the goods are in his possession or control (s. 135 (2)). Under the Hire-Purchase Act, where the owner or seller applied for an order for delivery and did not oppose the postponing of the operation of the order, many courts would make an order without any affirmative evidence that the goods were in the possession or control of the hirer or buyer. Such practice could no doubt be justified on the footing that since the requirement of possession or control was intended for the protection of the owner or seller, it was open to him to waive the requirement; and no doubt the same practice will be followed in dealing with s. 135 (2) of the Consumer Credit Act.

## TRANSFER ORDER

[**22.31**] The second type of order that may be made under s. 133 (1) is a transfer order. This is the type of order previously provided by s. 35 (4) (*c*) of the Hire-Purchase Act 1965, and commonly known as a "split" order. By such an order, the court transfers to the debtor the creditor's title to certain goods and directs return of the remainder of the goods to the creditor. However, as under the Hire-Purchase Act, the court can make a transfer order only where the sum paid by the debtor exceeds the part of the total price referable to the transferred goods by an amount equal to at least one-third of the unpaid balance of the total price (s. 133 (3)). The object of this provision is to compensate the creditor for having to accept the return of used goods under the order. For the purpose of s. 133, the part of the total price referable to any goods is the part assigned to those goods by the agreement or (if no such assignment is made) the part determined by the court to be reasonable (s. 133 (7)). In practice, an agreement comprising several goods will usually show a single *total price*, and only the *cash* price of each article will be separately stated. In determining for the purposes of s. 133 how much of the total price has been paid ("the paid-up sum"), the court may—

(*a*) treat any sum paid by the debtor, or owed by the creditor, in relation to the goods as part of the paid-up sum;

(*b*) deduct any sum owed by the debtor in relation to the goods (otherwise than as part of the total price) from the paid-up sum,

and make corresponding reductions in amounts so owed (s. 133 (2)).

[**22.32**] The above provisions may be illustrated by a simple example. Let us suppose that a hire-purchase agreement is made comprising a gas cooker and a refrigerator at a total price of £400, that this is apportioned, either in the agreement (which is unlikely) or by the court as to £225 to the cooker and £175 to the refrigerator, and that the debtor has made payments totalling £250. The court can order transfer of the refrigerator to the debtor, since the payments he has made exceed the price referable to the refrigerator by £75, and this is more than one-third of the unpaid balance of the total price (viz. £50). The court cannot order transfer of the cooker to the debtor, since the excess of payments over the price referable to the cooker is only £25, which is less than one-third of the unpaid balance of the total price. Whilst the court cannot reduce the one-third margin in favour of the creditor the margin may be greater than one-third and in practice will almost invariably be so, since it will only be by coincidence that payments exceed the price referable to the transferred goods by exactly one-third of the unpaid balance of the total price. Under the Hire-Purchase Act, there was no power to order the creditor to refund any excess of payments by the debtor over and above the one-third margin. In theory, the court can deal with this under s. 135 (1) (*a*) of the Consumer Credit Act by making such refund a condition of the transfer order; but since transfer orders are unusual and are not likely to appeal to the creditor, such a condition would in practice be likely to produce a stalemate.

[**22.33**] Notwithstanding the making of a transfer order, the debtor may at any time before the goods enter the possession of the creditor, on payment of the balance of the total price and the fulfillment of any other necessary conditions, claim the goods ordered to be returned to the creditor (s. 133 (4)).

DEBTOR'S FAILURE TO RETURN GOODS

[**22.34**] By s. 133 (6) if, in contravention of a return order or transfer order, any goods to which the order relates are not returned to the creditor, the court, on the application of the creditor, may—

(*a*) revoke so much of the order as relates to those goods, and

(*b*) order the debtor to pay the creditor the unpaid portion of so much of the total price as is referable to those goods.

The computation of the part of the total price referable to the goods is made in conformity with s. 133 (7) (see para. [**21.31**]).

SUSPENDED ORDERS IN RELATION TO CONSUMER HIRE AGREEMENTS

[**22.35**] The court's power to suspend the operation of an order is not restricted to orders under s. 133 but extends to any order made by the court in relation to a regulated agreement. However, in the case of a consumer hire agreement the court cannot use its power of suspension so as to extend the hirer's right to possession beyond the contractual period of hire (s. 135 (3)).

VARIATION OF ORDERS

[**22.36**] The court's power under s. 129 (6) to vary a time order has already been noted (see para. [**22.20**]). In addition, the court may vary a suspension or condition imposed by s. 135 (1), upon application by any person thereby affected (s. 135 (4)).

EXTORTIONATE CREDIT BARGAINS

[**22.37**] The court has long had an equitable jurisdiction to set aside harsh and unconscionable bargains, but this power has in the main been devoted to upsetting sales at an undervalue by poor or uninformed vendors, and improvident bargains made by expectant heirs or reversioners, and has rarely been invoked successfully in the last half century. Section 1 of the Money-lenders Act 1900 conferred on the court in any proceedings by a moneylender for recovery of the loan or enforcement of a security, or in any proceedings by a buyer or surety for relief, power to re-open the transaction where there was evidence that the interest or other charges were excessive and that the transaction was harsh and unconscionable or otherwise such that a court of equity would give relief. This provision was later strengthened by s. 10 (1) of the Moneylenders Act 1927, which created a presumption that interest was excessive, and the transaction harsh and unconscionable, if the rate of interest exceeded 48 per cent. *per annum*. Hence where interest was above 48 per cent., the onus was on the lender to refute that presumption; in other cases, the onus lay on the borrower to show that the interest was excessive.

[**22.38**] The utility of the above provisions in the consumer credit field was limited, since quite apart from the fact that moneylenders could usually advance a justification for their charges in terms of risk and the relatively small amount of the loan, borrowers normally failed to defend proceedings brought against them. Moreover the statutory provisions were confined to moneylending transactions within the Moneylenders Act. They did not catch other forms of credit, such as hire-purchase or instalment sale agreements; nor did they control loan transactions where the lender did not carry on moneylending as a business or was deemed by s. 6 of the Act of 1900 not to be carrying on the business of moneylending, *e.g.* because he was a banker.

[**22.39**] The only other legal control over interest rates was that imposed by the Pawnbrokers' Act, which laid down a tariff of charges that could be made by pawnbrokers.

[**22.40**] The Crowther Committee, whilst recommending retention of the 48 per cent. formula in the Moneylenders Act 1927, as opposed to the fixing of an inflexible ceiling rate, advocated that this should be extended over the whole field of consumer credit, and that the consumer should be protected from consistent overcharging in various other ways, as by use of the licensing system and by a requirement that a lender regularly charging more than 48 per cent. *per annum* should send quarterly returns to the consumer credit commissioner (see Crowther Report, paragraph 6.6.9).

[**22.41**] The Consumer Credit Act, though adopting the first part of the Crowther Committee's recommendations by extending control of extortionate credit bargains to cover all types of credit agreement with an individual as debtor, abandons the 48 per cent. formula altogether. What the Act does is to provide guidelines for the court in determining whether a credit bargain is extortionate, but to put the onus of showing that the credit bargain is not extortionate on the creditor in all cases (however low the rate of interest or charge) where the debtor or a surety asserts in proceedings that the bargain is extortionate (see para. [**22.51**]).

### THE POWER TO RE-OPEN

[**22.42**] If the court finds a credit bargain extortionate, it may re-open the credit agreement so as to do justice between the parties (s. 137 (1)). For this purpose, "credit agreement" means any agreement between an individual ("the debtor") and any other person ("the creditor") by which the creditor provides the debtor with credit of any amount (s. 137 (2) (*a*)). It is important to note that, in contrast to other provisions of the Act, the court's powers under s. 137 are not confined to regulated agreements but apply to all credit agreements of any kind—whether exempt agreements or agreements which are otherwise outside the Act altogether, *e.g.* because the credit exceeds £5,000—where the debtor is an individual. "Individual", it will be recalled, includes a partnership and an unincorporated association (s. 189 (1)). But only *credit* agreements can be re-opened. There is no power to re-open *hire* agreements under s. 137, though the court can provide substantial relief under s. 132 as regards goods comprised in a consumer hire agreement which are repossessed by or ordered to be returned to the owner (see para. [**22.23**]). There is no power to grant any relief to the hirer under a hiring agreement which is not a consumer hire agreement.

[**22.43**] By s. 137 (1) (*b*), "credit bargain"—

(i) where no transaction other than the credit agreement is to be taken into account in computing the total charge for credit, means the credit agreement, or

(ii) where one or more other transactions are to be so taken into account, means the credit agreement and those other transactions taken together.

Hence in determining whether a credit *agreement* is to be re-opened, the court looks not only at that agreement but at all other agreements to be taken into account in computing the total charge for credit, *e.g.* the maintenance and insurance contracts entered into pursuant to a term of the credit agreement where the debtor is not free to choose the insurer or the supplier of the maintenance service (see paras. [**3.17**]–[**3.18**]). The purpose of bringing such associated contracts within the definition of "credit bargain" is, of course, to enable the court to take account of the total charge for credit, whether the charge arises wholly under the credit agreement or partly under that agreement and partly under the ancillary contract or contracts. Section 137 (1) speaks only of re-opening the credit *agreement*; but s. 137 (2) empowers the court, in re-opening the agreement, to set aside the whole or part of any obligation imposed on the debtor or a surety by the credit bargain or any related agreement (see para. [**22.51**]). The words "related agreement" are not defined.

### HOW THE COURT'S JURISDICTION IS INVOKED

[**22.44**] By s. 139 (1) the credit agreement may be re-opened under the above provisions:

(*a*) on an application for the purpose made by the debtor or any surety to the High Court or county court; or

(*b*) at the instance of the debtor or a surety in any proceedings to which the debtor and creditor are parties, being proceedings to enforce the credit agreement, any security relating to it, or any linked transaction; or

(*c*) at the instance of the debtor or a surety in other proceedings in any court where the amount paid or payable under the credit agreement is relevant.

### WHEN A CREDIT BARGAIN IS EXTORTIONATE

[**22.45**] By s. 138 (1) a credit bargain is extortionate if it—

(*a*) requires the debtor or a relative of his to make payments (whether unconditionally, or on certain contingencies) which are grossly exorbitant, or

(*b*) otherwise grossly contravenes ordinary principles of fair dealing.

The words "(whether unconditionally or otherwise)" in s. 138 (1) (*a*) make it clear that the court can look not only at the primary obligations of the debtor but at provisions for default as well; and if these impose liabilities which are grossly exorbitant or otherwise grossly contravene the ordinary principles of fair dealing, the agreement will be extortionate even if the primary obligations are reasonable. The Act, though laying down certain guidelines discussed in the following paragraphs, sensibly does not attempt to define "grossly exorbitant" or "grossly contravenes the ordinary principles of fair dealing". In relation to default provisions, these words would seem to require a degree of unfairness rather greater than would, for example, be sufficient to attract the rule against penalties (see para. [**21.7**]). The requirement that the exorbitance or contravention of ordinary principles of fair dealing shall be gross helps to overcome the difficulty of utilising standard rates of charge not geared to the personal characteristics of any individual debtor (see para. [**22.49**]).

GUIDELINES

[**22.46**] These are laid down in sub-ss. (2)–(5) of s. 138, which provide as follows:

"(2) In determining whether a credit bargain is extortionate, regard shall be had to such evidence as is adduced concerning—

(*a*) interest rates prevailing at the time it was made,
(*b*) the factors mentioned in subsections (3) to (5), and
(*c*) any other relevant considerations.

(3) Factors applicable under subsection (2) in relation to the debtor include—

(*a*) his age, experience, business capacity and state of health; and
(*b*) the degree to which, at the time of making the credit bargain, he was under financial pressure, and the nature of that pressure.

(4) Factors applicable under subsection (2) in relation to the creditor include—

(*a*) the degree of risk accepted by him, having regard to the value of any security provided;
(*b*) his relationship to the debtor; and
(*c*) whether or not a colourable cash price was quoted for any goods or services included in the credit bargain.

(5) Factors applicable under subsection (2) in relation to a linked transaction include the question how far the transaction was reasonable required for the protection of debtor or creditor, or was in the interest of the debtor."

[**22.47**] The court is only *obliged* to take into account those factors listed above on which evidence is adduced, though it remains *entitled* to take account of other matters, *e.g.* facts of which it can take judicial cognisance and which therefore do not require to be established by evidence.

[**22.48**] The statutory provisions do not indicate in which direction a particular factor should incline a court to move. In some cases, this is not difficult to infer. It may be assumed, for example, that if the debtor is immature, senile, mentally unstable or lacking in business experience, this will go to support a contention that the credit bargain is extortionate, for the court may then be ready to assume that a high rate of charge was imposed not so much because the debtor was a poor risk but because the creditor was taking advantage of the debtor's mental state or ability or lack of experience.

But what if the debtor suffers physical ill-health or is under acute financial pressure? On the one hand, these are conditions which make him particularly vulnerable to acceptance of a harsh agreement; but on the other hand, it is these self-same conditions that may generate a pressing need for financial assistance, whilst making it difficult for the debtor to obtain credit because of his poor income prospects. Such is sometimes the case, for example, where a householder who is heavily in debt borrows money at higher rates not for some extravagance but to pay the electricity bill and thus avoid disconnection of the electricity supply. Is the existence of pressures of this kind to be taken as strengthening the likelihood that the credit bargain is extortionate or, on the contrary, as showing because of the need and the risks involved the interest rate, though high, is not unreasonable? No hard and fast rules can be laid down. Clearly the existence of a particular factor may sway the court in either direction, and the court must simply assess the totality of the evidence and form a value judgment as to whether, taking account of all the circumstances, the bargain is or is not extortionate.

[**22.49**] There is a potential difficulty for credit grantors in that as a rule tariffs of interest rates and finance charges are constructed not according to the personal characteristics or finances of a particular debtor (since the assessment of a separate rate for each individual transaction would be quite impracticable for all except the smallest credit granting institutions) but on the basis of external factors, *e.g.* the cost of money, the nature of the goods to be acquired with a purchase money credit (such as hire-purchase or conditional sale) and whether such goods are new or second-hand. Inevitably, therefore, there will be some debtors on whom, by reason of the factors mentioned in s. 138 (3), rates fixed by a standard tariff will bear more hardly than in the case of other debtors. The court should, it is submitted, seek to avoid a result in which the use of standard charges which are reasonable in themselves is jeopardised because of the prospect that particular debtors may, on account of their own personal circumstances, find their specific agreements burdensome to them. In short, in deciding whether the presence of one of the factors mentioned in s. 138 makes a credit bargain extortionate, the court should consider whether such factor influenced the rate of charge or the other terms of the credit bargain. If it did not, then in general it would seem reasonable to hold that the credit bargain is not made extortionate by reason only of that factor. This approach, which leaves credit-granting institutions free to continue the convenient practice of establishing and maintaining standard rates, is consistent with the requirement built into s. 138 (1) that for a credit bargain to be extortionate, the charges must be "grossly exorbitant" or the agreement must otherwise "grossly" contravene the ordinary principles of fair dealing.

[**22.50**] The particular factors referred to in s. 138 (2)–(4) do not call for further comment, except in relation to the factor mentioned in s. 138 (4) (*c*), namely "whether or nor a colourable cash price was quoted for any goods or services included in the credit bargain". This factor was mentioned in order to alert the court to the possibility that part of an apparently reasonable credit charge may in fact be concealed in an inflated cash price, as where goods are sold on credit sale at a specified cash price greater than would ordinarily be charged by a person selling goods of the like description for cash (cf. s. 45 of the

Act, discussed in paras. [**6.13**] *et seq.*). The effect of inflating the cash price is twofold. First, it enables the creditor to receive the same return while reducing the charges component of the total price. Secondly, it reduces the proportion which such charges bear to the cash price, so that the stated rate of charge is still more misleading.

### ONUS OF PROOF

[**22.51**] If, in proceedings referred to in s. 141 (1), the debtor or any surety alleges that the credit bargain is extortionate it is for the creditor to prove the contrary (s. 171 (5)). This provision applies however low the rate of interest or charge and even if it is a rate which makes the credit agreement an exempt agreement under regulations made pursuant to s. 16 (5) (*b*).

### NATURE OF RELIEF GIVEN

[**22.52**] Section 139 (2) provides as follows:

"In reopening the agreement, the court may, for the purpose of relieving the debtor or a surety from payment of any sum in excess of that fairly due and reasonable, by order—

(*a*) direct accounts to be taken, or (in Scotland) an accounting to be made, between any persons,
(*b*) set aside the whole or part of any obligation imposed on the debtor or a surety by the credit bargain or any related agreement,
(*c*) require the creditor to repay the whole or part of any sum paid under the credit bargain or any related agreement by the debtor or a surety, whether paid to the creditor or any other person,
(*d*) direct the return to the surety of any property provided for the purposes of the security, or
(*e*) alter the terms of the credit agreement or any security instrument."

An order may be made under s. 139 (2) notwithstanding that its effect is to place a burden on the creditor in respect of an advantage unfairly enjoyed by another person who is a party to a linked transaction (s. 139 (3)). An illustration of the effect of this provision is given in paragraph [**19.14**].

[**22.53**] An order under section 139 (2) is not to alter the effect of any judgment (s. 139 (4)). Hence, once the creditor has obtained judgment against the debtor for recovery of a loan or enforcement of a security, the debtor is obliged to meet the judgment and cannot secure his discharge by reliance on s. 139 (2). Such a principle is necessary in order to ensure the finality of judicial proceedings. But the court retains its normal power, by virtue of statutes, rules of court and its inherent jurisdiction, to set aside a judgment in a proper case, as where it is a judgment entered in default of appearance (R.S.C. Order 13, r. 9) or defence (R.S.C. Order 19, r. 9; C.C.R. Order 37, r. 3) or given in the absence of the defendant (R.S.C. Order 35, r. 2; C.C.R., Order 37, r. 2) or set aside consequent on an order for a new trial (R.S.C. Order 59, r. 11; County Courts Act 1959, s. 113 (1); C.C.R. Order 37, r. 1).

UNREGULATED CREDIT AGREEMENTS

[**22.54**] Section 140 provides that where the credit agreement is not a regulated agreement expressions used in ss. 137–139 which, apart from s. 140, apply only to regulated agreements, are to be construed as nearly as may be as if the credit agreement were a regulated agreement. The drafting of this section is defective, since there is only one expression used in ss. 137–139 which is peculiar to a *regulated* agreement, namely a "linked transaction", but there are several expressions applicable only to *consumer credit* or *consumer hire* agreements (which are not necessarily regulated agreements, since they may be exempt under s. 16), *i.e.* "creditor", "debtor", "security" and "surety". Obviously the court must employ in relation to these expressions the same approach as is required by s. 140 in relation to linked transactions.

SELECTION OF COUNTY COURT BY CREDITOR

[**22.55**] Section 49 of the Hire-Purchase Act 1965 provided that actions by the owner or seller for recovery of protected goods or actions for recovery of goods brought before one-third of the hire-purchase price or total purchase price had been paid or tendered, were to be brought into the county court district in which the hirer or buyer "resides or carries on business, or resided or carried on business at the date on which he last made a payment under the hire-purchase agreement or conditional sale agreement". No such provisions are contained in the Consumer Credit Act, and the place of commencement of proceedings is left to be governed by Order 2 of the County Court Rules.

DECLARATORY ORDERS

[**22.56**] In addition to its general power to grant declarations (which unless otherwise provided by statute is exercisable only where the declaration is claimed as ancillary to a claim that is otherwise within the county court's jurisdiction—*De Vries* v. *Smallridge*, [1928] 1 K.B. 482), the county court may make various declaratory orders under s. 142 of the Consumer Credit Act, which provides as follows:

"(1) Where under any provision of this Act a thing can be done by a creditor or owner on an enforcement order only, and either—

(*a*) the court dismisses (except on technical grounds only) an application for enforcement order, or

(*b*) where no such application has been made or such an application has been dismissed on technical grounds only, an interested party applies to the court for a declaration under this subsection,

the court may if it thinks just make a declaration that the creditor or owner is not entitled to do that thing, and thereafter no application for an enforcement order in respect of it shall be entertained.

(2) Where—

(*a*) a regulated agreement or linked transaction is cancelled under section 69 (1), or becomes subject to section 69 (2), or

(*b*) a regulated agreement is terminated under section 91,

and an interested party applies to the court for a declaration under this subsection, the court may make a declaration to that effect."

# CHAPTER 23

# ANCILLARY CREDIT BUSINESSES

## THE CONTROL

[**23.1**] Part X of the Consumer Credit Act regulates various kinds of ancillary credit business whose activities are connected to the provision of credit or hire facilities to individuals. The broad effect of Part X is:

(i) to subject all these forms of business to the licensing provisions of Part III of the Act;
(ii) to impose in relation to certain classes of ancillary credit business the same kind of requirements and restrictions as to the seeking of business as are imposed in relation to consumer credit and consumer hire businesses by Part IV of the Act;
(iii) to restrict to the sum of £1 brokerage fees recoverable by credit-brokers in cases where no credit agreement ensues within six months after the introduction effected by the credit-broker;
(iv) to provide for regulations as to ancillary credit agreements;
(v) to provide the consumer with various forms of protection in relation to information filed with credit reference agencies.

## "ANCILLARY CREDIT BUSINESS"

[**23.2**] By s. 145 (1) an ancillary credit business is any business insofar as it comprises or relates to—

(*a*) credit brokerage,
(*b*) debt-adjusting,
(*c*) debt-counselling,
(*d*) debt-collecting, or
(*e*) the operation of a credit reference agency.

Each of these forms of activity is defined, and we shall examine the definitions in the following paragraphs.

## CREDIT BROKERAGE

[**23.3**] Credit brokerage is in essence the effecting of introductions of individuals seeking credit or goods on rental to those whose business involves the grant of consumer credit or consumer hire facilities or who themselves carry on business as credit-brokers. The definition of credit brokerage contained in s. 145 (2)–(4) is so framed as to control not only introductions to creditors and owners extending such facilities under regulated agreements but also introductions to creditors and owners offering those facilities under certain classes of exempt agreement and certain types of unregulated agreement.

[**23.4**] Credit-brokers within the statutory definition cover not only the traditional type of loan and mortgage broker but a vast range of other credit intermediaries, including motor dealers and retail shops and stores who introduce retail customers to finance houses for hire-purchase, credit sale, conditional sale or rental facilities or personal loans; solicitors who regularly engage in negotiating advances for non-corporate clients; and estate agents who as part of their business introduce prospective house purchasers to building societies or other prospective mortgagees. There are two qualifications. First, barristers, and solicitors engaging in contentious business, are not on that account to be treated as carrying on the business of credit brokerage or indeed any ancillary business (s. 146 (1), (2)). Secondly, s. 146 (5) provides that for the purposes of s. 145 (2), introductions effected by an individual by canvassing off trade premises either debtor-creditor-supplier agreements falling within s. 12 (*a*) or regulated consumer hire agreements shall be disregarded if—

(*a*) the introductions are not effected by him in the capacity of an employee, and
(*b*) he does not by any other method effect introductions falling within s. 145 (2).

Hence agents engaged by check traders to canvass trading check applications are not on that account credit-brokers, nor are housewives who as part-time agents for mail-order companies canvass applications from those wishing to acquire goods on credit sale from the companies concerned.

DEBT-ADJUSTING

[**23.5**] Section 145 (5) provides as follows:

"Subject to section 146 (6), debt-adjusting is, in relation to debts due under consumer credit agreements or consumer hire agreements—

(*a*) negotiating with the creditor or owner, on behalf of the debtor or hirer, terms for the discharge of a debt, or
(*b*) taking over, in return for payments by the debtor or hirer, his obligation to discharge a debt, or
(*c*) any similar activity concerned with the liquidation of a debt."

Again, the scope of this definition is much wider than appears at first sight. It covers not only those whose main business is that of debt-adjustment but (subject to s. 146 (6)—see para. [**23.10**]) solicitors and accountants who negotiate on behalf of clients in respect of debts owed by such clients to third parties, and banks who as part of their business provide overdrafts to customers in replacement of overdrafts previously outstanding from such customers to other banks.

[**23.6**] As with credit brokerage, there are certain exemptions. A barrister engaged for clients in negotiating settlement of debts is not a credit-broker

(s. 146 (1)); nor is a solicitor *insofar as he is thereby engaging in contentious business* (s. 146 (2)). This qualification largely stultifies the exemption given to solicitors. It means that solicitors whose negotiations on behalf of the debtors are successful in avoiding proceedings require to be licensed as debt-adjustors to conduct such negotiations, whereas solicitors conducting negotiations on behalf of the debtor in respect of debts which are or become the subject of an action are not thereby acting as debt-adjustors and do not require to be licensed! Further exemptions from the definition of debt-adjusting are contained in s. 146 (6) (see para. [**23.10**]).

DEBT-COUNSELLING

[**23.7**] Subject to s. 146 (6) (see para. [**23.10**]), debt-counselling is the giving of advice to debtors or hirers about the liquidation of debts due under consumer credit agreements or consumer hire agreements (s. 145 (6)). First this covers any debt-counsellor who regularly advises for reward, whether he be a full-time debt-counsellor, a solicitor (if advising in relation to non-contentious business), an accountant or a banker. Secondly, by virtue of the definition of "business" in s. 189 (1) of the Act, the term "debt-counsellor" includes those whose *profession* is the giving of advice of the kind above mentioned. It is immaterial that such advice is given without fee or other reward. Thus, Citizens' Advice Bureaux, Neighbourhood Law Centres and other free legal advice organisations are debt-counsellors within the Act even though giving advice without charge. But such organisations are likely to qualify for a group licence under s. 22 (1) (*b*). See also para. [**23.11**].

DEBT-COLLECTORS

[**23.8**] Subject to s. 146 (6) (see para. [**23.10**]), debt-collecting is the taking of steps to procure payment of debts due under consumer credit agreements or consumer hire agreements (s. 145 (7)). Once more, this definition is not confined to the commercial debt-collection organisation but covers, for example, solicitors collecting debts for clients without recourse to proceedings and professional receivers and liquidators of companies (but not trustees in bankruptcy—see para. [**23.10**]). Also within the term "debt-collector" are those who collect debts which they have purchased (see para. [**23.10**]).

CREDIT REFERENCE AGENCIES

[**23.9**] A credit reference agency is a person ("person" includes a company—see Interpretation Act 1889, s. 19) carrying on a business comprising the furnishing of persons with information relevant to the financial standing of individuals, being information collected by the agency for that purpose (s. 145 (8)). It is only those furnishing information *collected for that purpose* who are within the statutory definition. Hence a bank supplying references is not a credit reference agency, even though such activity is the normal part of its business, since the information in its possession concerning the customer is not collected for the purpose of being supplied to third parties. Indeed, a bank is under a duty not to disclose any information about a customer to a third party without the consent of the customer.

FURTHER EXEMPTIONS

**[23.10]** Section 146 (6) provides that it is not debt-adjusting, debt-counselling or debt-collecting for a person to do anything in relation to a debt arising under an agreement if—

(*a*) he is the creditor or owner under the agreement, otherwise than by virtue of an assignment, or
(*b*) he is the creditor or owner under the agreement by virtue of an assignment made in connection with the transfer to the assignee of any business other than a debt-collecting business, or
(*c*) he is the supplier in relation to the agreement, or
(*d*) he is a credit-broker who has acquired the business of the person who was the supplier in relation to the agreement, or
(*e*) he is a person prevented by sub-s. (4) from being treated as a credit-broker, and the agreement was made in consequence of an introduction (whether made by him or another person) which, under sub-s. (4), is to be disregarded.

It should be observed that the exemption in favour of the creditor or owner is confined to the original creditor or owner or one who becomes such by operation of law (*e.g.* on death or bankruptcy of the original creditor or owner) as opposed to assignment of the debt. Those who buy debts at a discount and in due course proceed to collect in the debts thereby become debt-collectors. These include not only commercial buyers of bad debts but also finance houses discounting hire-purchase, instalment sale and rental agreements from dealers; factors who factor debts outstanding from sole traders or partnerships; professional receivers appointed by debenture holders (this would seem to be so even though they are as a matter of law agents of the mortgagor company to whom the debts are owed); and professional liquidators (since the property of a company in liquidation, including debts owed to it, remains vested in the company and does not pass to the liquidator so as to make him the creditor by operation of law). The licence required by the professional liquidator as a debt-collector is, of course, quite distinct from any licence required by the company of which he is appointed liquidator in respect of the consumer credit or ancillary credit activities of that company. On the other hand, the professional trustee in bankruptcy does not become a debt-collector solely by reason of collecting in debts due to the bankrupt's estate, since he becomes the creditor otherwise than by assignment, the property of the bankrupt vesting in him automatically by operation of law under the provisions of s. 18 of the Bankruptcy Act 1914.

LICENSING OF ANCILLARY CREDIT BUSINESS

**[23.11]** The provisions of Part III (except s. 40) apply to an ancillary credit business as they apply to a consumer credit business (s. 147 (1)). It is likely that certain categories of ancillary credit business will qualify for a group licence, *e.g.* solicitors engaged in debt-counselling or debt-collecting.

AGREEMENT FOR SERVICES OF UNLICENSED TRADER

[**23.12**] An agreement for the services of a person carrying on an ancillary credit business (the "trader"), if made when the trader was unlicensed, is enforceable against the other party (the "customer") only where the Director has made an order under s. 148 (2) which applies to the agreement (s. 148 (1)). The trader or his successor in title may apply to the Director for an order that agreements within s. 148 (1) are to be treated as if made when the trader was licensed (s. 148 (2)). Before refusing an application in the terms in which it is made the Director must, under s. 148 (3), give the trader reasons for the intended refusal and invite representations in accordance with s. 34. See paras. [**5.38**] *et seq.*, as to the similar procedure in regard to applications by those carrying on a consumer credit or consumer hire business. Section 148 (4) provides that in determining whether or not to make an order under s. 148 (2) in respect of any period the Director shall consider, in addition to any other relevant factors—

(*a*) how far, if at all, customers under agreements made by the trader during that period were prejudiced by the trader's conduct,
(*b*) whether or not the Director would have been likely to grant a licence covering that period on an application by the trader, and
(*c*) the degree of culpability for the failure to obtain a licence.

By s. 148 (5), if the Director thinks fit, he may in an order under s. 148 (2)—

(*a*) limit the order to specified agreements, or agreements of a specified description or made at a specified time;
(*b*) make the order conditional on the doing of specified acts by the trader.

REGULATED AGREEMENTS MADE ON INTRODUCTION OF UNLICENSED CREDIT-BROKER

[**23.13**] It behoves creditors to ensure that credit-brokers from whom they obtain business are duly licensed. Section 149 (1) and (2) provides as follows:

"(1) A regulated agreement made by a debtor or hirer who, for the purpose of making that agreement, was introduced to the creditor or owner by an unlicensed credit-broker is enforceable against the debtor or hirer only where—

(*a*) on the application of the credit-broker, the Director has made an order under section 148 (2) in respect of a period including the time when the introduction was made, and the order does not (whether in general terms or specifically) exclude the application of this paragraph to the regulated agreement, or
(*b*) the Director has made an order under subsection (2) which applies to the agreement.

(2) Where during any period individuals were introduced to a person carrying on a consumer credit business or consumer hire business by an unlicensed credit-broker for the purpose of making regulated agreements with the person carrying on that business, that person or his successor in title may apply to the Director for an order that regulated agreements so made are to be treated as if the credit-broker had been licensed at the time of the introduction."

The procedure to be adopted where the Director is minded to refuse the application, the factors he is to take into account and the limitations and conditions he may impose in any order he makes, follow the language of s. 148 (3)–(5), with the omission of s. 148 (4) (*b*).

APPEALS

[**23.14**] A disappointed applicant is given a right of appeal to the Secretary of State, and thence on a point of law to the High Court, pursuant to s. 41 as applied by s. 150. See generally paras [**5.51**] *et seq.*

SEEKING BUSINESS

[**23.15**] Sections 151–154 broadly apply the provisions of Part IV (relating to advertising, canvassing, quotations, the display of information and regulations for the conduct of business) to the seeking of business by those engaged in the business of credit brokerage, debt-adjusting and debt-cancelling. Section 154 makes it an offence to canvass off trade premises (as defined by s. 153) the services of a person carrying on a business of credit brokerage, debt-adjusting or debt-cancelling.

BROKERAGE FEES

[**23.16**] Evidence was given to the Crowther Committee of serious abuses in the charging of commission by brokers for supposedly undertaking to endeavour to procure a loan, knowing that there was little or no prospect of their succeeding. Perhaps the most remarkable case was the charging of a £20 survey fee to arrange the survey of a council house tenanted by the debtor to see if this would be suitable security for a second (!) mortgage! Section 155 tackles this problem by providing that if within six months following the introduction of an individual to a prospective creditor the introduction does not result in the individual's entry into a relevant agreement (as defined by the section) the whole of the brokerage fee except for the sum of £1 shall cease to be payable or, as the case may be, shall be recoverable, by the individual.

ENTRY INTO AGREEMENTS

[**23.17**] Regulations may make provision, in relation to agreements entered into in the course of a business of credit brokerage, debt-adjusting or debt-counselling, corresponding, with such modifications as the Secretary of State thinks fit, to the provision which is or may be made by or under s. 55, 60, 61, 62, 63, 65, 127, 179 or 180 in relation to agreements to which those sections apply (s. 156).

CREDIT RECORDS

[**23.18**] The Crowther Committee devoted much attention to problems arising in connection with credit records, and in particular the difficulties facing a consumer who did not know why he was being refused credit facilities and against whom adverse information might have been filed that was in some way erroneous or indeed should have been filed not against him at all but against some other person with whom he had been confused (see Crowther Report, paras. 9.1.9–9.1.28). Further study of these problems was made by the Younger Committee on Privacy, which recommended (*inter alia*) that an individual should have a legally enforceable right of access to information held about him by a credit reference agency (see *Report of the Committee on Privacy* (Cmnd. 5012, July 1972), Chapter 9, and in particular paragraph 275).

[**23.19**] The recommendation of the Younger Committee has been adopted in strengthened form by the Consumer Credit Act, which confers on an individual the following rights:

(i) The right to obtain from a creditor, owner or negotiator (and from a prospective creditor or owner) the name and address of any credit reference agency from whom the former has, during antecedent negotiations, applied for information about the individual's credit standing (s. 157 (1)—see para. [**23.20**]);

(ii) The right to obtain from the credit reference agency a copy of the file relating to him, on tender of prescribed particulars and a fee of 25p (s. 158 (1)—see paras. [**23.21**] *et seq.*);

(iii) The right to require erroneous information on the file to be removed or amended (s. 159—see paras. [**23.23**] *et seq.*).

In addition, regulations under s. 26 of the Act (as applied by s. 147 (1)) may include provisions regulating the collection and dissemination of information by credit reference agencies (s. 147 (2)).

DISCLOSURE OF NAME AND ADDRESS OF AGENCY

[**23.20**] Section 157 provides as follows:

"(1) A creditor, owner or negotiator, within the prescribed period after receiving a request in writing to that effect from the debtor or hirer, shall give him notice of the name and address of any credit reference agency from which the creditor, owner or negotiator has, during the antecedent negotiations, applied for information about his financial standing.

(2) Subsection (1) does not apply to a request received more than 28 days after the termination of the antecedent negotiations, whether on the making of the regulated agreement or otherwise.

(3) If the creditor, owner or negotiator fails to comply with subsection (1) he commits an offence."

"Creditor" and "owner" include a prospective creditor and a prospective owner, and "debtor or hirer" includes a prospective debtor or hirer (s. 189 (1)).

SUPPLY OF COPY OF FILE

[**23.21**] Subject to s. 160 (see para. [**23.22**]) a credit reference agency, within the prescribed period after receiving a request in writing to that effect from any individual (the "consumer") and such particulars as the agency may reasonably require to enable them to identify the file, and a fee of 25p, must give the consumer a copy of the file relating to him kept by the agency (s. 158 (1)). By "file" is meant, in relation to an individual, all the information about him kept by a credit reference agency, regardless of how the information is stored, and "copy of the file", as respects information not in plain English, means a transcript reduced into plain English (s. 158 (5)). This latter provision is designed to cover, for example, information which is in coded form or which consists of expressions or abbreviations familiar to those in the trade but not readily comprehensible by others. When giving a copy of the file, the agency must also give the consumer a statement in the prescribed form of his rights under s. 159 (s. 158 (2)), relating to the correction of wrong information (see para. [**23.23**]). If the agency does not keep a file relating to the consumer it must give him notice of that fact, but need not return any money paid (s. 158 (3)). If the agency contravenes any provision of s. 158 it commits an offence (s. 158 (4)).

[**23.22**] The above provisions, if left in unqualified form, might seriously have hampered the ability of a credit reference agency to provide an effective service to its subscribers concerning business consumers, *i.e.* debtors or hirers who were sole traders or partnerships. The particular difficulty envisaged by the trade was that since supply of a copy of the complete file would almost inevitably reveal the agency's sources of information, those sources, having given the information in confidence, might decline to provide such information in the future. To deal with this situation, s. 160 provides an alternative procedure as regards the business consumer, by empowering the Director, on application by the agency, to direct that the business consumer, instead of being given a copy of the file, shall be given only such information included in or based on entries in the file as the Director may direct. By s. 160 (1) the Director may only accede to such an application if he is satisfied—

(*a*) that compliance with s. 158 in the case of consumers who carry on a business would adversely affect the service provided to its customers by the agency, and

(*b*) that, having regard to the methods employed by the agency and to any other relevant factors, it is probable that consumers carrying on a business would not be prejudiced by the making of the direction.

The business consumer dissatisfied with the information he receives may ask the Director to direct that a copy of the file be sent to the Director, who may then disclose to the consumer such information on the file as the Director thinks fit (s. 160 (4)).

## CORRECTION OF WRONG INFORMATION

[**23.23**] Section 159 contains elaborate provisions entitling the consumer to give a notice to the credit reference agency requiring incorrect information on the file to be removed or amended and to be notified by the agency within twenty-eight days of such notice of the action it has taken (s. 159 (1), (2)). Where the entry has not been removed the consumer may, within the time laid down in s. 159 (3), require a corrective notice not exceeding two hundred words to be added to the file. The agency must then either give notice that it intends to comply or apply to the Director for an order waiving or relaxing compliance on the ground that the proposed notice of correction is incorrect or unjustly defames any person or is frivolous or scandalous or is for any other reason unsuitable (s. 159 (5)). Similarly, the consumer who has not received notice from the agency within the permitted time confirming its receipt of the corrective notice or intention to comply with it may apply to the Director (*ibid.*). In either such case the Director may make such order on the application as he thinks fit (*ibid.*). Non-compliance with such an order within the time therein specified is an offence (s. 159 (6)).

DEFAMATION AND QUALIFIED PRIVILEGE

**[23.24]** If a credit reference agency publishes (*i.e.* communicates to a third party) a defamatory statement concerning a consumer which is untrue, then if the statement is in writing the consumer may (subject to certain defences) sue for damages for libel, even if he has suffered no special damage; and if the statement is oral, the consumer may (subject to the same defences) sue for damages for slander on showing that he has suffered special damage or that the imputation is made against him in the way of his business or office or conveys that he has committed a criminal offence or suffers from an existing contagious or infectious disease or, in the case of a woman, that she is unchaste.

**[23.25]** Among the various defences to an action for defamation are justification and qualified privilege. Justification is a plea that the defamatory statement complained of is true; and if this be the case, it is a complete defence to a civil claim for libel, though not to a prosecution for criminal libel. Even if the defamatory statement is untrue, the defendant may be able to defeat the plaintiff's claim by establishing that the statement was made on an occasion of qualified privilege. The principal classes of statement attracting qualified privilege, apart from reports of Parliamentary, judicial and certain other public proceedings and professional communications between solicitor and client, are (i) statements made by the defendant under a legal, moral or social duty to communicate them and so made to a person having a corresponding interest or duty to receive the statements; and (ii) statements made by the defendant in the protection of some lawful interest and made to a third party who has a corresponding legal, moral or social duty to protect that interest. But in both cases, the privilege is qualified only, and accordingly subsists only so far as the defamatory statement is made honestly and without "malice" (*i.e.* improper motivation) and the publication of it is no wider than is reasonable for the fulfilment of the duty or the protection of the interest in question.

**[23.26]** Whether trade protection societies and other credit reference agencies are entitled to plead qualified privilege in answer to a claim based on their publication to third parties of defamatory statements concerning individuals on their files has never been finally settled. In *Macintosh* v. *Dun*, [1908] A.C. 390, the Judicial Committee of the Privy Council held that the privilege was not available to a trade protection society which carried on business as such for profit, whether its income was derived from subscriptions or from charges made on the occasion of each supply of information. The distinction drawn in this case between protection societies who (while making charges to cover their expenses) do not conduct business for profit and provide information as a service to their subscribers and protection societies operating as commercial concerns selling information to any who wish to buy it derived support from dicta in judgments of the House of Lords in *London Association for Protection of Trade* v. *Greenlands, Ltd.*, [1916] 2 A.C. 15. Nevertheless, *Macintosh* v. *Dun* (which is of persuasive authority only in an English Court) almost certainly overstated the case if it decided that the profit motive inevitably and in all circumstances negates the existence of a social or legal duty to communicate. Plainly a duty of communication imposed by statute must be observed; and even at common law, the communication made by the defendant may be made pursuant to a duty to do so, despite the fact that he carries on the business of disseminating information for profit. See *Watt* v. *Longsdon*, [1930] 1 K.B. 130, *per* Scrutton, L.J., at p. 148. We take up this matter further in paragraph [**23.29**].

[**23.27**] The Younger Report (para. 275), in recommending that a person refused credit on the basis of an agency report should be entitled to have details of the filed information and its sources, went on to say:

> " 'A pre-requisite of these arrangements would be the extension of qualified privilege to profit-seeking, commercial credit bureaux. A convenient moment for providing this protection would arise when the Faulks Committee on the law of defamation reports.' "

[**23.28**] The Consumer Credit Act, though implementing that part of the Younger Committee's recommendations calling for disclosure of the filed information to the consumer, contains no provision extending qualified privilege to publications of credit reference agencies run for profit. The first version of the Consumer Credit Bill had in fact provided for qualified privilege to apply to the publication of any defamatory matter relating to the financial standing of an individual where published to a licensed credit reference agency for the purposes of its business or published by such an agency in the course of its business. But as a result of opposition in Committee, this provision was dropped. It is thus clear that the absence of any provision in the Consumer Credit Act extending qualified privilege to defamatory statements published by organisations conducted for profit is a deliberate policy decision, not merely a postponement of consideration of the matter pending the report of the Faulks Committee.

[**23.29**] What, then, is now the position of a credit reference agency controlled by the Consumer Credit Act? No difficulty arises concerning supply to the Director of a copy of the file in accordance with a direction made under s. 160 (4). This is mandatory, and manifestly attracts qualified privilege, even if the agency business be conducted for profit. It is equally clear that despatch to the consumer of information on his file containing statements defamatory of a third party does not attract qualified privilege by reason of any duty imposed by the Consumer Credit Act, since the duty is to supply a copy of "the file" and by s. 158 (5) this means, in relation to the individual who asks for it, all the information *about him*, but does not extend to information concerning others. But what are the rights of the consumer as regards defamatory statements made *about him* by or to a creditor reference agency run for profit? No duty is imposed *by the Act* to supply such information. It is, however, submitted that despite *Macintosh* v.

*Dun* such a communication, if made to a prospective credit grantor or other person having a legitimate interest in receiving it, is to be considered made on a privileged occasion. Time and again, the courts have rightly criticised a creditor for failing to make proper enquiries concerning the financial position of the debtor before giving him credit. The failure to pursue such enquiries not only makes the creditor the author of his own misfortune but produces highly undesirable social consequences through the extension of credit to those who are not creditworthy and lack either the ability or the will to repay what they borrow. The public interest therefore requires that information held by reputable agencies concerning the financial standing of prospective debtors should be readily available to prospective creditors. Equally, it is in the public interest that such agencies shall be able to perform their function by collecting necessary information from reputable sources without thereby rendering the providers of such information liable in damages for defamatory statements honestly made. The reputability of credit reference agencies engaged in the consumer credit sector will be secured by the licensing provisions of the Consumer Credit Act, as applied by s. 147, which also empowers regulations made under s. 26 of the Act to regulate the collection and dissemination of information by credit reference agencies. It is therefore submitted that information honestly and without malice published by a licensed credit reference agency to a prospective creditor or prospective owner, or to a negotiator, or published to a licensed credit reference agency by a reputable source, attracts qualified privilege even if the agency business is conducted for profit.

# CHAPTER 24

# OFFENCES AND ENFORCEMENT

## OFFENCES

[**24.1**] The Act creates thirty-five offences. These, with mode of prosecution and penalty, are tabulated in the Second Schedule to the Act. They include not only offences referred to in the preceding chapters but infringement of regulations (s. 167 (2)), impersonation and obstruction of enforcement authority officers, and supply of false information to such officers, in contravention of the provisions of Part XI discussed in the present chapter. The Act also makes it an offence (in s. 7) to supply false information to the Director. The duty of enforcement and the power to prosecute for offences are conferred on the Director and on local weights and measures authorities (see paras. [**24.8**] *et seq.*).

## DEFENCES

[**24.2**] Section 168 provides as follows:

"(1) In any proceedings for an offence under this Act it is a defence for the person charged to prove—

(*a*) that his act or omission was due to a mistake, or to reliance on information supplied to him, or to an act or omission by another person, or to an accident or some other cause beyond his control, and

(*b*) that he took all reasonable precautions and exercised all due diligence to avoid such an act or omission by himself or any person under his control.

(2) If in any case the defence provided by subsection (1) involves the allegation that the act or omission was due to an act or omission by another person or to reliance on information supplied by another person, the person charged shall not, without leave of court, be entitled to rely on that defence unless, within a period ending seven clear days before the hearing, he has served on the prosecutor a notice giving such information identifying or assisting in the identification of that other person as was then in his possession."

This section reproduces almost verbatim s. 24 of the Trade Descriptions Act 1968, though the first line of s. 168 (1) (*a*) refers to "his act or omission" rather than "the commission of the offence" in order to avoid the paradox of predicating an offence when, by reason of the defence given, there is no offender. The controversial decision of the House of Lords in *Tesco Supermarkets, Ltd.* v. *Nattrass*, [1972] A.C. 153; [1971] 2 All E.R. 127, establishes that a company charged with an offence may be able to treat even one of its own employees as "another person" within s. 168 (1) (*a*) where the employee is not a director or other person of such seniority or responsibility as to represent the controlling mind and will of the company but is merely a junior executive or employee (whether or not exercising supervisory functions) who is the instrument for executing company policy as dictated by his superiors. Hence if a company institutes an effective system to avoid the commission of an offence, delegating to competent employees the duty to see that the system is scrupulously adhered to by junior staff, an infringing act or omission committed by a junior member of the staff does not defeat a defence under s. 168 (1) even if resulting from failure of the superior employee to exercise proper supervision. The company is entitled to contend that such employee, as well as the junior he was supposed to supervise, is "another person" within s. 168 (1) (*a*) and that accordingly it is not the company that has failed to exercise due diligence within s. 168 (1) (*b*). Similar principles apply to any large-scale organisation, even if not in corporate form.

[**24.3**] By "mistake" in s. 168 (1) (*a*) is meant the mistake of the person charged, not of some other person (*Birkenhead and District Co-operative Society, Ltd.* v. *Roberts*, [1970] 3 All E.R. 391). Hence if the act or omission which is the subject of the prosecution is alleged to be due to the default of a third party, the defendant cannot avoid the requirements of s. 168 (2) by relying on that default as a "mistake" of the third party attracting a distinct head of defence. The combined effect of this decision and that of the House of Lords in *Tesco Supermarkets, Ltd.* v. *Nattrass*, *supra*, would seem to be that a company prosecuted for the mistaken act or omission of an executive or employee who does not represent the controlling mind and will of the company, and is thus "another person" within s. 168 (1) (*a*), cannot plead that act or omission as a "mistake" within s. 168 (1) (*a*) but must rely fairly and squarely on the defence of "act or default of another person" and for that purpose comply with the requirements of s. 168 (2).

[**24.4**] The purpose of s. 168 (2) is to enable the prosecution to test the validity of the defence of "act or default of another person" by calling that other person as a witness. The subsection has the incidental effect that if the act or omission of such person resulting in the act or omission of the defendant is itself an offence under the Act, that other person can be identified and prosecuted for that offence. It should, however, be noted that s. 23 of the Trade Descriptions Act 1968 (which provides that where the commission by any person of an offence under the Act is due to the act of default of another, that other shall be guilty of an offence) has no counterpart in the Consumer Credit Act. Accordingly the mere fact that the act or omission of A causes B to omit an act required by the statutory provisions or to perform an act prohibited by such provisions, does not of itself make A guilty of an offence. It must be shown that A himself contravened a specific provision of the Consumer Credit Act, either as a principal or as an accomplice under criminal law through aiding and abetting or counselling and procuring the offence or as one who consents to or connives at the offence within s. 169 (see para. [**24.5**]).

OFFENCES BY BODY CORPORATE

**[24.5]** Section 169 of the Act provides that where at any time a body corporate commits an offence under the Act with the consent or connivance of, or because of neglect by, any individual, the individual commits the like offence if at that time—

(*a*) he is a director, manager, secretary or similar officer of the body corporate, or
(*b*) he is purporting to act as such an officer, or
(*c*) the body corporate is managed by its members, of whom he is one.

This provision is the counterpart of s. 20 (1) of the Trade Descriptions Act 1968. By "manager" is meant one who manages the affairs of the company, not, for example, the manager of a particular shop or store in a chain of shops or stores owned by the company. See the decision of the Divisional Court in *Tesco Supermarkets, Ltd.* v. *Nattrass*, [1972] A.C. 153; [1970] 3 All E.R. 357, which on this point was not challenged in the House of Lords.

NO FURTHER SANCTIONS FOR BREACH OF ACT

**[24.6]** A breach of any requirement made (otherwise than by any court) by or under the Act incurs no civil or criminal sanction as being such a breach, except to the extent (if any) expressly provided by or under the Act (s. 170 (1)). This provision does not prevent the grant of an injunction, or the making of an order of certiorari, mandamus or prohibition (s. 170 (3)).

NOTIFICATION OF CONVICTIONS TO DIRECTOR

**[24.7]** The original version of the Consumer Credit Bill conferred on the Court power to endorse the licence of a person convicted by that Court of an offence under the Act. This provision was subsequently dropped. Section 166 merely provides that where a person is convicted of an offence or has a judgment given against him by or before any court in the United Kingdom and it appears to the court—

(*a*) having regard to the functions of the Director under this Act, that the conviction or judgment should be brought to the Director's attention, and
(*b*) that it may not be brought to his attention unless arrangements for that purpose are made by the court,

the court may make such arrangements notwithstanding that the proceedings have been finally disposed of.

ENFORCEMENT OF ACT

**[24.8]** A specific duty to enforce the Act is imposed on "the enforcement authorities", i.e. the Director and local weights and measures authorities (s. 161 (1)). Consequent on the re-organisation of local government effected by the Local Government Act 1972, the number of local weights and measures authorities (as defined by s. 201 (2) and (3) of that Act) has been reduced to 36, and the area of each such authority has in consequence been greatly increased.

[**24.9**] Whereas under the Weights and Measures Act 1963, a local weights and measures authority must appoint weights and measures inspectors to perform the functions of the authority in its area, no such requirement applies to functions of local weights and measures authorities under the Trade Descriptions Act or the Consumer Credit Act. Hence whilst in most cases such authorities will no doubt delegate the task of enforcement of the Consumer Credit Act to weights and measures inspectors, as they have done in relation to their functions under the Trade Descriptions Act, they are not obliged to do so, and may empower any officer of the authority to enforce the provisions of the Consumer Credit Act.

[**24.10**] It has been a common practice for local weights and measures authorities to combine or make joint arrangements in exercising their functions under the Weights and Measures Act 1963 and the Trade Descriptions Act 1968, in reliance on powers previously contained in s. 37 of the Weights and Measures Act. The powers conferred by s. 37 have now been brought to an end by s. 201 (5) of the Local Government Act 1972, but that Act empowers any local authority (including, of course, a local authority which is a weights and measures authority) to arrange for the discharge of any of its functions by another local authority (s. 101 (1) (*b*)), and for two or more authorities to discharge any of their functions jointly (s. 101 (5)) and for that purpose to appoint joint committees (s. 102 (1)). Hence local weights and measures authorities continue to have ample powers to act in concert in the performance of their functions, including those imposed upon them by the Consumer Credit Act.

### LOCAL ENFORCEMENT

[**24.11**] In general, prosecutions by a local enforcement authority will be confined to contraventions arising within the area of the authority, though an authority is technically not debarred from launching a prosecution in respect of an offence committed in the area of another authority. Offences of a purely local character will usually be left by the Director to the initiative of local enforcement authorities, whilst his own staff will deal mainly with more widespread contraventions—*e.g.* advertising infringements in national newspapers—and with cases (whether local or otherwise) which in his opinion raise important questions of general policy. To ensure that the Director is kept in the picture as to local enforcement, and to avoid a multiplicity of prosecutions by different authorities arising from the same act of infringement committed in different areas, s. 161 (2) of the Consumer Credit Act (borrowing from s. 30 (2) of the Trade Descriptions Act 1968) provides as follows:

> "Where a local weights and measures authority in England or Wales propose to institute proceedings for an offence under this Act (other than an offence under section 162 (6), 165 (1) or (2) or 174 (5)) it shall, as between the authority and the Director, be the duty of the authority to give the Director notice of the intended proceedings, together with a summary of the facts on

which the charges are to be founded, and postpone institution of the proceedings until either—

(*a*) 28 days have expired since that notice was given, or

(*b*) the Director has notified them of receipt of the notice and summary."

[**24.12**] The duty to give notice to the Director is a duty only as between the authority and the Director, so that non-compliance with s. 161 (2) cannot be set up as a defence to a prosecution. It should also be noted that the local enforcement authority does not require the *consent* of the Director to institute proceedings. It suffices that the Director has been notified of the intended prosecution and given a summary of the facts and that such notification and summary were given at least twenty-eight days prior to the institution of proceedings or have been acknowledged by the Director. The Director does not appear to have any power under the Act to require a local enforcement authority to prosecute or to desist from an intended prosecution, unless such power can be inferred from s. 1 (1) (*c*) of the Act, which seems doubtful. However, every local weights and measures authority is obliged, whenever the Director requires, to report to him in such form and with such particulars as he requires on the exercise of their functions under the Act (s. 161 (3)). Moreover, the Director (or indeed anyone) can make a complaint to the Secretary of State that the functions of a local weights and measures authority under the Act are not being properly discharged in any area, and the Secretary of State may thereupon order a local inquiry, the results of which must be reported back to the Secretary of State and published by him with such observations on it (if any) as he thinks fit (s. 161 (4), (5)).

### POWERS OF ENTRY, INSPECTION AND SEIZURE

[**24.13**] As under the Weights and Measures Act and the Trade Descriptions Act, wide powers are conferred on a duly authorised officer of an enforcement authority to inspect goods, enter any premises (other than those used only as a dwelling), require the production of books and documents and take copies, and seize and detain goods (s. 162 (1)). Banks are not exempt from subjection to these provisions; but a barrister or solicitor cannot be compelled to produce a document containing a privileged communication made by or to him in that capacity, nor can the powers conferred by s. 162 be used to seize any such document in his possession (s. 162 (7)). The enforcement provisions relate to suspected *breaches* of the Act, thus covering purely civil breaches as well as criminal offences.

[**24.14**] Section 163 (1) provides that where in exercising his powers under s. 163 an officer of an enforcement authority seizes and detains goods and their owner suffers loss by reason of—

(*a*) that seizure, or

(*b*) the loss, damage or deterioration of the goods during detention,

then, unless the owner is convicted of an offence under the Act committed in relation to the goods, the authority shall compensate him for the loss so suffered. Any dispute as to the right to or amount of any compensation under s. 163 (1) is to be determined by arbitration (s. 163 (2)). Such an arbitration is governed by the Arbitration Act 1950, and involves reference to a single arbitrator (*ibid.*, ss. 6, 31 (1)). If a party fails to concur in the appointment of an arbitrator, or the arbitrator refuses to act, and such failure or refusal continues for seven days after service of a notice to the other party, or to the arbitrator, as the case may be, to appoint or concur in the appointment of the arbitrator, an arbitrator may be appointed by the High Court or a Judge thereof (*ibid.*, s. 10).

[**24.15**] Section 164 of the Act, like s. 27 of the Trade Descriptions Act provides that an enforcement authority may—

(*a*) make, or authorise any of their officers to make on their behalf, such purchases of goods; and

(*b*) authorise any of their officers to procure the provision of such services or facilities or to enter into such agreements or other transactions,

as may appear to them expedient for determining whether any provisions made by or under the Act are being complied with. The power to test goods extends to goods seized under the Act, and in that event the person from whom they are seized must be informed of the test results (s. 164 (3)). Where any test leads to proceedings under the Act, the enforcement authority must, under s. 164 (4)—

(*a*) if the goods were purchased, inform the person they were purchased from of the test results, and

(*b*) allow any person against whom the proceedings are taken to have the goods tested on his behalf if it is reasonably practicable to do so.

### OBSTRUCTION OF AUTHORISED OFFICER

[**24.16**] It is an offence wilfully to obstruct an officer of an enforcement authority acting in pursuance of the Act or to fail to comply with any requirement properly made by such an officer under s. 162 of the Act or give such an officer (so acting) other assistance or information he may reasonably require in performing his functions under the Act (s. 165 (1)). The giving of information knowing it to be false is also an offence (s. 165 (2)). But a person cannot be required to answer any question or give any information if to do so might incriminate that person or (where that person is married) the husband or wife of that person (s. 165 (3)).

[**24.17**] Wide though the provisions are, they are not unlimited. An offence is committed only where the officer is, in one of the ways indicated above, obstructed in the performance of his functions under the Act. Hence if, for example, an authorised officer calls for the production of books when reasonably suspecting that a particular act has been committed and in the erroneous belief that such an act would contravene the statutory provisions when as a matter of law it would not, refusal to produce the books to him would not be an offence (see, for example, *John* v. *Matthew*, [1970] 2 Q.B. 443; [1970] 2 All E.R. 643, a decision on s. 29 (1) (*a*) of the Trade Descriptions Act 1968).

### FALSE INFORMATION TO THE DIRECTOR

[**24.18**] A person who, in connection with any application or request to the Director under the Act, or in response to any invitation or requirement of the

Director under the Act, knowingly or recklessly gives information to the Director which, in a material particular, is false or misleading, commits an offence (s. 7).

CONSUMER ADVICE POWERS OF LOCAL AUTHORITIES

[**24.19**] By s. 201 (8) of the Local Government Act 1972, a local weights and measures authority may make, or assist in the making of, arrangements to provide advice to or for the benefit of consumers of goods and services within the area of the authority. This is a very useful provision which many authorities are expected to invoke.

# CHAPTER 25

# OTHER DUTIES OF THE DIRECTOR

### THE ROLE OF THE DIRECTOR

[**25.1**] The Act confers extensive powers, and imposes many duties, on the Director General of Fair Trading. The Director himself has, of course, other heavy tasks to perform under the Fair Trading Act 1973, and although he remains responsible for the operation of the Consumer Credit Act and the performance of the duties imposed on him by it, these matters will largely be delegated to a full-time director appointed by him for that purpose. Nevertheless, the Director himself will doubtless wish to keep an overall view of activities under the Consumer Credit Act and to take or influence major policy decisions relating to its administration and enforcement.

### GENERAL FUNCTIONS OF THE DIRECTOR

[**25.2**] Two of the most important functions of the Director are administration of the licensing system and supervision of enforcement of the Act. These duties are spelled out in s. 1 (1) of the Act, which provides as follows:

"It is the duty of the Director General of Fair Trading ('the Director')—

(*a*) to administer the licensing system set up by this Act,
(*b*) to exercise the adjudicating functions conferred on him by this Act in relation to the issue, renewal, variation, suspension and revocation of licences, and other matters,
(*c*) generally to superintend the working and enforcement of the Act, and regulations made under it, and
(*d*) where necessary or expedient, himself to take steps to enforce this Act, and regulations so made."

But crucial though these functions are, they are by no means the sole functions of the Director. Other important duties are imposed on him by ss. 1 (2) and 4.

[**25.3**] By s. 1 (2):

"It is the duty of the Director, so far as it appears to him to be practicable and having regard both to the national interest and the interests of persons carrying on business to which this Act applies and their customers, to keep under review and from time to time advise the Secretary of State about—

(*a*) social and commercial developments in the United Kingdom and elsewhere relating to the provision of credit or bailment or (in Scotland) hiring of goods to individuals, and related activities; and (*b*) the working and enforcement of this Act and orders and regulations made under it."

The reference to the national interest envisages that the Director shall have regard to the effect of consumer credit on the national economy, thereby obliquely involving him in the assessment of the effect of terms control operated under the Hire-Purchase and Credit Sale Agreements (Control) Order 1973 and the Control of Hiring Order 1973. Additional functions may be conferred on the Director by the Secretary of State (s. 2 (1)), who may give general directions indicating considerations to which the Director should have particular regard in carrying out his functions under the Act, and specific directions on any matter connected with the carrying out by the Director of those functions (s. 2 (2)).

[**25.4**] Section 4 requires the Director to arrange for the dissemination, in such form and manner as he considers appropriate, of such information and advice as it may appear to him expedient to give to the public in the United Kingdom about the operation of the Act, the credit facilities to him, and other matters within the scope of his functions under the Act. This is an extremely important aspect of the Director's work, enabling the Director to engage in activities designed to educate the consumer in relation to credit matters (a task the need for which was emphasised in the Crowther Report) and to provide information to Citizens' Advice Bureaux and other advisory organisations which can be passed on by them to members of the public consulting them

[**25.5**] Under s. 125 (1) of the Fair Trading Act 1973, the Director is required, as soon as practicable after the end of the year 1974 and of each subsequent calendar year, to make to the Secretary of State a report on his activities, and the activities of the Advisory Committee and of the Commission, during that year. Every such report must include a general survey of developments during the year to which it relates, in respect of matters falling within the scope of the Director's duties under any enactment (s. 125 (2), including, of course, the Consumer Credit Act, and must set out any directions given to the Director under s. 2 (2) of the Consumer Credit Act during that year (Fair Trading Act, s. 125 (2) as amended by Consumer Credit Act, s. 5).

### POWER TO VARY OR REVOKE DETERMINATIONS

[**25.6**] By s. 183 of the Consumer Credit Act, the Director may vary or revoke any determination or direction made or given by him under the Act, other than Part III or Part III as applied by s. 147. Within s. 183 are for example, directions under ss. 60 (3) and 101 (8) and determinations under ss. 64 (4) and 74 (3).

# CHAPTER 26

# TRANSITIONAL PROVISIONS

## COMMENCEMENT, AMENDMENTS AND REPEALS

[**26.1**] The commencement and transitional provisions of the Act are contained in the Third Schedule to the Act, and amendments to and repeals of other legislation are contained in the Fourth and Fifth Schedules respectively. The Act will be brought into operation in phases, on days to be appointed by order of the Secretary of State; and any such order must include a provision amending the Third Schedule so as to insert an express reference to the day appointed (s. 192 (2)). Similarly, the Secretary of State may by order provide for the coming into operation of the amendments contained in the Fourth Schedule, and the repeals contained in the Fifth Schedule, and these amendments and repeals will have effect only as provided by an order so made (s. 192 (4)).

[**26.2**] Except as otherwise provided by the Third Schedule, the provisions of the Act came into operation on its passing, that is, on the (Third Schedule, Note). The transitional provisions are discussed in the following paragraphs. Unless otherwise indicated, paragraph numbers given in parentheses are the numbers of the relevant paragraphs of the Third Schedule.

## THE NORMAL RULE

[**26.3**] The general principle embodied in the Third Schedule is that agreements, and acts and events occurring in relation to agreements and to parties to agreements, will not attract a provision of the Act if made, done or occurring:

(*a*) in the case of a provision becoming operative on the passing of the Act, before the passing of the Act; and

(*b*) in the case of a provision coming into force on an appointed day, before that day.

The Third Schedule (save where it wishes to do otherwise—see paras. [**26.5**]–[**26.6**]) achieves this result:

(i) by a general provision in paragraph 1 that an agreement made before the day appointed for the purposes of that paragraph is not a regulated agreement within the meaning of the Act, and that in the Act a "prospective regulated agreement" does not include a prospective agreement which, if made as expected, would be made before the day appointed for the purposes of that paragraph;

(ii) by omitting, in the paragraph providing for an appointed day in relation to a particular section, any reference to agreements made, etc., before that appointed day; and

(iii) by omitting any provision giving retrospective effect to those provisions of the Act coming into force on the passing of the Act.

The combined effect of (i) and (ii) is that where a transitional paragraph dealing with a section of the Act refers to a regulated agreement or a prospective regulated agreement without adding words indicating retrospective effect (see para. [**26.5**]), it necessarily confines the scope of that section to agreements or prospective agreements, and matters done in relation to agreements or prospective agreements, made on or after the day appointed for the purpose of the transitional paragraph in question or (in some cases) the day appointed for the purpose of paragraph 1 of the Third Schedule. Similarly, a provision of the Act which is not deferred to an appointed day but comes into operation on the passing of the Act has no retrospective effect, since neither in the body of the Act nor in the Third Schedule is any retrospective effect given to any such provision.

[**26.4**] Sections of the Act coming into operation on appointed days but having no effect on, or in relation to, agreements made before the appointed days in question (or in some cases, before the day appointed for the purposes of paragraph 1 of the Third Schedule) include the following:

(*a*) Part III of the Act, relating to licensing (see also para. [**5.62**]).

(*b*) Section 19, as regards transactions linked to consumer credit or consumer hire agreements made before the day appointed under paragraph 1 of the Third Schedule (but the position is otherwise as regards linked transactions made before that day in relation to a regulated agreement as defined by the Act and made on or after that day—see para. [**26.6**]).

(*c*) Section 56, as regards antecedent negotiations in relation to consumer credit or consumer hire agreements made before the day appointed under paragraph 1 (see para. 12 (1)).

(*d*) Section 75, relating to the liability of a creditor for misrepresentations and breaches by the supplier. By virtue of paragraph 1 of the Third Schedule, this does not impose any liability on a creditor under a credit agreement made before the day appointed for the purposes of paragraph 1.

(*e*) Sections 90 and 91, relating to protected goods. These sections will thus not apply to goods comprised in a hire-purchase or conditional sale agreement made before the day appointed for the purposes of Part VII of the Act, so that in relation to such agreements the restrictions on repossession imposed by those sections will not apply (see para. 35).

(*f*) Section 93, which restricts default interest under a regulated consumer credit agreement to the contract rate. This will not apply to agreements made before the day appointed for the purposes of Part VII of the Act (see para. 35).

(*g*) Sections 99–101, relating to the right of termination of a hirer or buyer under a hire-purchase, conditional sale or hiring agreement, and his liability on termination. These will not apply to the agreements made before the day appointed for the purposes of Part VII (para. 5).

(*h*) Section 102, relating to agency for receiving notices of rescission. This will similarly not apply to agreements made before such appointed day (see para. 35).

(*i*) Sections 105 and 106 relating to securities and 123–125, relating to negotiable instruments. By virtue of paragraph 1 of the Third Schedule, these sections will not affect securities or negotiable instruments given in relation to a credit or hire agreement made before the day appointed for the purposes of paragraph 1.

[**26.5**] There are, however, a number of provisions which, by virtue of the Third Schedule, have an impact on agreements made before those provisions are brought into operation, and the effect of the Third Schedule in such cases is that the agreements in question are affected even if made before the passing of the Act. The Third Schedule employs two different formulae to achieve this result:

(i) A provision that a given section of the Act (when brought into operation on the appointed day) shall apply to, or in relation to, an agreement "whenever made";

(ii) A provision that a given section of the Act (when brought into operation on the appointed day) shall apply "to an agreement made before the day appointed for the purposes of this paragraph where the agreement would have been a regulated agreement if made on that day."

Except that formula (i) is not necessarily confined to agreements that would have been regulated agreements, the two formulae produce the same result, namely of applying the stated section not only to agreements made before the relevant appointed day but even to agreements made before the passing of the Act. Formula (ii) achieves this just as effectively as formula (i), since in effect it applies the section in question to any agreement, *whenever made*, where it would have been a regulated agreement if made on the day appointed for the purpose of that section.

[**26.6**] Among the provisions of the Act which are given retrospective effect in this way by the Third Schedule are the following sections, which in each case, on being brought into operation, apply to, or in relation to, agreements whenever made:

(*a*) Section 19 (other than s. 19 (3)), as regards transactions linked to a regulated agreement or prospective regulated agreement as defined by paragraph 1 of the Third Schedule (see para. 2).

(*b*) Section 20, relating to regulations as to the total charge for credit (see para. 4).

(*c*) Section 51 (3), conferring an exemption from s. 51 (1) in relation to unsolicited credit-tokens (see para. 11 (2)).

(*d*) Section 76, dealing with notices to be served before a creditor or owner, exercises certain contractual rights otherwise than by reason of breach (para. 16 (2)).

(*e*) Sections 83 and 84 (restricting the debtor's liability for misuse by others of credit facilities or credit-tokens), as regards losses suffered by the creditor on or after the day appointed for the purposes of those sections (para. 20).

(*f*) Section 85, relating to the creditor's duty to supply documents on issue of new credit-tokens (para. 21 (2)).

(*g*) Section 86, imposing restrictions on exercise of remedies arising by reason of the death of the debtor or hirer (para. 22 (2)).

(*h*) Sections 87 and 88, relating to default notices (para. 35).

(*i*) Section 92, relating to entry on premises for the purpose of repossessing goods comprised in a hire-purchase or conditional sale agreement (para. 35).

(*j*) Sections 94–97, relating to rebates for early settlement (para. 35).

(*k*) Section 98, requiring at least seven days' notice before termination of an agreement otherwise than for default (para. 35).

(*l*) Sections 107–109, requiring information to be supplied to sureties (para. 37 (2)).

(*m*) Section 110, requiring a copy of a security instrument to be supplied to a debtor or hirer (*ibid.*).

(*n*) Section 111, relating to service of a copy of a default notice on a surety (para. 38 (2)).

(*o*) Sections 137–140, relating to extortionate credit bargains (para. 42).

# CHAPTER 27

# MISCELLANEA

A concluding assortment for those who have stayed the course!

ONUS OF PROOF

[**27.1**] Section 171 provides as follows:

"(1) If an agreement contains a term signifying that in the opinion of the parties section 10 (3) (*b*) (iii) does not apply to the agreement, it shall be taken not to apply unless the contrary is proved.

(2) It shall be assumed in any proceedings, unless the contrary is proved, that when a person initiated a transaction as mentioned in section 19 (1) (*c*) he knew the principal agreement had been made, or contemplated that it might be made.

(3) Regulations under section 44 or 52 may make provision as to the onus of proof in any proceedings to enforce the regulations.

(4) In proceedings brought by the creditor under a credit-token agreement—

(*a*) it is for the creditor to prove that the credit-token was lawfully supplied to the debtor, and was accepted by him, and

(*b*) if the debtor alleges that any use made of the credit-token was not authorised by him, it is for the creditor to prove either—

(i) that the use was so authorised, or

(ii) that the use occurred before the creditor had been given notice under section 84 (3).

(5) In proceedings under section 50 (1) in respect of a document received by a minor at any school or other educational establishment for minors, it is for the person sending it to him at that establishment to prove that he did not know or suspect it to be such an establishment.

(6) In proceedings under section 119 (1) it is for the pawnee to prove that he had reasonable cause to refuse to allow the pawn to be redeemed.

(7) If, in proceedings referred to in section 139 (1), the debtor or any surety alleges that the credit bargain is extortionate it is for the creditor to prove the contrary."

Of these various provisions, the last subsection, relating to extortionate bargains, is likely to occasion the most difficulty (see paras [**22.3**] *et seq.*).

BINDING NATURE OF STATEMENTS AND NOTICES

[**27.2**] The effect of s. 172 (1) is that subject to the power of the court to give relief under s. 172 (see para. [**27.3**]), a statement by a creditor or owner is binding on him if given under—

sections 77 (1), 78 (1) and 79 (1) (provision of information to debtors and hirers);

section 97 (1) (information to debtor as to figure for early settlement);

sections 107 (1), 108 (1) (*c*), 109 (1) (*c*) (provision of information to sureties).

By section 172 (2) a notice given by a trader to a customer in compliance with s. 103 (1) (*b*) (relating to termination statements) or asserting under s. 103 that the customer is not indebted to him, is binding on the trader, subject, again, to the provisions of s. 172 (3) (see para. [**27.3**]).

[**27.3**] The provisions of s. 172 could operate very harshly on a creditor or trader sending a statement or notice understating the indebtedness of the debtor or customer or erroneously stating that no sum was outstanding. Errors of this kind are inevitable in the light of human frailty, coupled with the enormous volume of credit business and the problems of feeding information into, and extracting information from, the computers that have become the standby of the modern financial world. Some margin of error is allowed for in the sections listed in s. 172 (1), since these sections only require the creditor's statement to show specified amounts "according to the information to which it is practicable for him to refer". This allows a certain amount of latitude where, for example, the creditor would have difficulty in furnishing information that was completely up to date, but it does not cover errors in accounts. Section 172 (3) deals with this problem by empowering the court, when a statement or notice relied on in proceedings is shown to be incorrect, to direct such relief (if any) to be given to the creditor or owner from the operation of s. 172 (1) and (2) as appears to the court to be just.

### NO CONTRACTING OUT OF ACT

[**27.4**] Section 173 of the Act deals with contracting out. The marginal note misleadingly describes the effect of the section as forbidding contracting out. This is true only in the sense that a contract term inconsistent with a provision for the protection of the debtor or hirer or his relative is void (s. 173 (1)). The inclusion of a void exclusion clause is not as yet a criminal offence, though it may become an offence if the Secretary of State makes an order under s. 22 of the Fair Trading Act 1973, on a reference by the Director under ss. 14 and 17 of that Act, prohibiting misleading exclusion clauses, as he is empowered to do (see *ibid.*, Sixth Schedule, paragraphs 1, 3). Nothing in s. 173 (1) prevents a thing being done in relation to any person which would ordinarily require an order of the court or the Director if that person gives his consent at the time (s. 173 (3)).

### CONFIDENTIALITY OF INFORMATION

[**27.5**] Section 174 contains provisions prohibiting the disclosure of information obtained under or by virtue of the Act about any individual or any business except with the consent of the individual or of the person for the time being carrying on the business (s. 174 (1)). Certain exceptions to this rule are made by s. 174 (3). Disclosure of information in contravention of s. 174 is an offence (s. 174 (5)).

DUTY OF DEEMED AGENTS

[**27.6**] Section 175 provides that where under the Act a person is deemed to receive a notice or payment as agent of the creditor or owner under a regulated agreement, he shall be deemed to be under a contractual duty to the creditor or owner to transmit the notice, or remit the payment, to him forthwith. The effect of this enigmatic provision is obscure. It is a general principle of agency law that where an agent receives notice of a fact which he owes a duty to communicate to his principal, the latter is deemed to have received notice of that fact as from the time when he would have received notice if the agent had duly performed his duty to communicate (*Proudfoot* v. *Montefiore* (1867), L.R. 2 Q.B. 511). But it is far from clear how this principle is to be applied in relation to those provisions of the Consumer Credit Act to which s. 175 is relevant. There is no provision in the Act at all making any person a deemed agent of the creditor or owner to receive a payment, so that the reference to payment in s. 175 appears to be totally without effect. There are only three provisions by which a person is deemed to receive a notice as agent of the creditor or owner, namely ss. 57 (3), 69 (6) and 102 (1), relating respectively to the debtor's or hirer's withdrawal from a prospective regulated agreement, cancellation of a regulated agreement and asserted right of rescission of a regulated agreement otherwise than by service of a notice of cancellation. Section 69 (7) provides that "whether or not it is actually received by him, a notice of cancellation sent by post to a person shall be deemed to be served on him at the time of posting". (This section does not apply to notice of withdrawal (see para. [**8.10**]).) It is scarcely conceivable that the Act intended to cut down the protection formerly available to the debtor or hirer by restricting the operation of s. 69 (7) to a notice posted to the creditor or owner personally, so as to exclude posting to the deemed agent under ss. 69 (6) and 57 (4); for the consequence of this would be that a notice of cancellation posted by the debtor to the deemed agent would not be considered given to him until received by him, and if it failed to arrive then it would not constitute notice to the creditor or owner. A notice under s. 102 is not deemed to be given at the time of posting, so that as regards such a notice the principle in *Proudfoot* v. *Montefiore* could be invoked. The effect would be that the principal would be deemed to have received the notice at the time he would have received it if it had been transmitted by the agent "forthwith". This does not mean instantaneously—for the law does not command the impossible—but at the earliest available moment. The same applies to a notice under s. 57 (1).

[**27.7**] It is therefore submitted that in relation to a notice of cancellation served under s. 69 of the Act, s. 175 does not change what has always been assumed to be the effect of s. 12 of the Hire-Purchase Act 1965, that notice to the deemed agent is notice to the creditor or owner and therefore if sent by post takes effect when posted to the agent. If this be right, the only effect of s. 172 in relation to a notice of cancellation (as opposed to a notice of withdrawal) would seem to be to confer on a creditor or owner who suffers loss through failure of the deemed agent to perform his deemed contractual duty a right to damages as for breach of contract.

SERVICE OF DOCUMENTS

[**27.8**] Section 176 sets out detailed rules as to the method of service of documents required to be served under the Act. Subsections (5) and (6) have the effect (*inter alia*) that a default notice given after the death of the debtor or hirer is validly served if addressed to him, even if the creditor or owner knows that he has died (and see para. [**21.12**]). These are self-explanatory, and the only comment that needs to be made is that (save in the case of s. 176 (5)) s. 176 deals only with the *mode* of service, not the deemed *time* of service. As previously noted, a notice of cancellation under s. 69, if sent by post, is deemed to be served at the time of posting (see para. [**27.6**]). Other notices sent by post, *e.g.* a notice of withdrawal under s. 57, are governed by s. 26 of the Interpretation Act 1889, which provides that where an Act authorises or requires a document to be served by post, whether the expression "serve" or the expression "give" or "send", or any other expression, is used, then unless the contrary intention appears the service shall be deemed to be effected by properly addressing, prepaying and posting a letter containing the document. The same section goes on to state that unless the contrary is proved, service is deemed to have been effected at the time at which the letter would be delivered in the ordinary course of post. It has, however, been held that evidence to rebut the presumption of service in the ordinary course of post is admissible only where the time of service, as opposed to the mere fact of service, is relevant, so that as regards statutory provisions which require or authorise service of a document by post but do not stipulate the time at or by which this has to be received, evidence that the document was enclosed in a prepaid letter properly addressed and posted establishes service for the purpose of such provisions, and the addressee cannot rely on the second limb of s. 26 (*i.e.* the words "unless the contrary is proved") to rebut the deemed service, which is effective even if the document goes astray in the post and never reaches the addressee (*Moody* v. *Godstone Rural District Council*, [1966] 2 All E.R. 696).

REGULATIONS AND ORDERS

[**27.9**] Sections 179–182 empower regulations to be made:

(*a*) as to the form and contents of credit-cards, trading checks and other such "secondary documents" (s. 179);

(*b*) as to the form, content and supply of copies of documents referred to in the Act (s. 180);

(*c*) amending the Act so as to increase or reduce sums mentioned in various provisions, including the £5,000 limit of application of the Act (s. 181) (but such regulations require an affirmative resolution of each House of Parliament (s. 181 (2));

(*d*) to differentiate between cases and classes of case in any regulations made (s. 182).

# APPENDIX A

# A NOTE ON TRUTH IN LENDING

## INTRODUCTION

[**A.1**] In its *Report on Consumer Credit* (Cmnd. 4596, March 1971), the Crowther Committee strongly recommended that in consumer credit advertisements and agreements the cost of the credit, covering not only the pure interest element but all other borrowing costs (including those to be incurred by the borrower under ancillary contracts for services where the borrower was not free to choose his own supplier of such services) should be stated in terms of a true annual percentage rate, thus enabling the borrower more readily to compare the cost of borrowing from one lender with the cost of borrowing from another, and to evaluate the relative costs of different forms of credit and of contracts of different payment periods.

[**A.2**] This recommendation will be implemented by regulations to be made under ss. 20 (1), 44 (1) and 60 (1) of the Consumer Credit Act; and the proposed content of the regulations, with formulae, is set out in Appendices I and II to the White Paper on *Reform of the Law on Consumer Credit* (Cmnd. 5427, September 1973). Crucial to the computation of a rate, as well as to the calculation of the £5,000 ceiling fixed by the Act, is the definition of the total charge for credit, that is, a sum calculated in accordance with regulations made under s. 20 (1) of the Act (see s. 189 (1) and Chapter 3, paras. [**3.17**]–[**3.18**]).

[**A.3**] This Note explains briefly what is meant by a true annual percentage rate and the different purposes served by the various formulae set out in paragraphs 9.4 and 11.4 of the above-mentioned Appendices. For greater detail, the reader should refer to Appendix IV to the Crowther Report and to R. M. Goode, *Hire-Purchase Law and Practice* (2nd edn.), Appendix A.

## THE FLAT RATE AND THE EFFECTIVE RATE

[**A.4**] It has for many years been common, when quoting a rate of interest or charge, to quote a flat rate, that is, a rate which is applied to the original loan figure, even where the loan is to be repaid by instalments and will thus not be outstanding in full throughout the agreed period for repayment. A flat rate may be an add-on rate or a discount rate. An add-on rate is that which is applied to the sum actually handed over to the borrower, or applied for his benefit, as where the borrower borrows £100 and repays by instalments over twelve months the total sum of £110, producing a flat rate of 10 per cent. A discount rate is a flat rate applied to a figure from which the amount of the discount is deducted at the outset, as where a loan of £100 is repayable by instalments over twelve months at a discount of 10 per cent. deducted from the advance, so that the sum the borrower receives is only £90. The discount rate is 10 per cent., but the equivalent add-on rate is $\frac{10}{90} \times 100$, *i.e.* 11.1 per cent., since the true amount of the loan is not £100 but £90.

[**A.5**] Both the add-on rate and the discount rate are seriously misleading (the latter more so than the former), since the stated rate takes no account of the diminution of the principal indebtedness through repayment by instalments but is geared throughout to the original advance (in the case of the add-on rate) or the original advance before deduction of the discount (in the case of the discount rate). Since the average amount outstanding throughout a loan contract providing for repayment by equal instalments at equal intervals is only one-half of the original advance plus one-half of one instalment, the effective annual rate (before compounding—see para. [**A.7**]) is nearly double the flat rate.

## THE ACTUARIALLY COMPUTED RATE

[**A.6**] Since interest (and we shall use this term for convenience, whilst making it clear that we are thereby referring to the cost to the borrower, not the net return to the lender) is a function of funds in use, it is axiomatic that interest must reduce as the principal indebtedness diminishes. There are any number of methods, of varying degrees of accuracy, by which interest may be notionally spread over a contract so as to reflect reductions in the principal indebtedness (a reasonably accurate method, if the loan period is not too long and the rate not too high, is that incorporated in the First Schedule to the Advertisements (Hire-Purchase) Act 1967), but there can be only one "true" rate, and that is a rate computed actuarially on the basis that the ratio of interest to funds in use, *i.e.* at the service of the borrower, is completely constant throughout the repayment period. The contract may, of course, be expressed to provide that interest shall be taken by the creditor in full at the outset (in which event it is in truth a discount) or shall be collected with the final instalment of principal or shall be spread evenly across the contract period; but such a provision is merely a convenient method of expressing the payment obligation and cannot alter the mathematical concept of interest, so that a stated rate computed on the basis of accrual of interest by any of such methods will not in fact be a true rate. For an illustration of a true rate computation, in which the ratio of accrued interest to principal outstanding at the end of each payment period is uniform throughout the contract, see M. R. Neifeld, *Neifeld's Guide to Instalment Computations* (Mack Publishing Co., Easton, Pennsylvania), p. 176, showing an interest spread table which is reproduced in R. M. Goode, *op. cit.*, p. 1004, Table 5.

## THE NOMINAL ANNUAL RATE

[**A.7**] A common method of arriving at an effective annual rate is to compute the rate for one payment period, utilising an actuarial spread, and then to multiply the period rate by the number of payment periods in a year. Thus if the actuarially calculated period rate is, for example, 1 per cent. per month, this is converted to produce an annual rate of 12 per cent. per year. This annual rate is known as the nominal annual rate, and is that used in Tables prepared by the United States Federal Reserve Board under Regulation Z, pursuant to the Consumer Credit Protection Act. Such a rate, though relatively accurate where the contract term is limited in duration and the frequency of payments is not too great, is not suitable in other cases for comparing rates payable under contracts of different length and payment frequency, since it fails to take account of the fact that a borrower who pays interest of 1 per cent. a month at the end of each month is parting with the use of the money represented by his interest payments earlier than the borrower who pays interest of 12 per cent. a year at the end of each year. The greater the payment frequency, the greater becomes the disparity between the nominal annual rate and a rate which takes this factor into account.

### THE ANNUAL RATE WITH ANNUAL COMPOUNDING

[**A.8**] To produce a true comparison between a rate of interest where interest is paid annually and a rate where interest is paid at the end of a different interval of time, it is necessary to introduce a compounding factor into the calculation, and thereby to compute what rate has to be paid by the borrower who pays interest at the end of a year in order for him to be paying the same effective rate as the borrower who pays interest at a different time or times. Use of compound interest tables would show, for example, that the true rate of interest paid by the borrower who pays 1 per cent. a month at the end of each month is not 12 per cent. *per annum* but 12·68 per cent. *per annum*, and that a borrower paying 3/13 per cent. a week at the end of each week would be paying a true annual rate of 12·76 per cent. If the nominal annual rate understates interest to the extent of 0·68 per cent. and 0·76 per cent. respectively when interest is pitched at this relatively modest level, the magnitude of the discrepancy when much higher rates and contract terms are involved becomes apparent. It is for this reason that a true picture can be provided only if a compounding factor is built into the calculation when the period rate is converted into the annual rate. This is so not only in relation to loans repayable by instalments but even in relation to single-repayment loans, where the period at the end of which the loan is to be repaid is greater or less than a year. It is only in the case of a loan for exactly a year repayable with interest at the end of the year that a simple interest formula will produce a completely accurate rate.

[**A.9**] The rates of 12·68 per cent. and 12·76 per cent. given in the above illustration represent the annual rate compounded annually. The phrase "compounded annually" denotes the yardstick by reference to which the period rate is being converted is a year. In other words, the annual rate compounded annually tells us what rate of interest a borrower paying at the end of a year would have to pay in order to be paying the equivalent of the borrower who pays the period rate per period. There is no mathematical magic in annual compounding. One could, for example, convert a monthly rate to the equivalent of an annual rate compounded semi-annually. The effective rate would then represent the rate which a debtor paying interest at half-yearly intervals would have to pay in order to be paying the same annual rate as the borrower who pays the contract period rate per period. But annual compounding is the conventional basis for comparison in the financial world, and is the basis employed in the Appendices to the White Paper. Unlike the nominal annual rate, it produces a true comparison between rates of interest charged under contracts of different length and/or different payment frequency.

## THE USE OF FORMULAE

[**A.10**] There is no mathematical formula by which the one true rate can be deduced from a stated amount of interest if the loan is repayable by more than three instalments; and for any loan other than a single-repayment loan the formula for the computation is extremely complex. Where more than three instalments are involved, the rate cannot be extracted by formula with complete precision since the equation that has to be set up contains an unknown quantity which makes the equation insoluble unless the rate desired to be ascertained is known in advance. An approximation can be obtained by eliminating the component from the formula on the basis that its quantity is so small as to make no significant difference to the result. But this is true only where the term of the contract is relatively short, and even then only up to a certain level of interest. Where these two conditions do not prevail, a completely true rate can be produced only by trial and error, by assuming a given rate as an approximation and then, if this is found to produce a figure above or below the actual amount of interest, adjusting the selected rate by a series of approximations so as to come ever closer to the right result. This can be done without undue difficulty by computer to any required degree of accuracy.

## RATE COMPUTATION IN REVOLVING CREDIT

[**A.11**] It will be obvious that in the case of revolving credit (or running-account credit, as it is termed in the Consumer Credit Act) a true rate in the sense predicated above cannot be stated in advance, since the actual rate of interest paid by the borrower depends on the manner in which he chooses to use the credit facility. A good illustration, in relation to a budget account, will be found in paragraph 6.5.20 of the Crowther Report:

> "Thus, in the case of an account on which charges are fixed on the balance carried forward from the end of the previous account period, it is theoretically open to the customer to secure one month's credit at no charge at all by making all his purchases on the first day of each account period and paying off his indebtedness on the last day of that period. On the other hand, if such a customer were to make his purchases on the last day of the account period, he would incur the full credit charge for that period without having enjoyed any credit at all. It follows from this that the actual cost of borrowing as a rate per cent cannot be stated for revolving accounts as it can for non-revolving instalment credit; and that the statement of a range of rates, from maximum to minimum, will not assist either, since the range will be from infinity to zero—a statement which would not be particularly helpful to the consumer."

[**A.12**] The White Paper adopts the solution advocated in paragraph 6.5.21 of the Crowther Report, namely to require the creditor to state in advance the basis of calculation of the credit charge (*e.g.* 1 per cent. per month on the balance outstanding at the end of the month) and the effective annual equivalent of the quoted period rate, on the basis of annual compounding. In other words, instead of computing the actual rate in fact paid by the customer after he has utilised the credit facility, one takes the period rate which is used as the basis of calculation of the charge and converts this into a true annual rate compounded annually, as described in paragraphs [**A.8**] and [**A.9**].

[**A.13**] With these explanatory remarks, the functions served by the formulae given in the Appendices to the White Paper should now become clear. The formulae are set out in paragraphs 9.4. and 11.4 of the Appendices (the two sets of formulae being identical) and are reproduced below.

*Formulae*—The annual percentage rate of charge would be:

(i) in all agreements of fixed-sum credit other than those mentioned in paragraphs (ii)–(iv) below, that at which the sum of the present values as at the date when the credit was made of repayments to be made by the debtor was equal to the amount borrowed. [For this purpose the present value at an annual rate of charge of i per cent of a sum payable in r years time would be taken to be that sum divided by $\left(1 + \frac{i}{100}\right)^r$, where r is expressed in complete years and/or fractions of a year.]*

(ii) in all agreements of fixed-sum credit where the instalments were of equal size and were to be repaid at equal intervals and the term of the credit did not exceed 48 months, it would be calculated by the following formula:

$$\frac{200\,md}{p\,(n+1) + \frac{d}{3}\,(n - 3m + 2)}$$

(iii) in all agreements of fixed-sum credit repayable in a lump sum (principal, interest and all charges), it would be calculated by the following formula:

$$100\left[\left(1 + \frac{d}{p}\right)^{\frac{1}{t}} - 1\right]$$

(iv) in all agreements of fixed-sum credit where the rate of charge/interest was computed on the balance outstanding but there was no pre-determined length of contract, repayment period or amount of instalment, the effective annual equivalent of the quoted period rate would have to be shown, calculated by the following formula:

$$100\left[\left(1 + \frac{x}{100}\right)^{y} - 1\right]$$

* "r" is an index and can be expressed as "the r[th] power of one-hundredth of that rate increased by unity".

(v) in all agreements of running-account credit the basis of the calculation of the period rate of charge would have to be shown, together with the effective annual equivalent of the period rate on the basis of annual compounding, calculated by the following formula:

$$100\left[\left(1+\frac{x}{100}\right)^{y}-1\right]$$

In the formulae quoted above:

m = number of instalments per annum
n = total number of instalments
p = amount borrowed
d = the charge for credit in cash terms calculated in accordance with paragraph 10
t = the term of the credit in years
x = period rate charged
y = number of periods in a year.

Taking each of the above in turn:

(i) is not in truth a formula for calculation of the true rate (since as we have seen, the perfect answer for a loan repayable by more than three instalments cannot be derived by formula—see para. [**A.10**]) but is an equation by which the accuracy of the stated rate can be tested. The equation will only be satisfied if the stated rate is correct. In other words, the sum of the present values (as at the date of the credit) of repayments to be made by the debtor at the stated rate will be equal to the amount borrowed only if the rate stated is a completely accurate figure.

(ii) is an approximation which produces the required degree of accuracy (*i.e.* accuracy within the tolerance to be permitted by the regulations) so long as the term of the credit does not exceed 48 months and also (though the White Paper omits this second important qualification) so long as that rate is not above a certain level (see para. [**A.10**]). The interaction between the two conditions (length of term and level of rate) will be taken into account when regulations are made. Subject to this, formula (ii) provides an appropriate short-cut within the two conditions stated.

(iii) is a formula for a loan to be repaid in a lump sum. Being a single-repayment loan, it is susceptible of a formula which will give a precise rate, and this is what is done by formula (iii), adoption of which would satisfy the equation in formula (i). Formula (iii) is more complex than the simple interest formula familiar to the schoolboy, which would not give an accurate result since, just as in the case of a loan repayable by instalments, a compounding factor has to be built into the formula to reflect the fact that the rate paid by one who repays in a lump sum at the end of a year is different from the rate paid by one who repays in a lump sum at the end of some other payment period (see para. [**A.8**]).

(iv) and (v), though dealing with different types of contract, embody the same formula, which is a formula for converting a stated period rate into the effective annual rate on the basis of annual compounding (see para. [**A.12**].

RATE TABLES

[**A.14**] The publication of official rate tables is under consideration. It is unfortunate that the Act makes no provision to confer on the Director General of Fair Trading power to approve and authorise the use of other rate tables prepared by or for credit-granting institutions. Such a power is conferred on the Federal Reserve Board by the Consumer Credit Protection Act, and is extremely useful in enabling a creditor to utilise tables constructed to reflect the duration, size and payment spread of transactions typical in his particular business.

# APPENDIX B

## REFORM OF THE LAW ON CONSUMER CREDIT, APPENDIX III

### REBATES FOR EARLY SETTLEMENT

THE RIGHT

1. Subject to the exceptions set out in paragraph 4 below, a debtor under an agreement for consumer credit for which any charge was made would be entitled to a minimum rebate of the charge for credit whenever full repayment of the credit was made, offered or required (no matter by whom and no matter whether by voluntary request, acceleration by contractual liability or court action) at a date earlier than originally anticipated in the contract. **[B.1]**

2. The "charge for credit" referred to above would include all the elements of charge to be included in the rate of charge calculations to be disclosed in an agreement, but with the one exception that in calculating the rebate creditors might, if they so wished, deduct from the charge any element that was payable as a registration fee for a mortgage of land or any other fee payable to the Land Registry. **[B.2]**

3. The refinancing by the original or a linked creditor (to be defined) of an existing indebtedness should be deemed to constitute an early settlement for the purpose of qualification for the rebate. **[B.3]**

EXCEPTIONS

4. There would be no requirement to provide a rebate in the following transactions:

(i) any fixed-sum credit facility where the amount of the credit was less than £30; or

(ii) any fixed-sum credit facility where the contractual life of the credit was 26 weeks or less. The fact that credit was expressed as being payable or repayable on demand should not render it as credit for a period of less than 26 weeks if the agreement, implicitly or explicitly, also included a provision either that the creditor at his discretion might permit payment by instalments over a period in excess of 26 weeks or the debtor had a contractual right to extend the date of repayment of the credit or part of the credit to a date beyond 26 weeks. **[B.4]**

5. Excluded from these rebate provisions by the definition in paragraph 1 would be:

(i) any fixed-sum credit transaction where the credit price was the same as the cash price; or

(ii) any running-account system which might only be used for restricted-use credit where the price charged to the consumer for the purchase under the facility was the cash price and no additional charge whatsoever was made for credit, the servicing of the account, the credit facility or any other items whatsoever; or

(iii) any credit facility where the debtor had the option of paying in full or by instalments and where the charge for credit was regularly added to the amount outstanding and repayments deducted, so that the total balance (principal and charges) outstanding at any time was known. (See also paragraph 19 below.) **[B.5]**

FORMULAE

6. Subject to paragraphs 8 and 10 below, the rebate would be ascertained by calculating, as at the date the credit was made, the sum of the products, for each instalment, of the amount of the instalments and the length of time before that instalment fell due; then making a similar calculation as at the date of repayment (or at such later date as might be permitted (see paragraph 18)); the ratio of the second amount to the first should then be applied to the total charge for credit to give the rebate. **[B.6]**

7. For example, if a credit of £100 was repayable by two instalments, one of £50 after six months from the date of contract and one of £60 after eight months from the date of contract and the debtor wished to repay after three months, the rebate (ignoring the loading factor in paragraph 18 below) would be:

$$\frac{£50 \times 3 + £60 \times 5}{£50 \times 6 + £60 \times 8} \times £10 \text{ (the total charge for credit)}$$

or $\frac{450}{780}$ of the total charge for credit of £10. **[B.7]**

8. Where the credit was repayable in equal instalments at regular intervals the rebate would be calculated by using "the Rule of 78"; viz. if there were originally n instalments and the debtor wished to pay the remaining instalments in one lump sum t intervals before the date of the final instalment (or such later date as might be permitted (see paragraph 18)), the rebate to which he would be entitled would be $\frac{t(t + 1)}{n(n + 1)}$ times the total charge for credit. **[B.8]**

9. For example, if credit of £100 was repayable by 11 monthly instalments of £10 and the debtor wished to repay at the end of the fifth month, n would be 11 and t would be 6, so that the rebate (ignoring the loading factor in paragraph 18 below) would be:

$$\frac{6(6 + 1)}{11(11 + 1)} \times £10 \text{ (the total charge for credit)}$$

or $\frac{42}{132}$ or $\frac{7}{22}$ of the total charge for credit of £10. **[B.9]**

10. Where repayment of the credit was envisaged by a lump sum (principal plus charge for credit) repayable at the end of an agreed period, the rebate would

be calculated by using the formula $\frac{a}{b}$ times the total charge for credit, where a = the period of the credit outstanding (or such later date as might be permitted (see para. 18)) and b = the original period of the credit. [**B.10**]

11. For example, if credit of £100 was repayable in 12 months' time with an interest charge of £10 and the debtor wished to pay after three months had elapsed, a would be 9 and b would be 12 so that the rebate (ignoring the loading factor in paragraph 18 below) would be:

$$\frac{9}{12} \times £10 \text{ (the total charge for credit).}$$ [**B. 11**]

RULES FOR THE APPLICATION OF THE FORMULAE

12. *Determination of Regular Contracts*—Any fixed-sum credit that was not repayable in equal payments might for these purposes be considered to be repayable by equal payments when the variation in repayments was not more than £5 or 20 per cent. of the amount payable in respect of any of the other instalments, whichever of these two amounts were the lesser. [**B.12**]

13. Any fixed-sum credit, repayable in quarterly, monthly or weekly instalments, where the length of time between the granting of the credit and the final repayment date was not an exact number of quarters, months or weeks, might, for these purposes, be considered as being for the nearer exact number. [**B.13**]

14. *Date of Quotation*—Save in credit repayable in a lump sum (where the rebate quotation would have to be calculated on the date the request was received) the rebate quotation would be calculated from the instalment due date nearest the date when the request was received (or the contractual liability became effective or on such date as a court might order). [**B.14**]

15. For example, in a monthly instalment contract, a request received on or before the 15th day following an instalment date should be treated as made on that instalment date; a request received on or after the 16th day following an instalment date should be treated as made on the next instalment date. [**B.15**]

16. *Variable Rate of Charge*—Where the rate of charge in the agreement was variable, the rebate would be calculated on the rate prevailing on the date the request for early settlement was received. [**B.16**]

17. *Date of Settlement*—Subject to paragraph 14, any settlement quotation would have to be based upon the state of the account between the parties on the day the quotation was made and would be binding on the parties for 21 days after it had been given. [**B.17**]

DEDUCTIONS

18. *Loading Factor*—Except for re-financing credit creditors might, if they so wished, calculate the rebate from a date three months after the date of quotation (see paragraph 14), but, if the agreement required notice of termination, such notice period would have to be included in this three months. [**B.18**]

REDEMPTION FEES OR PENALTIES

19. In any credit facility where the charge for credit was regularly added to the amount outstanding and repayments deducted (so that the total balance (principal and charges) outstanding at any time was known and where the debtor had the option of paying in full or by instalments) he would be entitled at any time to pay the full amount outstanding at that date with no penalty, additional charge or charge for advance interest. [**B.19**]

20. The charging of a fee for a quotation for redemption or early settlement, no matter how expressed, would not be permitted. [**B.20**]

VARIATIONS

21. Any creditor operating a credit scheme (other than one exempted under paragraph 4 above) to which because of its method of operation the above rules could not apply or where it would be inequitable to apply them would be required to provide a rebate for early settlement provision acceptable to the Consumer Credit Commissioner. [**B.21**]

# APPENDIX C

# CONSUMER CREDIT ACT 1974

(1974 c. 39)

## ARRANGEMENT OF SECTIONS

### PART I

### DIRECTOR GENERAL OF FAIR TRADING



### PART II

### CREDIT AGREEMENTS, HIRE AGREEMENTS AND LINKED TRANSACTIONS



### PART III

### LICENSING OF CREDIT AND HIRE BUSINESSES

*Licensing principles*



*Issue of licences*

*Renewal, variation, suspension and revocation of licences*



*Miscellaneous*



PART IV

SEEKING BUSINESS

*Advertising*



*Canvassing etc.*



*Miscellaneous*



PART V

ENTRY INTO CREDIT OR HIRE AGREEMENTS

*Preliminary matters*



*Making the agreement*

*Cancellation of certain agreements within cooling-off period*



*Exclusion of certain agreements from Part V*



PART VI

MATTERS ARISING DURING CURRENCY OF CREDIT OR HIRE AGREEMENTS



PART VII

DEFAULT AND TERMINATION

*Default notices*



*Further restriction of remedies for default*



*Early payment by debtor*



*Termination of agreements*

## Part VIII

## Security

### *General*



### *Pledges*



### *Negotiable instruments*



### *Land mortgages*



## Part IX

## Judicial Control

### *Enforcement of certain regulated agreements and securities*



### *Extension of time*



### *Protection of property pending proceedings*



### *Hire and hire-purchase etc. agreements*



### *Supplemental provisions as to orders*

*An Act to establish for the protection of consumers a new system, administered by the Director General of Fair Trading, of licensing and other control of traders concerned with the provision of credit, or the supply of goods on hire or hire-purchase, and their transactions, in place of the present enactments regulating moneylenders, pawnbrokers and hire-purchase traders and their transactions; and for related matters.* [31*st July* 1974]

NORTHERN IRELAND

This Act applies (s. 193 (2), *post*), subject to certain special provisions in s. 191, *post*.

## PART I

## DIRECTOR GENERAL OF FAIR TRADING

### 1. General functions of Director

(1) It is the duty of the Director General of Fair Trading ("the Director")—

(*a*) to administer the licensing system set up by this Act,

(*b*) to exercise the adjudicating functions conferred on him by this Act in relation to the issue, renewal, variation, suspension and revocation of licences, and other matters,

(*c*) generally to superintend the working and enforcement of this Act, and regulations made under it, and

(*d*) where necessary or expedient, himself to take steps to enforce this Act, and regulations so made.

(2) It is the duty of the Director, so far as appears to him to be practicable and having regard both to the national interest and the interests of persons carrying on businesses to which this Act applies and their customers, to keep under review and from time to time advise the Secretary of State about—

(*a*) social and commercial developments in the United Kingdom and elsewhere relating to the provision of credit or bailment or (in Scotland) hiring of goods to individuals, and related activities; and

(*b*) the working and enforcement of this Act and orders and regulations made under it. [**C.1**]

DIRECTOR GENERAL OF FAIR TRADING

That official is appointed under the Fair Trading Act 1973, s. 1 (43 Halsbury's Statutes (3rd edn.) 1624).

LICENSING SYSTEM

See ss. 21 *et seq.* as to the licensing of credit and hire businesses, and ss. 145 *et seq.* as to the licensing of "ancillary credit business".

OTHER MATTERS

For adjudicating functions conferred on the Director and relating to matters other than licensing see, in particular, ss. 40, 60, 64, 74 (3), 101 (8), 148 and 149.

DEFINITIONS

For "credit", see s. 9, *post*.

For "business", "goods" and "individual", see s. 189 (1), *post*.

## 2. Powers of Secretary of State

(1) The Secretary of State may by order—

(*a*) confer on the Director additional functions concerning the provision of credit or bailment or (in Scotland) hiring of goods to individuals, and related activities, and

(*b*) regulate the carrying out by the Director of his functions under this Act.

(2) The Secretary of State may give general directions indicating considerations to which the Director should have particular regard in carrying out his functions under this Act, and may give specific directions on any matter connected with the carrying out by the Director of those functions.

(3) The Secretary of State, on giving any directions under subsection (2), shall arrange for them to be published in such manner as he thinks most suitable for drawing them to the attention of interested persons.

(4) With the approval of the Secretary of State and the Treasury, the Director may charge, for any service or facility provided by him under this Act, a fee of an amount specified by general notice (the "specified fee").

(5) Provision may be made under subsection (4) for reduced fees, or no fees

at all, to be paid for certain services or facilities by persons of a specified description, and references in this Act to the specified fee shall, in such cases, be construed accordingly.

(6) An order under subsection (1) (*a*) shall be made by statutory instrument and shall be of no effect unless a draft of the order has been laid before and approved by each House of Parliament.

(7) References in subsection (2) to the functions of the Director under this Act do not include the making of a determination to which section 41 or 150 (appeals from Director to Secretary of State) applies. [C.2]

FUNCTIONS

For the functions of the Director, see s. 1 and the notes thereto, *ante*.

STATUTORY INSTRUMENT

For provisions as to statutory instruments generally, see the Statutory Instruments Act 1946 (32 Halsbury's Statutes (3rd edn.) 668).

ORDERS UNDER THIS SECTION

No orders had been made under this section up to the date of going to press.

For general provisions as to orders under this Act, see s. 182 (2), (4), *post*.

DEFINITIONS

For "credit", see s. 9, *post*.

For "Director", "general notice", "goods" and "individual", see s. 189 (1), *post*.

## 3. Supervision by Council on Tribunals

The Tribunals and Inquiries Act 1971 is amended as follows (the amendments bringing the adjudicating functions of the Director under this Act under the supervision of the Council on Tribunals)—

(*a*) in section 8 (2), insert "5A" after "paragraph";

(*b*) in section 19 (4), insert "or the Director General of Fair Trading referred to in paragraph 5A" after "or 46";

(*c*) in Schedule 1, after paragraph 5, insert—

"Credit consumer

5A. The Director General of Fair Trading, in respect of his functions under the Consumer Credit Act 1974 (c. 39), and any member of the Director's staff authorised to exercise those functions under paragraph 7 of Schedule 1 to the Fair Trading Act 1973." [C.3]

DIRECTOR GENERAL OF FAIR TRADING

That official is appointed under the Fair Trading Act 1973, s. 1 (43 Halsbury's Statutes (3rd edn.) 1624). He is not subject to supervision by the Council on Tribunals in respect of his functions under that Act.

FUNCTIONS

For the functions of the Director under this Act, see ss. 1, 2 (1) and the notes thereto, *ante*.

TRIBUNALS AND INQUIRIES ACT 1971, SS. 8 (2), 19 (4), SCH. 1

See 41 Halsbury's Statutes (3rd edn.) 254, 264, 265.

FAIR TRADING ACT 1973, SCH. 1, PARA. 7

See 43 Halsbury's Statutes (3rd edn.) 1743.

## 4. Dissemination of information and advice

The Director shall arrange for the dissemination, in such form and manner as he considers appropriate, of such information and advice as it may appear to him expedient to give to the public in the United Kingdom about the operation of this Act, the credit facilities available to them, and other matters within the scope of his functions under this Act. **[C.4]**

DIRECTOR
For meaning, see s. 189 (1), *post*.

## 5. Annual and other reports

At the end of subsection (2) of section 125 (annual and other reports of Director) of the Fair Trading Act 1973 insert "and shall set out any directions given to the Director under section 2 (2) of the Consumer Credit Act 1974 during that year". **[C.5]**

DIRECTOR
For meaning, see the Fair Trading Act 1973, s. 1 (1) (43 Halsbury's Statutes (3rd edn.) 1624).

FAIR TRADING ACT 1973, S. 125 (2)
See 43 Halsbury's Statutes (3rd edn.) 1729.

## 6. Form etc. of applications

(1) An application to the Director under this Act is of no effect unless the requirements of this section are satisfied.

(2) The application must be in writing, and in such form, and accompanied by such particulars, as the Director may specify by general notice, and must be accompanied by the specified fee.

(3) After giving preliminary consideration to an application, the Director may by notice require the applicant to furnish him with such further information relevant to the application as may be described in the notice, and may require any information furnished by the applicant (whether at the time of the application or subsequently) to be verified in such manner as the Director may stipulate.

(4) The Director may by notice require the applicant to publish details of his application at a time or times and in a manner specified in the notice. **[C.6]**

WRITING
This includes printing, lithography, photography and other modes of representing or reproducing words in a visible form (Interpretation Act 1889, s. 20 (32 Halsbury's Statutes (3rd edn.) 450)).

BY NOTICE
As to the service of notices, see s. 176, *post*.

DEFINITIONS
For "Director" and "general notice", see s. 189 (1), *post*; by virtue of that section, for "specified fee", see s. 2 (4), (5), *ante*.

**7. Penalty for false information**

A person who, in connection with any application or request to the Director under this Act, or in response to any invitation or requirement of the Director under this Act, knowingly or recklessly gives information to the Director which, in a material particular, is false or misleading, commits an offence. **[C.7]**

PERSON

Unless the contrary intention appears, this includes a body corporate (Interpretation Act 1889, ss. 2, 19 (32 Halsbury's Statutes (3rd edn.) 435, 449)).

DIRECTOR

For meaning, see s. 189 (1), *post*.

KNOWINGLY

There is authority for saying that, where a person deliberately refrains from making inquiries the result of which he might not care to have, this constitutes in law actual knowledge of the facts in question; see *Knox* v. *Boyd*, 1941 S.C. (J) 82, at p. 86, and *Taylor's Central Garages* (*Exeter*), *Ltd.* v. *Roper* (1951), 115 J.P. 445, at pp. 449, 450, *per* Devlin, J.; and see also *Mallon* v. *Allon*, [1964] 1 Q.B. 385; [1963] 3 All E.R. 843, at p. 394 and p. 847, respectively. However, mere neglect to ascertain what would have been found out by making reasonable inquiries is not tantamount to knowledge; see *Taylor's Central Garages* (*Exeter*), *Ltd.* v. *Roper*, *ubi supra*, *per* Devlin, J., and cf. *London Computator, Ltd.* v. *Seymour*, [1944] 2 All E.R. 11; but see also *Mallon* v. *Allon*, *ubi supra*.

RECKLESSLY

On the meaning of this expression, see, in particular, *Derry* v. *Peek* (1889), 14 App. Cas. 337; [1886–90] All E.R. Rep. 1; *Williams Brothers Direct Supply Stores, Ltd.* v. *Cloote* (1944), 60 T.L.R. 270; *R.* v. *Bates*, [1952] 2 All E.R. 842 (on appeal *sub. nom. R.* v *Russell*, [1953] 1 W.L.R. 77; 97 Sol. Jo. 12); *R.* v. *Mackinnon*, [1959] 1 Q.B. 150; [1958] 3 All E.R. 657; *R.* v. *Grunwald*, [1963] 1 Q.B. 935; [1960] 3 All E.R. 380; and *Shawinigan, Ltd.* v. *Vokins & Co., Ltd.*, [1961] 3 All E.R. 396.

FALSE

Something may be false on account of what it omits even though it is literally true; see *R.* v. *Lord Kylsant*, [1932] 1 K.B. 442; [1931] All E.R. Rep. 179, and *R.* v. *Bishirgian*, [1936] 1 All E.R. 586; and cf. *Curtis* v. *Chemical Cleaning and Dyeing Co., Ltd.*, [1951] 1 All E.R. 631; [1951] 1 K.B. 805, C.A., at p. 634 and p. 809, respectively, *per* Denning, L.J.

MATERIAL PARTICULAR

A particular may be material on the ground that it renders more credible another statement; see *R.* v. *Tyson* (1867), L.R. 1 C.C.R. 107.

## PART II

### CREDIT AGREEMENTS, HIRE AGREEMENTS AND LINKED TRANSACTIONS

**8. Consumer credit agreements**

(1) A personal credit agreement is an agreement between an individual "(the debtor") and any other person ("the creditor") by which the creditor provides the debtor with credit of any amount.

(2) A consumer credit agreement is a personal credit agreement by which the creditor provides the debtor with credit not exceeding £5,000.

(3) A consumer credit agreement is a regulated agreement within the meaning of this Act if it is not an agreement (an "exempt agreement") specified in or under section 16. **[C.8]**

GENERAL NOTE

The terms defined by this section demarcate the ambit of the whole Act. Subsection (1) defines "personal credit agreement" and the crucial point here is that the debtor must be an "individual". As defined by s. 189 (1), *post*, this includes a partnership but not a corporation. The creditor, on the other hand, is a "person" in the ordinary legal sense, which includes corporations. Certain particular categories of personal credit agreement are defined by ss. 10, 11, *post*, and no provision of this Act applies to agreements which are not personal credit agreements.

Subsection (2) identifies, by reference to a limit of value, those personal credit agreements which are "consumer credit agreements", and sub-s. (3) defines as "regulated agreements" all those consumer credit agreements which are not exempted by s. 16, *post*. Most of the provisions of this Act are confined in their application to consumer credit agreements and many are confined to regulated agreements. Generally speaking, therefore, the credit agreements which fall wholly or largely outside the scope of the Act are (i) those in which the debtor is a company, (ii) those involving loans of more than £5,000 and (iii) those exempted by s. 16.

For examples illustrating the use of the terms defined by this section, see Sch. 2, paras. 5–7, 15, 19, 21, *post*.

INDIVIDUAL

For meaning, see s. 189 (1), *post*. As to the case of an agreement with two or more debtors, some of whom are not "individuals", see s. 185 (4), *post*.

PERSON

Unless the contrary intention appears, this includes any body of persons, corporate or unincorporate (Interpretation Act 1889, s. 19 (32 Halsbury's Statutes (3rd edn.) 449)).

CREDIT

For meaning, see s. 9 (1), *post*.

NOT EXCEEDING

For the application of this provision to running accounts, see s. 10 (3), *post*.

£5,000

This amount may be amended by order under s. 181, *post*.

REGULATED AGREEMENT

Agreements made before the day appointed under Sch. 3, para. 1 (1), *post*, are not regulated agreements; see that sub-paragraph.

## 9. Meaning of credit

(1) In this Act "credit" includes a cash loan, and any other form of financial accommodation.

(2) Where credit is provided otherwise than in sterling it shall be treated for the purposes of this Act as provided in sterling of an equivalent amount.

(3) Without prejudice to the generality of subsection (1), the person by whom goods are bailed or (in Scotland) hired to an individual under a hire-purchase agreement shall be taken to provide him with fixed-sum credit to finance the transaction of an amount equal to the total price of the goods less the aggregate of the deposit (if any) and the total charge for credit.

(4) For the purposes of this Act, an item entering into the total charge for credit shall not be treated as credit even though time is allowed for its payment. [C.9]

GENERAL NOTE

This section defines "credit", which is the basic subject matter of the whole Act. The general definition in sub-s. (1) is in the widest terms and sub-s. (3) makes it specifically clear that all hire-purchase agreements involve credit within the meaning of the Act. Consequentially, hire-purchase agreements are now to be governed by Parts V, VI, VII and IX of this Act, and the Hire-Purchase Act 1965 (30 Halsbury's Statutes (3rd edn.) 61) is prospectively repealed by s. 192 (3), (4), and Sch. 5, *post*. The principal significance of sub-s. (4) lies in the fact that the amount of credit provided by any agreement has to be calculated for the purposes of s. 8 (1), *ante*, and s. 17 (1), *post*. In this calculation, the creditor's charges are to be omitted, as illustrated by Sch. 2, paras. 10, 19, *post*. For other illustrations relevant to this section, see also paras. 16 and 21 of that Schedule.

DEFINITIONS

For "cash", "deposit", "goods", "hire-purchase agreement", "individual", "total charge for credit" and "total price", see s. 189 (1), *post*.

For "fixed-sum credit", see s. 10 (1) (*b*), *post*.

## 10. Running-account credit and fixed-sum credit

(1) For the purposes of this Act—

(*a*) running-account credit is a facility under a personal credit agreement whereby the debtor is enabled to receive from time to time (whether in his own person, or by another person) from the creditor or a third party cash, goods and services (or any of them) to an amount or value such that, taking into account payments made by or to the credit of the debtor, the credit limit (if any) is not at any time exceeded; and

(*b*) fixed-sum credit is any other facility under a personal credit agreement whereby the debtor is enabled to receive credit (whether in one amount or by instalments).

(2) In relation to running-account credit, "credit limit" means, as respects any period, the maximum debit balance which, under the credit agreement, is allowed to stand on the account during that period, disregarding any term of the agreement allowing that maximum to be exceeded merely temporarily.

(3) For the purposes of section 8 (2), running-account credit shall be taken not to exceed the amount specified in that subsection ("the specified amount") if—

(*a*) the credit limit does not exceed the specified amount; or

(*b*) whether or not there is a credit limit, and if there is, notwithstanding that it exceeds the specified amount,—

(i) the debtor is not enabled to draw at any one time an amount which, so far as (having regard to section 9 (4)) it represents credit, exceeds the specified amount, or

(ii) the agreement provides that, if the debit balance rises above a given amount (not exceeding the specified amount), the rate of the total charge for credit increases or any other condition favouring the creditor or his associate comes into operation, or

(iii) at the time the agreement is made it is probable, having regard to the terms of the agreement and any other relevant considerations, that the debit balance will not at any time rise above the specified amount. **[C.10]**

GENERAL NOTE

This section divides personal credit agreements into those which provide "running-account credit", as defined in sub-s. (1) (*a*) above, and those which provide "fixed-sum credit", which are all others. This distinction is important, firstly, because of the questions which arise in determining whether a running-account credit agreement falls within the £5,000 limit under s. 8 (2), *ante*. These questions are answered by sub-s. (3) above by reference to the "credit limit" as defined in sub-s. (2) or alternatively by reference to the tests in sub-s. (3) (*b*) (i), (ii) and (iii). It is important to note that the tests in sub-s. (3) (*b*) are not applicable only in the absence of a credit limit. If one of these tests is satisfied, the agreement will be taken to be within the £5,000 limit notwithstanding the existence of a credit limit in excess of £5,000.

For further consequences flowing from the distinction between running-account and fixed-sum credit see, in particular, ss. 77, 78, 107 and 108, *post*, which make different provision as to the information to be supplied by the creditor in the two cases.

For illustrations of the use of the terms defined by this section, and of the operation of the provisions of sub-s. (3) (*b*), see Sch. 2, paras. 6, 7, 9, 10, 15–19 and 22, *post*.

DEFINITIONS

For "associate", see s. 184, *post*.

For "cash", "creditor", "debtor", "goods" and "total charge for credit", see s. 189 (1), *post*.

For "credit", see s. 9, *ante*.

For "personal credit agreement", see s. 8 (1), *ante*.

## 11. Restricted-use credit and unrestricted-use credit

(1) A restricted-use credit agreement is a regulated consumer credit agreement—

(*a*) to finance a transaction between the debtor and the creditor, whether forming part of that agreement or not, or

(*b*) to finance a transaction between the debtor and a person (the "supplier") other than the creditor, or

(*c*) to refinance any existing indebtedness of the debtor's, whether to the creditor or another person,

and "restricted-use credit" shall be construed accordingly.

(2) An unrestricted-use credit agreement is a regulated consumer credit agreement not falling within subsection (1), and "unrestricted-use credit" shall be construed accordingly.

(3) An agreement does not fall within subsection (1) if the credit is in fact provided in such a way as to leave the debtor free to use it as he chooses, even though certain uses would contravene that or any other agreement.

(4) An agreement may fall within subsection (1) (*b*) although the identity of the supplier is unknown at the time the agreement is made. **[C.11]**

GENERAL NOTE

This section divides personal credit agreements into restricted-use credit agreements (defined by sub-s. (1) subject to sub-ss. (2) and (3)) and unrestricted-use credit agreements, which are all others. The result of sub-s. (2) would appear to be that any arrangement by which the debtor has the borrowed money paid over to him is an unrestricted-use agreement, regardless of any term governing the use to which the money ought to be put. Subsection (3) covers such contracts as those relating to credit cards, by which the cardholder can obtain goods from any one of a large number of suppliers and credit is furnished by way of a payment of money by the creditor to the supplier, to be reimbursed at a later date by the debtor.

The importance of this distinction lies principally in the different provisions for the consequences of cancellation made by ss. 71 and 72, *post*. Note also the exclusion of certain restricted-use agreements from provisions of Part V by s. 74 (2), *post*. For illustrations of the use of the terms defined by this section, see Sch. 2, paras. 8, 10, 12, 13, 14, 16, 17 and 18, *post*.

PERSON

See the note to s. 8, *ante*.

DEFINITIONS

For "credit" see s. 9, *ante*.

For "creditor", "debtor" and "finance", see s. 189 (1), *post*.

For "regulated consumer credit agreement", see s. 8 (2), (3), *ante*.

## 12. Debtor-creditor-supplier agreements

A debtor-creditor-supplier agreement is a regulated consumer credit agreement being—

(*a*) a restricted-use credit agreement which falls within section 11 (1) (*a*), or

(*b*) a restricted-use credit agreement which falls within section 11 (1) (*b*) and is made by the creditor under pre-existing arrangements, or in contemplation of future arrangements, between himself and the supplier, or

(*c*) an unrestricted-use credit agreement which is made by the creditor under pre-existing arrangements between himself and a person (the "supplier") other than the debtor in the knowledge that the credit is to be used to finance a transaction between the debtor and the supplier. [C.12]

GENERAL NOTE

This section defines "debtor-creditor-supplier agreement", which is to be contrasted with the term "debtor-creditor agreement", defined by s. 13, *post*. The difference may be summarised thus: in a debtor-creditor agreement, a supplier of goods and services either does not feature at all or features without the existence of arrangements between himself and the creditor, whereas in a debtor-creditor-supplier agreement the supplier is either the same person as the creditor or a party to arrangements (actual or anticipated) between himself and the creditor. As to the significance of these definitions, note in particular s. 48 (prohibition of canvassing debtor-creditor agreements), ss. 71, 72 (cancellation), and s. 75 (liability of creditor for breaches by supplier), *post*.

For illustrations of the use of these terms, see Sch. 2, paras. 8, 16, 17, 18, *post*.

PERSON

See the note to s. 8, *ante*.

PRE-EXISTING ARRANGEMENTS; FUTURE ARRANGEMENTS

For provisions as to the construction of these provisions, see s. 187, *post*.

DEFINITIONS

For "credit", see s. 9, *ante*.

For "creditor", "debtor", "finance" and "supplier", see s. 189 (1), *post*.

For "regulated consumer credit agreement", see s. 8 (2), (3), *ante*.

For "unrestricted-use credit agreement", see s. 11 (2), *ante*.

## 13. Debtor-creditor agreements

A debtor-creditor agreement is a regulated consumer credit agreement being—

(*a*) a restricted-use credit agreement which falls within section 11 (1) (*b*) but is not made by the creditor under pre-existing arrangements, or in contemplation of future arrangements, between himself and the supplier, or

(*b*) a restricted-use credit agreement which falls within section 11 (1) (*c*), or

(*c*) an unrestricted-use credit agreement which is not made by the creditor under pre-existing arrangements between himself and a person (the "supplier") other than the debtor in the knowledge that that the credit is to be used to finance a transaction between the debtor and the supplier. **[C.13]**

GENERAL NOTE

See the General Note to s. 12, *ante*.

PERSON

See the note to s. 8, *ante*.

PRE-EXISTING ARRANGEMENTS; FUTURE ARRANGEMENTS

For provisions as to the construction of these provisions, see s. 187, *post*.

DEFINITIONS

For "credit", see s. 9, *ante*.
For "creditor", "debtor", "finance" and "supplier", see s. 189 (1), *post*.
For "regulated consumer credit agreement", see s. 8 (2), (3), *ante*.
For "unrestricted-use credit agreement", see s. 11 (2), *ante*.

### 14. Credit-token agreements

(1) A credit-token is a card, check, voucher, coupon, stamp, form, booklet or other document or thing given to an individual by a person carrying on a consumer credit business, who undertakes—

(*a*) that on the production of it (whether or not some other action is also required) he will supply cash, goods and services (or any of them) on credit, or

(*b*) that where, on the production of it to a third party (whether or not any other action is also required), the third party supplies cash, goods and services (or any of them), he will pay the third party for them (whether or not deducting any discount or commission), in return for payment to him by the individual.

(2) A credit-token agreement is a regulated agreement for the provision of credit in connection with the use of a credit-token.

(3) Without prejudice to the generality of section 9 (1), the person who gives to an individual an undertaking falling within subsection (1) (*b*) shall be taken to provide him with credit drawn on whenever a third party supplies him with cash, goods or services.

(4) For the purposes of subsection (1), use of an object to operate a machine provided by the person giving the object or a third party shall be treated as the production of the object to him. **[C.14]**

GENERAL NOTE

This section defines "credit-token" and "credit-token agreement", which are the subjects of special provisions under ss. 51, 66, 84 and 85, *post*. Paragraph (*a*) of sub-s. (1), read with sub-s. (4), covers vouchers used to operate cash dispensing machines if they supply cash "on credit". This presumably excludes cases where the customer's current account is immediately debited.

Paragraph (*b*) of sub-s. (1) covers a wide range of credit card and trading check schemes. The use of the word "individual" in sub-s. (1) should be noted. This term does not include a corporation.

For illustrations of the use of these terms, see Sch. 2, paras. 3, 14, 16, 22, *post*.

PERSON

See the note to s. 8, *ante*.

DEFINITIONS

For "cash", "consumer credit business", "goods", "individual" and "regulated agreement", see s. 189 (1), *post.*

For "credit", see s. 9, *ante.*

### 15. Consumer hire agreements

(1) A consumer hire agreement is an agreement made by a person with an individual (the "hirer") for the bailment or (in Scotland) the hiring of goods to the hirer, being an agreement which—

(*a*) is not a hire-purchase agreement, and

(*b*) is capable of subsisting for more than three months, and

(*c*) does not require the hirer to make payments exceeding £5,000.

(2) A consumer hire agreement is a regulated agreement if it is not an exempt agreement. **[C.15]**

GENERAL NOTE

This section defines "consumer hire agreement" and brings such agreements, unless exempted by s. 16, *post,* within the category of "regulated agreements". The result is that, unless so exempted, they are subject to numerous provisions of Parts V, VI, VII and IX, *post.* For provisions applying specifically to regulated consumer hire agreements, see ss. 79, 102, 132, *post.*

For an illustration of the use of this term, see Sch. 2, para. 20, *post.*

PERSON

See the note to s. 8, *ante.*

£5,000

This amount may be amended by order under s. 181, *post.*

IS A REGULATED AGREEMENT

See, however, Sch. 3, para. 1 (1), *post,* which excludes agreements made before the day appointed for the purposes of that sub-paragraph.

DEFINITIONS

For "exempt agreement", "goods", "hire-purchase agreement", "hirer" and "individual", see s. 189 (1), *post.*

### 16. Exempt agreements

(1) This Act does not regulate a consumer credit agreement where the creditor is a local authority or building society, or a body specified, or of a description specified, in an order made by the Secretary of State, being—

(*a*) an insurance company,

(*b*) a friendly society,

(*c*) an organisation of employers or organisation of workers,

(*d*) a charity,

(*e*) a land improvement company, or

(*f*) a body corporate named or specifically referred to in any public general Act.

(2) Subsection (1) applies only where the agreement is—

(*a*) a debtor-creditor-supplier agreement financing—

(i) the purchase of land, or

(ii) the provision of dwellings on any land, and secured by a land mortgage on that land; or (*b*) a debtor-creditor agreement secured by any land mortgage; or

(*c*) a debtor-creditor-supplier agreement financing a transaction which is a linked transaction in relation to—

(i) an agreement falling within paragraph (*a*), or

(ii) an agreement falling within paragraph (*b*) financing—

(*aa*) the purchase of any land, or

(*bb*) the provision of dwellings on any land,

and secured by a land mortgage on the land referred to in paragraph (*a*) or, as the case may be, the land referred to in sub-paragraph (ii).

(3) The Secretary of State shall not make, vary or revoke an order—

(*a*) under subsection (1) (*a*) without consulting the Minister of the Crown responsible for insurance companies,

(*b*) under subsection (1) (*b*) or (*c*) without consulting the Chief Registrar of Friendly Societies,

(*c*) under subsection (1) (*d*) without consulting the Charity Commissioners, or

(*d*) under subsection (1) (*e*) or (*f*) without consulting any Minister of the Crown with responsibilities concerning the body in question.

(4) An order under subsection (1) relating to a body may be limited so as to apply only to agreements by that body of a description specified in the order.

(5) The Secretary of State may by order provide that this Act shall not regulate other consumer credit agreements where—

(*a*) the number of payments to be made by the debtor does not exceed the number specified for that purpose in the order, or

(*b*) the rate of the total charge for credit does not exceed the rate so specified, or

(*c*) an agreement has a connection with a country outside the United Kingdom.

(6) The Secretary of State may by order provide that this Act shall not regulate consumer hire agreements of a description specified in the order where—

(*a*) the owner is a body corporate authorised by or under any enactment to supply electricity, gas or water, and

(*b*) the subject of the agreement is a meter or metering equipment,

or where the owner is the Post Office or the Kingston upon Hull City Council.

(7) Nothing in this section affects the application of sections 137—140 (extortionate credit bargains).

(8) In the application of this section to Scotland subsection (3) (*c*) shall not have effect.

(9) In the application of this section to Northern Ireland subsection (3) shall have effect as if any reference to a Minister of the Crown were a reference to a Northern Ireland department, any reference to the Chief Registrar of Friendly Societies were a reference to the Registrar of Friendly Societies for Northern

Ireland, and any reference to the Charity Commissioners were a reference to the Department of Finance for Northern Ireland. **[C.16]**

GENERAL NOTE

This section provides for certain agreements to be exempted from the provisions of this Act, other than ss. 137–140, *post*. Under sub-ss. (1)–(4), exemption will be given to land mortgage agreements in which the creditors are local authorities, building societies or bodies belonging to the other categories mentioned in sub-s. (1) (*a*) (i)–(vi), and specified in orders to be made by the Secretary of State.

Orders under sub-s. (5) may establish further categories of exempt agreements, defined by reference either to the number of payments or to the rate of charges or to the fact that they have a foreign element. Orders under sub-s. (6) may further exempt hire agreements relating to certain equipment let by public utilities.

ORGANISATION OF EMPLOYERS OR ORGANISATION OF WORKERS

These terms are not defined in this Act. The definitions in the Industrial Relations Act 1971, ss. 61 (1), 62 (1) (41 Halsbury's Statutes (3rd edn.) 2219, 2220) are applicable only for the purposes of that Act but may afford some guidance.

NORTHERN IRELAND DEPARTMENT

Those departments take the place of the former ministries of the Government of Northern Ireland; see the Northern Ireland Constitution Act 1973, s. 7 (5) (43 Halsbury's Statutes (3rd edn.) 1187).

DEFINITIONS

For "building society", "charity", "debtor", "friendly society", "insurance company", "land improvement company", "land mortgage", "local authority", "owner", and "total charge for credit", see s. 189 (1), *post*.

For "consumer credit agreement", see s. 8 (2), *ante*, and for "consumer hire agreement", see s. 15 (1), *ante*.

For "credit", see s. 9, *ante*.

For "debtor-creditor agreement", see s. 13, *ante*, and for "debtor-creditor-supplier agreement", see s. 12, *ante*.

ORDERS UNDER THIS SECTION

No orders had been made under this section up to the time of going to press.

For general provisions as to orders under this Act, see s. 182 (1), (2), (4), *post*.

### 17. Small agreements

(1) A small agreement is—

(*a*) a regulated consumer credit agreement for credit not exceeding £30, other than a hire-purchase or conditional sale agreement; or

(*b*) a regulated consumer hire agreement which does not require the hirer to make payments exceeding £30,

being an agreement which is either unsecured or secured by a guarantee or indemnity only (whether or not the guarantee or indemnity is itself secured).

(2) Section 10 (3) applies for the purposes of subsection (1) as it applies for the purposes of section 8 (2).

(3) Where—

(*a*) two or more small agreements are made at or about the same time between the same parties, and

(*b*) it appears probable that they would instead have been made as a single agreement but for the desire to avoid the operation of provisions of this Act which would have applied to that single agreement but, apart from this subsection, are not applicable to small agreements, this Act applies to the small agreements as if they were regulated agreements other than small agreements.

(4) If, apart from this subsection, subsection (3) does not apply to any agreements but would apply if, for any party or parties to any of the agreements, there were substituted an associate of that party, or associates of each of those parties, as the case may be, then subsection (3) shall apply to the agreements. **[C.17]**

GENERAL NOTE

This section defines "small agreement". The general test is a £30 limit of value, but no hire-purchase agreement and no agreement secured by a pledge falls within the definition. Subsections (3) and (4) contain provisions against the evasion of the Act by dividing larger transactions artificially into small agreements. Small agreements fall outside some, but by no means all, of the regulatory provisions of this Act (see, e.g., s. 74 (2), *post*).

For illustrations of the use of this term, see Sch. 2, paras. 16, 17, 22, *post*.

NOT EXCEEDING

For the application of this provision to running-account credit see, by virtue of sub-s. (2) above, s. 10 (3), *ante*.

£30

This amount may be amended by order under s. 181, *post*.

GUARANTEE OR INDEMNITY

These terms are not defined. Guarantees are contracts by which a third party undertakes to make good any loss sustained by the creditor as a result of default by the principal debtor; see 18 Halsbury's Laws (3rd edn.) 411 *et seq*. Contracts of guarantee (into which the guarantor or surety usually enters at the request of the debtor) are distinguished from contracts of insurance, by which the creditor arranges, quite independently of the debtor, to be covered against the risk of default (see *ibid*., 415). It is not thought, however, that the existence of a contract of insurance covering the transaction would take it outside the definition of "small agreement". The reason is that a debt covered by insurance is not a secured debt in the ordinary meaning of those words (and see the definition of "security" in s. 189 (1), *post*). An indemnity is an undertaking as to loss which is a primary liability, not dependent on the default of the principal debtor.

DEFINITIONS

For "associate", see s. 184, *post*.

For "conditional sale agreement", "deposit", "hire-purchase agreement" and "hirer", see s. 189 (1), *post*.

For "consumer credit agreement", see s. 8 (2), *ante*, and for "consumer hire agreement", see s. 15, *ante*.

For "credit", see s. 9, *ante*.

## 18. Multiple agreements

(1) This section applies to an agreement (a "multiple agreement") if its terms are such as—

(*a*) to place a part of it within one category of agreement mentioned in this Act, and another part of it within a different category of agreement so mentioned, or within a category of agreement not so mentioned, or

(*b*) to place it, or a part of it, within two or more categories of agreement so mentioned.

(2) Where a part of an agreement falls within subsection (1), that part shall be treated for the purposes of this Act as a separate agreement.

(3) Where an agreement falls within subsection (1) (*b*), it shall be treated

as an agreement in each of the categories in question, and this Act shall apply to it accordingly.

(4) Where under subsection (2) a part of a multiple agreement is to be treated as a separate agreement, the multiple agreement shall (with any necessary modifications) be construed accordingly; and any sum payable under the multiple agreement, if not apportioned by the parties, shall for the purposes of proceedings in any court relating to the multiple agreement be apportioned by the court as may be requisite.

(5) In the case of an agreement for running-account credit, a term of the agreement allowing the credit limit to be exceeded merely temporarily shall not be treated as a separate agreement or as providing fixed-sum credit in respect of the excess.

(6) This Act does not apply to a multiple agreement so far as the agreement relates to goods if under the agreement payments are to be made in respect of the goods in the form of rent (other than a rent-charge) issuing out of land. **[C.18]**

GENERAL NOTE

This section deals with the problem of agreements which fall partly within one of the definitions in this Act and partly within another (or partly outside them all), or which fall, wholly or in part, under two or more definitions at once. Such agreements are defined by sub-s. (1) as "multiple agreements". By sub-ss. (2) and (4), parts of agreements which fall under different definitions are to be treated as separate agreements and construed accordingly, and sums payable may be apportioned accordingly. By sub-s. (3), an agreement falling under two or more definitions is to receive the treatment appropriate to each. Subsections (5) and (6) make exceptions for temporary waiver of credit limits and for agreements by which goods are paid for by rent issuing out of land.

For examples of multiple agreements, see Sch. 2, paras. 16, 18, *post*.

CATEGORY OF AGREEMENT

For the principal categories of agreement mentioned in this Act, see ss. 8, 10, 11, 12, 13, 14, 15, 16 and 17, *ante*.

RENT ISSUING OUT OF LAND

Note the exclusion of a rentcharge (as to which, see 32 Halsbury's Laws (3rd edn.) 527 *et seq*.). Thus sub-s. (6) does not exclude the case where chattels are included in a sale of land in consideration of a rentcharge, and in such a case, that part of the agreement which relates to goods might be held to be a credit-sale agreement as defined by s. 189 (1), *post*. Subsection (6) does, however, exclude the possibility that furniture included in a lease of premises might be held to be the subject of a consumer hire agreement as defined by s. 15, *ante*.

DEFINITIONS

For "credit limit", see s. 10 (2), *ante*.

For "fixed-sum credit" and "running-account credit", see s. 10 (1), *ante*.

For "court", "goods" and "land", see s. 189 (1), *post*.

## 19. Linked transactions

(1) A transaction entered into by the debtor or hirer, or a relative of his, with any other person ("the other party"), except one for the provision of security, is a linked transaction in relation to an actual or prospective regulated agreement (the "principal agreement") of which it does not form part if—

(*a*) the transaction is entered into in compliance with a term of the principal agreement; or

(*b*) the principal agreement is a debtor-creditor-supplier agreement and the transaction is financed, or to be financed, by the principal agreement; or

(*c*) the other party is a person mentioned in subsection (2), and a person so mentioned initiated the transaction by suggesting it to the debtor or hirer, or his relative, who enters into it—

(i) to induce the creditor or owner to enter into the principal agreement, or

(ii) for another purpose related to the principal agreement, or

(iii) where the principal agreement is a restricted-use credit agreement, for a purpose related to a transaction financed, or to be financed, by the principal agreement.

(2) The persons referred to in subsection (1) (*c*) are—

(*a*) the creditor or owner, or his associate;

(*b*) a person who, in the negotiation of the transaction, is represented by a credit-broker who is also a negotiator in antecedent negotiations for the principal agreement;

(*c*) a person who, at the time the transaction is initiated, knows that the principal agreement has been made or contemplates that it might be made.

(3) A linked transaction entered into before the making of the principal agreement has no effect until such time (if any) as that agreement is made.

(4) Regulations may exclude linked transactions of the prescribed description from the operation of subsection (3). **[C.19]**

COMMENCEMENT

As to the commencement of sub-s. (3), see Sch. 3, para. 3, *post*, and the note "Appointed days" to Part II of that Schedule.

GENERAL NOTE

This section defines "linked transactions", which are transactions connected with actual or prospective regulated agreements in one of the ways described in sub-s. (1) (*a*), (*b*) and (*c*). Transactions for the provision of security do not under any circumstances fall within the definition. By virtue of sub-s. (3) above (subject to exceptions made by regulations under sub-s. (4)), a linked transaction cannot come into effect before the principal agreement. A linked transaction is further subject to various regulatory provisions of this Act; see, e.g., ss. 57 (1), 69 (1), 70 (1), 96, 171 (1), *post*.

For an illustration of the operation of this definition, see Sch. 2, para. 11, *post*.

TRANSACTION

This includes transactions entered into before the appointed day under Sch. 3, para. 1 (1), *post*; see para. 2 (1) of that Schedule.

PROSPECTIVE REGULATED AGREEMENT

This does not include an agreement which, if made as expected, would have been made before the appointed day under Sch. 3, para. 1 (1), *post*; see para. 1 (2) of that Schedule.

PERSON

See the note to s. 8, *ante*.

KNOWS . . . OR CONTEMPLATES

As to the onus of proof of this issue, see s. 171 (1), *post*.

DEFINITIONS

For "antecedent negotiations" and "negotiator", see s. 56 (1), *post*.

For "associate", see s. 184, *post*. For "credit broker", "creditor", "debtor", "finance", "hirer", "owner", "prescribed", "regulated agreement", "regulations", "relative" and "security", see s. 189 (1), *post*.

For "debtor-creditor-supplier agreement", see s. 12, *ante*, and for "restricted-use credit", see s. 11 (1), *ante*. As to "principal agreement", note sub-s. (1) above.

REGULATIONS UNDER THIS SECTION

No regulations had been made under this section up to the time of going to press.

For general provisions as to regulations under this Act, see s. 183 (1)–(3), *post*.

## 20. Total charge for credit

(1) The Secretary of State shall make regulations containing such provisions as appear to him appropriate for determining the true cost to the debtor of the credit provided or to be provided under an actual or prospective consumer credit agreement (the "total charge for credit"), and regulations so made shall prescribe—

(*a*) what items are to be treated as entering into the total charge for credit, and how their amount is to be ascertained;

(*b*) the method of calculating the rate of the total charge for credit.

(2) Regulations under subsection (1) may provide for the whole or part of the amount payable by the debtor or his relative under any linked transaction to be included in the total charge for credit, whether or not the creditor is a party to the transaction or derives benefit from it. [**C.20**]

GENERAL NOTE

This section enables regulations to be made for determining the true cost to the debtor of the credit provided under a consumer credit agreement. The regulations will provide a definition of the term "total charge for credit", which is used in numerous provisions of this Act (as to disclosure of the total charge for credit, note in particular s. 60 (1) (*b*), *post*). Sub-s. (2) enables amounts payable under linked transactions to be included in the total charge for credit.

ACTUAL OR PROSPECTIVE CONSUMER CREDIT AGREEMENT

This section applies to agreements whenever made; see Sch. 3, para. 4, *post*.

DEFINITIONS

For "credit", see s. 9, *ante*.

For "creditor", "debtor", "regulations" and "relative", see s. 189 (1), *post*.

For "consumer credit agreement", see s. 8 (2), *ante*.

REGULATIONS UNDER THIS SECTION

No regulations had been made under this section up to the time of going to press.

For general provisions as to regulations under this Act, see s. 182 (1)–(3), *post*.

## PART III

## LICENSING OF CREDIT AND HIRE BUSINESSES

EXTENSION OF PART III

This Part of this Act (ss. 21–42), except s. 40, applies to ancillary credit businesses as it applies to consumer credit businesses; see s. 147 (1), *post*.

### *Licensing principles*

## 21. Businesses needing a licence

(1) Subject to this section, a licence is required to carry on a consumer credit business or consumer hire business.

(2) A local authority does not need a licence to carry on a business.

(3) A body corporate empowered by a public general Act naming it to carry on a business does not need a licence to do so. [**C.21**]

COMMENCEMENT

See Sch. 3, paras. 5, 44, *post*, and the notes "Appointed days" to Parts III and X of that Schedule.

LICENCE

Licences are either standard licences or group licences; see s. 22, *post*. For the scope of licences, see ss. 23, 24, *post*. As to their issue, renewal, variation, suspension and revocation, see ss. 25–33, *post*.

REQUIRED

Unlicensed trading is an offence under s. 39, *post*. The further consequence of carrying on business without a licence is that certain agreements made in the course of that business are enforceable only to the extent provided by s. 40, *post*. In view of the provisions of s. 170 (1), *post*, there is no room for any implication that transactions by an unlicensed trader are absolutely void. An injunction to restrain unlicensed trading appears to be a possibility; see s. 170 (3), *post*, and 32 Halsbury's Statutes (3rd edn.) 401.

CARRY ON BUSINESS

Occasional transactions do not amount to the carrying on of a business; see s. 189 (2), *post*. It is thought, however, that the provisions of that subsection do not invalidate the point made by Lord Esher, M.R., in *Re Griffin, Ex parte Board of Trade* (1890), 60 L.J.Q.B. 235, at p. 237, that if there is evidence of the requisite intent, a single transaction can be proved to be the beginning of the carrying on of a business. Cf. also *Cornelius* v. *Phillips*, [1918] A.C. 199; [1916–1917] All E.R. Rep. 685.

CONSUMER CREDIT BUSINESS

For meaning, see s. 189 (1), *post*. The provisions of this Part of this Act (except s. 40) apply to an ancillary credit business as they apply to a consumer credit business; see s. 142 (1), *post*.

DEFINITIONS

For "business", "consumer hire business" and "local authority", see s. 189 (1), *post*.

## 22. Standard and group licences

(1) A licence may be—

(*a*) a standard licence, that is a licence, issued by the Director to a person named in the licence on an application made by him, which, during the prescribed period, covers such activities as are described in the licence, or

(*b*) a group licence, that is a licence, issued by the Director (whether on the application of any person or of his own motion), which, during such period as the Director thinks fit or, if he thinks fit, indefinitely, covers such persons and activities as are described in the licence.

(2) A licence is not assignable or, subject to section 37, transmissible on death or in any other way.

(3) Except in the case of a partnership or an unincorporated body of persons, a standard licence shall not be issued to more than one person.

(4) A standard licence issued to a partnership or an unincorporated body of persons shall be issued in the name of the partnership or body.

(5) The Director may issue a group licence only if it appears to him that the

public interest is better served by doing so than by obliging the persons concerned to apply separately for standard licences.

(6) The persons covered by a group licence may be described by general words, whether or not coupled with the exclusion of named persons, or in any other way the Director thinks fit.

(7) The fact that a person is covered by a group licence in respect of certain activities does not prevent a standard licence being issued to him in respect of those activities or any of them.

(8) A group licence issued on the application of any person shall be issued to that person, and general notice shall be given of the issue of any group licence (whether on application or not). **[C.22]**

LICENCE
For the businesses which require a licence, see s. 21, *ante*. For the scope of licences, see ss. 23, 24, *post*, and as to their issue, renewal, variation, suspension and revocation, see ss. 25–33, *post*.

PERSON
See the note to s. 8, *ante*.

APPLICATION
As to the determination of applications, see ss. 25, 27, *post*, and as to appeal to the Secretary of State, see s. 41, *post*.

PRESCRIBED PERIOD
I.e., prescribed by regulations; see s. 189 (1), *post*. Nothing had been prescribed for the purposes of sub-s. (1) (*a*) up to the time of going to press.

ISSUED
This section applies also to the renewal of licences; see s. 29 (3), *post*.

EXCLUSION OF NAMED PERSONS
For procedural provisions on this point, see s. 28, *post*, and as to appeal, see s. 41, *post*.

DEFINITIONS
For "Director", and "general notice", see s. 189 (1), *post*.

## 23. Authorisation of specific activities

(1) Subject to this section, a licence to carry on a business covers all lawful activities done in the course of that business, whether by the licensee or other persons on his behalf.

(2) A licence may limit the activities it covers, whether by authorising the licensee to enter into certain types of agreement only, or in any other way.

(3) A licence covers the canvassing off trade premises of debtor-creditor-supplier agreements or regulated consumer hire agreements only if, and to the extent that, the licence specifically so provides; and such provision shall not be included in a group licence.

(4) Regulations may be made specifying other activities which, if engaged in by or on behalf of the person carrying on a business, require to be covered by an express term in his licence. **[C.23]**

LICENCE
For the businesses which require a licence, see s. 21, *ante*. For the types of licence which may be issued, see s. 22 (1), *ante*.

COVERS
It follows from the definition of "licensed" in s. 189 (1), *post*, that if a licensee performs an act which his licence does not cover, he is not licensed in relation to that act. As to the consequences of unlicensed trading, see the note "Required" to s. 21, *ante*.

PERSON
See the note to s. 8, *ante*.

CANVASSING . . . OFF TRADE PREMISES
For the meaning of these words, see s. 48, *post* (applied by s. 152, *post*, to certain ancillary credit businesses).

DEFINITIONS
For "business", "licence", "licensee" and "regulated agreement", see s. 189 (1), *post*. For "group licence", see s. 22 (1) (*b*), *ante*.

### 24. Control of name of business

A standard licence authorises the licensee to carry on a business under the name or names specified in the licence, but not under any other name. **[C.24]**

AUTHORITIES
Cf. the note "Covers" to s. 23, *ante*.

CARRY ON BUSINESS
See the note to s. 21, *ante*.

NOT UNDER ANY OTHER NAME
Contravention is an offence; see s. 39 (2), *post*.

DEFINITIONS
For "business", "licence" and "licensee", see s. 189 (1), *post*. For "standard licence", see s. 22 (1) (*a*), *ante*.

### 25. Licensee to be a fit person

(1) A standard licence shall be granted on the application of any person if he satisfies the Director that—

(*a*) he is a fit person to engage in activities covered by the licence, and
(*b*) the name or names under which he applies to be licensed is or are not misleading or otherwise undesirable.

(2) In determining whether an applicant for a standard licence is a fit person to engage in any activities, the Director shall have regard to any circumstances appearing to him to be relevant, and in particular any evidence tending to show that the applicant, or any of the applicant's employees, agents or associates (whether past or present) or, where the applicant is a body corporate, any person appearing to the Director to be a controller of the body corporate or an associate of any such person, has—

(*a*) committed any offence involving fraud or other dishonesty, or violence,
(*b*) contravened any provision made by or under this Act, or by or under any other enactment regulating the provision of credit to individuals or other transactions with individuals,
(*c*) practised discrimination on grounds of sex, colour, race or ethnic or natural origins in, or in connection with, the carrying on of any business, or

(*d*) engaged in business practices appearing to the Director to be deceitful or oppressive, or otherwise unfair or improper (whether unlawful or not).

(3) In subsection (2), "associate", in addition to the persons specified in section 184, includes a business associate. **[C.25]**

APPLICATION

For procedure in determining applications, see s. 27, *post*, and as to appeal to the Secretary of State, see s. 41, *post*. This section applies to the renewal of licences as to their issue; see s. 29 (3), *post*.

PERSON

See the note to s. 8, *ante*.

IF HE SATISFIES

The onus is on the applicant to satisfy the Director of his fitness and sub-s. (2) above confers a wide discretion upon the Director as to the matters which he takes into consideration. It is thought that the Director is bound to observe the principles of natural justice; see, e.g., *Ridge* v. *Baldwin*, [1964] A.C. 40; [1963] 2 All E.R. 66, H.L., and *R.* v. *Gaming Board for Great Britain, ex parte Benaim*, [1970] 2 All E.R. 528, C.A. The Director's duty to afford a hearing to the applicant is dealt with by ss. 27 and 34, *post*, and compliance with those sections will presumably be sufficient as a general rule.

COVERED

For the scope of licences, see ss. 23, 24, *ante*.

CONTRAVENED . . . THIS ACT

Provisions of this Act which create offences are listed in Sch. 1, *post*. *Quaere* whether the word "contravened" applies to non-compliance with provisions to which no criminal sanction is attached. It is thought that it would.

OTHER ENACTMENT REGULATING THE PROVISION OF CREDIT, ETC.

Enactments which clearly fall within the words "regulating the provision of credit" are the Money-Lenders Act 1900 (22 Halsbury's Statutes (3rd edn.) 693), the Moneylenders Act 1927 (22 Halsbury's Statutes (3rd edn.) 700), and the Hire-Purchase Act 1965 (30 Halsbury's Statutes (3rd edn.) 61) (all repealed by s. 192 (3) and Sch. 5, *post*). Of these, however, only the Act of 1965 could be said (by virtue of s. 4 thereof (30 Halsbury's Statutes (3rd edn.) 65)) to be confined to the provision of credit "to individuals".

NATIONAL ORIGINS

This is not the same thing as nationality; see *London Borough of Ealing* v. *Race Relations Board*, [1972] A.C. 342; [1972] 1 All E.R. 105, H.L.

CARRYING ON OF ANY BUSINESS

Occasional transactions do not amount to the carrying on of a business; see s. 189 (2), *post*.

DEFINITIONS

For "associate", see s. 184, *post*, with sub-s. (2) above.

For "business", "controller", "Director", "individual" and "licence", see s. 189 (1), *post*.

For "credit", see s. 9, *ante*.

For "standard licence", see s. 22 (1) (*a*), *ante*.

## 26. Conduct of business

Regulations may be made as to the conduct by a licensee of his business, and may in particular specify—

(*a*) the books and other records to be kept by him, and

(*b*) the information to be furnished by him to persons with whom he does business or seeks to do business, and the way it is to be furnished. **[C.26]**

EXTENSION
For further provisions which may be made by regulations under this section with regard to the seeking of business and to credit reference agencies, see ss. 54, 147 (2), *post.*

DEFINITIONS
For "business" and "licensee", see s. 189 (1), *post.*

REGULATIONS UNDER THIS SECTION
No regulations had been made under this section up to the time of going to press.
For general provisions as to regulations under this Act, see s. 182 (1)–(3), *post.*

*Issue of licences*

## 27. Determination of applications

(1) Unless the Director determines to issue a licence in accordance with an application he shall, before determining the application, by notice—

(*a*) inform the applicant, giving his reasons, that, as the case may be, he is minded to refuse the application, or to grant it in terms different from those applied for, describing them, and

(*b*) invite the applicant to submit to the Director representations in support of his application in accordance with section 34.

(2) If the Director grants the application in terms different from those applied for then, whether or not the applicant appeals, the Director shall issue the licence in the terms approved by him unless the applicant by notice informs him that he does not desire a licence in those terms. **[C.27]**

DETERMINES
For the grounds on which a determination is to be made, see s. 25, *ante.*

ISSUE
This section applies also to the renewal of a licence; see s. 29 (3), *post.*

GIVING HIS REASONS
It has been held that an arbitrator's reasons must be "proper, adequate reasons which . . . deal with the substantial points which have been raised" (*Re Poyser and Mills' Arbitration*, [1963] 1 All E.R. 612, at p. 616). That statement, however, cannot be literally applied to the present case, where there has been no hearing and no points have been raised. The important question here is whether the Director may simply state that he is not satisfied of the applicant's fitness (s. 25 (1) (*a*), *ante*) or is bound to go on to mention the circumstances to which he has had regard in that connection (s. 25 (2), *ante*). It is thought that the applicant is entitled to be given such statement of reasons as will afford him reasonable notice of the case he has to meet, so that he can direct written or oral representations to the points in issue.

APPEALS
I.e., to the Secretary of State under s. 41, *post.*

DEFINITIONS
For "Director", "licence" and "notice", see s. 189 (1), *post.*

## 28. Exclusion from group licence

Where the Director is minded to issue a group licence (whether on the application of any person or not), and in doing so to exclude any person from the group by name, he shall, before determining the matter,—

(*a*) give notice of that fact to the person proposed to be excluded, giving his reasons, and

(*b*) invite that person to submit to the Director representations against his exclusion in accordance with section 34. **[C.28]**

EXCLUDE ANY PERSON . . . BY NAME

For the Director's power to do this, see s. 22 (6), *ante*. As to the case of renewal of a group licence, see s. 29 (3), *post*.

PERSON

See the note to s. 8, *ante*.

GIVING HIS REASONS

See the note to s. 27, *ante*.

DEFINITIONS

For "give" and "notice", see s. 189 (1), *post*.
For "group licence", see s. 22 (1) (*b*), *ante*.

*Renewal, variation, suspension and revocation of licences*

## 29. Renewal

(1) If the licensee under a standard licence, or the original applicant for, or any licensee under, a group licence of limited duration, wishes the Director to renew the licence, whether on the same terms (except as to expiry) or on varied terms, he must, during the period specified by the Director by general notice or such longer period as the Director may allow, make an application to the Director for its renewal.

(2) The Director may of his own motion renew any group licence.

(3) The preceding provisions of this Part apply to the renewal of a licence as they apply to the issue of a licence, except that section 28 does not apply to a person who was already excluded in the licence up for renewal.

(4) Until the determination of an application under subsection (1) and, where an appeal lies from the determination, until the end of the appeal period, the licence shall continue in force, notwithstanding that apart from this subsection it would expire earlier.

(5) On the refusal of an application under this section, the Director may give directions authorising a licensee to carry into effect agreements made by him before the expiry of the licence.

(6) General notice shall be given of the renewal of a group licence. **[C.29]**

PRECEDING PROVISIONS OF THIS PART

I.e., ss. 21–28, *ante*.

PERSON

See the note to s. 8, *ante*.

APPEAL

I.e., to the Secretary of State under s. 41, *post*. Such appeal lies either against a refusal to renew a licence or against a refusal to give directions under sub-s. (5) above.

DEFINITIONS

For "appeal period", "Director", "general notice" and "licensee", see s. 189 (1), *post*.
For "group licence" and "standard licence", see s. 22 (1), *ante*.

### 30. Variation by request

(1) On an application made by the licensee, the Director may if he thinks fit by notice to the licensee vary a standard licence in accordance with the application.

(2) In the case of a group licence issued on the application of any person, the Director, on an application made by that person, may if he thinks fit by notice to that person vary the terms of the licence in accordance with the application; but the Director shall not vary a group licence under this subsection by excluding a named person, other than the person making the request, unless that named person consents in writing to his exclusion.

(3) In the case of a group licence from which (whether by name or description) a person is excluded, the Director, on an application made by that person, may if he thinks fit, by notice to that person, vary the terms of the licence so as to remove the exclusion.

(4) Unless the Director determines to vary a licence in accordance with an application he shall, before determining the application, by notice—

(*a*) inform the applicant, giving his reasons, that he is minded to refuse the application, and

(*b*) invite the applicant to submit to the Director representations in support of his application in accordance with section 34.

(5) General notice shall be given that a variation of a group licence has been made under this section. **[C.30]**

MAY IF HE THINKS FIT
These words confer a wide discretion on the Director. As to his duty to observe the principles of natural justice, cf. the note "If he satisfies" to s. 25, *ante*. An appeal against refusal lies to the Secretary of State under s. 41, *post*.

PERSON
See the note to s. 8, *ante*.

EXCLUDED
For power to exclude persons from group licences, see s. 22 (6), *ante*.

GIVING HIS REASONS
See the note to s. 27, *ante*.

DEFINITIONS
For "Director", "general notice", "licensee" and "notice", see s. 189 (1), *post*. For "group licence" and "standard licence", see s. 22 (1), *ante*.

### 31. Compulsory variation

(1) Where at a time during the currency of a licence the Director is of the opinion that, if the licence had expired at that time, he would, on an application for its renewal or further renewal on the same terms (except as to expiry), have been minded to grant the application but on different terms, and that therefore the licence should be varied, he shall proceed as follows.

(2) In the case of a standard licence the Director shall, by notice—

(*a*) inform the licensee of the variations the Director is minded to make in the terms of the licence, stating his reasons, and

(*b*) invite him to submit to the Director representations as to the proposed variations in accordance with section 34.

(3) In the case of a group licence the Director shall—

(*a*) give general notice of the variations he is minded to make in the terms of the licence, stating his reasons, and

(*b*) in the notice invite any licensee to submit to him representations as to the proposed variations in accordance with section 34.

(4) In the case of a group licence issued on application the Director shall also—

(*a*) inform the original applicant of the variations the Director is minded to make in the terms of the licence, stating his reasons, and

(*b*) invite him to submit to the Director representations as to the proposed variations in accordance with section 34.

(5) If the Director is minded to vary a group licence by excluding any person (other than the original applicant) from the group by name the Director shall, in addition, take the like steps under section 28 as are required in the case mentioned in that section.

(6) General notice shall be given that a variation of any group licence has been made under this section.

(7) A variation under this section shall not take effect before the end of the appeal period. [C.31]

GENERAL NOTE

Though this section nowhere states in so many words that the Director has a discretion to vary the terms of a licence at any time during its currency, that seems to be clearly implied. Subsection (1) states the condition on which the machinery of the section may be put into motion, i.e., that the Director should be of the opinion there described. Subsections (2)–(5) prescribe the procedure to be followed in various cases for the purpose of inviting representations from interested parties. Subsections (6) and (7) then make provisions for the event that a variation is made. The proposition which is left to be implied is that if, after considering any representations made to him, the Director is still of the opinion described in sub-s. (1), he has power to vary the licence.

RENEWAL

For provisions as to renewal, see s. 29, *ante*.

PERSON

See the note to s. 8, *ante*.

APPEAL

An appeal lies to the Secretary of State against the variation of a licence under this section; see s. 41, *post*.

DEFINITIONS

For "appeal period", "Director", "general notice", "licensee" and "notice", see s. 189 (1), *post*.

For "group licence" and "standard licence", see s. 22 (1), *ante*.

## 32. Suspension and revocation

(1) Where at a time during the currency of a licence the Director is of the opinion that if the licence had expired at that time he would have been minded not to renew it, and that therefore it should be revoked or suspended, he shall proceed as follows.

(2) In the case of a standard licence the Director shall, by notice—

(*a*) inform the licensee that, as the case may be, the Director is minded to revoke the licence, or suspend it until a specified date or indefinitely, stating his reasons, and

(*b*) invite him to submit representations as to the proposed revocation or suspension in accordance with section 34.

(3) In the case of a group licence the Director shall—

(*a*) give general notice that, as the case may be, he is minded to revoke the licence, or suspend it until a specified date or indefinitely, stating his reasons, and

(*b*) in the notice invite any licensee to submit to him representations as to the proposed revocation or suspension in accordance with section 34.

(4) In the case of a group licence issued on application the Director shall also—

(*a*) inform the original applicant that, as the case may be, the Director is minded to revoke the licence, or suspend it until a specified date or indefinitely, stating his reasons, and

(*b*) invite him to submit representations as to the proposed revocation or suspension in accordance with section 34.

(5) If he revokes or suspends the licence, the Director may give directions authorising a licensee to carry into effect agreements made by him before the revocation or suspension.

(6) General notice shall be given of the revocation or suspension of a group licence.

(7) A revocation or suspension under this section shall not take effect before the end of the appeal period.

(8) Except for the purposes of section 29, a licensee under a suspended licence shall be treated, in respect of the period of suspension, as if the licence had not been issued; and where the suspension is not expressed to end on a specified date it may, if the Director thinks fit, be ended by notice given by him to the licensee or, in the case of a group licence, by general notice. **[C.32]**

GENERAL NOTE

As in the case of s. 31, *ante* (see the General Note thereto), this section contains no express words conferring the power which is clearly implied in its provisions (in this case, the power to revoke or suspend a licence). Subsection (1) provides that if the Director is of the opinion there described, he shall set the procedure of the section in motion. Subsections (2)–(4) provide procedures for different cases, with a view to affording interested parties an opportunity to make representations. Subsections (5)–(8) go on to deal with various consequences of revocation or suspension. What must obviously be implied is that if, after considering any representations made to him, the Director is still of the opinion described in sub-s. (1), he has a discretion to revoke or suspend the licence.

NOT TO RENEW IT

As to renewal, see s. 29, *ante*. By virtue of s. 29 (3), the grounds for refusal to issue a licence under s. 25, *ante*, are also grounds for refusal to renew it.

STATING HIS REASONS

See the note "Giving his reasons" to s. 27, *ante*.

APPEAL

An appeal lies to the Secretary of State under s. 41, *post*, against the revocation or suspension of a licence, or against a refusal to give directions under sub-s. (5) above.

DEFINITIONS
For "appeal period", "Director", "general notice", "licensee" and "notice", see s. 189 (1), *post.*
For "group licence" and "standard licence", see s. 22 (1), *ante.*

## 33. Application to end suspension

(1) On an application made by a licensee the Director may, if he thinks fit, by notice to the licensee end the suspension of a licence, whether the suspension was for a fixed or indefinite period.

(2) Unless the Director determines to end the suspension in accordance with the application he shall, before determining the application, by notice—

(*a*) inform the applicant, giving his reasons, that he is minded to refuse the application, and

(*b*) invite the applicant to submit to the Director representations in support of his application in accordance with section 34.

(3) General notice shall be given that a suspension of a group licence has been ended under this section.

(4) In the case of a group licence issued on application—

(*a*) the references in subsection (1) to a licensee include the original applicant;

(*b*) the Director shall inform the original applicant that a suspension of a group licence has been ended under this section. [C.33]

MAY IF HE THINKS FIT
These words confer a wide discretion on the Director. As to his duty to observe the principles of natural justice, cf. the note "If he satisfies" to s. 25, *ante.* An appeal against refusal lies to the Secretary of State under s. 41, *post.*

SUSPENSION
A licence may be suspended under s. 32, *ante.*

GIVING HIS REASONS
See the note to s. 27, *ante.*

DEFINITIONS
For "Director", "general notice", "licence", "licensee" and "notice", see s. 189 (1), *post.*
For "group licence", see s. 22 (1), *ante.*

*Miscellaneous*

## 34. Representations to Director

(1) Where this section applies to an invitation by the Director to any person to submit representations, the Director shall invite that person, within 21 days after the notice containing the invitation is given to him or published, or such longer period as the Director may allow,—

(*a*) to submit his representations in writing to the Director, and

(*b*) to give notice to the Director, if he thinks fit, that he wishes to make representations orally,

and where notice is given under paragraph (*b*) the Director shall arrange for the oral representations to be heard.

(2) In reaching his determination the Director shall take into account any representations submitted or made under this section.

(3) The Director shall give notice of his determination to the persons who were required to be invited to submit representations about it or, where the invitation to submit representations was required to be given by general notice, shall give general notice of the determination. **[C.34]**

WHERE THIS SECTION APPLIES
This section is applied by ss. 27, 28, 30, 31, 32, 33, *ante*, and ss. 40, 148, 149, *post*.

PERSON
See the note to s. 8, *ante*.

DEFINITIONS
For "Director", "general notice", "give" and "notice", see s. 189 (1), *post*.

### 35. The register

(1) The Director shall establish and maintain a register, in which he shall cause to be kept particulars of—

(*a*) applications not yet determined for the issue, variation or renewal of licences, or for ending the suspension of a licence;
(*b*) licences which are in force, or have at any time been suspended or revoked, with details of any variation of the terms of a licence;
(*c*) decisions given by him under this Act, and any appeal from those decisions; and
(*d*) such other matters (if any) as he thinks fit.

(2) The Director shall give general notice of the various matters required to be entered in the register, and of any change in them made under subsection (1) (*d*).

(3) Any person shall be entitled, on payment of the specified fee—

(*a*) to inspect the register during ordinary office hours and take copies of any entry, or
(*b*) to obtain from the Director a copy, certified by the Director to be correct, of any entry in the register.

(4) The Director may, if he thinks fit, determine that the right conferred by subsection (3) (*a*) shall be exercisable in relation to a copy of the register instead of or in addition to, the original.

(5) The Director shall give general notice of the place or places where, and times when the register or a copy of it may be inspected. **[C.35]**

COMMENCEMENT
See Sch. 3, para. 6, *post*, and the note "Appointed days" to Part III of that Schedule.

APPLICATIONS
As to the applications referred to in sub-s. (1) (*a*), see ss. 25 (issue), 29 (renewal), 30 (variation) and 33 (ending suspension), *ante*.

APPEAL
Appeals may be brought against decisions of the Director under s. 41, *post*.

SPECIFIED FEE

For power to specify fees, see s. 2 (4), (5), *ante*.

COPIES

For power to prescribe the form, etc., of copies, see s. 180, *post*.

NOTIFICATION OF CHANGES

For the duty of licensees to notify changes in registered information, see s. 36, *post*

**36. Duty to notify changes**

(1) Within 21 working days after a change takes place in any particulars entered in the register in respect of a standard licence or the licensee under section 35 (1) (*d*) (not being a change resulting from action taken by the Director), the licensee shall give the Director notice of the change; and the Director shall cause any necessary amendment to be made in the register.

(2) Within 21 working days after—

(*a*) any change takes place in the officers of—

(i) a body corporate, or an unincorporated body of persons, which is the licensee under a standard licence, or

(ii) a body corporate which is a controller of a body corporate which is such a licensee, or

(*b*) a body corporate which is such a licensee becomes aware that a person has become or ceased to be a controller of the body corporate, or

(*c*) any change takes place in the members of a partnership which is such a licensee, (including a change on the amalgamation of the partnership with another firm, or a change whereby the number of partners is reduced to one),

the licensee shall give the Director notice of the change.

(3) Within 14 working days after any change takes place in the officers of a body corporate which is a controller of another body corporate which is a licensee under a standard licence, the controller shall give the licensee notice of the change.

(4) Within 14 working days after a person becomes or ceases to be a controller of a body corporate which is a licensee under a standard licence, that person shall give the licensee notice of the fact.

(5) Where a change in a partnership has the result that the business ceases to be carried on under the name, or any of the names, specified in a standard licence the licence shall cease to have effect.

(6) Where the Director is given notice under subsection (1) or (2) of any change, and subsection (5) does not apply, the Director may by notice require the licensee to furnish him with such information, verified in such manner, as the Director may stipulate. **[C.36]**

COMMENCEMENT

See Sch. 3, para. 6, *post*, and the note "Appointed days" to Part III of that Schedule.

WITHIN 21 DAYS; WITHIN 14 DAYS

The date of the change is to be excluded from the computation; see *Goldsmiths' Co.* v. *West Metropolitan Rail Co.*, [1904] 1 K.B. 1; [1900–3] All E.R. Rep. 667.

OFFICERS

In the Companies Act 1948, s. 455 (1) (5 Halsbury's Statutes (3rd edn.) 430) "officer" is defined as including a director, manager or secretary. It is thought that this is an acceptable definition for the present purpose, provided that "manager" is understood to mean a person with responsibilities in relation to the company as a whole and not a mere subordinate such as a branch manager (cf. the discussion of a branch manager's position in *Tesco Supermarkets Ltd.* v. *Nattrass*, [1971] 2 All E.R. 127, H.L.). An auditor has been held to be an officer for certain purposes (*Re London and General Bank*, [1895] 2 Ch. 166, C.A.) but it seems doubtful whether an auditor is intended to be included here.

OFFENCES

Failure to comply with this section is an offence; see s. 39 (3), *post*.

DEFINITIONS

For "controller", "Director", "give", "licence", "licensee", "notice", "register" and "working day", see s. 189 (1), *post*.

For "standard licence", see s. 22 (1), *ante*.

**37. Death, bankruptcy etc. of licensee**

(1) A licence held by one individual terminates if he—

(*a*) dies, or

(*b*) is adjudged bankrupt, or

(*c*) becomes a patient within the meaning of Part VIII of the Mental Health Act 1959.

(2) In relation to a licence held by one individual, or a partnership or other unincorporated body of persons, or a body corporate, regulations may specify other events relating to the licensee on the occurrence of which the licence is to terminate.

(3) Regulations may—

(*a*) provide for the termination of a licence by subsection (1), or under subsection (2), to be deferred for a period not exceeding 12 months and

(*b*) authorise the business of the licensee to be carried on under the licence by some other person during the period of deferment, subject to such conditions as may be prescribed.

(4) This section does not apply to group licences. [**C.37**]

ONE INDIVIDUAL

Although "individual" is defined by s. 189 (1), *post*, as including a partnership, it seems that in this section "one individual" is used in contradistinction to a partnership or association.

ADJUDGED BANKRUPT

As to orders adjudging a person bankrupt, see the Bankruptcy Act 1914, s. 18 (3 Halsbury's Statutes (3rd edn.) 60).

PERSON

See the note to s. 8, *ante*.

DEFINITIONS

For "business", "individual", "licence", "licensee" and "regulations", see s. 189 (1), *post*.

For "group licence", see s. 22 (1), *ante*.

MENTAL HEALTH ACT 1959, PART VIII

I.e., ss. 100–121 of that Act (25 Halsbury's Statutes (3rd edn.) 129 *et seq.*).

REGULATIONS UNDER THIS SECTION

No regulations had been made for the purposes of this section up to the time of going to press.

For general provisions as to regulations under this Act, see s. 182 (1)–(3), *post*.

NORTHERN IRELAND

For provisions having effect instead of sub-s. (1) above, see s. 38 (2), *post*.

## 38. Application of s. 37 to Scotland and Northern Ireland

(1) In the application of section 37 to Scotland the following shall be substituted for paragraphs (*b*) and (*c*) of subsection (1)—

"(*b*) has his estate sequestrated, or

(*c*) becomes incapable of managing his own affairs."

(2) In the application of section 37 to Northern Ireland the following shall be substituted for subsection (1)—

"(1) A licence held by one individual terminates if—

(*a*) he dies, or

(*b*) he is adjudged bankrupt or his estate and effects vest in the official assignee under section 349 of the Irish Bankrupt and Insolvent Act 1857, or

(*c*) a declaration is made under section 15 of the Lunacy Regulation (Ireland) Act 1871 that he is of unsound mind and incapable of managing his person or property, or an order is made under section 68 of that Act in consequence of its being found that he is of unsound mind and incapable of managing his affairs.".

ONE INDIVIDUAL

See the note to s. 37, *ante*.

LICENCE

For meaning, see s. 189 (1), *post*.

IRISH BANKRUPT AND INSOLVENT ACT 1857

20 & 21 Vict. c. 60.

LUNACY REGULATION (IRELAND) ACT 1871

34 & 35 Vict. c. 22.

## 39. Offences against Part III

(1) A person who engages in any activities for which a licence is required when he is not a licensee under a licence covering those activities commits an offence.

(2) A licensee under a standard licence who carries on business under a name not specified in the licence commits an offence.

(3) A person who fails to give the Director or a licensee notice under section 36 within the period required commits an offence. **[C.39]**

PERSON

See the note to s. 7, *ante*.

LICENCE . . . REQUIRED

For the activities for which a licencei s required, see s. 21, *ante*, and that section as extended by s. 147 (1), *post*.

COVERING

**For the scope of licences, see ss. 23, 24, *ante*.**

CARRIES ON BUSINESS

**See the note to s. 21, *ante*.**

OFFENCE

**As to notification of convictions to the Director, see s. 166, *post*. For mode of prosecution and penalties, see s. 167 (1) and Sch. 1, *post*. For special defences, see s. 168, *post*. As to offences by bodies corporate, see s. 169, *post*.**

DEFINITIONS

**For "business", "Director", "give", "licence", "licensee" and "notice", see s. 189 (1), *post*. For "standard licence", see s. 22 (1), *ante*.**

## 40. Enforcement of agreements made by unlicensed trader

(1) A regulated agreement, other than a non-commercial agreement, if made when the creditor or owner was unlicensed, is enforceable against the debtor or hirer only where the Director has made an order under this section which applies to the agreement.

(2) Where during any period an unlicensed person (the "trader") was carrying on a consumer credit business or consumer hire business, he or his successor in title may apply to the Director for an order that regulated agreements made by the trader during that period are to be treated as if he had been licensed.

(3) Unless the Director determines to make an order under subsection (2) in accordance with the application, he shall, before determining the application, by notice—

(*a*) inform the applicant, giving his reasons, that, as the case may be, he is minded to refuse the application, or to grant it in terms different from those applied for, describing them, and

(*b*) invite the applicant to submit to the Director representations in support of his application in accordance with section 34.

(4) In determining whether or not to make an order under subsection (2) in respect of any period the Director shall consider, in addition to any other relevant factors—

(*a*) how far, if at all, debtors or hirers under regulated agreements made by the trader during that period were prejudiced by the trader's conduct,

(*b*) whether or not the Director would have been likely to grant a licence covering that period on an application by the trader, and

(*c*) the degree of culpability for the failure to obtain a licence.

(5) If the Director thinks fit, he may in an order under subsection (2)—

(*a*) limit the order to specified agreements, or agreements of a specified description or made at a specified time;

(*b*) make the order conditional on the doing of specified acts by the applicant. [C.40]

COMMENCEMENT

See Sch. 3, para. 7, *post*, and the note "Appointed days" to Part III of that Schedule.

GENERAL NOTE

This section deals with the consequences, so far as civil liabilities are concerned, of trading without the licence required by this Part of this Act. This section must be read in the light of s. 170 (1), *post*, which provides that a breach of the Act incurs no civil or criminal sanction except as expressly provided. Therefore there is no room for the usual implication that transactions in contravention of the Act are *ipso facto* void and this section deals exhaustively with the question of unlicensed trading.

It must also be read in the light of s. 173, *post*. Subsection (1) of that section prohibits contracting out of the provisions of this Act, so that it will not avail an unlicensed trader to insert terms in his contracts to the effect that they shall be enforceable notwithstanding the provisions of the Act. Section 173 (3), however, provides that the consent of the other party, given at the time when enforcement is sought, is an adequate substitute for the Director's order.

Subject to that, this section renders the agreements of an unlicensed trader unenforceable unless the Director has made an order under this section (sub-s. (1)). Subsections (2) and (3) provide for applications for the Director's order and for the applicant to be afforded an opportunity to be heard.

Subsection (4) enumerates the factors to be considered by the Director and sub-s. (5) empowers him to make conditional orders or orders limited to particular agreements or periods of time.

SUB-S. (1) ENFORCEABLE

For consequences relative to any security provided in connection with the agreement, see s. 113, *post*.

ONLY

See, however, s. 173 (3), *post* (summarised in the General Note above).

SUB-S. (2): PERSON

See the note to s. 8, *ante*.

CONSUMER CREDIT BUSINESS

For meaning, see s. 189 (1), *post*. The extension of this Part of this Act to ancillary credit businesses by s. 147 (1), *post*, does not include this section. For comparable provisions relating to ancillary credit businesses, see s. 148, *post*.

SUB-S. (3): DETERMINES

It is thought that the Director must observe the principles of natural justice; cf. the note "If he satisfies" to s. 25, *ante*.

GIVING HIS REASONS

See the note to s. 27, *ante*.

SUB-S. (4): LIKELY TO GRANT A LICENCE

For factors to be taken into account when the Director considers whether to grant a licence, see s. 25, *ante*.

APPEAL

An appeal lies to the Secretary of State against refusal of an order under this section; s. 41, *post*.

DEFINITIONS

For "business", "consumer credit business", "consumer hire business", "creditor", "debtor", "Director", "hirer", "licence", "licensed", "non-commercial agreement", "notice", "owner", "regulated agreement" and "unlicensed", see s. 189 (1), *post*.

For "trader", see sub-s. (2) above.

## 41. Appeals to Secretary of State under Part III

(1) If, in the case of a determination by the Director such as is mentioned in column 1 of the table set out at the end of this section, a person mentioned in relation to that determination in column 2 of the table is aggrieved by the determination he may, within the prescribed period, and in the prescribed manner, appeal to the Secretary of State.

(2) Regulations may make provision as to the persons by whom (on behalf

of the Secretary of State) appeals under this section are to be heard, the manner in which they are to be conducted, and any other matter connected with such appeals.

(3) On an appeal under this section, the Secretary of State may give such directions for disposing of the appeal as he thinks just, including a direction for the payment of costs by any party to the appeal.

(4) A direction under subsection (3) for payment of costs may be made a rule of the High Court on the application of the party in whose favour it is given.

(5) In Scotland a direction under subsection (3) for payment of expenses may be enforced in like manner as a recorded decree arbitral.

TABLE

| *Determination* | *Appellant* |
|---|---|
| Refusal to issue, renew or vary licence in accordance with terms of application. | The applicant. |
| Exclusion of person from group licence. | The person excluded. |
| Refusal to give directions in respect of a licensee under section 29 (5) or 32 (5). | The licensee. |
| Compulsory variation, or suspension or revocation, of standard licence. | The licensee. |
| Compulsory variation, or suspension or revocation, of group licence. | The original applicant or any licensee. |
| Refusal to end suspension of licence in accordance with terms of application. | The applicant. |
| Refusal to make order under section 40 (2) in accordance with terms of application. | The applicant. |

**[C.41]**

PERSON
See the note to s. 8, *ante*.

MAY GIVE SUCH DIRECTIONS
The Secretary of State must act fairly and judicially. He must not tie his hands by policy decisions which preclude the proper consideration of both sides of a case, but this does not mean that he may not have a policy on relevant matters; see *Stringer* v. *Minister of Housing and Local Government*, [1971] 1 All E.R. 65. In that case it was also decided that under the Town and Country Planning Act 1971 (41 Halsbury's Statutes (3rd edn.) 1571) the Secretary of State may exercise his appellate jurisdiction even though the order appealed against is a nullity. The position may be the same under this section, but there are material differences in the wording of the relevant provisions.

EXTENSION
A further entry is added to the Table by s. 152, *post*.

FURTHER APPEAL
A further appeal lies to the High Court on a point of law; see s. 42, *post*.

DEFINITIONS
For "Director", "prescribed" and "regulations", see s. 189 (1), *post*.

REGULATIONS UNDER THIS SECTION
No regulations had been made under this section up to the time of going to press.
For general provisions as to regulations under this Act, see s. 182 (1)–(3), *post*.

**42. Further appeal on point of law**

(1) In section 13 of the Tribunals and Inquiries Act 1971 (subsection (1) of which provides that on a point of law an appeal shall lie to the High Court from a decision of any tribunal mentioned in that subsection or the tribunal may be required to state a case for the opinion of the High Court), insert the following new subsection after subsection (5)—

"(5A) Subsection (1) of this section shall apply to a decision of the Secretary of State on an appeal under section 41 of the Consumer Credit Act 1974 from a determination of the Director General of Fair Trading as it applies to a decision of any of the tribunals mentioned in that subsection, but with the substitution for the reference to a party to proceedings of a reference to any person who had a right to appeal to the Secretary of State (whether or not he has exercised that right); and accordingly references in subsections (1) and (3) of this section to a tribunal shall be construed, in relation to such an appeal, as references to the Secretary of State."

(2) In subsection (6) (*a*) of the said section 13 (application to Scotland), after the word "commissioners" there shall be inserted the words "or on an appeal under section 41 of the Consumer Credit Act 1974 by a company registered in Scotland or by any other person whose principal or prospective principal place of business in the United Kingdom is in Scotland".

(3) In subsection (7) of the said section 13 (application to Northern Ireland) after "subsection (1) of this section" insert "and in relation to a decision of the Secretary of State on an appeal under section 41 of the Consumer Credit Act 1974 by a company registered in Northern Ireland or by any other person whose principal or prospective principal place of business in the United Kingdom is in Northern Ireland. [C.42]

GENERAL NOTE

This section amends the Tribunals and Inquiries Act 1971, s. 13 (41 Halsbury's Statutes (3rd edn.) 258) so as to allow an appeal on a point of law to the High Court from the Secretary of State acting under s. 41, *ante*. Proceedings may take the form of a simple appeal, or of a case stated for the opinion of the High Court (s. 13 (1) of the Act of 1971). The matter comes before a Divisional Court of the Q.B.D. and procedure is governed by R.S.C. Ords. 55–57 and Ord. 94, ss. 8, 9. The decision of the High Court is appealable to the Court of Appeal by virtue of s. 13 (2) of the Act of 1971.

HAD A RIGHT TO APPEAL

For the persons who have such a right, see the Table at the end of s. 41, *ante*. The new sub-s. (5A) above evidently envisages that the appeal to the High Court may be brought by a potential appellant under s. 41, *ante*, who has not actually appealed under that section. This cannot mean that an appeal may lie directly from the Director to the High Court, by-passing the Secretary of State, for it is clear that sub-s. (5A) applies only to "a decision of the Secretary of State". The case envisaged must therefore be that one licensee under a group licence has appealed to the Secretary of State and another licensee under the same licence wishes (though not a party to the proceedings before the Secretary of State) to take the matter further, to the High Court.

PRINCIPAL PLACE OF BUSINESS

As to what is a "place of business", see *Lord Advocate* v. *Huron* and *Erie Loan and Savings Co.*, 1911 S.C. 612. Cf. also the decisions on the expression "principal office" in *Garton* v. *Great Western Rail Co.* (1858), E.B. & E. 837, and *Palmer* v. *Caledonian Rail Co.*, [1892] 1 Q.B. 823.

TRIBUNALS AND INQUIRIES ACT 1971, S. 13

See 41 Halsbury's Statutes (3rd edn.) 258.

## Part IV

## Seeking Business

### *Advertising*

### 43. Advertisements to which Part IV applies

(1) This Part applies to any advertisement, published for the purposes of a business carried on by the advertiser, indicating that he is willing—

(*a*) to provide credit, or

(*b*) to enter into an agreement for the bailment or (in Scotland) the hiring of goods by him.

(2) An advertisement does not fall within subsection (1) if the advertiser does not carry on—

(*a*) a consumer credit business or consumer hire business, or

(*b*) a business in the course of which he provides credit to individuals secured on land, or

(*c*) a business which comprises or relates to unregulated agreements where—

(i) the proper law of the agreement is the law of a country outside the United Kingdom, and

(ii) if the proper law of the agreement were the law of a part of the United Kingdom it would be a regulated agreement.

(3) An advertisement does not fall within subsection (1) (*a*) if it indicates—

(*a*) that the credit must exceed £5,000, and that no security is required, or the security is to consist of property other than land, or

(*b*) that the credit is available only to a body corporate.

(4) An advertisement does not fall within subsection (1) (*b*) if it indicates that the advertiser is not willing to enter into a consumer hire agreement.

(5) The Secretary of State may by order provide that this Part shall not apply to other advertisements of a description specified in the order. [C.43]

COMMENCEMENT

See Sch. 3, para. 8, *post*, and the note "Appointed days" to Part IV of that Schedule.

THIS PART

I.e., ss. 43–51.

CARRY ON

See the note "Carry on business" to s. 21, *ante*.

£5,000

This amount is subject to amendment under s. 181, *post*.

DEFINITIONS

For "advertisement", "advertiser", "business", "consumer credit business", "consumer hire business", "goods", "individual", "land" and "security", see s. 189 (1), *post*.

For "consumer hire agreement" see s. 15, *ante*, and for "credit", see s. 9, *ante*.

ORDERS UNDER THIS SECTION

No orders had been made under this section up to the time of going to press.

For general provisions as to orders under this Act, see s. 182 (1), (2), (4), *post*.

## 44. Form and content of advertisements

(1) The Secretary of State shall make regulations as to the form and content of advertisements to which this Part applies, and the regulations shall contain such provisions as appear to him appropriate with a view to ensuring that, having regard to its subject-matter and the amount of detail included in it, an advertisement conveys a fair and reasonably comprehensive indication of the nature of the credit or hire facilities offered by the advertiser and of their true cost to persons using them.

(2) Regulations under subsection (1) may in particular—

(*a*) require specified information to be included in the prescribed manner in advertisements, and other specified material to be excluded;

(*b*) contain requirements to ensure that specified information is clearly brought to the attention of persons to whom advertisements are directed, and that one part of an advertisement is not given insufficient or excessive prominence compared with another. **[C.44]**

COMMENCEMENT

See Sch. 3, para. 8, *post*, and the note "Appointed days" to Part IV of that Schedule.

TO WHICH THIS PART APPLIES

For the advertisements to which this Part (ss. 43–51) applies, see s. 43, *ante*. This section and ss. 45–47 are applied to a further category of advertisements by s. 151 (1), *post*, and this section and ss. 46, 47 are applied to a further category of advertisements by s. 151 (2), *post* (see also s. 151 (3)–(5), *post*).

ADVERTISEMENT

For meaning, see s. 189 (1), *post*.

REGULATIONS

For meaning, see s. 189 (1), *post*. Regulations under this section may include provision as to onus of proof (s. 171 (3), *post*) and contravention is an offence (s. 167 (2), *post*). For general provisions as to regulations under this Act, see s. 182 (1)–(3), *post*.

No regulations had been made under this section up to the time of going to press.

## 45. Prohibition of advertisement where goods etc. not sold for cash

If an advertisement to which this Part applies indicates that the advertiser is willing to provide credit under a restricted-use credit agreement relating to goods or services to be supplied by any person, but at the time when the advertisement is published that person is not holding himself out as prepared to sell the goods or provide the services (as the case may be) for cash, the advertiser commits an offence. **[C.45]**

COMMENCEMENT

See Sch. 3, para. 8, *post*, and the note "Appointed days" to Part IV of that Schedule.

TO WHICH THIS PART APPLIES

See the note to s. 44, *ante*.

ADVERTISER

For meaning, see s. 189 (1), *post*. For other persons who are also guilty of an offence when an advertiser contravenes this section, see s. 47( 1), *post*.

PERSON

See the note to s. 8, *ante*.

OFFENCE
As to notification of convictions to the Director, see s. 166, *post.* For mode of prosecution and penalties, see s. 167 (1) and Sch. 1, *post.* For special defences, see s. 168, *post.* As to offences by bodies corporate, see s. 169, *post.*

DEFINITIONS
For "advertisement", "cancellable agreement", "cash", "goods" and "payment", see s. 189 (1), *post.*
For "credit", see s. 9, *ante*; for "notice of cancellation", see s. 69 (1), *post,* and for "restricted-use credit agreement" see s. 11 (1), *ante.*

### 46. False or misleading advertisements

(1) If an advertisement to which this Part applies conveys information which in a material respect is false or misleading the advertiser commits an offence.

(2) Information stating or implying an intention on the advertiser's part which he has not got is false. **[C.46]**

COMMENCEMENT
See Sch. 3, para. 8, *post,* and the note "Appointed days" to Part IV of that Schedule.

ADVERTISEMENT
For meaning, see s. 189 (1), *post.*

TO WHICH THIS PART APPLIES
See the note to s. 44, *ante.*

FALSE
See the note to s. 7, *ante,* and note also the provisions of sub-s. (2) above.

MATERIAL RESPECT
See the note "Material particular" to s. 7, *ante.*

ADVERTISER
For meaning, see s. 189 (1), *post.* For other persons who are also guilty of an offence when an advertiser contravenes this section, see s. 47 (1), *post.*

OFFENCE
As to notification of convictions to the Director, see s. 166, *post.* For mode of prosecution and penalties, see s. 167 (1) and Sch. 1, *post.* For special defences, see s. 168, *post.* As to offences by bodies corporate, see s. 169, *post.*

### 47. Advertising infringements

(1) Where an advertiser commits an offence against regulations made under section 44 or against section 45 or 46, or would be taken to commit such an offence but for the defence provided by section 168, a like offence is committed by—

(*a*) the publisher of the advertisement, and
(*b*) any person who, in the course of a business carried on by him, devised the advertisement, or a part of it relevant to the first-mentioned offence, and
(*c*) where the advertiser did not procure the publication of the advertisement, the person who did procure it.

(2) In proceedings for an offence under subsection (1) (*a*) it is a defence for the person charged to prove that—

(*a*) the advertisement was published in the course of a business carried on by him, and

(*b*) he received the advertisement in the course of that business, and did not know and had no reason to suspect that its publication would be an offence under this Part. **[C.47]**

COMMENCEMENT

See Sch. 3, para. 8, *post*, and the note "Appointed days" to Part IV of that Schedule.

OFFENCE

For the offence of contravening regulations under s. 44, *ante*, see s. 167 (2), *post*. For offences against ss. 45, 46, *ante*, see ss. 45 (1), 46 (1) respectively. See also the note to s. 46, *ante*.

PUBLISHER

This term is not defined. The meaning of "publish" has often been considered for the purposes of the law of libel (see *Pullman* v. *Hill & Co.*, [1891] 1 Q.B. 524, C.A., and other cases cited in 24 Halsbury's Laws (3rd edn.) 33–41) and of the law of copyright (see *Boucicault* v. *Chatterton* (1876), 5 Ch.D. 267, C.A., and *McFarlane* v. *Hulton*, [1899] 1 Ch. 884, at p. 888). If the definitions in these cases are to be adopted, there will often be more than one publisher of an advertisement (e.g., in the case of a newspaper advertisement, the printer and proprietor of the newspaper, a shopkeeper who sells it over the counter and a newsvendor who hawks it in the street are all publishers for the purposes of the law of libel). The use, however, of the words "the publisher" instead of "any person who publishes" may suggest that in this section the legislature envisages a single person who is principally responsible for the publication (e.g., the newspaper proprietor).

PERSON

See the note to s. 7, *ante*.

CARRIED ON

See the note "Carry on business" to s. 24, *ante*.

IT IS A DEFENCE

The matters to be proved by the defendant need be proved on balance of probability only; see *R.* v. *Carr-Briant*, [1943] 2 All E.R. 156, and *R.* v. *Dunbar*, [1957] 2 All E.R. 737.

THIS PART

I.e., ss. 43–54.

DEFINITIONS

For "advertisement", "advertiser" and "business", see s. 189 (1), *post*.

*Canvassing etc.*

**48. Definition of canvassing off trade premises (regulated agreements)**

(1) An individual (the "canvasser") canvasses a regulated agreement off trade premises if he solicits the entry (as debtor or hirer) of another individual (the "consumer") into the agreement by making oral representations to the consumer, or any other individual, during a visit by the canvasser to any place (not excluded by subsection (2)) where the consumer, or that other individual, as the case may be, is, being a visit—

(*a*) carried out for the purpose of making such oral representations to individuals who are at that place, but

(*b*) not carried out in response to a request made on a previous occasion.

(2) A place is excluded from subsection (1) if it is a place where a business is carried on (whether on a permanent or temporary basis) by—

(*a*) the creditor or owner, or

(*b*) a supplier, or

(*c*) the canvasser, or the person whose employee or agent the canvasser is, or

(*d*) the consumer. [C.48]

COMMENCEMENT
See Sch. 3, para. 8, *post*, and the note "Appointed days" to Part IV of that Schedule.

CARRIED ON
See the note "Carry on business" to s. 24, *ante*.

REQUEST
By reason of the provisions of s. 49 (2), *post*, the request should be in writing.

OFFENCE
It is an offence to canvass certain agreements off trade premises; see s. 49 (1), *post*.

DEFINITIONS
For "business", "creditor", "debtor", "hirer", "individual", "owner", "regulated agreement" and "supplier", see s. 189 (1), *post*.
For "canvasser" and "consumer", see sub-s. (1) above.

## 49. Prohibition of canvassing debtor-creditor agreements off trade premises

(1) It is an offence to canvass debtor-creditor agreements off trade premises.

(2) It is also an offence to solicit the entry of an individual (as debtor) into a debtor-creditor agreement during a visit carried out in response to a request made on a previous occasion, where—

(*a*) the request was not in writing signed by or on behalf of the person making it, and

(*b*) if no request for the visit had been made, the soliciting would have constituted the canvassing of a debtor-creditor agreement off trade premises.

(3) Subsections (1) and (2) do not apply to any soliciting for an agreement enabling the debtor to overdraw on a current account of any description kept with the creditor, where—

(*a*) the Director has determined that current accounts of that description kept with the creditor are excluded from subsections (1) and (2), and

(*b*) the debtor already keeps an account with the creditor (whether a current account or not).

(4) A determination under subsection (3) (*a*)—

(*a*) may be made subject to such conditions as the Director thinks fit, and

(*b*) shall be made only where the Director is of opinion that it is not against the interests of debtors.

(5) If soliciting is done in breach of a condition imposed under subsection (4) (*a*), the determination under subsection (3) (*a*) does not apply to it. [C.49]

COMMENCEMENT
See Sch. 3, para. 9, *post*, and the note "Appointed days" to Part IV of that Schedule.

CANVASS
Section 189 (1), *post*, directs that this term is to be "construed in accordance with ss. 48 and 153". It is thought, however, that only s. 48, *ante*, is relevant to its meaning in this section.

OFF TRADE PREMISES
For the meaning of this expression, see s. 48, *ante*.

OFFENCE
As to notification of convictions to the Director, see s. 166, *post*. For mode of prosecution and penalties, see s. 167 (1) and Sch. 1, *post*. For special defences, see s. 168, *post*. As to offences by bodies corporate, see s. 169, *post*.

WRITING
See the note to s. 6, *ante*.

DEFINITIONS
For "creditor", "debtor", "Director" and "individual", see s. 189 (1), *post*.
For "credit", see s. 9, *ante*, and for "debtor-creditor agreement", see s. 13, *ante*.

## 50. Circulars to minors

(1) A person commits an offence who, with a view to financial gain, sends to a minor any document inviting him to—

(*a*) borrow money, or
(*b*) obtain goods on credit or hire, or
(*c*) obtain services on credit, or
(*d*) apply for information or advice on borrowing money or otherwise obtaining credit, or hiring goods.

(2) In proceedings under subsection (1) in respect of the sending of a document to a minor, it is a defence for the person charged to prove that he did not know, and had no reasonable cause to suspect, that he was a minor.

(3) Where a document is received by a minor at any school or educational establishment for minors, a person sending it to him at that establishment knowing or suspecting it to be such an establishment shall be taken to have reasonable cause to suspect that he is a minor. [C.50]

COMMENCEMENT
See Sch. 3, para. 10, *post*, and the note "Appointed days" to Part IV of that Schedule.

PERSON
See the note to s. 7, *ante*.

OFFENCE
As to the notification of convictions to the Director, see s. 166, *post*. For mode of prosecution and penalties, see s. 167 (1) and Sch. 1, *post*. For special defences, see s. 168, *post*. As to offences by bodies corporate, see s. 169, *post*.

KNOW; KNOWING
Cf. the note "Knowingly" to s. 7, *ante*. As to the onus of proof of knowledge or suspicion for the purposes of sub-s. (3) above, see s. 171 (5), *post*.

MINOR
I.e., a person under the age of eighteen; see the Family Law Reform Act 1969, s. 1 (1), (2) (17 Halsbury's Statutes (3rd edn.) 792).

DEFINITIONS
For "goods" and "individual", see s. 189 (1), *post*.
For "credit", see s. 9, *ante*.

**51. Prohibition of unsolicited credit-tokens**

(1) It is an offence to give a person a credit-token if he has not asked for it.

(2) To comply with subsection (1) a request must be contained in a document signed by the person making the request, unless the credit-token agreement is a small debtor-creditor-supplier agreement.

(3) Subsection (1) does not apply to the giving of a credit-token to a person—

(*a*) for use under a credit-token agreement already made, or

(*b*) in renewal or replacement of a credit-token previously accepted by him under a credit-token agreement which continues in force, whether or not varied. **[C.51]**

COMMENCEMENT

See Sch. 3, para. 11, *post*, and the note "Appointed days" to Part IV of that Schedule.

OFFENCE

As to notification of convictions to the Director, see s. 166, *post*. For mode of prosecution and penalties, see s. 167 (1) and Sch. 1, *post*. For special defences, see s. 168, *post*. As to offences by bodies corporate, see s. 169, *post*.

PERSON

See the note to s. 8, *ante*.

SIGNED

In the case of a body corporate, sealing is equivalent to signature; see s. 189 (3), *post*. See also s. 185 (5), *post*, as to signature on behalf of a body corporate. For decisions on signature by means of a mark, initials, rubber stamps, etc., see 8 Halsbury's Laws (3rd edn.) 105.

DEFINITIONS

For "credit-token", see s. 14 (1), *ante*. For "credit-token agreement", see s. 189 (1), *post*.

For "debtor-creditor-supplier agreement", see s. 12, *ante*, and for "small agreement", see s. 17 (1), *ante*.

*Miscellaneous*

**52. Quotations**

(1) Regulations may be made—

(*a*) as to the form and content of any document (a "quotation") by which a person who carries on a consumer credit business or consumer hire business, or a business in the course of which he provides credit to individuals secured on land, gives prospective customers information about the terms on which he is prepared to do business;

(*b*) requiring a person carrying on such a business to provide quotations to such persons and in such circumstances as are prescribed.

(2) Regulations under subsection (1) (*a*) may in particular contain provisions relating to quotations such as are set out in relation to advertisements in section 44. **[C.52]**

COMMENCEMENT

See Sch. 3, para. 8, *post*, and the note "Appointed days" to Part IV of that Schedule.

PERSON
See the note to s. 8, *ante*.

CARRIES ON
See the note "Carry on business" to s. 24, *ante*.

CONSUMER CREDIT BUSINESS
For meaning, see s. 189 (1), *post*. This section and ss. 53, 54, *post*, apply to a business of credit brokerage, debt-adjusting or debt-counselling as they apply to a consumer credit business; see s. 152 (1), *post*. See also s. 152 (2), *post*, as to the extended application of this section and s. 53.

DEFINITIONS
For "business", "consumer hire business", "individual", "land", "prescribed" and "regulations", see s. 189 (1), *post*.
For "credit", see s. 9. *ante*.

REGULATIONS
Contravention is an offence; see s. 167 (2), *post*. Regulations may include provisions as to onus of proof; see s. 171 (2), *post*. For general provisions as to regulations under this Act, see s. 182 (1)–(3), *post*.
No regulations had been made under this section up to the time of going to press.

## 53. Duty to display information

Regulations may require a person who carries on a consumer credit business or consumer hire business, or a business in the course of which he provides credit to individuals secured on land, to display in the prescribed manner, at any premises where the business is carried on to which the public have access, prescribed information about the business. **[C.53]**

COMMENCEMENT
See Sch. 3, para. 8, *post*, and the note "Appointed days" to Part IV of that Schedule.

PERSON
See the note to s. 8, *ante*.

CARRIES ON
See the note "Carry on business" to s. 24, *ante*.

CONSUMER CREDIT BUSINESS
See the note to s. 52, *ante*.

DEFINITIONS
For "business", "consumer hire business", "individual", "land", "prescribed" and "regulations", see s. 189 (1), *post*.
For "credit", see s. 9, *ante*.

REGULATIONS
Contravention is an offence; see s. 167 (2), *post*. For general provisions as to regulations under this Act, see s. 182 (1)–(3), *post*.
No regulations had been made under this section up to the time of going to press.

## 54. Conduct of business regulations

Without prejudice to the generality of section 26, regulations under that section may include provisions further regulating the seeking of business by a licensee who carries on a consumer credit business or a consumer hire business. **[C.54]**

COMMENCEMENT
See Sch. 3, para. 8, *post*, and the note "Appointed days" to Part IV of that Schedule.

CONSUMER CREDIT BUSINESS
See the note to s. 52, *ante*.

DEFINITIONS
For "business", "consumer hire business", "licensee" and "regulations", see s. 189 (1), *post*.

REGULATIONS
Contravention is an offence; see s. 167 (2), *post*. For general provisions as to regulations under this Act, see s. 182 (1)–(3), *post*.

No regulations had been made under s. 26 as extended by this section up to the time of going to press.

## PART V

## ENTRY INTO CREDIT OR HIRE AGREEMENTS

*Preliminary matters*

### 55. Disclosure of information

(1) Regulations may require specified information to be disclosed in the prescribed manner to the debtor or hirer before a regulated agreement is made.

(2) A regulated agreement is not properly executed unless regulations under subsection (1) were complied with before the making of the agreement. [C.55]

REGULATED AGREEMENT
For meaning, see s. 189 (1), *post*. This section does not apply to non-commercial agreements or (in such cases as the Director determines) to debtor-creditor agreements conferring the right to overdraw on a current account and agreements to finance indebtedness on the death of a debtor; see s. 74 (1), (3), *post*. See also the note "Further exclusion" to that section.

NOT PROPERLY EXECUTED
For the consequences of improper execution, see s. 65, *post*. In view of the provisions of s. 170 (1), *post*, it seems that regulations under this section cannot impose any other sanction for non-compliance with their provisions.

DEFINITIONS
For "debtor", "hirer", "prescribed" and "regulations", see s. 189 (1), *post*.

REGULATIONS UNDER THIS SECTION
No regulations had been made under this section up to the time of going to press.

For general provisions as to regulations under this Act, see s. 182 (1)–(3), *post*.

### 56. Antecedent negotiations

(1) In this Act "antecedent negotiations" means any negotiations with the debtor or hirer—

(*a*) conducted by the creditor or owner in relation to the making of any regulated agreement, or

(*b*) conducted by a credit-broker in relation to goods sold or proposed to be sold by the credit-broker to the creditor before forming the subject-matter of a debtor-creditor-supplier agreement within section 12 (*a*), or

(*c*) conducted by the supplier in relation to a transaction financed or proposed to be financed by a debtor-creditor-supplier agreement within section 12 (*b*) or (*c*), and "negotiator" means the person by whom negotiations are so conducted with the debtor or hirer.

(2) Negotiations with the debtor in a case falling within subsection (1) (*b*) or (*c*) shall be deemed to be conducted by the negotiator in the capacity of agent of the creditor as well as in his actual capacity.

(3) An agreement is void if, and to the extent that, it purports in relation to an actual or prospective regulated agreement—

(*a*) to provide that a person acting as, or on behalf of, a negotiator is to be treated as the agent of the debtor or hirer, or

(*b*) to relieve a person from liability for acts or omissions of any person acting as, or on behalf of, a negotiator.

(4) For the purposes of this Act, antecedent negotiations shall be taken to begin when the negotiator and the debtor or hirer first enter into communication (including communication by advertisement), and to include any representations made by the negotiator to the debtor or hirer and any other dealings between them. **[C.56]**

COMMENCEMENT

See Sch. 3, para. 12, *post*, and the note "Appointed days" to Part V of that Schedule.

PROHIBITION OF CONTRACTING OUT

Terms contained in regulated agreements or linked transactions are void if inconsistent with provisions for the protection of debtors, hirers, their relatives or sureties in this Act or regulations thereunder; see s. 173 (1), *post*.

DEEMED TO BE . . . AGENT

For the duties of the agent towards the creditor, see s. 175, *post*.

DEFINITIONS

For "advertisement", "credit-broker", "creditor", "debtor", "finance", "goods", "hirer", "owner", "regulated agreement", "representation" and "supplier", see s. 189 (1), *post*.

For "debtor-creditor-supplier agreement", see s. 12, *ante*.

For "negotiator", see sub-s. (1) above.

## 57. Withdrawal from prospective agreement

(1) The withdrawal of a party from a prospective regulated agreement shall operate to apply this Part to the agreement, any linked transaction and any other thing done in anticipation of the making of the agreement as it would apply if the agreement were made and then cancelled under section 69.

(2) The giving to a party of a written or oral notice which, however expressed, indicates the intention of the other party to withdraw from a prospective regulated agreement operates as a withdrawal from it.

(3) Each of the following shall be deemed to be the agent of the creditor or owner for the purpose of receiving a notice under subsection (2)—

(*a*) a credit-broker or supplier who is the negotiator in antecedent negotiations, and

(*b*) any person who, in the course of a business carried on by him, acts on behalf of the debtor or hirer in any negotiations for the agreement.

(4) Where the agreement, if made, would not be a cancellable agreement, subsection (1) shall nevertheless apply as if the contrary were the case. **[C.57]**

COMMENCEMENT
See Sch. 3, para. 13, *post*, and the note "Appointed days" to Part V of that Schedule.

GENERAL NOTE
The effect of sub-s. (1) above is to apply the provisions of this Part about the consequences of the cancellation of an agreement to the case in which a party withdraws from an agreement before its conclusion. The provisions so applied are, in particular, those of ss. 70–73, *post*. Certain persons are deemed by sub-s. (3) to be the agents of the creditor or owner for the purpose of receiving a notice of withdrawal. At common law, it would be a question of fact whether such persons were agents and in many cases they would not be.

Subsection (4) makes it clear that sub-s. (1) is not confined to such agreements as would be cancellable under s. 67, *post*, if they were concluded.

PROHIBITION OF CONTRACTING OUT
See the note to s. 56, *ante*.

REGULATED AGREEMENT
For meaning, see s. 189 (1), *post*. By virtue of s. 74, *post*, this section and ss. 58–73, *post*, are not applicable to the following regulated agreements:
(i) non-commercial agreements,
(ii) if the Director so determines under s. 74 (3), debtor-creditor agreements conferring the right to overdraw on a current account, and agreements to finance payments due upon the death of a person, and
(iii) small debtor-creditor-supplier agreements for restricted-use credit.
See also the note "Further exclusion" to s. 74, *post*.

THIS PART
I.e., ss. 55–74.

DEEMED TO BE THE AGENT
For the agent's duties to the creditor or owner, see s. 175, *post*.

DEFINITIONS
For "cancellable agreement", "business", "credit-broker", "creditor", "debtor", "hirer", "owner" and "supplier", see s. 189 (1), *post*.
For "antecedent negotiations" and "negotiator", see s. 56, *ante*.
For "linked transaction", see s. 19 (1), *ante*.

## 58. Opportunity for withdrawal from prospective land mortgage

(1) Before sending to the debtor or hirer, for his signature, an unexecuted agreement in a case where the prospective regulated agreement is to be secured on land (the "mortgaged land"), the creditor or owner shall give the debtor or hirer a copy of the unexecuted agreement which contains a notice in the prescribed form indicating the right of the debtor or hirer to withdraw from the prospective agreement, and how and when the right is exercisable, together with a copy of any other document referred to in the unexecuted agreement.

(2) Subsection (1) does not apply to—

(*a*) a restricted-use credit agreement to finance the purchase of the mortgaged land, or
(*b*) an agreement for a bridging loan in connection with the purchase of the mortgaged land or other land. **[C.58]**

COMMENCEMENT
See Sch. 3, para. 13, *post*, and the note "Appointed days" to Part V of that Schedule.

PROHIBITION OF CONTRACTING OUT
See the note to s. 56, *ante*.

REGULATED AGREEMENT
See the note to s. 57, *ante*.

COPY
For power to make regulations prescribing the form, etc., of copies, see s. 180, *post*.

PRESCRIBED FORM
I.e., prescribed by regulations (s. 189 (1), *post*). Nothing had been prescribed for the purposes of this section up to the time of going to press.

RIGHT . . . TO WITHDRAW
No such right is expressly conferred upon debtors and hirers by this Act. Since, however, regulated agreements must be in writing and signed (s. 61 (1), *post*) and no agreement binding a person to enter as debtor or hirer into a regulated agreement is enforceable (s. 59 (1), *post*), it must always be the case that until he has signed a written agreement, the debtor or hirer is free to withdraw.

HOW AND WHEN THE RIGHT IS EXERCISABLE
The provisions of s. 57 (2)–(4), *ante*, would seem to be relevant here.

FURTHER PROVISIONS
For provisions as to the proper execution of agreements to which this section applies, see s. 61 (2), (3), *post*.

DEFINITIONS
For "creditor", "debtor", "finance", "give", "hirer", "land", "notice" "owner", "regulated agreement" and "unexecuted agreement", see s. 189 (1), *post*.
For "restricted-use credit", see s. 11 (1), *ante*.

## 59. Agreement to enter future agreement void

(1) An agreement is void if, and to the extent that, it purports to bind a person to enter as debtor or hirer into a prospective regulated agreement.

(2) Regulations may exclude from the operation of subsection (1) agreements such as are described in the regulations. [C.59]

COMMENCEMENT
See Sch. 3, para. 13, *post*, and the note "Appointed days" to Part V of that Schedule.

REGULATED AGREEMENT
See the note to s. 57, *ante*.

DEFINITIONS
For "debtor", "hirer" and "regulations", see s. 189 (1), *post*.

REGULATIONS UNDER THIS SECTION
No regulations had been made under this section up to the time of going to press.
For general provisions as to regulations under this Act, see s. 182 (1)–(3), *post*.

*Making the agreement*

## 60. Form and content of agreements

(1) The Secretary of State shall make regulations as to the form and content of documents embodying regulated agreements, and the regulations shall contain such provisions as appear to him appropriate with a view to ensuring that the debtor or hirer is made aware of—

(*a*) the rights and duties conferred or imposed on him by the agreement, (*b*) the amount and rate of the total charge for credit (in the case of a consumer credit agreement),

(*c*) the protection and remedies available to him under this Act, and

(*d*) any other matters which, in the opinion of the Secretary of State, it is desirable for him to know about in connection with the agreement.

(2) Regulations under subsection (1) may in particular—

(*a*) require specified information to be included in the prescribed manner in documents, and other specified material to be excluded;

(*b*) contain requirements to ensure that specified information is clearly brought to the attention of the debtor or hirer, and that one part of a document is not given insufficient or excessive prominence compared with another.

(3) If, on an application made to the Director by a person carrying on a consumer credit business or a consumer hire business, it appears to the Director impracticable for the applicant to comply with any requirement of regulations under subsection (1) in a particular case, he may, by notice to the applicant, direct that the requirement be waived or varied in relation to such agreements, and subject to such conditions (if any), as he may specify, and this Act and the regulations shall have effect accordingly.

(4) The Director shall give a notice under subsection (3) only if he is satisfied that to do so would not prejudice the interests of debtors or hirers. **[C.60]**

PROHIBITION OF CONTRACTING OUT
See the note to s. 56, *ante*.

REGULATED AGREEMENT
See the note to s. 57, *ante*, but see also s. 74 (4), *post*, which applies regulations under this section to certain written regulated agreements to which they would otherwise be inapplicable by virtue of s. 74 (1) or (2).

REQUIRE; REQUIREMENTS
The consequence of failure to comply with the requirements of regulations under this section will be that the agreement is not properly executed; see s. 61 (1) (*a*), *post*. For the further consequences of that, see s. 65, *post*. In view of the provisions of s. 170 (1), *post*, it seems that regulations under this section cannot provide for any further sanction for non-compliance.

PERSON
See the note to s. 8, *ante*.

DEFINITIONS
For "consumer credit business", "consumer hire business", "debtor", "Director", "give", "hirer", "notice", "prescribed", "regulations", and "total charge for credit", see s. 189 (1), *post*.
For "embodying", see s. 189 (4), *post*.

REGULATIONS UNDER THIS SECTION
No regulations had been made under this section up to the time of going to press.
For general provisions as to regulations under this Act, see s. 182 (1)–(3), *post*.

## 61. Signing of agreement

(1) A regulated agreement is not properly executed unless—

(*a*) a document in the prescribed form itself containing all the prescribed terms and conforming to regulations under section 60 (1) is signed in the prescribed manner both by the debtor or hirer and by or on behalf of the creditor or owner, and

(*b*) the document embodies all the terms of the agreement, other than implied terms, and

(*c*) the document is, when presented or sent to the debtor or hirer for signature, in such a state that all its terms are readily legible.

(2) In addition, where the agreement is one to which section 58 (1) applies, it is not properly executed unless—

(*a*) the requirements of section 58 (1) were complied with, and

(*b*) the unexecuted agreement was sent, for his signature, to the debtor or hirer by post not less than seven days after a copy of it was given to him under section 58 (1), and

(*c*) during the consideration period, the creditor or owner refrained from approaching the debtor or hirer (whether in person, by telephone or letter, or in any other way) except in response to a specific request made by the debtor or hirer after the beginning of the consideration period, and

(*d*) no notice of withdrawal by the debtor or hirer was received by the creditor or owner before the sending of the unexecuted agreement.

(3) In subsection (2) (*c*), "the consideration period" means the period beginning with the giving of the copy under section 58 (1) and ending—

(*a*) at the expiry of seven days after the day on which the unexecuted agreement is sent, for his signature, to the debtor or hirer, or

(*b*) on its return by the debtor or hirer after signature by him,

whichever first occurs.

(4) Where the debtor or hirer is a partnership or an unincorporated body of persons, subsection (1) (*a*) shall apply with the substitution for "by the debtor or hirer" of "by or on behalf of the debtor or hirer". [**C.61**]

COMMENCEMENT

See Sch. 3, para. 13, *post*, and the note "Appointed days" to Part V of that Schedule.

PROHIBITION OF CONTRACTING OUT

See the note to s. 56, *ante*.

REGULATED AGREEMENT

See the note to s. 57, *ante*.

NOT PROPERLY EXECUTED

For the consequences of improper execution, see ss. 65, 127 (3), *post*.

PRESCRIBED

I.e., prescribed by regulations; see s. 189 (1), *post*. Nothing had been prescribed for the purposes of sub-s. (1) above up to the time of going to press.

SIGNED

See the note to s. 51, *ante*.

BY THE DEBTOR OR HIRER

Note the absence of the words "or on behalf of" and the exclusion by s. 185 (3), *post*, of the provisions of s. 185 (1) (*b*). It seems that each debtor or hirer must sign in person.

TO WHICH S. 58 (1) APPLIES
Note that the scope of s. 58 (1), *ante*, is limited by s. 58 (2).

NOT LESS THAN SEVEN DAYS
It is thought that seven clear days must be allowed, exclusive both of the date of delivery of the copy and of the date of sending of the agreement for signature; see *R.* v. *Turner* [1910] 1 K.B. 346, and *Re Hector Whaling, Ltd.*, [1936] Ch. 208; [1935] All E.R. Rep. 302, but see also *Schnabel* v. *Allard*, [1967] 1 Q.B. 627; [1966] 3 All E.R. 816, C.A.

NO NOTICE OF WITHDRAWAL . . . WAS RECEIVED
By virtue of s. 57, *ante*, the giving of a notice of withdrawal is effective to operate as a withdrawal of the debtor or hirer from a prospective agreement. Therefore, if nothing further happened, there could be no agreement and the provisions of this section would be superfluous. The case envisaged by sub-s. (2) (*d*) above must be that, having sent a notice of withdrawal, the debtor or hirer changes his mind again and subsequently signs the agreement. Then, if the notice of withdrawal was received by the creditor or owner prior to the dispatch of the agreement for signature (but not otherwise) the notice of withdrawal continues to vitiate the agreement notwithstanding the subsequent change of mind. There would appear to be no way in which this obstacle can be overcome and a prospective creditor would be well advised to treat any notice of withdrawal which he receives as final, no matter what subsequent communications may pass between the parties.

DEFINITIONS
For "creditor", "debtor", "hirer", "notice", "owner", "regulations", and "unexecuted agreement", see s. 189 (1), *post*.
For "consideration period", see sub-s. (3) above.

## 62. Duty to supply copy of unexecuted agreement

(1) If the unexecuted agreement is presented personally to the debtor or hirer for his signature, but on the occasion when he signs it the document does not become an executed agreement, a copy of it, and of any other document referred to in it, must be there and then delivered to him.

(2) If the unexecuted agreement is sent to the debtor or hirer for his signature, a copy of it, and of any other document referred to in it, must be sent to him at the same time.

(3) A regulated agreement is not properly executed if the requirements of this section are not observed. [**C.62**]

COMMENCEMENT
See Sch. 3, para. 13, *post*, and the note "Appointed days" to Part V of that Schedule.

PROHIBITION OF CONTRACTING OUT
See the note to s. 56, *ante*.

THE UNEXECUTED AGREEMENT
For definition, see s. 189 (1), *post*. For categories of agreement which are excluded, see the note "Regulated agreement" to s. 57, *ante*.

SIGNS
See the note "Signed" to s. 51, *ante*.

COPY
For power to prescribe the form of copies, see s. 180, *post*. For matters to be included in the copy in certain cases, see s. 64 (1), *post*.

REGULATED AGREEMENT
See the note to s. 57, *ante*.

NOT PROPERLY EXECUTED
For the consequences of improper execution, see ss. 65, 127 (4), *post.*

OFFENCE
In the case of a regulated agreement to take an article in pawn, non-compliance with this section or ss. 63, 64, *post,* is an offence; see s. 115, *post.*

DEFINITIONS
For "debtor", "executed agreement" and "hirer", see s. 189 (1), *post.*

**63. Duty to supply copy of executed agreement**

(1) If the unexecuted agreement is presented personally to the debtor or hirer for his signature, and on the occasion when he signs it the document becomes an executed agreement, a copy of the executed agreement, and of any other document referred to in it, must be there and then delivered to him.

(2) A copy of the executed agreement, and of any other document referred to in it, must be given to the debtor or hirer within the seven days following the making of the agreement unless—

(*a*) subsection (1) applies, or

(*b*) the unexecuted agreement was sent to the debtor or hirer for his signature and, on the occasion of his signing it, the document became an executed agreement.

(3) In the case of a cancellable agreement, a copy under subsection (2) must be sent by post.

(4) In the case of a credit-token agreement, a copy under subsection (2) need not be given within the seven days following the making of the agreement if it is given before or at the time when the credit-token is given to the debtor.

(5) A regulated agreement is not properly executed if the requirements of this section are not observed. [C.63]

COMMENCEMENT
See Sch. 3, para. 13, *post,* and the note "Appointed days" to Part V of that Schedule.

PROHIBITION OF CONTRACTING OUT
See the note to s. 56, *ante.*

THE UNEXECUTED AGREEMENT
For definition, see s. 189 (1), *post.* For categories of agreement which are excluded, see the note "Regulated agreement" to s. 57, *ante.*

SIGNS
See the note "Signed" to s. 51, *ante.*

COPY
For power to prescribe the form of copies, see s. 181, *post.* For matters to be included in the copy in certain cases, see s. 64 (1), *post.*

REGULATED AGREEMENT
See the note to s. 57, *ante.*

NOT PROPERLY EXECUTED
See the note to s. 62, *ante.*

OFFENCE
See the note to s. 62, *ante.*

DEFINITIONS
For "cancellable agreement", "credit-token agreement", "debtor", "executed agreement", "give", and "hirer", see s. 189 (1), *post*.
For "credit-token", see s. 14 (1), *ante*.

**64. Duty to give notice of cancellation rights**

(1) In the case of a cancellable agreement, a notice in the prescribed form indicating the right of the debtor or hirer to cancel the agreement, how and when that right is exercisable, and the name and address of a person to whom notice of cancellation may be given,—

(*a*) must be included in every copy given to the debtor or hirer under section 62 or 63, and

(*b*) except where section 63 (2) applied, must also be sent by post to the debtor or hirer within the seven days following the making of the agreement.

(2) In the case of a credit-token agreement, a notice under subsection (1) (*b*) need not be sent by post within the seven days following the making of the agreement if either—

(*a*) it is sent by post to the debtor or hirer before the credit-token is given to him, or

(*b*) it is sent by post to him together with the credit-token.

(3) Regulations may provide that except where section 63 (2) applied a notice sent under subsection (1) (*b*) shall be accompanied by a further copy of the executed agreement, and of any other document referred to in it.

(4) Regulations may provide that subsection (1) (*b*) is not to apply in the case of agreements such as are described in the regulations, being agreements made by a particular person, if—

(*a*) on an application by that person to the Director, the Director has determined that, having regard to—

(i) the manner in which antecedent negotiations for agreements with the applicant of that description are conducted, and

(ii) the information provided to debtors or hirers before such agreements are made,

the requirement imposed by subsection (1) (*b*) can be dispensed with without prejudicing the interests of debtors or hirers; and

(*b*) any conditions imposed by the Director in making the determination are complied with.

(5) A cancellable agreement is not properly executed if the requirements of this section are not observed. **[C.64]**

COMMENCEMENT
See Sch. 3, para. 13, *post*, and the note "Appointed days" to Part V of that Schedule.

PROHIBITION OF CONTRACTING OUT
See the note to s. 56, *ante*.

AGREEMENT
For agreements excluded from the ambit of this section by s. 74; *post*, see the note "Regulated agreement" to s. 57, *ante*.

PRESCRIBED
I.e., prescribed by regulations; see s. 189 (1), *post*. Nothing had been prescribed for the purposes of sub-s. (1) above up to the time of going to press.

RIGHT . . . TO CANCEL
As to that right, see s. 69, *post*.

MUST BE; SHALL BE
The only consequences of non-compliance are as stated in sub-s. (5) above and in the note "Offence" to s. 62, *ante* (see s. 170 (1), *post*, for the exclusion of any implied provision as to other sanctions).

NOT PROPERLY EXECUTED
See the note to s. 62, *ante*.

OFFENCE
See the note to s. 62, *ante*.

DEFINITIONS
For "antecedent negotiations", see s. 56 (1), *ante*.
For "cancellable agreement", "creditor", "credit-token agreement", "debtor", "Director", "executed agreement", "hirer", "notice" and "regulations", see s. 189 (1), *post*.
For "credit-token", see s. 14 (1), *ante*.

REGULATIONS UNDER THIS SECTION
No regulations had been made under this section up to the time of going to press.
For general provisions as to regulations under this Act, see s. 182 (1)–(3), *post*.

## 65. Consequences of improper execution

(1) An improperly-executed regulated agreement is enforceable against the debtor or hirer on an order of the court only.

(2) A retaking of goods or land to which a regulated agreement relates is an enforcement of the agreement. **[C.65]**

COMMENCEMENT
See Sch. 3, para. 13, *post*, and the note "Appointed days" to Part V of that Schedule.

GENERAL NOTE
Sections 61–64, *ante*, contain provisions to the effect that under various circumstances, agreements are "not properly executed". This section provides for the consequences which follow from those provisions. An improperly executed agreement is enforceable against the debtor or hirer only upon an order of the court. The full significance of this provision can be understood only in the light of s. 127, *post*, which governs the granting or refusal of an order under this section. The general principle is that the order should be granted unless there exists a reason for refusing it under s. 127, *post*. The court has a general discretion under s. 127 (1) to refuse an order on the ground that prejudice was caused by the irregularity in question, and certain particular irregularities are grounds for refusal under s. 127 (3) or (4) (see further the "General Note" to that section). There are further powers to couple an order with an extension of time (s. 129, *post*) to grant it conditionally or suspend it (s. 135, *post*) and to include in it provision for varying the agreement (s. 136, *post*).

REGULATED AGREEMENT
See the note to s. 57, *ante*.

ENFORCEABLE
As to the enforcement of securities in cases governed by this section, see s. 113 (2), *post*.

ONLY
A court order is not necessary if the debtor or hirer consents, at the time when enforcement is sought, to the enforcement of the agreement; see s. 173 (3), *post*. Any

agreement, however, by which the debtor or hirer bound himself in advance to give such consent would be void by virtue of s. 173 (1), *post.*

DEFINITIONS
For "court", "debtor", "goods", "hirer" and "land", see s. 189 (1), *post.*

## 66. Acceptance of credit-tokens

(1) The debtor shall not be liable under a credit-token agreement for use made of the credit-token by any person unless the debtor had previously accepted the credit-token, or the use constituted an acceptance of it by him.

(2) The debtor accepts a credit-token when—

(*a*) it is signed, or
(*b*) a receipt for it is signed, or
(*c*) it is first used,

either by the debtor himself or by a person who, pursuant to the agreement, is authorised by him to use it. **[C.66]**

COMMENCEMENT
See Sch. 3, para. 14, *post,* and the note "Appointed days" to Part V of that Schedule.

PROHIBITION OF CONTRACTING OUT
See the note to s. 56, *ante.*

CREDIT-TOKEN AGREEMENT
For meaning, see s. 189 (1), *post.* For agreements which are excluded from the provisions of this section, see the note "Regulated agreement" to s. 57, *ante.*

ACCEPTED
As to onus of proof of this issue, see s. 171 (4), *post.*

PERSON
See the note to s. 8, *ante.*

SIGNED
See the note to s. 51, *ante.*

DEFINITIONS
For "credit-token", see s. 14 (1), *ante.*
For "debtor", see s. 189 (1), *post.*

*Cancellation of certain agreements within cooling-off period*

## 67. Cancellable agreements

A regulated agreement may be cancelled by the debtor or hirer in accordance with this Part if the antecedent negotiations included oral representations made when in the presence of the debtor or hirer by an individual acting as, or on behalf of, the negotiator, unless—

(*a*) the agreement is secured on land, or is a restricted-use credit agreement to finance the purchase of land or is an agreement for a bridging loan in connection with the purchase of land, or
(*b*) the unexecuted agreement is signed by the debtor or hirer at premises at which any of the following is carrying on any business (whether on a permanent or temporary basis)—
(i) the creditor or owner;

(ii) any party to a linked transaction (other than the debtor or hirer or a relative of his);

(iii) the negotiator in any antecedent negotiations. **[C.67]**

COMMENCEMENT
See Sch. 3, para. 13, *post*, and the note "Appointed days" to Part V of that Schedule.

PROHIBITION OF CONTRACTING OUT
See the note to s. 56, *ante*.

REGULATED AGREEMENT
See the note to s. 57, *ante*.

THIS PART
I.e., ss. 55–74. See, in particular, ss. 68 (period allowed for cancellation), 69 (notice of cancellation) and 70–73 (consequences of cancellation), *post*.

SIGNED
See the note to s. 51, *ante*.

CARRYING ON BUSINESS
See the note "Carry on business" to s. 24, *ante*.

DEFINITIONS
For "antecedent negotiations" and "negotiator", see s. 56 (1), *ante*.
For "business", "creditor", "debtor", "finance", "hirer", "individual", "land", "owner", "relative", "representation" and "unexecuted agreement", see s. 189 (1), *post*.
For "linked transaction", see s. 19 (1), *ante*.
For "restricted-use credit", see s. 11 (1), *ante*.

## 68. Cooling-off period

The debtor or hirer may serve notice of cancellation of a cancellable agreement between his signing of the unexecuted agreement and—

(*a*) the end of the fifth day following the day on which he received a copy under section 63 (2) or a notice under section 64 (1) (*b*), or

(*b*) if (by virtue of regulations made under section 64 (4)) section 64 (1) (*b*) does not apply, the end of the fourteenth day following the day on which he signed the unexecuted agreement.

COMMENCEMENT
See Sch. 3, para. 13, *post*, and the note "Appointed days" to Part V of that Schedule.

PROHIBITION OF CONTRACTING OUT
See the note to s. 56, *ante*.

SERVE
For provisions as to service of notices, see ss. 69 (5), 176, *post*. See also the definition in s. 189 (1), *post*.

NOTICE OF CANCELLATION
As to the contents of the notice, see s. 69, *post*.

DEFINITIONS
For "cancellable agreement", "debtor", "hirer", "notice" and "unexecuted agreement", see s. 189 (1), *post*.

## 69. Notice of cancellation

(1) If within the period specified in section 68 the debtor or hirer under a cancellable agreement serves on—

(*a*) the creditor or owner, or
(*b*) the person specified in the notice under section 64 (1), or
(*c*) a person who (whether by virtue of subsection (6) or otherwise) is the agent of the creditor or owner,

a notice (a "notice of cancellation") which, however expressed and whether or not conforming to the notice given under section 64 (1), indicates the intention of the debtor or hirer to withdraw from the agreement, the notice shall operate—

(i) to cancel the agreement, and any linked transaction, and
(ii) to withdraw any offer by the debtor or hirer, or his relative, to enter into a linked transaction.

(2) In the case of a debtor-creditor-supplier agreement for restricted use credit financing—

(*a*) the doing of work or supply of goods to meet an emergency, or
(*b*) the supply of goods which, before service of the notice of cancellation, had by the act of the debtor or his relative become incorporated in any land or thing not comprised in the agreement or any linked transaction, subsection (1) shall apply with the substitution of the following for paragraph (i)—

"(i) to cancel only such provisions of the agreement and any linked transaction as—

(*aa*) relate to the provision of credit, or
(*bb*) require the debtor to pay an item in the total charge for credit, or
(*cc*) subject the debtor to any obligation other than to pay for the doing of the said work, or the supply of the said goods".

(3) Except so far as is otherwise provided, references in this Act to the cancellation of an agreement or transaction do not include a case within subsection (2).

(4) Except as otherwise provided by or under this Act, an agreement or transaction cancelled under subsection (1) shall be treated as if it had never been entered into.

(5) Regulations may exclude linked transactions of the prescribed description from subsection (1) (i) or (ii).

(6) Each of the following shall be deemed to be the agent of the creditor or owner for the purpose of receiving a notice of cancellation—

(*a*) a credit-broker or supplier who is the negotiator in antecedent negotiations, and
(*b*) any person who, in the course of a business carried on by him, acts on behalf of the debtor or hirer in any negotiations for the agreement.

(7) Whether or not it is actually received by him, a notice of cancellation sent by post to a person shall be deemed to be served on him at the time of posting. **[C.69]**

COMMENCEMENT
See Sch. 3, para. 13, *post*, and the note "Appointed days" to Part V of that Schedule.

PROHIBITION OF CONTRACTING OUT

See the note to s. 56, *ante*.

SERVES

For provisions as to service of notices, see s. 176, *post*. See also the definition in s. 189 (1), *post*, and note the provisions of sub-s. (5) above.

PERSON

See the note to s. 8, *ante*.

EXCEPT AS OTHERWISE PROVIDED

For other provisions as to the position after cancellation, see ss. 70–73, *post*. For the effect of cancellation on securities, see s. 113 (3), *post*.

DEEMED TO BE THE AGENT

For the duties of the agent to the creditor or owner, see s. 175, *post*.

CARRIED ON

See the note "carry on business' to s. 24, *ante*.

DECLARATION BY COURT

For the court's jurisdiction to declare that an agreement has been cancelled under this section, see s. 142 (2), *post*.

DEFINITIONS

For "antecedent negotiations" and "negotiator", see s. 56 (1), *ante*.

For "business", "cancellable agreement", "credit-broker", "creditor", "debtor", "hirer", "notice", "owner", "prescribed", "regulations" and "relative", see s. 189 (1), *post*.

For "debtor-creditor-supplier agreement", see s. 12, *ante*.

For "linked transaction", see s. 19 (1), *ante*.

For "restricted-use credit", see s. 11 (1), *ante*.

REGULATIONS UNDER THIS SECTION

No regulations had been made under this section up to the time of going to press.

For general provisions as to regulations under this Act, see s. 182 (1)–(3), *post*.

## 70. Cancellation: recovery of money paid by debtor or hirer

(1) On the cancellation of a regulated agreement, and of any linked transaction,—

(*a*) any sum paid by the debtor or hirer, or his relative, under or in contemplation of the agreement or transaction, including any item in the total charge for credit, shall become repayable, and

(*b*) any sum, including any item in the total charge for credit, which but for the cancellation is, or would or might become, payable by the debtor or hirer, or his relative, under the agreement or transaction shall cease to be, or shall not become, so payable, and

(*c*) in the case of a debtor-creditor-supplier agreement falling within section 12 (*b*), any sum paid on the debtor's behalf by the creditor to the supplier shall become repayable to the creditor.

(2) If, under the terms of a cancelled agreement or transaction, the debtor or hirer, or his relative, is in possession of any goods, he shall have a lien on them for any sum repayable to him under subsection (1) in respect of that agreement or transaction, or any other linked transaction.

(3) A sum repayable under subsection (1) is repayable by the person to whom it was originally paid, but in the case of a debtor-creditor-supplier agreement falling within section 12 (*b*) the creditor and the supplier shall be under

a joint and several liability to repay sums paid by the debtor, or his relative, under the agreement or under a linked transaction falling within section 19 (1) (*b*) and accordingly, in such a case, the creditor shall be entitled, in accordance with rules of court, to have the supplier made a party to any proceedings brought against the creditor to recover any such sums.

(4) Subject to any agreement between them, the creditor shall be entitled to be indemnified by the supplier for loss suffered by the creditor in satisfying his liablity under subsection (3), including costs reasonably incurred by him in defending proceedings instituted by the debtor.

(5) Subsection (1) does not apply to any sum which, if not paid by a debtor, would be payable by virtue of section 71 and applies to a sum paid or payable by a debtor for the issue of a credit-token only where the credit-token has been returned to the creditor or surrendered to a supplier.

(6) If the total charge for credit includes an item in respect of a fee or commission charged by a credit-broker, the amount repayable under subsection (1) in respect of that item shall be the excess over £1 of the fee or commission.

(7) If the total charge for credit includes any sum payable or paid by the debtor to a credit-broker otherwise than in respect of a fee or commission charged by him, that sum shall for the purposes of subsection (6) be treated as if it were such a fee or commission.

(8) So far only as is necessary to give effect to section 69 (2), this section applies to an agreement or transaction within that subsection as it applies to a cancelled agreement or transaction. **[C.70]**

COMMENCEMENT

See Sch. 3, para. 13, *post*, and the note "Appointed days" to Part V of that Schedule.

PROHIBITION OF CONTRACTING OUT

See the note to s. 56, *ante*.

SUB-S. (1): CANCELLATION

For the right of cancellation and the time and manner of its exercise, see ss. 67–69, *ante*.

REGULATED AGREEMENT

See the note to s. 57, *ante*.

SUB-S. (2): LIEN

This presumably means a legal rather than an equitable lien. For the distinction between the two and the law as to liens generally, see 24 Halsbury's Laws (3rd edn.) 142 *et seq*.

SUB-S. (3): PERSON

See the note to s. 8, *ante*.

RULES OF COURT

See the definition in s. 189 (1), *post*. At the time of going to press, the County Court Rules contain no provision made expressly for the purposes of this Act, but for general provisions as to third party procedure, see C.C.R. Ord. 12.

SUB-S. (7): £1

This amount is subject to amendment by order under s. 181 (1), *post*.

DEFINITIONS
For "credit-broker", "creditor", "debtor", "goods", "hirer", "relative", "supplier" and "total charge for credit", see s. 189 (1), *post*.
For "credit-token", see s. 14 (1), *ante*.
For "debtor-creditor-supplier agreement", see s. 12, *ante*.

**71. Cancellation: repayment of credit**

(1) Notwithstanding the cancellation of a regulated consumer credit agreement, other than a debtor-creditor-supplier agreement for restricted-use credit, the agreement shall continue in force so far as it relates to repayment of credit and payment of interest.

(2) If, following the cancellation of a regulated consumer credit agreement, the debtor repays the whole or a portion of a credit—

(*a*) before the expiry of one month following service of the notice of cancellation, or

(*b*) in the case of a credit repayable by instalments, before the date on which the first instalment is due,

no interest shall be payable on the amount repaid.

(3) If the whole of a credit repayable by instalments is not repaid on or before the date specified in subsection (2) (*b*), the debtor shall not be liable to repay any of the credit except on receipt of a request in writing in the prescribed form, signed by or on behalf of the creditor, stating the amounts of the remaining instalments (recalculated by the creditor as nearly as may be in accordance with the agreement and without extending the repayment period), but excluding any sum other than principal and interest.

(4) Repayment of a credit, or payment of interest, under a cancelled agreement shall be treated as duly made if it is made to any person on whom, under section 69, a notice of cancellation could have been served, other than a person referred to in section 69 (6) (*b*). **[C.71]**

COMMENCEMENT
See Sch. 3, para. 13, *post*, and the note "Appointed days" to Part V of that Schedule.

PROHIBITION OF CONTRACTING OUT
See the note to s. 56, *ante*.

CANCELLATION
For the right of cancellation and the time and manner of its exercise, see ss. 67–69, *ante*.

REGULATED AGREEMENT
See the note to s. 57, *ante*.

NOTICE OF CANCELLATION
As to that notice, see s. 69, *ante*.

WRITING
See the note to s. 6, *ante*.

PRESCRIBED FORM
I.e., prescribed by regulations; see s. 189 (1), *post*. Nothing had been prescribed for the purposes of sub-s. (3) above up to the time of going to press.

SIGNED
See the note to s. 51, *ante*.

SECURITY

If a cancelled agreement was secured, the duties imposed on the debtor or hirer by this section or s. 72, *post*, are not enforceable until the creditor has carried out the duties regarding the security which are imposed on him by s. 106, *post*; see s. 113 (5), *post*.

DEFINITIONS

For "credit", see s. 9, *ante*.
For "creditor" and "debtor", see s. 189 (1), *post*.
For "debtor-creditor-supplier agreement", see s. 12, *ante*, and for "restricted-use credit", see s. 11 (1), *ante*.

## 72. Cancellation: return of goods

(1) This section applies where any agreement or transaction relating to goods, being—

(*a*) a restricted-use debtor-creditor-supplier agreement, a consumer hire agreement, or a linked transaction to which the debtor or hirer under any regulated agreement is a party, or

(*b*) a linked transaction to which a relative of the debtor or hirer under any regulated agreement is a party.

is cancelled after the debtor or hirer (in a case within paragraph (*a*)) or the relative (in a case within paragraph (*b*)) has acquired possession of the goods by virtue of the agreement or transaction.

(2) In this section—

(*a*) "the possessor" means the person who has acquired possession of the goods as mentioned in subsection (1),

(*b*) "the other party" means the person from whom the possessor acquired possession, and

(*c*) "the pre-cancellation period" means the period beginning when the possessor acquired possession and ending with the cancellation.

(3) The possessor shall be treated as having been under a duty throughout the pre-cancellation period—

(*a*) to retain possession of the goods, and

(*b*) to take reasonable care of them.

(4) On the cancellation, the possessor shall be under a duty, subject to any lien, to restore the goods to the other party in accordance with this section, and meanwhile to retain possession of the goods and take reasonable care of them.

(5) The possessor shall not be under any duty to deliver the goods except at his own premises and in pursuance of a request in writing signed by or on behalf of the other party and served on the possessor either before, or at the time when, the goods are collected from those premises.

(6) If the possessor—

(*a*) delivers the goods (whether at his own premises or elsewhere) to any person on whom, under section 69, a notice of cancellation could have been served (other than a person referred to in section 69 (6) (*b*)), or

(*b*) sends the goods at his own expense to such a person,

he shall be discharged from any duty to retain the goods or deliver them to any person.

(7) Where the possessor delivers the goods as mentioned in subsection (6) (*a*), his obligation to take care of the goods shall cease; and if he sends the goods as mentioned in subsection (6) (*b*), he shall be under a duty to take reasonable care to see that they are received by the other party and not damaged in transit, but in other respects his duty to take care of the goods shall cease.

(8) Where, at any time during the period of 21 days following the cancellation, the possessor receives such a request as is mentioned in subsection (5), and unreasonably refuses or unreasonably fails to comply with it, his duty to take reasonable care of the goods shall continue until he delivers or sends the goods as mentioned in subsection (6), but if within that period he does not receive such a request his duty to take reasonable care of the goods shall cease at the end of that period.

(9) The preceding provisions of this section do not apply to—

(*a*) perishable goods, or

(*b*) goods which by their nature are consumed by use and which, before the cancellation, were so consumed, or

(*c*) goods supplied to meet an emergency, or

(*d*) goods which, before the cancellation had become incorporated in any land or thing not comprised in the cancelled agreement or a linked transaction.

(10) Where the address of the possessor is specified in the executed agreement, references in this section to his own premises are to that address and no other.

(11) Breach of a duty imposed by this section is actionable as a breach of statutory duty. [**C.72**]

COMMENCEMENT
See Sch. 3, para. 13, *post*, and the note "Appointed day" to Part V of that Schedule.

PROHIBITION OF CONTRACTING OUT
See the note to s. 56, *ante*.

SUB-S. (1): ANY AGREEMENT
For agreements excepted from the provisions of this Part, see the note "Regulated agreement" to s. 57, *ante*.

CANCELLED
For the right of cancellation and the time and manner of its exercise, see ss. 67–69, *ante*.

SUB-S. (2): PERSON
See the note to s. 8, *ante*.

SUB-S. (3): REASONABLE CARE
These are the same words which are used to describe the common-law duty of a bailee for reward, and in that case the onus is on the bailee to show that any loss or damage to the goods took place without fault on his part. See *Morris* v. *C. W. Martin & Sons, Ltd.*, [1966] 1 Q.B. 716; [1965] 2 All E.R. 725, where the law on this point is summarised by Lord Denning, M.R., at pp. 726, 731 respectively, and see further 2 Halsbury's Laws (4th edn.) 711–716.

SUB-S. (4): SUBJECT TO ANY LIEN
A debtor or hirer may have a lien under s. 70 (2), *ante*, or s. 73 (5), *post*, for any sums repayable to him under s. 70 (1) or goods returnable to him under s. 73 (2). For the bailee's lien at common law, see 2 Halsbury's Laws (4th edn.) 719.

SUB-S. (5): WRITING
See the note to s. 6, *ante*.

SIGNED
See the note to s. 51, *ante*.

SERVED
For provisions as to service of documents, see s. 176, *post*, and see also the definition in s. 189 (1), *post*.

SUB-S. (8): 21 DAYS FOLLOWING
See the note "Within 21 days" to s. 36, *ante*.

SUB-S. (9): INCORPORATED IN ANY LAND
For cases on the annexation of chattels to land as fixtures, see 23 Halsbury's Laws (3rd edn.) 489–494.

SUB-S. (11): ACTIONABLE AS A BREACH OF STATUTORY DUTY
As to the remedies for breaches of statutory duty, see the Preliminary Note to the title Statutes, Vol. 32, p. 401.

SECURITY
See the note to s. 71, *ante*.

DEFINITIONS
For "consumer hire agreement" see s. 15, *ante*.
For "debtor", "executed agreement", "goods", "hirer", "land", "regulated agreement" and "relative", see s. 189 (1), *post*.
For "debtor-creditor-supplier agreement", see s. 12, *ante*.
For "linked transaction", see s. 19 (1), *ante*.
For "other party", "possessor" and "pre-cancellation period", see sub-s. (2) above.

## 73. Cancellation: goods given in part-exchange

(1) This section applies on the cancellation of a regulated agreement where, in antecedent negotiations, the negotiator agreed to take goods in part-exchange (the "part-exchange goods") and those goods have been delivered to him.

(2) Unless, before the end of the period of ten days beginning with the date of cancellation, the part-exchange goods are returned to the debtor or hirer in a condition substantially as good as when they were delivered to the negotiator, the debtor or hirer shall be entitled to recover from the negotiator a sum equal to the part-exchange allowance (as defined in subsection (7) (*b*)).

(3) In the case of a debtor-creditor-supplier agreement within section 12 (*b*), the negotiator and the creditor shall be under a joint and several liability to pay to the debtor a sum recoverable under subsection (2).

(4) Subject to any agreement between them, the creditor shall be entitled to be indemnified by the negotiator for loss suffered by the creditor in satisfying his liability under subsection (3), including costs reasonably incurred by him in defending proceedings instituted by the debtor.

(5) During the period of ten days beginning with the date of cancellation, the debtor or hirer, if he is in possession of goods to which the cancelled agreement relates, shall have a lien on them for—

(*a*) delivery of the part-exchange goods, in a condition substantially as good as when they were delivered to the negotiator, or

(*b*) a sum equal to the part-exchange allowance;

and if the lien continues to the end of that period it shall thereafter subsist only as a lien for a sum equal to the part-exchange allowance.

(6) Where the debtor or hirer recovers from the negotiator or creditor, or both of them jointly, a sum equal to the part-exchange allowance, then, if the title of the debtor or hirer to the part-exchange goods has not vested in the negotiator, it shall so vest on the recovery of that sum.

(7) For the purposes of this section—

(*a*) the negotiator shall be treated as having agreed to take goods in part-exchange if, in pursuance of the antecedent negotiations, he either purchased or agreed to purchase those goods or accepted or agreed to accept them as part of the consideration for the cancelled agreement, and

(*b*) the part-exchange allowance shall be the sum agreed as such in the antecedent negotiations or, if no such agreement was arrived at, such sum as it would have been reasonable to allow in respect of the part-exchange goods if no notice of cancellation had been served.

(8) In an action brought against the creditor for a sum recoverable under subsection (2), he shall be entitled, in accordance with rules of court, to have the negotiator made a party to the proceedings. **[C.73]**

COMMENCEMENT
See Sch. 3, para. 13, *post*, and the note "Appointed day" to Part V of that Schedule

PROHIBITION OF CONTRACTING OUT
See the note to s. 56, *ante*.

SUB-S. (1): CANCELLATION
For the right of cancellation and the time and manner of its exercise, see ss. 67–69, *ante*

REGULATED AGREEMENT
See the note to s. 57, *ante*.

SUB-S. (2): BEGINNING WITH THE DATE
The date of cancellation is to be included in the computation; see *Trow* v. *Ind Coope (West Midlands) Ltd.*, [1967] 2 Q.B. 909; [1967] 2 All E.R. 900, C.A.

SUB-S. (5): LIEN
See the note to s. 70 (2), *ante*.

SUB-S. (8): RULES OF COURT
See the note to s. 70 (3), *ante*.

DEFINITIONS
For "antecedent negotiations" and "negotiator", see s. 56 (1), *ante*.
For "creditor", "debtor", "goods" and "hirer", see s. 189 (1), *post*
For "debtor-creditor-supplier agreement", see s. 12, *ante*.

*Exclusion of certain agreements from Part V*

## 74. Exclusion of certain agreements from Part V

(1) This Part (except section 56) does not apply to—

(*a*) a non-commercial agreement, or

(*b*) a debtor-creditor agreement enabling the debtor to overdraw on a current account, or (*c*) a debtor-creditor agreement to finance the making of such payments arising on, or connected with, the death of a person as may be prescribed.

(2) This Part (except sections 55 and 56) does not apply to a small debtor-creditor-supplier agreement for restricted-use credit.

(3) Subsection (1) (*b*) or (*c*) applies only where the Director so determines, and such a determination—

(*a*) may be made subject to such conditions as the Director thinks fit, and
(*b*) shall be made only if the Director is of opinion that it is not against the interests of debtors.

(4) If any term of an agreement falling within subsection (1) (*b*) or (*c*) or (2) is expressed in writing, regulations under section 60 (1) shall apply to that term (subject to section 60 (3)) as if the agreement were a regulated agreement not falling within subsection (1) (*b*) or (*c*) or (2). **[C.74]**

THIS PART
I.e., ss. 55–74.

WRITING
See the note to s. 6, *ante*.

FURTHER EXCLUSION
This Part (except s. 56) does not apply by virtue of s. 82 (2), *post*, to an agreement for running-account credit as varied by a merely temporary waiver of a credit limit; see s. 82 (4), *post*.

DEFINITIONS
For "debtor", "Director" and "non-commercial agreement", see s. 189 (1), *post*.
For "debtor-creditor agreement", see s. 13, *ante*, for "debtor-creditor-supplier agreement", see s. 12, *ante*, and for "restricted-use credit", see s. 11 (1), *ante*.

## PART VI

## MATTERS ARISING DURING CURRENCY OF CREDIT OR HIRE AGREEMENTS

### 75. Liability of creditor for breaches by supplier

(1) If the debtor under a debtor-creditor-supplier agreement falling within section 12 (*b*) or (*c*) has, in relation to a transaction financed by the agreement, any claim against the supplier in respect of a misrepresentation or breach of contract, he shall have a like claim against the creditor, who, with the supplier, shall accordingly be jointly and severally liable to the debtor.

(2) Subject to any agreement between them, the creditor shall be entitled to be indemnified by the supplier for loss suffered by the creditor in satisfying his liability under subsection (1), including costs reasonably incurred by him in defending proceedings instituted by the debtor.

(3) Subsection (1) does not apply to a claim—

(*a*) under a non-commercial agreement, or
(*b*) so far as the claim relates to any single item to which the supplier has attached a cash price not exceeding £30 or more than £10,000.

(4) This section applies notwithstanding that the debtor, in entering into the transaction, exceeded the credit limit or otherwise contravened any term of the agreement.

(5) In an action brought against the creditor under subsection (1) he shall be entitled, in accordance with rules of court, to have the supplier made a party to the proceedings. [C.75]

COMMENCEMENT

See Sch. 3, para. 15, *post*, and the note "Appointed days" to Part VI of that Schedule.

GENERAL NOTE

This section applies to all debtor-creditor-supplier agreements in which the creditor and the supplier are not one and the same person. Thus, for example, it applies to the ordinary tripartite arrangement between a seller, a purchaser and a finance house regarding a purchase-loan transaction and it applies to credit card and trading check transactions. It gives the purchaser a right of action against the creditor (i.e., in the examples just mentioned, the finance house, the credit card company or the trading check company) wherever he complains of misrepresentation or breach of contract on the part of the seller ("the supplier" in the terminology of this Act). The liability of creditor and supplier is joint and several, so that the purchaser can choose to sue either or both of them. If he sues the creditor, an indemnity may be claimed by the creditor from the supplier and the supplier may be joined as a defendant. Thus the court will be able to decide in a single action where the ultimate liability lies. It should be noted that while there can be no contracting out of the liability to the purchaser (see s. 173 (1), *post*), the right of indemnity of the creditor against the supplier is subject to alteration by agreement between them (sub-s. (2) above).

Subsection (4) above seems to present some difficulties. It presumably cannot apply to a case where, owing to the debtor's contravention of the agreement, the creditor has in fact refused to finance the transaction (because sub-s. (1) is in terms confined to "a transaction financed by the agreement"). Where, however, the creditor has waived the irregularity to the extent that he has provided credit, sub-s. (4) prevents him from saying that the irregularity takes the transaction outside the section. But does sub-s. (4) prevent the creditor from counterclaiming for breach of contract and assessing his damages at the amount for which he has been rendered liable under this section? To construe sub-s. (4) as depriving the creditor, by mere implication, of all remedy for a breach of contract would be going very far. Yet if the creditor can counterclaim in this way, the operation of this section will produce no practical effect and sub-s. (4) will be rendered nugatory.

PROHIBITION OF CONTRACTING OUT

See the note to s. 56, *ante*.

ANY CLAIM . . . A LIKE CLAIM

Fraudulent misrepresentation, innocent misrepresentation and breach of contract all give rise to claims for damages and the application of this section to such claims presents no difficulty (as to damages for misrepresentation, see the Misrepresentation Act 1907, s. 2 (22 Halsbury's Statutes (3rd edn.) 676).

In some cases, however, the alternative remedy of rescission of the contract will be open to the purchaser (as to that remedy in cases of misrepresentation, see s. 1 of the Act of 1967 (22 Halsbury's Statutes (3rd edn.) 675). In such a case, it would seem that, even though the creditor may not be a party to the contract of which rescission is sought, he can nevertheless be made the defendant in an action claiming rescission and repayment of whatever deposit or instalments may have been paid. Should the plaintiff in such an action tender return of the goods to the creditor or to the supplier? If the supplier is bankrupt, this may be a very important question, but the section provides no clear answer. A creditor discharging his statutory liability under s. 75 and having a right to indemnity against the supplier would in principle be subrogated to the debtor's rights against the supplier, but these would add little to the creditor's statutory right of indemnity and would not give him any claim over goods revesting on the supplier as the result of the debtor's rescission.

A third type of claim which the purchaser may have against the supplier is for specific delivery, if the breach of contract consists of a failure to deliver. Though the words of the section on the face of them cover such a claim, the court's discretion to refuse the equitable remedy of specific performance in an inappropriate case is presumably unaffected, and if the creditor does not have the goods in his possession, an order compelling him to deliver them would clearly be inappropriate (cf. cases in 36 Halsbury's Laws (3rd edn.) 318). It may be, however, that the creditor would be ordered either to procure specific performance by the supplier, or to pay damages if he fails to do so.

INDEMNIFIED
On the analogy of the rules governing a surety's right to be indemnified by the principal debtor (for which, see 18 Halsbury's Laws (3rd edn.) 474 *et seq.*), it is submitted that the creditor's right arises only after he has paid the claim, and that he is entitled to pay without consulting the supplier, if he is convinced on reasonable grounds that there is no defence to the claim.

£30; £10,000
These amounts are subject to amendment by order under s. 181 (1), *post.*

RULES OF COURT
See the note to s. 70 (3), *ante.*

DEFINITIONS
For "credit limit", see s. 10 (2), *ante.*
For "creditor", "debtor", "finance", "non-commercial agreement" and "supplier", see s. 189 (1), *post.*
For "debtor-creditor-supplier agreement", see s. 12, *ante.*

## 76. Duty to give notice before taking certain action

(1) The creditor or owner is not entitled to enforce a term of a regulated agreement by—

(*a*) demanding earlier payment of any sum, or
(*b*) recovering possession of any goods or land, or
(*c*) treating any right conferred on the debtor or hirer by the agreement as terminated, restricted or deferred,

except by or after giving the debtor or hirer not less than seven days' notice of his intention to do so.

(2) Subsection (1) applies only where—

(*a*) a period for the duration of the agreement is specified in the agreement, and
(*b*) that period has not ended when the creditor or owner does an act mentioned in subsection (1),

but so applies notwithstanding that, under the agreement, any party is entitled to terminate it before the end of the period so specified.

(3) A notice under subsection (1) is ineffective if not in the prescribed form.

(4) Subsection (1) does not prevent a creditor from treating the right to draw on any credit as restricted or deferred and taking such steps as may be necessary to make the restriction or deferment effective.

(5) Regulations may provide that subsection (1) is not to apply to agreements described by the regulations.

(6) Subsection (1) does not apply to a right of enforcement arising by reason of any breach by the debtor or hirer of the regulated agreement. **[C.76]**

COMMENCEMENT

See Sch. 3, para. 16, *post*, and the note "Appointed days" to Part VI of that Schedule.

GENERAL NOTE

This section requires seven days' written notice in the prescribed form to be given by the creditor before taking certain steps to enforce the contract. The steps in question are enumerated in sub-s. (1) (*a*) to (*c*), but para. (*c*) is limited by sub-s. (4). The latter subsection saves the right of the creditor to take such steps as prohibiting the further use of a credit card or ceasing to honour cheques on an overdrawn account, without waiting for the expiry of the seven days' notice.

Subsection (6) excludes cases where the right of enforcement arises out of a breach of contract. Such cases fall under the provisions of ss. 87, 88, *post*, which require a very similar "default notice" to be served. In practice, the steps mentioned in sub-s. (1) will normally be available only in cases of breach.

PROHIBITION OF CONTRACTING OUT

See the note to s. 56, *ante*.

NOT LESS THAN SEVEN DAYS

See the note to s. 61, *ante*.

PRESCRIBED FORM

I.e., prescribed by regulations; see s. 189 (1), *post*. Nothing had been prescribed for the purposes of sub-s. (3) above up to the time of going to press.

NOTICE TO SURETY

When a notice is given under this section, a copy must be served upon any surety (if a different person from the debtor or hirer); see s. 111, *post*.

DEFINITIONS

For "credit", see s. 9, *ante*.
For "creditor", "debtor", "give", "goods", "hirer", "land", "notice", "regulated agreement", and "regulations", see s. 189 (1), *post*.

REGULATIONS UNDER THIS SECTION

No regulations had been made for the purposes of sub-s. (5) above up to the time of going to press.

For general provisions as to regulations under this Act, see s. 182 (1)–(3), *post*.

## 77. Duty to give information to debtor under fixed-sum credit agreement

(1) The creditor under a regulated agreement for fixed-sum credit, within the prescribed period after receiving a request in writing to that effect from the debtor and payment of a fee of 15 new pence, shall give the debtor a copy of the executed agreement (if any) and of any other document referred to in it, together with a statement signed by or on behalf of the creditor showing, according to the information to which it is practicable for him to refer—

(*a*) the total sum paid under the agreement by the debtor;

(*b*) the total sum which has become payable under the agreement by the debtor but remains unpaid, and the various amounts comprised in that total sum, with the date when each became due; and

(*c*) the total sum which is to become payable under the agreement by the debtor, and the various amounts comprised in that total sum, with the date, or mode of determining the date, when each becomes due.

(2) If the creditor possesses insufficient information to enable him to ascertain the amounts and dates mentioned in subsection (1) (*c*), he shall be taken to comply with that paragraph if his statement under subsection (1) gives the basis on which, under the regulated agreement, they would fall to be ascertained.

(3) Subsection (1) does not apply to—

(*a*) an agreement under which no sum is, or will or may become, payable by the debtor, or

(*b*) a request made less than one month after a previous request under that subsection relating to the same agreement was complied with.

(4) If the creditor under an agreement fails to comply with subsection (1)—

(*a*) he is not entitled, while the default continues, to enforce the agreement; and

(*b*) if the default continues for one month he commits an offence.

(5) This section does not apply to a non-commercial agreement. [**C.77**]

COMMENCEMENT
See Sch. 3, para. 17, *post*, and the note "Appointed days" to Part VI of that Schedule.

PRESCRIBED PERIOD
I.e., prescribed by regulations; see s. 189 (1), *post*. Nothing had been prescribed for the purposes of sub-s. (1) above up to the time of going to press.

WRITING
See the note to s. 6, *ante*.

15 NEW PENCE
This amount is subject to amendment by order under s. 181 (1), *post*.

COPY
For power to prescribe the form of copies, see s. 180, *post*.

STATEMENT
As to the binding effect of statements furnished under this section or ss. 78 (1), 79 (1), *post*, see s. 172 (1), (3), *post*.

SIGNED
See the note to s. 51, *ante*.

OFFENCE
As to notification of convictions to the Director, see s. 166, *post*. For penalties and mode of prosecution, see s. 167 (1) and Sch. 1, *post*. For special defences, see s. 168, *post*. As to offences by bodies corporate, see s. 169, *post*.

DEFINITIONS
For "creditor", "debtor", "executed agreement", "give", "non-commercial agreement", and "regulated agreement", see s. 189 (1), *post*.
For "fixed-sum credit", see s. 10 (1) (*b*), *ante*.

**78. Duty to give information to debtor under running-account credit agreement**

(1) The creditor under a regulated agreement for running-account credit, within the prescribed period after receiving a request in writing to that effect from the debtor and payment of a fee of 15 new pence, shall give the debtor a copy of the executed agreement (if any) and of any other document referred to in it, together with a statement signed by or on behalf of the creditor showing, according to the information to which it is practicable for him to refer—

(*a*) the state of the account, and

(*b*) the amount, if any, currently payable under the agreement by the debtor to the creditor, and (*c*) the amounts and due dates of any payments which, if the debtor does not draw further on the account, will later become payable under the agreement by the debtor to the creditor.

(2) If the creditor possesses insufficient information to enable him to ascertain the amounts and dates mentioned in subsection (1) (*c*), he shall be taken to comply with that paragraph if his statement under subsection (1) gives the basis on which, under the regulated agreement, they would fall to be ascertained.

(3) Subsection (1) does not apply to—

(*a*) an agreement under which no sum is, or will or may become, payable by the debtor, or

(*b*) a request made less than one month after a previous request under that subsection relating to the same agreement was complied with.

(4) Where running-account credit is provided under a regulated agreement, the creditor shall give the debtor statements in the prescribed form, and with the prescribed contents—

(*a*) showing according to the information to which it is practicable for him to refer, the state of the account at regular intervals of not more than twelve months, and

(*b*) where the agreement provides, in relation to specified periods, for the making of payments by the debtor, or the charging against him of interest or any other sum, showing according to the information to which it is practicable for him to refer the state of the account at the end of each of those periods during which there is any movement in the account.

(5) A statement under subsection (4) shall be given within the prescribed period after the end of the period to which the statement relates.

(6) If the creditor under an agreement fails to comply with subsection (1)—

(*a*) he is not entitled, while the default continues, to enforce the agreement; and

(*b*) if the default continues for one month he commits an offence.

(7) This section does not apply to a non-commercial agreement, and subsections (4) and (5) do not apply to a small agreement. [C.78]

COMMENCEMENT

See Sch. 3, para. 17, *post*, and the note "Appointed days" to Part VI of that Schedule.

PRESCRIBED PERIOD, FORM, CONTENTS

I.e., prescribed by regulations; see s. 189 (1), *post*. Nothing had been prescribed for the purposes of sub-ss. (1) and (4) above up to the time of going to press.

WRITING

See the note to s. 6, *ante*.

15 NEW PENCE; COPY; STATEMENT; OFFENCE

See the notes to s. 77, *ante*.

SIGNED

See the note to s. 51, *ante*.

SHALL GIVE THE DEBTOR

As a general rule, this means each of the debtors, if there are two or more; see s. 185 (1), *post.* For the power of a joint debtor to dispense with the obligation to furnish statements under sub-s. (4) above to him, see s. 185 (2), *post.*

DEFINITIONS

For "creditor", "debtor", "executed agreement", "give", "non-commercial agreement" and "regulated agreement", see s. 189 (1), *post.*

For "running account credit", see s. 10 (1) (*a*), *ante.*

For "small agreement", see s. 17 (1), *ante.*

## 79. Duty to give hirer information

(1) The owner under a regulated consumer hire agreement, within the prescribed period after receiving a request in writing to that effect from the hirer and payment of a fee of 15 new pence, shall give to the hirer a copy of the executed agreement and of any other document referred to in it, together with a statement signed by or on behalf of the owner showing, according to the information to which it is practicable for him to refer, the total sum which has become payable under the agreement by the hirer but remains unpaid and the various amounts comprised in that total sum, with the date when each became due.

(2) Subsection (1) does not apply to—

(*a*) an agreement under which no sum is, or will or may become, payable by the hirer, or

(*b*) a request made less than one month after a previous request under that subsection relating to the same agreement was complied with.

(3) If the owner under an agreement fails to comply with subsection (1)—

(*a*) he is not entitled, while the default continues, to enforce the agreement; and

(*b*) if the default continues for one month he commits an offence.

(4) This section does not apply to a non-commercial agreement. **[C.79]**

COMMENCEMENT

See Sch. 3, para. 17, *post*, and the note "Appointed days" to Part VI of that Schedule.

PRESCRIBED PERIOD

I.e., prescribed by regulations; see s. 189 (1), *post.* Nothing had been prescribed for the purposes of sub-s. (1) above up to the time of going to press.

WRITING

See the note to s. 6, *ante.*

15 NEW PENCE; COPY; STATEMENT; OFFENCE

See the notes to s. 77, *ante.*

SIGNED

See the note to s. 51, *ante.*

DEFINITIONS

For "consumer hire agreement", see s. 15, *ante.*

For "give", "hirer", "non-commercial agreement", "owner" and "regulated agreement", see s. 189 (1), *post.*

## 80. Debtor or hirer to give information about goods

(1) Where a regulated agreement, other than a non-commercial agreement, requires the debtor or hirer to keep goods to which the agreement relates in his

possession or control, he shall, within seven working days after he has received a request in writing to that effect from the creditor or owner, tell the creditor or owner where the goods are.

(2) If the debtor or hirer fails to comply with subsection (1), and the default continues for 14 days, he commits an offence. **[C.80]**

COMMENCEMENT

See Sch. 3, para. 17, *post*, and the note "Appointed days" to Part VI of that Schedule.

WITHIN SEVEN . . . DAYS

See the note "Within 21 days" to s. 36, *ante*.

WRITING

See the note to s. 6, *ante*.

OFFENCE

As to notification of convictions to the Director, see s. 166, *post*. For penalties and mode of prosecution, see s. 167 (1) and Sch. 1, *post*. For special defences, see s. 168, *post*.

DEFINITIONS

For "creditor", "debtor", "goods", "hirer", "non-commercial agreement", "owner", "regulated agreement" and "working day", see s. 189 (1), *post*.

## 81. Appropriation of payments

(1) Where a debtor or hirer is liable to make to the same person payments in respect of two or more regulated agreements, he shall be entitled, on making any payment in respect of the agreements which is not sufficient to discharge the total amount then due under all the agreements, to appropriate the sum so paid by him—

(*a*) in or towards the satisfaction of the sum due under any one of the agreements, or

(*b*) in or towards the satisfaction of the sums due under any two or more of the agreements in such proportions as he thinks fit.

(2) If the debtor or hirer fails to make any such appropriation where one or more of the agreements is—

(*a*) a hire-purchase agreement or conditional sale agreement, or

(*b*) a consumer hire agreement, or

(*c*) an agreement in relation to which any security is provided,

the payment shall be appropriated towards the satisfaction of the sums due under the several agreements respectively in the proportions which those sums bear to one another. **[C.81]**

COMMENCEMENT

See Sch. 3, para. 18, *post*; and the note "Principal appointed day" to Part VI of that Schedule.

PERSON

See the note to s. 8, *ante*.

DEFINITIONS

For "conditional sale agreement", "debtor", "hire-purchase agreement", "hirer", "regulated agreement" and "security", see s. 189 (1), *post*.

For "consumer hire agreement", see s. 15, *ante*.

**82. Variation of agreements**

(1) Where, under a power contained in a regulated agreement, the creditor or owner varies the agreement, the variation shall not take effect before notice of it is given to the debtor or hirer in the prescribed manner.

(2) Where an agreement (a "modifying agreement") varies or supplements an earlier agreement, the modifying agreement shall for the purposes of this Act be treated as—

(*a*) revoking the earlier agreement, and

(*b*) containing provisions reproducing the combined effect of the two agreements,

and obligations outstanding in relation to the earlier agreement shall accordingly be treated as outstanding instead in relation to the modifying agreement.

(3) If the earlier agreement is a regulated agreement but (apart from this subsection) the modifying agreement is not then, unless the modifying agreement is for running-account credit, it shall be treated as a regulated agreement.

(4) If the earlier agreement is a regulated agreement for running-account credit, and by the modifying agreement the creditor allows the credit limit to be exceeded but intends the excess to be merely temporary, Part V (except section 56) shall not apply to the modifying agreement.

(5) If—

(*a*) the earlier agreement is a cancellable agreement, and

(*b*) the modifying agreement is made within the period applicable under section 68 to the earlier agreement,

then, whether or not the modifying agreement would, apart from this subsection, be a cancellable agreement, it shall be treated as a cancellable agreement in respect of which a notice may be served under section 68 not later than the end of the period applicable under that section to the earlier agreement.

(6) Except under subsection (5), a modifying agreement shall not be treated as a cancellable agreement.

(7) This section does not apply to a non-commercial agreement. [C.82]

COMMENCEMENT

See Sch. 3, para. 19, *post*, and the note "Appointed days" to Part VI of that Schedule.

GENERAL NOTE

Subsection (1) of this section requires notice to be given of unilateral variations of regulated agreements. The remainder of the section deals with the application of this Act in cases where an agreement is varied or supplemented by a subsequent agreement. By sub-s. (2), the later agreement is to be treated as containing provisions reproducing the combined effect of the later and earlier agreements. It would seem to follow that the combined provisions must be embodied in a document with regard to which any applicable formalities (e.g., those of ss. 61, 62 and 63, *ante*) must be gone through *de novo*, and if this is not done the whole agreement will become "not properly executed", even though the proper procedure was originally observed.

An exception is, however, made by sub-s. (4) above for cases of variation by the merely temporary waiver of a credit limit, and sub-s. (7) excepts non-commercial agreements. Subsection (5) makes it clear that in the case of a cancellable agreement modified within the period allowed for cancellation, the right of cancellation may still be exercised within the original period.

PRESCRIBED MANNER
I.e., prescribed by regulations; see s. 189 (1), *post*. Nothing had been prescribed for the purposes of sub-s. (1) above up to the time of going to press.

PART V
I.e., ss. 55–74, *ante*.

DEFINITIONS
For "credit limit", see s. 10 (2), *ante*.
For "creditor", "debtor", "give", "hirer", "non-commercial agreement", "notice", "owner" and "regulated agreement", see s. 189 (1), *post*.
For "running account credit", see s. 10, *ante*.
For "modifying agreement", see sub-s. (2) above.

### 83. Liability for misuse of credit facilities

(1) The debtor under a regulated consumer credit agreement shall not be liable to the creditor for any loss arising from use of the credit facility by another person not acting, or to be treated as acting, as the debtor's agent.

(2) This section does not apply to a non-commercial agreement or to any loss in so far as it arises from misuse of an instrument to which section 4 of the Cheques Act 1957 applies. [C.83]

COMMENCEMENT
See Sch. 3, para. 20, *post*, and the note "Appointed days" to Part VI of that Schedule.

PROHIBITION OF CONTRACTING OUT
See the note to s. 56, *ante*.

EXCEPTIONS
For cases excepted from the operation of this section, see s. 84, *post*.

TO BE TREATED AS ACTING
This Act contains no provisions by which any person is to be treated as acting as the debtor's agent. This reference must therefore be to cases of ostensible authority or agency by estoppel at common law, as to which, see 1 Halsbury's Laws (4th edn,) 434.

MISUSE OF AN INSTRUMENT, ETC.
The purpose of this provision of sub-s. (2) is to save the protection accorded to bankers by the Bills of Exchange Act 1882, s. 80 (3 Halsbury's Statutes (3rd edn.) 231) and the Cheques Act 1957, ss 1, 4 (3 Halsbury's Statutes (3rd edn.) 238, 241).

DEFINITIONS
For "consumer credit agreement", see s. 8 (1), *ante*.
For "creditor", "debtor", "non-commercial agreement" and "regulated agreement", see s. 189 (1), *post*.

CHEQUES ACT 1957, S. 4
See 3 Halsbury's Statutes (3rd edn.) 241.

### 84. Misuse of credit-tokens

(1) Section 83 does not prevent the debtor under a credit-token agreement from being made liable to the extent of £30 (or the credit limit if lower) for loss to the creditor arising from use of the credit-token by other persons during a period beginning when the credit-token ceases to be in the possession of any authorised person and ending when the credit-token is once more in the possession of an authorised person.

(2) Section 83 does not prevent the debtor under a credit-token agreement

from being made liable to any extent for loss to the creditor from use of the credit-token by a person who acquired possession of it with the debtor's consent.

(3) Subsections (1) and (2) shall not apply to any use of the credit-token after the creditor has been given oral or written notice that it is lost or stolen, or is for any other reason liable to misuse.

(4) Subsections (1) and (2) shall not apply unless there are contained in the credit-token agreement in the prescribed manner particulars of the name, address and telephone number of a person stated to be the person to whom notice is to be given under subsection (3).

(5) Notice under subsection (3) takes effect when received, but where it is given orally, and the agreement so requires, it shall be treated as not taking effect if not confirmed in writing within seven days.

(6) Any sum paid by the debtor for the issue of the credit-token, to the extent (if any) that it has not been previously offset by use made of the credit-token, shall be treated as paid towards satisfaction of any liability under subsection (1) or (2).

(7) The debtor, the creditor, and any person authorised by the debtor to use the credit-token shall be authorised persons for the purposes of subsection (1).

(8) Where two or more credit-tokens are given under one credit-token agreement, the preceding provisions of this section apply to each credit-token separately. **[C.84]**

COMMENCEMENT

See Sch. 3, paras. 12, 13, 15, *post*, and the note "Principal appointed day" to Part VI of that Schedule.

£30

This figure is subject to amendment by order under s. 182 1), *post*.

WRITTEN

See the note "Writing" to s. 6, *ante*.

PRESCRIBED MANNER

I.e., prescribed by regulations; see s. 189 (1), *post*. Nothing had been prescribed for the purposes of sub-s. (4) above up to the time of going to press.

ONUS OF PROOF

As to the onus of proof on questions of authorised use, and of use prior to notice under sub-s. (3) above, see s. 172 (3), *post*.

DEFINITIONS

For "creditor", "credit-token agreement", "debtor", "give" and "notice", see s. 189 (1), *post*.

For "credit-token", see s.14 (1), *ante*. As to "authorised person", note the provisions of sub-s. (7) above.

## 85. Duty on issue of new credit-tokens

(1) Whenever, in connection with a credit-token agreement, a credit-token (other than the first) is given by the creditor to the debtor, the creditor shall give the debtor a copy of the executed agreement (if any) and of any other document referred to in it.

(2) If the creditor fails to comply with this section—

(*a*) he is not entitled, while the default continues, to enforce the agreement; and

(*b*) if the default continues for one month he commits an offence.

(3) This section does not apply to a small agreement. **[C.85]**

COMMENCEMENT

See Sch. 3, para. 21, *post*, and the note "Appointed days" to Part VI of that Schedule.

COPY

For power to prescribe the form of copies, see s. 180, *post*.

OFFENCE

As to notification of convictions to the Director, see s. 166, *post*. For penalties and mode of prosecution, see s. 167 (1) and Sch. 1, *post*. For special defences, see s. 168, *post*. As to offences by bodies corporate, see s. 169, *post*.

DEFINITIONS

For "creditor", "credit-token agreement", "debtor", "executed agreement", "give" and "small agreement", see s. 189 (1), *post*.

**86. Death of debtor or hirer**

(1) The creditor or owner under a regulated agreement is not entitled, by reason of the death of the debtor or hirer, to do an act specified in paragraphs (*a*) to (*e*) of section 87 (1), if at the death the agreement is fully secured.

(2) If at the death of the debtor or hirer a regulated agreement is only partly secured or is unsecured, the creditor or owner is entitled, by reason of the death of the debtor or hirer, to do an act specified in paragraphs (*a*) to (*e*) of section 87 (1) on an order of the court only.

(3) This section applies in relation to the termination of an agreement only where—

(*a*) a period for its duration is specified in the agreement, and

(*b*) that period has not ended when the creditor or owner purports to terminate the agreement,

but so applies notwithstanding that, under the agreement, any party is entitled to terminate it before the end of the period so specified.

(4) This section does not prevent the creditor from treating the right to draw on any credit as restricted or deferred and taking such steps as may be necessary to make the restriction or deferment effective.

(5) This section does not affect the operation of any agreement providing for payment of sums—

(*a*) due under the regulated agreement, or

(*b*) becoming due under it on the death of the debtor or hirer,

out of the proceeds of a policy of assurance on his life.

(6) For the purposes of this section an act is done by reason of the death of the debtor or hirer if it is done under a power conferred by the agreement which is—

(*a*) exercisable on his death, or
(*b*) exercisable at will and exercised at any time after his death. **[C.86]**

COMMENCEMENT
See Sch. 3, para. 22, *post*, and the note "Appointed days" to Part VI of that Schedule.

PROHIBITION OF CONTRACTING OUT
See the note to s. 56, *ante*.

FULLY-SECURED; PARTLY SECURED
These terms are not defined, but the word "secured" is presumably to be construed in accordance with the definition of "security" in s. 189 (1), *post*. If there is a contract of indemnity or guarantee or a bill, note, etc. covering the whole amount of the debt, the agreement is presumably "fully-secured". In the case of a mortgage or pledge, the question arises whether the true value of the land mortgaged or chattel pledged has to be taken into consideration in order to discover whether the agreement is fully or only partly secured. If so, the case is similar to that under the Bankruptcy Act 1914, s. 4 (2) (3 Halsbury's Statutes (3rd edn.) 45), where a secured creditor, upon giving an estimate of the value of his security and showing that it does not cover the whole amount due to him, is permitted to petition as if he were an unsecured creditor for the difference. A similar estimate could be given by the creditor when applying for an order under sub-s. (2) above. A possible alternative view is that if the mortgage or pledge is expressed to be given in respect of the whole debt, the agreement is to be considered as fully secured, even if the actual value of the security is insufficient to cover the whole debt. Note that certain types of security are prohibited by s. 123 (3), *post*, but contravention of that section renders the securities not absolutely void, but enforceable upon an order of the court only (s. 124 (2), *post*). It is thought that the existence of such a security suffices to render the agreement "secured" for the purposes of this section.

ON AN ORDER OF THE COURT ONLY
For the rules governing the making or refusal of such an order, see s. 128, *post*. For further powers exercisable by the court on an application for an enforcement order, see ss. 129, 135, 136 and 142, *post*.
*Quaere* whether the consent of the deceased's personal representatives could take the place of a court order by virtue of s. 173 (3), *post*.

DEFINITIONS
For "court", "creditor", "debtor", "hirer", "owner" and "regulated agreement", see s. 189 (1), *post*.
For "credit", see s. 9, *ante*

## PART VII

### DEFAULT AND TERMINATION

*Default notices*

### 87. Need for default notice

(1) Service of a notice on the debtor or hirer in accordance with section 88 (a "default notice") is necessary before the creditor or owner can become entitled, by reason of any breach by the debtor or hirer of a regulated agreement,—

(*a*) to terminate the agreement, or
(*b*) to demand earlier payment of any sum, or
(*c*) to recover possession of any goods or land, or
(*d*) to treat any right conferred on the debtor or hirer by the agreement as terminated, restricted or deferred, or
(*e*) to enforce any security.

(2) Subsection (1) does not prevent the creditor from treating the right to draw upon any credit as restricted or deferred and taking such steps as may be necessary to make the restriction or deferment effective.

(3) The doing of an act by which a floating charge becomes fixed is not enforcement of a security.

(4) Regulations may provide that subsection (1) is not to apply to agreements described by the regulations. **[C.87]**

COMMENCEMENT

See Sch. 3, para. 23, *post*, and the note "Appointed days" to Part VII of that Schedule.

GENERAL NOTE

This section and ss. 88, 89, *post*, establish a new code governing the enforcement by the creditor of terms in a regulated agreement by which remedies are provided for the breach of the agreement. None of the steps listed in paras. (*a*)–(*e*) of sub-s. (1) above may be taken unless a default notice has been served. The only step which may be taken immediately after the breach has occurred is to prevent the debtor from making further drawings of credit (thus, for example, the creditor could refuse to honour further cheques on an overdrawn account); see sub-s. (2) above. As respects all other steps, a period of at least seven days must be allowed, during which the debtor may be given the opportunity either to remedy his default or to pay damages by way of compensation for it; see s. 88 (1), (2), (5), *post*. If this opportunity is taken, the breach of contract is cured and it obviously follows that no further steps may be taken by the creditor; see s. 89, *post*. In the case of a breach which is not capable of remedy, it is not compulsory for the creditor to allow an opportunity for the payment of damages (see s. 88 (1) (*c*), *post*), and if he does not, then so far as the provisions of these sections go, he will be able to proceed with steps for enforcement at the end of the seven days, whatever the debtor does in the meantime. The debtor may, however, take advantage of the seven days' notice to apply for a "time order" under s. 129, *post*, or (in an appropriate case) to seek relief under ss. 137–139, *post*.

Subsection (3) above provides that an act by which a floating charge becomes fixed is not enforcement of a security. Where such an act does not fall under any other provision of sub-s. (1) above, it will not be within ss. 87–89 at all.

Subsection 88 (3), *post*, deals with the situation which arises when one breach of contract brings provisions into operation and those provisions are in turn breached. Suppose, for example, that an agreement provides for the whole amount of a loan to become due and payable immediately upon failure to pay any instalment. In such a case, default notice must be served in respect of the non-payment of the instalment only; it cannot treat non-payment of the whole amount as a breach at that stage. If, however, the debtor does nothing to rectify the position and the obligation to pay the whole amount comes into force at the end of the period of notice, no further default notice is required for the enforcement of that obligation.

PROHIBITION OF CONTRACTING OUT

See the note to s. 56, *ante*.

SERVICE

For provisions as to the service of notices, see s. 176, *post*, and see also the definition of "serve on" in s. 189 (1), *post*.

NOTICE

See the definition in s. 189 (1), *post*. For the contents of a default notice, see s. 88 (1) (2), (6), *post*.

THIS PART

I.e., ss. 87–103.

BY WHICH A FLOATING CHARGE BECOMES FIXED

The agreement itself may specify what these acts are. For the general law, see 7 Halsbury's Laws (4th edn.) 493.

FURTHER PROVISIONS

For the effect of a default notice, see ss. 88, 89, *post*. For further provisions restricting the right to re-possess goods or land, see ss. 90–93, *post*. As to the notice required for the taking of steps mentioned in sub-s. (1) above, otherwise than by reason of breach of contract, see s. 76, *ante*, and s. 98, *post*. As to enforcement of securities generally, see Part VIII (ss. 105–127), *post*.

DEFINITIONS

For "creditor", "debtor", "goods", "hirer", "land", "owner", "regulated agreement", "regulations" and "security", see s. 189 (1), *post*.

REGULATIONS UNDER THIS SECTION

No regulations had been made for the purposes of sub-s. (3) above up to the time of going to press.

For general provisions as to regulations under this Act, see s. 182 (1)–(3), *post*.

## 88. Contents and effect of default notice

(1) The default notice must be in the prescribed form and specify—

(*a*) the nature of the alleged breach;

(*b*) if the breach is capable of remedy, what action is required to remedy it and the date before which that action is to be taken;

(*c*) if the breach is not capable of remedy, the sum (if any) required to be paid as compensation for the breach, and the date before which it is to be paid.

(2) A date specified under subsection (1) must not be less than seven days after the date of service of the default notice, and the creditor or owner shall not take action such as is mentioned in section 87 (1) before the date so specified or (if no requirement is made under subsection (1)) before those seven days have elapsed.

(3) The default notice must not treat as a breach failure to comply with a provision of the agreement which becomes operative only on breach of some other provision, but if the breach of that other provision is not duly remedied or compensation demanded under subsection (1) is not duly paid, or (where no requirement is made under subsection (1)) if the seven days mentioned in subsection (2) have elapsed, the creditor or owner may treat the failure as a breach and section 87 (1) shall not apply to it.

(4) The default notice must contain information in the prescribed terms about the consequences of failure to comply with it.

(5) A default notice making a requirement under subsection (1) may include a provision for the taking of action such as is mentioned in section 87 (1) at any time after the restriction imposed by subsection (2) will cease, together with a statement that the provision will be ineffective if the breach is duly remedied or the compensation duly paid. **[C.88]**

COMMENCEMENT

See Sch. 3, para. 23, *post*, and the note "Appointed days" to Part VII of that Schedule.

GENERAL NOTE

See the General Note to s. 87, *ante*.

PRESCRIBED FORM; PRESCRIBED TERMS

I.e., prescribed by regulations; see s. 189 (1), *post*. Nothing had been prescribed for the purposes of sub-ss. (1) or (5) above up to the time of going to press.

SPECIFY

The courts may be expected to require that these matters should be specified unambiguously and with a reasonable degree of particularity. Cf. decisions on notices to quit under the Agricultural Holdings Act 1948, s. 24, Vol. 1, p. 707, such as *Budge* v. *Hicks*, [1951] 2 K.B. 335; [1951] 2 All E.R. 245, and *Cowan* v. *Wrayford*, [1953] 2 All E.R. 1138, and see also *Eshun* v. *Moorgate Mercantile Co., Ltd.*, [1971] 2 All E.R. 402, (default notice under Hire-Purchase Act 1965).

CAPABLE OF REMEDY

These words seem on the face of them to impose an objective test, that is to say, the question is whether the breach can in fact be remedied, not merely whether the creditor regards it as remediable. The question is important, since if para. (*b*) of sub-s. (1) applies, the creditor *must* specify remedial action, whereas under para. (*c*) it is optional for him to specify an amount to be paid as compensation. A notice might well be held to be a nullity if it specified no remedial action and the court came to the conclusion that the breach was capable of remedy.

NOT . . . LESS THAN SEVEN DAYS

See the note to s. 61, *ante*.

SERVICE

See the note to s. 87, *ante*.

DEFINITIONS

For "creditor", and "owner", see s. 189 (1), *post*.
For "default notice", see s. 87 (1), *ante*.

## 89. Compliance with default notice

If before the date specified for that purpose in the default notice the debtor or hirer takes the action specified under section 88 (1) (*b*) or (*c*) the breach shall be treated as not having occurred. **[C.89]**

COMMENCEMENT

See Sch. 3, para. 23, *post*, and the note "Appointed days" to Part VII of that Schedule.

GENERAL NOTE

See the General Note to s. 87, *ante*.

TAKES THE ACTION SPECIFIED

It is thought that subject to the *de minimis* rule, the creditor may rely upon a partial failure to comply with the notice; see *Price* v. *Romilly*, [1960] 3 All E.R. 429. A notice specifying remedial action which the creditor is not entitled to require, together with other action to which he is entitled, might well be held to be a good notice, but in that case partial compliance would obviously be sufficient; see *Shepherd* v. *Lomas*, [1963] 2 All E.R. 902.

THE BREACH

This must mean the breach to which the notice related, as specified therein (see s. 88 (1) (*a*), *ante*).

DEFINITIONS

For "debtor" and "hirer", see s. 189 (1), *post*.
For "default notice", see s. 87 (1), *ante*.

*Further restriction of remedies for default*

## 90. Retaking of protected hire-purchase etc. goods

(1) At any time when—

(*a*) the debtor is in breach of a regulated hire-purchase or a regulated conditional sale agreement relating to goods, and (*b*) the debtor has paid to the creditor one-third or more of the total price of the goods, and

(*c*) the property in the goods remains in the creditor,

the creditor is not entitled to recover possession of the goods from the debtor except on an order of the court.

(2) Where under a hire-purchase or conditional sale agreement the creditor is required to carry out any installation and the agreement specifies, as part of the total price, the amount to be paid in respect of the installation (the "installation charge") the reference in subsection (1) (*b*) to one third of the total price shall be construed as a reference to the aggregate of the installation charge and one-third of the remainder of the total price.

(3) In a case where—

(*a*) subsection (1) (*a*) is satisfied, but not subsection (1) (*b*), and

(*b*) subsection (1) (*b*) was satisfied on a previous occasion in relation to an earlier agreement, being a regulated hire-purchase or regulated conditional sale agreement, between the same parties, and relating to any of the goods comprised in the later agreement (whether or not other goods were also included),

subsection (1) shall apply to the later agreement with the omission of paragraph (*b*).

(4) If the later agreement is a modifying agreement subsection (3) shall apply with the substitution, for the second reference to the later agreement, of a reference to the modifying agreement.

(5) Subsection (1) shall not apply, or shall cease to apply, to an agreement if the debtor has terminated, or terminates, the agreement.

(6) Where subsection (1) applies to an agreement at the death of the debtor, it shall continue to apply (in relation to the possessor of the goods) until the grant of probate or administration, or (in Scotland) confirmation (on which the personal representative would fall to be treated as the debtor).

(7) Goods falling within this section are in this Act referred to as "protected goods". [C.90]

COMMENCEMENT

See Sch. 3, para. 24, *post*, and the note "Appointed days" to Part VII of that Schedule

GENERAL NOTE

This section provides for the retaking under a hire-purchase or conditional sale agreement of "protected goods", i.e., goods in respect of which at least one-third of the total purchase price has been paid. This section, read with ss. 131, 133, *post* (powers of the court), substantially re-enacts, with drafting amendments and certain changes of terminology, the provisions of the Hire-Purchase Act 1965, ss. 33, 34 (1), 35, 37 and 55 (1) (*b*) (30 Halsbury's Statutes (3rd edn.) 91–94, 106) (repealed by s. 192 (3) and Sch. 5, *post*). The only innovation of substance is made by s. 133 (5), *post*, which gives the debtor an absolute right to pay his arrears and claim the goods at any time before they enter the possession of the creditor. Under the Act of 1965, the same result might be achieved in the discretion of the court, exercising its powers under s. 39 (30 Halsbury's Statutes (3rd edn.) 95).

PROHIBITION OF CONTRACTING OUT

See the note to s. 56, *ante*.

NOT ENTITLED

See, however, s. 173 (3), *post*, as to the sufficiency of the debtor's consent, given at the time when possession is recovered. In view of that provision, it is thought that certain decisions on former hire-purchase legislation are applicable under this section. These are *Mercantile Credit Co., Ltd.* v. *Cross*, [1965] 1 All E.R. 577, C.A. (Act not contravened by letter requiring re-delivery of goods and voluntarily complied with by debtor) and *Bentinck, Ltd.* v. *Cromwell Engineering Co.*, [1971] 1 All E.R. 33, C.A. (owner may take possession of goods abandoned by hirer). See also *Smart Brothers, Ltd.* v. *Ross*, [1943] A.C. 84; [1942] 2 All E.R. 282, H.L. For the consequences of contravention of this section, see s. 91, *post*.

ORDER OF THE COURT

For the power of the court and the principles on which they are to be exercised, see ss. 131, 133, *post*. As to evidence of adverse possession, see s. 134, *post*, and for supplemented provisions as to orders, ss. 135, 136, *post*.

DEFINITIONS

For "conditional sale agreement", "court", "creditor", "debtor", "goods", "hire-purchase agreement", "installation", "regulated agreement" and "total price", see s. 189 (1), *post*.

For "modifying agreement", see s. 82 (2), *ante*.

## 91. Consequences of breach of s. 90

If goods are recovered by the creditor in contravention of section 90—

(*a*) the regulated agreement, if not previously terminated, shall terminate, and

(*b*) the debtor shall be released from all liability under the agreement, and shall be entitled to recover from the creditor all sums paid by the debtor under the agreement. [C.91]

COMMENCEMENT

See Sch. 3, para. 24, *post*, and the note "Appointed days" to Part VII of that Schedule.

GENERAL NOTE

This section provides for the termination of agreements when goods have been repossessed in contravention of s. 90, *ante*. It is substantially a re-enactment of the Hire-Purchase Act 1965, s. 34 (2) (30 Halsbury's Statutes (3rd edn.) 92) (repealed by s. 192 (3) and Sch. 5, *post*).

SHALL TERMINATE

As to the avoidance of securities in that event, see s. 113 (3), *post*. As to the effect on linked transactions, see s. 96, *post*.

DECLARATION BY COURT

For the court's jurisdiction to declare that an agreement has been terminated under this section, see s. 142 (2), *post*.

DEFINITIONS

For "creditor", "debtor", "goods" and "regulated agreement", see s. 189 (1), *post*.

## 92. Recovery of possession of goods or land

(1) Except under an order of the court, the creditor or owner shall not be entitled to enter any premises to take possession of goods subject to a regulated hire-purchase agreement, regulated conditional sale agreement or regulated consumer hire agreement.

(2) At any time when the debtor is in breach of a regulated conditional sale agreement relating to land, the creditor is entitled to recover possession of the

land from the debtor, or any person claiming under him, on an order of the court only.

(3) An entry in contravention of subsection (1) or (2) is actionable as a breach of statutory duty. **[C.92]**

COMMENCEMENT
See Sch. 3, para. 25, *post*, and the note "Appointed days" to Part VII of that Schedule.

ORDER OF THE COURT
See the note to s. 90, *ante*.

PREMISES
Though this word is capable of meaning real property of any kind, including unenclosed land, it is also used in a narrower sense to mean only buildings, enclosures and their curtilages; see *Gardiner* v. *Sevenoaks Rural District Council*, [1950] 2 All E.R. 84, at p. 85; *Bracey* v. *Read*, [1963] Ch. 88, at p. 92; [1962] 3 All E.R. 472, at p. 475; *R.* v. *Hastings Licensing Justices*, [1968] 2 All E.R. 270, at p. 271. It is thought that the narrower meaning is to be preferred in the present context.

ACTIONABLE AS A BREACH OF STATUTORY DUTY
For the remedies available see 32 Halsbury's Statutes (3rd edn.) 401.

DEFINITIONS
For "conditional sale agreement", "court", "creditor", "debtor", "goods", "hire-purchase agreement", "land", "owner" and "regulated agreement", see s. 189 (1), *post*. For "consumers hire agreement", see s. 15, *ante*.

## 93. Interest not to be increased on default

The debtor under a regulated consumer credit agreement shall not be obliged to pay interest on sums which, in breach of the agreement, are unpaid by him at a rate—

(*a*) where the total charge for credit includes an item in respect of interest, exceeding the rate of that interest, or

(*b*) in any other case, exceeding what would be the rate of the total charge for credit if any items included in the total charge for credit by virtue of section 20 (2) were disregarded. **[C.93]**

COMMENCEMENT
See Sch. 3, para. 26, *post*, and the note "Appointed days" to Part VII of that Schedule.

PROHIBITION OF CONTRACTING OUT
See the note to s. 56, *ante*.

DEFINITIONS
For "consumer credit agreement", see s. 8 (1), *ante*. For "debtor", "regulated agreement" and "total charge for credit", see s. 189 (1), *post*.

*Early payment by debtor*

## 94. Right to complete payments ahead of time

(1) The debtor under a regulated consumer credit agreement is entitled at any time, by notice to the creditor and the payment to the creditor of all amounts payable by the debtor to him under the agreement (less any rebate allowable under section 95), to discharge the debtor's indebtedness under the agreement.

(2) A notice under subsection (1) may embody the exercise by the debtor of any option to purchase goods conferred on him by the agreement, and deal with any other matter arising on, or in relation to, the termination of the agreement. **[C.94]**

COMMENCEMENT
See Sch. 3, para. 27, *post,* and the note "Appointed days" to Part VII of that Schedule.

PROHIBITION OF CONTRACTING OUT
See the note to s. 56, *ante.*

NOTICE
See the definition in s. 189 (1), *post.*

AMOUNTS PAYABLE
For the debtor's right to obtain a statement of these amounts, see s. 97, *post.*

DISCHARGE
As to rebates of charges, see s. 95, *post.* For the effect on linked transactions, see s. 96, *post.*

DEFINITIONS
For "consumer credit agreement", see s. 8 (1), *ante.*
For "creditor", "debtor", "goods" and "regulated agreement", see s. 189 (1), *post.*

## 95. Rebate on early settlement

(1) Regulations may provide for the allowance of a rebate of charges for credit to the debtor under a regulated consumer credit agreement where, under section 94, on refinancing, on breach of the agreement, or for any other reason, his indebtedness is discharged or becomes payable before the time fixed by the agreement, or any sum becomes payable by him before the time so fixed.

(2) Regulations under subsection (1) may provide for calculation of the rebate by reference to any sums paid or payable by the debtor or his relative under or in connection with the agreement (whether to the creditor or some other person), including sums under linked transactions and other items in the total charge for credit. **[C.95]**

COMMENCEMENT
See Sch. 3, para. 27, *post,* and the note "Appointed days" to Part VII of that Schedule.

DEFINITIONS
For "consumer credit agreement", see s. 8 (1), *ante.*
For "credit", see s. 9, *ante.*
For "debtor", "regulated agreement", "regulations", "relative" and "total charge for credit", see s. 189 (1), *post.*
For "linked transaction", see s. 19 (1), *ante.*

REGULATIONS UNDER THIS SECTION
No regulations had been made under this section up to the time of going to press.
For general provisions as to regulations under this Act, see s. 182 (1)–(3), *post.*

## 96. Effect on linked transactions

(1) Where for any reason the indebtedness of the debtor under a regulated consumer credit agreement is discharged before the time fixed by the agreement, he, and any relative of his, shall at the same time be discharged from any liability under a linked transaction, other than a debt which has already become payable.

(2) Subsection (1) does not apply to a linked transaction which is itself an agreement providing the debtor or his relative with credit.

(3) Regulations may exclude linked transactions of the prescribed description from the operation of subsection (1). **[C.96]**

COMMENCEMENT
See Sch. 3, para. 27, *post,* and the note "Appointed days" to Part VII of that Schedule.

PROHIBITION OF CONTRACTING OUT
See the note to s. 56, *ante.*

DEFINITIONS
For "consumer credit agreement", see s. 8 (1), *ante.* For "credit", see s. 9, *ante.* For "debtor", "prescribed", "regulated agreement", "regulations" and "relative", see s. 189 (1), *post.* For "linked transaction", see s. 19 (1), *ante.*

REGULATIONS UNDER THIS SECTION
No regulations had been made for the purposes of sub-s. (3) above up to the time of going to press.
For general provisions as to regulations under this Act, see s. 182 (1)–(3), *post.*

## 97. Duty to give information

(1) The creditor under a regulated consumer credit agreement, within the prescribed period after he has received a request in writing to that effect from the debtor, shall give the debtor a statement in the prescribed form indicating, according to the information to which it is practicable for him to refer, the amount of the payment required to discharge the debtor's indebtedness under the agreement, together with the prescribed particulars showing how the amount is arrived at.

(2) Subsection (1) does not apply to a request made less than one month after a previous request under that subsection relating to the same agreement was complied with.

(3) If the creditor fails to comply with subsection (1)—

(*a*) he is not entitled, while the default continues, to enforce the agreement; and

(*b*) if the default continues for one month he commits an offence. **[C.97]**

COMMENCEMENT
See Sch. 3, para. 27, *post,* and the note "Appointed days" to Part VII of that Schedule.

PRESCRIBED PERIOD; PRESCRIBED FORM; PRESCRIBED PARTICULARS
I.e., prescribed by regulations; see s. 189 (1), *post.* Nothing had been prescribed for the purposes of sub-s. (1) above up to the time of going to press.

WRITING
See the note to s. 6, *ante.*

STATEMENT
As to the binding effect of a statement given under this section, see s. 172 (1), (3), *post.*

OFFENCE
As to notification of convictions to the Director, see s. 166, *post.* For penalties and mode of prosecution, see s. 167 (1) and Sch. 1, *post.* For special defences, see s. 168, *post.* As to offences by bodies corporate, see s. 169, *post.*

*Termination of agreements*

**98. Duty to give notice of termination (non-default cases)**

(1) The creditor or owner is not entitled to terminate a regulated agreement except by or after giving the debtor or hirer not less than seven days' notice of the termination.

(2) Subsection (1) applies only where—

(*a*) a period for the duration of the agreement is specified in the agreement, and

(*b*) that period has not ended when the creditor or owner does an act mentioned in subsection (1),

but so applies notwithstanding that, under the agreement, any party is entitled to terminate it before the end of the period so specified.

(3) A notice under subsection (1) is ineffective if not in the prescribed form.

(4) Subsection (1) does not prevent a creditor from treating the right to draw on any credit as restricted or deferred and taking such steps as may be necessary to make the restriction or deferment effective.

(5) Regulations may provide that subsection (1) is not to apply to agreements described by the regulations.

(6) Subsection (1) does not apply to the termination of a regulated agreement by reason of any breach by the debtor or hirer of the agreement. **[C.98]**

COMMENCEMENT

See Sch. 3, para. 28, *post*, and the note "Appointed days" to Part VII of that Schedule.

GENERAL NOTE

This section requires at least seven days' written notice in the prescribed form to be given by the creditor when he terminates a regulated agreement. By sub-s. (6), cases of breach of contract are excluded; such cases are dealt with by ss. 87–89, *ante*. This section does not apply to cases where an agreement comes to an end by effluxion of time in accordance with its original terms; see sub-s. (2) above. In such cases, no positive act of termination by the creditor is normally required. This section is, therefore, concerned with cases where the agreement gives the creditor a power to terminate the agreement at his discretion. Such cases might be thought to fall also within s. 76, but that section is presumably aimed at termination of a specific right of the debtor or hirer rather than termination of the agreement as a whole.

PROHIBITION OF CONTRACTING OUT

See the note to s. 56, *ante*.

NOT LESS THAN SEVEN DAYS

See the note to s. 61, *ante*.

PRESCRIBED FORM

I.e., prescribed by regulations; see s. 189 (1), *post*. Nothing had been prescribed for the purposes of sub-s. (2) above up to the time of going to press.

DEFINITIONS

For "credit", see s. 9, *ante*

For "creditor", "debtor", "give", "hirer", "notice", "owner", "regulated agreement" and "regulations", see s. 189 (1), *post*.

REGULATIONS UNDER THIS SECTION

No regulations had been made for the purposes of sub-s. (4) above up to the time of going to press.

For general provisions as to regulations under this Act, see s. 182 (1)–(3), *post.*

## 99. Right to terminate hire-purchase etc. agreements

(1) At any time before the final payment by the debtor under a regulated hire-purchase or regulated conditional sale agreement falls due, the debtor shall be entitled to terminate the agreement by giving notice to any person entitled or authorised to receive the sums payable under the agreement.

(2) Termination of an agreement under subsection (1) does not affect any liability under the agreement which has accrued before the termination.

(3) Subsection (1) does not apply to a conditional sale agreement relating to land after the title to the land has passed to the debtor.

(4) In the case of a conditional sale agreement relating to goods, where the property in the goods, having become vested in the debtor, is transferred to a person who does not become the debtor under the agreement, the debtor shall not thereafter be entitled to terminate the agreement under subsection (1).

(5) Subject to subsection (4), where a debtor under a conditional sale agreement relating to goods, terminates the agreement under this section after the property in the goods has become vested in him, the property in the goods shall thereupon vest in the person (the "previous owner") in whom it was vested immediately before it became vested in the debtor:

Provided that if the previous owner has died, or any other event has occurred whereby that property, if vested in him immediately before that event, would thereupon have vested in some other person, the property shall be treated as having devolved as if it had been vested in the previous owner immediately before his death or immediately before that event, as the case may be. **[C.99]**

COMMENCEMENT

See Sch. 3, para. 29, *post,* and the note "Appointed days" to Part VII of that Schedule.

GENERAL NOTE

This section gives a right of termination to the hirer or buyer under a regulated hire-purchase or conditional sale agreement. It is substantially a re-enactment of provisions of the Hire-Purchase Act 1965; sub-ss. (1), (3) and (4) correspond to s. 27 (1)–(3) of that Act (30 Halsbury's Statutes (3rd edn.) 85) and sub-s. (3) contains a provision formerly in s. 28 (1) of that Act (30 Halsbury's Statutes (3rd edn.) 86). The Act of 1965 is repealed by s. 192 (3) and Sch. 5, *post.*

PROHIBITION OF CONTRACTING OUT

See the note to s. 56, *ante.*

PERSON

See the note to s. 8, *ante.*

LIABILITY

As to the liabilities of the debtor or hirer, other than those saved by sub-s. (2) above, see s. 100, *post.*

DEFINITIONS

For "conditional sale agreement", "debtor", "give", "goods", "hire-purchase agreement", "land" and "regulated agreement", see s. 189 (1), *post.*

**100. Liability of debtor on termination of hire-purchase etc. agreement**

(1) Where a regulated hire-purchase or regulated conditional sale agreement is terminated under section 99 the debtor shall be liable, unless the agreement provides for a smaller payment, or does not provide for any payment, to pay to the creditor the amount (if any) by which one-half of the total price exceeds the aggregate of the sums paid and the sums due in respect of the total price immediately before the termination.

(2) Where under a hire-purchase or conditional sale agreement the creditor is required to carry out any installation and the agreement specifies, as part of the total price, the amount to be paid in respect of the installation (the "installation charge") the reference in subsection (1) to one-half of the total price shall be construed as a reference to the aggregate of the installation charge and one-half of the remainder of the total price.

(3) If in any action the court is satisfied that a sum less than the amount specified in subsection (1) would be equal to the loss sustained by the creditor in consequence of the termination of the agreement by the debtor, the court may make an order for the payment of that sum in lieu of the amount specified in subsection (1).

(4) If the debtor has contravened an obligation to take reasonable care of the goods or land, the amount arrived at under subsection (1) shall be increased by the sum required to recompense the creditor for that contravention, and subsection (2) shall have effect accordingly.

(5) Where the debtor, on the termination of the agreement, wrongfully retains possession of goods to which the agreement relates, then, in any action brought by the creditor to recover possession of the goods from the debtor, the court, unless it is satisfied that having regard to the circumstances it would not be just to do so, shall order the goods to be delivered to the creditor without giving the debtor an option to pay the value of the goods. **[C.100]**

COMMENCEMENT

See Sch. 3, para. 30, *post*, and the note "Appointed days" to Part VII of that Schedule.

GENERAL NOTE

This section deals with the consequences of terminating an agreement under s. 99, *ante*. Like that section, it is substantially a re-enactment of provisions of the Hire-Purchase Act 1965; sub-ss. (1) and (3)–(5) correspond to s. 28 (1)–(4) of the Act of 1965 (30 Halsbury's Statutes (3rd edn.) 86) and sub-s. (2) to s. 55 (1) (*a*) of that Act (30 Halsbury's Statutes (3rd edn.) 106). The Act of 1965 is repealed by s. 192 (3) and Sch. 5, *post*.

PROHIBITION OF CONTRACTING OUT

See the note to s. 56, *ante*.

LOSS SUSTAINED BY THE CREDITOR

As to the computation of that loss, cf. the Sale of Goods Act 1893, s. 50 (30 Halsbury's Statutes (3rd edn.) 36).

OBLIGATION TO TAKE REASONABLE CARE

This must mean a contractual obligation, as no such obligation is imposed by this Act. See, further, the note "Reasonable care" to s. 72, *ante*.

DEFINITIONS

For "conditional sale agreement", "court", "creditor", "debtor", "goods", "hire-purchase agreement", "installation", "land", "regulated agreement" and "total price", see s. 189 (1), *post*.

## 101. Right to terminate hire agreement

(1) The hirer under a regulated consumer hire agreement is entitled to terminate the agreement by giving notice to any person entitled or authorised to receive the sums payable under the agreement.

(2) Termination of an agreement under subsection (1) does not affect any liability under the agreement which has accrued before the termination.

(3) A notice under subsection (1) shall not expire earlier than eighteen months after the making of the agreement, but apart from that the minimum period of notice to be given under subsection (1), unless the agreement provides for a shorter period, is as follows.

(4) If the agreement provides for the making of payments by the hirer to the owner at equal intervals, the minimum period of notice is the length of one interval or three months, whichever is less.

(5) If the agreement provides for the making of such payments at differing intervals, the minimum period of notice is the length of the shortest interval or three months, whichever is less.

(6) In any other case, the minimum period of notice is three months.

(7) This section does not apply to—

(*a*) any agreement which provides for the making by the hirer of payments which in total (and without breach of the agreement) exceed £300 in any year, or

(*b*) any agreement where—

(i) goods are bailed or (in Scotland) hired to the hirer for the purposes of a business carried on by him, or the hirer holds himself out as requiring the goods for those purposes, and

(ii) the goods are selected by the hirer, and acquired by the owner for the purposes of the agreement at the request of the hirer from any person other than the owner's associate, or

(*c*) any agreement where the hirer requires, or holds himself out as requiring, the goods for the purpose of bailing or hiring them to other persons in the course of a business carried on by him.

(8) If, on an application made to the Director by a person carrying on a consumer hire business, it appears to the Director that it would be in the interest of hirers to do so, he may by notice to the applicant direct that this section shall not apply to consumer hire agreements made by the applicant, and subject to such conditions (if any) as the Director may specify, this Act shall have effect accordingly.

(9) In the case of a modifying agreement, subsection (3) shall apply with the substitution, for "the making of the agreement" of "the making of the original agreement". **[C.101]**

COMMENCEMENT
See Sch. 3, para 31, *post*, and the note "Appointed days" to Part VII of that Schedule.

PERSON
See the note to s. 8, *ante*.

PROHIBITION OF CONTRACTING OUT
See the note to s. 56, *ante*.

£300
This amount is subject to amendment by order under s. 181 (1), *post*.

CARRIED ON
See the note "Carry on business" to s. 24, *ante*.

APPLICATION
For general provisions as to applications to the Director, see s. 6, *ante*. As to the offence of furnishing false information, etc., see s. 7, *ante*.

IF . . . IT APPEARS TO THE DIRECTOR
As to the duty of the Director to observe the principles of natural justice, cf. the note "If he satisfies" to s. 25, *ante*.

DEFINITIONS
For "associate", see s. 184, *post*. For "business", "Director", "give", "goods", "hirer", "notice" and "owner", see s. 189 (1), *post*.
For "consumer hire agreement", see s. 15, *ante*.
For "modifying agreement", see s. 82 (2), *ante*.

## 102. Agency for receiving notice of rescission

(1) Where the debtor or hirer under a regulated agreement claims to have a right to rescind the agreement, each of the following shall be deemed to be the agent of the creditor or owner for the purpose of receiving any notice rescinding the agreement which is served by the debtor or hirer—

(*a*) a credit-broker or supplier who was the negotiator in antecedent negotiations, and
(*b*) any person who, in the course of a business carried on by him, acted on behalf of the debtor or hirer in any negotiations for the agreement.

(2) In subsection (1) "rescind" does not include—

(*a*) service of a notice of cancellation, or
(*b*) termination of an agreement under section 99 or 101, or by the exercise of a right or power in that behalf expressly conferred by the agreement. **[C.102]**

COMMENCEMENT
See Sch. 3, para. 32, *post*, and the note "Appointed days" to Part VII of that Schedule.

PROHIBITION OF CONTRACTING OUT
See the note to s. 56, *ante*.

RESCIND
Note the provisions of sub-s. (2), in the light of which this term can only refer to rescission on such grounds as misrepresentation, undue influence, duress, etc.

DEEMED TO BE THE AGENT
For the duty of the agent towards the creditor or owner, see s. 175, *post*.

CARRIED ON
See the note "Carry on business" to s. 24, *ante*.

CANCELLATION
For the right of cancellation, see ss. 67–69, *ante*.

DEFINITIONS
For "antecedent negotiations" and "negotiator", see s. 56 (1), *ante*.
For "business", "credit-broker", "creditor", "debtor", "hirer", "notice", "regulated agreement" and "serve", see s. 189 (1), *post*.
For "notice of cancellation", see s. 69 (1), *ante*.

**103. Termination statements**

(1) If an individual (the "customer") serves on any person (the "trader") a notice—

(*a*) stating that—

(i) the customer was the debtor or hirer under a regulated agreement described in the notice, and the trader was the creditor or owner under the agreement, and

(ii) the customer has discharged his indebtedness to the trader under the agreement, and

(iii) the agreement has ceased to have any operation; and

(*b*) requiring the trader to give the customer a notice, signed by or on behalf of the trader, confirming that those statements are correct,

the trader shall, within the prescribed period after receiving the notice, either comply with it or serve on the customer a counter-notice stating that, as the case may be, he disputes the correctness of the notice or asserts that the customer is not indebted to him under the agreement.

(2) Where the trader disputes the correctness of the notice he shall give particulars of the way in which he alleges it to be wrong.

(3) Subsection (1) does not apply in relation to any agreement if the trader has previously complied with that subsection on the service of a notice under it with respect to that agreement.

(4) Subsection (1) does not apply to a non-commercial agreement.

(5) If the trader fails to comply with subsection (1), and the default continues for one month, he commits an offence. [**C.103**]

COMMENCEMENT
See Sch. 3, para. 33, *post*, and the note "Appointed days" to Part VII of that Schedule

SERVES
For provisions as to service of notices, see s. 176, *post*. See also the definition in s. 189 (1), *post*.

PERSON
See the note to s. 8, *ante*.

NOTICE
See the definition in s. 189 (1), *post*. A notice served under sub-s. (1) (*b*) above is binding on the trader by virtue of s. 172 (2), *post*, subject to s. 172 (3), *post*.

PRESCRIBED PERIOD
I.e., prescribed by regulations; see s. 189 (1), *post*. Nothing had been prescribed for the purposes of sub-s. (1) above up to the time of going to press.

OFFENCE
As to the notification of convictions to the Director, see s. 166, *post*. For penalties and mode of prosecution, see s. 167 (1) and Sch. 1, *post*. For special defences, see s. 168, *post*. As to offences by bodies corporate, see s. 169, *post*.

DEFINITIONS
For "debtor", "hirer", "individual", "non-commercial agreement" and "regulated agreement", see s. 189 (1), *post*.
As to "customer" and "trader", note the provisions of sub-s. (1) above.

**104. Goods not to be treated as subject to landlord's hypothec in Scotland**

Goods comprised in a hire-purchase agreement or goods comprised in a conditional sale agreement which have not become vested in the debtor shall not be treated in Scotland as subject to the landlord's hypothec—

(*a*) during the period between the service of a default notice in respect of the goods and the date on which the notice expires or is earlier complied with; or

(*b*) if the agreement is enforceable on an order of the court only, during the period between the commencement and termination of an action by the creditor to enforce the agreement. **[C.104]**

COMMENCEMENT
See Sch. 3, para. 34, *post*, and the note "Appointed days" to Part VII of the Schedule.

SERVICE
For provisions as to service of notices, see s. 176, *post*. See also the definition in s. 189 (1), *post*.

DEFAULT NOTICE
For provisions as to default notices, see ss. 87–89, *ante*.

DEFINITIONS
For "goods", "hire-purchase agreement", "conditional sale agreement", "debtor", "court" and "creditor", see s. 189 (1), *post*.

## PART VIII

## SECURITY

### *General*

**105. Form and content of securities**

(1) Any security provided in relation to a regulated agreement shall be expressed in writing.

(2) Regulations may prescribe the form and content of documents ("security instruments") to be made in compliance with subsection (1).

(3) Regulations under subsection (2) may in particular—

(*a*) require specified information to be included in the prescribed manner in documents, and other specified material to be excluded;

(*b*) contain requirements to ensure that specified information is clearly brought to the attention of the surety, and that one part of a document is not given insufficient or excessive prominence compared with another.

(4) A security instrument is not properly executed unless—

(*a*) a document in the prescribed form, itself containing all the prescribed terms and conforming to regulations under subsection (2), is signed in the prescribed manner by or on behalf of the surety, and (*b*) the document embodies all the terms of the security, other than implied terms, and

(*c*) the document, when presented or sent for the purpose of being signed by or on behalf of the surety, is in such a state that its terms are readily legible, and

(*d*) when the document is presented or sent for the purpose of being signed by or on behalf of the surety there is also presented or sent a copy of the document.

(5) A security instrument is not properly executed unless—

(*a*) where the security is provided after, or at the time when, the regulated agreement is made, a copy of the executed agreement, together with a copy of any other document referred to in it, is given to the surety at the time the security is provided, or

(*b*) where the security is provided before the regulated agreement is made, a copy of the executed agreement, together with a copy of any other document referred to in it, is given to the surety within seven days after the regulated agreement is made.

(6) Subsection (1) does not apply to a security provided by the debtor or hirer.

(7) If—

(*a*) in contravention of subsection (1) a security is not expressed in writing, or

(*b*) a security instrument is improperly executed,

the security (so far as provided in relation to a regulated agreement) is enforceable against the surety on an order of the court only.

(8) If an application for an order under subsection (7) is dismissed (except on technical grounds only) section 106 (ineffective securities) shall apply to the security.

(9) Regulations under section 60 (1) shall include provision requiring documents embodying regulated agreements also to embody any security provided in relation to a regulated agreement by the debtor or hirer. **[C.105]**

COMMENCEMENT

See Sch. 3, para. 36, *post*, and the note "Appointed days" to Part VIII of that Schedule.

PROHIBITION OF CONTRACTING OUT

See the note to s. 56, *ante*.

SUB-S. (1): SHALL BE EXPRESSED

The only consequence of non-compliance is that provided for by sub-s. (7) above; see s. 170 (1), *post*, as to the exclusion of any implication of further sanctions for breach of this provision.

WRITING

See the note to s. 6, *ante*.

SUB-S. (4): NOT PROPERLY EXECUTED

The consequences of improper execution are set out in sub-s. (7) above; see s. 170 (1) *post*, as to the exclusion of any implication of further sanctions for improper execution.

COPY

For power to prescribe the form, etc., of copies, see s. 180, *post*.

WITHIN SEVEN DAYS
See the note "Within 21 days" to s. 36, *ante*.

SIGNED
See the note to s. 51, *ante*.

SUB-S. (6): ON AN ORDER OF THE COURT ONLY
For the principles on which the court is to proceed, see ss. 127 (1), (2), *post*. For further powers of the court, see ss. 129, 130, 135, 136 and 142, *post*. A court order is not necessary if the surety consents to enforcement at the time when enforcement is sought (s. 173 (3), *post*), but any advance consent would be hit by s. 173 (1), *post*.

SUB-S. (7): ON TECHNICAL GROUNDS ONLY
An application is to be taken as so dismissed if the court so certifies; see s. 189 (5), *post*.

SAVING FOR REGISTERED CHARGES
Certain registered charges of which the proprietor has no notice of any defect in his title are exempted from the provisions of this Act by s. 177, *post*.

DEFINITIONS
For "court", "debtor", "executed agreement", "give", "hirer", "prescribed", "regulated agreement", "regulations", "security" and "surety", see s. 189 (1), *post*.
For "embodied", see s. 189 (1), (4), *post*.

REGULATIONS UNDER THIS SECTION
No regulations had been made under this section up to the time of going to press.
For general provisions as to regulations under this Act, see s. 182 (1)–(3), *post*.

**106. Ineffective securities**

Where, under any provision of this Act, this section is applied to any security provided in relation to a regulated agreement, then, subject to section 177 (saving for registered charges),—

(*a*) the security, so far as it is so provided, shall be treated as never having effect;

(*b*) any property lodged with the creditor or owner solely for the purposes of the security as so provided shall be returned by him forthwith;

(*c*) the creditor or owner shall take any necessary action to remove or cancel an entry in any register, so far as the entry relates to the security as so provided; and

(*d*) any amount received by the creditor or owner on realisation of the security shall, so far as it is referable to the agreement, be repaid to the surety. [**C.106**]

WHERE . . . THIS SECTION IS APPLIED
This section is applied by s. 105 (8), *ante*, and s. 113 (3)–(6), *post*.

DEFINITIONS
For "creditor", "owner", "regulated agreement", "security" and "surety", see s. 189 (1), *post*.

**107. Duty to give information to surety under fixed-sum credit agreement**

(1) The creditor under a regulated agreement for fixed-sum credit in relation to which security is provided, within the prescribed period after receiving a request in writing to that effect from the surety and payment of a fee of 15 new pence, shall give to the surety (if a different person from the debtor)—

(*a*) a copy of the executed agreement (if any) and of any other document referred to in it;

(*b*) a copy of the security instrument (if any); and

(*c*) a statement signed by or on behalf of the creditor showing, according to the information to which it is practicable for him to refer,—

(i) the total sum paid under the agreement by the debtor,

(ii) the total sum which has become payable under the agreement by the debtor but remains unpaid, and the various amounts comprised in that total sum, with the date when each became due, and

(iii) the total sum which is to become payable under the agreement by the debtor, and the various amounts comprised in that total sum, with the date, or mode of determining the date, when each becomes due.

(2) If the creditor possesses insufficient information to enable him to ascertain the amounts and dates mentioned in subsection (1) (*c*) (iii), he shall be taken to comply with that sub-paragraph if his statement under subsection (1) (*c*) gives the basis on which, under the regulated agreement, they would fall to be ascertained.

(3) Subsection (1) does not apply to—

(*a*) an agreement under which no sum is, or will or may become, payable by the debtor, or

(*b*) a request made less than one month after a previous request under that subsection relating to the same agreement was complied with.

(4) If the creditor under an agreement fails to comply with subsection (1)—

(*a*) he is not entitled, while the default continues, to enforce the security so far as provided in relation to the agreement; and

(*b*) if the default continues for one month he commits an offence.

(5) This section does not apply to a non-commercial agreement. **[C.107]**

COMMENCEMENT

See Sch. 3, para. 37, *post*, and the note "Appointed days" to Part VIII of that Schedule.

15 NEW PENCE

This amount and the similar amounts referred to in ss. 108 (1), 109 (1) and 110 (1), *post*, are subject to amendment by order under s. 181 (1), *post*.

PRESCRIBED PERIOD

I.e., prescribed by regulations; see s. 189 (1), *post*. Nothing had been prescribed for the purposes of sub-s. (1) above or of ss. 108 (1), 109 (1) or 110 (1), *post*, up to the time of going to press.

WRITING

See the note to s. 6, *ante*.

COPY

For power to prescribe the form, etc., of copies, see s. 180, *post*.

STATEMENT

As to the binding effect of statements given under sub-s. (1) above or ss. 108 (1), 109 (1), *post*, see s. 172 (1), (3), *post*.

SIGNED
See the note to s. 51, *ante*.

OFFENCE
As to notification of convictions to the Director, see s. 166, *post*. For penalties and mode of prosecution, see s. 167 (1) and Sch. 1, *post*. For special defences, see s. 168, *post*. As to offences by bodies corporate, see s. 169, *post*.

DEFINITIONS
For "creditor", "debtor", "executed agreement", "give", "non-commercial agreement", "regulated agreement", "security" and "surety", see s. 189 (1), *post*.
For "fixed-sum credit", see s. 10 (1), *ante*.
For "security instrument", see s. 105 (2), *ante*.

**108. Duty to give information to surety under running-account credit agreement**

(1) The creditor under a regulated agreement for running-account credit in relation to which security is provided, within the prescribed period after receiving a request in writing to that effect from the surety and payment of a fee of 15 new pence, shall give to the surety (if a different person from the debtor)—

(*a*) a copy of the executed agreement (if any) and of any other document referred to in it;

(*b*) a copy of the security instrument (if any); and

(*c*) a statement signed by or on behalf of the creditor showing, according to the information to which it is practicable for him to refer,—

(i) the state of the account, and

(ii) the amount, if any, currently payable under the agreement by the debtor to the creditor, and

(iii) the amounts and due dates of any payments which, if the debtor does not draw further on the account will later become payable under the agreement by the debtor to the creditor.

(2) If the creditor possesses insufficient information to enable him to ascertain the amounts and dates mentioned in subsection (1) (*c*) (iii), he shall be taken to comply with that sub-paragraph if his statement under subsection (1) (*c*) gives the basis on which, under the regulated agreement, they would fall to be ascertained.

(3) Subsection (1) does not apply to—

(*a*) an agreement under which no sum is, or will or may become, payable by the debtor, or

(*b*) a request made less than one month after a previous request under that subsection relating to the same agreement was complied with.

(4) If the creditor under an agreement fails to comply with subsection (1)—

(*a*) he is not entitled, while the default continues, to enforce the security (so far as provided in relation to the agreement); and

(*b*) if the default continues for one month he commits an offence.

(5) This section does not apply to a non-commercial agreement. **[C.108]**

COMMENCEMENT
See Sch. 3, para. 37, *post*, and the note "Appointed days" to Part VIII of that Schedule.

15 NEW PENCE; PRESCRIBED PERIOD; COPY; STATEMENT; OFFENCE
See the notes to s. 107, *ante*.

WRITING
See the note to s. 6, *ante.*

SIGNED
See the note to s. 51, *ante.*

DEFINITIONS
For "creditor", "debtor", "executed agreement", "give", "non-commercial agreement", "regulated agreement", "security" and "surety", see s. 189 (1), *post.*
For "running-account credit", see s. 10, *ante.* For "security instrument", see s. 105 (2), *ante.*

## 109. Duty to give information to surety under consumer hire agreement

(1) The owner under a regulated consumer hire-agreement in relation to which security is provided, within the prescribed period after receiving a request in writing to that effect from the surety and payment of a fee of 15 new pence, shall give to the surety (if a different person from the hirer) —

(*a*) a copy of the executed agreement and of any other document referred to in it;
(*b*) a copy of the security instrument (if any); and
(*c*) a statement signed by or on behalf of the owner showing, according to the information to which it is practicable for him to refer, the total sum which has become payable under the agreement by the hirer but remains unpaid and the various amounts comprised in that total sum, with the date when each became due.

(2) Subsection (1) does not apply to—

(*a*) an agreement under which no sum is, or will or may become, payable by the hirer, or
(*b*) a request made less than one month after a previous request under that subsection relating to the same agreement was complied with.

(3) If the owner under an agreement fails to comply with subsection (1)—

(*a*) he is not entitled, while the default continues, to enforce the security (so far as provided in relation to the agreement); and
(*b*) if the default continues for one month he commits an offence.

(4) This section does not apply to a non-commercial agreement. [C.109]

COMMENCEMENT
See Sch. 3, para. 37, *post,* and the note "Appointed days" to Part VIII of that Schedule.

15 NEW PENCE; PRESCRIBED PERIOD; COPY; STATEMENT; OFFENCE
See the notes to s. 107, *ante.*

WRITING
See the note to s. 6, *ante.*

SIGNED
See the note to s. 51, *ante.*

DEFINITIONS
For "consumer hire agreement", see s. 15, *ante.*
For "executed agreement", "give", "hirer", "non-commercial agreement", "regulated agreement", "security" and "surety", see s. 189 (1), *post.*
For "security instrument", see s. 105 (2), *ante.*

### 110. Duty to give information to debtor or hirer

(1) The creditor or owner under a regulated agreement, within the prescribed period after receiving a request in writing to that effect from the debtor or hirer and payment of a fee of 15 new pence, shall give the debtor or hirer a copy of any security instrument executed in relation to the agreement after the making of the agreement.

(2) Subsection (1) does not apply to—

(*a*) a non-commercial agreement, or

(*b*) an agreement under which no sum is, or will or may become, payable by the debtor or hirer, or

(*c*) a request made less than one month after a previous request under subsection (1) relating to the same agreement was complied with.

(3) If the creditor or owner under an agreement fails to comply with subsection (1)—

(*a*) he is not entitled, while the default continues, to enforce the security (so far as provided in relation to the agreement); and

(*b*) if the default continues for one month he commits an offence. [**C.110**]

COMMENCEMENT

See Sch. 3, para. 37, *post*, and the note "Appointed days" to Part VIII of that Schedule.

15 NEW PENCE; PRESCRIBED PERIOD; COPY; OFFENCE

See the notes to s. 107, *ante*.

WRITING

See the note to s. 6, *ante*.

SIGNED

See the note to s. 51, *ante*.

DEFINITIONS

For "creditor", "debtor", "give", "hirer", "non-commercial agreement", "regulated agreement" and "security", see s. 189 (1), *post*.

For "security instrument", see s. 105 (2), *ante*.

### 111. Duty to give surety copy of default etc. notice

(1) When a default notice or a notice under section 76 (1) or 98 (1) is served on a debtor or hirer, a copy of the notice shall be served by the creditor or owner on any surety (if a different person from the debtor or hirer).

(2) If the creditor or owner fails to comply with subsection (1) in the case of any surety, the security is enforceable against the surety (in respect of the breach or other matter to which the notice relates) on an order of the court only. [**C.111**]

COMMENCEMENT

See Sch. 3, para. 38, *post*, and the note "Appointed days" to Part VIII of that Schedule.

COPY

For power to prescribe the form, etc., of copies, see s. 180, *post*.

SERVE

For provisions as to the service of documents, see s. 176, *post*. See also the definition in s. 189 (1), *post*.

ON AN ORDER OF THE COURT ONLY

See the note to s. 105 (6), *ante*.

DEFINITIONS

For "court", "creditor", "debtor", "hirer", "notice", "security" and "surety", see s. 189 (1), *post*.

For "default notice", see s. 86 (1), *ante*.

## 112. Realisation of securities

Subject to section 121, regulations may provide for any matters relating to the sale or other realisation, by the creditor or owner, of property over which any right has been provided by way of security in relation to an actual or prospective regulated agreement, other than a non-commercial agreement. **[C.112]**

DEFINITIONS

For "creditor", "non-commercial agreement", "owner", "regulated agreement", "regulations" and "security", see s. 189 (1), *post*.

REGULATIONS UNDER THIS SECTION

No regulations had been made under this section up to the time of going to press.

For general provisions as to regulations under this Act, see s. 182 (1)–(3), *post*.

## 113. Act not to be evaded by use of security

(1) Where a security is provided in relation to an actual or prospective regulated agreement, the security shall not be enforced so as to benefit the creditor or owner, directly or indirectly, to an extent greater (whether as respects the amount of any payment or the time or manner of its being made) than would be the case if the security were not provided and any obligations of the debtor or hirer, or his relative, under or in relation to the agreement were carried out to the extent (if any) to which they would be enforced under this Act.

(2) In accordance with subsection (1), where a regulated agreement is enforceable on an order of the court or the Director only, any security provided in relation to the agreement is enforceable (so far as provided in relation to the agreement) where such an order has been made in relation to the agreement, but not otherwise.

(3) Where—

(*a*) a regulated agreement is cancelled under section 69 (1) or becomes subject to section 69 (2), or

(*b*) a regulated agreement is terminated under section 91, or

(*c*) in relation to any agreement an application for an order under section 40 (2), 65 (1), 124 (1) or 149 (2) is dismissed (except on technical grounds only), or

(*d*) a declaration is made by the court under section 142 (1) (refusal of enforcement order) as respects any regulated agreement,

section 106 shall apply to any security provided in relation to the agreement.

(4) Where subsection (3) (*d*) applies and the declaration relates to a part only of the regulated agreement, section 106 shall apply to the security only so far as it concerns that part.

(5) In the case of a cancelled agreement, the duty imposed on the debtor or hirer by section 71 or 72 shall not be enforceable before the creditor or owner has

discharged any duty imposed on him by section 106 (as applied by subsection (3) (*a*)).

(6) If the security is provided in relation to a prospective agreement or transaction the security shall be enforceable in relation to the agreement or transaction only after the time (if any) when the agreement is made; and until that time the person providing the security shall be entitled, by notice to the creditor or owner, to require that section 106 shall thereupon apply to the security.

(7) Where an indemnity is given in a case where the debtor or hirer is a minor, or is otherwise not of full capacity, the reference in subsection (1) to the extent to which his obligations would be enforced shall be read in relation to the indemnity as a reference to the extent to which they would be enforced if he were of full capacity.

(8) Subsections (1) to (3) also apply where a security is provided in relation to an actual or prospective linked transaction, and in that case—

(*a*) references to the agreement shall be read as references to the linked transaction, and

(*b*) references to the creditor or owner shall be read as references to any person (other than the debtor or hirer, or his relative) who is a party, or prospective party, to the linked transaction. **[C.113]**

COMMENCEMENT

No provision is made as to the commencement of this section, but note the provisions of Sch. 3, para. 1, *post*, as to regulated agreements.

PROHIBITION OF CONTRACTING OUT

See the note to s. 56, *ante*.

SUB-S. (1): SHALL NOT BE ENFORCED

In relation to several categories of case, the consequences of this general principle in sub-s. (1) are spelled out in detail in sub-ss. (2)–(7) above. The question then arises whether there are any cases covered by sub-s. (1) but not by the subsections which follow. It is thought that there are. Several sections of this Act provide that an agreement shall not be enforced while the creditor is in default in the provision of information required by the Act (see, e.g., ss. 77 (4) (*a*), 78 (6) (*a*), 79 (3) (*a*), *ante*). Subsection (1) above would appear to affect the enforcement of securities in cases falling under those provisions. It will be noted that with respect to such cases there is no provision applying s. 106, *ante*, and therefore no express provision to the effect that the creditor should return property lodged with him for the purposes of the security. Such provision has been held to be implied in the enactments as to unenforceable securities in the Moneylenders Act 1927 (22 Halsbury's Statutes (3rd edn.) 700) (repealed by s. 192 (3) and Sch. 5, *post*); see *Kasumu* v. *Baba-Egbe*, [1956] A.C. 539; [1956] 3 All E.R. 266, P.C., followed in *Barclay* v. *Prospect Mortgages, Ltd.*, [1974] 2 All E.R. 672. Cases falling under ss. 77–79, *ante*, and sub-s. (1) above may, however, be distinguishable on the ground that the unenforceability of the principal obligation is temporary and remediable.

SUB-S. (2): ENFORCEABLE UPON AN ORDER OF THE COURT OR THE DIRECTOR ONLY

For provisions to this effect, see ss. 40 (agreements of unlicensed trader), 65 (improperly executed agreements) and 86 (2) (enforcement after death of debtor), *ante*, and ss. 124 (1) (negotiable instruments unlawfully taken) and 149 (2) (agreements of unlicensed credit-broker), *post*.

SUB-S. (3): ON TECHNICAL GROUNDS ONLY

For the power of the court or the Director to certify that an application is so dismissed, see s. 189 (5), *post*.

SUB-S. (7): MINOR
I.e., a person under the age of eighteen; see the Family Law Reform Act 1969 s. 1 (1), (2) (17 Halsbury's Statutes (3rd edn.) 792).

SAVING FOR REGISTERED CHARGES
For a saving of the rights of a proprietor of certain registered charges, if he has no notice of any defect in his title, see s. 177, *post*.

DEFINITIONS
For "court", "creditor", "debtor", "Director", "hirer", "owner", "regulated agreement", "relative" and "security", see s. 189 (1), *post*.
For "linked transaction", see s. 19 (1), *ante*.

*Pledges*

### 114. Pawn-receipts

(1) At the time he receives the article, a person who takes any article in pawn under a regulated agreement shall give to the person from whom he receives it a receipt in the prescribed form (a "pawn-receipt").

(2) A person who takes any article in pawn from an individual whom he knows to be, or who appears to be and is, a minor commits an offence.

(3) This section and sections 115 to 122 do not apply to—

(*a*) a pledge of documents of title, or
(*b*) a non-commercial agreement. [C.114]

COMMENCEMENT
As to the commencement of sub-s. (1), see Sch. 3, para. 39, *post*, and the note "Appointed days" to Part VIII of that Schedule.

GENERAL NOTE
This section and ss. 115–122, *post*, contain provisions regulating the taking and redemption of pawns. They replace provisions of the Pawnbrokers Act 1872, as amended (24 Halsbury's Statutes (3rd edn.) 703), which is repealed by s. 192 (3) and Sch. 5, *post*. The term "pawn-receipt" used in these provisions replaces the term "pawn-ticket" used in the Act of 1872. Some of these provisions are similar to those of the Act of 1872, but there are many changes.

PERSON
See the note to s. 8, *ante*.

SHALL GIVE
Contravention is an offence; see s. 115, *post*.

MINOR
I.e., a person under the age of eighteen; see the Family Law Reform Act 1969, s. 1 (1), (2) (17 Halsbury's Statutes (3rd edn.) 792).

PRESCRIBED FORM
I.e., prescribed by regulations; see s. 189 (1), *post*. Nothing had been prescribed for the purposes of sub-s. (1) above up to the time of going to press.

OFFENCE
As to the notification of convictions to the Director, see s. 166, *post*. For penalties and mode of prosecution, see s. 167 (1) and Sch. 1, *post*. For special defences, see s. 168, *post*. As to offences by bodies corporate, see s. 169, *post*.

DOCUMENT OF TITLE
The term is not defined in this Act, but see definitions in the Factors Act, 1889, s. 1 (1 Halsbury's Statutes (3rd edn.) 95, and the Forgery Act 1913, s. 18 (1) (8 Halsbury's Statutes (3rd edn.) 269). It may be taken to include title deeds of land and documents

such as bills of lading which are used in the ordinary course of business as proof of the possession or control of goods (see *Ramdas Vithaldas Durbar* v. *Amerchand & Co.* (1916), 85 L.J.P.C. 214, at p. 215). But the term does not include the logbook of a car; see *Bishopsgate Motor Finance Corporation, Ltd.* v. *Transport Brakes Ltd.*, [1949] 1 All E.R. 37, at p. 46.

DEFINITIONS
For "individual", "non-commercial agreement", "pawn" and "regulated agreement", see s. 189 (1), *post*.

### 115. Penalty for failure to supply copies of pledge agreement, etc.

If the creditor under a regulated agreement to take any article in pawn fails to observe the requirements of sections 62 to 64 or 114 (1) in relation to the agreement he commits an offence. [C.115]

COMMENCEMENT
See Sch. 3, para. 39, *post*, and the note "Appointed days" to Part VIII of that Schedule.

EXCLUSIONS
This section does not apply to pledges of documents of title or to non-commercial agreements; see s. 114 (3), *ante*.

OFFENCE
See the note to s. 115, *ante*.

DEFINITIONS
For "creditor", "pawn" and "regulated agreement", see s. 189 (1), *post*.

### 116. Redemption period

(1) A pawn is redeemable at any time within six months after it was taken.

(2) Subject to subsection (1), the period within which a pawn is redeemable shall be the same as the period fixed by the parties for the duration of the credit secured by the pledge, or such longer period as they may agree.

(3) If the pawn is not redeemed by the end of the period laid down by subsections (1) and (2) (the "redemption period"), it nevertheless remains redeemable until it is realised by the pawnee under section 121, except where under section 120 (1) (*a*) the property in it passes to the pawnee.

(4) No special charge shall be made for redemption of a pawn after the end of the redemption period, and charges in respect of the safe keeping of the pawn shall not be at a higher rate after the end of the redemption period than before. [C.116]

COMMENCEMENT
See Sch. 3, para. 39, *post*, and the note "Appointed days" to Part VIII of that Schedule.

PROHIBITION OF CONTRACTING OUT
See the note to s. 56, *ante*.

EXCLUSIONS
This section does not apply to pledges of documents of title or to non-commercial agreements; see s. 114 (3), *ante*.

REDEEMABLE
For redemption procedure, see ss. 117, 118, *post*. For the offence of refusal to redeem, see s. 119, *post*. As to realisation of pawns not redeemed, see ss. 120, 121, *post*.

WITHIN SIX MONTHS
I.e., calendar months (Interpretation Act 1889, s. 3 (32 Halsbury's Statutes (3rd edn.) 436)). See also the note "Within 21 days" to s. 36, *ante*.

DEFINITIONS
For "credit", see s. 9, *ante*.
For "pawn" and "pawnee", see s. 189 (1), *post*.

### 117. Redemption procedure

(1) On surrender of the pawn-receipt, and payment of the amount owing, at any time when the pawn is redeemable, the pawnee shall deliver the pawn to the bearer of the pawn-receipt.

(2) Subsection (1) does not apply if the pawnee knows or has reasonable cause to suspect that the bearer of the pawn-receipt is neither the owner of the pawn nor authorised by the owner to redeem it.

(3) The pawnee is not liable to any person in tort or delict for delivering the pawn where subsection (1) applies, or refusing to deliver it where the person demanding delivery does not comply with subsection (1) or, by reason of subsection (2), subsection (1) does not apply. [**C.117**]

COMMENCEMENT
See Sch. 3, para. 39, *post*, and the note "Appointed days" to Part VIII of that Schedule.

EXCLUSIONS
This section does not apply to pledges of documents of title, or to non-commercial agreements; see s. 114 (3), *ante*.

PAWN-RECEIPT
For meaning, see s. 114 (1), *ante*. For the modified application of this section to cases where the pawn-receipt cannot be produced, see s. 118 (2), *post*.

REDEEMABLE
For the time during which a pawn is redeemable, see s. 116 (1)–(3), *ante*.

SHALL DELIVER
For the offence of refusal without reasonable cause to allow redemption, see s. 119 (1), *post*. Failure to deliver may also amount to theft (see the Theft Act 1968) (8 Halsbury's Statutes (3rd edn.) 782)).

DELICT
This is a term of Scots law.

DEFINITIONS
For "pawn", "pawnee" and "payment", see s. 189 (1), *post*.

### 118. Loss etc. of pawn-receipt

(1) A person (the "claimant") who is not in possession of the pawn-receipt but claims to be the owner of the pawn, or to be otherwise entitled or authorised to redeem it, may do so at any time when it is redeemable by tendering to the pawnee in place of the pawn-receipt—

(*a*) a statutory declaration made by the claimant in the prescribed form, and with the prescribed contents, or

(*b*) where the pawn is security for fixed-sum credit not exceeding £15 or running-account credit on which the credit limit does not exceed £15, and the pawnee agrees, a statement in writing in the prescribed form, and with the prescribed contents, signed by the claimant.

(2) On compliance by the claimant with subsection (1), section 117 shall apply as if the decaration or statement were the pawn-receipt, and the pawn-receipt itself shall become inoperative for the purposes of section 117. [C.118]

COMMENCEMENT
See Sch. 3, para. 39, *post*, and the note "Appointed days" to Part VIII of that Schedule.

EXCLUSIONS
This section does not apply to pledges of documents of title or to non-commercial agreements; see s. 114 (3), *ante*.

PERSON
See the note to s. 8, *ante*.

REDEEMABLE
For the time during which a pawn is redeemable, see s. 116 (1)–(3), *ante*.

PRESCRIBED FORM AND CONTENTS
I.e., prescribed by regulations; see s. 189 (1), *post*. Nothing had been prescribed for the purposes of sub-s. (1) above up to the time of going to press.

£15
The amounts mentioned in sub-s. (1) (*b*) above and in s. 120 (1) (*a*), *post*, are subject to amendment by order under s. 181 (1), *post*.

WRITING
See the note to s. 6, *ante*.

SIGNED
See the note to s. 51, *ante*.

DEFINITIONS
For "credit limit", "fixed-sum credit" and "running-account credit", see s. 10, *ante*. For "pawn" and "pawnee", see s. 189 (1), *post*. For "pawn-receipt", see s. 114 (1), *ante*.

STATUTORY DECLARATION
General provisions as to such declarations are contained in the Statutory Declarations Act 1835 (12 Halsbury's Statutes (3rd edn.) 804) s. 12 of which (repealed by s. 192 (3) and Sch. 5, *post*) formerly applied to pawnbrokers. The making of a false statement in a statutory declaration is an offence under the Perjury Act 1911, s. 5 (8 Halsbury's Statutes (3rd edn.) 245).

## 119. Unreasonable refusal to deliver pawn

(1) If a person who has taken a pawn under a regulated agreement refuses without reasonable cause to allow the pawn to be redeemed, he commits an offence.

(2) On the conviction in England or Wales of a pawnee under subsection (1) where the offence does not amount to theft, section 28 (orders for restitution) of the Theft Act 1968, and any provision of the Theft Act 1968 relating to that section, shall apply as if the pawnee had been convicted of stealing the pawn.

(3) On the conviction in Northern Ireland of a pawnee under subsection (1) where the offence does not amount to theft, section 27 (orders for restitution) of the Theft Act (Northern Ireland) 1969, and any provision of the Theft Act (Northern Ireland) 1969 relating to that section, shall apply as if the pawnee had been convicted of stealing the pawn. [C.119]

COMMENCEMENT
See Sch. 3, para. 39, *post*, and the note "Appointed days" to Part VIII of that Schedule.

EXCLUSIONS
This section does not apply to pledges of documents of title or to non-commercial agreements; see s. 11 (3), *ante*.

PERSON
See the note to s. 7, *ante*.

REASONABLE CAUSE
As to onus of proof, see s. 171 (6), *post*.

REDEEMED
For the time during which a pawn is redeemable, see s. 116 (1)–(3), *ante*. For redemption procedure, see ss. 117, 118, *ante*.

OFFENCE
As to notification of convictions to the Director, see s. 166, *post*. For penalties and mode of prosecution, see s. 167 (1) and Sch. 1, *post*. For special defences, see s. 168, *post*. As to offences by bodies corporate, see s. 169, *post*.

AMOUNT TO THEFT
As to the possibility that the offence will amount to theft, note in particular the provisions of the Theft Act 1968, s. 3 (1) (8 Halsbury's Statutes (3rd edn.) 784).

DEFINITIONS
For "pawn", "pawnee" and "regulated agreement", see s. 189 (1), *post*.

THEFT ACT 1968, S. 28
See 8 Halsbury's Statutes (3rd edn.) 800.

THEFT ACT (NORTHERN IRELAND) 1969
1969 c. 16 (N.I.).

## 120. Consequence of failure to redeem

(1) If at the end of the redemption period the pawn has not been redeemed—

(*a*) notwithstanding anything in section 113, the property in the pawn passes to the pawnee where the redemption period is six months and the pawn is security for fixed-sum credit not exceeding £15 or running-account credit on which the credit limit does not exceed £15; or

(*b*) in any other case the pawn becomes realisable by the pawnee.

(2) Where the debtor or hirer is entitled to apply to the court for a time order under section 129, subsection (1) shall apply with the substitution, for "at the end of the redemption period" of "after the expiry of five days following the end of the redemption period". **[C.120]**

COMMENCEMENT
See Sch. 3, para. 39, *post*, and the note "Appointed days" to Part VIII of that Schedule,

PROHIBITION OF CONTRACTING OUT
See the note to s. 56, *ante*.

EXCLUSIONS
This section does not apply to pledges of documents of title or to non-commercial agreements; see s. 114 (3), *ante*.

£15
See the note to s. 118, *ante*.

REALISABLE
For realisation procedure, see s. 121, *post*.

DEFINITIONS
For "credit limit", "fixed-sum credit" and "running-account credit", see s. 10, *ante*.
For "debtor", "hirer", "pawn", "pawnee" and "security", see s. 189 (1), *post*.
For "redemption period", see s. 116 (3), *ante*.
For "time order", see s. 129 (1), *post*.

## 121. Realisation of pawn

(1) When a pawn has become realisable by him, the pawnee may sell it, after giving to the pawnor (except in such cases as may be prescribed) not less than the prescribed period of notice of the intention to sell, indicating in the notice the asking price and such other particulars as may be prescribed.

(2) Within the prescribed period after the sale takes place, the pawnee shall give the pawnor the prescribed information in writing as to the sale, its proceeds and expenses.

(3) Where the net proceeds of sale are not less than the sum which, if the pawn had been redeemed on the date of the sale, would have been payable for its redemption, the debt secured by the pawn is discharged and any surplus shall be paid by the pawnee to the pawnor.

(4) Where subsection (3) does not apply, the debt shall be treated as from the date of sale as equal to the amount by which the net proceeds of sale fall short of the sum which would have been payable for the redemption of the pawn on that date.

(5) In this section the "net proceeds of sale" is the amount realised (the "gross amount") less the expenses (if any) of the sale.

(6) If the pawnor alleges that the gross amount is less than the true market value of the pawn on the date of sale, it is for the pawnee to prove that he and any agents employed by him in the sale used reasonable care to ensure that the true market value was obtained, and if he fails to do so subsections (3) and (4) shall have effect as if the reference in subsection (5) to the gross amount were a reference to the true market value.

(7) If the pawnor alleges that the expenses of the sale were unreasonably high, it is for the pawnee to prove that they were reasonable, and if he fails to do so subsections (3) and (4) shall have effect as if the reference in subsection (5) to expenses were a reference to reasonable expenses. **[C.121]**

COMMENCEMENT
See Sch. 3, para. 39, *post*, and the note "Appointed days" to Part VIII of that Schedule.

PROHIBITION OF CONTRACTING OUT
See the note to s. 56, *ante*.

EXCLUSIONS
This section does not apply to pledges of documents of title or to non-commercial agreements; see s. 114 (3), *ante*.

REALISABLE
As to the time when pawns become realisable, see s. 120 (1), *ante*.

PRESCRIBED PERIOD; PRESCRIBED INFORMATION
I.e., prescribed by regulations; see s. 189 (1), *post*. Nothing had been prescribed for the purposes of sub-ss. (1) and (2) above up to the time of going to press.

DEFINITIONS
For "pawn", "pawnee" and "pawnor", see s. 189 (1), *post.*

## 122. Order in Scotland to deliver pawn

(1) As respects Scotland where—

(*a*) a pawn is either—

(i) an article which has been stolen, or

(ii) an article which has been obtained by fraud, and a person is convicted of any offence in relation to the theft or, as the case may be, the fraud; or

(*b*) a person is convicted of an offence under section 119 (1);

the court by which that person is so convicted may order delivery of the pawn to the owner or the person otherwise entitled thereto.

(2) A court making an order under subsection (1) (*a*) for delivery of a pawn may make the order subject to such conditions as to payment of the debt secured by the pawn as it thinks fit. [**C.122**]

COMMENCEMENT
See Sch. 3, para. 39, *post,* and the note "Appointed days" to Part VIII of that Schedule.

EXCLUSIONS
This section does not apply to pledges of documents of title or to non-commercial agreements; see s. 114 (3), *ante.*

PERSON
See the note to s. 8, *ante.*

DEFINITIONS
For "pawn", "court", "owner" and "payment", see s. 189 (1), *post.*

*Negotiable instruments*

## 123. Restrictions on taking and negotiating instruments

(1) A creditor or owner shall not take a negotiable instrument, other than a bank note or cheque, in discharge of any sum payable—

(*a*) by the debtor or hirer under a regulated agreement, or

(*b*) by any person as surety in relation to the agreement.

(2) The creditor or owner shall not negotiate a cheque taken by him in discharge of a sum payable as mentioned in subsection (1), except to a banker (within the meaning of the Bills of Exchange Act 1882).

(3) The creditor or owner shall not take a negotiable instrument as security for the discharge of any sum payable as mentioned in subsection (1).

(4) A person takes a negotiable instrument as security for the discharge of a sum if the sum is intended to be paid in some other way, and the negotiable instrument is to be presented for payment only if the sum is not paid in that way.

(5) This section does not apply where the regulated agreement is a non-commercial agreement.

(6) The Secretary of State may by order provide that this section shall not

apply where the regulated agreement has a connection with a country outside the United Kingdom. [C.123]

COMMENCEMENT

See Sch. 3, para. 40, *post*, and the note "Appointed days" to Part VIII of that Schedule.

SHALL NOT TAKE; SHALL NOT NEGOTIATE

For the consequences of contravention, see ss. 124, 125, *post*.

NEGOTIABLE INSTRUMENT

The meaning of this term was considered in *Crouch* v. *Credit Foncier of England, Ltd.* (1873), L.R. 8 Q.B. 374, at pp. 381, 382. It includes bills of exchange (which are defined in the Bills of Exchange Act 1882, s. 3 (3 Halsbury's Statutes (3rd edn.) 191)) and promissory notes (defined in *ibid.*, s. 83 (3 Halsbury's Statutes (3rd edn.) 232).

CHEQUE

The essential features of a cheque are that it is drawn on a banker and payable on demand; see the definition in the Bills of Exchange Act 1882, s. 73 (3 Halsbury's Statutes (3rd edn.) 229). Though a post-dated cheque is similar in its effect to a promissory note and in modern practice has largely taken the place of the promissory note, there is nothing irregular about post-dating (see s. 13 of the Act of 1882 (3 Halsbury's Statutes (3rd edn.) 197)) and it seems clear that a post-dated cheque still falls within the meaning of the word "cheque". Therefore, provided that there is no contravention of sub-s. (2) or (3) above, a post-dated cheque may lawfully be taken.

PERSON

See the note to s. 8, *ante*.

NEGOTIATE

For the meaning of this term, see the Bills of Exchange Act 1882, s. 31 (3 Halsbury's Statutes (3rd edn.) 205).

DEFINITIONS

For "creditor", "debtor", "hirer", "non-commercial agreement", "owner", "regulated agreement" and "surety", see s. 189 (1), *post*.

As to "take as security", note the provisions of sub-s. (4) above.

BILLS OF EXCHANGE ACT 1882

For the meaning of "banker" in that Act, see s. 2 thereof (3 Halsbury's Statutes (3rd edn.) 190).

ORDERS UNDER THIS SECTION

No orders had been made for the purposes of sub-s. (6) above up to the time of going to press. For general provisions as to orders under this Act, see s. 182 (1), (2), (4), *post*.

## 124. Consequences of breach of s. 123

(1) After any contravention of section 123 has occurred in relation to a sum payable as mentioned in section 123 (1) (*a*), the agreement under which the sum is payable is enforceable against the debtor or hirer on an order of the court only.

(2) After any contravention of section 123 has occurred in relation to a sum payable by any surety, the security is enforceable on an order of the court only.

(3) Where an application for an order under subsection (2) is dismissed (except on technical grounds only) section 106 shall apply to the security. [C.124]

COMMENCEMENT

See Sch. 3, para. 40, *post*, and the note "Appointed days" to Part VIII of that Schedule.

ON AN ORDER OF THE COURT ONLY

For the principles on which the court is to proceed, see s. 127 (1), (2), *post*. For further powers of the court, see ss. 129, 130, 135, 136 and 142, *post*. A court order is not necessary if the debtor or surety consents to enforcement at the time when enforcement is sought (see s. 173 (3), *post*) but any advance consent would be hit by s. 173 (1), *post*.

ON TECHNICAL GROUNDS ONLY

For the power of the court to certify that an application is so dismissed, see s. 189 (5), *post*.

DEFINITIONS

For "court", "debtor", "hirer", "security" and "surety", see s. 189 (1), *post*.

## 125. Holders in due course

(1) A person who takes a negotiable instrument in contravention of section 123 (1) or (3) is not a holder in due course and is not entitled to enforce the instrument.

(2) Where a person negotiates a cheque in contravention of section 123 (2), his doing so constitutes a defect in his title within the meaning of the Bills of Exchange Act 1882.

(3) If a person mentioned in section 123 (1) (*a*) or (*b*) ("the protected person") becomes liable to a holder in due course of an instrument taken from the protected person in contravention of section 123 (1) or (3), or taken from the protected person and negotiated in contravention of section 123 (2), the creditor or owner shall indemnify the protected person in respect of that liability.

(4) Nothing in this Act affects the rights of the holder in due course of any negotiable instrument. **[C.125]**

COMMENCEMENT

See Sch. 3, para. 40, *post*, and the note "Appointed days" to Part VIII of that Schedule.

PERSON

See the note to s. 8, *ante*.

NEGOTIABLE INSTRUMENT; NEGOTIATES; CHEQUE

See the notes to s. 123, *ante*.

HOLDER IN DUE COURSE

For meaning, see the Bills of Exchange Act 1882, s. 29 (1) (3 Halsbury's Statutes (3rd edn.) 204). For the rights of a holder in due course see, in particular, s. 38 (2) of that Act (3 Halsbury's Statutes (3rd edn.) 209).

DEFECT IN HIS TITLE

It is one of the requirements of the definition of a holder in due course (see the provisions cited above) that the person in question should have no notice of any defect in the title of the person from whom he took the instrument. Therefore the result of sub-s. (2) above is that if the person to whom the cheque is negotiated has notice of the contravention of s. 123 (2), he cannot be a holder in due course. It further follows that any defence which could have been raised against the original payee of the cheque can be raised against the holder.

BECOMES LIABLE TO A HOLDER IN DUE COURSE

There is nothing in ss. 123, 124, *ante*, or in this section which renders either the negotiable instruments referred to in these sections or any transfer thereof from one person to another null and void. Therefore a person who takes such instruments from the original payee for value and in good faith may be a holder in due course, notwithstanding the fact that s. 123 has been contravened. In that case, the original debtor, hirer or surety will be liable to pay the holder in due course and cannot raise against him any of the defences which he could have raised against the original creditor. Subsection (3) above gives him a claim for indemnity against the original creditor in that event.

DEFINITIONS
For "creditor" and "owner", see s. 189 (1), *post.*

BILLS OF EXCHANGE ACT 1882
See 3 Halsbury's Statutes (3rd edn.) 188.

*Land mortgages*

### 126. Enforcement of land mortgages

A land mortgage securing a regulated agreement is enforceable (so far as provided in relation to the agreement) on an order of the court only. **[C.126]**

COMMENCEMENT
See Sch. 3, para. 41, *post,* and the note "Appointed days" to Part VIII of that Schedule.

ON AN ORDER OF THE COURT ONLY
Section 127, *post,* makes no provision for the dismissal of an application for an order. Therefore it seems that the only purpose of this provision is to provide an opportunity for the exercise of the powers of the court, under ss. 129, 130, 131, 135, 136 and 142, *post.* A court order is not necessary if the debtor consents to enforcement at the time when enforcement is sought (see s. 173 (3), *post*) but any advance consent would be hit by s. 173 (1), *post.*

ON TECHNICAL GROUNDS ONLY
For the power of the court to certify that an application is so dismissed, see s. 189 (5), *post.*

DEFINITIONS
For "court", "land mortgage" and "regulated agreement", see s. 189 (1), *post.*

## PART IX

## JUDICIAL CONTROL

*Enforcement of certain regulated agreements and securities*

### 127. Enforcement orders in cases of infringement

(1) In the case of an application for an enforcement order under—

(*a*) section 65 (1) (improperly executed agreements), or

(*b*) section 105 (7) (*a*) or (*b*) (improperly executed security instruments), or

(*c*) section 111 (2) (failure to serve copy of notice on surety), or

(*d*) section 124 (1) or (2) (taking of negotiable instrument in contravention of section 123),

the court shall dismiss the application if, but (subject to subsections (3) and (4)) only if, it considers it just to do so having regard to—

(i) prejudice caused to any person by the contravention in question, and the degree of culpability for it; and

(ii) the powers conferred on the court by subsection (2) and sections 135 and 136.

(2) If it appears to the court just to do so, it may in an enforcement order reduce or discharge any sum payable by the debtor or hirer, or any surety, so as to compensate him for prejudice suffered as a result of the contravention in question.

(3) The court shall not make an enforcement order under section 65 (1) if section 61 (1) (*a*) (signing of agreements) was not complied with unless a document (whether or not in the prescribed form and complying with regulations under section 60 (1)) itself containing all the prescribed terms of the agreement was signed by the debtor or hirer (whether or not in the prescribed manner).

(4) The court shall not make an enforcement order under section 65 (1) in the case of a cancellable agreement if—

(*a*) a provision of section 62 or 63 was not complied with, and the creditor or owner did not give a copy of the executed agreement, and of any other document referred to in it, to the debtor or hirer before the commencement of the proceedings in which the order is sought, or

(*b*) section 64 (1) was not complied with.

(5) Where an enforcement order is made in a case to which subsection (3) applies, the order may direct that the regulated agreement is to have effect as if it did not include a term omitted from the document signed by the debtor or hirer. [**C.127**]

COMMENCEMENT

See Sch. 3, para. 43, *post*, and the note "Appointed days" to Part IX of that Schedule.

GENERAL NOTE

This section contains the rules governing the refusal of enforcement orders on grounds of contraventions of the requirements of this Act. Subsection (1) directs the court to make any of the relevant contraventions a ground of refusal if it considers it just to do so, having regard to prejudice caused by the contravention, culpability for it and the court's power under sub-s. (2) above and ss. 135, 136, *post*. The intention presumably is that if prejudice has been caused, the court will endeavour to remedy that prejudice by exercise of its powers under the provisions cited, and will refuse an order if the prejudice cannot be thus remedied.

The effect of sub-s. (3) above is that s. 61 (1) (*a*), *ante*, is mandatory in so far as it requires the existence of a written and signed agreement containing the prescribed terms, but contraventions of the further requirements of s. 61 can be condoned. The effect of sub-s. (4) above similarly is that the provisions of ss. 62, 63 and 64 (1), *ante*, are mandatory in the case of cancellable agreements, but not otherwise, but contravention of s. 62 or 63 may be condoned if a copy of the agreement and other necessary documents was given to the debtor before the commencement of proceedings. Subsection (5) above deals with the case where the signed document omits a term of the agreement other than one of the prescribed terms (the subsection cannot apply to the omission of a prescribed term because such an omission is fatal by virtue of sub-s. (3)). In that case, the court may order that the agreement is to have effect without the term omitted from the signed document.

PERSON

See the note to s. 8, *ante*.

PRESCRIBED FORM, TERMS, MANNER

See the note "Prescribed" to s. 61, *ante*.

SIGNED

See the note to s. 51, *ante*.

BY THE DEBTOR OR HIRER

This apparently means by all the debtors or hirers if there are more than one; note the exclusion by s. 185 (3), *post*, of s. 185 (1) (*b*).

DEFINITIONS

For "cancellable agreement", "court", "creditor", "debtor", "enforcement order", "executed agreement", "hirer", "prescribed", "regulated agreement", "regulations" and "surety", see s. 189 (1), *post*.

### 128. Enforcement orders on death of debtor or of hirer

The court shall make an order under section 86 (2) if, but only if, the creditor or owner proves that he has been unable to satisfy himself that the present and future obligations of the debtor or hirer under the agreement are likely to be discharged. **[C.128]**

COMMENCEMENT

See Sch. 3, para. 43, *post*, and the note "Appointed days" to Part IX of that Schedule.

DEFINITIONS

For "creditor", "owner" and "regulated agreement", see s. 189 (1), *post*.

*Extension of time*

### 129. Time orders

(1) If it appears to the court just to do so—

(*a*) on an application for an enforcement order; or

(*b*) on an application made by a debtor or hirer under this paragraph after service on him of—

(i) a default notice, or

(ii) a notice under section 76 (1) or 98 (1); or

(*c*) in an action brought by a creditor or owner to enforce a regulated agreement or any security, or recover possession of any goods or land to which a regulated agreement relates,

the court may make an order under this section (a "time order").

(2) A time order shall provide for one or both of the following, as the court considers just—

(*a*) the payment by the debtor or hirer or any surety of any sum owed under a regulated agreement or a security by such instalments, payable at such times, as the court, having regard to the means of the debtor or hirer and any surety, considers reasonable;

(*b*) the remedying by the debtor or hirer of any breach of a regulated agreement (other than the non-payment of money) within such period as the court may specify. **[C.129]**

COMMENCEMENT

See Sch. 3, para. 43, *post*, and the note "Appointed days" to Part IX of that Schedule.

GENERAL NOTE

This section gives the court wide powers to make orders known as time orders. These are of two kinds, described in sub-s. (2) above, namely, orders giving the debtor time for payment and orders giving him time in which to remedy a breach of contract not relating to the payment of money. Subsection (1) above enumerates the occasions on which the court has jurisdiction to make time orders. It will be observed that the categories of agreement to which this section applies vary according to the paragraph of sub-s. (1) under which jurisdiction arises. Thus para. (*c*) of sub-s. (1) applies to all regulated agreements. The application of para. (*a*), however, is limited by the application of those provisions of this Act which require enforcement orders to be sought. The most important of those provisions, s. 65, *ante*, applies to regulated agreements with the exceptions mentioned in s. 74, *ante*. Again, para. (*b*) is limited by the ambit of ss. 87 (default notices), 76 and 98, *ante*, and those sections apply to regulated agreements with exceptions to be made by regulations under ss. 76 (4), 87 (3) and 98 (4), *ante*. In this connection, note the provisions of s. 130 (3), *post*.

MAY MAKE AN ORDER
For certain cases in which an order giving time for payment may not be made, see s. 130 (3), *post.* For the consequences of a time order as respects goods in the possession of the debtor or hirer, see s. 130 (4), *post.* For power to vary or revoke the order, see s. 130 (6), *post.* For further powers exercisable in the case of hire-purchase or conditional sale agreements, see s. 133, *post,* and for further provisions which may be included in orders generally, see ss. 135, 136, *post.*

ANY SUM OWED
In certain cases, this may include sums not yet payable; see s. 130 (2), *post.*

HAVING REGARD TO THE MEANS
Evidence of means may be dispensed with in certain cases where the debtor has made an offer to pay; see s. 130 (1), *post.*

EXTENSION OF A PERIOD
For special provisions governing breach of contract and enforcement measures during the extended period, see s. 130 (5), *post.*

DEFINITIONS
For "court", "creditor", "debtor", "enforcement order", "goods", "hirer", "land", "owner", "regulated agreement", "security" and "surety", see s. 189 (1), *post.*
For "default notice", see s. 87 (1), *ante.*

**130. Supplemental provisions about time orders**

(1) Where in accordance with rules of court an offer to pay any sum by instalments is made by the debtor or hirer and accepted by the creditor or owner, the court may in accordance with rules of court make a time order under section 129 (2) (*a*) giving effect to the offer without hearing evidence of means.

(2) In the case of a hire-purchase or conditional sale agreement only, a time order under section 129 (2) (*a*) may deal with sums which, although not payable by the debtor at the time the order is made, would if the agreement continued in force, become payable under it subsequently.

(3) A time order under section 129 (2) (*a*) shall not be made where the regulated agreement is secured by a pledge if, by virtue of regulations made under section 76 (5), 87 (4) or 98 (5), service of a notice is not necessary for enforcement of the pledge.

(4) Where, following the making of a time order in relation to a regulated hire-purchase or conditional sale agreement or a regulated consumer hire agreement, the debtor or hirer is in possession of the goods, he shall be treated (except in the case of a debtor to whom the creditor's title has passed) as a bailee or (in Scotland) a custodier of the goods under the terms of the agreement, notwithstanding that the agreement has been terminated.

(5) Without prejudice to anything done by the creditor or owner before the commencement of the period specified in a time order made under section 129 (2) (*b*) ("the relevant period")—

(*a*) he shall not while the relevant period subsists take in relation to the agreement any action such as is mentioned in section 87 (1);

(*b*) where—

(i) a provision of the agreement ("the secondary provision") becomes operative only on breach of another provision of the agreement ("the primary provision"), and

(ii) the time order provides for the remedying of such a breach of the primary provision within the relevant period,

he shall not treat the secondary provision as operative before the end of that period;

(*c*) if while the relevant period subsists the breach to which the order relates is remedied it shall be treated as not having occurred.

(6) On the application of any person affected by a time order, the court may vary or revoke the order. [**C.130**]

COMMENCEMENT

See Sch. 3, para. 43, *post*, and the note "Appointed days" to Part IX of that Schedule.

RULES OF COURT

At the time of going to press, there are no rules made expressly for the purposes of this section. See, however, C.C.R. Ord. 9, r. 1, for the procedure generally applicable where a defendant admits liability and offers to pay by instalments.

PERSON

See the note to s. 8, *ante*.

DEFINITIONS

For "conditional sale agreement", "court", "creditor", "debtor", "goods", "hire-purchase agreement", "hirer", "owner", "pledge", "regulated agreement" and "regulations", see s. 189 (1), *post*.

For "consumer hire agreement", see s. 15, *ante*.

For "time order", see s. 129 (1), *ante*.

*Protection of property pending proceedings*

## 131. Protection orders

The court, on the application of the creditor or owner under a regulated agreement, may make such orders as it thinks just for protecting any property of the creditor or owner, or property subject to any security, from damage or depreciation pending the determination of any proceedings under this Act, including orders restricting or prohibiting use of the property or giving directions as to its custody. [**C.131**]

COMMENCEMENT

See Sch. 3, para. 43, *post*, and the note "Appointed days" to Part IX of that Schedule.

DEFINITIONS

For "court", "creditor", "owner" and "regulated agreement", see s. 189 (1), *post*.

*Hire and hire-purchase etc. agreements*

## 132. Financial relief for hirer

(1) Where the owner under a regulated consumer hire agreement recovers possession of goods to which the agreement relates otherwise than by action, the hirer may apply to the court for an order that—

(*a*) the whole or part of any sum paid by the hirer to the owner in respect of the goods shall be repaid, and

(*b*) the obligation to pay the whole or part of any sum owed by the hirer to the owner in respect of the goods shall cease, and if it appears to the court just to do so, having regard to the extent of the enjoyment of the goods by the hirer, the court shall grant the application in full or in part.

(2) Where in proceedings relating to a regulated consumer hire agreement the court makes an order for the delivery to the owner of goods to which the agreement relates the court may include in the order the like provision as may be made in an order under subsection (1). **[C.132]**

COMMENCEMENT
See Sch. 3, para. 43, *post*, and the note "Appointed days" to Part IX of that Schedule.

DEFINITIONS
For "consumer hire agreement", see s. 15, *ante*.
For "court", "goods", "hirer" and "regulated agreement", see s. 189 (1), *post*.

**133. Hire-purchase etc. agreements: special powers of court**

(1) If, in relation to a regulated hire-purchase or conditional sale agreement, it appears to the court just to do so—

(*a*) on an application for an enforcement order or time order; or

(*b*) in an action brought by the creditor to recover possession of goods to which the agreement relates, the court may—

(i) make an order (a "return order") for the return to the creditor of goods to which the agreement relates;

(ii) make an order (a "transfer order") for the transfer to the debtor of the creditor's title to certain goods to which the agreement relates ("the transferred goods"), and the return to the creditor of the remainder of the goods.

(2) In determining for the purposes of this section how much of the total price has been paid ("the paid-up sum"), the court may—

(*a*) treat any sum paid by the debtor, or owed by the creditor, in relation to the goods as part of the paid-up sum;

(*b*) deduct any sum owed by the debtor in relation to the goods (otherwise than as part of the total price) from the paid-up sum,

and make corresponding reductions in amounts so owed.

(3) Where a transfer order is made, the transferred goods shall be such of the goods to which the agreement relates as the court thinks just; but a transfer order shall be made only where the paid-up sum exceeds the part of the total price referable to the transferred goods by an amount equal to at least one-third of the unpaid balance of the total price.

(4) Notwithstanding the making of a return order or transfer order, the debtor may at any time before the goods enter the possession of the creditor, on payment of the balance of the total price and the fulfilment of any other necessary conditions, claim the goods ordered to be returned to the creditor.

(5) When, in pursuance of a time order or under this section, the total price of goods under a regulated hire-purchase agreement or regulated conditional sale agreement is paid and any other necessary conditions are fulfilled, the creditor's title to the goods vests in the debtor.

(6) If, in contravention of a return order or transfer order, any goods to which the order relates are not returned to the creditor, the court, on the application of the creditor, may—

(*a*) revoke so much of the order as relates to those goods, and

(*b*) order the debtor to pay the creditor the unpaid portion of so much of the total price as is referable to those goods.

(7) For the purposes of this section, the part of the total price referable to any goods is the part assigned to those goods by the agreement or (if no such assignment is made) the part determined by the court to be reasonable. **[C.133]**

COMMENCEMENT

See Sch. 3, para. 43, *post*, and the note "Appointed days" to Part IX of that Schedule.

GENERAL NOTE

See the General Note to s. 90, *ante*.

MAKE AN ORDER

For further provisions which may be included in orders, see ss. 135, 136, *post*.

DEFINITIONS

For "conditional sale agreement", "court", "creditor", "debtor", "enforcement order", "goods", "hire-purchase agreement", "regulated agreement", "security" and "total price", see s. 189 (1), *post*.

For "paid up sum", "return order", "transfer order" and "transferred goods", see sub-ss. (1) and (2) above.

For "time order", see s. 129 (1), *ante*.

**134. Evidence of adverse detention in hire-purchase etc. cases**

(1) Where goods are comprised in a regulated hire-purchase agreement, regulated conditional sale agreement or regulated consumer hire agreement, and the creditor or owner—

(*a*) brings an action or makes an application to enforce a right to recover possession of the goods from the debtor or hirer, and

(*b*) proves that a demand for the delivery of the goods was included in the default notice under section 88 (5), or that, after the right to recover possession of the goods accrued but before the action was begun or the application was made, he made a request in writing to the debtor or hirer to surrender the goods,

then, for the purposes of the claim of the creditor or owner to recover possession of the goods, the possession of them by the debtor or hirer shall be deemed to be adverse to the creditor or owner.

(2) In subsection (1) "the debtor or hirer" includes a person in possession of the goods at any time between the debtor's or hirer's death and the grant of probate or administration, or (in Scotland) confirmation.

(3) Nothing in this section affects a claim for damages for conversion or (in Scotland) for delict. **[C.134]**

COMMENCEMENT

See Sch. 3, para. 43, *post*, and the note "Appointed days" to Part IX of that Schedule.

GENERAL NOTE

This section deals with the evidence by which the owner of goods may prove that the debtor's possession of the goods was adverse to him (which is an essential element in the owner's cause of action if he wishes to sue in trover or detinue). Subsections (1) and (3) above are substantially a re-enactment of the Hire-Purchase Act 1965, s 48 (30 Halsbury's Statutes (3rd edn.) 101) (repealed by s. 192 (3) and Sch. 5, *post*. Subsection (2) above re-enacts Sch. 3, para. 6 (5), to that Act, Vol. 30, p. 115 (similarly repealed).

REQUEST IN WRITING

A request for surrender of the goods is sufficient even if the debtor or hirer is told that if he pays off the arrears he may retain the goods; and the request need not be followed by attendance at the hirer's premises (*Smart Brothers, Ltd.* v. *Pratt*, [1940] 2 K.B. 498; [1940] 3 All E.R. 432). A request under this section is necessary where an enforcement order is required, since otherwise the debtor or hirer could plead that his continued posssesion was not adverse, sinc he was merely invoking his statutory rights (*ibid.*).

CONVERSION

As to the measure of damages for conversion where the defendant is the hirer under a hire-purchase agreement, see *Wickham Holdings, Ltd.* v. *Brooke House Motors, Ltd.*, [1967] 1 All E.R. 117, C.A., and *Belvoir Finance Co., Ltd.* v. *Stapleton*, [1970] 3 All E.R. 664, C.A.

DEFINITIONS

For "conditional sale agreement", "creditor", "debtor", "goods", "hire-purchase agreement" and "regulated agreement", see s. 189 (1), *post*.
For "consumer hire agreement", see s. 15, *ante*.
For "default notice", see s. 87 (1), *ante*.

*Supplemental provisions as to orders*

## 135. Power to impose conditions, or suspend operation of order

(1) If it considers it just to do so, the court may in an order made by it in relation to a regulated agreement include provisions—

(*a*) making the operation of any term of the order conditional on the doing of specified acts by any party to the proceedings;

(*b*) suspending the operation of any term of the order either—

(i) until such time as the court subsequently directs, or

(ii) until the occurrence of a specified act or omission.

(2) The court shall not suspend the operation of a term requiring the delivery up of goods by any person unless satisfied that the goods are in his possession or control.

(3) In the case of a consumer hire agreement, the court shall not so use its powers under subsection (1) (*b*) as to extend the period for which, under the terms of the agreement, the hirer is entitled to possession of the goods to which the agreement relates.

(4) On the application of any person affected by a provision included under subsection (1), the court may vary the provision. **[C.135]**

COMMENCEMENT

See Sch. 3, para. 43, *post*, and the note "Appointed days" to Part IX of that Schedule.

DEFINITIONS

For "consumer hire agreement", see s. 15, *ante*. For "court", "goods" and "regulated agreement", see s. 189 (1), *post*.

## 136. Power to vary agreements and securities

The court may in an order made by it under this Act include such provision as it considers just for amending any agreement or security in consequence of a term of the order. **[C.136]**

COMMENCEMENT

See Sch. 3, para. 43, *post*, and the note "Appointed days" to Part IX of that Schedule.

DEFINITIONS

For "court" and "security", see s. 189 (1), *post*.

*Extortionate credit bargains*

## 137. Extortionate credit bargains

(1) If the court finds a credit bargain extortionate it may reopen the credit agreement so as to do justice between the parties.

(2) In this section and sections 138 to 140,—

(*a*) "credit agreement" means any agreement between an individual (the "debtor") and any other person (the "creditor") by which the creditor provides the debtor with credit of any amount, and

(*b*) "credit bargain"—

(i) where no transaction other than the credit agreement is to be taken into account in computing the total charge for credit, means the credit agreement, or

(ii) where one or more other transactions are to be so taken into account, means the credit agreement and those other transactions, taken together. **[C.137]**

COMMENCEMENT

See Sch. 3, para. 42, *post*, and the note "Appointed days" to Part IX of that Schedule.

GENERAL NOTE

This section and ss. 138–140, *post*, give power to the courts to re-open extortionate credit bargains. These provisions replace the Moneylenders Act 1900, s.1 (22 Halsbury's Statutes (3rd edn.) 693), as amended by the Moneylenders Act 1927, s. 10 (22 Halsbury's Statutes (3rd edn.) 715) (both repealed by s. 192 (3) and Sch. 5, *post*). The main differences between these provisions and the replaced provisions are that:

(i) the replaced provisions applied only to loans made by money lenders within the meaning of the Act of 1900, and to certain transactions of pawnbrokers, whereas the present provisions apply to all "credit agreements" as defined by sub-s. (2) (*a*) above;

(ii) the presumption in s. 10 (1) of the Act of 1927, that any interest charge over 48% per annum is excessive, is not reproduced in these provisions.

The term "extortionate" is used in these provisions instead of "harsh and unconscionable" but presumably means much the same thing. The provisions of s. 138, *post*, as to the factors to be taken into account by the court, and of s. 139, *post*, as to the action which the court may take, are broadly in line with the cases under the replaced provisions.

FINDS

For the proceedings in which such finding may be made, see s. 139 (1), *post*. The onus of proof is on the creditor; see s. 171 (7), *post*.

EXTORTIONATE

As to when credit bargains are extortionate, see s. 138, *post*.

AGREEMENT

This section and ss. 138–140, *post*, apply to agreements and transactions whenever made; see Sch. 3, para. 42, *post*.

DEFINITIONS
For "credit", see s. 9, *ante*. For "individual" and "total charge for credit", see s. 189 (1), *post*. See also s. 140, *post*, and the notes thereto.

**138. When bargains are extortionate**

(1) A credit bargain is extortionate if it—

(*a*) requires the debtor or a relative of his to make payments (whether unconditionally, or on certain contingencies) which are grossly exorbitant, or

(*b*) otherwise grossly contravenes ordinary principles of fair dealing.

(2) In determining whether a credit bargain is extortionate, regard shall be had to such evidence as is adduced concerning—

(*a*) interest rates prevailing at the time it was made,

(*b*) the factors mentioned in subsections (3) to (5), and

(*c*) any other relevant considerations.

(3) Factors applicable under subsection (2) in relation to the debtor include—

(*a*) his age, experience, business capacity and state of health; and

(*b*) the degree to which, at the time of making the credit bargain, he was under financial pressure, and the nature of that pressure.

(4) Factors applicable under subsection (2) in relation to the creditor include—

(*a*) the degree of risk accepted by him, having regard to the value of any security provided;

(*b*) his relationship to the debtor; and

(*c*) whether or not a colourable cash price was quoted for any goods or services included in the credit bargain.

(5) Factors applicable under subsection (2) in relation to a linked transaction include the question how far the transaction was reasonably required for the protection of debtor or creditor, or was in the interest of the debtor. [C.138]

COMMENCEMENT
See Sch. 3, para. 42, *post*, and the note "Appointed days" to Part IX of that Schedule.

GENERAL NOTE
See the General Note to s. 137, *ante*.

CREDIT BARGAIN
For meaning, see s. 137 (2) (*b*), *ante*. This section applies to agreements and transactions whenever made; see Sch. 3, para. 42, *post*.

OTHER RELEVANT CONSIDERATIONS
Under the Moneylenders Act 1900, s. 1 (22 Halsbury's Statutes (3rd edn.) 695) it was held that the failure of the lender adequately to explain the transaction to the borrower was a ground for holding that the transaction was harsh and unconscionable; see, e.g., *Halsey* v. *Wolfe*, [1915] 2 Ch. 330. *Quaere* whether that is a relevant consideration under this section, in view of the elaborate provisions made elsewhere in this Act for the provision of information to debtors.

FACTORS . . . IN RELATION TO THE DEBTOR
For decisions on similar factors under the replaced provisions, see *Samuel* v. *Newbold*,

[1906] A.C. 461; [1904–7] All E.R. Ref. 693; *Poncione* v. *Higgins* (1904), 21 T.C.R. 11; *Glaskie* v. *Griffin* (194), 111 L.T. 712.

DEGREE OF RISK . . . VALUE OF SECURITY

For decisions on these factors under the replaced provisions, see *Kruse* v. *Seeley*, [1924] 1 Ch. 136; *Verner-Jeffreys* v. *Pinto*, [1929] 1 Ch. 401; [1928] All E.R. Rep. 81; *Reading Trust Ltd.* v. *Spero*, [1930] 1 K.B. 492; [1929] All E.R. Rep. 405.

DEFINITIONS

For "creditor" and "debtor", see s. 137 (2) (*a*), *ante*.
For "goods", "relative" and "security", see s. 189 (1), *post*.
For "linked transaction", see s. 19 (1), *ante*.
See also s. 140, *post*, and the notes thereto.

## 139. Reopening of extortionate agreements

(1) A credit agreement may, if the court thinks just, be reopened on the ground that the credit bargain is extortionate—

(*a*) on an application for the purpose made by the debtor or any surety to the High Court, county court or sheriff court; or

(*b*) at the instance of the debtor or a surety in any proceedings to which the debtor and creditor are parties, being proceedings to enforce the credit agreement, any security relating to it, or any linked transaction; or

(*c*) at the instance of the debtor or a surety in other proceedings in any court where the amount paid or payable under the credit agreement is relevant.

(2) In reopening the agreement, the court may, for the purpose of relieving the debtor or a surety from payment of any sum in excess of that fairly due and reasonable, by order—

(*a*) direct accounts to be taken, or (in Scotland) an accounting to be made, between any persons,

(*b*) set aside the whole or part of any obligation imposed on the debtor or a surety by the credit bargain or any related agreement,

(*c*) require the creditor to repay the whole or part of any sum paid under the credit bargain or any related agreement by the debtor or a surety, whether paid to the creditor or any other person,

(*d*) direct the return to the surety of any property provided for the purposes of the security, or

(*e*) alter the terms of the credit agreement or any security instrument.

(3) An order may be made under subsection (2) notwithstanding that its effect is to place a burden on the creditor in respect of an advantage unfairly enjoyed by another person who is a party to a linked transaction.

(4) An order under subsection (2) shall not alter the effect of any judgment.

(5) In England and Wales, an application under subsection (1) (*a*) shall be brought only in the county court in the case of—

(*a*) a regulated agreement, or

(*b*) an agreement (not being a regulated agreement) under which the creditor provides the debtor with fixed-sum credit not exceeding £750 or running-account credit on which the credit limit does not exceed £750.

(6) In Scotland an application under subsection (1) (*a*) may be brought in the sheriff court for the district in which the debtor or surety resides or carries on business.

(7) In Northern Ireland an application under subsection (1) (*a*) may be brought in the county court in the case of—

(*a*) a regulated agreement, or

(*b*) an agreement (not being a regulated agreement) under which the creditor provides the debtor with fixed-sum credit not exceeding £300 or running-account credit on which the credit limit does not exceed £300. **[C.139]**

COMMENCEMENT

See Sch. 3, para. 42, *ante*, and the note "Appointed days" to Part IX of that Schedule.

GENERAL NOTE

See the General Note to s. 137, *ante*.

CREDIT AGREEMENT; CREDIT BARGAIN

For meanings, see s. 137 (2), *ante*. This section applies to agreements whenever made; see Sch. 3, para. 42, *post*.

IS EXTORTIONATE

The onus of proof is on the creditor; see s. 171 (7), *post*.

OTHER PROCEEDINGS

Bankruptcy proceedings in relation to the debtor's estate would seem to fall within the description in sub-s. (1) (*c*) above. The case of bankruptcy was expressly mentioned in the Moneylenders Act 1900, s. 1 (3) (22 Halsbury's Statutes (3rd edn.) 694) and the Moneylenders Act 1927, s. 10 (4) (22 Halsbury's Statutes (3rd edn.) 715) (both repealed by s. 192 (3) and Sch. 5, *post*), which also gave the debtor's trustee in bankruptcy *locus standi* to initiate proceedings. Under this section, however, it seems that the trustee cannot do so.

ALTER THE TERMS

Reduction of the interest rate was a common course of action under the replaced provisions; see, e.g., *Verner-Jeffreys* v. *Pinto*, [1929] 1 Ch. 401; *Collings* v. *Charles Bradbury, Ltd.*, [1936] 3 All E.R. 369. For other forms of relief which have been granted, see other cases cited in the note "may re-open the transaction" (22 Halsbury's Statutes (3rd edn.) 696).

DEFINITIONS

For "creditor" and "debtor", see s. 137 (2) (*a*), *ante*.

For "regulated agreement", "security" and "surety", see s. 189 (1), *post*.

For "fixed-sum credit" and "running-account credit", see s. 10, *ante*.

For "linked transaction", see s. 19 (1), *ante*.

See also s. 140, *post*, and the notes thereto.

## 140. Interpretation of sections 137 to 139

Where the credit agreement is not a regulated agreement, expressions used in sections 137 to 139 which, apart from this section, apply only to regulated agreements, shall be construed as nearly as may be as if the credit agreement were a regulated agreement. **[C.140]**

CREDIT AGREEMENT

For meaning, see s. 137 (2) (*a*), *ante*, and the note "Agreement" to that section.

REGULATED AGREEMENT

For meaning, see s. 189 (1), *post*.

EXPRESSIONS . . . WHICH . . . APPLY ONLY TO REGULATED AGREEMENTS
The interpretation of this section presents some difficulty, as the only expression used in ss. 137–139, *ante*, which applies only to regulated agreements, is "linked transaction" (see s. 19 (1), *ante*). The expressions "security" and "total charge for credit", however, are defined with exclusive reference to consumer credit agreements (see s. 20 (1), *ante*, and s. 189 (1), *post*) and the definition of "surety" is limited by that of "security". Since ss. 137–139 are not confined to consumer credit agreements, some provision for a wider application of all the expressions mentioned seems to be required (cf. the definitions of "creditor" and "debtor" in s. 139 (2) (*a*), *ante*, which here replace those in s. 189 (1), *post*). Perhaps the necessary provision can be found in the opening words of s. 189 (1), *post*, considered in conjunction with this section.

*Miscellaneous*

## 141. Jurisdiction and parties

(1) In England and Wales, the county court shall have jurisdiction to hear and determine—

(*a*) any action by the creditor or owner to enforce a regulated agreement or any security relating to it;

(*b*) any action to enforce any linked transaction against the debtor or hirer or his relative;

and such an action shall not be brought in any other court.

(2) Where an action or application is brought in the High Court which, by virtue of this Act, ought to have been brought in the county court it shall not be treated as improperly brought, but shall be transferred to the county court.

(3) In Scotland the sheriff court for the district in which the debtor or hirer resides or carries on business, or resided or carried on business at the date on which he last made a payment under the agreement, shall have jurisdiction to hear and determine any action falling within subsection (1) and such an action shall not be brought in any other court.

(4) In Northern Ireland the county court shall have jurisdiction to hear and determine any action or application falling within subsection (1).

(5) Except as may be provided by rules of court, all the parties to a regulated agreement, and any surety, shall be made parties to any proceedings relating to the agreement. [**C.141**]

COMMENCEMENT
See Sch. 3, para. 43, *post*, and the note "Appointed days" to Part IX of that Schedule.

THE COUNTY COURT SHALL HAVE JURISDICTION
"The county court" means a county court established under the County Courts Act 1959; see the Interpretation Act 1889, s. 6 (32 Halsbury's Statutes (3rd edn.) 437), as construed in accordance with s. 205 (4) of the Act of 1959 (7 Halsbury's Statutes (3rd edn.) 425). This section enables county courts to hear actions which would otherwise be beyond their jurisdiction by virtue of the limit of amount in s. 39 (1), as amended, of the Act of 1959 (7 Halsbury's Statutes (3rd edn.) 326). It does not affect the territorial limits of jurisdiction of any particular county court, for which, see C.C.R. Ord. 2, r. 1. Note that this Act does not re-enact the Hire-Purchase Act 1965, s. 49 (1) (30 Halsbury's Statutes (3rd edn.) 102) (repealed by s. 192 (3) and Sch. 5, *post*) which required certain actions on hire-purchase agreements to be brought in a particular county court.

RULES OF COURT
At the time of going to press, there are no rules made expressly for the purposes of sub-s.

(5) above. Note, however, the provision of C.C.R. Ord. 5, r. 6, that no action is to be defeated by reason of the non-joinder of parties.

DEFINITIONS

For "creditor", "debtor", "hirer", "owner", "regulated agreement", "relative" and "security", see s. 189 (1), *post*.

NORTHERN IRELAND

For further provisions as to county court rules and as to appeals from county courts, see ss. 143, 144, *post*.

### 142. Power to declare rights of parties

(1) Where under any provision of this Act a thing can be done by a creditor or owner on an enforcement order only, and either—

(*a*) the court dismisses (except on technical grounds only) an application for an enforcement order, or

(*b*) where no such application has been made or such an application has been dismissed on technical grounds only, an interested party applies to the court for a declaration under this subsection,

the court may if it thinks just make a declaration that the creditor or owner is not entitled to do that thing, and thereafter no application for an enforcement order in respect of it shall be entertained.

(2) Where—

(*a*) a regulated agreement or linked transaction is cancelled under section 69 (1), or becomes subject to section 69 (2), or

(*b*) a regulated agreement is terminated under section 91,

and an interested party applies to the court for a declaration under this subsection, the court may make a declaration to that effect. **[C.142]**

COMMENCEMENT

See Sch. 3, para. 43, *post*, and the note "Appointed days" to Part IX of that Schedule.

ON TECHNICAL GROUNDS ONLY

For the court's power to certify that an application has been so dismissed, see s. 189 (5), *post*.

DEFINITIONS

For "creditor", "debtor", "enforcement order", "hirer", "owner", "regulated agreement" and "surety", see s. 189 (1), *post*.

*Northern Ireland*

### 143. Jurisdiction of county court in Northern Ireland

Without prejudice to any provision which may be made by rules of court made in relation to county courts in Northern Ireland such rules may provide—

(*a*) that any action or application such as is mentioned in section 141 (4) which is brought against the debtor or hirer in the county court may be brought in the county court for the division in which the debtor or hirer resided or carried on business at the date on which he last made a payment under the regulated agreement;

(*b*) that an application by a debtor or hirer or any surety under section 129 (1) (*b*), 132 (1), 139 (1) (*a*) or 142 (1) (*b*) which is brought in the county court may be brought in the county court for the division in which the debtor, or, as the case may be, the hirer or surety resides or carries on business;

(*c*) for service of process on persons outside Northern Ireland. [C.143]

COMMENCEMENT

See Sch. 3, para. 43, *post*, and the note "Appointed days" to Part IX of that Schedule.

COUNTY COURT; DIVISION

As to county courts in Northern Ireland and their divisions, see the County Courts Act (Northern Ireland) 1959 c. 25 (N.I.).

DEFINITIONS

For "debtor", "hirer", "regulated agreement" and "surety", see s. 189 (1), *post*.

**144. Appeal from county court in Northern Ireland**

Any person dissatisfied—

(*a*) with an order, whether adverse to him or in his favour, made by a county court in Northern Ireland in the exercise of any jurisdiction conferred by this Act, or

(*b*) with the dismissal or refusal by such a county court of any action or application instituted by him under the provisions of this Act,

shall be entitled to appeal from the order or from the dismissal or refusal as if the order, dismissal or refusal had been made in exercise of the jurisdiction conferred by Part III of the County Courts Act (Northern Ireland) 1959 and the appeal brought under the County Court Appeals Act (Northern Ireland) 1964 and sections 2 (cases stated by county court judge) and 3 (cases stated by assize judge or High Court on appeal from county court) of the last mentioned Act shall apply accordingly. [C.144]

COMMENCEMENT

See Sch. 3, para. 43, *post*, and the note "Appointed days" to Part IX of that Schedule.

COUNTY COURT

See the note to s. 145, *ante*.

JURISDICTION CONFERRED BY THIS ACT

See ss. 133, 144, *ante*.

COUNTY COURTS ACT (NORTHERN IRELAND) 1959

1959 c. 25 (N.I.).

COUNTY COURT APPEALS ACT (NORTHERN IRELAND) 1964

1964 c. 3.

## Part X

## Ancillary Credit Businesses

### *Definitions*

**145. Types of ancillary credit business**

(1) An ancillary credit business is any business so far as it comprises or relates to—

(*a*) credit brokerage,

(*b*) debt-adjusting,
(*c*) debt-counselling,
(*d*) debt-collecting, or
(*e*) the operation of a credit reference agency.

(2) Subject to section 146 (5), credit brokerage is the effecting of introductions—

(*a*) of individuals desiring to obtain credit—

(i) to persons carrying on businesses to which this sub-paragraph applies, or

(ii) in the case of an individual desiring to obtain credit to finance the acquisition or provision of a dwelling occupied or to be occupied by himself or his relative, to any person carrying on a business in the course of which he provides credit secured on land, or

(*b*) of individuals desiring to obtain goods on hire to persons carrying on businesses to which this paragraph applies, or

(*c*) of individuals desiring to obtain credit, or to obtain goods on hire, to other credit-brokers.

(3) Subsection (2) (*a*) (i) applies to—

(*a*) a consumer credit business,

(*b*) a business which comprises or relates to consumer credit agreements being, otherwise than by virtue of section 16 (5) (*a*), exempt agreements,

(*c*) a business which comprises or relates to unregulated agreements where—

(i) the proper law of the agreement is the law of a country outside the United Kingdom, and

(ii) if the proper law of the agreement were the law of a part of the United Kingdom it would be a regulated consumer credit agreement.

(4) Subsection (2) (*b*) applies to—

(*a*) a consumer hire business,

(*b*) a business which comprises or relates to unregulated agreements where—

(i) the proper law of the agreement is the law of a country outside the United Kingdom, and

(ii) if the proper law of the agreement were the law of a part of the United Kingdom it would be a regulated consumer hire agreement.

(5) Subject to section 146 (6), debt-adjusting is, in relation to debts due under consumer credit agreements or consumer hire agreements,—

(*a*) negotiating with the creditor or owner, on behalf of the debtor or hirer, terms for the discharge of a debt, or

(*b*) taking over, in return for payments by the debtor or hirer, his obligation to discharge a debt, or

(*c*) any similar activity concerned with the liquidation of a debt.

(6) Subject to section 146 (6), debt-counselling is the giving of advice to

debtors or hirers about the liquidation of debts due under consumer credit agreements or consumer hire agreements.

(7) Subject to section 146 (6), debt-collecting is the taking of steps to procure payment of debts due under consumer credit agreements or consumer hire agreements.

(8) A credit reference agency is a person carrying on a business comprising the furnishing of persons with information relevant to the financial standing of individuals, being information collected by the agency for that purpose. [**C.145**]

GENERAL NOTE

This section (read with s. 146, *post*, which contains a number of exceptions from its provisions) defines ancillary credit businesses and the five species thereof. The licensing system established by Part III, *ante*, is extended to ancillary credit business by s. 147, *post*, and further provisions for the control of such businesses are made by ss. 149–159, *post*.

PERSON

See the note to s. 8, *ante*.

EXCEPTIONS FOR LEGAL PRACTITIONERS

Barristers acting in that capacity and solicitors engaging in contentious business are excepted by s. 146 (1), (2), *post*.

DEFINITIONS

For "business", "consumer credit business", "consumer hire business", "creditor", "debtor", "goods", "hirer", "individual", and "owner", see s. 189 (1), *post*.

For "consumer credit agreement", see s. 8 (1), *ante*, for "consumer hire agreement" see s. 75, *ante*, and for "credit", see s. 9, *ante*.

## 146. Exceptions from section 145

(1) A barrister or advocate acting in that capacity is not to be treated as doing so in the course of any ancillary credit business.

(2) A solicitor engaging in contentious business (as defined in section 86 (1) of the Solicitors Act 1957) is not to be treated as doing so in the course of any ancillary credit business.

(3) A solicitor within the meaning of the Solicitors (Scotland) Act 1933 engaging in business done in or for the purposes of proceedings before a court or before an arbiter is not to be treated as doing so in the course of any ancillary credit business.

(4) A solicitor in Northern Ireland engaging in business done, whether as solicitor or advocate, in or for the purposes of proceedings begun before a court (including the Lands Tribunal for Northern Ireland) or before an arbitrator appointed under the Arbitration Act (Northern Ireland) 1937, not being business contained in section 2 of the Probates and Letters of Administration Act (Ireland) 1857, is not to be treated as doing so in the course of any ancillary credit business.

(5) For the purposes of section 145 (2), introductions effected by an individual by canvassing off trade premises either debtor-creditor-supplier agreements falling within section 12 (*a*) or regulated consumer hire agreements shall be disregarded if—

(*a*) the introductions are not effected by him in the capacity of an employee, and (*b*) he does not by any other method effect introductions falling within section 145 (2).

(6) It is not debt-adjusting, debt-counselling or debt-collecting for a person to do anything in relation to a debt arising under an agreement if—

(*a*) he is the creditor or owner under the agreement, otherwise than by virtue of an assignment, or

(*b*) he is the creditor or owner under the agreement by virtue of an assignment made in connection with the transfer to the assignee of any business other than a debt-collecting business, or

(*c*) he is the supplier in relation to the agreement, or

(*d*) he is a credit-broker who has acquired the business of the person who was the supplier in relation to the agreement, or

(*e*) he is a person prevented by subsection (5) from being treated as a credit-broker, and the agreement was made in consequence of an introduction (whether made by him or another person) which, under subsection (5), is to be disregarded. **[C.146]**

ADVOCATE
This term applies to Scotland.

ANCILLARY CREDIT BUSINESS
See s. 145, *ante*, for a list of such businesses.

CANVASSING OFF TRADE PREMISES
For meaning, see s. 48, *ante*.

DEFINITIONS
For "consumer credit business", "consumer hire business", "credit-broker", "creditor", "individual", "owner", "regulated agreement" and "supplier", see s. 189 (1), *post*.
For "consumer hire agreement", see s. 15, *ante*.
For "debt-adjusting", "debt-counselling" and "debt-collecting", see s. 145 (5)–(7), *ante*.
For "debtor-creditor-supplier agreement", see s. 12, *ante*.

SOLICITORS ACT 1957, S. 86 (1)
See 32 Halsbury's Statutes (3rd edn.) 86.

SOLICITORS (SCOTLAND) Act 1933
23 & 24 Geo. 5 c. 21.

*Licensing*

## 147. Application of Part III

(1) The provisions of Part III (except section 40) apply to an ancillary credit business as they apply to a consumer credit business.

(2) Without prejudice to the generality of section 26, regulations under that section (as applied by subsection (1)) may include provisions regulating the collection and dissemination of information by credit reference agencies. **[C.147]**

COMMENCEMENT
As to the commencement of s. 21 (1), *ante*, as applied by this section, see Sch. 3, para 44, *post*, and the note "Appointed days" to Part X of that Schedule.

PART III
I.e., ss. 21–42, *ante*.

DEFINITIONS
For "ancillary credit business", see s. 147, *ante*.
For "consumer credit business" and "regulations", see s. 189 (1), *post*.
For "credit reference agency", see s. 145 (8), *ante*.

REGULATIONS UNDER THIS SECTION
No regulations had been made under s. 26, *ante*, as extended by sub-s. (2) above, up to the time of going to press.

SUB-S. (2): ORDER
An order made under sub-s. (2) on the application of a credit-broker may contain provisions as to the applicability of s. 149, *post*; see s. 149 (1) (*a*).

## 148. Agreement for services of unlicensed trader

(1) An agreement for the services of a person carrying on an ancillary credit business (the "trader"), if made when the trader was unlicensed, is enforceable against the other party (the "customer") only where the Director has made an order under subsection (2) which applies to the agreement.

(2) The trader or his successor in title may apply to the Director for an order that agreements within subsection (1) are to be treated as if made when the trader was licensed.

(3) Unless the Director determines to make an order under subsection (2) in accordance with the application, he shall, before determining the application, by notice—

(*a*) inform the trader, giving his reasons, that, as the case may be, he is minded to refuse the application, or to grant it in terms different from those applied for, describing them, and
(*b*) invite the trader to submit to the Director representations in support of his application in accordance with section 34.

(4) In determining whether or not to make an order under subsection (2) in respect of any period the Director shall consider, in addition to any other relevant factors,—

(*a*) how far, if at all, customers under agreements made by the trader during that period were prejudiced by the trader's conduct,
(*b*) whether or not the Director would have been likely to grant a licence covering that period on an application by the trader, and
(*c*) the degree of culpability for the failure to obtain a licence.

(5) If the Director thinks fit, he may in an order under subsection (2)—

(*a*) limit the order to specified agreements, or agreements of a specified description or made at a specified time;
(*b*) make the order conditional on the doing of specified acts by the trader. [**C.148**]

GENERAL NOTE
Cf. the General Note to s. 40, *ante*.

SUB-S. (1): PERSON
See the note to s. 8, *ante*.

COMMENCEMENT
See Sch. 3, para. 45, *post*, and the note "Appointed days" to Part X of that Schedule.

ONLY

See, however, s. 173 (3), *post,* as to the sufficiency of the consent of the customer, given at the time when enforcement is sought.

SUB-S. (3): DETERMINES

It is thought that the Director must observe the principles of natural justice; cf. the note "If he satisfies" to s. 25, *ante.*

GIVING HIS REASONS

See the note to s. 27, *ante.*

SUB-S. (4): LIKELY TO GRANT A LICENCE

For factor to be taken into account when the Director considers whether to grant a licence, see s. 25, *ante.*

APPEAL

An appeal lies to the Secretary of State against refusal of an order; see s. 41, *ante,* as extended by s. 150, *post.*

DEFINITIONS

For "ancillary credit business", see s. 145, *ante.*

For business", see s. 145, *ante.*

For "Director", "licence", "licensed", "notice" and "unlicensed", see s. 189 (1), *post.* For "customer" and "trader", see sub-s. (1) above.

**149. Regulated agreements made on introductions by unlicensed credit-broker**

(1) A regulated agreement made by a debtor or hirer who, for the purpose of making that agreement, was introduced to the creditor or owner by an unlicensed credit-broker is enforceable against the debtor or hirer only where—

(*a*) on the application of the credit-broker, the Director has made an order under section 148 (2) in respect of a period including the time when the introduction was made, and the order does not (whether in general terms or specifically) exclude the application of this paragraph to the regulated agreement, or

(*b*) the Director has made an order under subsection (2) which applies to the agreement.

(2) Where during any period individuals were introduced to a person carrying on a consumer credit business or consumer hire business by an unlicensed credit-broker for the purpose of making regulated agreements with the person carrying on that business, that person or his successor in title may apply to the Director for an order that regulated agreements so made are to be treated as if the credit-broker had been licensed at the time of the introduction.

(3) Unless the Director determines to make an order under subsection (2) in accordance with the application, he shall, before determining the application, by notice—

(*a*) inform the applicant, giving his reasons, that, as the case may be, he is minded to refuse the application, or to grant it in terms different from those applied for, describing them, and

(*b*) invite the applicant to submit to the Director representations in support of his application in accordance with section 34.

(4) In determining whether or not to make an order under subsection (2) the Director shall consider, in addition to any other relevant factors—

(*a*) how far, if at all, debtors or hirers under regulated agreements to which the application relates were prejudiced by the credit-broker's conduct, and

(*b*) the degree of culpability of the applicant in facilitating the carrying on by the credit-broker of his business when unlicensed.

(5) If the Director thinks fit, he may in an order under subsection (2)—

(*a*) limit the order to specified agreements, or agreements of a specified description or made at a specified time;

(*b*) make the order conditional on the doing of specified acts by the applicant. **[C.149]**

COMMENCEMENT
See Sch. 3, para. 46, *post*, and the note "Appointed days" to Part X of that Schedule.

GENERAL NOTE
Cf. the General Note to s. 40. *ante*.

SUB-S. (1): ONLY
See, however, s. 173 (3), *post*, as to the sufficiency of the consent of the debtor or hirer, given at the time when enforcement is sought.

SUB-S. (2): PERSON
See the note to s. 8, *ante*.

SUB-S. (3): DETERMINES
It is thought that the Director must observe the principles of natural justice; cf. the note "If he satisfies" to s. 25, *ante*.

GIVING HIS REASONS
See the note to s. 27, *ante*.

APPEAL
An appeal lies to the Secretary of State against refusal of an order; see s. 41, *ante*, as extended by s. 150, *post*.

SECURITIES
As to the position of securities given in connection with an agreement which is unenforceable by virtue of this section, see s. 113, *ante*.

DEFINITIONS
For "consumer credit business", "consumer hire business", "credit-broker", "creditor", "debtor", "Director", "hirer", "individual", "licensed", "notice", "owner", "regulated agreement" and "unlicensed", see s. 189 (1), *post*.

**150. Appeals to Secretary of State against licensing decisions**

Section 41 (as applied by section 147 (1)) shall have effect as if the following entry were included in the table set out at the end—

| *Determination* | *Appellant* |
|---|---|
| Refusal to make order under section 148 (2) or 149 (2) in accordance with terms of application | The applicant |

**[C.150]**

GENERAL NOTE
The effect of this section is to give a right of appeal to persons aggrieved by the refusal of orders under ss. 148, 149, *ante*. See, further, the notes to s. 41, *ante*.

*Seeking business*

## 151. Advertisements

(1) Sections 44 to 47 apply to an advertisement published for the purposes of a business of credit brokerage carried on by any person, whether it advertises the services of that person or the services of persons to whom he effects introductions, as they apply to an advertisement to which Part IV applies.

(2) Sections 44, 46 and 47 apply to an advertisement, published for the purposes of a business carried on by the advertiser, indicating that he is willing to advise on debts, or engage in transactions concerned with the liquidation of debts, as they apply to an advertisement to which Part IV applies.

(3) The Secretary of State may by order provide that an advertisement published for the purposes of a business of credit brokerage, debt adjusting or debt counselling shall not fall within subsection (1) or (2) if it is of a description specified in the order.

(4) An advertisement does not fall within subsection (2) if it indicates that the advertiser is not willing to act in relation to consumer credit agreements and consumer hire agreements.

(5) In subsections (1) and (3) "credit brokerage" includes the effecting of introductions of individuals desiring to obtain credit to any person carrying on a business in the course of which he provides credit secured on land. [**C.151**]

COMMENCEMENT
See Sch. 3, para. 47, *post*, and the note "Appointed days" to Part X of that Schedule.

CARRIED ON
See the note "Carry on business" to s. 24, *ante*.

PERSON
See the note to s. 8, *ante*.

PART IV
I.e., ss. 43–54, *ante*.

DEFINITIONS
For "advertisement", "advertiser", "business", "individual" and "land", see s. 189 (1), *post*.

For "consumer credit agreement", see s. 8 (1), *ante*, and for "consumer hire agreement", see s. 15, *ante*. For "credit", see s. 9, *ante*. For "credit brokerage", see s. 145 (2), *ante*, with sub-s. (5) above. For "debt-adjusting" and "debt-counselling", see s. 145 (5), (6), *ante*.

ORDERS UNDER THIS SECTION
No orders had been made under sub-s. (3) above up to the time of going to press.

For general provisions as to orders under this Act, see s. 182 (1), (2), (4), *post*.

## 152. Application of sections 52 to 54 to credit brokerage etc.

(1) Sections 52 to 54 apply to a business of credit brokerage, debt-adjusting or debt-counselling as they apply to a consumer credit business.

(2) In their application to a business of credit brokerage, sections 52 and 53 shall apply to the giving of quotations and information about the business of any person to whom the credit-broker effects introductions as well as to the giving of quotations and information about his own business. [**C.152**]

PERSON
See the note to s. 8, *ante*.

DEFINITIONS
For "business", "consumer credit business" and "credit-broker", see s. 189 (1), *post*. For "credit brokerage", "debt-adjusting" and "debt-counselling", see s. 145 (2)–(6), *ante*.

## 153. Definition of canvassing off trade premises (agreements for ancillary credit services)

(1) An individual (the "canvasser") canvasses off trade premises the services of a person carrying on an ancillary credit business if he solicits the entry of another individual (the "consumer") into an agreement for the provision to the consumer of those services by making oral representations to the consumer, or any other individual, during a visit by the canvasser to any place (not excluded by subsection (2)) where the consumer, or that other individual, as the case may be, is, being a visit—

(*a*) carried out for the purpose of making such oral representations to individuals who are at that place, but

(*b*) not carried out in response to a request made on a previous occasion.

(2) A place is excluded from subsection (1) if it is a place where (whether on a permanent or temporary basis)—

(*a*) the ancillary credit business is carried on, or

(*b*) any business is carried on by the canvasser or the person whose employee or agent the canvasser is, or by the consumer. [**C.153**]

PERSON
See the note to s. 8, *ante*.

CARRYING ON; CARRIED ON
See the note "Carry on business" to s. 24, *ante*.

OFFENCE
It is an offence to canvass the services of certain persons off trade premises; see s. 154, *post*.

DEFINITIONS
For "ancillary credit business", see s. 145, *ante*.
For "business" and "individual", see s. 189 (1), *post*.

## 154. Prohibition of canvassing certain ancillary credit services off trade premises

It is an offence to canvass off trade premises the services of a person carrying on a business of credit-brokerage, debt-adjusting or debt-counselling. [**C.154**]

OFFENCE
As to notification of convictions to the Director, see s. 166, *post*. For penalties and mode of prosecution, see s. 167 (1) and Sch. 1, *post*. For special defences, see s. 168, *post*. As to offences by bodies corporate, see s. 169, *post*.

DEFINITIONS
For "business", see s. 189 (1), *post*. For "canvass off trade premises", see s. 153, *ante*.
For "credit brokerage", "debt-adjusting" and "debt-counselling", see s. 145 (2)–(6), *ante*.

**155. Right to recover brokerage fees**

(1) The excess over £1 of a fee or commission for his services charged by a credit-broker to an individual to whom this subsection applies shall cease to be payable or, as the case may be, shall be recoverable by the individual if the introduction does not result in his entering into a relevant agreement within the six months following the introduction (disregarding any agreement which is cancelled under section 69 (1) or becomes subject to section 69 (2)).

(2) Subsection (1) applies to an individual who sought an introduction for a purpose which would have been fulfilled by his entry into—

(*a*) a regulated agreement, or

(*b*) in the case of an individual such as is referred to in section 145 (2) (*a*) (ii), an agreement for credit secured on land, or

(*c*) an agreement such as is referred to in section 145 (3) (*b*) or (*c*) or (4) (*b*).

(3) An agreement is a relevant agreement for the purposes of subsection (1) in relation to an individual if it is an agreement such as is referred to in subsection (2) in relation to that individual.

(4) In the case of an individual desiring to obtain credit under a consumer credit agreement, any sum payable or paid by him to a credit-broker otherwise than as a fee or commission for the credit-broker's services shall for the purposes of subsection (1) be treated as such a fee or commission if it enters, or would enter, into the total charge for credit. **[C.155]**

PROHIBITION OF CONTRACTING OUT
See the note to s. 56, *ante.*

£1
This amount is subject to amendment by order under s. 181 (1), *post.*

WITHIN THE SIX MONTHS FOLLOWING
I.e., calendar months (Interpretation Act 1889, s. 3 (32 Halsbury's Statutes (3rd edn.) 436), the date of the introduction being excluded from the computation (*Goldsmiths' Co.* v. *West Metropolitan Rail. Co.*, [1904] 1 K.B. 1; [1900–3] All E.R. Rep. 667).

DEFINITIONS
For "consumer credit agreement", see s. 8 (1), *ante,* and for "consumer hire agreement", see s. 15, *ante.* For "credit", see s. 9, *ante.* For "credit-broker", "goods", "individual" and "total charge for credit", see s. 189 (1), *post.*

*Entry into agreements*

**156. Entry into agreements**

Regulations may make provision, in relation to agreements entered into in the course of a business of credit brokerage, debt-adjusting or debt-counselling, corresponding, with such modifidations as the Secretary of State thinks fit, to the provision which is or may be made by or under sections 55, 60, 61, 62, 63, 65, 127, 179 or 180 in relation to agreements to which those sections apply. **[C.156]**

DEFINITIONS
For "business" and "regulations", see s. 189 (1), *post.*
For "credit brokerage", "debt-adjusting" and "debt-counselling", see s. 145 (2)–(6), *ante.*

REGULATIONS UNDER THIS SECTION

No regulations had been made under this section up to the time of going to press.

For general provisions as to regulations under this Act, see s. 181 (1)–(3), *post*.

*Credit reference agencies*

## 157. Duty to disclose name etc. of agency

(1) A creditor, owner or negotiator, within the prescribed period after receiving a request in writing to that effect from the debtor or hirer, shall give him notice of the name and address of any credit reference agency from which the creditor, owner or negotiator has, during the antecedent negotiations, applied for information about his financial standing.

(2) Subsection (1) does not apply to a request received more than 28 days after the termination of the antecedent negotiations, whether on the making of the regulated agreement or otherwise.

(3) If the creditor, owner or negotiator fails to comply with subsection (1) he commits an offence. **[C.157]**

COMMENCEMENT

See Sch. 3, para. 48, *post*, and the note "Appointed days" to Part X of that Schedule.

PRESCRIBED PERIOD

I.e., prescribed by regulations; see s. 189 (1), *post*. Nothing had been prescribed for the purposes of sub-s. (1) above up to the time of going to press.

WRITING

See the note to s. 6, *ante*.

SHALL GIVE

It is thought that criminal proceedings under sub-s. (3) above are the only remedy for non-compliance, subject to the court's power to grant a mandatory injunction (see s. 170 (1), (3)).

28 DAYS AFTER

Cf. the note "Within 21 days" to s. 36, *ante*.

OFFENCE

As to notification of convictions to the Director, see s. 166, *post*. For penalties and mode of prosecution, see s. 167 (1) and Sch. 1, *post*. For special defences, see s.168, *post*. As to offences by bodies corporate, see s. 169, *post*.

DEFINITIONS

For "antecedent negotiations" and "negotiator", see s. 56 (1), *ante*.

For "creditor", "debtor", "give", "hirer", "notice", "owner" and "regulated agreement", see s. 189 (1), *post*.

For "credit reference agency", see s. 145 (8), *ante*.

## 158 Duty of agency to disclose filed information

(1) A credit reference agency, within the prescribed period after receiving—

(*a*) a request in writing to that effect from any individual (the "consumer") and

(*b*) such particulars as the agency may reasonably require to enable them to identify the file, and

(*c*) a fee of 25 new pence,

shall give the consumer a copy of the file relating to him kept by the agency.

(2) When giving a copy of the file under subsection (1), the agency shall also give the consumer a statement in the prescribed form of his rights under section 159.

(3) If the agency does not keep a file relating to the consumer it shall give him notice of that fact, but need not return any money paid.

(4) If the agency contravenes any provision of this section it commits an offence.

(5) In this Act "file", in relation to an individual, means all the information about him kept by a credit reference agency, regardless of how the information is stored and "copy of the file", as respects information not in plain English, means a transcript reduced into plain English. [**C.158**]

COMMENCEMENT
See Sch. 3, para. 48, *post*, and the note "Appointed days" to Part X of that Schedule.

PRESCRIBED PERIOD; PRESCRIBED FORM
I.e., prescribed by regulations; see s. 189 (1), *post*. Nothing had been prescribed for the purposes of sub-s. (1) or (2) above up to the time of going to press.

WRITING
See the note to s. 6, *ante*.

25 NEW PENCE
This amount is subject to amendment by order under s. 181 (1), *post*.

SHALL GIVE
It is thought that criminal proceedings under sub-s. (4) above are the only remedy for non-compliance; see s. 170 (1), *post*.

OFFENCE
See the note to s. 157, *ante*.

FURTHER RIGHTS OF CONSUMER
For the right of the consumer to require the correction of wrong information, see s. 159, *post*.

DEFINITIONS
For "credit reference agency", see s. 145 (8), *ante*.
For "give" and "individual", see s. 189 (1), *post*.
For "consumer", "copy" and "file", see sub-ss. (1), (5), above.

## 159. Correction of wrong information

(1) A consumer given information under section 158 who considers that an entry in his file is incorrect, and that if it is not corrected he is likely to be prejudiced, may give notice to the agency requiring it either to remove the entry from the file or amend it.

(2) Within 28 days after receiving a notice under subsection (1), the agency shall by notice inform the consumer that it has—

(*a*) removed the entry from the file, or
(*b*) amended the entry, or
(*c*) taken no action,

and if the notice states that the agency has amended the entry it shall include a copy of the file so far as it comprises the amended entry.

(3) Within 28 days after receiving a notice under subsection (2) or, where no

such notice was given, within 28 days after the expiry of the period mentioned in subsection (2), the consumer may, unless he has been informed by the agency that it has removed the entry from his file, serve a further notice on the agency requiring it to add to the file an accompanying notice of correction (not exceeding 200 words) drawn up by the consumer, and include a copy of it when furnishing information included in or based on that entry.

(4) Within 28 days after receiving a notice under subsection (3), the agency, unless it intends to apply to the Director under subsection (5), shall by notice inform the consumer that it has received the notice under subsection (3) and intends to comply with it.

(5) If—

(*a*) the consumer has not received a notice under subsection (4) within the time required, or

(*b*) it appears to the agency that it would be improper for it to publish a notice of correction because it is incorrect, or unjustly defames any person, or is frivolous or scandalous, or is for any other reason unsuitable,

the consumer or, as the case may be, the agency may, in the prescribed manner and on payment of the specified fee, apply to the Director, who may make such order on the application as he thinks fit.

(6) If a person to whom an order under this section is directed fails to comply with it within the period specified in the order he commits an offence. **[C.159]**

THE AGENCY
I.e., a credit reference agency to which a request under s. 158, *ante*, has been directed.

WITHIN 28 DAYS
See the note "Within 21 days" to s. 36, *ante*.

SHALL . . . INFORM
In view of the provisions of s. 170 (1), *post*, it is thought that the consumer's only remedies for non-compliance with sub-s. (2) or (4) are further proceedings as provided for by sub-ss. (3) and (5) respectively.

SERVE
For provisions as to the service of documents, see s. 176, *post*. See also the definition in s. 189 (1), *post*.

PRESCRIBED MANNER
I.e., prescribed by regulations; see s. 189 (1), *post*. Nothing had been prescribed for the purposes of sub-s. (5) above up to the time of going to press.

SPECIFIED FEE
I.e., specified by the Director under s. 6, *ante*. See that section generally as to applications to the Director.

OFFENCE
See the note to s. 157, *ante*.

PERSON
See the note to s. 7, *ante*.

DEFINITIONS
For "consumer", "copy" and "file", see s. 158 (1), (5), *ante*.
For "Director", "give" and "notice", see s. 189 (1), *post*.

**160. Alternative procedure for business consumers**

(1) The Director, on an application made by a credit reference agency, may direct that this section shall apply to the agency if he is satisfied—

(*a*) that compliance with section 158 in the case of consumers who carry on a business would adversely affect the service provided to its customers by the agency, and

(*b*) that, having regard to the methods employed by the agency and to any other relevant factors, it is probable that consumers carrying on a business would not be prejudiced by the making of the direction.

(2) Where an agency to which this section applies receives a request, particulars and a fee under section 158 (1) from a consumer who carries on a business, and section 158 (3) does not apply, the agency, instead of complying with section 158, may elect to deal with the matter under the following subsections.

(3) Instead of giving the consumer a copy of the file, the agency shall within the prescribed period give notice to the consumer that it is proceeding under this section, and by notice give the consumer such information included in or based on entries in the file as the Director may direct, together with a statement in the prescribed form of the consumer's rights under subsections (4) and (5).

(4) If within 28 days after receiving the information given him under subsection (3), or such longer period as the Director may allow, the consumer—

(*a*) gives notice to the Director that he is dissatisfied with the information, and

(*b*) satisfies the Director that he has taken such steps in relation to the agency as may be reasonable with a view to removing the cause of his dissatisfaction, and

(*c*) pays the Director the specified fee,

the Director may direct the agency to give the Director a copy of the file, and the Director may disclose to the consumer such of the information on the file as the Director thinks fit.

(5) Section 159 applies with any necessary modifications to information given to the consumer under this section as it applies to information given under section 158.

(6) If an agency making an election under subsection (2) fails to comply with subsection (3) or (4) it commits an offence. [**C.160**]

PRESCRIBED

I.e., prescribed by regulations; see s. 189 (1), *post*. Nothing had been prescribed for the purposes of this section up to the time of going to press.

WITHIN 28 DAYS

See the note to s. 36, *ante*.

OFFENCE

See the note to s. 157, *ante*.

DEFINITIONS

For "business" and "Director", see s. 189 (1), *post*.
For "consumer", "copy" and "file", see s. 158 (1), (5), *ante*.
For "credit reference agency", see s. 145 (8), *ante*.

## Part XI

### Enforcement of Act

**161. Enforcement authorities**

(1) The following authorities ("enforcement authorities") have a duty to enforce this Act and regulations made under it—

(*a*) the Director,

(*b*) in Great Britain, the local weights and measures authority,

(*c*) in Northern Ireland, the Department of Commerce for Northern Ireland.

(2) Where a local weights and measures authority in England or Wales propose to institute proceedings for an offence under this Act (other than an offence under section 162 (6), 165 (1) or (2) or 174 (5)) it shall, as between the authority and the Director, be the duty of the authority to give the Director notice of the intended proceedings, together with a summary of the facts on which the charges are to be founded, and postpone institution of the proceedings until either—

(*a*) 28 days have expired since that notice was given, or

(*b*) the Director has notified them of receipt of the notice and summary.

(3) Every local weights and measures authority shall, whenever the Director requires, report to him in such form and with such particulars as he requires on the exercise of their functions under this Act.

(4) Where a complaint is made to the Secretary of State that all or any of the functions of a local weights and measures authority under this Act are not being properly discharged in any area, or he is of the opinion that an investigation should be made relating to the proper discharge of those functions in any area, he may cause a local inquiry to be held, and section 250 (2) to (5) of the Local Government Act 1972 (evidence and costs at local inquiries), but subsection (4) (costs of department) of that section only in a case where the Secretary of State so directs, shall apply as if the inquiry were held in pursuance of section 250 (1) of that Act.

(5) The person holding an inquiry under subsection (4) shall make a written report of the results to the Secretary of State, who shall publish it together with such observations on it (if any) as he thinks fit.

(6) In the application of subsection (4) to Scotland, for the references to section 250 (2) to (5) of the Local Government Act 1972, subsection (4) of that section and section 250 (1) of that Act there shall be substituted respectively references to section 210 (4) to (8) of the Local Government (Scotland) Act 1973, subsection (7) of that section and section 210 (1) of that Act. **[C.161]**

LOCAL WEIGHTS AND MEASURES AUTHORITY

For the authorities on whom this function is conferred in England and Wales, see the Local Government Act 1972, s. 201 (2) (42 Halsbury's Statutes (3rd edn.) 1030).

FURTHER PROVISIONS

For power of entry, search and seizure of goods and documents by officers of enforcement authorities, see s. 162, *post*. For power to make test purchases, etc., see s. 164, *post*. As to obstruction of authorised officers, see s. 165, *post*.

LOCAL GOVERNMENT ACT 1972, S. 250
See 42 Halsbury's Statutes (3rd edn.) 1974.

## 162. Powers of entry and inspection

(1) A duly authorised officer of an enforcement authority, at all reasonable hours and on production, if required, of his credentials, may—

(*a*) in order to ascertain whether a breach of any provision of or under this Act has been committed, inspect any goods and enter any premises (other than premises used only as a dwelling);

(*b*) if he has reasonable cause to suspect that a breach of any provision of or under this Act has been committed, in order to ascertain whether it has been committed, require any person—

(i) carrying on, or employed in connection with, a business to produce any books or documents relating to it; or

(ii) having control of any information relating to a business recorded otherwise than in a legible form to provide a document containing a legible reproduction of the whole or any part of the information,

and take copies of, or of any entry in, the books or documents;

(*c*) if he has reasonable cause to believe that a breach of any provision of or under this Act has been committed, seize and detain any goods in order to ascertain (by testing or otherwise) whether such a breach has been committed;

(*d*) seize and detain any goods, books or documents which he has reason to believe may be required as evidence in proceedings for an offence under this Act;

(*e*) for the purpose of exercising his powers under this subsection to seize goods, books or documents, but only if and to the extent that it is reasonably necessary for securing that the provisions of this Act and of any regulations made under it are duly observed, require any person having authority to do so to break open any container and, if that person does not comply, break it open himself.

(2) An officer seizing goods, books or documents in exercise of his powers under this section shall not do so without informing the person he seizes them from.

(3) If a justice of the peace, on sworn information in writing, or, in Scotland, a sheriff or a magistrate or justice of the peace, on evidence on oath,—

(*a*) is satisfied that there is reasonable ground to believe either—

(i) that any goods, books or documents which a duly authorised officer has power to inspect under this section are on any premises and their inspection is likely to disclose evidence of a breach of any provision of or under this Act; or

(ii) that a breach of any provision of or under this Act has been, is being or is about to be committed on any premises; and

(*b*) is also satisfied either—

(i) that admission to the premises has been or is likely to be refused and that notice of intention to apply for a warrant under this subsection has been given to the occupier; or

(ii) that an application for admission, or the giving of such a notice, would defeat the object of the entry or that the premises are unoccupied or that the occupier is temporarily absent and it might defeat the object of the entry to wait for his return,

the justice or, as the case may be, the sheriff or magistrate may by warrant under his hand, which shall continue in force for a period of one month, authorise an officer of an enforcement authority to enter the premises (by force if need be).

(4) An officer entering premises by virtue of this section may take such other persons and equipment with him as he thinks necessary; and on leaving premises entered by virtue of a warrant under subsection (3) shall, if they are unoccupied or the occupier is temporarily absent, leave them as effectively secured against trespassers as he found them.

(5) Regulations may provide that, in cases described by the regulations, an officer of a local weights and measures authority is not to be taken to be duly authorised for the purposes of this section unless he is authorised by the Director.

(6) A person who is not a duly authorised officer of an enforcement authority, but purports to act as such under this section, commits an offence.

(7) Nothing in this section compels a barrister, advocate or solicitor to produce a document containing a privileged communication made by or to him in that capacity or authorises the seizing of any such document in his possession. **[C.162]**

SUB-S. (1): SEIZE AND DETAIN

As to compensation for loss suffered by the owner of goods seized, see s. 163, *post*. For power to test such goods, see s. 164 (3), *post*.

SUB-S. (3): WRITING

See the note to s. 6, *ante*.

SUB-S. (5): LOCAL WEIGHTS AND MEASURES AUTHORITY

See the note to s. 161, *ante*.

SUB-S. (6): OFFENCE

As to notification of convictions to the Director, see s. 166, *post*. For penalties and mode of prosecution, see s. 167 (1) and Sch. 1, *post*. For special defences, see s. 168, *post*. As to offences by bodies corporate, see s. 169, *post*.

SUB-S. (7): ADVOCATE

This term applies to Scotland.

PRIVILEGED COMMUNICATION

As to legal professional privilege, see 12 Halsbury's Laws (3rd edn.) 39.

OBSTRUCTION AND NON-COMPLIANCE

As to the offences of obstructing an authorised officer and wilfully failing to comply with requirements under this section, see s. 165, *post*.

PROHIBITION OF DISCLOSURE

Information obtained under this Act may not be disclosed without consent, except for particular purposes; see s. 174, *post*.

DEFINITIONS

For "enforcement authority", see s. 181 (1), *ante*.
For "goods" and "regulations", see s. 189 (1), *post*.

REGULATIONS UNDER THIS SECTION

No regulations had been made for the purposes of sub-s. (5) above up to the time of going to press.

For general provisions as to regulations under this Act, see s. 182 (1)–(3), *post.*

### 163. Compensation for loss

(1) Where, in exercising his powers under section 162, an officer of an enforcement authority seizes and detains goods and their owner suffers loss by reason of—

(*a*) that seizure, or

(*b*) the loss, damage or deterioration of the goods during detention,

then, unless the owner is convicted of an offence under this Act committed in relation to the goods, the authority shall compensate him for the loss so suffered.

(2) Any dispute as to the right to or amount of any compensation under subsection (1) shall be determined by arbitration. **[C.163]**

ARBITRATION

With certain exceptions, Part I of the Arbitration Act 1950 applies; see s. 31 of that Act (2 Halsbury's Statutes (3rd edn.) 459).

DEFINITIONS

For "enforcement authority", see s. 161 (1), *ante.*

For "goods", see s. 189 (1), *post.*

### 164. Power to make test purchases etc.

(1) An enforcement authority may—

(*a*) make, or authorise any of their officers to make on their behalf, such purchases of goods; and

(*b*) authorise any of their officers to procure the provision of such services or facilities or to enter into such agreements or other transactions,

as may appear to them expedient for determining whether any provisions made by or under this Act are being complied with.

(2) Any act done by an officer authorised to do it under subsection (1) shall be treated for the purposes of this Act as done by him as an individual on his own behalf.

(3) Any goods seized by an officer under this Act may be tested, and in the event of such a test he shall inform the person mentioned in section 162 (2) of the test results.

(4) Where any test leads to proceedings under this Act, the enforcement authority shall—

(*a*) if the goods were purchased, inform the person they were purchased from of the test results, and

(*b*) allow any person against whom the proceedings are taken to have the goods tested on his behalf if it is reasonably practicable to do so. **[C.164]**

TREATED . . . AS DONE BY HIM AS AN INDIVIDUAL

The significance of this provision is that if any agreement entered into by the officer were to be treated as entered into by him as an agent of the enforcement authority, the agreement could not be a consumer credit agreement or a consumer hire agreement (see the definitions in ss. 8, 15, *ante*).

DEFINITIONS

For "enforcement authority", see s. 161 (1), *ante*.

For "goods" and "individual", see s. 189 (1), *post*.

## 165. Obstruction of authorised officers

(1) Any person who—

(*a*) wilfully obstructs an officer of an enforcement authority acting in pursuance of this Act; or

(*b*) wilfully fails to comply with any requirement properly made to him by such an officer under section 162; or

(*c*) without reasonable cause fails to give such an officer (so acting) other assistance or information he may reasonably require in performing his functions under this Act,

commits an offence.

(2) If any person, in giving such information as is mentioned in subsection (1) (*c*), makes any statement which he knows to be false, he commits an offence.

(3) Nothing in this section requires a person to answer any question or give any information if to do so might incriminate that person or (where that person is married) the husband or wife of that person. **[C.165]**

PERSON

See the note to s. 7, *ante*.

WILLFULY OBSTRUCTS

Obstruction need not involve physical violence; see, in particular, *Borrow* v. *Howland* (1896), 74 L.T. 787, and *Hinchcliffe* v. *Sheldon*, [1955] 3 All E.R. 406. In fact there is authority for saying that anything which makes it more difficult for a person to carry out his duty amounts to obstruction; see *Hinchcliffe* v. *Sheldon*, *supra*. Yet standing by and doing nothing is not obstruction unless there is a legal duty to act; see *Swallow* v. *London County Council*, [1916] 1 K.B. 224; [1914–15] All E.R. Rep. 403; and contrast *Baker* v. *Ellison*, [1914] 2 K.B. 762; but see *Rice* v. *Connolly*, [1966] 2 Q.B. 414; [1966] 2 All E.R. 649. However, a positive act does not cease to be obstructive just because it is lawful in itself; see *Ingleton* v. *Dibble*, [1972] 1 All E.R. 275.

Obstruction must, however, to be an offence under this section, be wilful; and an act is done wilfully if it is deliberate and intentional, not accidental or inadvertent, but so that the mind of the person who does the act goes with it; see *R.* v. *Senior*, [1899] 1 Q.B. 283; [1895–9] All E.R. Rep. 511, *per* Lord Russell of Killowen, at pp. 290, 291 and p. 514, respectively. See also *R.* v. *Walker* (1934), 24 Cr. App. Rep. 117; *Eaton* v. *Cobb*, [1950] 1 All E.R. 1016; *Arrowsmith* v. *Jenkins*, [1963] 2 Q.B. 561; [1963] 2 All E.R. 210; *Rice* v. *Connolly*, *supra*; and *Ingleton* v. *Dibble*, *supra*.

ENFORCEMENT AUTHORITY

For meaning, see s. 161 (1), *ante*.

KNOWS

See the note "Knowingly" to s. 7, *ante*.

FALSE

See the note to s. 7, *ante*.

OFFENCE

As to notification of convictions to the Director, see s. 166, *post*. For penalties and mode of prosecution, see s. 167 (1) and Sch. 1, *post*. For special defences, see s. 168, *post*. As to offences by bodies corporate, see s. 169, *post*.

INCRIMINATE

For cases on the common-law privilege against self-incrimination, see 12 Halsbury's Laws (3rd edn.) 50.

HUSBAND; WIFE

There is nothing to suggest that these words are intended to include anyone other than a party to a marriage recognised by the law. If an alleged marriage took place in England, it must comply with the relevant statutes (in particular, the Marriage Act 1949 (17 Halsbury's Statutes (3rd edn.) 44). If it took place elsewhere, it must comply as to formalities with the law of the place of celebration and as to substantial validity with the law of the parties' domicile (see 7 Halsbury's Laws (3rd edn.) 91–94) or alternatively with the Foreign Marriage Acts 1892 to 1947 (17 Halsbury's Statutes (3rd edn.) 16 *et seq.*).

It has in the past been held that polygamy is so fundamentally contrary to the policy of the English Law that a polygamous marriage will never be recognised, even though valid by the laws of the place of celebration and of the parties' domicile (see, e.g., *Hyde* v. *Hyde and Woodmansee* (1866) L.R. 1 P. & D. 130). The Matrimonial Proceedings (Polygamous Marriages) Act 1972 (42 Halsbury's Statutes (3rd Edn.) 760) now affords recognition for some purposes to such marriages. Though the Act of 1972 does not expressly affect the construction of a provision such as sub-s. (3) above, it may be that the courts will now take a different view of the questions of public policy involved and will give general recognition to foreign polygamous marriages which satisfy the general rules for the recognition of foreign marriages.

## 166. Notification of convictions and judgments to Director

Where a person is convicted of an offence or has a judgment given against him by or before any court in the United Kingdom and it appears to the court—

(*a*) having regard to the functions of the Director under this Act, that the conviction or judgment should be brought to the Director's attention, and

(*b*) that it may not be brought to his attention unless arrangements for that purpose are made by the court,

the court may make such arrangements notwithstanding that the proceedings have been finally disposed of. **[C.166]**

PERSON

See the note to s. 8, *ante*.

UNITED KINGDOM

I.e., Great Britain and Northern Ireland; see the Royal and Parliamentary Titles Act 1927 (6 Halsbury's Statutes (3rd edn.) 520).

DIRECTOR

For meaning, see s. 189 (1), *post*.

## 167. Penalties

(1) An offence under a provision of this Act specified in column 1 of Schedule 1 is triable in the mode or modes indicated in column 3, and on conviction is punishable as indicated in column 4 (where a period of time indicates the maximum term of imprisonment, and a monetary amount indicates the maximum fine, for the offence in question).

(2) A person who contravenes any regulations made under section 44, 52, 53, or 112, or made under section 26 by virtue of section 54, commits an offence. **[C.167]**

**168. Defences**

(1) In any proceedings for an offence under this Act it is a defence for the person charged to prove—

(*a*) that his act or omission was due to a mistake, or to reliance on information supplied to him, or to an act or omission by another person, or to an accident or some other cause beyond his control, and

(*b*) that he took all reasonable precautions and exercised all due diligence to avoid such an act or omission by himself or any person under his control.

(2) If in any case the defence provided by subsection (1) involves the allegation that the act or omission was due to an act or omission by another person or to reliance on information supplied by another person, the person charged shall not, without leave of the court, be entitled to rely on that defence unless, within a period ending seven clear days before the hearing, he has served on the prosecutor a notice giving such information identifying or assisting in the identification of that other person as was then in his possession. **[C.168]**

IT IS A DEFENCE
See the note to s. 47, *ante*.

PERSON
See the note to s. 7, *ante*.

MISTAKE
It is thought that this must mean a mistaken belief in a state of facts which, if true, would have rendered the defendant's conduct lawful; cf. the authorities on mistake as a defence at common law, discussed in 10 Halsbury's Laws (3rd edn.) 284.

ACT OR OMISSION BY ANOTHER PERSON
It has been held that the words "act or default" in a similar provision mean only a wrongful act or default; see *Noss Farm Products Ltd.* v. *Lilico*, [1945] 2 All E.R. 609. The present provision may, however, be distinguishable in that it contains no requirement that an information should be laid against the other person. A manager employed by the defendant may be "another person" for the purposes of this section; see *Tesco Supermarkets, Ltd.* v. *Nattrass*, [1972] A.C. 153; [1971] 2 All E.R. 127.

ALL DUE DILIGENCE
In the case of a large firm, if an adequate system for avoiding contraventions has been adopted by senior management, the firm may succeed in proving that it exercised all due diligence, notwithstanding a failure of supervision on the part of a junior manager; see *Tesco Supermarkets, Ltd.* v. *Nattrass*, [1972] A.C. 153; [1971] 2 All E.R. 127.

SERVED
For provisions as to the service of documents, see s. 176, *post*. See also the definition in s. 189 (1), *post*.

NOTICE
For meaning, see s. 189 (1), *post*.

**169. Offences by bodies corporate**

Where at any time a body corporate commits an offence under this Act with the consent or connivance of, or because of neglect by, any individual, the individual commits the like offence if at that time—

(*a*) he is a director, manager, secretary or similar officer of the body corporate, or (*b*) he is purporting to act as such an officer, or

(*c*) the body corporate is managed by its members, of whom he is one. **[C.169]**

BODY CORPORATE COMMITS

Where an offence is committed by an agent of a corporation under such circumstances that his act and his knowledge or intent can be said to be those of the corporation, the offence is committed by the corporation; see *Director of Public Prosecutions* v. *Kent and Sussex Contractors, Ltd.*, [1944] K.B. 146; [1944] 1 All E.R. 110, and *R.* v. *I.C.R. Haulage, Ltd.*, [1944] K.B. 551; [1944] 1 All E.R. 691.

CONSENT

There is authority for saying that this presupposes knowledge: see *Re Caughey, Ex parte Ford* (1876), 1 Ch. D. 521, C.A., at p. 528, *per* Jessel, M.R., and *Lamb* v. *Wright & Co.*, [1924] 1 K.B. 857; [1924] All E.R. Rep. 220, at p. 864 and p. 223, respectively. It is thought, however, that actual knowledge is not necessary; cf. *Knox* v. *Boyd*, [1941] S.C. (J.) 82, at p. 86, and *Taylor's Central Garages* (*Exeter*), *Ltd.* v. *Roper* (1951), 115 J.P. 445, at pp. 449, 450, *per* Devlin, J.; and see also, in particular, *Mallon* v. *Allon*, [1963] 3 All E.R. 843; [1964] 1 Q.B. 385, at p. 847 and p. 394, respectively.

CONNIVANCE

There are many decisions on the meaning of this word in matrimonial law, see *Godfrey* v. *Godfrey*, [1965] A.C. 444; [1964] 3 All E.R. 154, H.L., especially the speech of Lord Guest, in which earlier decisions are reviewed. It would seem that an element of encouragement is essential. The word has been used in a number of statutes in the same context as in this section, but there is little authority as to its meaning in this context. See Glanville Williams *Criminal Law: The General Part*, para. 222, and *Gregory* v. *Walker* (1912), 77 J.P. 55; 29 T.L.R. 51.

NEGLECT

This term, in the words of Simonds, J. (as he then was) in *Re Hughes, Rea* v. *Black*, [1943] Ch. 296; [1943] 2 All E.R. 269, at p. 298 and p. 271, respectively, "in its legal connotation implies failure to perform a duty of which the person knows or ought to know." This, it is thought, is also the meaning that the expression has in the present context.

## 170. No further sanctions for breach of Act

(1) A breach of any requirement made (otherwise than by any court) by or under this Act shall incur no civil or criminal sanction as being such a breach, except to the extent (if any) expressly provided by or under this Act.

(2) In exercising his functions under this Act the Director may take account of any matter appearing to him to constitute a breach of a requirement made by or under this Act, whether or not any sanction for that breach is provided by or under this Act and, if it is so provided, whether or not proceedings have been brought in respect of the breach.

(3) Subsection (1) does not prevent the grant of an injunction, or the making of an order of certiorari, mandamus or prohibition or as respects Scotland the grant of an interdict or of an order under section 91 of the Court of Session Act 1868 (order for specific performance of statutory duty). **[C.170]**

FUNCTIONS UNDER THIS ACT

For functions to which the provisions of sub-s. (2) may be particularly relevant, see ss. 25, 31, 32, 40 (2) and 149 (2), *ante*.

DIRECTOR

For meaning, see s. 189 (1), *post*.

INJUNCTION
As to injunction as a remedy for contraventions of statutory duties, see 32 Halsbury's Statutes (3rd edn.) 402.

COURT OF SESSION ACT 1868
31 & 32 Vict. c. 100.

**171. Onus of proof in various proceedings**

(1) If an agreement contains a term signifying that in the opinion of the parties section 10 (3) (*b*) (iii) does not apply to the agreement, it shall be taken not to apply unless the contrary is proved.

(2) It shall be assumed in any proceedings, unless the contrary is proved, that when a person initiated a transaction as mentioned in section 19 (1) (*c*) he knew the principal agreement had been made, or contemplated that it might be made.

(3) Regulations under section 44 or 52 may make provision as to the onus of proof in any proceedings to enforce the regulations.

(4) In proceedings brought by the creditor under a credit-token agreement—

(*a*) it is for the creditor to prove that the credit-token was lawfully supplied to the debtor, and was accepted by him, and

(*b*) if the debtor alleges that any use made of the credit-token was not authorised by him, it is for the creditor to prove either—

(i) that the use was so authorised, or

(ii) that the use occurred before the creditor had been given notice under section 84 (3).

(5) In proceedings under section 50 (1) in respect of a document received by a minor at any school or other educational establishment for minors, it is for the person sending it to him at that establishment to prove that he did not know or suspect it to be such an establishment.

(6) In proceedings under section 119 (1) it is for the pawnee to prove that he had reasonable cause to refuse to allow the pawn to be redeemed.

(7) If, in proceedings referred to in section 139 (1), the debtor or any surety alleges that the credit bargain is extortionate it is for the creditor to prove the contrary. [C.171]

PERSON
See the note to s. 8, *ante*.

DEFINITIONS
For "creditor", "credit-token agreement", "debtor", "pawn", "pawnee" and "regulations", see s. 189 (1), *post*.
For "credit bargain", see s. 137 (2), *ante*.
For "credit-token", see s. 14 (1), *ante*.
For "principal agreement", see s. 19 (1), *ante*.

**172. Statements by creditor or owner to be binding**

(1) A statement by a creditor or owner is binding on him if given under—

section 77 (1),
section 78 (1),

section 79 (1),
section 97 (1),
section 107 (1) (*c*),
section 108 (1) (*c*), or
section 109 (1) (*c*).

(2) Where a trader—

(*a*) gives a customer a notice in compliance with section 103 (1) (*b*), or

(*b*) gives a customer a notice under section 103 (1) asserting that the customer is not indebted to him under an agreement,

the notice is binding on the trader.

(3) Where in proceedings before any court—

(*a*) it is sought to rely on a statement or notice given as mentioned in subsection (1) or (2), and

(*b*) the statement or notice is shown to be incorrect,

the court may direct such relief (if any) to be given to the creditor or owner from the operation of subsection (1) or (2) as appears to the court to be just. [**C.172**]

DEFINITIONS

For "creditor" and "owner", see s. 189 (1), *post*. For "trader", see s. 103 (1), *ante*.

### 173. Contracting-out forbidden

(1) A term contained in a regulated agreement or linked transaction, or in any other agreement relating to an actual or prospective regulated agreement or linked transaction, is void if, and to the extent that, it is inconsistent with a provision for the protection of the debtor or hirer or his relative or any surety contained in this Act or in any regulation made under this Act.

(2) Where a provision specifies the duty or liability of the debtor or hirer or his relative or any surety in certain circumstances, a term is inconsistent with that provision if it purports to impose, directly or indirectly, an additional duty or liability on him in those circumstances.

(3) Notwithstanding subsection (1), a provision of this Act under which a thing may be done in relation to any person on an order of the court or the Director only shall not be taken to prevent its being done at any time, with that person's consent given at that time but the refusal of such consent shall not give rise to any liability. [**C.173**]

DEFINITIONS

For "court", "debtor", "Director", "hirer", "regulated agreement", "regulation" "relative" and "surety", see s. 189 (1), *post*.

For "linked transaction", see s. 19 (1), *ante*.

## Part XII

## Supplemental

### 174. Restrictions on disclosure of information

(1) No information obtained under or by virtue of this Act about any individual shall be disclosed without his consent.

(2) No information obtained under or by virtue of this Act about any business shall be disclosed except, so long as the business continues to be carried on, with the consent of the person for the time being carrying it on.

(3) Subsections (1) and (2) do not apply to any disclosure of information made—

(*a*) for the purpose of facilitating the performance of any functions under this Act, the Trade Descriptions Act 1968 or Part II or III or section 125 (annual and other reports of Director) of the Fair Trading Act 1973 of the Secretary of State, any other Minister, any enforcement authority or any Northern Ireland department, or

(*b*) in connection with the investigation of any criminal offence or for the purposes of any criminal proceedings, or

(*c*) for the purposes of any civil proceedings brought under or by virtue of this Act or under Part III of the Fair Trading Act 1973.

(4) Nothing in subsections (1) and (2) shall be construed—

(*a*) as limiting the particulars which may be entered in the register; or

(*b*) as applying to any information which has been made public as part of the register.

(5) Any person who discloses information in contravention of this section commits an offence. **[C.174]**

PERSON
See the note to s. 8, *ante*.

OFFENCE
As to notification of convictions to the Director, see s. 166, *ante*. For penalties and mode of prosecution, see s. 167 (1), *ante*, and Sch. 1, *post*. For special defences, see s. 168, *ante*. As to offences by bodies corporate, see s. 169, *ante*.

DEFINITIONS
For "business", "individual" and "register", see s. 189 (1), *post*. For "enforcement authority", see s. 161 (1), *ante*.

TRADE DESCRIPTIONS ACT 1968
See 37 Halsbury's Statutes (3rd edn.) 948.

FAIR TRADING ACT 1973, PARTS II, III
I.e., ss. 13–33 and 34–43 of that Act (43 Halsbury's Statutes (3rd edn.) 1635 *et seq.*).

### 175. Duty of persons deemed to be agents

Where under this Act a person is deemed to receive a notice or payment as agent of the creditor or owner under a regulated agreement, he shall be deemed to be under a contractual duty to the creditor or owner to transmit the notice, or remit the payment, to him forthwith. **[C.175]**

PERSON
See the note to s. 8, *ante*.

DEFINITIONS
For "creditor", "notice", "owner", "payment" and "regulated agreement", see s. 189 (1), *post*.

**176. Service of documents**

(1) A document to be served under this Act by one person ("the server") on another person ("the subject") is to be treated as properly served on the subject if dealt with as mentioned in the following subsections.

(2) The document may be delivered or sent by post to the subject, or addressed to him by name and left at his proper address.

(3) For the purposes of this Act, a document sent by post to, or left at, the address last known to the server as the address of a person shall be treated as sent by post to, or left at, his proper address.

(4) Where the document is to be served on the subject as being the person having any interest in land, and it is not practicable after reasonable inquiry to ascertain the subject's name or address, the document may be served by—

(*a*) addressing it to the subject by the description of the person having that interest in the land (naming it), and

(*b*) delivering the document to some responsible person on the land or affixing it, or a copy of it, in a conspicuous position on the land.

(5) Where a document to be served on the subject as being a debtor, hirer or surety, or as having any other capacity relevant for the purposes of this Act, is served at any time on another person who—

(*a*) is the person last known to the server as having that capacity, but

(*b*) before that time had ceased to have it,

the document shall be treated as having been served at that time on the subject.

(6) Anything done to a document in relation to a person who (whether to the knowledge of the server or not) has died shall be treated for the purposes of subsection (5) as service of the document on that person if it would have been so treated had he not died.

(7) Neither of the following enactments (which provide for the vesting of the estate of an intestate in the Probate Judge) shall be construed as authorising service on the Probate Judge of any document which is to be served under this Act—

section 9 of the Administration of Estates Act 1925;
section 3 of the Administration of Estates Act (Northern Ireland) 1955.

(8) References in the preceding subsections to the serving of a document on a person include the giving of the document to that person. **[C.176]**

PERSON
See the note to s. 8, *ante*.

BY POST
This provision brings into operation the provision of the Interpretation Act 1889, s. 26 (32 Halsbury's Statutes (3rd edn.) 452) that service is deemed to be effected by properly addressing, prepaying and posting a letter containing the document and, unless the contrary is proved, to be effected at the time when the letter would be delivered in the ordinary course of post. For decisions on that section, see the notes thereto.

DEFINITIONS
For "creditor", "debtor", "hirer" and "surety", see s. 189 (1), *post*.

ADMINISTRATION OF ESTATES ACT 1925, S. 9
See 13 Halsbury's Statutes (3rd edn.) 46.

ADMINISTRATION OF ESTATES ACT (NORTHERN IRELAND) 1955
1955 c. 24 (N.I.).

**177. Saving for registered charges**

(1) Nothing in this Act affects the rights of a proprietor of a registered charge (within the meaning of the Land Registration Act 1925), who—

(*a*) became the proprietor under a transfer for valuable consideration without notice of any defect in the title arising (apart from this section) by virtue of this Act, or

(*b*) derives title from such a proprietor.

(2) Nothing in this Act affects the operation of section 104 of the Law of Property Act 1925 (protection of purchaser where mortgagee exercises power of sale).

(3) Subsection (1) does not apply to a proprietor carrying on a business of debt-collecting.

(4) Where, by virtue of subsection (1), a land mortgage is enforced which apart from this section would be treated as never having effect, the original creditor or owner shall be liable to indemnify the debtor or hirer against any loss thereby suffered by him.

(5) In the application of this section to Scotland for subsections (1) to (3) there shall be substituted the following subsections—

"(1) Nothing in this Act affects the rights of a creditor in a heritable security who—

(*a*) became the creditor under a transfer for value without notice of any defect in the title arising (apart from this section) by virtue of this Act; or

(*b*) derives title from such a creditor.

(2) Nothing in this Act affects the operation of section 41 of the Conveyancing (Scotland) Act 1924 (protection of purchasers), or of that section as applied to standard securities by section 32 of the Conveyancing and Feudal Reform (Scotland) Act 1970.

(3) Subsection (1) does not apply to a creditor carrying on a business of debt collecting.".

(6) In the application of this section to Northern Ireland—

(*a*) any reference to the proprietor of a registered charge (within the meaning of the Land Registration Act 1925) shall be construed as a reference to the registered owner of a charge under the Local Registration of Title (Ireland) Act 1891 or Part IV of the Land Registration Act (Northern Ireland) 1970, and

(*b*) for the reference to section 104 of the Law of Property Act 1925 there shall be substituted a reference to section 21 of the Conveyancing and Law of Property Act 1881 and section 5 of the Conveyancing Act 1911. [C.177]

REGISTERED CHARGE
This term is not defined by the Land Registration Act 1925, but see, as to registration of charges under that Act, ss. 25, 26 thereof (27 Halsbury's Statutes (3rd edn.) 807, 809).

TREATED AS NEVER HAVING EFFECT
For relevant provisions see, in particular, s. 106, *ante*.

LAND REGISTRATION ACT 1925
See 27 Halsbury's Statutes (3rd edn.) 778.

LAW OF PROPERTY ACT 1925, S. 104
See 27 Halsbury's Statutes (3rd edn.) 510.

LOCAL REGISTRATION OF TITLE (IRELAND) ACT 1891
54 & 55 Vict. c. 66.

LAND REGISTRATION ACT (NORTHERN IRELAND) 1970
1970 c. 18 (N.I.).

CONVEYANCING AND LAW OF PROPERTY ACT 1881
See 27 Halsbury's Statutes (3rd edn.) 330 (s. 21, however, has been repealed as to England and Wales and is not printed in this work).

CONVEYANCING ACT 1911
1 & 2 Geo. 5 c. 37; repealed as to England and Wales.

### 178. Local Acts

The Secretary of State or the Department of Commerce for Northern Ireland may by order make such amendments or repeals of any provision of any local Act as appears to the Secretary of State or, as the case may be, the Department, necessary or expedient in consequence of the replacement by this Act of the enactments relating to pawnbrokers and money-lenders. [**C.178**]

*Regulations, orders, etc.*

### 179. Power to prescribe form etc. of secondary documents

(1) Regulations may be made as to the form and content of credit-cards, trading-checks, receipts, vouchers and other documents or things issued by creditors, owners or suppliers under or in connection with regulated agreements or by other persons in connection with linked transactions, and may in particular—

(*a*) require specified information to be included in the prescribed manner in documents, and other specified material to be excluded;

(*b*) contain requirements to ensure that specified information is clearly brought to the attention of the debtor or hirer, or his relative, and that one part of a document is not given insufficient or excessive prominence compared with another.

(2) If a person issues any document or thing in contravention of regulations under subsection (1) then, as from the time of the contravention but without prejudice to anything done before it, this Act shall apply as if the regulated agreement had been improperly executed by reason of a contravention of regulations under section 60 (1). [**C.179**]

GENERAL NOTE
No orders had been made under this section up to the time of going to press. In so far as such orders are local, they will not be noted in this work.
For general provisions as to orders under this Act, see s. 182 (1), (2), (4), *post*.

**180. Power to prescribe form etc. of copies**

(1) Regulations may be made as to the form and content of documents to be issued as copies of any executed agreement, security instrument or other document referred to in this Act, and may in particular—

(*a*) require specified information to be included in the prescribed manner in any copy, and contain requirements to ensure that such information is clearly brought to the attention of a reader of the copy;

(*b*) authorise the omission from a copy of certain material contained in the original, or the inclusion of such material in condensed form.

(2) A duty imposed by any provision of this Act (except section 35) to supply a copy of any document—

(*a*) is not satisfied unless the copy supplied is in the prescribed form and conforms to the prescribed requirements;

(*b*) is not infringed by the omission of any material, or its inclusion in condensed form, if that is authorised by regulations;

and references in this Act to copies shall be construed accordingly.

(3) Regulations may provide that a duty imposed by this Act to supply a copy of a document referred to in an unexecuted agreement or an executed agreement shall not apply to documents of a kind specified in the regulations. **[C.180]**

IMPROPERLY EXECUTED

For the consequences of improper execution, see s. 65, *ante*.

DEFINITION

For "creditor", "debtor", "hirer", "owner", "regulated agreement", "regulation", "relative" and "supplier", see s. 189 (1), *post*.

For "linked transaction", see s. 19 (1), *ante*.

REGULATIONS UNDER THIS SECTION

No regulations had been made under this section up to the time of going to press.

For general provisions as to regulations under this Act, see s. 182 (1), (2), (4), *post*.

**181. Power to alter monetary limits etc.**

(1) The Secretary of State may by order made by statutory instrument amend, or further amend, any of the following provisions of this Act so as to reduce or increase a sum mentioned in that provision, namely, sections 8 (2), 15 (1) (*c*), 17 (1), 43 (3) (*a*), 70 (6), 75 (3) (*b*), 77 (1), 78 (1), 79 (1), 84 (1), 101 (7) (*a*), 107 (1), 108 (1), 109 (1), 110 (1), 118 (1) (*b*), 120 (1) (*a*), 139 (5) and (7), 155 (1) and 158 (1) (*c*).

(2) An order under subsection (1) amending section 8 (2), 15 (1) (*c*), 17 (1), 43 (3) (*a*), 75 (3) (*b*) or 139 (5) (*b*) or (7) (*b*) shall be of no effect unless a draft of the order has been laid before and approved by each House of Parliament. **[C.181]**

DEFINITIONS

For "executed agreement", "prescribed", "regulations" and "unexecuted agreement", see s. 189 (1), *post*.

For "security instrument", see s. 105 (2), *ante*.

REGULATIONS UNDER THIS SECTION

No regulations had been made under this section up to the time of going to press.

For general provisions as to regulations under this Act, see s. 182 (1), (2), (4), *post*.

**182. Regulations and orders**

(1) Any power of the Secretary of State to make regulations or orders under this Act, except the power conferred by sections 2 (1) (*a*), 181 and 192, shall be exercisable by statutory instrument subject to annulment in pursuance of a resolution of either House of Parliament.

(2) Where a power to make regulations or orders is exercisable by the Secretary of State by virtue of this Act, regulations or orders made in the exercise of that power may—

(*a*) make different provision in relation to different cases or classes of case, and

(*b*) exclude certain cases or classes of case, and

(*c*) contain such transitional provisions as the Secretary of State thinks fit.

(3) Regulations may provide that specified expressions, when used as described by the regulations, are to be given the prescribed meaning, notwithstanding that another meaning is intended by the person using them.

(4) Any power conferred on the Secretary of State by this Act to make orders includes power to vary or revoke an order so made. [**C.182**]

LAID BEFORE . . . PARLIAMENT

For the meaning of this provision, see the Laying of Documents before Parliament (Interpretation) Act 1948 (32 Halsbury's Statutes (3rd edn.) 677).

ORDERS UNDER THIS SECTION

No orders had been made under this section up to the time of going to press.

For general provisions as to orders under this Act, see s. 182 (1), (2), (4), *post*.

**183. Determinations etc. by Director**

The Director may vary or revoke any determination or direction made or given by him under this Act (other than Part III, or Part III as applied by section 147). [**C. 183**]

STATUTORY INSTRUMENT

See the note to s. 2, *ante*.

POWER TO REVOKE

That power is implied in the case of regulations (but not in the case of orders) by virtue of the Interpretation Act 1889, s. 32 (3) (32 Halsbury's Statutes (3rd edn.) 454).

*Interpretation*

**184. Associates**

(1) A person is an associate of an individual if that person is the individual's husband or wife, or is a relative, or the husband or wife of a relative, of the individual or of the individual's husband or wife.

(2) A person is an associate of any person with whom he is in partnership, and of the husband or wife or a relative of any individual with whom he is in partnership.

(3) A body corporate is an associate of another body corporate—

(*a*) if the same person is a controller of both, or a person is a controller of one and persons who are his associates, or he and persons who are his associates, are the controllers of the other; or

(*b*) if a group of two or more persons is a controller of each company, and the groups either consist of the same persons or could be regarded as consisting of the same persons by treating (in one or more cases) a member of either group as replaced by a person of whom he is an associate.

(4) A body corporate is an associate of another person if that person is a controller of it or if that person and persons who are his associates together are controllers of it.

(5) In this section "relative" means brother, sister, uncle, aunt, nephew, niece, lineal ancestor or lineal descendant, and references to a husband or wife include a former husband or wife and a reputed husband or wife; and for the purposes of this subsection a relationship shall be established as if any illegitimate child, step-child or adopted child of a person had been a child born to him in wedlock. **[C.184]**

PERSON
See the note to s. 8, *ante*.

PARTNERSHIP
For a definition of partnership and for rules for determining whether a partnership exists, see the Partnership Act 1890, ss. 1, 2 (24 Halsbury's Statutes (3rd edn.) 501, 502).

DEFINITIONS
For "controller" and "individual", see s. 189 (1), *post*.
As to "husband", "relative" and "wife", note the provisions of sub-s. (5) above.

### 185. Agreement with more than one debtor or hirer

(1) Where an actual or prospective regulated agreement has two or more debtors or hirers (not being a partnership or an unincorporated body of persons)—

(*a*) anything required by or under this Act to be done to or in relation to the debtor or hirer shall be done to or in relation to each of them; and

(*b*) anything done under this Act by or on behalf of one of them shall have effect as if done by or on behalf of all of them.

(2) Notwithstanding subsection (1) (*a*), where running-account credit is provided to two or more debtors jointly, any of them may by a notice signed by him (a "dispensing notice") authorise the creditor not to comply in his case with section 78 (4) (giving of periodical statement of account); and the dispensing notice shall have effect accordingly until revoked by a further notice given by the debtor to the creditor:

Provided that:

(*a*) a dispensing notice shall not take effect if previous dispensing notices are operative in the case of the other debtor, or each of the other debtors, as the case may be;

(*b*) any dispensing notices operative in relation to an agreement shall cease to have effect if any of the debtors dies.

(3) Subsection (1) (*b*) does not apply for the purposes of section 61 (1) (*a*) or 127 (3).

(4) Where a regulated agreement has two or more debtors or hirers (not being a partnership or an unincorporated body of persons), section 86 applies to the death of any of them.

(5) An agreement for the provision of credit, or the bailment or (in Scotland) the hiring of goods, to two or more persons jointly where—

(*a*) one or more of those persons is an individual, and

(*b*) one or more of them is a body corporate,

is a consumer credit agreement or consumer hire agreement if it would have been one had they all been individuals; and the body corporate or bodies corporate shall accordingly be included among the debtors or hirers under the agreement.

(6) Where subsection (5) applies, references in this Act to the signing of any document by the debtor or hirer shall be construed in relation to a body corporate as referring to a signing on behalf of the body corporate. **[C.185]**

PARTNERSHIP
See the note to s. 184, *ante*.

SIGNED
See the note to s. 51, *ante*, and note the provisions of sub-s. (5) above.

DEFINITIONS
For "consumer credit agreement", see s. 8 (2), *ante*, and for "consumer hire agreement", see s. 15, *ante*.
For "credit", see s. 9, *ante*.
For "creditor", "debtor", "give", "hirer", "individual", "notice" and "regulated agreement", see s. 189 (1), *post*.
For "dispensing notice", see sub-s. (1) above.
For "running-account credit", see s. 10. *ante*.

### 186. Agreement with more than one creditor or owner

Where an actual or prospective regulated agreement has two or more creditors or owners, anything required by or under this Act to be done to, or in relation to, or by, the creditor or owner shall be effective if done to, or in relation to, or by, any one of them. **[C. 186]**

DEFINITIONS
For "creditor", "owner" and "regulated agreement", see s. 189 (1), *post*.

### 187. Arrangements between creditor and supplier

(1) A consumer credit agreement shall be treated as entered into under pre-existing arrangements between a creditor and a supplier if it is entered into in accordance with, or in furtherance of, arrangements previously made between persons mentioned in subsection (4) (*a*), (*b*) or (*c*).

(2) A consumer credit agreement shall be treated as entered into in contemplation of future arrangements between a creditor and a supplier if it is entered into in the expectation that arrangements will subsequently be made between persons mentioned in subsection (4) (*a*), (*b*) or (*c*) for the supply of cash,

goods and services (or any of them) to be financed by the consumer credit agreement.

(3) Arrangements shall be disregarded for the purposes of subsection (1) or (2) if—

(*a*) they are arrangements for the making, in specified circumstances, of payments to the supplier by the creditor, and

(*b*) the creditor holds himself out as willing to make, in such circumstances, payments of the kind to suppliers generally.

(4) The persons referred to in subsections (1) and (2) are—

(*a*) the creditor and the supplier;

(*b*) one of them and an associate of the other's;

(*c*) an associate of one and an associate of the other's.

(5) Where the creditor is an associate of the supplier's, the consumer credit agreement shall be treated, unless the contrary is proved, as entered into under pre-existing arrangements between the creditor and the supplier. **[C.187]**

SHALL BE TREATED

I.e., for the purposes of the definitions of "debtor-creditor agreement" and "debtor creditor-supplier agreement" in ss. 12, 13, *ante.*

PERSONS

See the note to s. 8, *ante.*

DEFINITIONS

For "associate", see s. 184, *ante.*
For "consumer credit agreement", see s. 8 (2), *ante.*
For "cash", "creditor", "goods" and "supplier", see s. 189 (1), *post.*

### 188. Examples of use of new terminology

(1) Schedule 2 shall have effect for illustrating the use of terminology employed in this Act.

(2) The examples given in Schedule 2 are not exhaustive.

(3) In the case of conflict between Schedule 2 and any other provision of this Act, that other provision shall prevail.

(4) The Secretary of State may by order amend Schedule 2 by adding further examples or in any other way. **[C.188]**

ORDERS UNDER THIS SECTION

No orders had been made for the purposes of sub-s. (4) above up to the time of going to press.
For general provisions as to orders under this Act, see s. 182 (1), (2), (4), *ante.*

### 189. Definitions

(1) In this Act, unless the context otherwise requires—

"advertisement" includes every form of advertising, whether in a publication, by television or radio, by display of notices, signs, labels, showcards or goods, by distribution of samples, circulars, catalogues, price lists or other material, by exhibition of pictures, models or films, or in any other way, and references to the publishing of advertisements shall be construed accordingly;

"advertiser" in relation to an advertisement, means any person indicated by the advertisement as willing to enter into transactions to which the advertisement relates;

"ancillary credit business" has the meaning given by section 145 (1);

"antecedent negotiations" has the meaning given by section 56;

"appeal period" means the period beginning on the first day on which an appeal to the Secretary of State may be brought and ending on the last day on which it may be brought or, if it is brought, ending on its final determination, or abandonment;

"assignment", in relation to Scotland, means assignation;

"associate" shall be construed in accordance with section 184;

"bill of sale" has the meaning given by section 4 of the Bills of Sale Act 1878 or, for Northern Ireland, by section 4 of the Bills of Sale (Ireland) Act 1879;

"building society" has the meaning given by section 1 of the Building Societies Act 1962, and includes a Northern Ireland society as defined by section 134 (4) of that Act;

"business" includes profession or trade, and references to a business apply subject to subsection (2);

"cancellable agreement" means a regulated agreement which, by virtue of section 67, may be cancelled by the debtor or hirer;

"canvass" shall be construed in accordance with sections 48 and 153;

"cash" includes money in any form;

"charity" means as respects England and Wales a charity registered under the Charities Act 1960 or an exempt charity (within the meaning of that Act), and as respects Scotland and Northern Ireland an institution or other organisation established for charitable purposes only ("organisation" including any persons administering a trust and "charitable" being construed in the same way as if it were contained in the Income Tax Acts);

"conditional sale agreement" means an agreement for the sale of goods or land under which the purchase price or part of it is payable by instalments, and the property in the goods or land is to remain in the seller (notwithstanding that the buyer is to be in possession of the goods or land) until such conditions as to the payment of instalments or otherwise as may be specified in the agreement are fulfilled;

"consumer credit agreement" has the meaning given by section 8 and includes a consumer credit agreement which is cancelled under section 69 (1), or becomes subject to section 69 (2), so far as the agreement remains in force;

"consumer credit business" means any business so far as it comprises or relates to the provision of credit under regulated consumer credit agreements;

"consumer hire agreement" has the meaning given by section 15;

"consumer hire business" means any business so far as it comprises or relates to the bailment or (in Scotland) the hiring of goods under regulated consumer hire agreements;

"controller", in relation to a body corporate, means a person—

(*a*) in accordance with whose directions or instructions the directors of the body corporate or of another body corporate which is its controller (or any of them) are accustomed to act, or

(*b*) who, either alone or with any associate or associates, is entitled to exercise or control the exercise of, one third or more of the voting power at any general meeting of the body corporate or of another body corporate which is its controller;

"copy" shall be construed in accordance with section 180;

"costs", in relation to Scotland, means expenses;

"court" means in relation to England and Wales the county court, in relation to Scotland the sheriff court and in relation to Northern Ireland the High Court or the county court;

"credit" shall be construed in accordance with section 9;

"credit-broker" means a person carrying on a business of credit brokerage;

"credit brokerage" has the meaning given by section 145 (2);

"credit limit" has the meaning given by section 10 (2);

"creditor" means the person providing credit under a consumer credit agreement or the person to whom his rights and duties under the agreement have passed by assignment or operation of law, and in relation to a prospective consumer credit agreement, includes the prospective creditor;

"credit reference agency" has the meaning given by section 145 (8);

"credit-sale agreement" means an agreement for the sale of goods, under which the purchase price or part of it is payable by instalments, but which is not a conditional sale agreement;

"credit-token" has the meaning given by section 14 (1);

"credit-token agreement" means a regulated agreement for the provision of credit in connection with the use of a credit-token;

"debt-adjusting" has the meaning given by section 145 (5);

"debt-collecting" has the meaning given by section 145 (7);

"debt-counselling" has the meaning given by section 145 (6);

"debtor" means the individual receiving credit under a consumer credit agreement or the person to whom his rights and duties under the agreement have passed by assignment or operation of law, and in relation to a prospective consumer credit agreement includes the prospective debtor;

"debtor-creditor agreement" has the meaning given by section 13;

"debtor-creditor-supplier agreement" has the meaning given by section 12;

"default notice" has the meaning given by section 87 (1);

"deposit" means any sum payable by a debtor or hirer by way of deposit or down-payment, or credited or to be credited to him on account of any deposit or down-payment, whether the sum is to be or has been paid to the creditor or owner or any other person, or is to be or has been discharged by a payment of money or a transfer or delivery of goods or by any other means;

"Director" means the Director General of Fair Trading;

"electric line" has the meaning given by the Electric Lighting Act 1882 or, for Northern Ireland, the Electricity Supply (Northern Ireland) Order 1972;

"embodies" and related words shall be construed in accordance with subsection (4);

"enforcement authority" has the meaning given by section 161 (1);

"enforcement order" means an order under section 65 (1), 105 (7) (*a*) or (*b*), 111 (2) or 124 (1) or (2);

"executed agreement" means a document, signed by or on behalf of the parties, embodying the terms of a regulated agreement, or such of them as have been reduced to writing;

"exempt agreement" means an agreement specified in or under section 16;

"finance" means to finance wholly or partly, and "financed" and "refinanced" shall be construed accordingly;

"file" and "copy of the file" have the meanings given by section 158 (5);

"fixed-sum credit" has the meaning given by section 10 (1) (*b*);

"friendly society" means a society registered under the Friendly Societies Acts 1896 to 1971 or a society within the meaning of the Friendly Societies Act (Northern Ireland) 1970;

"future arrangements" shall be construed in accordance with section 187;

"general notice" means a notice published by the Director at a time and in a manner appearing to him suitable for securing that the notice is seen within a reasonable time by persons likely to be affected by it;

"give" means deliver or send by post to;

"goods" has the meaning given by section 62 (1) of the Sale of Goods Act 1893;

"group licence" has the meaning given by section 22 (1) (*b*);

"High Court" means Her Majesty's High Court of Justice, or the Court of Session in Scotland or the High Court of Justice in Northern Ireland;

"hire-purchase agreement" means an agreement, other than a conditional sale agreement, under which—

(*a*) goods are bailed or (in Scotland) hired in return for periodical payments by the person to whom they are bailed or hired, and

(*b*) the property in the goods will pass to that person if the terms of the agreement are complied with and one or more of the following occurs—

(i) the exercise of an option to purchase by that person,

(ii) the doing of any other specified act by any party to the agreement,

(iii) the happening of any other specified event;

"hirer" means the individual to whom goods are bailed or (in Scotland) hired under a consumer hire agreement, or the person to whom his rights and duties under the agreement have passed by assignment or operation of law, and in relation to a prospective consumer hire agreement includes the prospective hirer;

"individual" includes a partnership or other unincorporated body of persons not consisting entirely of bodies corporate;

"installation" means—

(*a*) the installing of any electric line or any gas or water pipe,

(*b*) the fixing of goods to the premises where they are to be used, and the alteration of premises to enable goods to be used on them,

(*c*) where it is reasonably necessary that goods should be constructed or erected on the premises where they are to be used, any work carried out for the purpose of constructing or erecting them on those premises;

"insurance company" has the meaning given by section 33 (1) of the Insurance Companies Act 1958, and includes such a company as defined by section 72 (1) of the Insurance Companies Act (Northern Ireland) 1968, but does not include a friendly society or an organisation of workers or organisation of employers;

"judgment" includes an order or decree made by any court;

"land", includes an interest in land, and in relation to Scotland includes heritable subjects of whatever description;

"land improvement company" means an improvement company as defined by section 7 of the Improvement of Land Act 1899;

"land mortgage" includes any security charged on land;

"licence" means a licence under Part III (including that Part as applied to ancillary credit businesses by section 147);

"licensed", in relation to any act, means authorised by a licence to do the act or cause or permit another person to do it;

"licensee", in the case of a group licence, includes any person covered by the licence;

"linked transaction" has the meaning given by section 19 (1);

"local authority", in relation to England and Wales, means the Greater London Council, a county council, a London borough council, a district council, the Common Council of the City of London, or the Council of the Isles of Scilly, and in relation to Scotland, means a regional, islands or district council, and, in relation to Northern Ireland, means a district council;

"minor", in relation to Scotland, includes pupil;

"modifying agreement" has the meaning given by section 82 (2);

"mortgage", in relation to Scotland, includes any heritable security;

"multiple agreement" has the meaning given by section 18 (1);

"negotiator" has the meaning given by section 56 (1);

"non-commercial agreement" means a consumer credit agreement or a consumer hire agreement not made by the creditor or owner in the course of a business carried on by him;

"notice" means notice in writing;

"notice of cancellation" has the meaning given by section 69 (1);

"owner" means a person who bails or (in Scotland) hires out goods under a consumer hire agreement or the person to whom his rights and duties under the agreement have passed by assignment or operation of law, and in relation to a prospective consumer hire agreement, includes the prospective bailor or person from whom the goods are to be hired;

"pawn" means any article subject to a pledge;
"pawnee" and "pawnor" include any person to whom the rights and duties of the original pawnee or the original pawnor, as the case may be, have passed by assignment or operation of law;
"pawn-receipt" has the meaning given by section 114;
"payment" includes tender;
"personal credit agreement" has the meaning given by section 8 (1);
"pledge" means the pawnee's rights over an article taken in pawn;
"pre-existing arrangements" shall be construed in accordance with section 187;
"prescribed" means prescribed by regulations made by the Secretary of State;
"principal agreement" has the meaning given by section 19 (1);
"protected goods" has the meaning given by section 90 (7);
"quotation" has the meaning given by section 52 (1) (*a*);
"redemption period" has the meaning given by section 116 (3);
"register" means the register kept by the Director under section 35;
"regulated agreement" means a consumer credit agreement, or consumer hire agreement, other than an exempt agreement, and "regulated" and "unregulated" shall be construed accordingly;
"regulations" means regulations made by the Secretary of State;
"relative", except in section 184, means a person who is an associate by virtue of section 184 (1);
"representation" includes any condition or warranty, and any other statement or undertaking, whether oral or in writing;
"restricted-use credit agreement" and "restricted-use credit" have the meanings given by section 11 (1);
"rules of court", in relation to Northern Ireland means, in relation to the High Court, rules made under section 7 of the Northern Ireland Act 1962, and, in relation to any other court, rules made by the authority having for the time being power to make rules regulating the practice and procedure in that court;
"running-account credit" shall be construed in accordance with section 10;
"security", in relation to an actual or prospective consumer credit agreement or consumer hire agreement, or any linked transaction, means a mortgage, charge, pledge, bond, debenture, indemnity, guarantee, bill, note or other right provided by the debtor or hirer, or at his request (express or implied), to secure the carrying out of the obligations of the debtor or hirer under the agreement;
"security instrument" has the meaning given by section 105 (2);
"serve on" means deliver or send by post to;
"signed" shall be construed in accordance with subsection (3);
"small agreement" has the meaning given by section 17 (1), and "small" in relation to an agreement within any category shall be construed accordingly;
"specified fee" shall be construed in accordance with section 2 (4) and (5);
"standard licence" has the meaning given by section 22 (1) (*a*);
"supplier" has the meaning given by section 11 (1) (*b*) or 12 (*c*) or 13 (*c*) or,

in relation to an agreement falling within section 11 (1) (*a*), means the creditor, and includes a person to whom the rights and duties of a supplier (as so defined) have passed by assignment or operation of law, or (in relation to a prospective agreement) the prospective supplier;

"surety" means the person by whom any security is provided, or the person to whom his rights and duties in relation to the security have passed by assignment or operation of law;

"technical grounds" shall be construed in accordance with subsection (5);

"time order" has the meaning given by section 129 (1);

"total charge for credit" means a sum calculated in accordance with regulations under section 20 (1);

"total price" means the total sum payable by the debtor under a hire-purchase agreement or a conditional sale agreement, including any sum payable on the exercise of an option to purchase, but excluding any sum payable as a penalty or as compensation or damages for a breach of the agreement;

"unexecuted agreement" means a document embodying the terms of a prospective regulated agreement, or such of them as it is intended to reduce to writing;

"unlicensed" means without a licence but applies only in relation to acts for which a licence is required;

"unrestricted-use credit agreement" and "unrestricted-use credit" have the meanings given by section 11 (2);

"working day" means any day other than—

(*a*) Saturday or Sunday.

(*b*) Christmas Day or Good Friday,

(*c*) a bank holiday within the meaning given by section 1 of the Banking and Financial Dealings Act 1971.

(2) A person is not to be treated as carrying on a particular type of business merely because occasionally he enters into transactions belonging to a business of that type.

(3) Any provision of this Act requiring a document to be signed is complied with by a body corporate if the document is sealed by that body.

This subsection does not apply to Scotland.

(4) A document embodies a provision if the provision is set out either in the document itself or in another document referred to in it.

(5) An application dismissed by the court or the Director shall, if the court or the Director (as the case may be) so certifies, be taken to be dismissed on technical grounds only.

(6) Except in so far as the context otherwise requires, any reference in this Act to an enactment shall be construed as a reference to that enactment as amended by or under any other enactment, including this Act.

(7) In this Act, except where otherwise indicated—

(*a*) a reference to a numbered Part, section or Schedule is a reference to the Part or section of, or the Schedule to, this Act so numbered, and (*b*) a reference in a section to a numbered subsection is a reference to the subsection of that section so numbered, and

(*c*) a reference in a section, subsection or Schedule to a numbered paragraph is a reference to the paragraph of that section, subsection or Schedule so numbered. **[C.189]**

APPLIED TO THE SECRETARY OF STATE

For the right of appeal, see ss. 41, 150, *ante*.

BUSINESS

It has been said that "the word, 'business' . . . means almost anything which is an occupation, as distinguished from a pleasure—anything which is an occupation or duty which requires attention is a business': (*Rolls* v. *Miller* (1884), 27 Ch. D. 71, C.A., *per* Lindley, L.J., at p. 88). In other cases, however, it has been pointed out that there is a difference between "business" in this very broad sense and "business" meaning a regularly conducted commercial enterprise; see *Inland Revenue Comrs.* v. *Marine Steam Turbine Co. Ltd.*, [1920] 1 K.B. 193, at pp. 202–204, and *Lord Advocate* v. *Glasgow Corpn.*, 1958 S.L.T. 2, at p. 8. The reference to "profession" in the definition indicates that the activity need not be gainful and that the broader sense of the word "business" is to be adopted.

It is clear that a business does not cease to be such merely because it makes a loss (*Re Ogilby, Ogilby* v. *Wentworth-Stanley*, [1942] Ch. 288) and even activities intended permanently to be carried on at a loss have been held to be businesses (*Rolls* v. *Miller*, *supra; South-West Suburban Water Co.* v. *St. Marylebone Guardians*, [1904] 2 K.B. 174 at p. 180).

In connection with the provisions of sub-s. (2) above, see also the note "Carry on business" to s. 21, *ante*.

PROPERTY . . . IS TO REMAIN IN THE SELLER

Whether this is the case or not is a question of the intention of the parties; see the Sale of Goods Act 1890, s. 17 (30 Halsbury's Statutes (3rd edn.) 17).

LAND

The definition given above is not inconsistent with that in the Interpretation Act 1889, s. 3 (32 Halsbury's Statutes (3rd edn.) 436) to which reference should therefore also be made.

PART III

I.e., ss. 21–42, *ante*.

LOCAL AUTHORITY

For the constitutions and areas of jurisdiction of the bodies mentioned in this definition with regard to England and Wales, see the London Government Act 1963 (20 Halsbury's Statutes (3rd edn.) 690) and the Local Government Act 1972, (42 Halsbury's Statutes (3rd edn.) 841).

WRITING

See the note to s. 6, *ante*.

BY POST

See the note to s. 177, *ante*.

REGULATED AGREEMENT

An agreement made before the principal appointed day for the purposes of Sch. 3, *post*, is not a regulated agreement; see Sch. 3, para. 1 (1), *post*.

BILLS OF SALE ACT 1878

See 3 Halsbury's Statutes (3rd edn.) 245.

BILLS OF SALE (IRELAND) ACT 1879

42 & 43 Vict. c. 50.

BUILDING SOCIETIES ACT 1962, SS. 1, 134 (4)

See 3 Halsbury's Statutes (3rd edn.) 315, 414.

CHARITIES ACT 1960

See 3 Halsbury's Statutes (3rd edn.) 589.

INCOME TAX ACTS
For meaning, see the Income and Corporation Taxes Act 1970, s. 526 (1) (33 Halsbury's Statutes (3rd edn.) 681).

ELECTRIC LIGHTING ACT 1882
See 11 Halsbury's Statutes (3rd edn.) 849.

ELECTRICITY SUPPLY (NORTHERN IRELAND) ORDER 1972
S.I. 1972 No. 1072.

FRIENDLY SOCIETIES ACTS 1896 TO 1971
For the Acts which may be cited by this collective title, see the Friendly Societies Act 1896 (14 Halsbury's Statutes (3rd edn.) 259), and see further the Friendly Societies Act 1971, s. 15 (1) (41 Halsbury's Statutes (3rd edn.) 596).

FRIENDLY SOCIETIES ACT (NORTHERN IRELAND) 1970
1970 c. 31 (N.I.).

SALE OF GOODS ACT 1890, S. 62 (1)
See 30 Halsbury's Statutes (3rd edn.) 42.

INSURANCE COMPANIES ACT 1958, S. 31 (1)
See 5 Halsbury's Statutes (3rd edn.) 326.

INSURANCE COMPANIES ACT (NORTHERN IRELAND) 1968
1968 c. 6 (N.I.).

IMPROVEMENT OF LAND ACT 1899, S. 7
See 18 Halsbury's Statutes (3rd edn.) 157.

NORTHERN IRELAND ACT 1962, S. 7
See 23 Halsbury's Statutes (3rd edn.) 950.

POST OFFICE ACT 1969, S. 24 (1)
See 25 Halsbury's Statutes (3rd edn.) 497.

BANKING AND FINANCIAL DEALINGS ACT 1971, S. 1
See 41 Halsbury's Statutes (3rd edn.) 1554.

## 190. Financial provisions

(1) There shall be defrayed out of money provided by Parliament—

(*a*) all expenses incurred by the Secretary of State in consequence of the provisions of this Act;

(*b*) any expenses incurred in consequence of those provisions by any other Minister of the Crown or Government department;

(*c*) any increase attributable to this Act in the sums payable out of money so provided under the Superannuation Act 1972 or the Fair Trading Act 1973.

(2) Any fees received by the Director under this Act shall be paid into the Consolidated Fund. [**C.190**]

SUPERANNUATION ACT 1972
See 42 Halsbury's Statutes (3rd edn.) 1423.

FAIR TRADING ACT, 1973.
See 43 Halsbury's Statutes (3rd edn.) 1618.

NORTHERN IRELAND
As to expenditure by Northern Ireland departments, see s. 191 (1), *post*.

**191. Special provisions as to Northern Ireland**

(1) The Director may make arrangements with the Department of Commerce for Northern Ireland for the Department, on his behalf,—

(*a*) to receive applications, notices and fees;

(*b*) to maintain, and make available for inspection and copying copies of entries in the register; and

(*c*) to provide certified copies of entries in the register,

to the extent that seems to him desirable for the convenience of persons in Northern Ireland.

(2) The Director shall give general notice of any arrangements made under subsection (1).

(3) Nothing in this Act shall authorise any Northern Ireland department to incur any expenses attributable to the provisions of this Act until provision has been made for those expenses to be defrayed out of money appropriated for the purpose.

(4) The power of the Department of Commerce for Northern Ireland to make an order under section 178 shall be exercisable by statutory rule for the purposes of the Statutory Rules Act (Northern Ireland) 1958, and any such order shall be subject to negative resolution within the meaning of the Interpretation Act (Northern Ireland) 1954 as if it were a statutory instrument within the meaning of that Act.

(5) In this Act "enactment" includes an enactment of the Parliament of Northern Ireland or the Northern Ireland Assembly, and "Act" shall be construed in a corresponding manner; and (without prejudice to section 188 (4)) any reference in this Act to such an enactment shall include a reference to any enactment re-enacting it with or without modifications.

(6) Section 38 of the Interpretation Act 1889 (effect of repeals) shall have the same operation in relation to any repeal by this Act of an enactment of the Parliament of Northern Ireland as it has in relation to the repeal of an Act of the Parliament of the United Kingdom, references in that section of the Act of 1889 to Acts and enactments being construed accordingly. [**C.191**]

PARLIAMENT OF IRELAND; NORTHERN IRELAND ASSEMBLY

For the abolition of the Parliament and the powers of the Assembly, see the Northern Ireland Constitution Act 1973, ss. 2–6, 31 (43 Halsbury's Statutes (3rd edn.) 1183–1186, 1206). By virtue of the Northern Ireland (Temporary Provisions) Act 1972, s. 1 (3) (42 Halsbury's Statutes (3rd edn.) 1406) this reference to enactments of the Parliament also includes a reference to Orders in Council under the Act of 1972.

INTERPRETATION ACT 1889, S. 38

See 32 Halsbury's Statutes (3rd edn.) 457.

**192. Transitional and commencement provisions, amendments and repeals**

(1) The provisions of Schedule 3 shall have effect for the purposes of this Act.

(2) The appointment of a day for the purposes of any provision of Schedule 3 shall be effected by an order of the Secretary of State made by statutory instrument; and any such order shall include a provision amending Schedule 3 so as to insert an express reference to the day appointed.

(3) Subject to subsection (4)—

(*a*) the enactments specified in Schedule 4 shall have effect subject to the amendments specified in that Schedule (being minor amendments or amendments consequential on the preceding provisions of this Act), and

(*b*) the enactments specified in Schedule 5 are hereby repealed to the extent shown in column 3 of that Schedule.

(4) The Secretary of State shall by order made by statutory instrument provide for the coming into operation of the amendments contained in Schedule 4 and the repeals contained in Schedule 5, and those amendments and repeals shall have effect only as provided by an order so made. **[C.192]**

STATUTORY INSTRUMENT
See the note to s. 2, *ante*.

ORDERS UNDER THIS SECTION
No orders had been made under this section up to the time of going to press.
For general provisions as to orders under this Act, see s. 182 (1), (2), (4), *ante*.

### 193. Short title and extent

(1) This Act may be cited as the Consumer Credit Act 1974.

(2) This Act extends to Northern Ireland. **[C.193]**

## SCHEDULE 1

Section 167

### Prosecution and Punishment of Offences

| 1<br>*Section* | 2<br>*Offence* | 3<br>*Mode of prosecution* | 4<br>*Imprisonment or fine* |
|---|---|---|---|
| 7 .. | Knowingly or recklessly giving false information to Director. | (*a*) Summarily.<br>(*b*) On indictment | £400.<br>2 years or a fine or both. |
| 39 (1) .. | Engaging in activities requiring a licence when not a licensee. | (*a*) Summarily.<br>(*b*) On indictment. | £400.<br>2 years or a fine or both. |
| 39 (2) .. | Carrying on business under a name not specified in licence. | (*a*) Summarily.<br>(*b*) On indictment. | £400.<br>2 years or a fine or both. |
| 39 (3) .. | Failure to notify changes in registered particulars. | (*a*) Summarily.<br>(*b*) On indictment. | £400.<br>2 years or a fine or both. |
| 45 .. | Advertising credit where goods etc. not available for cash. | (*a*) Summarily.<br>(*b*) On indictment. | £400.<br>2 years or a fine or both. |
| 46 (1) .. | False or misleading advertisements. | (*a*) Summarily.<br>(*b*) On indictment. | £400.<br>2 years or a fine or both. |
| 47 (1) .. | Advertising infringements. | (*a*) Summarily.<br>(*b*) On indictment. | £400.<br>2 years or a fine or both. |
| 49 (1) .. | Canvassing debtor-creditor agreements off trade premises. | (*a*) Summarily.<br>(*b*) On indictment. | £250.<br>1 year or a fine or both. |
| 49 (2) .. | Soliciting debtor-creditor agreements during visits made in response to previous oral requests. | (*a*) Summarily.<br>(*b*) On indictment. | £200.<br>1 year or a fine or both. |
| 50 (1) .. | Sending circulars to minors. | (*a*) Summarily.<br>(*b*) On indictment. | £400.<br>1 year or a fine or both. |
| 51 (1) .. | Supplying unsolicited credit-tokens. | (*a*) Summarily.<br>(*b*) On indictment. | £400.<br>2 years or a fine or both. |
| 77 (4) .. | Failure of creditor under fixed-sum credit agreement to supply copies of documents etc. | Summarily. | £200. |
| 78 (6) .. | Failure of creditor under running-account credit agreement to supply copies of documents etc. | Summarily. | £200. |
| 79 (3) .. | Failure of owner under consumer hire agreement to supply copies of documents etc. | Summarily. | £200. |
| 80 (2) .. | Failure to tell creditor or owner whereabouts of goods. | Summarily. | £50. |
| 85 (2) .. | Failure of creditor to supply copy of credit-token agreement. | Summarily. | £200. |

| 1<br>*Section* | 2<br>*Offence* | 3<br>*Mode of prosecution* | 4<br>*Imprisonment or fine* |
|---|---|---|---|
| 97 (3) .. | Failure to supply debtor with statement of amount required to discharge agreement. | Summarily. | £50. |
| 103 (5) .. | Failure to deliver notice relating to discharge of agreements. | Summarily. | £50. |
| 107 (4) .. | Failure of creditor to give information to surety under fixed-sum credit agreement. | Summarily. | £200. |
| 108 (4) .. | Failure of creditor to give information to surety under running-account credit agreement. | Summarily. | £200. |
| 109 (3) .. | Failure of owner to give information to surety under consumer hire agreement. | Summarily. | £200. |
| 110 (3) .. | Failure of creditor or owner to supply a copy of any security instrument to debtor or hirer. | Summarily. | £200. |
| 114 (2) .. | Taking pledges from minors. | (*a*) Summarily.<br>(*b*) On indictment. | £400.<br>1 year or a fine or both. |
| 115 .. | Failure to supply copies of a pledge agreement or pawn-receipt. | Summarily. | £200. |
| 119 (1) .. | Unreasonable refusal to allow pawn to be redeemed. | Summarily. | £200. |
| 154 .. | Canvassing ancillary credit services off trade premises. | (*a*) Summarily.<br>(*b*) On indictment. | £200.<br>1 year or a fine or both. |
| 157 (3) .. | Refusal to give name etc. of credit reference agency. | Summarily. | £200. |
| 158 (4) .. | Failure of credit reference agency to disclose filed information. | Summarily. | £200. |
| 159 (6) .. | Failure of credit reference agency to correct information. | Summarily. | £200. |
| 160 (6) .. | Failure of credit reference agency to comply with section 160 (3) or (4). | Summarily. | £200. |
| 162 (6) .. | Impersonation of enforcement authority officers. | (*a*) Summarily.<br>(*b*) On indictment. | £400.<br>2 years or a fine or both. |
| 165 (1) .. | Obstruction of enforcement authority officers. | Summarily. | £200. |
| 165 (2) .. | Giving false information to enforcement authority officers. | (*a*) Summarily.<br>(*b*) On indictment. | £400.<br>2 years or a fine or both. |
| 167 (2) .. | Contravention of regulations under section 44, 52, 53, 54 or 112. | (*a*) Summarily.<br>(*b*) On indictment. | £400.<br>2 years or a fine or both. |
| 174 (5) .. | Wrongful disclosure of information. | (*a*) Summarily.<br>(*b*) On indictment. | £400.<br>2 years or a fine or both. |

GENERAL NOTE
For definitions of expressions used in column 2, see the notes to the respective sections in column 1.

## SCHEDULE 2

Section 188 (1)

### EXAMPLES OF USE OF NEW TERMINOLOGY

### PART I

### LIST OF TERMS

| *Term* | *Defined in section* | *Illustrated by example(s)* |
|---|---|---|
| Advertisement | 189 (1) | 2 |
| Advertiser | 189 (1) | 2 |
| Antecedent negotiations | 56 | 1, 2, 3, 4 |
| Cancellable agreement | 67 | 4 |
| Consumer credit agreement | 8 | 5, 6, 7, 15, 19, 21 |
| Consumer hire agreement | 15 | 20, 24 |
| Credit | 9 | 16, 19, 21 |
| Credit-broker | 189 (1) | 2 |
| Credit limit | 10 (2) | 6, 7, 19, 22, 23 |
| Creditor | 189 (1) | 1, 2, 3, 4 |
| Credit-sale agreement | 189 (1) | 5 |
| Credit-token | 14 | 3, 14, 16 |
| Credit-token agreement | 14 | 3, 14, 16, 22 |
| Debtor-creditor agreement | 13 | 8, 16, 17, 18 |
| Debtor-creditor-supplier agreement | 12 | 8, 16 |
| Fixed-sum credit | 10 | 9, 10, 17, 23 |
| Hire-purchase agreement | 189 (1) | 10 |
| Individual | 189 (1) | 19, 24 |
| Linked transaction | 19 | 11 |
| Modifying agreement | 82 (2) | 24 |
| Multiple agreement | 18 | 16, 18 |
| Negotiator | 56 (1) | 1, 2, 3, 4 |
| Personal credit agreement | 8 (1) | 19 |
| Pre-existing arrangements | 187 | 8, 21 |
| Restricted-use credit | 11 | 10, 12, 13, 14, 16 |
| Running-account credit | 10 | 15, 16, 18, 23 |
| Small agreement | 17 | 16, 17, 22 |
| Supplier | 189 (1) | 3, 14 |
| Total charge for credit | 20 | 5, 10 |
| Total price | 189 (1) | 10 |
| Unrestricted-use credit | 11 | 8, 12, 16, 17, 18 |

**[C.195]**

### PART II

## EXAMPLES

### EXAMPLE 1

*Facts*. Correspondence passes between an employee of a moneylending company (writing on behalf of the company) and an individual about the terms on which the company would grant him a loan under a regulated agreement.

*Analysis*. The correspondence constitutes antecedent negotiations falling within section 56 (1) (*a*), the moneylending company being both creditor and negotiator.

**[C.196]**

EXAMPLE 2

*Facts.* Representations are made about goods in a poster displayed by a shopkeeper near the goods, the goods being selected by a customer who has read the poster and then sold by the shopkeeper to a finance company introduced by him (with whom he has a business relationship). The goods are disposed of by the finance company to the customer under a regulated hire-purchase agreement.

*Analysis.* The representations in the poster constitute antecedent negotiations falling within section 56 (1) (*b*), the shopkeeper being the credit-broker and negotiator and the finance company being the creditor. The poster is an advertisement and the shopkeeper is the advertiser. [**C.197**]

EXAMPLE 3

*Facts.* Discussions take place between a shopkeeper and a customer about goods the customer wishes to buy using a credit-card issued by the D Bank under a regulated agreement.

*Analysis.* The discussions constitute antecedent negotiations falling within section 56 (1) (*c*), the shopkeeper being the supplier and negotiator and the D Bank the creditor. The credit-card is a credit-token as defined in section 14 (1), and the regulated agreement under which it was issued is a credit-token agreement as defined in section 14 (2). [**C.198**]

EXAMPLE 4

*Facts.* Discussions take place and correspondence passes between a secondhand car dealer and a customer about a car, which is then sold by the dealer to the customer under a regulated conditional sale agreement. Subsequently, on a revocation of that agreement by consent, the car is resold by the dealer to a finance company introduced by him (with whom he has a business relationship), who in turn dispose of it to the same customer under a regulated hire-purchase agreement.

*Analysis.* The discussions and correspondence constitute antecedent negotiations in relation both to the conditional sale agreement and the hire-purchase agreement. They fall under section 56 (1) (*a*) in relation to the conditional sale agreement, the dealer being the creditor and the negotiator. In relation to the hire-purchase agreement they fall within section 56 (1) (*b*), the dealer continuing to be treated as the negotiator but the finance company now being the creditor. Both agreements are cancellable if the discussions took place when the individual conducting the negotiations (whether the "negotiator" or his employee or agent) was in the presence of the debtor, unless the unexecuted agreement was signed by the debtor at trade premises (as defined in section 67 (*b*)). If the discussions all took place by telephone however, or the unexecuted agreement was signed by the debtor on trade premises (as so defined) the agreements are not cancellable. [**C.199**]

EXAMPLE 5

*Facts.* E agrees to sell to F (an individual) an item of furniture in return for 24 monthly instalments of £10 payable in arrear. The property in the goods passes to F immediately.

*Analysis.* This is a credit-sale agreement (see definition of "credit-sale agreement" in section 189 (1)). The credit provided amounts to £240 less the amount which, according to regulations made under section 20 (1), constitutes the total charge for credit. (This amount is required to be deducted by section 9 (4)). Accordingly the agreement falls within section 8 (2) and is a consumer credit agreement. [**C.200**]

EXAMPLE 6

*Facts.* The G Bank grants H (an individual) an unlimited overdraft, with an increased rate of interest on so much of any debit balance as exceeds £2,000.

*Analysis.* Although the overdraft purports to be unlimited, the stipulation for increased interest above £2,000 brings the agreement within section 10 (3) (*b*) (ii) and it is a consumer credit agreement. [**C.201**]

EXAMPLE 7

*Facts.* J is an individual who owns a small shop which usually carries a stock worth about £1,000. K makes a stocking agreement under which he undertakes to provide on short-term credit the stock needed from time to time by J without any specified limit.

*Analysis.* Although the agreement appears to provide unlimited credit, it is probable, having regard to the stock usually carried by J, that his indebtedness to K will not at any time rise above £5,000. Accordingly the agreement falls within section 10 (3) (*b*) (iii) and is a consumer credit agreement. [**C.202**]

EXAMPLE 8

*Facts.* U, a moneylender, lends £500 to V (an individual) knowing he intends to use it to buy office equipment from W. W introduced V to U, it being his practice to introduce customers needing finance to him. Sometimes U gives W a commission for this and sometimes not. U pays the £500 direct to V.

*Analysis.* Although this appears to fall under section 11 (1) (*b*) it is excluded by section 11 (3) and is therefore (by section 11 (2)) an unrestricted-use credit agreement. Whether it is a debtor-creditor agreement (by section 13 (*c*)) or a debtor-creditor-supplier agreement (by section 12 (*c*)) depends on whether the previous dealings between U and W amount to "pre-existing arrangements", that is whether the agreement can be taken to have been entered into "in accordance with, or in furtherance of" arrangements previously made between U and W, as laid down in section 187 (1). [**C.203**]

EXAMPLE 9

*Facts.* A agrees to lend B (an individual) £4,500 in nine monthly instalments of £500.

*Analysis.* This is a cash loan and is a form of credit (see section 9 and definition of "cash" in section 189 (1)). Accordingly it falls within section 10 (1) (*b*) and is fixed-sum credit amounting to £4,500. [**C.204**]

EXAMPLE 10

*Facts.* C (in England) agrees to bail goods to D (an individual) in return for periodical payments. The agreement provides for the property in the goods to pass to D on payment of a total of £7,500 and the exercise by D of an option to purchase. The sum of £7,500 includes a down-payment of £1,000. It also includes an amount which, according to regulations made under section 20 (1), constitutes a total charge for credit of £1,500.

*Analysis.* This is a hire-purchase agreement with a deposit of £1,000 and a total price of £7,500 (see definitions of "hire-purchase agreement", "deposit" and "total price" in section 189 (1)). By section 9 (3), it is taken to provide credit amounting to £7,500—(£1,500 + £1,000), which equals £5,000. Under section 8 (2), the agreement is therefore a consumer credit agreement, and under sections 9 (3) and 11 (1) it is a restricted-use credit agreement for fixed-sum credit. A similar result would follow if the agreement by C had been a hiring agreement in Scotland. [**C.205**]

EXAMPLE 11

*Facts.* X (an individual) borrows £500 from Y (Finance). As a condition of the granting of the loan X is required—

(*a*) to execute a second mortgage on his house in favour of Y (Finance), and
(*b*) to take out a policy of insurance on his life with Y (Insurances).

In accordance with the loan agreement, the policy is charged to Y (Finance) as collateral security for the loan. The two companies are associates within the meaning of section 184 (3).

*Analysis.* The second mortgage is a transaction for the provision of security and accordingly does not fall within section 19 (1), but the taking out of the insurance policy is a linked transaction falling within section 19 (1) (*a*). The charging of the policy is a separate transaction (made between different parties) for the provision of security and again is excluded from section 19 (1). The only linked transaction is therefore the taking out of the insurance policy. If X had not been required by the loan agreement to take out the policy, but it had been done at the suggestion of Y (Finance) to induce them to enter into the loan agreement, it would have been a linked transaction under section 19 (1) (*c*) (i) by virtue of section 19 (2) (*a*) [**C.206**]

EXAMPLE 12

*Facts.* The N Bank agrees to lend O (an individual £2,000 to buy a car from P. To make sure the loan is used as intended, the N Bank stipulates that the money must be paid by it direct to P.

*Analysis.* The agreement is a consumer credit agreement by virtue of section 8 (2). Since it falls within section 11 (1) (*b*), it is a restricted-use credit agreement, P being the supplier. If the N Bank had not stipulated for direct payment to the supplier, section 11 (3) would have operated and made the agreement into one for unrestricted-use credit. [**C.207**]

EXAMPLE 13

*Facts.* Q, a debt-adjuster, agrees to pay off debts owed by R (an individual) to various moneylenders. For this purpose the agreement provides for the making of a loan by Q to R in return for R's agreeing to repay the loan by instalments with interest. The loan money is not paid over to R but retained by Q and used to pay off the moneylenders.

*Analysis.* This is an agreement to refinance existing indebtedness of the debtor's, and if the loan by Q does not exceed £5,000 is a restricted-use credit agreement falling within section 11 (1) (*c*). [**C.208**]

EXAMPLE 14

*Facts.* On payment of £1, S issues to T (an individual) a trading check under which T can spend up to £20 at any shop which has agreed, or in future agrees, to accept S's trading checkt.

*Analysis.* The trading check is a credit-token falling within section 14 (1) (*b*). The credit-token agreement is a restricted-use credit agreement within section 11 (1) (*b*), any shop in which the credit-token is used being the "supplier". The fact that further shops may be added after the issue of the credit-token is irrelevant in view of section 11 (4). **[C.209]**

EXAMPLE 15

*Facts.* A retailer, L, agrees with M (an individual) to open an account in M's name and, in return for M's promise to pay a specified minimum sum into the account each month and to pay a monthly charge for credit, agrees to allow to be debited to the account, in respect of purchases made by M from L, such sums as will not increase the debit balance at any time beyond the credit limit, defined in the agreement as a given multiple of the specified minimum sum.

*Analysis.* This agreement provides credit falling within the definition of running-account credit in section 10 (1) (*a*). Provided the credit limit is not over £5,000, the agreement falls within section 8 (2) and is a consumer credit agreement for running-account credit. **[C.210]**

EXAMPLE 16

*Facts.* Under an unsecured agreement, A (Credit), an associate of the A Bank, issues to B (an individual) a credit-card for use in obtaining cash on credit from A (Credit), to be paid by branches of the A Bank (acting as agent of A (Credit)), or goods or cash from suppliers or banks who have agreed to honour credit-cards issued by A (Credit). The credit limit is £30.

*Analysis.* This is a credit-token agreement falling within section 14 (1) (*a*) and (*b*). It is a regulated consumer credit agreement for running-account credit. Since the credit limit does not exceed £30, the agreement is a small agreement. So far as the agreement relates to goods it is a debtor-creditor-supplier agreement within section 12 (*b*), since it provides restricted-use credit under section 11 (1) (*b*). So far as it relates to cash it is a debtor-creditor agreement within section 13 (*c*) and the credit it provides is unrestricted-use credit. This is therefore a multiple agreement. In that the whole agreement falls within several of the categories of agreement mentioned in this Act, it is, by section 18 (3), to be treated as an agreement in each of those categories. So far as it is a debtor-creditor-supplier agreement providing restricted-use credit it is, by section 18 (2), to be treated as a separate agreement; and similarly so far as it is a debtor-creditor agreement providing unrestricted-use credit. (See also Example 22.) **[C.211]**

EXAMPLE 17

*Facts.* The manager of the C Bank agrees orally with D (an individual) to open a current account in D's name. Nothing is said about overdraft facilities. After maintaining the account in credit for some weeks, D draws a cheque in favour of E for an amount exceeding D's credit balance by £20. E presents the cheque and the Bank pay it.

*Analysis.* In drawing the cheque D, by implication, requests the Bank to grant him an overdraft of £20 on its usual terms as to interest and other charges. In deciding to honour the cheque, the Bank by implication accept the offer. This constitutes a regulated small consumer credit agreement for unrestricted-use, fixed-sum credit. It is a debtor-creditor agreement, and falls within section 74 (1) (*b*) if covered by a determination under section 74 (3). (Compare Example 18.) **[C.212]**

EXAMPLE 18

*Facts.* F (an individual) has had a current account with the G Bank for many years. Although usually in credit, the account has been allowed by the Bank to become overdrawn from time to time. The maximum such overdraft has been is about £1,000. No explicit agreement has ever been made about overdraft facilities. Now, with a credit balance of £500, F draws a cheque for £1,300.

*Analysis.* It might well be held that the agreement with F (express or implied) under which the Bank operates his account includes an implied term giving him the right to overdraft facilities up to say £1,000. If so, the agreement is a regulated consumer credit agreement for unrestricted-use, running-account credit. It is a debtor-creditor agreement, and falls within section 74 (1) (*b*) if covered by a direction under section 74 (3). It is also a multiple agreement, part of which (i.e. the part not dealing with the overdraft), as referred to in section 18 (1) (*a*), falls within a category of agreement not mentioned in this Act. (Compare Example 17.) [**C.213**]

EXAMPLE 19

*Facts.* H (a finance house) agrees with J (a partnership of individuals) to open an unsecured loan account in J's name on which the debit balance is not to exceed £7,000 (having regard to payments into the account made from time to time by J). Interest is to be payable in advance on this sum, with provision for yearly adjustments. H is entitled to debit the account with interest, a "setting-up" charge, and other charges. Before J has an opportunity to draw on the account it is initially debited with £2,250 for advance interest and other charges.

*Analysis.* This is a personal running-account credit agreement (see sections 8 (1) and 10 (1) (*a*), and definition of "individual" in section 189 (1)). By section 10 (2) the credit limit is £7,000. By section 9 (4) however the initial debit of £2,250, and any other charges later debited to the account by H, are not to be treated as credit even though time is allowed for their payment. Effect is given to this by section 10 (3). Although the credit limit of £7,000 exceeds the amount (£5,000) specified in section 8 (2) as the maximum for a consumer credit agreement, so that the agreement is not within section 10 (3) (*a*), it is caught by section 10 (3) (*b*) (i). At the beginning J can effectively draw (as credit) no more than £4,750, so the agreement is a consumer credit agreement. [**C.214**]

EXAMPLE 20

*Facts.* K (in England) agrees with L (an individual) to bail goods to L for a period of three years certain at £2,000 a year, payable quarterly. The agreement contains no provision for the passing of the property in the goods to L.

*Analysis.* This is not a hire-purchase agreement (see paragraph (*b*) of the definition of that term in section 189 (1)), and is capable of subsisting for more than three months. Paragraphs (*a*) and (*b*) of section 15 (1) are therefore satisfied, but paragraph (*c*) is not. The payments by L must exceed £5,000 if he conforms to the agreement. It is true that under section 101 L has a right to terminate the agreement on giving K three months' notice expiring not earlier than eighteen months after the making of the agreement, but that section applies only where the agreement is a regulated consumer hire agreement apart from the section (see subsection (1)). So the agreement is not a consumer hire agreement, though it would be if the hire charge were say £1,500 a year, or there were a "break" clause in it operable by either party before the hire charges exceeded £5,000. A similar result would follow if the agreement by K had been a hiring agreement in Scotland. [**C.215**]

### EXAMPLE 21

*Facts.* The P Bank decides to issue cheque cards to its customers under a scheme whereby the bank undertakes to honour cheques of up to £30 in every case where the payee has taken the cheque in reliance on the cheque card, whether the customer has funds in his account or not. The P Bank writes to the major retailers advising them of this scheme and also publicises it by advertising. The Bank issues a cheque card to Q (an individual), who uses it to pay by cheque for goods costing £20 bought by Q from R, a major retailer. At the time, Q has £500 in his account at the P Bank.

*Analysis.* The agreement under which the cheque card is issued to Q is a consumer credit agreement even though at all relevant times Q has more than £30 in his account. This is because Q is free to draw out his whole balance and then use the cheque card, in which case the Bank has bound itself to honour the cheque. In other words the cheque card agreement provides Q with credit, whether he avails himself of it or not. Since the amount of the credit is not subject to any express limit the cheque card can be used any number of times. It may be presumed however that section 10 (3) (*b*) (iii) will apply. The agreement is an unrestricted-use debtor-creditor agreement (by section 13 (*c*)). Although the P Bank wrote to R informing R of the P Bank's willingness to honour any cheque taken by R in reliance on a cheque card, this does not constitute pre-existing arrangements as mentioned in section 13 (*c*) because section 187 (3) operates to prevent it. The agreement is not a credit-token agreement within section 14 (1) (*b*) because payment by the P Bank to R, would be a payment of the cheque and not a payment for the goods. **[C.216]**

### EXAMPLE 22

*Facts.* The facts are as in Example 16. On one occasion B uses the credit-card in a way which increases his debit balance with A (Credit) to £40. A (Credit) writes to B agreeing to allow the excess on that occasion only, but stating that it must be paid off within one month.

*Analysis.* In exceeding his credit limit, B, by implication, requests A (Credit) to allow him a temporary excess (compare Example 17). A (Credit) is thus faced by B's action with the choice of treating it as a breach of contract or granting his implied request. He does the latter. If he had done the former, B would be treated as taking credit to which he was not entitled (see section 14 (3)) and, subject to the terms of his contract with A (Credit), would be liable to damages for breach of contract. As it is, the agreement to allow the excess varies the original credit-token agreement by adding a new term. Under section 10 (2), the new term is to be disregarded in arriving at the credit limit, so that the credit-token agreement at no time ceases to be a small agreement. By section 82 (2), the later agreement is deemed to revoke the original agreement and contain provisions reproducing the combined effect of the two agreements. By section 82 (4), this later agreement is exempted from Part V (except section 56). **[C.217]**

### EXAMPLE 23

*Facts.* Under an oral agreement made on 10th January, X (an individual) has an overdraft on his current account at the Y bank with a credit limit of £100. On 15th February, when his overdraft stands at £90, X draws a cheque for £25. It is the first time that X has exceeded his credit limit, and on 16th February the bank honours the cheque.

*Analysis.* The agreement of 10th January is a consumer credit agreement for running-account credit. The agreement of 15th–16th February varies the earlier agreement by adding a term allowing the credit limit to be exceeded merely temporarily. By section 82 (2) the later agreement is deemed to revoke the earlier agreement and reproduce the combined effect of the two agreements. By section 82 (4), Part V of this Act (except section 56) does not apply to the later agreement. By section 18 (5) a term allowing a merely temporary excess over the credit limit is not to be treated as a separate agreement, or as providing fixed-sum credit. The whole of the £115 owed to the bank by X on 16th February is therefore running-account credit. **[C.218]**

EXAMPLE 24

*Facts.* On 1st March 1975 Z (in England) enters into an agreement with A (an unincorporated body of persons) to bail to A equipment consisting of two components (component P and component Q). The agreement is not a hire-purchase agreement and is for a fixed term of 3 years, so paragraphs (*a*) and (*b*) of section 15 (1) are both satisfied. The rental is payable monthly at a rate of £2,400 a year, but the agreement provides that this is to be reduced to £1,200 a year for the remainder of the agreement if at any time during its currency A returns component Q to the owner Z. On 5th May 1976 A is incorporated as A Ltd., taking over A's assets and liabilities. On 1st March 1977, A Ltd. returns component Q. On 1st January 1978, Z and A Ltd. agree to extend the earlier agreement by one year, increasing the rental for the final year by £250 to £1,450.

*Analysis.* When entered into on 1st March 1975, the agreement is a consumer hire agreement. A falls within the definition of "individual" in section 189 (1) and if A returns component Q before 1st May 1976 the total rental will not exceed £5,000 (see section 15 (1) (*c*)). When this date is passed without component Q having been returned it is obvious that the total rental must now exceed £5,000. Does this mean that the agreement then ceases to be a consumer hire agreement? The answer is no, because there has been no change in the terms of the agreement, and without such a change the agreement cannot move from one category to the other. Similarly the fact that A's rights and duties under the agreement pass to a body corporate on 5th May 1976 does not cause the agreement to cease to be a consumer hire agreement (see the definition of "hirer" in section 189 (1)).

The effect of the modifying agreement of 1st January 1978 is governed by section 82 (2), which requires it to be treated as containing provisions reproducing the combined effect of the two actual agreements, that is to say as providing that—

(*a*) obligations outstanding on 1st January 1978 are to be treated as outstanding under the modifying agreement;

(*b*) the modifying agreement applies at the old rate of hire for the months of January and February 1978, and

(*c*) for the year beginning 1st March 1978 A Ltd. will be the bailee of component P at a rental of £1,450.

The total rental under the modifying agreement is £1,850. Accordingly the modifying agreement is a regulated agreement. Even if the total rental under the modifying agreement exceeded £5,000 it would still be regulated because of the provisions of section 82 (3). **[C.219]**

GENERAL NOTE

The examples given in this Schedule are intended merely as illustrations of the use of the various terms listed in Part I above. It must be permissible for a court to look at these illustrations for the purpose of construing the definitions of the terms, but s. 188 (2), (3), *ante*, makes it clear that the illustrations do not limit or contradict the natural meanings of the definitions.

DEFINITIONS

For "advertisement", "advertiser", "cancellable agreement", "cash", "credit sale agreement", "credit-token agreement", "creditor", "debtor", "hire-purchase agreement", "individual", "modifying agreement", "regulated agreement", "supplier" and "unexecuted agreement", see s. 189 (1), *ante*.

For "antecedent negotiations" and "negotiator", see s. 56 (1), *ante*.
For "consumer credit agreement", see s. 8 (2), *ante*.
For "consumer hire agreement", see s. 15, *ante*.
For "credit", see s. 9, *ante*.
For "credit-token", see s. 14 (1), *ante*.
For "debtor-creditor agreement" and "debtor-creditor-supplier agreement", see ss. 13, 12, *ante*.
For "fixed-sum credit" and "running-account credit", see s. 10, *ante*.
For "restricted-use credit" and "unrestricted-use credit", see s. 11 (1), *ante*.
For "small agreement", see s. 17 (1), *ante*.

## SCHEDULE 3

Section 193 (1)

### TRANSITIONAL AND COMMENCEMENT PROVISIONS

*Note*. Except as otherwise mentioned in this Schedule, the provisions of this Act come into operation on its passing, that is on 31st July 1974. **[C.220]**

### PART II OF ACT

### CREDIT AGREEMENTS, HIRE AGREEMENTS AND LINKED TRANSACTIONS

*Regulated agreements*

1.—(1) An agreement made before the day appointed for the purposes of this paragraph is not a regulated agreement within the meaning of this Act.

(2) In this Act "prospective regulated agreement" does not include a prospective agreement which, if made as expected, would be made before the day appointed for the purposes of this paragraph. **[C.221]**

*Linked transactions*

2. A transaction may be a linked transaction in relation to a regulated agreement or prospective regulated agreement even though the transaction was entered into before the day appointed for the purposes of paragraph 1. **[C.222]**

3. Section 19 (3) applies only to transactions entered into on or after the day appointed for the purposes of this paragraph. **[C.223]**

*Total charge for credit*

4. Section 20 applies to consumer credit agreements whenever made. **[C.224]**

APPOINTED DAYS

Days are to be appointed by order under s. 192 (2), *ante*. No such order had been made up to the time of going to press.

DEFINITIONS

For "consumer credit agreement", see s. 8 (2), *ante*.
For "linked transaction", see s. 19 (1), *ante*.
For "regulated agreement", see s. 189 (1), *ante*.

## Part III of Act

### Licensing of Credit and Hire Businesses

*Businesses needing a licence*

5.—(1) Section 21 does not apply to the carrying on of any description of consumer credit business or consumer hire business before the day appointed for the purposes of this paragraph in relation to a business of that description.

(2) Where the person carrying on any description of consumer credit business or consumer hire business applies for a licence before the day appointed for the purposes of this paragraph in relation to a business of that description, he shall be deemed to have been granted on that day a licence covering that business and continuing in force until the licence applied for is granted or, if the application is refused, until the end of the appeal period. [**C.225**]

*The register*

6. Sections 35 and 36 come into operation on the day appointed for the purposes of this paragraph. [**C.226**]

*Enforcement of agreements made by unlicensed trader*

7. Section 40 does not apply to a regulated agreement made in the course of any business before the day appointed for the purposes of paragraph 5 in relation to a business of that description. [**C.227**]

APPOINTED DAYS

Days are to be appointed by order under s. 192 (2), *ante*. No such order had been made up to the time of going to press.

DEFINITIONS

For "business", "consumer credit business", "consumer hire business", "licence" and "regulated agreement", see s. 189 (1), *ante*.

For "standard licence", see s. 22 (1) (*a*), *ante*.

## Part IV of Act

### Seeking business

*Advertisements*

8. Part IV does not apply to any advertisement published before the day appointed for the purposes of this paragraph. [**C.228**]

*Canvassing*

9. Section 49 comes into operation on the day appointed for the purposes of this paragraph. [**C.229**]

*Circulars to minors*

10. Section 50 comes into operation on the day appointed for the purposes of this paragraph. [**C.230**]

*Unsolicited credit-tokens*

11.—(1) Section 51 (1) does not apply to the giving of a credit-token before the day appointed for the purposes of this paragraph.

(2) In section 51 (3), "agreement" means an agreement whenever made. **[C.231]**

APPOINTED DAYS
Days are to be appointed by order under s. 192 (2), *ante*. No such order had been made up to the time of going to press.

DEFINITIONS
For "advertisement", see s. 189 (1), *ante*.
For "credit-token", see s. 14 (1), *ante*.

PART V OF ACT

ENTRY INTO CREDIT OR HIRE AGREEMENTS

*Antecedent negotiations*

12.—(1) Section 56 applies to negotiations in relation to an actual or prospective regulated agreement where the negotiations begin after the day appointed for the purposes of this paragraph.

(2) In section 56 (3), "agreement", where it first occurs, means an agreement whenever made. **[C.232]**

*General*

13. Sections 57 to 59, 61 to 65 and 67 to 73 come into operation on the day appointed for the purposes of this paragraph. **[C.233]**

14. Section 66 comes into operation on the day appointed for the purposes of this paragraph. **[C.234]**

REGULATED AGREEMENT
For meaning, see s. 189 (1), *ante*.

APPOINTED DAYS
Days are to be appointed by order under s. 192 (2), *ante*. No such order had been made up to the time of going to press.

PART VI OF ACT

MATTERS ARISING DURING CURRENCY OF CREDIT OR HIRE AGREEMENTS

*Liability of creditor for breaches by supplier*

15. Section 75 comes into operation on the day appointed for the purposes of this paragraph. **[C.235]**

*Duty to give notice*

16.—(1) Section 76 comes into operation on the day appointed for the purposes of this paragraph.

(2) Section 76 applies to an agreement made before the day appointed for the

purposes of this paragraph where the agreement would have been a regulated agreement if made on that day. [**C.236**]

*Duty to give information*

17.—(1) Sections 77 to 80 come into operation on the day appointed for the purposes of this paragraph.

(2) Sections 77 to 79 apply to an agreement made before the day appointed for the purposes of this paragraph where the agreement would have been a regulated agreement if made on that day. [**C.237**]

*Appropriation of payments*

18. Section 81 comes into operation on the day appointed for the purposes of this paragraph. [**C.238**]

*Variation of agreements*

19. Section 82 comes into operation on the day appointed for the purposes of this paragraph. [**C.239**]

*Misuse of credit facilities*

20.—(1) Sections 83 and 84 come into operation on the day appointed for the purposes of this paragraph.

(2) Subject to sub-paragraph (4), section 83 applies to an agreement made before the day appointed for the purposes of this paragraph where the agreement would have been a regulated consumer credit agreement if made on that day.

(3) Subject to sub-paragraph (4), section 84 applies to an agreement made before the day appointed for the purposes of this paragraph where the agreement would have been a credit-token agreement if made on that day.

(4) Sections 83 and 84 do not apply to losses arising before the day appointed for the purposes of this paragraph.

(5) Section 84 (4) shall be taken to be satisfied in relation to an agreement made before the day appointed for the purposes of this paragraph if, within 28 days after that day, the creditor gives notice to the debtor of the name, address and telephone number of a person stated in that notice to be the person to whom notice is to be given under section 84 (3). [**C.240**]

*Duty on issue of new credit-tokens*

21.—(1) Section 85 comes into operation on the day appointed for the purposes of this paragraph.

(2) Section 85 applies to an agreement made before the day appointed for the purposes of this paragraph where the agreement would have been a regulated agreement if made on that day. [**C.241**]

*Death of debtor or hirer*

22.—(1) Section 86 comes into operation on the day appointed for the purposes of this paragraph.

(2) Section 86 applies to an agreement made before the day appointed for the purposes of this paragraph where the agreement would have been a regulated agreement if made on that day. **[C.242]**

APPOINTED DAYS

Days are to be appointed by order under s. 192 (2), *ante*. No such order had been made up to the time of going to press.

DEFINITIONS

For "consumer credit agreement", see s. 8 (2), *ante*.

For "creditor", "credit-token agreement", "debtor", "give", "notice" and "regulated agreement", see s. 189 (1), *ante*.

## Part VII of Act

### Default and Termination

*Default notices*

23. Sections 87 to 89 come into operation on the day appointed for the purposes of this paragraph. **[C.243]**

*Retaking of goods and land*

24. Sections 90 and 91 come into operation on the day appointed for the purposes of this paragraph. **[C.244]**

25. Section 92 comes into operation on the day appointed for the purposes of this paragraph. **[C.245]**

*Interest on default*

26. Section 93 comes into operation on the day appointed for the purposes of this paragraph. **[C.246]**

*Early payment by debtor*

27. Sections 94 to 97 come into operation on the day appointed for the purposes of this paragraph. **[C.247]**

*Termination of agreements*

28. Section 98 comes into operation on the day appointed for the purposes of this paragraph. **[C.248]**

29. Section 99 comes into operation on the day appointed for the purposes of this paragraph. **[C.249]**

30. Section 100 comes into operation on the day appointed for the purposes of this paragraph. **[C.250]**

31. Section 101 comes into operation on the day appointed for the purposes of this paragraph. **[C.251]**

32. Section 102 comes into operation on the day appointed for the purposes of this paragraph. **[C.252]**

33. Section 103 comes into operation on the day appointed for the purposes of this paragraph. **[C.253]**

34. Section 104 comes into operation on the day appointed for the purposes of this paragraph. **[C.254]**

*Old agreements*

35. Part VII (except sections 90, 91, 93 and 99 to 102 and 104) applies to an agreement made before the day appointed for the purposes of this paragraph where the agreement would have been a regulated agreement if made on that day. **[C.255]**

PART VII
I.e., ss. 87–104, *ante*.

APPOINTED DAYS
Days are to be appointed by order under s. 192 (2), *ante*. No such order had been made up to the time of going to press.

REGULATED AGREEMENT
For meaning, see s. 189 (1), *ante*.

## PART VIII OF ACT

### SECURITY

*General*

36. Section 105 comes into operation on the day appointed for the purposes of this paragraph. **[C.256]**

37.—(1) Sections 107 to 110 come into operation on the day appointed for the purposes of this paragraph.

(2) Sections 107 to 110 apply to an agreement made before the day appointed for the purposes of this paragraph where the agreement would have been a regulated agreement if made on that day. **[C.257]**

38.—(1) Section 111 comes into operation on the day appointed for the purposes of this paragraph.

(2) Section 111 applies to an agreement made before the day appointed for the purposes of this paragraph where the agreement would have been a regulated agreement if made on that day. **[C.258]**

*Pledges*

39. Sections 114 to 122 come into operation on the day appointed for the purposes of this paragraph. **[C.259]**

*Negotiable instruments*

40. Sections 123 to 125 come into operation on the day appointed for the purposes of this paragraph. **[C.260]**

*Land mortgages*

41. Section 126 comes into operation on the day appointed for the purposes of this paragraph. **[C.261]**

APPOINTED DAYS
Days are to be appointed by order under s. 192 (2), *ante*. No such order had been made up to the time of going to press.

REGULATED AGREEMENT
For meaning, see s. 189 (1), *ante*.

## Part IX of Act

### Judicial Control

42. Sections 137 to 140 (extortionate credit bargains) come into operation on the day appointed for the purposes of this paragraph, and apply to agreements and transactions whenever made. **[C.262]**

43. Subject to paragraph 42, Part IX comes into operation on the day appointed for the purposes of this paragraph. **[C.263]**

PART IX

I.e., ss. 127–144, *ante*.

APPOINTED DAYS

Days are to be appointed by order under s. 192 (2), *ante*. No such order had been made up to the time of going to press.

## Part X of Act

### Ancillary Credit Businesses

*Licensing*

44.—(1) Section 21 (1) does not apply (by virtue of section 147 (1)) to the carrying on of any ancillary credit business before the day appointed for the purposes of this paragraph in relation to a business of that description.

(2) Where the person carrying on an ancillary credit business applies for a licence before the day appointed for the purposes of this paragraph in relation to a business of that description, he shall be deemed to have been granted on that day a licence covering that business and continuing in force until the licence applied for is granted or, if the application is refused, until the end of the appeal period. **[C.264]**

*Enforcement of agreements made by unlicensed trader*

45. Section 148 (1) does not apply to an agreement made in the course of any business before the day appointed for the purposes of paragraph 44 in relation to a business of that description. **[C.265]**

*Introductions by unlicensed credit-broker*

46. Section 149 does not apply to a regulated agreement made on an introduction effected in the course of any business if the introduction was effected before the day appointed for the purposes of paragraph 44 in relation to a business of that description. **[C.266]**

*Advertisements*

47. Subsections (1) and (2) of section 151 do not apply to any advertisement published before the day appointed for the purposes of this paragraph. **[C.267]**

*Credit reference agencies*

48. Sections 157 and 158 do not apply to a request received before the day appointed for the purposes of this paragraph. **[C.268]**

APPOINTED DAYS

Days are to be appointed by order under s. 192 (2), *ante*. No such order had been made up to the time of going to press.

DEFINITIONS

For "ancillary credit business" see s. 145, *ante*.

For "advertisement", "appeal period", "business", "licence" and "regulated agreement", see s. 189 (1), *ante*.

For "standard licence", see s. 22 (1) (*a*), *ante*.

## PART XII OF ACT

### SUPPLEMENTAL

### *Interpretation*

49.—(1) In the case of an agreement—

(*a*) which was made before the day appointed for the purposes of paragraph 17, and

(*b*) to which (by virtue of paragraph 17 (2)) section 78 (4) applies,

section 185 (2) shall have effect as respects a notice given before that day in relation to the agreement (whether given before or after the passing of this Act) as it would have effect if section 78 (4) had been in operation when the notice was given.

(2) Paragraph (1) applies to an agreement made on or after the day appointed for the purposes of paragraph 17 to provide credit on a current account opened before that day as it applies to an agreement made before that day. **[C.269]**

50. In section 189, the definition of "local authority" shall have effect in relation to matters arising before 16th May 1975 as if for the words "regional, islands or district council" there were substituted "a county council or town council". **[C.270]**

DAY APPOINTED FOR THE PURPOSES OF PARA. 17

See the note "Appointed days" to paras. 15–22 of this Schedule, *ante*.

PASSING OF THIS ACT

This Act was passed (i.e., received the Royal Assent) on 31st July, 1974.

## SCHEDULE 4

Section 192

### MINOR AND CONSEQUENTIAL AMENDMENTS

### PART I

### UNITED KINGDOM

### *Bills of Sale Act* (1878) *Amendment Act* 1882

1. The following section shall be inserted after section 7—

**"7A. Defaults under consumer credit agreements**

(1) Paragraph (1) of section 7 of this Act does not apply to a default relating to a bill of sale given by way of security for the payment of money under a regulated agreement to which section 87 (1) of the Consumer Credit Act 1974 applies—

(*a*) unless the restriction imposed by section 88 (2) of that Act has ceased to apply to the bill of sale; or

(*b*) if, by virtue of section 89 of that Act, the default is to be treated as not having occurred.

(2) Where paragraph (1) of section 7 of this Act does apply in relation to a bill of sale such as is mentioned in subsection (1) of this section, the proviso to that section shall have effect with the substitution of 'county court' for 'High Court'." [**C.271**]

*Factors Act* 1889

2. At the end of section 9 insert—

"For the purposes of this section—

(i) the buyer under a conditional sale agreement shall be deemed not to be a person who has bought or agreed to buy goods, and

(ii) 'conditional sale agreement' means an agreement for the sale of goods which is a consumer credit agreement within the meaning of the Consumer Credit Act 1974 under which the purchase price or part of it is payable by instalments, and the property in the goods is to remain in the seller (notwithstanding that the buyer is to be in possession of the goods) until such conditions as to the payment of instalments or otherwise as may be specified in the agreement are fulfilled." [**C.272**]

*Sale of Goods Act* 1893

3. In section 14 (as substituted by section 3 of the Supply of Goods (Implied Terms) Act 1973) for subsection (3) substitute—

"(3) Where the seller sells goods in the course of a business and the buyer, expressly or by implication, makes known—

(*a*) to the seller, or

(*b*) where the purchase price or part of it is payable by instalments and the goods were previously sold by a credit-broker to the seller, to that credit broker

any particular purpose for which the goods are being bought, there is an implied condition that the goods supplied under the contract are reasonably fit for that purpose, whether or not that is a purpose for which such goods are commonly supplied, except where the circumstances show that the buyer does not rely, or that it is unreasonable for him to rely, on the skill or judgment of the seller or credit-broker.

In this subsection 'credit-broker' means a person acting in the course of a business of credit brokerage carried on by him, that is a business of effecting introductions of individuals desiring to obtain credit—

(i) to persons carrying on any business so far as it relates to the provision of credit, or

(ii) to other persons engaged in credit brokerage." [**C.273**]

4. In section 25, at the end of subsection (2) insert—

"For the purposes of this section—

(i) the buyer under a conditional sale agreement shall be deemed not to be a person who has bought or agreed to buy goods, and

(ii) 'conditional sale agreement' means an agreement for the sale of goods which is a consumer credit agreement within the meaning of the Consumer Credit Act 1974 under which the purchase price or part of it is payable by instalments, and the property in the goods is to remain in the seller (notwithstanding that the buyer is to be in possession of the goods) until such conditions as to the payment of instalments or otherwise as may be specified in the agreement are fulfilled." **[C.274]**

*Law of Distress Amendment Act* 1908

5. The following section shall be inserted after section 4—

**"4A. Hire purchase etc. agreements**

(1) Goods—

(*a*) bailed under a hire-purchase agreement or a consumer hire agreement, or

(*b*) agreed to be sold under a conditional sale agreement,

are, where the relevant agreement has not been terminated, excluded from the application of this Act except during the period between the service of a default notice under the Consumer Credit Act 1974 in respect of the goods and the date on which the notice expires or is earlier complied with.

(2) Goods comprised in a bill of sale are excluded from the application of this Act except during the period between service of a default notice under the Consumer Credit Act 1974 in respect of goods subject to a regulated agreement under which a bill of sale is given by way of security and the date on which the notice expires or is earlier complied with.

(3) In this section—

'conditional sale agreement' means an agreement for the sale of goods under which the purchase price or part of it is payable by instalments, and the property in the goods is to remain in the seller (notwithstanding that the buyer is to be in possession of the goods) until such conditions as to the payment of instalments or otherwise as may be specified in the agreement are fulfilled;

'consumer hire agreement' has the meaning given by section 15 of the Consumer Credit Act 1974.

'hire-purchase agreement' means an agreement, other than a conditional sale agreement, under which—

(*a*) goods are bailed in return for periodical payments by the person to whom they are bailed, and

(*b*) the property in the goods will pass to that person if the terms of the agreement are complied with and one or more of the following occurs—

(i) the exercise of an option to purchase by that person,

(ii) the doing of any other specified act by any party to the agreement,

(iii) the happening of any other specified event; and

'regulated agreement' has the meaning given by section 189 (1) of the Consumer Credit Act 1974." **[C.275]**

PARAS. 3–5: GENERAL NOTE

The new sub-s. 14 (3) substituted in the Sale of Goods Act 1893 differs from the existing subsection in that in clause (*b*), the words "or credit-broker" at the end of the first paragraph and the whole of the second paragraph defining "credit-broker" are new. The amendments are directed to the common case where a dealer, having agreed to sell goods to a customer on credit, sells the goods to a finance house which in turn sells them to the customer. The effect is that if the customer has made known to the dealer the purpose for which he requires the goods, the implied condition of reasonable fitness attaches as if he had made that purpose known to the finance house.

In the case of a regulated agreement, the same result would follow from the provisions of s. 56 (2), *ante*. These new provisions in the Act of 1893, however, are not restricted to regulated agreements, but apply to all instalment sales of goods.

DEFINITIONS

For "consumer credit agreement", see s. 8 (2), *ante*.

For "default notice", see s. 87 (1), *ante*.

For "regulated agreement", see s. 189 (1), *ante*.

BILLS OF SALE ACT (1878) AMENDMENT ACT 1882, S. 7

See 3 Halsbury's Statutes (3rd edn.) 264.

FACTORS ACT 1889, S. 9

See 1 Halsbury's Statutes (3rd edn.) 100.

SALE OF GOODS ACT 1893, SS. 14, 25

For s. 14 as substituted by the Supply of Goods (Implied Terms) Act 1973, see 43 Halsbury's Statutes (3rd edn.) 1341. For s. 25, see 30 Halsbury's Statutes (3rd edn. 23).

LAW OF DISTRESS AMENDMENT ACT 1908, S. 4

See 9 Halsbury's Statutes (3rd edn.) 539.

*Bankruptcy Act* 1914

6. The following section shall be inserted after section 38—

**"38A. Hire purchase etc. agreements**

(1) Goods—

(*a*) bailed under a hire-purchase agreement or a consumer hire agreement, or

(*b*) agreed to be sold under a conditional sale agreement, or

(*c*) subject to a regulated agreement under which a bill of sale is given by way of security,

shall not be treated as the property of the bankrupt during the period between the service of a default notice under the Consumer Credit Act 1974 in respect of the goods and the date on which the notice expires or is earlier complied with.

(2) in this section—

'conditional sale agreement' means an agreement for the sale of goods under which the purchase price or part of it is payable by instalments, and the property in the goods is to remain in the seller (notwithstanding that the buyer is to be in possession of the goods) until such conditions as to the payment of instalments or otherwise as may be specified in the agreement are fulfilled;

'consumer hire agreement' has the meaning given by section 15 of the Consumer Credit Act 1974;

'hire-purchase agreement' means an agreement, other than a conditional sale agreement, under which—

(*a*) goods are bailed in return for periodical payments by the person to whom they are bailed, and

(*b*) the property in the goods will pass to that person if the terms of the agreement are complied with and one or more of the following occurs—

(i) the exercise of an option to purchase by that person,

(ii) the doing of any other specified act by any party to the agreement,

(iii) the happening of any other specified event; and

'regulated agreement' has the meaning given by section 189 (1) of the Consumer Credit Act 1974." **[C.276]**

*Compensation (Defence) Act* 1939

7. In section 13 after "hire-purchase agreement" insert "or a conditional sale agreement". **[C.277]**

8. In section 17 (1)—

(1) After the definition of "aircraft" insert—

" ' conditional sale agreement' means an agreement for the sale of goods which is a consumer credit agreement within the meaning of the Consumer Credit Act 1974 under which the purchase price or part of it is payable by instalments, and the property in the goods is to remain in the seller (notwithstanding that the buyer is to be in possession of the goods) until such conditions as to the payment of instalments or otherwise as may be specified in the agreement are fulfilled;", and

(2) for the definition of "hire-purchase agreement" substitute—

" 'hire-purchase agreement' means an agreement which is a consumer credit agreement within the meaning of the Consumer Credit Act 1974, other than a conditional sale agreement, under which—

(*a*) goods are bailed or (in Scotland) hired in return for periodical payments by the person to whom they are bailed or hired, and

(*b*) the property in the goods will pass to that person if the terms of the agreement are complied with and one or more of the following occurs—

(i) the exercise of an option to purchase by that person,

(ii) the doing of any other specified act by any party to the agreement,

(iii) the happening of any other specified event;" **[C.278]**

*Liability for War Damage (Miscellaneous Provisions) Act* 1939

9. In section 1 (3), for paragraphs (*a*) and (*b*) substitute—

"(*a*) a hire-purchase agreement or a conditional sale agreement within the meaning of the Consumer Credit Act 1974 being (in either case) a consumer credit agreement as defined by that Act; or

(*b*) a consumer hire agreement as defined by that Act." **[C.270]**

*Agriculture (Miscellaneous Provisions) Act* 1950

10. For section 1 (4) substitute—

"(4) A person in possession of a machine by virtue of a hire-purchase agreement or a conditional sale agreement shall for the purposes of this section be treated as the owner of the machine.

In this subsection—

'conditional sale agreement' means an agreement for the sale of goods under which the purchase price or part of it is payable by instalments, and the property in the goods is to remain in the seller (notwithstanding that the buyer is to be in possession of the goods) until such conditions as to the payment of instalments or otherwise as may be specified in the agreement are fulfilled; and

'hire-purchase agreement' means an agreement, other than a conditional sale agreement, under which—

(*a*) goods are bailed or (in Scotland) hired in return for periodical payments by the person to whom they are bailed or hired, and

(*b*) the property in the goods will pass to that person if the terms of the agreement are complied with and one or more of the following occurs—

(i) the exercise of an option to purchase by that person,

(ii) the doing of any other specified act by any party to the agreement,

(iii) the happening of any other specified event." **[C.280]**

*Rag Flock and Other Filling Materials Act* 1951

11. For section 10 (7) substitute—

"(7) References in this section to a sale or to selling include references to a bailment or (in Scotland) hiring under a hire-purchase agreement or to an agreement to sell under a conditional sale agreement.

In this subsection—

'conditional sale agreement' means an agreement for the sale of goods under which the purchase price or part of it is payable by instalments, and the property in the goods is to remain in the seller (notwithstanding that the buyer is to be in possession of the goods) until such conditions as to the payment of instalments or otherwise as may be specified in the agreement are fulfilled; and

'hire-purchase agreement' means an agreement other than a conditional sale agreement, under which—

(*a*) goods are bailed or (in Scotland) hired in return for periodical payments by the person to whom they are bailed or hired, and

(*b*) the property in the goods will pass to that person if the terms of the agreement are complied with and one or more of the following occurs—

(i) the exercise of an option to purchase by that person,

(ii) the doing of any other specified act by any party to the agreement,

(iii) the happening of any other specified event." **[C.281]**

DEFINITIONS

For "conditional sale agreement" and "hire-purchase agreement", see s. 189 (1), *ante*. For "consumer credit agreement", see s. 8 (2), *ante*, for "consumer hire agreement" see s. 15, *ante*, and for "default notice", see s. 87 (1), *ante*.

BANKRUPTCY ACT 1914, S. 38

See 3 Halsbury's Statutes (3rd edn.) 87.

COMPENSATION (DEFENCE) ACT 1939, SS. 13, 17 (1)

See 6 Halsbury's Statutes (3rd edn.) 94, 95.

LIABILITY FOR WAR DAMAGE (MISCELLANEOUS PROVISIONS) ACT 1939, S. 1 (3)

See 38 Halsbury's Statutes (3rd edn.) 534.

AGRICULTURE (MISCELLANEOUS PROVISIONS) ACT 1950, S. 1 (4)
See 1 Halsbury's Statutes (3rd edn.) 233.

RAG FLOCK AND OTHER FILLING MATERIALS ACT 1951, S. 10 (7)
See 26 Halsbury's Statutes (3rd edn.) 435.

*Reserve and Auxiliary Forces (Protection of Civil Interest) Act* 1951

12. In section 4 for subsections (4), (5) and (6), substitute—

"(4) Where the appropriate court refuses leave under section 4 (2) of this Act to take possession of goods subject to a hire-purchase agreement or a conditional sale agreement or to execute a judgment or order for delivery of such goods, or gives leave subject to restrictions and conditions, and the person to whom the goods are bailed, or, as the case may be, the buyer, before possession is taken or execution on the judgment or order completed, pays the total price, the creditor's title to the goods shall, notwithstanding any failure to pay the total price at the time required by the agreement, vest in that person.

(5) Where the creditor under a hire-purchase agreement or a conditional sale agreement has taken possession of the goods bailed or agreed to be sold under it, the appropriate court on an application under section 3 (1) (*c*) of this Act, may, if it thinks fit, deal with the case as if the creditor were proceeding to take possession of the goods and, if it makes an order under that paragraph, may direct accordingly that the goods be restored to the person to whom they were bailed or, as the case may be, the buyer; and if, after the creditor has taken possession of the goods, notice is given under that paragraph with respect to them, he shall not, so long as the notice is in force or any application in pursuance of the notice is undisposed of, deal with the goods in such a way as to prejudice the powers of the appropriate court under this subsection." **[C.282]**

13. For section 10 substitute—

**"10. Property in goods subject to hire-purchase agreement**

(1) Where the appropriate court refuses leave under section 8 (3) of this Act to take or resume possession of goods subject to a hire-purchase agreement or a conditional sale agreement or to do diligence on any decree for the delivery of such goods, or gives leave subject to restrictions and conditions, and the person to whom they are hired, or, as the case may be, the buyer before possession is taken or resumed or diligence is done, pays the total price, the creditors' title to the goods shall, notwithstanding any failure to pay the total price at the time required by the agreement, vest in that person.

(2) Where the creditor under a hire-purchase agreement or a conditional sale agreement has taken possession of the goods hired or agreed to be sold under it, the appropriate court on an application under section 9 (1) (*c*) of this Act may, if it thinks fit, deal with the case as if the creditor were proceeding to take possession of the goods and, if it makes an order under that paragraph, may direct accordingly that the goods be restored to the person to whom they were hired or, as the case may be, the buyer; and if, after the creditor has taken possession of the goods, notice is given under that paragraph with respect to them, he shall not, so long as the notice is in force or any application in pursuance of the notice is undisposed of, deal with the goods in such a way as to prejudice the powers of the appropriate court under this subsection." **[C.283]**

14. In section 64 (1)—

(1) After the definition of "compulsory national service" insert—

" 'conditional sale agreement' means an agreement for the sale of goods under which the purchase price or part of it is payable by instalments, and the property in the goods is to remain in the seller (notwithstanding that the buyer is to be in possession of the goods) until such conditions as to the payment of instalments or otherwise as may be specified in the agreement are fulfilled;

'creditor' means the person by whom goods are bailed or (in Scotland) hired under a hire-purchase agreement or, as the case may be, the seller under a conditional sale agreement, or the person to whom his rights and duties have passed by assignment or operation of the law;

'hire-purchase agreement' means an agreement, other than a conditional sale agreement, under which—

(*a*) goods are bailed or (in Scotland) hired in return for periodical payments by the person to whom they are bailed or hired, and

(*b*) the property in the goods will pass to that person if the terms of the agreement are complied with and one or more of the following occurs—

(i) the exercise of an option to purchase by that person,

(ii) the doing of any other specified act by any party to the agreement,

(iii) the happening of any other specified event;".

(2) After the definition of "short period of training" insert—

" 'total price' means the total sum payable by the person to whom goods are bailed or hired under a hire-purchase agreement or, as the case may be, the buyer under a conditional sale agreement including any sum payable on the exercise of an option to purchase but excluding any sum payable as a penalty or as compensation or damages for a breach of the agreement." **[C.284]**

RESERVE AND AUXILIARY FORCES (PROTECTION OF CIVIL INTERESTS) ACT 1951, SS. 4, 64 (1)

See 29 Halsbury's Statutes (3rd edn.) 723, 774.

*Clean Air Act* 1956

15. In section 14 for the words "a hire-purchase agreement for the letting to him" substitute—

"either—

(i) a conditional sale agreement for the sale to him, or

(ii) a hire-purchase agreement for the bailment or (in Scotland) hiring to him,". **[C.285]**

16. In section 34 (1)—

(*a*) after the definition of "chimney" insert—

" 'conditional sale agreement' means an agreement for the sale of goods under which the purchase price or part of it is payable by instalments, and the property in the goods is to remain in the seller (notwithstanding that the buyer is to be in possession of the goods) until such conditions as to the payment of instalments or otherwise as may be specified in the agreement are fulfilled;", and (*b*) for the definition of "hire-purchase agreement" substitute—

"hire-purchase agreement" means an agreement, other than a conditional sale agreement under which—

(*a*) goods are bailed or (in Scotland) hired in return for periodical payments by the person to whom they are bailed or hired, and

(*b*) the property in the goods will pass to that person if the terms of the agreement are complied with and one or more of the following occurs—

(i) the exercise of an option to purchase by that person,

(ii) the doing of any other specified act by any party to the agreement,

(iii) the happening of any other specified event;". **[C.286]**

*Restrictive Trade Practices Act* 1956

17. For section 26 (3) substitute—

"(3) In this Part of this Act any reference to selling goods includes a reference to bailing or (in Scotland) hiring goods under a hire-purchase agreement or to agreeing to sell the goods under a conditional sale agreement.

In this subsection—

(1) "conditional sale agreement" means an agreement for the sale of goods under which the purchase price or part of it is payable by instalments, and the property in the goods is to remain in the seller (notwithstanding that the buyer is to be in possession of the goods) until such conditions as to the payment of instalments or otherwise as may be specified in the agreement are fulfilled; and

(2) "hire-purchase agreement" means an agreement, other than a conditional sale agreement, under which—

(*a*) goods are bailed or (in Scotland) hired in return for periodical payments by the person to whom they are bailed or hired, and

(*b*) the property in the goods will pass to that person if the terms of the agreement are complied with and one or more of the following occurs—

(i) the exercise of an option to purchase by that person,

(ii) the doing of any other specified act by any party to the agreement,

(iii) the happening of any other specified event." **[C.287]**

*Housing Act* 1957

18. For section 94 substitute—

**"94. Power to provide furniture**

A local authority may fit out, furnish and supply any house erected, converted or acquired by them under section 92 of this Act with all requisite furniture, fittings and conveniences and may sell, or supply under a hire-purchase agreement or a conditional sale agreement, furniture to the occupants of houses provided by the local authority and for that purpose may buy furniture.

In this subsection—

(1) "conditional sale agreement" means an agreement for the sale of goods under which the purchase price or part of it is payable by instal-

ments, and the property in the goods is to remain in the seller (notwithstanding that the buyer is to be in possession of the goods) until such conditions as to the payment of instalments or otherwise as may be specified in the agreement are fulfilled; and

(2) "hire-purchase agreement" means an agreement, other than a conditional sale agreement, under which—

(*a*) goods are bailed in return for periodical payments by the person to whom they are bailed, and

(*b*) the property in the goods will pass to that person if the terms of the agreement are complied with and one or more of the following occurs—

(i) the exercise of an option to purchase by that person,

(ii) the doing of any other specified act by any party to the agreement,

(iii) the happening of any other specified event." **[C.288]**

CLEAN AIR ACT 1956, SS. 14, 34 (1)
See 26 Halsbury's Statutes (3rd edn.) 470, 485.

RESTRICTIVE TRADE PRACTICES ACT 1956, S. 26 (3)
See 37 Halsbury's Statutes (3rd edn.) 107.

HOUSING ACT 1957, S. 94
See 16 Halsbury's Statutes (3rd edn.) 188.

*County Courts Act* 1959

19. At the end of section 192 (2) (*c*) insert—
"(*d*) section 139 (5) (*b*) of the Consumer Credit Act 1974." **[C.289]**

*Consumer Protection Act* 1961

20. In section 2, for subsection (6) substitute—

"(6) If as respects goods of any class or description regulations under section 1 above so provide, subsections (1) to (3) above (other than subsection 3 (*d*) and (*e*)) shall apply in relation to goods of that class or description as if—

(*a*) references to selling or to a sale included references to—

(i) bailing or (in Scotland) hiring under a hire-purchase agreement, or

(ii) bailing or (in Scotland) hiring under a hire agreement, or

(iii) an agreement to sell under a conditional sale agreement; and

(*b*) the reference to a sale under a credit-sale agreement were a reference

(i) to a bailment, or a hiring under a hire-purchase agreement, or

(ii) to an agreement to sell under a conditional sale agreement.

Provided that subsections (1) and (2) above shall not apply—

(*a*) in a case of bailment or hiring under a hire agreement, where the bailment or hiring is incidental to an agreement under which payments are to be made in the form of rent issuing out of land;

(*b*) in a case of possession for the purpose of bailment or hiring under a hire agreement, where possession is for the purpose of a bailment or hiring which is incidental to an agreement under which payments are to be made in the form of rent issuing out of land;

(*c*) in any case of bailment or hire under a hire agreement, where the bailment or hiring was lawful at the time when it began." **[C.290]**

21. In section 5—

(1) After the definition of "component part" insert—

"conditional sale agreement" means an agreement for the sale of goods under which the purchase price or part of it is payable by instalments, and the property in the goods is to remain in the seller (notwithstanding that the buyer is to be in possession of the goods) until such conditions as to the payment of instalments or otherwise as may be specified in the agreement are fulfilled;

"hire agreement" means an agreement for the bailment or (in Scotland) the hiring of goods which is not a hire-purchase agreement;

(2) for the definition of "credit-sale agreement" substitute—

" 'credit sale agreement' means an agreement for the sale of goods, under which the purchase price or part of it is payable by instalments, but which is not a conditional sale agreement;"

(3) for the definition of "hire-purchase agreement" substitute—

" 'hire-purchase agreement' means an agreement, other than a conditional sale agreement, under which—

(*a*) goods are bailed or (in Scotland) hired in return for periodical payments by the person to whom they are bailed or hired, and

(*b*) the property in the goods will pass to that person if the terms of the agreement are complied with and one or more of the following occurs—

(i) the exercise of an option to purchase by that person,

(ii) the doing of any other specified act by any party to the agreement,

(iii) the happening of any other specified event;" **[C.291]**

COUNTY COURTS ACT 1959, S. 192 (2)
See 7 Halsbury's Statutes (3rd edn.) 419.

CONSUMER PROTECTION ACT 1961, SS. 2, 5
See 30 Halsbury's Statutes (3rd edn.) 48, 52.

*Hire Purchase Act* 1964

22. For Part III substitute the following (which reproduces the existing provisions of that Part subject only to changes in terminology)—

"PART III

TITLE TO MOTOR VEHICLES ON HIRE-PURCHASE OR CONDITIONAL SALE

**27. Protection of purchasers of motor vehicles**

(1) This section applies where a motor vehicle has been bailed or (in Scotland) hired under a hire-purchase agreement, or has been agreed to be sold under a conditional sale agreement, and, before the property in the vehicle has become vested in the debtor, he disposes of the vehicle to another person.

(2) Where the disposition referred to in subsection (1) above is to a private purchaser, and he is a purchaser of the motor vehicle in good faith without notice of the hire-purchase or conditional sale agreement (the 'relevant agreement') that disposition shall have effect as if the creditor's title to the vehicle has been vested in the debtor immediately before that disposition.

(3) Where the person to whom the disposition referred to in subsection (1) above is made (the 'original purchaser') is a trade or finance purchaser, then if the person who is the first private purchaser of the motor vehicle after that disposition (the 'first private purchaser') is a purchaser of the vehicle in good faith without notice of the relevant agreement, the disposition of the vehicle to the first private purchaser shall have effect as if the title of the creditor to the vehicle had been vested in the debtor immediately before he disposed of it to the original purchaser.

(4) Where, in a case within subsection (3) above—

(*a*) the disposition by which the first private purchaser becomes a purchaser of the motor vehicle in good faith without notice of the relevant agreement is itself a bailment or hiring under a hire-purchase agreement, and

(*b*) the person who is the creditor in relation to that agreement disposes of the vehicle to the first private purchaser, or a person claiming under him, by transferring to him the property in the vehicle in pursuance of a provision in the agreement in that behalf,

the disposition referred to in paragraph (*b*) above (whether or not the person to whom it is made is a purchaser in good faith without notice of the relevant agreement) shall as well as the disposition referred to in paragraph (*a*) above, have effect as mentioned in subsection (3) above.

(5) The preceding provisions of this section apply—

(*a*) notwithstanding anything in section 21 of the Sale of Goods Act 1893 (sale of goods by a person not the owner), but

(*b*) without prejudice to the provisions of the Factors Acts (as defined by section 62 (1) of the said Act of 1893) or of any other enactment enabling the apparent owner of goods to dispose of them as if he were the true owner.

(6) Nothing in this section shall exonerate the debtor from any liability (whether criminal or civil) to which he would be subject apart from this section; and, in a case where the debtor disposes of the motor vehicle to a trade or finance purchaser, nothing in this section shall exonerate—

(*a*) that trade or finance purchaser, or

(*b*) any other trade or finance purchaser who becomes a purchaser of the vehicle and is not a person claiming under the first private purchaser,

from any liability (whether criminal or civil) to which he would be subject apart from this section.

**28. Presumptions relating to dealings with motor vehicles**

(1) Where in any proceedings (whether criminal or civil) relating to a motor vehicle it is proved—

(*a*) that the vehicle was bailed or (in Scotland) hired under a hire-purchase agreement, or was agreed to be sold under a conditional sale agreement and

(*b*) that a person (whether a party to the proceedings or not) became a private purchaser of the vehicle in good faith without notice of the hire-purchase or conditional sale agreement (the 'relevant agreement'),

this section shall have effect for the purposes of the operation of section 27 of this Act in relation to those proceedings.

(2) It shall be presumed for those purposes, unless the contrary is proved, that the disposition of the vehicle to the person referred to in subsection (1) (*b*) above (the 'relevant purchaser') was made by the debtor.

(3) If it is proved that that disposition was not made by the debtor, then it shall be presumed for those purposes, unless the contrary is proved—

(*a*) that the debtor disposed of the vehicle to a private purchaser purchasing in good faith without notice of the relevant agreement, and

(*b*) that the relevant purchaser is or was a person claiming under the person to whom the debtor so disposed of the vehicle.

(4) If it is proved that the disposition of the vehicle to the relevant purchaser was not made by the debtor, and that the person to whom the debtor disposed of the vehicle (the 'original purchaser') was a trade or finance purchaser, then it shall be presumed for those purposes, unless the contrary is proved,—

(*a*) that the person who, after the disposition of the vehicle to the original purchaser, first became a private purchaser of the vehicle was a purchaser in good faith without notice of the relevant agreement, and

(*b*) that the relevant purchaser is or was a person claiming under the original purchaser.

(5) Without prejudice to any other method of proof, where in any proceedings a party thereto admits a fact, that fact shall, for the purposes of this section, be taken as against him to be proved in relation to those proceedings.

**29. Interpretation of Part III**

(1) In this Part of this Act—

'conditional sale agreement' means an agreement for the sale of goods under which the purchase price or part of it is payable by instalments, and the property in the goods is to remain in the seller (notwithstanding that the buyer is to be in possession of the goods) until such conditions as to the payment of instalments or otherwise as may be specified in the agreement are fulfilled;

'creditor' means the person by whom goods are bailed or (in Scotland) hired under a hire-purchase agreement or as the case may be, the seller under a conditional sale agreement or the person to whom his rights and duties have passed by assignment or operation of law;

'disposition' means any sale or contract of sale (including a conditional sale agreement), any bailment or (in Scotland) hiring under a hire-purchase agreement and any transfer of the property in goods in pursuance of a provision in that behalf contained in a hire-purchase agreement, and includes, any transaction purporting to be a disposition (as so defined), and 'dispose of' shall be construed accordingly;

'hire-purchase agreement' means an agreement, other than a conditional sale agreement, under which

(*a*) goods are bailed or (in Scotland) hired in return for periodical payments by the person to whom they are bailed or hired, and

(*b*) the property in the goods will pass to that person if the terms of the agreement are complied with and one or more of the following occurs—

(i) the exercise of an option to purchase by that person,
(ii) the doing of any other specified act by any party to the agreement,
(iii) the happening of any other specified events; and

'motor vehicle' means a mechanically propelled vehicle intended or adapted for use on roads to which the public has access.

(2) In this Part of this Act, 'trade or finance purchaser' means a purchaser who, at the time of the disposition made to him, carries on a business which consists, wholly or partly,—

(*a*) of purchasing motor vehicles for the purpose of offering or exposing them for sale, or
(*b*) of providing finance by purchasing motor vehicles for the purpose of bailing or (in Scotland) hiring them under hire-purchase agreements or agreeing to sell them under conditional sale agreements,

and 'private purchaser' means a purchaser who, at the time of the disposition made to him, does not carry on any such business.

(3) For the purposes of this Part of this Act a person becomes a purchaser of a motor vehicle if, and at the time when, a disposition of the vehicle is made to him; and a person shall be taken to be a purchaser of a motor vehicle without notice of a hire-purchase agreement or conditional sale agreement if, at the time of the disposition made to him, he has no actual notice that the vehicle is or was the subject of any such agreement.

(4) In this Part of this Act the 'debtor' in relation to a motor vehicle which has been bailed or hired under a hire-purchase agreement, or, as the case may be, agreed to be sold under a conditional sale agreement, means the person who at the material time (whether the agreement has before that time been terminated or not) is either—

(*a*) the person to whom the vehicle is bailed or hired under that agreement, or
(*b*) is, in relation to the agreement, the buyer,

including a person who at that time is, by virtue of section 130 (4) of the Consumer Credit Act 1974 treated as a bailee or (in Scotland) a custodier of the vehicle.

(5) In this Part of this Act any reference to the title of the creditor to a motor vehicle which has been bailed or (in Scotland) hired under a hire-purchase agreement, or agreed to be sold under a conditional sale agreement, and is disposed of by the debtor, is a reference to such title (if any) to the vehicle as, immediately before that disposition, was vested in the person who then was the creditor in relation to the agreement,". [**C.292**]

GENERAL NOTE

The changes in terminology made by this amendment are the substitution of "bailed" for "let", of "debtor" for "hirer or buyer" and of "creditor" for "owner or seller". Definitions of "conditional sale agreement" and "hire-purchase agreement", identical with those in s. 189 (1), *ante*, are substituted for a reference to the definitions in the Hire-Purchase Act 1965 (repealed by s. 192 (3), *ante*, and Sch. 5, *post*).

HIRE-PURCHASE ACT 1964, SS. 27–29

See 30 Halsbury's Statutes (3rd edn.) 55–59.

*Emergency Laws (Re-enactment and Repeals) Act* 1964

23. In section 1—

(1) In subsection (1) for "or credit-sale agreements, or under agreements for letting on hire" substitute "conditional sale agreements, credit-sale agreements or hire agreements".

(2) For subsection (2) substitute—

"(2) In this section—

'conditional sale agreement' means an agreement for the sale of any article under which the purchase price, or part of it is payable by instalments, and the property in the article is to remain in the seller (notwithstanding that the buyer is to be in possession of the article) until such conditions as to the payment of instalments or otherwise as may be specified in the agreement are fulfilled;

'credit-sale agreement' means an agreement for the sale of any article, under which the purchase price or part of it is payable by instalments, but which is not a conditional sale agreement;

'hire-purchase agreement' means an agreement, other than a conditional sale agreement under which—

(*a*) an article is bailed or (in Scotland) hired in return for periodical payments by the person to whom it is bailed or hired, and

(*b*) the property in the article will pass to that person if the terms of the agreement are complied with and one or more of the following occurs—

(i) the exercise of an option by that person;

(ii) the doing of any other specified act by any party to the agreement;

(iii) the happening of any other specified event; and

'hire agreement' means an agreement for the bailment or (in Scotland) the hiring of an article which is not a hire-purchase agreement." **[C.293]**

*Trading Stamps Act* 1964

24. In section 2, for subsection (1) substitute—

"(1) No person shall after the coming into force of this section issue any trading stamp, or cause any trading stamp to be issued, or deliver any trading stamp to any person in connection with the sale of any goods, the bailment or (in Scotland) the hiring of any goods under a hire-purchase agreement or the performance of any services, unless such trading stamp bears on its face in clear and legible characters a value expressed in or by reference to current coin of the realm." **[C.294]**

25. In section 3, for subsection (4) substitute—

"(4) In this section 'redeemable trading stamps' means trading stamps delivered after the coming into force of this section in accordance with a trading stamp scheme on or in connection with either—

(*a*) the purchase of any goods,

(*b*) the bailment or (in Scotland) the hiring of any goods under a hire-purchase agreement, or

(*c*) the obtaining of any services for money,

and 'the holder', in relation to such a trading stamp, means the person to whom it was so delivered or any person who holds it without notice of any defect in title." **[C.295]**

26. In section 10 (1)—

(1) after the definition of "cash value" insert—

" 'conditional sale agreement' means an agreement for the sale of goods under which the purchase price or part of it is payable by instalments, and the property in the goods is to remain in the seller (notwithstanding that the buyer is to be in possession of the goods) until such conditions as to the payment of instalments or otherwise as may be specified in the agreement are fulfilled;",

and

(2) after the definition of "goods" insert—

" 'hire-purchase agreement' means an agreement, other than a conditional sale agreement, under which—

(*a*) goods are bailed or (in Scotland) hired in return for periodical payments by the person to whom they are bailed or hired, and

(*b*) the property in the goods will pass to that person if the terms of the agreement are complied with and one or more of the following occurs—

(i) the exercise of an option to purchase by that person,

(ii) the doing of any other specified act by any party to the agreement,

(iii) the happening of any other specified event;".

(3) For the definition of "trading stamp" substitute—

" 'trading stamp' means a stamp which is, or is intended to be, delivered to any person on or in connection with either—

(i) the purchase of any goods, or

(ii) the bailment or (in Scotland) the hiring of any goods under a hire-purchase agreement,

(other than the purchase of a newspaper or other periodical of which the stamp forms part or in which it is contained) and is, or is intended to be, redeemable (whether singly or together with other such sums) by that or some other person:

Provided that a stamp shall not be deemed to be a trading stamp if—

(*a*) it is delivered or is intended to be delivered to a person (in this definition called 'the purchaser') on or in connection with the purchase of any goods by the purchaser, or the bailment or (in Scotland) the hiring to him of any goods, and

(*b*) it is intended to be, and is not, redeemable from any person other than—

(i) the person (in this definition called 'the seller') from whom the purchaser purchased those goods, or who bailed or hired those goods to him, or

(ii) any person from whom the seller (whether directly or indirectly) acquired those goods, and

(*c*) in the case where a business is carried on by six or more retail establishments, the stamp is one of a kind obtainable at no more than six of those retail establishments, and not obtainable by the public elsewhere, and the arrangements under which it is redeemable are entirely separate from arrangements under which any other stamps, whether trading stamps or not, are redeemable

and references in this definition to the purchase of goods include references to the obtaining of services for money;" [**C.296**]

EMERGENCY LAWS (RE-ENACTMENT AND REPEALS) ACT 1964, S. 1
See 38 Halsbury's Statutes (3rd edn.) 336.

TRADING STAMPS ACT 1964, SS. 2 (1), 3 (4), 10 (1)
See 37 Halsbury's Statutes (3rd edn.) 171, 172, 175.

*Housing (Scotland) Act* 1966

27. In section 140 (2), for the words from "as defined" onwards substitute "within the meaning of the Consumer Credit Act 1974." [**C.297**]

*Trade Descriptions Act* 1968

28. In section 28, insert the following new subsection after subsection (5)—

"(5A) Subsection (5) of this section does not apply to disclosure for a purpose specified in section 174 (3) of the Consumer Credit Act 1974." [**C.298**]

*Income and Corporation Taxes Act* 1970

29. In section 495, for subsection (7) substitute—

"(7) In this section—

'hire-purchase agreement' means an agreement, other than a conditional sale agreement, under which—

(*a*) goods are bailed or (in Scotland) hired in return for periodical payments by the person to whom they are bailed or hired, and

(*b*) the property in the goods will pass to that person if the terms of the agreement are complied with and one or more of the following occurs—

(i) the exercise of an option to purchase by that person,

(ii) the doing of any other specified act by any party to the agreement,

(iii) the happening of any other specified event; and

'conditional sale agreement' means an agreement for the sale of goods under which the purchase price or part of it is payable by instalments, and the property in the goods is to remain in the seller (notwithstanding that the buyer is to be in possession of the goods) until such conditions as to the payment of instalments or otherwise as may be specified in the agreement are fulfilled." [**C.299**]

*Administration of Justice Act* 1970

30. After section 38 insert the following new section—

"38A. This Part of this Act shall not apply to a mortgage securing an agreement which is a regulated agreement within the meaning of the Consumer Credit Act 1974." [**C.300**]

31. In section 54 (6) (*c*) after "36" insert "38A". [**C.301**]

*Vehicles (Excise) Act* 1971

32. In section 38 (1)—

(1) before the definition of "gas" insert—

" 'conditional sale agreement' means an agreement for the sale of a vehicle under which the purchase price or part of it is payable by instalments, and the property in the vehicle is to remain in the seller (notwithstanding that the buyer is to be in possession of the vehicle) until such conditions as to the payment of instalments or otherwise as may be specified in the agreement are fulfilled;"

(2) for the definition of "hackney carriage" substitute—

"hackney carriage" means a mechanically propelled vehicle standing or plying for hire and includes any mechanically propelled vehicle bailed or (in Scotland) hired under a hire agreement by a person whose trade it is to sell such vehicles or bail or hire them under hire agreements;

(3) after the definition of "hackney carriage" insert—

"hire agreement" means an agreement for the bailment or (in Scotland) the hiring of a vehicle which is not a hire-purchase agreement;

"hire-purchase agreement" means an agreement, other than a conditional sale agreement, under which—

(*a*) a vehicle is bailed or (in Scotland) hired in return for periodical payments by the person to whom it is bailed or hired, and

(*b*) the property in the vehicle will pass to that person if the terms of the agreement are complied with and one or more of the following occurs—

(i) the exercise of an option to purchase by that person,

(ii) the doing of any other specified act by any party to the agreement,

(iii) the happening of any other specified event;" **[C.302]**

*Industry Act* 1972

33. In section 6 (2)—

(1) After the definition of " 'capital expenditure,' or expenditure of a 'capital nature' " insert—

" 'conditional sale agreement' means an agreement for the sale of goods under which the purchase price or part of it is payable by instalments, and the property in the goods is to remain in the seller (notwithstanding that the buyer is to be in possession of the goods) until such conditions as to the payment of instalments or otherwise as may be specified in the agreement are fulfilled;" and

(2) For the definition of "hire-purchase agreement" substitute—

" 'hire-purchase agreement' " means an agreement, other than a conditional sale agreement, under which

(*a*) goods are bailed or (in Scotland) hired in return for periodical payments by the person to whom they are bailed or hired, and

(*b*) the property in the goods will pass to that person if the terms of the agreement are complied with and one or more of the following occurs—

(i) the exercise of an option to purchase by that person,

(ii) the doing of any other specified act by any party to the agreement,

(iii) the happening of any other specified event;". **[C.303]**

*Counter-Inflation Act* 1973

34. In section 21 (5)—

(*a*) for "total purchase price or hire-purchase price" substitute "total price"; and

(*b*) for the words from "This subsection" onwards substitute—

"In this subsection—

'conditional sale agreement' means an agreement for the sale of goods under which the purchase price or part of it is payable by instalments, and the property in the goods is to remain in the seller (notwithstanding that the buyer is to be in possession of the goods) until such conditions as to the payment of instalments or otherwise as may be specified in the agreement are fulfilled, and

'hire-purchase agreement' means an agreement, other than a conditional sale agreement, under which—

(*a*) goods are bailed or (in Scotland) hired in return for periodical payments by the person to whom they are bailed or hired, and

(*b*) the property in the goods will pass to that person if the terms of the agreement are complied with and one or more of the following occurs—

(i) the exercise of an option to purchase by that person,

(ii) the doing of any other specified act by any party to the agreement,

(iii) the happening of any other specified event; and

'total price' means the total sum payable by the person to whom goods are bailed or hired under a hire-purchase agreement or, as the case may be, the buyer under a conditional sale agreement including any sum payable on the exercise of an option to purchase but excluding any sum payable as a penalty or as compensation or damages for a breach of the agreement." **[C.304]**

REGULATED AGREEMENT

For meaning, see s. 189 (1), *ante*.

TRADE DESCRIPTIONS ACT 1968, S. 28

See 37 Halsbury's Statutes (3rd edn.) 968.

INCOME AND CORPORATION TAXES ACT 1970, S. 495 (7)

See 33 Halsbury's Statutes (3rd edn.) 652.

ADMINISTRATION OF JUSTICE ACT 1970, SS. 38, 54 (6)

See 40 Halsbury's Statutes (3rd edn.) 1061, 1063.

VEHICLES (EXCISE) ACT 1971, S. 38 (1)

See 41 Halsbury's Statutes (3rd edn.) 464.

INDUSTRY ACT 1972, S. 6 (2)

See 42 Halsbury's Statutes (3rd edn.) 2215.

*Supply of Goods (Implied Terms) Act* 1973

35. For sections 8 to 12 substitute the following sections (which reproduce the existing provisions of those sections subject only to changes in terminology)—

**"8. Implied terms as to title**

(1) In every hire-purchase agreement, other than one to which subsection (2) below applies, there is—

(*a*) an implied condition on the part of the creditor that he will have a right to sell the goods at the time when the property is to pass; and

(*b*) an implied warranty that—

(i) the goods are free, and will remain free until the time when the property is to pass, from any charge or encumbrance not disclosed or known to the person to whom the goods are bailed or (in Scotland) hired before the agreement is made, and

(ii) that person will enjoy quiet possession of the goods except so far as it may be disturbed by any person entitled to the benefit of any charge or encumbrance so disclosed or known.

(2) In a hire-purchase agreement, in the case of which there appears from the agreement or is to be inferred from the circumstances of the agreement an intention that the creditor should transfer only such title as he or a third person may have, there is—

(*a*) an implied warranty that all charges or encumbrances known to the creditor and not known to the person to whom the goods are bailed or hired have been disclosed to that person before the agreement is made; and

(*b*) an implied warranty that neither—

(i) the creditor; nor

(ii) in a case where the parties to the agreement intend that any title which may be transferred shall be only such title as a third person may have, that person; nor

(iii) anyone claiming through or under the creditor or that third person otherwise than under a charge or encumbrance disclosed or known to the person to whom the goods are bailed or hired, before the agreement is made;

will disturb the quiet possession of the person to whom the goods are bailed or hired.

**9. Bailing or hiring by description**

(1) Where under a hire-purchase agreement goods are bailed or (in Scotland) hired by description, there is an implied condition that the goods will correspond with the description, and if under the agreement the goods are bailed or hired by reference to a sample as well as a description, it is not sufficient that the bulk of the goods corresponds with the sample if the goods do not also correspond with the description.

(2) Goods shall not be prevented from being bailed or hired by description by reason only that, being exposed for sale, bailment or hire, they are selected by the person to whom they are bailed or hired.

**10. Implied undertakings as to quality or fitness**

(1) Except as provided by this section and section 11 below and subject to the provisions of any other enactment, including any enactment of the Parliament of Northern Ireland, or the Northern Ireland Assembly there is no implied condition or warranty as to the quality or fitness for any particular purpose of goods bailed or (in Scotland) hired under a hire-purchase agreement.

(2) Where the creditor bails or hires goods under a hire-purchase agree-

ment in the course of a business, there is an implied condition that the goods are of merchantable quality, except that there is no such condition—

(*a*) as regards defects specifically drawn to the attention of the person to whom the goods are bailed or hired before the agreement is made; or

(*b*) if that person examines the goods before the agreement is made, as regards defects which that examination ought to reveal.

(3) Where the creditor bails or hires goods under a hire-purchase agreement in the course of a business and the person to whom the goods are bailed or hired, expressly or by implication, makes known—

(*a*) to the creditor in the course of negotiations conducted by the creditor in relation to the making of the hire-purchase agreement, or

(*b*) to a credit-broker in the course of negotiations conducted by that broker in relation to goods sold by him to the creditor before forming the subject matter of the hire-purchase agreement,

any particular purpose for which the goods are being bailed or hired, there is an implied condition that the goods supplied under the agreement are reasonably fit for that purpose, whether or not that is a purpose for which such goods are commonly supplied, except where the circumstances show that the person to whom the goods are bailed or hired does not rely, or that it is unreasonable for him to rely, on the skill or judgment of the creditor or credit-broker.

(4) An implied condition or warranty as to quality or fitness for a particular purpose may be annexed to a hire-purchase agreement by usage.

(5) The preceding provisions of this section apply to a hire-purchase agreement made by a person who in the course of a business is acting as agent for the creditor as they apply to an agreement made by the creditor in the course of a business, except where the creditor is not bailing or hiring in the course of a business and either the person to whom the goods are bailed or hired knows that fact or reasonable steps are taken to bring it to the notice of that person before the agreement is made.

(6) In subsection (3) above and this subsection—

(*a*) 'credit-broker' means a person acting in the course of a business of credit brokerage;

(*b*) 'credit brokerage' means the effecting of introductions of individuals desiring to obtain credit—

(i) to persons carrying on any business so far as it relates to the provision of credit, or

(ii) to other persons engaged in credit brokerage.

**11. Samples**

Where under a hire-purchase agreement goods are bailed or (in Scotland) hired by reference to a sample, there is an implied condition—

(*a*) that the bulk will correspond with the sample in quality; and

(*b*) that the person to whom the goods are bailed or hired will have a reasonable opportunity of comparing the bulk with the sample; and

(*c*) that the goods will be free from any defect, rendering them unmerchantable, which would not be apparent on reasonable examination of the sample.

**12. Exclusion of implied terms and conditions**

(1) An express condition or warranty does not negative a condition or warranty implied by this Act unless inconsistent with it.

(2) A term of a hire-purchase agreement or any other agreement exempting from all or any of the provisions of section 8 above shall be void.

(3) A term of a hire-purchase agreement or any other agreement exempting from all or any of the provisions of sections 9, 10 or 11 above shall be void in the case of a consumer agreement and shall, in any other case, not be enforceable to the extent that it is shown that it would not be fair or reasonable to allow reliance on the term.

(4) In determining for the purpose of subsection (3) above whether or not reliance on any such term would be fair or reasonable regard shall be had to all the circumstances of the case and in particular to the following matters—

(*a*) the strength of the bargaining positions of the creditor and the person to whom the goods are bailed or hired relative to each other, taking into account, among other things, the availability of suitable alternative products and sources of supply;

(*b*) whether that person received an inducement to agree to the term or in accepting it had an opportunity of acquiring the goods or suitable alternatives without it from any source of supply;

(*c*) whether that person knew or ought reasonably to have known of the existence and extent of the term (having regard, among other things, to any custom of the trade and any previous course of dealing between the parties);

(*d*) where the term exempts from all or any of the provisions of section 9, 10 or 11 above if some condition is not complied with, whether it was reasonable at the time of the agreement to expect that compliance with that condition would be practicable;

(*e*) whether the goods were manufactured, processed or adapted to the special order of that person.

(5) Subsection (4) above shall not prevent the court from holding, in accordance with any rule of law, that a term which purports to exclude or restrict any of the provisions of sections 9, 10 and 11 above is not a term of the hire-purchase agreement.

(6) In this section 'consumer agreement' means a hire-purchase agreement where the creditor makes the agreement in the course of a business and the goods to which the agreement relates—

(*a*) are of a type ordinarily supplied for private use or consumption; and

(*b*) are bailed or (in Scotland) hired to a person who does not bail or hire them or hold himself out as bailing or hiring them in the course of a business.

(7) The onus of proving that a hire-purchase agreement is to be treated for the purposes of this section as not being a consumer agreement shall lie on the party so contending.

(8) Any reference in this section to a term exempting from all or any of the provisions of any section of this Act is a reference to a term which purports to exclude or restrict, or has the effect of excluding or restricting, the operation of all or any of the provisions of that section, or the exercise of a right conferred by any provision of that section, or any liability of the owner for breach of a condition or warranty implied by any provision of that section.

(9) It is hereby declared that any reference in this section to a term of an agreement includes a reference to a term which although not contained in an agreement is incorporated in the agreement by another term of the agreement." [C.305]

36. For sections 14 and 15 substitute the following sections (which reproduce the existing provisions of those sections subject only to changes in terminology)—

**"14. Special provisions as to conditional sale agreements**

(1) Section 11 (1) (*c*) of the principal Act (whereby in certain circumstances a breach of a condition in a contract of sale is treated only as a breach of warranty) shall not apply to conditional sale agreements which are agreements for consumer sales.

(2) In England and Wales and Northern Ireland a breach of a condition (whether express or implied) to be fulfilled by the seller under any such agreement shall be treated as a breach of warranty, and not as grounds for rejecting the goods and treating the agreement as repudiated, if (but only if) it would have fallen to be so treated had the condition been contained or implied in a corresponding hire-purchase agreement as a condition to be fulfilled by the creditor.

**15. Supplementary**

(1) In sections 8 to 14 above and this section—

'business' includes a profession and the activities of any government department (including a Northern Ireland department), local authority or statutory undertaker;

'buyer' and 'seller' includes a person to whom rights and duties under a conditional sale agreement have passed by assignment or operation of law;

'condition' and 'warranty', in relation to Scotland, mean stipulation, and any stipulation referred to in sections 8 (1) (*a*), 9, 10 and 11 above shall be deemed to be material to the agreement.

'conditional sale agreement' means an agreement for the sale of goods under which the purchase price or part of it is payable by instalments, and the property in the goods is to remain in the seller (notwithstanding that the buyer is to be in possession of the goods) until such conditions as to the payment of instalments or otherwise as may be specified in the agreement are fulfilled;

'consumer sale' has the same meaning as in section 55 of the principal Act, as amended by section 4 above;

'creditor' means the person by whom the goods are bailed or (in Scotland) hired under a hire-purchase agreement or the person to whom his rights and duties under the agreement have passed by assignment or operation of law; and

'hire-purchase agreement' means an agreement, other than a conditional sale agreement, under which—

(*a*) goods are bailed or (in Scotland) hired in return for periodical payments by the person to whom they are bailed or hired, and

(*b*) the property in the goods will pass to that person if the terms of the agreements are complied with and one or more of the following occurs—

(i) the exercise of an option to purchase by that person,

(ii) the doing of any other specified act by any party to the agreement,

(iii) the happening of any other specified event.

(2) Goods of any kind are of merchantable quality within the meaning of section 10 (2) above if they are as fit for the purpose or purposes for which goods of that kind are commonly bought as it is reasonable to expect having regard to any description applied to them, the price (if relevant) and all the other relevant circumstances; and in section 11 above 'unmerchantable' shall be construed accordingly.

(3) In section 14 (2) above 'corresponding hire-purchase agreement' means, in relation to a conditional sale agreement, a hire-purchase agreement relating to the same goods as the conditional sale agreement and made between the same parties and at the same time and in the same circumstances and, as nearly as may be, in the same terms as the conditional sale agreement.

(4) Nothing in sections 8 to 13 above shall prejudice the operation of any other enactment including any enactment of the Parliament of Northern Ireland or the Northern Ireland Assembly or any rule of law whereby any condition or warranty, other than one relating to quality or fitness, is to be implied in any hire-purchase agreement." **[C.306]**

GENERAL NOTE

The changes in terminology made by this amendment are the substitution of "creditor" for "owner", of "person to whom the goods are bailed" for "hirer", of "bailed" for "let" and of references to credit-broker for references to persons by whom antecedent negotiations were conducted. Definitions of "credit-broker" and "credit-brokerage" are added to s. 10 of the Act of 1973, and definitions of "conditional sale agreement", "creditor" and "hire-purchase agreement" to s. 15. The subsections of s. 15 are renumbered because there is now no need for a separate subsection containing definitions for Northern Ireland (the former s. 15 (2)).

PARLIAMENT OF NORTHERN IRELAND; NORTHERN IRELAND ASSEMBLY

See the note to s. 191, *ante*.

SUPPLY OF GOODS (IMPLIED TERMS) ACT 1973, SS. 8–12, 14, 15

See 43 Halsbury's Statutes (3rd edn.) 1349–1355.

COUNTER-INFLATION ACT 1973, S. 21 (5)

See 43 Halsbury's Statutes (3rd edn.) 1601.

*Fair Trading Act* 1973

37. For section 138 (5) substitute—

"(5) In subsection (4) of this section, the following expressions have the meanings given by, or referred to in, section 189 of the Consumer Credit Act 1974—

"antecedent negotiations",
"conditional sale agreement",
"credit-sale agreement",
"hire-purchase agreement"." **[C.307]**

PART II

NORTHERN IRELAND

*Irish Bankrupt and Insolvent Act* 1857

38. The following section shall be inserted after section 313—

**"313A. Hire-purchase etc. agreements**

(1) Goods—

(*a*) bailed under a hire-purchase agreement or a consumer hire agreement, or

(*b*) agreed to be sold under a conditional sale agreement, or

(*c*) subject to a regulated agreement under which a bill of sale is given by way of security,

shall not during the period between—

(i) the service of a default notice under the Consumer Credit Act 1974 in respect of the goods, and

(ii) the date on which the notice expires or is earlier complied with,

be treated for the purposes of section 313 of this Act as goods which are by the consent and permission of the creditor, or (in the case of goods which are the subject of a consumer hire agreement) of the owner, in the possession, order or disposition of the person to whom they are bailed or agreed to be sold or who is the grantor of the bill of sale.

(2) In this section—

'conditional sale agreement' means an agreement for the sale of goods under which the purchase price or part of it is payable by instalments, and the property in the goods is to remain in the seller (notwithstanding that the buyer is to be in possession of the goods) until such conditions as to the payment of instalments or otherwise as may be specified in the agreement are fulfilled;

'consumer hire agreement' has the meaning given by section 15 of the Consumer Credit Act 1974;

'creditor' means the person bailing goods under a hire-purchase agreement or, as the case may be, the seller under a conditional sale agreement or the person providing credit under a regulated agreement, and includes the person to whom his rights and duties under the agreement have passed by assignment or operation of law;

'hire-purchase agreement' means an agreement, other than a conditional sale agreement, under which—

(*a*) goods are bailed or (in Scotland) hired in return for periodical payments by the person to whom they are bailed or hired, and

(*b*) the property in the goods will pass to that person if the terms of the agreement are complied with and one or more of the following occurs—

(i) the exercise of an option to purchase by that person,

(ii) the doing of any other specified act by any party to the agreement,

(iii) the happening of any other specified event. [**C.308**]

'owner' means a person who bails out goods under a consumer hire agreement or the person to whom his rights and duties under the agreement have been passed by assignment or operation of law; and

'regulated agreement' has the meaning given by section 189 of the Consumer Credit Act 1974."

*Bills of Sale (Ireland) Act* (1879) *Amendment Act* 1883

39. The following section shall be inserted after section 7:—

"7A. **Defaults under consumer credit agreements**

(1) Paragraph (1) of section 7 of this Act does not apply to a default relating to a bill of sale given by way of security for the payment of money under a regulated agreement to which section 87 (1) of the Consumer Credit Act 1974 applies:—

(*a*) unless the restriction imposed by section 88 (2) of that Act has ceased to apply to the bill of sale; or

(*b*) if, by virtue of section 89 of that Act, the default is to be treated as not having occurred.

(2) Where paragraph (1) of section 7 of this Act does apply in relation to a bill of sale such as is mentioned in subsection (1) of this section, the proviso to that section shall have effect with the insertion after 'High Court' of the words 'or county court'. [**C.309**]

*Liability for War Damage (Miscellaneous Provisions) Act (Northern Ireland)* 1939

40. In section 1 (3), for paragraphs (*a*) and (*b*) substitute—

"(*a*) a hire-purchase agreement or a conditional sale agreement within the meaning of the Consumer Credit Act 1974 being a consumer credit agreement as defined by that Act; or

(*b*) a consumer hire agreement within the meaning of that Act." [**C.310**]

*Clean Air Act (Northern Ireland)* 1964

41. In section 14 (4) for "a hire-purchase agreement for the letting to him" substitute— "either—

(i) a conditional sale agreement for the sale to him, or

(ii) a hire-purchase agreement for the bailment to him,". [**C.311**]

42. In section 43 (1)—

(*a*) after the definition of "chimney" insert—

" 'conditional sale agreement' means an agreement for the sale of goods under which the purchase price or part of it is payable by instalments, and the property in the goods is to remain in the seller (notwithstanding that the buyer is to be in possession of the goods) until such conditions as to the payment of instalments or otherwise as may be specified in the agreement are fulfilled;", and

(*b*) for the definition of "hire-purchase agreement" substitute—

" 'hire-purchase agreement' means an agreement, other than a conditional sale agreement, under which—

(*a*) goods are bailed in return for periodical payments by the person to whom they are bailed, and

(*b*) the property in the goods will pass to that person if the terms of the agreement are complied with and one or more of the following occurs—

(i) the exercise of an option to purchase by that person,

(ii) the doing of any other specified act by any party to the agreement,

(iii) the happening of any other specified event;". [**C.312**]

*Trading Stamps Act (Northern Ireland)* 1965

43. In section 2, for subsection (1) substitute—

"(1) No person shall after the coming into force of this section issue any trading stamp, or cause any trading stamp to be issued, or deliver any trading stamp to any person in connection with the sale of any goods, the bailment of any goods under a hire-purchase agreement or the performance of any services, unless such trading stamp bears on its face in clear and legible characters a value expressed in or by reference to current coin of the realm". **[C.313]**

44. In section 3, for subsection (4) substitute—

"(4) In this section 'redeemable trading stamps' means trading stamps delivered after the coming into force of this section in accordance with a trading stamp scheme on or in connection with either—

(*a*) the purchase of any goods,

(*b*) the bailment of any goods under a hire-purchase agreement, or

(*c*) the obtaining of any services for money,

and 'the holder', in relation to such a trading stamp, means the person to whom it was so delivered or any person who holds it without notice of any defect in title." **[C.314]**

45. In section 9—

(1) after the definition of "cash value" insert—

" 'conditional sale agreement' means an agreement for the sale of goods under which the purchase price or part of it is payable by instalments, and the property in the goods is to remain in the seller (notwithstanding that the buyer is to be in possession of the goods) until such conditions as to the payment of instalments or otherwise as may be specified in the agreement are fulfilled;", and

(2) after the definition of "goods" insert—

" 'hire-purchase agreement' means an agreement, other than a conditional sale agreement, under which—

(*a*) goods are bailed in return for periodical payments by the person to whom they are bailed, and

(*b*) the property in the goods will pass to that person if the terms of the agreement are complied with and one or more of the following occurs—

(i) the exercise of an option to purchase by that person,

(ii) the doing of any other specified act by any party to the agreement,

(iii) the happening of any other specified event;"

(3) For the definition of "trading stamp" substitute—

" 'trading stamp' means a stamp which is, or is intended to be, delivered to any person on or in connection with either—

(i) the purchase of any goods, or

(ii) the bailment of any goods under a hire-purchase agreement,

(other than the purchase of a newspaper or other periodical of which the stamp forms part or in which it is contained) and is, or is intended to be, redeemable (whether singly or together with other such sums) by that or some other person:

Provided that a stamp shall not be deemed to be a trading stamp if—

(*a*) it is delivered or is intended to be delivered to a person (in this definition called 'the purchaser') on or in connection with the purchase of any goods by the purchaser, or the bailment to him of any goods, and

(*b*) it is intended to be, and is not, redeemable from any person other than—

(i) the person (in this definition called 'the seller') from whom the purchaser purchased those goods or who bailed those goods to him, or

(ii) any person from whom the seller (whether directly or indirectly) acquired those goods, and

(*c*) in the case where a business is carried on by six or more retail establishments, the stamp is one of a kind obtainable at no more than six of those retail establishments, and not obtainable by the public elsewhere, and the arrangements under which it is redeemable are entirely separate from arrangements under which any other stamps, whether trading stamps or not, are redeemable,

and references in this definition to the purchase of goods include references to the obtaining of services for money." **[C.315]**

*Consumer Protection Act* (*Northern Ireland*) 1965

46. In section 2, for subsections (5) and (6) substitute—

"(5) If as respects goods of any class or description regulations under section 1 so provide, subsections (1) to (3) (other than subsection 3 (*d*) and (*e*)) shall apply subject to subsection (6) in relation to goods of that class or description as if—

(*a*) references to selling or to a sale included references to—

(i) bailing under a hire-purchase agreement, or

(ii) bailing under a hire agreement, or

(iii) an agreement to sell under a conditional sale agreement; and

(*b*) the reference to a sale under a credit-sale agreement were a reference

(i) to a bailment under a hire-purchase agreement, or

(ii) to an agreement to sell under a conditional sale agreement.

(6) Subsections (1) and (2) shall not apply—

(*a*) in a case of bailment under a hire agreement, where the bailment is incidental to an agreement under which payments are to be made in the form of rent issuing out of land;

(*b*) in a case of possession for the purpose of bailment under a hire agreement, where possession is for the purpose of a bailment which is incidental to an agreement under which payments are to be made in the form of rent issuing out of land;

(*c*) in any case of bailment under a hire agreement, where the bailment was lawful at the time when it began." **[C.316]**

47. In section 5—

(1) after the definition of "component part" insert—

" 'conditional sale agreement' " means an agreement for the sale of goods under which the purchase price or part of it is payable by instalments, and the property in the goods is to remain in the seller (notwithstanding that the buyer is to be in possession of the goods) until such conditions as to the payment of instalments or otherwise as may be specified in the agreement are fulfilled;

"'hire agreement' means an agreement for the bailment of goods which is not a hire-purchase agreement;"

(2) for the definition of "credit-sale agreement" substitute—

"'credit sale agreement' means an agreement for the sale of goods, under which the purchase price or part of it is payable by instalments, but which is not a conditional sale agreement;"

(3) for the definition of hire-purchase agreement substitute—

"'hire-purchase agreement' means an agreement, other than a conditional sale agreement, under which—

(*a*) goods are bailed in return for periodical payments by the person to whom they are bailed, and

(*b*) the property in the goods will pass to that person if the terms of the agreement are complied with and one or more of the following occurs—

(i) the exercise of an option to purchase by that person,

(ii) the doing of any other specified act by any party to the agreement,

(iii) the happening of any other specified event;". **[C.317]**

*Industrial Investment* (*General Assistance*) *Act* (*Northern Ireland*) 1966

48. In section 14 (1)—

(1) after the definition of "computer" insert—

"'conditional sale agreement' means an agreement for the sale of goods under which the purchase price or part of it is payable by instalments, and the property in the goods is to remain in the seller (notwithstanding that the buyer is to be in possession of the goods) until such conditions as to the payment of instalments or otherwise as may be specified in the agreement are fulfilled;" and

(2) for the definition of "hire-purchase agreement" substitute—

"'hire-purchase agreement' means an agreement, other than a conditional sale agreement, under which—

(*a*) goods are bailed in return for periodical payments by the person to whom they are bailed or hired, and

(*b*) the property in the goods will pass to that person if the terms of the agreement are complied with and one or more of the following occurs—

(i) the exercise of an option to purchase by that person,

(ii) the doing of any other specified act by any party to the agreement,

(iii) the happening of any other specified event;". **[C.318]**

*Hire-Purchase Act* (*Northern Ireland*) 1966

49. For Part VI substitute the following (which reproduces the existing provisions of that Part subject only to changes in terminology)—

"PART VI

TITLE TO MOTOR VEHICLES ON HIRE-PURCHASE OR CONDITIONAL SALE

**62. Protection of purchasers of motor vehicles**

(1) This section applies where a motor vehicle has been bailed under a hire-purchase agreement, or has been agreed to be sold under a conditional sale

agreement, and, before the property in the vehicle has become vested in the debtor, he disposes of the vehicle to another person.

(2) Where the disposition referred to in subsection (1) is to a private purchaser, and he is a purchaser of the motor vehicle in good faith without notice of the hire-purchase or conditional sale agreement (the 'relevant agreement') that disposition shall have effect as if the creditor's title to the vehicle had been vested in the debtor immediately before that disposition.

(3) Where the person to whom the disposition referred to in subsection (1) is made (the 'original purchaser') is a trade or finance purchaser, then if the person who is the first private purchaser of the motor vehicle after that disposition ('the first private purchaser') is a purchaser of the vehicle in good faith without notice of the relevant agreement, the disposition of the vehicle to the first private purchaser shall have effect as if the title of the creditor to the vehicle had been vested in the debtor immediately before he disposed of it to the original purchaser.

(4) Where, in a case within subsection (3)—

(*a*) the disposition by which the first private purchaser becomes a purchaser of the motor vehicle in good faith without notice of the relevant agreement is itself a bailment under a hire-purchase agreement, and

(*b*) the person who is the creditor in relation to that agreement disposes of the vehicle to the first private purchaser, or a person claiming under him, by transferring to him the property in the vehicle in pursuance of a provision in the agreement in that behalf,

the disposition referred to in paragraph (*b*) (whether or not the person to whom it is made is a purchaser in good faith without notice of the relevant agreement) shall, as well as the disposition referred to in paragraph (*a*), have effect as mentioned in subsection (3).

(5) The preceding provisions of this section apply—

(*a*) notwithstanding anything in section 21 of the Sale of Goods Act 1893 (sale of goods by a person not the owner), but

(*b*) without prejudice to the provisions of the Factors Act (as defined by section 62 (1) of the said Act of 1893) or of any other enactment enabling the apparent owner of goods to dispose of them as if he were the true owner.

(6) Nothing in this section shall exonerate the debtor from any liability (whether criminal or civil) to which he would be subject apart from this section; and, in a case where the debtor disposes of the motor vehicle to a trade or finance purchaser, nothing in this section shall exonerate—

(*a*) that trade or finance purchaser, or

(*b*) any other trade or finance purchaser who becomes a purchaser of the vehicle and is not a person claiming under the first private purchaser,

from any liability (whether criminal or civil) to which he would be subject apart from this section.

**63. Presumptions relating to dealings with motor vehicles**

(1) Where in any proceedings (whether criminal or civil) relating to a motor vehicle it is proved—

(*a*) that the vehicle was bailed under a hire-purchase agreement, or was agreed to be sold under a conditional sale agreement and (*b*) that a person (whether a party to the proceedings or not) became a private purchaser of the vehicle in good faith without notice of the hire-purchase or conditional sale agreement (the 'relevant agreement'),

this section shall have effect for the purpose of the operation of section 62 of this Act in relation to those proceedings.

(2) It shall be presumed for those purposes, unless the contrary is proved, that the disposition of the vehicle to the person referred to in subsection (1) (*b*) (the 'relevant purchaser') was made by the debtor.

(3) If it is proved that that disposition was not made by the debtor, then it shall be presumed for those purposes, unless the contrary is proved—

(*a*) that the debtor disposed of the vehicle to a private purchaser purchasing in good faith without notice of the relevant agreement, and

(*b*) that the relevant purchaser is or was a person claiming under the person to whom the debtor so disposed of the vehicle.

(4) If it is proved that the disposition of the vehicle to the relevant purchaser was not made by the debtor, and that the person to whom the debtor disposed of the vehicle (the 'original purchaser') was a trade or finance purchaser, then it shall be presumed for those purposes, unless the contrary is proved,—

(*a*) that the person who, after the disposition of the vehicle to the original purchaser, first became a private purchaser of the vehicle was a purchaser in good faith without notice of the relevant agreement, and

(*b*) that the relevant purchaser is or was a person claiming under the original purchaser.

(5) Without prejudice to any other method of proof, where in any proceedings a party thereto admits a fact, that fact shall, for the purposes of this section, be taken as against him to be proved in relation to those proceedings.

**64. Interpretation of Part VI and application to the Crown**

(1) In this Part—

'conditional sale agreement' means an agreement for the sale of goods under which the purchase price or part of it is payable by instalments, and the property in the goods is to remain in the seller (notwithstanding that the buyer is to be in possession of the goods) until such conditions as to the payment of instalments or otherwise as may be specified in the agreement are fulfilled;

'creditor' means the person by whom goods are bailed under a hire-purchase agreement or, as the case may be, the seller under a conditional sale agreement, or the person to whom his rights and duties have passed by assignment or operation of law;

'disposition' means any sale or contract of sale (including a conditional sale agreement), any bailment under a hire-purchase agreement and any transfer of the property in goods in pursuance of a provision in that behalf contained in a hire-purchase agreement, and includes any transaction purporting to be a disposition (as so defined), and 'dispose of' shall be construed accordingly;

'hire-purchase agreement' means an agreement, other than a conditional sale agreement, under which—

(*a*) goods are bailed in return for periodical payments by the person to whom they are bailed, and (*b*) the property in the goods will pass to that person if the terms of the agreement are complied with and one or more of the following occurs—

(i) the exercise of an option to purchase by that person,

(ii) the doing of any other specified act by any party to the agreement,

(iii) the happening of any other specified event; and

'motor vehicle' means a mechanically propelled vehicle intended or adapted for use on roads to which the public has access.

(2) In this Part 'trade or finance purchaser' means a purchaser who, at the time of the disposition made to him, carries on a business which consists, wholly or partly,—

(*a*) of purchasing motor vehicles for the purpose of offering or exposing them for sale, or

(*b*) of providing finance by purchasing motor vehicles for the purpose of bailing them under hire-purchase agreements or agreeing to sell them under conditional sale agreements,

and 'private purchaser' means a purchaser who, at the time of the disposition made to him, does not carry on any such business.

(3) For the purposes of this Part a person becomes a purchaser of a motor vehicle if, and at the time when, a disposition of the vehicle is made to him; and a person shall be taken to be a purchaser of a motor vehicle without notice of a hire-purchase agreement or conditional sale agreement if, at the time of the disposition made to him, he has no actual notice that the vehicle is or was the subject of any such agreement.

(4) In this Part the 'debtor',—

(*a*) in relation to a motor vehicle which has been bailed under a hire-purchase agreement or, as the case may be, agreed to be sold under a conditional sale agreement, means the person who at the material time (whether the agreement has before that time been terminated or not) either—

(*a*) is the person to whom the vehicle is bailed under that agreement or

(*b*) is, in relation to the agreement, the buyer, including a person who at that time is, by virtue of section 130 (4) of the Consumer Credit Act 1974 treated as a bailee of the vehicle;

(5) In this Part any reference to the title of the creditor to a motor vehicle which has been bailed under a hire-purchase agreement, or agreed to be sold under a conditional sale agreement, and is disposed of by the debtor, is a reference to such title (if any) to the vehicle as, immediately before that disposition, was vested in the person who then was the creditor in relation to the agreement.

(6) This Part binds the Crown to the full extent authorised or permitted by the constitutional laws of Northern Ireland." **[C.319]**

*Vehicles (Excise) Act (Northern Ireland)* 1972

50. In section 35 (1) substitute—

(1) before the definition of "gas" insert—

" 'conditional sale agreement' means an agreement for the sale of a vehicle under which the purchase price or part of it is payable by instalments, and the property in the vehicle is to remain in the seller (notwithstanding that the buyer is to be in possession of the vehicle) until such conditions as to the payment of instalments or otherwise as may be specified in the agreement are fulfilled;".

(2) for the definition of "hackney carriage" substitute—

" 'hackney carriage' means a mechanically propelled vehicle standing or plying for hire and includes any mechanically propelled vehicle bailed under a hire agreement by a person whose trade it is to sell such vehicles or bail them under hire agreements;"

(3) After the definition of "hackney carriage" insert—

" 'hire agreement' means an agreement for the bailment of a vehicle which is not a hire-purchase agreement;

'hire-purchase agreement' means an agreement, other than a conditional sale agreement, under which—

(*a*) a vehicle is bailed in return for periodical payments by the person to whom it is bailed, and

(*b*) the property in the vehicle will pass to that person if the terms of the agreement are complied with and one or more of the following occurs—

(i) the exercise of an option to purchase by that person,

(ii) the doing of any other specified act by any party to the agreement,

(iii) the happening of any other specified event;". **[C.320]**

*Miscellaneous Transferred Excise Duties Act* (*Northern Ireland*) 1972

51. In section 1 (2) for "VII" where first occurring substitute "V" and for "to VII" where secondly occurring substitute "and V". **[C.321]**

IRISH BANKRUPT AND INSOLVENT ACT 1857
20 & 21 Vict. c. 60.

BILLS OF SALE (IRELAND) ACT (1879) AMENDMENT ACT 1883
46 & 47 Vict. c. 7.

LIABILITY FOR WAR DAMAGE (MISCELLANEOUS PROVISIONS) ACT (NORTHERN IRELAND) 1939
1939 c. 36 (N.I.).

CLEAN AIR ACT (NORTHERN IRELAND) 1964
1964 c. 16 (N.I.).

TRADING STAMPS ACT (NORTHERN IRELAND) 1965
1965 c. 6 (N.I.).

CONSUMER PROTECTION ACT (NORTHERN IRELAND) 1965
1965 c. 14 (N.I.).

INDUSTRIAL INVESTMENT (GENERAL ASSISTANCE) ACT (NORTHERN IRELAND) 1966
1966 c. 41 (N.I.).

HIRE-PURCHASE ACT (NORTHERN IRELAND) 1966
1966 c. 42 (N.I.).

VEHICLES (EXCISE) ACT (NORTHERN IRELAND) 1972
1972 c. 10 (N.I.).

MISCELLANEOUS TRANSFERRED EXCISE DUTIES ACT (NORTHERN IRELAND) 1972

1972 c. 11 (N.I.). | | Section 192 (3) (*b*)

## SCHEDULE 5

### REPEALS

### PART I

### UNITED KINGDOM

| Chapter | Short Title | Extent of Repeal |
|---|---|---|
| 1835 (5 & 6 Will. 4.) c. 62 | Statutory Declarations Act 1835 | Section 12. |
| 1839 (2 & 3 Vict.) c. 47 | Metropolitan Police Act 1839 | Section 50. |
| 1839 (2 & 3 Vict.) c. 71 | Police Courts (Metropolis) Act 1839 | In section 27 the words "pawned, pledged" and the words "or of any person who shall have advanced money upon the credit of such goods". In section 28 the words "pawned, pledged or" (in each place). |
| 1872 (35 & 36 Vict.) c. 93 | Pawnbrokers Act 1872 | The whole Act. |
| 1875 (38 & 39 Vict.) c. 25 | Public Stores Act 1875 | In section 9 the words "or a pawnbroker" and "or to pawnbrokers". |
| 1891 (54 & 55 Vict.) c. 50 | Commissioners for Oaths Act 1891 | In section 1, the words "or the Pawnbrokers Act 1872". |
| 1892 (55 & 56 Vict.) c. 4 | Betting and Loans (Infants) Act 1892 | Sections 2 to 4. Section 6, except so far as it extends to Northern Ireland. In section 7, the definitions of "indictment" and "summary conviction". |
| 1892 (55 & 56 Vict.) c. 55 | Burgh Police (Scotland) Act 1892 | In section 453, the words "and all offences committed against the provisions of the Pawnbrokers Act, 1872". |
| 1894 (56 & 57 Vict.) c. 71 | Sale of Goods Act 1893 | Section 14 (6). |
| 1894 (56 & 57 Vict.) c. 73 | Local Government Act 1894 | Section 27 (1) (*b*). |
| 1897 (60 & 61 Vict.) c. 30 | Police (Property) Act 1897 | In section 1 (1), the words "or section thirty-four of the Pawnbrokers Act 1872". |
| 1900 (63 & 64 Vict.) c. 51 | Moneylenders Act 1900 | The whole Act. |
| 1908 (8 Edw. 7.) c. 53 | Law of Distress Amendment Act 1908 | In section 4 (1) the words "bill of sale, hire purchase agreement or". |

| Chapter | Short Title | Extent of Repeal |
|---|---|---|
| 1927 (17 & 18 Geo. 5.) c. 21 | Moneylenders Act 1927 | The whole Act. |
| 1933 (23 & 24 Geo. 5.) c. 12 | Children and Young Persons Act 1933 | Section 8. |
| 1937 (1 Edw. 8 & 1 Geo. 6.) c. 37 | Children and Young Persons (Scotland) Act 1937 | Section 19. |
| 1939 (2 & 3 Geo. 6.) c. 75 | Compensation (Defence) Act 1939 | In section 18 (1) the words from "the expression 'hire purchase agreement' " to "omitted". |
| 1939 (2 & 3 Geo. 6.) c. 102 | Liability for War Damage (Miscellaneous Provisions) Act 1939 | Sections 4 and 6 (*b*). |
| 1940 (3 & 4 Geo. 6.) c. 42 | Law Reform (Miscellaneous Provisions) (Scotland) Act 1940 | In section 4 (2), paragraphs (*b*) and (*c*). |
| 1945 (8 & 9 Geo. 6.) c. 16 | Limitation (Enemies and War Prisoners) Act 1945 | In section 2, the words "subsection (1) of section thirteen of the Moneylenders Act 1927".<br>In section 4, the words "subsection (1) of section thirteen of the Moneylenders Act 1927". |
| 1948 (11 & 12 Geo. 6.) c. 38 | Companies Act 1948 | Section 201 (2) (*c*). |
| 1949 (12 & 13 Geo. 6.) c. 47 | Finance Act 1949 | In section 15, subsections (1) to (3) and (6) to (8A). |
| 1952 (15 & 16 Geo. 6 & 1 Eliz. 2.) c. 44 | Customs and Excise Act 1952 | In section 313 (1) the words "or section fifteen of the Finance Act 1949". |
| 1956 (4 & 5 Eliz. 2.) c. 68 | Restrictive Trade Practices Act 1956 | Section 26 (4) from "and for the reference to a hire-purchase agreement" onwards.<br>Section 26 (5). |
| 1960 (8 & 9 Eliz. 2.) c. 24 | Pawnbrokers Act 1960 | The whole Act. |
| 1961 (9 & 10 Eliz. 2.) c. 36 | Finance Act 1961 | Section 11 (1) from "or section 15 of the Finance Act 1949" onwards. |
| 1964 c. 42 | Administration of Justice Act 1964 | Section 9 (3) (*b*). |
| 1964 c. 53 | Hire-Purchase Act 1964 | The whole Act, except Part III and section 37. |
| 1964 c. 60 | Emergency Laws (Re-enactment and Repeals) Act 1964 | Section 1 (4). |
| 1964 c. 71 | Trading Stamps Act 1964 | In section 10 (1) the definition of "purchase". |
| 1965 c. 66 | Hire Purchase Act 1965 | The whole Act. |
| 1965 c. 67 | Hire Purchase (Scotland) Act 1965 | The whole Act. |

| Chapter | Short Title | Extent of Repeal |
|---|---|---|
| 1966 c. 42 | Local Government Act 1966 | In Schedule 3, Part II, the entries relating to section 37 of the Pawnbrokers Act 1872 and section 1 (1) of the Moneylenders Act 1927. |
| 1966 c. 51 | Local Government (Scotland) Act 1966 | In Schedule 4, Part II, the entries relating to section 37 of the Pawnbrokers Act 1872 and section 1 (1) of the Moneylenders Act 1927. |
| 1967 c. 42 | Advertisements (Hire Purchase) Act 1967 | The whole Act. |
| 1967 c. 81 | Companies Act 1967 | Sections 123 to 125. |
| 1968 c. 60 | Theft Act 1968 | In Schedule 2, Part III, the entry relating to the Pawnbrokers Act 1872. |
| 1969 c. 19 | Decimal Currency Act 1969 | In Schedule 2, paragraph 2. |
| 1969 c. 48 | Post Office Act 1969 | In Schedule 4, paragraph 31. |
| 1971 c. 23 | Courts Act 1971 | In Schedule 9, Part I, the entries relating to the Pawnbrokers Act 1872 and the Moneylenders Act 1927. |
| 1972 c. 70 | Local Government Act 1972 | Section 213 (1) (*a*) and (*b*) and (3). |
| 1973 c. 65 | Local Government (Scotland) Act 1973 | In Schedule 27, paragraph 96. In Schedule 29, the entry relating to the Finance Act 1949. |

**[C.322]**

PART II

NORTHERN IRELAND

| Chapter | Short Title | Extent of Repeal |
|---|---|---|
| 1842 (5 & 6 Vict.) c. 75 | Charitable Pawn Offices (Ireland) Act 1842 | The whole Act. |
| 1933 c. 23 (N.I.) | Moneylenders Act (Northern Ireland) 1933 | The whole Act. |
| 1939 c. 36 (N.I.) | Liability for War Damage (Miscellaneous Provisions) Act (Northern Ireland) 1939 | In section 5 (1) the definition of "hire-purchase agreement". |
| 1949 c. 2 (N.I.) | Agriculture Act (Northern Ireland) 1949 | Section 7 (2). |
| 1954 c. 30 (N.I.) | Pawnbrokers Act (Northern Ireland) 1954 | The whole Act. |
| 1957 c. 19 (N.I.) | Betting and Lotteries Act (Northern Ireland) 1957 | Section 3 (1) (*j*). |
| 1960 c. 22 (N.I.) | Companies Act (Northern Ireland) 1960 | Section 192 (3) (*c*). |
| 1965 c. 6 (N.I.) | Trading Stamps Act (Northern Ireland) 1965 | In section 9 the definition of "purchase". |
| 1966 c. 42 (N.I.) | Hire-Purchase Act (Northern Ireland) 1966 | The whole Act except Part VI and section 68. |
| 1967 c. 29 (N.I.) | Increase of Fines Act (Northern Ireland) 1967 | In Part I of the Schedule the entries relating to the Moneylenders Act (Northern Ireland) 1933. |
| 1968 c. 28 (N.I.) | Criminal Justice (Miscellaneous Provisions) Act (Northern Ireland) 1968 | In Schedule 2 the entry relating to the Moneylenders Act (Northern Ireland) 1933. |
| 1969 c. 16 (N.I.) | Theft Act (Northern Ireland) 1969 | In Schedule 2 the entry relating to the Pawnbrokers Act (Northern Ireland) 1954. |
| 1969 c. 24 (N.I.) | Industrial and Provident Societies Act (Northern Ireland) 1969 | Section 96. |
| 1969 c. 27 (N.I.) | Moneylenders (Amendment) Act (Northern Ireland) 1969 | The whole Act. |
| 1969 c. 30 (N.I.) | Judgments (Enforcement) Act (Northern Ireland) 1969 | In Schedule 4 the amendments of the Hire-Purchase Act (Northern Ireland) 1966. |
| 1971 c. 13 (N.I.) | Licensing Act (Northern Ireland) 1971 | Section 2 (5) (*b*). |
| 1972 c. 11 (N.I.) | Miscellaneous Transferred Excise Duties Act (Northern Ireland) 1972 | Parts VI and VII. In Schedule 4 the entry relating to the Pawnbrokers Act (Northern Ireland) 1954. |

# INDEX



**All references are to paragraph numbers**

**All references are to paragraph numbers**

All references are to paragraph numbers

**All references are to paragraph numbers**